Systematic Theology for the New Apostolic Reformation:
An Exposition of Father-Son Theology

Second Edition

Dr. Harold R. Eberle

Systematic Theology for the New Apostolic Reformation:
An Exposition of Father-Son Theology

Second Edition

Dr. Harold R. Eberle

Worldcast Publishing
Yakima, Washington USA

Systematic Theology for the New Apostolic Reformation:
An Exposition of Father-Son Theology

© 2015 by Harold R. Eberle
First Edition, First Printing, July 2015, under the title: *Father-Son Theology*
Second Edition, First Printing, May 2016

Worldcast Publishing
P.O. Box 10653
Yakima, WA 98909-1653
(509) 248-5837
www.worldcastministries.com
office@worldcastministries.com

ISBN 978-1-882523-46-7
Cover by Chris Ritchie

Unless otherwise stated, all biblical quotations are taken from the NEW AMERICAN STANDARD BIBLE®, Copyright © 1960, 1962, 1963, 1968, 1971, 1972, 1973, 1975, 1977, 1995 by The Lockman Foundation. Used by permission. <u>Underlining</u> within Scripture quotations is the author's own.

ALL RIGHTS RESERVED

No part of this publication may be reproduced, stored in a retrieval system, or transmitted in any form or by any means—electronic, mechanical, photocopy, recording, or otherwise—without the express prior permission of Worldcast Publishing Company, with the exception of brief excerpts in magazine articles and/or reviews.

Requests for translating into other languages should be addressed to Worldcast Publishing.

What Others Are Saying

God is a loving Father who desires sons. From this premise, Harold Eberle develops a Hebraic/Judeo, Bible-based, systematic theology. While reading *Father-Son Theology* I would often find myself nodding as Eberle states positions I had long felt but had never seen clearly articulated. Father-Son theology challenges Classical/Reformed theology that has been infused by the ancient Greek dualistic worldview. Father-Son theology leads us to our God who is present with us and who loves us. This is a must-read for everyone who takes the Bible seriously.

    Dr. Tim Hamon
    CEO, Christian International
    Santa Rosa Beach, FL USA

In his *Father-Son Theology* Harold Eberle has taken on many of the strongholds of Greek philosophy that have influenced the Church in the West. He unfolds how the writings of Augustine gripped both Calvin and Luther and greatly influenced their understanding of the nature of God. Many of the ideas commonly accepted in Western theology, Harold contends, were derived from concepts of God that Augustine learned from the Greek philosophers. Eberle proposes a return to a more Hebrew—therefore a more biblical—worldview in interpreting the Scriptures. In my opinion, his call to a more relational theology with a focus on God's call to sonship is a much-needed challenge to many unbiblical concepts of the divine nature. Jesus came to reveal a Father who was and is relational.

    Pastor Joe McIntyre
    Senior Minister, Word of His Grace Church
    President, Kenyon's Gospel Publishing Society
    Bothell, WA, USA

Systematic Theology for the New Apostolic Reformation

Harold Eberle's *Father-Son Theology* is an important contribution that throughout makes us ask hard questions about whether or not some of our theological orientations are really foreign to what the Bible is saying and even contrary to the biblical material. Some of the sacred cows addressed do need to be killed. The book is elegantly written, clear, easy to comprehend, but deep. I find myself sometimes in agreement (most of the time), sometimes not, sometimes wanting to add other material that was not addressed, but always profitably challenged. The book restores a theology with a God who loves, acts, responds, has emotion, and is time related. It will cause quite a stir and should be widely read.

>Dr. Daniel Juster
>Director, *Tikkum International*
>Jerusalem, Israel

What an incredible read! Harold Eberle's understanding of Church history and the effects of broader culture over the centuries is incredible. This book challenges and questions so much of Western Christianity. The end result is a thought-provoking journey that should help you better understand the heart of God and the type of relationship He desires to have with you.

>Pastor Dave Edler
>Senior Pastor, Yakima Foursquare Church,
>Yakima, WA, USA

Father-Son Theology passionately declares faith in an understanding of God I have always longed for. Harold systematically addresses many classic theological issues that have challenged Christians throughout the ages and leads the reader into a new understanding of God as Father and what it means to be His sons and daughters. This book is a brilliant breakthrough in authentic biblical theology which has changed my theological perspective, my life, and ministry. I hope it melts your heart and transforms your mind as it has mine.

>Dr. Bill Starr, D. Min., MAC, CDP
>Chaplain, Sundown M Ranch
>Selah, WA, USA

What Others Are Saying

I write this endorsement not only as a fellow author, but also as an Eberle aficionado. Over the last decade I have devoured all 30+ books that Harold has written, multiple times. I have had the honor of teaching side-by-side with him countless times and through our writings we have become two of the main lightning rods for optimistic eschatology. That being said, this Eberle book in your hands is likely the one to be referred to again and again over the next 100 years.

Martin Luther changed the world with his 95 Thesis, John Calvin did it again with *Institutes*, and Harold Eberle will dramatically shift the cold distant view of God to the correct view of a loving Father bringing forth sons through his work, *Father-Son Theology*. So get comfy in your armchair, brew 50 gallons of coffee and prepare to change your perspective to a biblical view of God.

> Dr. Jonathan Welton
> Best-Selling Author of *School of the Seers* and *Raptureless*
> Founder, The Welton Academy
> Rochester, NY, USA

Very often, the study of theology has been based on splitting the Bible, and even God Himself, into a list of "categories" or "attributes." But the Bible itself is very different. It is not a list of subjects; it is a book of stories, poetry, songs and letters—it's all about relationships and real life. God reveals Himself as a Father who is seeking a living relationship with His children—a personal, knowable God. Often, discussions about a "relationship with God" are lacking in any theological foundation, and discussions about theology can be cold and clinical and void of any feeling of "relationship." Harold Eberle has bridged this gap in our learning, relating, and journey of faith. Here he has presented a clear, biblical, and meaningful theology that will enable you to grow in your understanding of the Scriptures in a way which is personal, relatable, and inspiring. Thank you, Harold, for helping to redefine theology and bring it back to its biblical basis—God is a loving Father who sent His Son to bring many children into His family!

> Dr. Martin Trench, D. Th.
> Lead Pastor, Gateway Alliance Church
> Edmonton, Canada

Systematic Theology for the New Apostolic Reformation

It is refreshing to read a systematic theology that comes from the starting point that we are created in the image of God who is relational, loving, and for us the way a father is toward a son. What we believe about the nature of God and the nature of humans affects everything: how we live, read Scripture, view ourselves, and treat others. There is not an area of life unaffected by how we view God and thus ourselves in relation to God. Harold Eberle is a passionate seeker of truth, a voracious student of the Bible and the history of Christianity. He is driven by an immense desire for people to know the love of God.

>Catherine Skurja, MFT
>Adjunct professor, George Fox Evangelical Seminary
>Author of *Paradox Lost*
>Portland, OR, USA

Jesus didn't just teach on man's relationship with God, he modeled it. By addressing His Father as our Father, He showed us how to relate to the Creator of the Universe. Father-Son Theology builds on this profound unity between a Father and a son, with all of creation to shape and explore.

>James Bryson
>Writer and Editor
>Sharpsburg, Maryland, USA

In Dr. Eberle's twelve volume tome, he embraces the style of writing suited to a standard systematic theology, in that he discusses the Godhead and other key theological topics, but does so from a perspective of covenantal (New Covenant) revelation . . . with a major focus on the wonderful and dynamic relationship between the Father and the Son, and of course, does not leave out the dynamic work of Holy Spirit in our daily life. This is an outstanding, scholarly work; I highly recommend it for personal growth and a continuous resource for deep and meaningful study.

>Dr. Stan E. DeKoven, Ph.D., MFT
>President, Vision International University
>Ramona, CA, USA

What Others Are Saying

This book is both remarkable and daring. Remarkable in its size and thoroughness; daring in its claim that the Father-Son paradigm is the centerpiece of our theology. My deep and deepening conviction is that the whole of ultimate reality is the Kingdom of our God Who, among all His names, makes it clear that He wishes to be called FATHER.

This is a safe read because Harold Eberle is a safe man, a scholar, a theologian, a philosopher and much more. It probably would not be difficult to find something with which the reader would not totally agree in this work. There is likely no book in print of which this cannot be said. I suggest that when and if you encounter such an experience, you lay the point in question aside and read on. Often, hanging out with a doubt leads to a theft of valid certainties to be encountered later.

I recently met Harold Eberle after years of hearing his name repeatedly across a wide spectrum of contemporary Christianity. Read this book and you will likely be returning to it again and again for the rest of your life.

Jack Taylor
Dimensions Ministries
Melbourne, Florida

God started as a loving Father determined to have sons, and He will finish as a loving Father with sons.

Contents

Foreword 1
Preface 9
Acknowledgments 13
Introduction 15
Prolegomenon 21

Volume I: The Nature of God 27
   Section A: The Cornerstone of Father-Son Theology 29
   Section B: God of Creation 35
   Section C: God of Abraham 55
   Section D: God of the Old Testament 65
   Section E: God of Jesus 75
   Section F: God of the Greek Philosophers 81
   Section G: God of Classical Theology 93
   Section H: Two Views in Conflict 109
   Section I: Building on the Biblical View of God 131

Volume II: God's Involvement with this World 145
   Section A: God's Involvement from the Reformed View 147
   Section B: God's Involvement from the Father-Son View 153
   Section C: Cooperative Relationships 167
   Section D: Theodicy 171
   Section E: Father-God's Knowledge of the World 177
   Section F: Father-God Is Bigger and Greater 189

Volume III: The Nature of Creation 191
   Section A: The Who and What of Creation 193
   Section B: The Why of Creation 211
   Section C: Natural Theology 215
   Section D: Spiritual Aspects of Creation 219
   Section E: Angelology 223
   Section F: Creation and Time 227
   Section G: Theology and Science 251

Systematic Theology for the New Apostolic Reformation

Volume IV: The Nature of Humanity 263
   Section A: Classical/Reformed View of Humanity 267
   Section B: How People Are Like God 277
   Section C: The Original Blessing 287
   Section D: Separated from God? 293
   Section E: The Original Sin 315
   Section F: Rethinking Original Sin 325
   Section G: Born Sinful and Condemned? 333
   Section H: How Good or Bad Are People? 337
   Section I: The Pelagian Controversy 347
   Section J: The Triune Nature 357
   Section K: The Soul of a Person 365
   Section L: The Heart of a Person 371
   Section M: The Will of a Person 379

Volume V: Evil, Sin, and Suffering 389
   Section A: Classical View of Evil, Death, and Suffering 391
   Section B: The Best World in Which to Raise Sons 399
   Section C: God's Role in Causing Pain and Suffering 407
   Section D: Satan's Origin and Role 415
   Section E: Humanity as a Source of Evil 433
   Section F: Sin as Something People Do 439
   Section G: Transgressions and Iniquities 457
   Section H: Outside Influences of Sin and Evil 461
   Section I: Why Is There Pain, Suffering, and Death? 467

Volume VI: Soteriology 477
   Section A: Saved from What? 479
   Section B: The Covenantal View of the Atonement 489
   Section C: Salvation via the Life of Jesus 509
   Section D: Becoming Children of God 523
   Section E: What Is the Gospel? 529
   Section F: What Is the Proper Response to the Gospel? 533
   Section G: What Is Necessary for Salvation? 537
   Section H: *Sola Gratia* 545
   Section I: *Sola Fide* 565

Contents

Volume VII: Ecclesiology and Basilology 581
    Section A: Distinction Between the Church and Kingdom 583
    Section B: The *Ecclesia* 587
    Section C: The Kingdom of God 611
    Section D: Gospel of Salvation or Gospel of Kingdom? 621

Volume VIII: General Eschatology 627
    Section A: Dispensational or Progressive View? 629
    Section B: The Millennial Reign of Jesus 635
    Section C: Kingdom Theology 641
    Section D: The Revelation of Daniel 9 649
    Section E: Futurism, Partial Preterism, or Full Preterism? 667
    Section F: The Book of Revelation 675

Volume IX: Personal Eschatology 687
    Section A: Old Testament Saints After Death 689
    Section B: New Testament Saints After Death 693
    Section C: Our Eternal Destination 701
    Section D: What Is Hell? 711

Volume X: The Trinity and Christology 733
    Section A: Biblical Witness to the Trinity 735
    Section B: Jesus as Fully God 741
    Section C: Jesus as Fully Man 749
    Section D: Who Is Jesus? 753

Volume XI: Pneumatology 757
    Section A: Person of the Holy Spirit 759
    Section B: Works of the Holy Spirit 763
    Section C: Anointing of the Holy Spirit 773
    Section D: Gifts of the Holy Spirit 779
    Section E: Gift of Tongues 783
    Section F: Prophetic Gifts 791
    Section G: Divine Healing 797

Systematic Theology for the New Apostolic Reformation

Volume XII: The Christian Life 805
    Section A: Living as Children 807
    Section B: Healthy Relationships 813
    Section C: Prayer 817
    Section D: Worship 823
    Section E: The Victorious Life 831
    Section F: Mature Sons of God 853

Conclusion 861
Appendix A: Major Differences Charted 865
Appendix B: The Unholy Union with Western Philosophy 869
Bibliography 877
Other Books by Harold R. Eberle 883
On-line Bible College 888

Foreword

Let me set the context for this foreword with two very important and interrelated theological observations.

First, God is a God who reveals Himself and interacts with human beings in the times and seasons of His choice. The Bible says, *"Blessed be the name of God forever and ever, for wisdom and might are His. And He changes the times and the seasons . . ."* (Dan. 2:20-21). It goes on to say that God gives wisdom to the wise and knowledge to the understanding. Obviously, those to whom God gives this wisdom and knowledge would be those who recognize and embrace the new season which God brings. There would be no reason for God to release new revelation to those who choose to remain in the old season.

Secondly, the Holy Spirit continually speaks to the churches. Seven times in the Book of Revelation we read, *"He who has an ear, let him hear what the Spirit says to the churches"* (e.g., Rev. 2:7, 11, 17). It is well to note that "says" is in the present tense. This admonition does not refer to hearing what the Spirit said (past tense) to the churches, but rather what He is now saying to the churches. I am not in the least diminishing the importance of understanding what the Spirit has already said, beginning with the Old Testament and the New Testament, which we regard as the authoritative Word of God. Unfortunately, however, some church leaders today have decided that when the Holy Spirit finished inspiring the written Word of God, He no longer revealed new things to the churches. His activities ever since, according to them, have been concerned simply with illuminating for the people of God what He already has said.

My friend, Harold Eberle, is one who is thoroughly rooted in the Scriptures, but who also has ears to hear what the Spirit is now saying to the churches in this new season. Among other things, he believes that

Systematic Theology for the New Apostolic Reformation

God has raised up prophets to be special recipients of God's word for new seasons such as this one. To go back to Daniel 2 for a moment, it says that God *"reveals deep and secret things"* (Dan. 2:22). This brings to mind Amos 3:7, *"Surely the Lord God does nothing, unless He reveals His secret to His servants, the prophets."* Lest anyone might think that prophets are exclusively an Old Testament phenomenon, we also need to keep in mind that the New Testament clearly says, *"And God has appointed these in the church: first apostles, second prophets . . ."* (1 Cor. 12:28).

Only with this as a background would Eberle undertake the formidable task of writing a systematic theology for the New Apostolic Reformation (NAR). "New Apostolic Reformation" is simply a label meant to describe the new season of God in which the churches currently find themselves. "Systematic theology" reflects a tradition carried on by thinkers throughout every century of Christian history. We think of famous systematic theologians such as Tertullian and Saint Augustine and Thomas Aquinas. More familiar to us in the Protestant tradition would be Martin Luther and John Calvin and John Wesley. Innumerable theologies have been written elaborating on the Protestant Reformation. Harold Eberle is fully aware of them, and he holds firmly to basic Reformation principles such as the authority of Scripture, justification by faith, and the priesthood of all believers. However, we must keep in mind that the Protestant Reformation was one of God's former seasons, albeit an extremely important one. We are now in a new season, God has continued to speak, and consequently we need new systematic theologies. While Eberle's is one of the first written for the New Apostolic Reformation, it certainly will not be the last.

Theology

At this point, I would like to raise a crucial question: What, exactly, is "theology"?

Admitting that there are many respectable answers to this question, I would like to offer mine. Theology is a human attempt to describe God's Word and God's works in a reasonable and systematic way.

Look at that phrase, "a human attempt." Theologians of integrity freely admit that there is an essential difference between their writings and the inspired word of God, the Holy Scriptures. The Scriptures, in their intended meaning, cannot be contradicted. However, systematic theologies, since

Foreword

they are "human attempts" not only can, but inevitably will, be contradicted. By nature, they are bound to stimulate discussion and debate. Some of their critics will be highly intelligent and deeply devoted Christian leaders. In fact, it is not unheard of that certain criticisms will be so well-taken that the theologians themselves will modify their views.

If I were so inclined, I believe that I could find some things in every systematic theology with which I am acquainted that I could intelligently criticize. This applies to the systematic theology that you now hold in your hands. I am well aware of the inherent danger of penning a foreword for a systemic theology like this one. It would be easy for uninformed readers to assume that because I am doing the foreword, I agree with every one of Harold Eberle's conclusions. This would be a wrong assumption. I am serving notice that I do not agree with every theological nuance in this book. But what I do affirm is Harold Eberle's right and responsibility to make his best "human attempt" to interpret what the Spirit is saying to the churches in the season of the New Apostolic Reformation. I also affirm that Eberle, through the years, has proven to be one of the most astute theological thinkers of our generation. I am certainly not alone in agreeing that Eberle's theology is respectable and worthy of careful consideration.

History

Now let's offer a bit of historical perspective.

I have been using the term "New Apostolic Reformation" (NAR). Where did it come from?

One of the most distinctive characteristics of the NAR is apostolic government. Jesus began this process by labeling the chief leaders among His disciples "apostles" (see Luke 6:13). The Book of Acts tells us that Jesus, at His ascension, *"gave some to be apostles, some prophets, some evangelists, and some pastors and teachers"* (Eph. 4:11). Then, as I mentioned before, a divine order is revealed when we read: *"God has appointed these in the church: first apostles, second prophets, third teachers . . ."* (1 Cor. 12:28). For two or three hundred years after Jesus left, the church functioned with this form of government. Then, for reasons that I do not need to delineate at this point, church government became more bureaucratic and legalistic. This was characteristic of Christianity, both Catholic and Protestant, for 1700 or 1800 years.

Systematic Theology for the New Apostolic Reformation

From this point on I will concentrate on the Protestant stream. Both before and after the Protestant Reformation, Christianity for the most part, particularly in the Western world, had taken the form of state churches. This means that governments of nations would decide what the religion of the citizens of that nation would be. If you were born in Switzerland, for example, you were expected to be Reformed. If you were Spanish, you were Catholic. Citizens of Sweden were Lutheran, citizens of England were Anglicans, and so on. Then, denominational government, with which most of us are familiar today, didn't begin until the 1700s when Protestant Europeans settled America and soon discovered that the new nation they were forming refused to establish a state church, while respecting the exercise of the differing religions of its citizens. Eventually those branches of Protestantism began to be called "denominations."

Soon afterward, in the early 1800s, the modern missionary movement saw church-planting missionaries from Europe and America launched into many of the non-Christian nations of the world. Not surprisingly, these nations were unprepared to embrace state Christian churches, so the only option missionaries had was to gather their churches into denominations. Even so, Anglican churches planted in Nigeria looked very much like their counterparts in England. The same with German Lutheran churches in South Africa or American Congregational churches in China or Scottish Presbyterian churches in India.

And, more apropos to this book and to the NAR, none of these denominational churches, whether in America or in non-Christian nations, adopted biblical apostolic government. Consequently, denominational governments of whatever nature dominated world Protestantism for around 400 years. And this sets the historical stage for the emergence of the New Apostolic Reformation.

The New Apostolic Reformation

Two very significant developments for world Christianity took place around 1900. The first was the emergence of the African Independent Church Movement and the second was the Azusa Street Revival, bringing the birth of Pentecostalism.

The African Independent Church Movement was sparked when some second-generation African church leaders began to observe that the mission churches planted by Western missionaries of whatever denomination did not look and feel very African. The mission churches closely resembled

Foreword

churches in the Western nations that had sent the missionaries. Most of them, for example, even prohibited drums in their services. Some of these African leaders were bold enough to step outside the boundaries of traditional missionary Christianity and begin their own more culturally contextualized churches, complete with drums. The resulting African Independent Church Movement soon outgrew the mission churches, and today it dominates the sub-Saharan African religious scene. By and large, these vigorous independent churches intuitively took on biblical apostolic government. They were the precursors of the New Apostolic Reformation.

At about the same time, Pentecostalism began to take root in the United States. This clearly marked one of God's new seasons for the church. Its main distinguishing characteristic was its emphasis on the person and work of the Holy Spirit, both individually and corporately. Because it reinstated biblical practices such as baptism in the Holy Spirit, speaking in tongues, prophecy, supernatural signs and wonders, and the like, most traditional denominational leaders either ignored or actively opposed Pentecostalism, particularly during the first half of the 20th century.

Around 1970, an offshoot of this new season of Pentecostalism called the Independent Charismatic Movement emerged. Pentecostalism had, for the most part, retained traditional denominational structure and government. Some Pentecostal leaders found this too restrictive and even unbiblical, so they launched out and started independent churches, many of which adopted biblical apostolic government. A number of them even developed apostolic networks which became functional substitutes for denominations. They were also precursors of the New Apostolic Reformation.

Simultaneously, God was raising up two other significant manifestations of this new season. Without pausing for details I will simply mention the Chinese Rural House Church Movement and the Latin American Grassroots Church Movement. Like African Independent Churches and U.S. Independent Charismatics, a significant number of these new movements also chose to follow biblical apostolic principles. When taken together, an impressive number of innovative characteristics had appeared in all four of these movements and collectively they, and others following in their stream, comprise the pioneers of the New Apostolic Reformation.

This is the context for which Harold Eberle has provided his systematic theology.

Systematic Theology for the New Apostolic Reformation

Systematic Theologies

It would be worthwhile to note that systematic theologies for the Pentecostal Movement and the Charismatic Movement have been done as well. As would be expected, there have been many theologies written, but two of them, if I am not mistaken, have stood the test of time and become classics in their own right. One is Stanley Horton's *Systematic Theology: A Pentecostal Perspective* and the other is Rodman Williams' *Renewal Theology: Systematic Theology from a Charismatic Perspective*. Both of these books are excellent representatives of their respective movements. I applaud both of them for their thoroughness, their documentation, and their clarity of thought. However, as I said earlier, all theology is a "human attempt," and it would be predictable that a later theology such as Eberle's might disagree with them from time to time. I have not attempted to count the number of these differences, but I would like to highlight two which for me personally are particularly significant.

Initial physical evidence. I admire Harold Eberle's courage in breaking from the well-entrenched Pentecostal-Charismatic view that the initial physical evidence of being baptized in the Holy Spirit is speaking in tongues. Simply put, if you have ever spoken in tongues you know that you have been baptized in the Holy Spirit, but if you have never spoken in tongues, you know that the baptism in the Spirit is something you should continue to seek. I imagine that almost everyone who reads this would know some tongues speakers who do not regularly exhibit the fruit of the Spirit, while others are characterized by the fruit of the Spirit who have never spoken in tongues. This calls into question the classical doctrine.

Open Theism. Most systematic theologies of the past assume that because God is omniscient and unchangeable, He has foreknowledge of everything that ever happens or will happen. This is not the place to fully argue the matter, but as you read on, Eberle will describe his point of view that God is sovereign enough to limit His own omniscience if and when He chooses to do so. That means He leaves the outcome of certain things up to human decisions, which helps to explain the numerous biblical references to God changing His mind. How important is this? In my opinion, it is the fifth most important doctrinal advance since Jesus' death and resurrection. The first four would be that Gentiles can be saved without circumcision, justification by faith, the use of means to save the heathen, and the Pentecostal view of the person and work of the Holy Spirit.

Foreword

A Gift of God

I believe that by now you will have caught some of my excitement in seeing this book released. It is a gift of God for this new season in the body of Christ. It will enable all of us to move toward fulfilling the mandate in Romans 12:2: *"be transformed by the renewing of your mind."* Agree or disagree, you will find this book stimulating reading. I speak for many when I say, "Thank you, Harold Eberle!"

C. Peter Wagner, Ph.D., Th.M.
V. P. and Ambassadorial Apostle of Global Spheres, Inc.
Chancellor Emeritus of the Wagner Leadership Institute

Preface

The systematic theology taught in these pages is called Father-Son theology because it is built on the foundational truth that we should see God as Father and ourselves as sons of God.

This work is written for the consideration of leaders with whom I fellowship. In particular, for those within the New Apostolic Reformation which is a current worldwide move of God in which leaders believe the orthodox Christian doctrines laid out in the Apostles' Creed, but also that the ministries of apostle and prophet are valid ministries in the modern Church. This movement is also known for its belief in the gifts of the Holy Spirit, including tongues, prophecy, and divine healing, as valid works of God today. Plus, leaders within the New Apostolic Reformation teach that Jesus was enthroned over God's Kingdom 2,000 years ago when He sat down at the right hand of God. Now Jesus desires to work with His people to establish His Kingdom throughout the whole earth.

Of course, other teachers have set out to write a systematic theology, but this one is unique in several ways. Most significantly, this one is built on:

1. An understanding of God as Father

2. A concept of God developed from the Bible as it is understood in the Hebraic/Judeo culture in which it was written

3. A biblical understanding of the spiritual and natural realms being fully integrated, rather than a dualistic[1] understanding that sees the spiritual world separate from the natural world

4. A relational understanding of God's involvement with this world rather than a legal understanding

---

[1] Here and throughout this book, I will be using the words "dualistic" and "dualism" in the most common sense, referring to a system consisting of two contrasting parts.

Systematic Theology for the New Apostolic Reformation

Building a systematic theology on these distinctives may sound harmless, but it is actually a challenge upon the dominant theological view of Western Christianity.

I will show how Western Christianity has been profoundly influenced by the ancient Greek philosophers. In particular, our modern concept of God has been influenced by Plato, Aristotle, and Plotinus,[2] primarily through the work of Augustine. The resulting concept of God is called the "Classical" view of God. It has been termed "Classical" because it developed during the period historians refer to as Classical antiquity, i.e., the period when the ancient Greek and Roman Empires ruled the region around the Mediterranean Sea. This view is also referred to as "Classical" because it has become the well-established standard throughout Western Christianity.

Throughout this book we will be contrasting the Classical view of God with a more biblical view of God. Identifying the differences is not the result of new discoveries. Many Christians have attempted to expose the errors that we will be discussing. Way back in the 16th century, the famous French mathematician, scientist, and philosopher, Blaise Pascal wrote:

> *God of Abraham, God of Isaac, God of Jacob, not of the philosophers and the intellectuals. The God of Jesus Christ.*[3]

After a night of deep encounter with God, Pascal sewed a note with these words into the liner of his coat, and always transferred the note when he changed clothes. Throughout Church history there have been other noted Christians who have shared in Pascal's disillusionment with the God of the philosophers and intellectuals.

Although others have tried to point out the related errors, little progress has been made in actually changing the historic Church. This is partly because the foundation of Western civilization was laid down by the ancient Greek philosophers. With Greek thought deeply embedded in Western civilization, extracting the thoughts related to God requires radical surgery.

Extracting those thoughts has also been difficult because Western Christianity has been married to Western philosophy for almost 2,000

---

2 It is possible that Plotinus was not Greek, even though he is considered a philosopher of late antiquity and he built on the foundation of Plato,
3 Blaise Pascal. *Oeuvres complètes*. (Paris: Seuil, 1960), p. 618; Pascal also wrote this in his celebrated *Pensées*.

Preface

years. The theologians and philosophers holding the positions of authority within institutions of higher learning have been unmoved in their views about God. As a result, the thoughts of the ancient Greek philosophers have been yoked with Christian thought to this day.

That yoking has yielded a form of godliness that denies the power inherent in biblical Christianity. This will become very evident in the body of this work. You will see how the form of Christianity that we have inherited in the Western world is distorted and hinders modern Christians from knowing God, experiencing His presence, and seeing His power.

In Volume I of this book, we will examine relevant Bible passages so readers can clearly see the difference between the Classical view of God and a more biblical view of God. Then, we will consider the logical implications in all of the major areas of Christian thought, including:

Vol. II	God's Involvement with this World
Vol. III	The Nature of Creation
Vol. IV	The Nature of Humanity
Vol. V	Evil, Sin, and Suffering
Vol. VI	Soteriology (Study of Salvation)
Vol. VII	Ecclesiology and Basilology (Study of the Church and Kingdom)
Vol. VIII	General Eschatology (Study of End Times)
Vol. IX	Personal Eschatology (What Happens to People After Death)
Vol. X	The Trinity and Christology
Vol. XI	Pneumatology (Study of the Holy Spirit)
Vol. XII	The Christian Life

Anyone who alters their view of God will find their understanding of all the subjects mentioned above shifting accordingly.

I have written books on almost all of the major areas of Christian thought mentioned above. Those books are used by Church leaders around the world. The systematic theology that you are about to read is a compilation of those studies, presented in an easy-to-understand, logical progression of thought.

Throughout this book, Father-Son theology will be contrasted with Classical theology. This is because some form of Classical theology is taught in most Bible colleges and seminaries in the Western world. As a result, Christians in the Western world have already been trained in Classical theology, whether or not they realize it. With Classical theology

Systematic Theology for the New Apostolic Reformation

as an already established standard, it will serve as a reference point with which we can contrast the view of Father-Son theology. It is also important in the sense of seeing what we are up against.

Asking you to consider the advantages of Father-Son theology over and against Classical theology is a significant request. It is actually calling for a revolution, something young zealots envision, while seasoned thinkers know that even incremental changes are difficult to achieve.

It took the Church 1,500 years to rid herself of the teaching of the Greek-Egyptian astronomer, Ptolemy, who taught that the sun revolved around Earth. It also took the Church 1,400 years to rid herself of the condemnation that Plato and Aristotle put on business and commerce.[4] Then the Church took 1,800 years to rid herself of Plato and Aristotle's thoughts justifying slavery. Even today the Roman Catholic Church has been unable to purge herself of the ancient understanding that natural pleasures should be shunned—a view that contributes to Roman Catholic asceticism, calling for vows of poverty and celibacy among some of their clergy. So it should not surprise us if the whole Church unknowingly clings too tightly to other ideas laid down by the ancient Greek forefathers of Western civilization.

Yet, almost every other field of human understanding has gone through a revolution in recent years. Of course, theology is different than all other fields of study in that experts in this field consider the thoughts of leaders who lived 500, 1000, and even 1,500 years ago as sanctioned by the historic Church. That makes change more difficult. Honoring the Church in its historical development is right and necessary, yet, that honor often results in a reverence that muffles voices calling for change. Hope remains in the fact that today Christians who are deeply in love with the Church are asking questions. They are aware that there are some fundamental changes that need to take place. Perhaps we are ready for a revolution. Yes, I am sure of it. *"A cloud as small as a man's hand is coming up from the sea"* (1 Kings 18:44).

---

[4] For more information on this, see my book entitled, *Compassionate Capitalism, a Judeo-Christian Ethic.*

Acknowledgments

It is impossible to name all of the people who have added their insights into this work and into my life. However, the following people deserve special mention.

One of the most gifted leaders I know is Pastor Dave Edler, who has shepherded my family for many years. Dr. C. Peter Wagner was an inspiration long before I met him personally. Now I consider Peter a spiritual father at a distance. Dr. Stan DeKoven has been a friend. I am grateful Stan allowed me to submit an earlier version of Father-Son theology for my doctoral thesis under his oversight. Anthony Delatorre has faithfully served as the administrator of my ministry and fully supported me with his heart. Rev. Bill Starr, D. Min., painstakingly edited these pages for errors and encouraged me when I thought this project would never get done. James Bryson is my copy editor, hardest critic, and strongest contributor. I am grateful that James does not allow me to leave any thought unfinished or poorly communicated. Jerry Denton is my final proofreader. Jerry is brilliant and I am so glad he stepped into my life. The entire staff of Bethel Church in Redding, California, have served as a beacon of light for me and the Church worldwide. I am grateful for all of these, but my wife, Linda, is my joy, my song, and the anchor of my heart.

Although each of these have added their suggestions and help, this does not mean they each agree with everything that I have written. Any errors in this book are my own responsibility, but I am deeply thankful for those who helped me see key issues in a clearer light.

Introduction

Welcome to Father-Son theology.

Theology refers to the study of God, but in the broader sense, theology includes the study of God's relations with this world and all of its implications. For many Christians, such as myself, theology has always been the most exciting and rewarding study.

One of the problems with learning theology is the communication gap between professional theologians and the average Christian who is simply hungry to understand God. But theology does not have to be difficult to understand. As Albert Einstein said, "You do not really understand something unless you can explain it to your grandmother." Of course, I have met some pretty sharp grandmothers, but this book has been written in simple language so all grandmothers can understand.

It also delves deep and progresses quickly enough to captivate the attention of those already studied in the field. It is written as a textbook which may be used for personal study or in a theology classroom. It defines theological terms (with new terms identified in **bold letters**) and introduces readers to the historic Church's major doctrines, along with biblical truths at the forefront of current Christian thought.

Systematic theology is meant to be a broad overview of all areas of Christian thought. This allows serious Bible students to step back and objectively see if what they have learned in different areas is logically consistent. For example, Christians are able to determine if what they believe about God's nature corresponds with their understanding of creation or if what they know about God's involvement with this world is logically consistent with their understanding of salvation. Believing that God is the source of all truth, Christians can affirm that all truths discovered in one area are consistent with truths held in another area.

Systematic Theology for the New Apostolic Reformation

This process provides an unshakable foundation for all future study, proclamation of the gospel, and teachings upon which people can build their lives. The systematic theology taught herein is a serious attempt to provide that unshakable foundation.

Systematic theology has always served as an anchor for the historic Church. Without moving that anchor there can be no major changes within Christianity. Different branches of Christianity have experienced revivals, but none of those have impacted society so as to produce lasting reformation. One of the primary reasons is because every revival has been on a leash held by leaders who are anchored in a specific systematic theology. Without those leaders changing their systematic theology, revivals will always be tethered and, therefore limited.

For lasting reformation of society the Church must pull the anchor and reposition herself. To develop Father-Son theology, we will be pulling up the Church's historic anchor in the Classical view of God and replanting it in the Hebraic-biblical concept of God. This will be fully explained in coming pages.

For now I want to give you a preview of Father-Son theology, but I cannot accomplish this using the same terminology that has been used in theology for hundreds of years. Readers familiar with theology may expect me to compare Father-Son theology to Calvinism, Arminianism, evangelicalism, liberalism, fundamentalism, or any number of other "isms," but simply using such terms forces our dialogue down the same rabbit trails that have been chased for hundreds of years. Rather than rehashing the same arguments, we need to think in new categories which will require different terminology. In this endeavor, allow me to give you a preview of Father-Son theology by comparing it to categories that are much more relevant and understandable to Christians in the modern world.

During 35+ years of ministry I have met thousands of ministers and taught in hundreds of churches of many different denominations. I have observed the strengths and weaknesses of various ways of thinking and theological perspectives. All of the churches at which I minister attempt to follow the teachings of the Bible, however, their views and theological perspectives vary widely. I can summarize the major views of different Christian groups into four distinct categories according to four different worldviews:

Introduction

1. Salvation worldview
2. Pentecostal/Charismatic worldview
3. Kingdom worldview
4. Father-Son worldview

Allow me to offer brief, generalized descriptions.

A church or a group of Christians who hold to the *Salvation worldview* build their understanding of the world starting with the fall of Adam and Eve. From there all of their theological thoughts flow. They see God's primary work in the world as fixing the problem of sin through the death of Jesus. All who accept Jesus as Savior are saved. The Christian's role is foremost to help other people get saved. The role of the Holy Spirit is to convict people of sin, helping to fulfill the goal of getting people saved and populating heaven.

Christians with the *Pentecostal/Charismatic worldview* start at the same point as those with the Salvation worldview—the fall of Adam and Eve. They see the death of Jesus as God's primary work in the world, but they also emphasize how Jesus poured out the Holy Spirit upon humanity. Therefore, people can be saved and baptized in the Holy Spirit.[5] The primary role of Christians is to help others get saved and be baptized in the Holy Spirit so they can be joyful, effective while on earth, and exercise the gifts of the Holy Spirit.[6] The primary role of the Holy Spirit is to give gifts to and empower Christians. The end goal is to populate heaven.

Christians with a *Kingdom worldview* start building their theological perspective with God's commission to Adam and Eve to fill and subdue the earth. From this starting point their thoughts flow. Of course, they see that Jesus died for the sins of humanity, but Jesus also resurrected from the grave, ascended into heaven, and sat down at the right hand of the throne of God. Each step was key in establishing the Kingdom of God. As Jesus rose from the dead, He conquered death. As He ascended into heaven, everything was placed under His feet. When Jesus sat down at the right hand of Father-God, He was given authority over everything in heaven and on earth. Of course, Christians who hold to the other worldviews believe that Jesus rose, ascended, and sat down at the right hand of God, but they do not see the significance of these events in establishing the Kingdom of God. The establishment of the Kingdom is key for churches with a Kingdom worldview because followers see themselves as not only

---

5 Baptism in the Holy Spirit is explained in XI:B.
6 The gifts of the Holy Spirit are discussed in XI:D, E, F, and G.

Systematic Theology for the New Apostolic Reformation

saved, but now enabled to fulfill the first commission to fill and subdue the earth. This gives *all* Christians a mission in the world to establish the will of King Jesus in whatever area of influence they are called. The role of the Holy Spirit is seen primarily as guiding and empowering Christians to share the gospel and establish the Kingdom on earth.

There is truth to be found in each of these worldviews, but most of my own work in churches is helping those with a Salvation or Pentecostal/Charismatic worldview embrace a Kingdom worldview. That is a significant change for most Christians today.

However, it is the *Father-Son worldview* that I believe is the most mature, biblically accurate worldview. The Father-Son worldview does not start building from the fall of Adam and Eve nor from God's commission to fill and subdue earth. It reaches back to God's original intention to have sons. Of course, it recognizes that God commissioned Adam and Eve and that they sinned. However, God's redemption plan is seen as a parenthesis in His overall plan to raise sons. Jesus not only resurrected, ascended, sat down at the right hand of God, and poured out the Holy Spirit, but He also established a new covenant in which all who believe in Him are swept into His victory. All believers are joined to Jesus, and then, forgiven and given a new heart and spirit. They are being transformed from glory to glory. Now the goal includes getting others saved, helping them receive the baptism in the Holy Spirit, and establishing the Kingdom of God on earth, but Father-Son theology envisions more than that. The ultimate goal is to raise sons for God, a Bride for Jesus, and a temple for the Spirit to indwell.

This work is not meant to be the final word on Father-Son theology. My hope is that many others will teach and write on this subject. I am sure others will see things from different perspectives and add their insights. Most importantly, I hope Father-Son theology will open a dialogue among Christian leaders who are determined to develop a more biblical, relational, relevant, powerful, and mature understanding of Christianity.

• • •

Readers familiar with theology will recognize some similarities between Father-Son theology and Open Theism. **Open Theism** is a theological perspective that recognizes God as having open relationships with people. By "open," adherents mean that God is open for the input

Introduction

of people, and therefore, some of the future is open, that is, some of the future will be formed as a result of cooperative relationships between God and humanity.

I am grateful to the Open theists[7] who in recent years have battled to introduce the related concepts to the Church. I am convinced that Open Theism offers a more biblically accurate view of God than Classical theology does, i.e., I agree with Open theists about the relational aspect of God's nature. Yet, this book is not limited to that perspective. The primary focus of this book is that God is not only relational, but interactive with Christians as a Father with His sons.

• • •

Father-Son theology is not a variation of Arminianism.

Christians trained in Calvinism tend to label any theological view that questions God's divine predestination of all things as Arminianism. Hence, adherents of Father-Son theology may be accused of being Arminian, but that is far from the truth. Arminian theology developed in the late 16th century as leaders began pointing out biblical concepts that they saw as inconsistent with Calvinism. As a consequence, Arminianism was reactionary to Calvinism, yet it was still built on the same Classical view of God upon which Calvinism was built.

Father-Son theology is not built on the Classical view of God. It goes all the way back to the foundation laid in the first three centuries of the Church. Father-Son theology develops a concept of God directly from the biblical revelation, then it follows the implications through every major area of Christian thought.

• • •

Some readers may react negatively to the title, "Father-Son theology." Using male terminology (Father-Son) may cause concern for those who long for a gender-neutral theology. I recognize the gender bias that can result, but the term *Father* is not a culturally conditioned term. It is a proper name for God given by divine revelation (Matt. 6:9). It is fundamental to our understanding of the Trinity, and Jesus instructs His followers to call God, "Father."

---

[7] Some modern adherents and authors of Open Theism include Clark Pinnock, Greg Boyd, Richard Rice, John Sanders, and Paul Fiddes.

Systematic Theology for the New Apostolic Reformation

Within Father-Son theology, the term *Son* must be understood as male when speaking of Jesus Christ, who is the only begotten Son of God. However, son(s) should be understood as without gender when speaking of all children of God.

• • •

Several of my friends who are Bible scholars/teachers read through earlier versions of this book, and I appreciate all of their suggestions and comments. One of my friends suggested that I may be too passionate about ridding Christianity of the influence of the ancient Greek philosophers, Plato, Aristotle, and Plotinus. My friend is probably correct. I am determined to incinerate the residue of those philosophers and then blow away the dust!

• • •

The contents of this book are divided into the following three categories:

    Volume
      Section
        Point

When referencing any passage in this book, I will offer a Roman numeral to refer to the number of the volume, followed by a capital letter referring to the section, and an Arabic numeral to reference the point. For example, X:B:56 refers to Volume 10, Section B, and point number 56.

When I reference certain passages of this book in footnotes, I am not suggesting that readers should read all of those referenced passages. They are simply being noted for readers who need more clarification concerning the topic being discussed.

• • •

The Old and New Testaments will be referenced as OT and NT respectively.

Prolegomenon

Traditionally, a systematic theology starts with a **prolegomenon**. A prolegomenon for a systematic theology offers an explanation concerning the basis for determining truth. Father-Son theology builds on the truths revealed in the OT and NT.

Often the prolegomenon is the longest portion of a systematic theology because the basis of truth should determine all of the conclusions throughout the entire systematic theology. However, I am not going to offer a lengthy prolegomenon. I have chosen to simply offer a brief description concerning how I value the Bible along with an explanation of the Bible's progressive revelation.

I have accepted the apostle Paul's evaluation that *"all Scripture is inspired by God . . ."* (2 Tim. 3:16). Although Paul probably had the Hebrew Scripture (OT) in mind when he wrote this, I accept the view of the historic Church that both the OT and NT are inspired by God. *Inspired* literally means "breathed upon," and in the context of Scripture we are saying that God inspired the original writers to write what they wrote.

God's inspiration gives the Scripture divine authority.

However, I find that people who accept the inspiration of Scripture, as I do, often miss the value inherent in the Scripture simply because of its human authorship. In the Holy Book we have over a thousand years of documentation concerning God's interactions with this world, along with the thoughts of various individuals and their understanding of the ways of God. Contributing to those thoughts are some of the most influential people in history, such as Abraham, Moses, Elijah, David, Solomon, Isaiah, Daniel, Matthew, Mark, Luke, John, Peter, and Paul.

Please do not misunderstand what I am saying here. Christians value the Scripture above all else because of God's inspiration. However, even

Systematic Theology for the New Apostolic Reformation

without that inspiration, the collection of writings that we know as the Bible are also invaluable because of the historic figures who contributed to those writings. If we had a similar collection of the writings of other great historical leaders—such as Julius Caesar, Napoleon Bonaparte, Mahatma Gandhi, George Washington, Winston Churchill, and so forth—each explaining their understanding of God and how He influenced them, that collection would be priceless. It would be studied and dissected by scholars around the world.

The Bible is such a collection. Yet, Christians recognize that all of the authors of the Bible wrote about the one true God. Those authors did not disagree or argue with one another concerning who that One God is. They recorded how and what God communicated with them. They wrote of their experiences with God and testified to miracles that they accredited to the One God. The consistency is astounding when we realize that about 40 authors over the course of 1,500 years contributed to the Bible.

Their understanding of God has been preserved and passed on to us so successfully that today it is the Book in more homes and hearts than any other book.

The Bible is also the Book that records the actions and words of Jesus Christ, who has the largest following of any leader in human history.[8] This is the Jesus with whom millions have fallen in love. What we know about Him is written on those Holy Pages.[9]

We also value the Bible because it is the foundation for Christianity. Paul explained that the Church is built on the foundation of the apostles and prophets, with Jesus Christ as the cornerstone (Eph. 2:20). If, indeed, we want to keep the Church firmly established upon that foundation, we must pay close attention to the writings of the apostles. The writings we have today of Jesus' original apostles are in the NT.[10]

Still, the Bible has been challenged more than any other book. Scholars have torn it to pieces, professors have ridiculed it, leaders have banned it, and revolutionaries have burned it. Perhaps the greatest challenges in recent history come from those who say the Holy Book is filled with human errors.

---

8 Some may disagree with this point, claiming instead that Abraham has the largest following since he is considered a forefather of Christianity, Judaism, and Islam. Indeed, Abraham is the forefather of a greater number, but people do not follow Abraham in the sense of listening to and following his teachings.

9 This statement is not meant to negate the personal revelation of Jesus to individuals and throughout history.

10 Of course, in making this statement I am agreeing with the historic Church concerning which books belong in the canon of Scripture.

Prolegomenon

Karl Barth, the late Swiss Reformed theologian, dismissed all such criticism by simply glorying in the fact that God can speak through the Bible even if its human authors were inept. God has been speaking to people through those Holy Pages for generations, and He continues to speak today.

However, our use of the Bible deserves more than a simple dismissal of the critics' talk. Evangelical[11] teachers typically categorize their evaluation and use of the Bible under one of two headings: **inerrant** or **infallible**. If we say the Bible is **inerrant**, we are saying that it is without any errors, including scientific and historical accuracy. Many teachers will qualify their belief in inerrancy, saying the manuscripts written by the original human authors were without error, but the scribes who recopied the manuscripts time and again may have made some errors. Teachers who point this out, may still hold to inerrancy, but they are applying the term to the original manuscripts, called the **autographs**.

If we say the Bible is **infallible**, we are saying that it is accurate in matters pertaining to Christian faith and living. In other words, teachers who say the Bible is infallible do not necessarily take the Bible as literally as those who hold to the inerrancy of the Bible, but they believe there are no errors on subjects related to Christian doctrine.

At this point, I will set a pattern that will be used several times in this book by *not* identifying this work with inerrancy or infallibility. The reason is because those terms come out of Western thought rather than Hebraic thought. This will be fully discussed later,[12] but for now we can say that Hebraic thought is foundational to the worldview in which the Bible was written.

Instead of identifying my use of the Bible with either inerrancy or infallibility, I will use terminology that has recently become popular among Bible teachers who hold to the validity of the Scriptures. I take the Bible **seriously**. Using this terminology gets right to the appropriation of the Book we claim to believe. If we take the Bible seriously, then we must value it as authoritative and apply it to our own lives.

It is important not only to note the value I place upon Scripture, but also to acknowledge Scripture's **progressive revelation**. By this I am acknowledging that all sections of the Bible are inspired by God, however,

---

11 The word *evangelical* means different things in different parts of the world. Here I am referring to Christians who believe the Bible is inspired by God and, therefore, believe that a person must be born again to be saved.
12 Discussed in I:H:69.

Systematic Theology for the New Apostolic Reformation

the sections that were written later offer fuller revelation compared to earlier sections. For this reason the NT should be used to better understand and interpret the OT. The fullest revelation that we have of God is in Jesus Christ.

This progressive understanding has become especially significant at this time because of current debates about the nature of God. In particular, there are many Christian teachers (some who are part of the present grace movement and some who are pacifists associated with Anabaptists) who want to present God as having no judgment in His heart, and therefore, they want to develop their understanding of God independently of those OT passages that portray God as violent and judgmental. They focus on passages such as 1 John 4:8 which tells us that *"God is love."* In contrast, there are other Christian teachers who hold to the wrath of God as a central characteristic in their understanding of God. Indeed, this is a problem that must be addressed.

Today Christians who want to focus only on the love of God sometimes accuse the teachers who emphasize God's wrath as reading the Bible as "flat." By **flat**, they mean the Bible is like a flat plane with all revelation on the same level of authority. In contrast to flat, a teacher may think of the NT as **elevated** above the OT in the sense of being of higher authority and significance.

In reality, no mature Christian actually reads the Bible as completely flat. Christians who know the Bible agree that Jesus Christ is the fullest revelation of God and that truths such as the gospel are more clearly revealed in the NT. However, different Christians do value the OT revelation differently. Rather than accuse anyone of reading the Bible as flat, it is more accurate to acknowledge that Christians are spread across the spectrum concerning how they value the OT with respect to the NT. At one end of the spectrum are those who see God as the violent destroyer who is found in some passages of the OT. At the other end of the spectrum are those who elevate the revelation of God in Jesus to the exclusion of God as He is revealed in the OT.

In Father-Son theology, the God of the OT is the God of the NT. However, Jesus is the clearest, most perfect revelation of Father-God. Those who have come to believe in Jesus can understand this. They have become children of God and are learning to see God as Father.

To understand this perspective, it is helpful to envision a human father who has a family with several children. This father loves and dotes

Prolegomenon

over his children. At the same time, this father is a soldier in the army. This father never talks to his children about his work as a soldier, and they have never seen him on the battlefield. The only father they know is the one who loves and cares for them. Comparatively, we can say that God is Father. All who accept His Son come to know God as their Father. We wish all people knew Him this way.

In comparing God to this soldier/father, I am implying that God reveals Himself differently at different times and to different people. However, God does not change in nature. The God of the OT is the God of the NT. Furthermore, the revelation of God as love does not eliminate His revelation as a consuming fire. He is the one and only God. We want the world to know that God is a consuming fire, but anyone can experience His fatherly love if they approach Him through Jesus.

I pray that the discussions to follow will reveal God as Father. I trust that you will see more clearly your own identity as a child of God.

In the pages that follow, I will endeavor to take the truths revealed in the Bible and show you new vantage points from which you can examine them. I want to separate the truth of Scripture from wrong interpretations that we Western Christians have embraced because of the cultural biases that we share. It is not my intent to communicate anything beyond what was written by the human authors whom God inspired. I simply want to show you what they intended when they wrote what they wrote. I will be offering my best attempt to say what the Bible says and emphasize what the Bible emphasizes.

I also hope I can impart my love for the Scriptures. I not only take the Scriptures seriously, but I have given my life to understanding and communicating the truths revealed therein. Of course, your interest in reading this book reveals that you too are a lover of God's Word. I pray that our shared love will yield a clearer understanding of our Father who is the Author of those Words.

Volume I
The Nature of God

Our beginning point determines our ending point. With systematic theology the beginning point is God (assuming we have already established that our source of truth is the Bible). How we understand God determines everything that we understand about His interactions with this world. Therefore, the foundation laid in this volume will influence all of the subjects addressed in the rest of this book.

In Volume I, Section A, we will determine what was in God's heart—His intentions and plans—*before* He created the world. This will provide us with a cornerstone for Father-Son theology. Then we will develop a biblical view of God by examining relevant Bible passages.

Acknowledging the progressive revelation of God in the Scriptures, we will start with Genesis. Then we will build one truth upon another as God is revealed in the Holy Pages. We will break our biblical study of the nature of God into four sections:

> Section B: God of Creation
> Section C: God of Abraham
> Section D: God of the Old Testament
> Section E: God of Jesus

The compilation of our study of these areas will provide us with a solid foundation for Father-Son theology.

After laying that foundation, I will explain the God of Classical theology. I will begin by discussing how the ancient Greek philosophers developed their concept of god. Then we will discover how some of the

Systematic Theology for the New Apostolic Reformation

thoughts of the ancient philosophers were incorporated into early Christianity. After that I will explain how the Classical view of God is contrary to the biblical revelation. We will finish this first volume by discussing the importance of building our theology upon the biblical view of God. These discussions will be broken into the following sections:

> Section F: God of the Greek Philosophers
> Section G: God of Classical Theology
> Section H: Two Views in Conflict
> Section I: Building on the Biblical View of God

Only after these foundations have been laid will we be able to go on in Volumes II through XII to build Father-Son theology. I am confident that you will see how one's concept of God determines one's theology. The Classical view of God leads to Classical theology, and the biblical view of God leads to Father-Son theology.

> Classical View of God ⟶ Classical Theology
> Biblical View of God ⟶ Father-Son theology

Section A
The Cornerstone of Father-Son Theology

What do we know about God's existence before creation? Was He peaceful and happy? Was He creating other worlds or stoically positioned in a realm of nothingness? Was He planning for the future or thinking about us? We like to envision God with the best of everything, in a state of perfection—whatever that is. However, the Bible reveals very little about God's conditions or state before Genesis 1:1.

Many Church leaders have warned of the futility of conjecturing about this subject. Augustine, Luther, and Calvin each made reference to a well-known statement whose origin is unknown: "God was preparing hell for those who pry too deep." What was He doing? We do not know. In what state did He exist? We don't know.

Although little is revealed in the Bible about this subject, what is revealed has profound implications upon all of systematic theology.

Point 1: God Determined to Have Sons

Paul wrote about God's existence before creation, describing God's intentions, heart, and plans:

> ... He chose us in Him before the foundation of the world, that we should be holy and blameless before Him. In love He predestined us to adoption as sons through Jesus Christ to Himself....
> (Eph. 1:4-5)

God foreordained that He would have sons (I will use this term without reference to gender). His foreordination was done "in love." God foreordained

Systematic Theology for the New Apostolic Reformation

that His sons will be holy and blameless before Him. He foreordained that this would be accomplished through Jesus Christ.

<u>God's Intentions</u>
1. To have sons
2. Motivated by love
3. His sons will be holy and blameless
4. To accomplish this through Jesus

Before we complete this study, we will see the outcome of God's creation, which will be sons who are holy and blameless. *God started as a loving Father determined to have sons, and He will finish as a loving Father with sons.* This is the cornerstone for Father-Son theology.[13]

<u>Cornerstone for Father-Son Theology</u>
God determined in love to have sons.

Some readers may want to challenge this as the cornerstone because Paul wrote that Jesus is the cornerstone of the Church. Indeed, when we discuss the Church in Volume VII, we will see that Jesus is the reference point for all that is built and accomplished in the Church, but here we are establishing the reference point for all of creation and the work of God throughout history. That reference point is the heart of God—His heart to have sons.

Point 2: The Cornerstone of Classical Theology

Classical theology has a different cornerstone than Father-Son theology does. It is founded on the idea that God is timeless. **Timeless** means that there is nothing related to time in the nature of God. Further, He exists outside of time.

<u>The Cornerstone for Classical Theology</u>
God is timeless.

---

13 Books offering similar views include: C. Baxter Kruger, *God Is For Us* (Jackson, MS: Perichoresis Press, 2000); and DeVern Fromke, *Ultimate Intention* (Shoals, IN: Sure Foundation, 1963).

The Cornerstone of Father-Son Theology

As we continue, we will see that most of the attributes assigned to God by Classical theologians are determined from this attribute of timelessness. Like a cornerstone in a building under construction, timelessness is the reference point for understanding who God is in Classical theology.

In Section F, we will study how the concept of timelessness originated with the ancient Greek philosophers, most prominently Plato and Aristotle. We do not need to reject the concept of timelessness simply because it had a non-Christian origin, but we must study the Scriptures to see if, indeed, it is a biblical concept.

Well-known theologians in history, such as Augustine, Anselm, Aquinas, Luther, and Calvin, took the biblical references that God is "eternal" (*aiónios*, in Greek) to mean that God is timeless. Yet the Greek word *aión* is a noun meaning an "age," "era," or "dispensation of time." The corresponding adjective, *aiónios*, means "age-long." The words *aión* and *aiónios* carry no indication concerning how long the age is. The reader or translator has to decide how long any one age is. For example, Paul wrote about Jesus:

> ... who gave Himself for our sins so that He might rescue us from this present evil age [aiónios] ....
>
> (Gal. 1:4)

Here Paul used the Greek word *aiónios* to refer to the age in which he was living. Obviously, this is not referring to a timeless age.

In coming pages we will discuss more about God's nature as it is related to time, but for now we can say that an increasing number of theologians and philosophers have been arguing that God does not live in a timeless age or state. He is **temporal**, meaning He exists in time.[14] Theologians and philosophers have been unable to settle this issue because no one knows for sure. The Bible does not tell us if God is timeless. As the Bible scholar Oscar Cullmann wrote:

> ... the New Testament never speculates about God's eternal being, and since it is concerned primarily with God's redemptive activity, it does not make a philosophical, qualitative distinction between time and eternity.[15]

---

14 For an excellent book offering four views of God's relations to time, see: Gregory E. Ganssle, ed., *God and Time* (Downers Grove, IL: Inter Varsity Press, 2001).
15 Oscar Cullmann, *Christ and Time* (Philadelphia: The Westminster Press: 1964), p. 10-11.

Systematic Theology for the New Apostolic Reformation

God is definitely eternal in the sense that He always existed and always will exist. However, any Bible scholar, theologian, or philosopher who is honest will admit that it cannot be proven scripturally nor philosophically that God is timeless. That is only an assumption.

Point 3: No More Time?

Many Christians have searched the Bible to find evidence of a timeless world in which God dwells. An often quoted verse is Revelation 10:6, where the KJV says that *"there should be time no longer."* From this verse, some Christians have concluded that there is a world where time does not exist.

In reality, no one familiar with the biblical languages would come to that conclusion. Any serious study reveals that Revelation 10:6 is speaking of impending destruction. The writer was warning about the destruction described in the Book of Revelation that was about to be released.

We can make a comparative use of the phrase "no more time" by talking about Noah's flood. When the rains began to fall, Noah could have said to his family to get into the boat because there was no more time. By saying, this, Noah would not have been announcing the end of time. He was simply saying that there would be no more time until the flood came.

Similarly in Revelation 10:6, we read about an angel who was specifically telling John about a time at which judgment would be released. Recognizing this, many translations, such as the NASV, translate the meaning of this verse more clearly by saying *"there will be no more delay."* To confirm this understanding, we can look at Hebrews 10:37, where similar terminology is used. The point is that Revelation 10:6 is *not* saying that there will be an age when time does not exist.

There is no verse in the Bible that talks about a timeless world. Nor is there any verse that states or implies that God is timeless.

Point 4: Building on the Correct Cornerstone

Please note that I am not saying that God is not timeless. I am merely saying that we do not know. The Bible does not reveal this. Before God created this world, He may have existed in an age that was timeless. Even now He may exist outside of time, but it is also possible that He exists

The Cornerstone of Father-Son Theology

in His own dimension of time. He may exist in an age with cyclic time. He may transcend time.[16] He may contain time. He may be above time. He may exist in some dimension of time that we do not understand. We simply do not know. No one knows.

Admitting that we do not know is the first step to learning.

For 1,500 years most Church leaders "knew" that the sun revolved around Earth. Martin Luther boldly argued for the geocentric universe, and he tried to prove it by quoting Joshua 10:13, where we are told that *"the sun stood still,"* which implies that the sun normally moves.[17] John Calvin also "knew" that the sun revolved around Earth,[18] and to prove it, he quoted Psalm 93:1b: *"Indeed, the world is firmly established, it will not be moved."* Clinging to these thoughts, Luther and Calvin were unable to seriously consider any alternative view.

The same principle applies to our understanding of God's nature. So long as people "know" that God is timeless, they will have difficulty seriously considering any other possibilities. So admitting that one does not know God's existence in relation to time is the starting point for learning about this subject.

Readers familiar with theology know that removing the cornerstone of timelessness completely undermines Classical theology. Timelessness is an assumption that Classical theology needs. Therefore, Christians committed to Classical theology may want to stop reading here. I know it is difficult to abandon ideas that are seated at the foundation of one's thought processes. So I understand how readers may struggle to let go of the assumption that God is timeless.

Let me compare it to another idea deeply seated in some branches of Christianity where I have found Christians struggling to let go. Many times I have taught in church settings about eschatology (one's understanding of end times). I have a victorious eschatology, and I do not envision an Antichrist playing a major role in the future as some Christians do. Hence, some Christians who listen to me teach on this subject get defensive. Some have even thought that I am "taking away their Antichrist." Of course, no one can take away anyone's Antichrist. What they are really sensing is that a pillar in their thoughts is being shaken and it is not easy to rethink all of

---

16 Transcending time is different than being timeless. This is explained in III:F:168.
17 This is from the record of Luther's dinner-table conversations, entitled, *Tablebook (Tischreden).*
18 John Calvin. *Commentary on the Book of Psalms,* vol. IV, (Grand Rapids, MI: Eerdmans Pub., 1949), p. 5f.

Systematic Theology for the New Apostolic Reformation

the implications. It is not "their Antichrist" that they want, but their sense of security in their present understanding.

For those who are adventurous truth-seekers, you are about to see how one's concept of God being timeless or temporal leads to specific implications. After you see those implications you will be able to make an informed decision concerning God's nature relative to time. This is true because an idea is true if the implications of that idea are true. Likewise an idea is false if the implications of that idea are false. Anytime you are eager to see the implications of God's nature related to time, you can jump ahead to the end of this book and find Appendix A, where a chart succinctly outlines the implications that are thoroughly developed throughout the body of this book.

For now we are going to set aside the Classical cornerstone of timelessness. We have another cornerstone upon which we can build. As the apostle Paul explained, God determined to have sons who will be holy and blameless before Him. This is not an assumption. The Bible clearly tells us that God determined to have sons and to accomplish this through Jesus Christ. These intentions of God came out of His love. This is the cornerstone for Father-Son theology. Let's build on it.

Section B
God of Creation

Now we can proceed to develop our concept of God from the Bible. In this section we will study His revelation in Genesis chapters 1 through 9, from creation through Noah's flood. We may add supporting truths from other Bible passages, but we will follow the progression of thought as Genesis presents it to us.

Since we are now laying the foundation, we must be careful to cling to the biblical revelation. If our foundation is solid, then our systematic theology will be solid. If our foundation is consistent with the Bible, then Father-Son theology will be consistent with the Bible. So let's be careful students of the Word.

Point 5: God, the Creator, Is Elohim

Genesis 1:1 tells us:

In the beginning God created the heavens and the earth.
(Gen. 1:1)

This reveals that God is the Creator.

In this verse, the word *God* has been translated from the Hebrew word *Elohim*. This Hebrew word is used over 2,500 times in the OT, and it can refer to deities (plural) or God (singular). When it is used to refer to deities, the verb following *Elohim* is plural. In Genesis 1:1, the verb *created* is singular so *Elohim* has been translated as God.

Systematic Theology for the New Apostolic Reformation

When some Bible teachers read Genesis 1:1, they emphasize the fact that *Elohim* is plural and then suggest that this is hinting at the Christian view of three Persons in one God. Indeed, there may be a hint of that truth, but there is not enough in this one word to develop that doctrine. In Volume X, we will be affirming the Christian belief in the Trinity.

It is worth noting again that God is eternal in the sense that He always existed and He will always exist (e.g., Rev. 1:8 ; Ps. 90:2 ; 1 Tim. 1:17). God may have existed in some timeless age before creation. He may exist in some timeless realm outside of creation even now. However, the Bible does not tell us. We don't know. What we do know from the Bible is that God created the heavens and earth.

God Created the Heavens and Earth

Timeless? **GOD** **Timeless?**

Creation

We can further deduce from Genesis 1:1 that God is powerful. He created the universe with His spoken Word and destroyed humanity (except Noah and his family) with a flood. God's power is an aspect of His nature which is prominent throughout Scripture.

God of Creation

Point 6: A Spiritual Realm that Is Part of Creation

God created the *heavens*. Notice that the word *heavens* is plural. God created the natural heaven that we see when we look up into the sky (including the clouds, planets, and stars). He also created a heavenly realm that is spiritual. Among other things, angels and demons exist in that spiritual realm. Paul explained:

> *For by Him all things were created, both in the heavens and on earth, visible and invisible, whether thrones or dominions or rulers or authorities....*
>
> (Col. 1:16)

We will discuss these invisible rulers and authorities later, but for now it is important to note that there is a spiritual heaven that is part of creation.

Although it is impossible to accurately diagram the relationship between the spiritual and natural realms, it is helpful to envision the spiritual realm hidden behind the natural realm. God created both and both are part of creation.

The Natural Realm Superimposed upon the Spiritual Realm

GOD

Spiritual Realm

Natural Realm

Systematic Theology for the New Apostolic Reformation

The spiritual realm that is part of creation is governed by space and time. We can know this by seeing how created beings within the spiritual realm act and interact. Consider how the angels move around. If there were no space limitations in the spiritual realm where they exist, then those angels would be omnipresent. If there were no time limitations, then it would be impossible for angels to be in one location one minute and a different location a minute later. If the spiritual realm that is within creation was timeless, there could be no before and after.

Consider Satan. He is not omnipresent. We also know that he is limited in space and time, because one day in the future Satan will be cast into the Lake of Fire. If there were no time limitations in the spiritual realm in which he exists, then Satan who is a created spiritual being could never be confined in hell. He would just move into another time and place. By examining how spiritual beings act within the spiritual realm, we can see how the spiritual realm in which angels and demons exist is governed by space and time.

Seeing the spiritual realm behind the natural realm is helpful, but some people may conclude that there is distance between the two realms. In reality, they fill the same space, so we should envision them together.

THE SPIRITUAL AND NATURAL REALMS FILL THE SAME SPACE

GOD

God of Creation

Point 7: God's Spirit Is Temporal within Creation

The second verse in the Bible tells us:

> ... *the Spirit of God was moving over the surface of the waters.*
> (Gen. 1:2)

This reveals an aspect of God called "the Spirit," and that Spirit can move through space. The Hebrew word translated as "moving" can also be translated as "hovering" or "brooding," offering us an image much like a hen brooding over her eggs.

To the careful student, this reveals a world of information that influences all areas of theology. This is true because Genesis 1:2 is the first mention of God's existence *within creation*. And what do we learn from this verse? God, at least through His Spirit, entered into creation.

GOD'S SPIRIT ENTERED CREATION

Systematic Theology for the New Apostolic Reformation

God's Spirit not only entered creation, but we also see that His Spirit has the ability to be in a certain location in relation to earth. Plus, God's Spirit can move about and hover over specific aspects of His creation. This idea of God's Spirit being in a certain location at a certain time can be identified in numerous Bible passages. For example, Jesus ascended into heaven and poured out the Spirit upon humanity (Acts 2:33). There are also several passages in the OT and NT where we see the Spirit of God coming upon certain individuals.

This truth is extremely important in theology. This is because the Holy Spirit could never occupy a certain location at a certain time if it was timeless within creation. To see this, imagine a timeless Spirit entering into this world. If, indeed, the Spirit was timeless, then He would instantly flood the past, present, and future. If the Spirit was timeless, He could never be limited in time or space. Since the Bible reveals the Spirit at certain locations at certain times, we must conclude that God's Spirit is *temporal within creation*.

Notice that we are not saying anything about the Spirit's existence *outside of creation*. As we have noted, the Bible does not tell us in what state God existed or exists outside of creation. However, within creation the Bible reveals God's Spirit as entering into space and time.

Point 8: God Himself Entered into Creation

Not only God's Spirit, but God entered into creation. God spoke through Jeremiah:

> *Do I not fill the heavens and the earth?*
>
> (Jer. 23:24)

So in what form did God enter creation? John 4:24 tells us that God is spirit, so His existence within creation is not in physical form. Of course, there are some passages in the Bible where we see God manifesting in physical form (Gen. 32:28-30), however, on a continual basis God's existence within creation is in spiritual form. He entered *into* and *fills* creation.[19]

---

[19] It is possible that the terminology "entered into creation" is wrong, because God may have existed in creation from the beginning, rather than entered into it.

God of Creation

GOD ENTERED AND FILLS CREATION

Point 9: God's Throne Room within Creation

The Bible reveals that God has a throne room within creation. He may also have a throne room outside of creation, but the throne room talked about in the Bible is subject to changes related to space and time.

To see this, think about the created beings that go in and out of God's throne room. Job 1:6-12 shows us Satan entering and later leaving the throne room. Genesis 28:12 describes a ladder on which the angels ascend and descend between earth and heaven. Such movements necessitate change. One minute an angel is in the throne room and the next minute it is not in the throne room. In a timeless realm, there is never one minute followed by another minute. So if these Bible passages are accurate depictions of God's throne room, then we have to conclude that space and time do exist there.

For more evidence of this, consider when John was taken into God's throne room (Rev. 4:1-2). John watched Jesus break the seals on a book, *one*

Systematic Theology for the New Apostolic Reformation

at a time (Rev. 4:5-6). John also watched many other events taking place in the throne room as recorded throughout the Book of Revelation.

Most significantly, Jesus ascended into the throne room and sat down at the right hand of God. That was a change. This is important because nothing can change in a timeless realm. So if we accept the fact that Jesus entered into the throne room of God and took His place as King and Lord, then we must recognize that that throne room is governed by time.

We will discuss this more fully later, but now we can say that those who take the Bible seriously must conclude that there is a spiritual realm that is part of creation. That spiritual realm is governed by time. Within that spiritual realm, God has a throne room.

Point 10: God Is Revealed as Temporal within Creation

God fills creation, and He limits Himself within creation. For example, when God manifested in a burning bush to Moses, He limited His manifestation to that little area in and around the bush. When God spoke over Jesus, "This is My beloved Son," He limited the sound of His voice to those who heard Him. If God had not limited the sound of His voice in space and time, that exact same voice would be at the exact same volume every second of every day throughout eternity in every corner of the universe.

So the Bible reveals how God entered creation, and He limited Himself within space and time.

This raises the question, "Why would God enter into space and time?" The Bible does not give us a clear answer to this, but it is certainly in keeping with His goals and nature. God wants sons. He wants relationship with His sons. God is like a natural father who stoops down to the level of his children to talk to them.

This is in keeping with the revelation of God in Christ Jesus. The Word of God became flesh and dwelt among us because He loves us. Like Father, like Son. We can understand how the Father acts by looking at the Son. Jesus is motivated by love. Father-God is motivated by love. Knowing this, we can say that God entered into space and time because He loves.

I hate to repeat, but I must reassure readers who are determined to defend the idea that God is timeless. Father-Son theology does not deny the timelessness of God outside of creation. Here we are recognizing how God entered into creation and within creation He limited Himself.

God of Creation

Point 11: God Interacts with Humanity from within Creation

We have now identified a fundamental difference between Father-Son theology and Classical theology. Rather than seeing God's actions that are recorded in the Bible as Him acting from a timeless dimension outside of creation, we must see His actions as Him acting from *within* creation. Why? *Because He is within creation.*

GOD RELATES TO HUMANITY FROM WITHIN CREATION

This fundamental difference determines much of how we understand the Bible and God's involvement with this world. If Christians trained in Classical theology accept the truth that God acts from within creation and continue to meditate on the implications, their theology will shift away from Classical theology. They will discover their Classical theological training as a logical progression of thought, but if one domino is knocked down, many other dominoes will also fall. If Christians accept the biblical revelation that God acts in time, then their understanding will shift concerning the nature of humanity, the nature of sin and evil, the atonement, the gospel, the victorious Christian life, and most other theological subjects.

As we continue, you will see the sum of the facts that we have already established provides a foundation that will determine much of what is written in the rest of this book.

Systematic Theology for the New Apostolic Reformation

<u>Father-Son Theology</u>
Cornerstone: God determined in love to have sons.
Foundational in the Nature of God:
    Creator
    Eternal (has always existed and always will exist)
    Powerful
    His Spirit Is Temporal within Creation
    Exists in a Spiritual Realm that Fills the Natural Realm
    Entered into Space and Time
    Limited Himself within Creation
    Acts from within Creation

Classical theology is built on a different cornerstone and foundation. We will examine the Classical foundation in Sections F and G, but now we will continue laying the foundation of Father-Son theology.

Point 12: God Is Like Us in Some Fashion

Genesis 1:26 says:

> *Then God said, "Let Us make man in Our image, according to Our likeness . . . ."*

We see in this verse a correlation between God's nature and ours. We are created in God's image. In some ways we are as God. This implies that we can look at people and get an idea of God's nature.

Of course, we know that humanity fell into sin, and hence, what we see in each other today may be different than what was seen in our original parents. Yet, we must not think of ourselves as totally estranged from God's image, because other Bible verses indicate that we still bear His image (e.g., Gen. 9:6 ; 1 Cor. 11:7 ; Jas. 3:9). Humans—even after the fall—are still God's image-bearers.

To what degree are we similar to God?

Great thinkers in Church history have often noted that humans are similar to God in the sense that we were created to rule over earth as God rules over all. Certainly that is one aspect of our image-bearing nature, but there must be more.

God of Creation

Paul inferred more when he talked with the philosophers and other leaders in Athens. He explained:

> *Being then the children of God, we ought not to think that the Divine Nature is like gold or silver or stone, an image formed by the art and thought of man.*
>
> (Acts 17:29)

Paul was examining the nature of humanity, and from this he drew conclusions about the nature of God. He was making the argument that God is more like us than He is like a man-made statue.

In what other ways are God's nature and our nature similar?

Father-Son theology and Classical theology vary greatly on this subject. The related issues are so important we will be touching on this subject throughout this book, especially in Volume IV when we discuss the nature of humanity.

For now we can say that Father-Son theology recognizes much more similarity between God and humanity than Classical theology does. This is true because the foundation of Father-Son theology is that God wants sons. He did not create some strange creatures that walk on two legs so He can someday change them into His image. Instead, God created humanity in His image from the start.

GOD ENTERED INTO CREATION AND CREATED ADAM IN HIS IMAGE

Systematic Theology for the New Apostolic Reformation

Point 13: God Is Relational and Social

In the Garden of Eden, God walked and talked with Adam and Eve. This reaffirms the nearness of God to His creation, but it also reveals God's relational nature. Throughout the OT, we learn of God's continued dealings with the Hebrew people. Then, in the NT we see the great demonstration of His love as He sent His Son to die and reconcile humanity to Himself. Finally, in the end, we have the vision of God spending eternity with His people. The obvious characteristics revealed about God are that He cares about humanity and wants to be involved.

God is relational and social.

Please recognize these as true characteristics of God's nature. When we talk about a specific human being, we often will describe him or her as either social or reclusive. We may explain that one person is outgoing and fun-loving, while another person is an introvert. As we identify the characteristics of God as revealed in Scripture, we recognize that He repeatedly reaches out to people. God is not a Creator who started the world and left humankind to run things while He watches from a distance. The Bible reveals to us a God who wants to be involved with humanity.

Point 14: God Is Personal and Responsive to Individuals

God is not only relational and social, but He is personal and responsive. This is revealed as we read about God's interactions with Cain and Abel. When they brought their offerings to the Lord, God's response is eye-opening:

> *And the Lord had regard for Abel and for his offering; but for Cain and for his offering He had no regard.*
> (Gen. 4:4b-5a)

God had different responses to each of these brothers.

When God looks at humanity, He sees individuals. Some people wrongly envision God's relationship to humanity as they would think of a human looking at an ant mound, not distinguishing one ant from another. That image is erroneous. God is involved and interactive.

God of Creation

Point 15: God Is Judge

One way God is involved in this world is as a Judge.

However, the Hebraic-biblical understanding of a judge is different than that which is envisioned by modern people in the Western world. Westerners tend to think in legal terms with a judge who rules from the bench in a courtroom and declares people as guilty or innocent. In contrast, the ancient Hebrew people thought of a judge as a leader who delivered the oppressed from their oppressors. This is especially evident in the Book of Judges, where we read about God raising up judges to lead the Hebrews out of oppression. We can also describe a judge in biblical terms by saying a judge corrects injustice and sets things straight.

This understanding of God as a judge is evident with Noah's flood. Of course, people were punished and suffered for their sins, but the focus of God as a Hebraic-biblical judge was to correct the course of civilization. Humanity was moving in the wrong direction, and God intervened to put things back on course.

GOD IS JUDGE

The Hebraic-biblical concept of a judge helps us understand God's judgment of Sodom and Gomorrah. God's focus was not to identify the sins of individuals and then punish them for their actions. That would be a Western understanding of a judge. Instead, God saw that humanity had gotten so far off course that correction was required. God intervened to set things straight and save humanity from further destruction.

Even when we think of God judging all of humanity in the end, we should think of God "setting things straight." Paul explained that every person will see the *"revelation of the righteous judgment of God, who will render to each person according to his deeds"* (Rom. 2:5-6). People will be rewarded in the sense of justice being accomplished and every person finally receiving exactly what they deserve.

Point 16: God Acts in Mercy

Even though God administers justice, He also acts in mercy.

For example, God was merciful in sparing Noah and his family. Further, Peter explained that God patiently waited during the period of the construction of the ark (120 years), giving the people the opportunity to repent (1 Peter 3:20). Then after the flood, God promised that He would never again destroy the earth even if humanity became as evil again (Gen. 8:21). This means God would not destroy humanity, even if justice would dictate that they be destroyed. God made a promise to be merciful.

This truth, that God is both just and merciful, is consistent throughout the Scripture.

Point 17: God Is Sovereign

The One who created the universe is sovereign over His creation (1 Tim. 6:15). This includes His sovereignty over humanity.

God's **sovereignty** *means He can do whatever He wants to do, whenever He wants; He has no higher authority to whom He must answer.*

One important aspect of God's sovereignty is that He can be both just and merciful at the same time. This is a simple statement, but it is profound and it will influence much of our theology as we continue.

When people act in justice they act one way, but when they act in mercy they act a different way. For example, a just judge enforces the law, but if that judge is merciful, he may lessen the punishment that the law dictates. Notice that for human behavior, justice and mercy dictate two different actions.

God of Creation

Not so with God. He can act in mercy and still be just because He is sovereign. Paul explained this in Romans 9, where he quoted the words God spoke to Moses:

> *I will have mercy on whom I have mercy, and I will have compassion on whom I have compassion.*
> (Rom. 9:15)

Paul argued that acting in mercy does not make God unjust (Rom. 9:14). God is so high in authority above humanity, that He can destroy people or bless people. He can do whatever He wants whenever He wants. God owes no one an explanation for what He does. There is no authority to whom He must answer. Because He is sovereign, God can have mercy and still be just at the same time.

Point 18: God Is an Emotional Being

One more characteristic about the nature of God that is revealed in the beginning chapters of Genesis is that God is an emotional Being. This is not meant in the sense that He is emotional as a child, but He is an emotional Being in the sense of One who experiences and is moved by emotions. (Before the end of this section, we will discuss how this is incompatible with Classical theology.)

God's emotional nature is evident when we read of God's dealings with people in the days of Noah.

> *The Lord was sorry that He had made man on the earth, and He was grieved in His heart.*
> (Gen. 6:6)

God felt sorrow. He grieved. Furthermore, God's emotions stirred Him to act.

There are many examples throughout the Bible of God experiencing emotions—a full array of them. Some of the most startling emotional expressions are those associated with His responses to humanity's sin. God can get angry. We can also read about positive emotions, such as how God rejoices over His people (Is. 62:5) and takes pleasure in their obedience and prosperity (Deut. 30:9 ; Ps. 35:27). This is part of who God is.

Systematic Theology for the New Apostolic Reformation

The implications of this characteristic of God are far-reaching. When we acknowledge the emotional side of God's nature, we must recognize it as good. What, then, does that say about the emotional makeup of human beings who are made in the image of God? In the culture of which I am a part, as a North American Christian, we often look negatively on emotions. We are especially critical of people who allow their emotions to strongly influence their behavior. Historically, Western Christianity has portrayed God as unemotional, and corresponding to that belief, Western society has tended to think a stoic lifestyle is more spiritual, mature, and godlike.

In reality, the biblical view of God leads us to conclude that emotions are okay. In fact, people who completely suppress their emotions are not healthy. This does not validate every emotional or impulsive action. We are simply noting that people who show no emotions are falling short of the God-like image.

As we accept God's nature as emotional, relational, social, and personal, we recognize similarities between God's nature and human nature. Of course, there are many ways in which God is unlike humans. For example, He is the eternal, sovereign Judge over all creation. So then, we can identify some ways in which God and humanity are alike and other ways in which they are different.

Point 19: What We Know about the God of Creation

There are other characteristics and revelations about the nature of God that can be found in the first few chapters of Genesis, but we have selected those that are obvious and have a significant impact upon all of our systematic theology.

> <u>Father-Son Theology</u>
> Cornerstone: God determined in love to have sons.
> Foundational in the Nature of God:
> > Creator
> > Eternal (has always existed and always will exist)
> > Powerful
> > His Spirit Is Temporal within Creation
> > Exists in a Spiritual Realm that Fills the Natural Realm

God of Creation

> Entered into Space and Time
> Limited Himself within Creation
> Acts from within Creation
> Relational and Social
> Personal and Responsive
> Judge
> Acts in Mercy
> Sovereign (can do whatever He wants, whenever He wants)
> Emotional

Point 20: Classical Theology Says Anthropomorphisms

Before we complete this section, it will be worth taking a moment to contrast what we have already learned with the Classical view of God. Most importantly, Classical theologians do not believe that God can experience emotional variation. In fact, they do not believe that God can change in any way. The theological term for this is **immutability**.

Classical theologians must hold to the immutability of God because they have decided that God is timeless outside of and within creation. If God is timeless, then He would always have all of time standing before Him, and therefore, He could never have any new information come before Him to which He could respond. If, indeed, God is timeless, then all of His decisions were settled in eternity past. Therefore, God could never experience change nor change in anyway. As William Lane Craig, professor of theology at Talbot School of Theology, described an immutable God, "He never thinks successive thoughts, He never performs successive activities, He never undergoes even the most trivial alteration."[20] This is what is implied with the label "timeless."

John Calvin (1509–1564) was committed to the doctrine of God being timeless outside of and within creation. Being consistent with this, Calvin explained the Bible passages that talk about God showing anger or any emotion as follows:

> Therefore whenever we hear that God is angered, we ought not to imagine any emotion in him but rather to consider that this expression has been taken for our own human

---

20 William Lane Craig, *Time and Eternity* (Wheaton, IL: Crossway, 2001), p. 30.

experience ... what he had from eternity foreseen, approved and decreed, he pursues in uninterrupted tenor ....[21]

By "uninterrupted tenor," Calvin was referring to God continuing without the slightest rise or fall of emotions.

Classical theologians agree with Calvin on this issue. Whenever the Bible reports God showing emotions, they explain those reports as figures of speech called **anthropomorphisms**. By this, Classical theologians are saying that any Bible passages where God is shown acting or feeling as humans act or feel are the Bible writer's way of explaining God in human terms so that we can understand.

Another Classical theologian, Thomas Aquinas (1225–1274), explained God's emotions in these terms:

> ... a human figure of speech ... for instance in the account of the Flood ....[22]

In order to be consistent, Classical theologians must reject as literal all of the Bible's accounts of God experiencing emotional changes or experiencing change in any way.

Augustine (354–430) is the Church leader most known for developing his theology based on the timelessness of God and, therefore, the corresponding idea that God cannot change or experience emotional variation. As we study his reasoning in Sections F and G, we will see how Augustine envisioned God relating to this natural world from His timeless world rather than from the time-governed realm of the spirit. The implications became the foundation for Classical theology.

Point 21: God Is Temporal within Creation

If we accept the Bible's reports of God experiencing emotional changes and if we remain logically consistent with this truth, then we have to reject the concept of God's timelessness within creation. Here we see again a clear demarcation between Classical theology and Father-Son

---

21 John Calvin, *Institutes of the Christian Religion*, trans. Ford Lewis Battles, ed. John T. McNeil (Philadelphia: Westminster Press, 1960), 1:227 (1.17.13).
22 Thomas Aquinas, *Summa Theologiae*, trans. Thomas Gilby (London: Spottiswoode, 1966), 1a.19.7.

God of Creation

theology. Classical theology clings to its assumption of God's timelessness outside of and within creation. In contrast, Father-Son theology is open to the possibility that God is timeless outside of creation, but sees God as temporal within creation—and God acting from within creation.

This means that God can experience emotions. When the Bible tells us that God grieved in the days of Noah, that was not an anthropomorphism as Classical theologians must insist. When God is reported as being angry, He truly was angry. Those reports in the Bible are not figures of speech. They really happened.

This is confirmed when we study Jesus. He is God made flesh. As such, He entered into creation. Therefore, Jesus was able to experience emotions. For example, when some women were mourning for Lazarus who had died, Jesus wept (John 11:33-35). Jesus entered into time and experienced time with the people around Him. He was able to feel what they felt. So also, the Bible reveals that Father-God entered into creation. Therefore, He was and is able to experience emotional changes.

Volume I
The Nature of God

Section C
God of Abraham

God revealed Himself to Abraham and his descendants. We will study that revelation in this section. First, we will look at the covenantal relationship that God formed with Abraham. Then we will glance at some of the resulting interactions between God and Abraham's descendants.

Point 22: God Is a Covenant-Maker

God made a covenant with Abraham and his descendants. This means that God was not only willing to relate to people, but He was willing to enter into deeper, committed relationships. We can compare this to a person who is not only willing to have friends, but he is also willing to get married to the right individual. In a parallel fashion, God loves people and is willing to commit to individuals in covenant relationships.

Point 23: God Acts According to His Covenants

When God made a covenant, He was committing to relate to people in a specific manner. God stated, "I will be your God and you will be My people." In this statement, God was (among other things) committing to stand by His covenant people and protect them.

One of the passages that makes this evident is Genesis 20, where Abraham traveled with his wife Sarah into the land of the Negev. Abraham feared King Abimelech who ruled in that area, and so he told Sarah to tell everyone that she was his sister, rather than his wife. Abraham reasoned

Systematic Theology for the New Apostolic Reformation

that the king would be good to him, because his wife was very beautiful. Seeing her beauty, King Abimelech took Abraham's wife to be his own, but before the king had relations with Sarah, God appeared to the king in a dream and warned him not to touch her or He would kill him and his entire family (Gen. 20:1-7).

The thought of God killing the king may seem unfair to us, because we know that King Abimelech was deceived by Abraham, but God had a covenant with Abraham. God was committed to protect Abraham. If God did not protect Abraham, then God would have been unrighteous, because righteousness entailed, among other things, the keeping of one's covenants. Yet, God did not want to kill King Abimelech, so He gave the king a warning in a dream. Indeed, King Abimelech heeded the warning and did not sin, but if he had, God would have killed him and his family.

This is a pattern that we see throughout the OT where God acted in accordance with the covenants He made. This helps us understand many of His actions as recorded in the OT. To the critic, it seems that God was unfair, treating different people by different standards. Indeed, that is exactly what God did in OT times. Such favoritism is unavoidable when a person is a covenant-maker and a covenant-keeper. By definition, a covenant-maker favors covenant-partners.

Point 24: Covenant Partners Work Together

The Hebraic understanding of covenant entails two parties committing to work together in the sense of making decisions together. For this reason, God conferred with Abraham before He destroyed Sodom and Gomorrah. God said: *"Shall I hide from Abraham what I am about to do . . . ?"* (Gen. 18:17). Abraham knew that he had a covenant with God, so he dared to reason with God: *"Wilt You indeed sweep away the righteous with the wicked?"* (Gen. 18:23b). God honored His covenant with Abraham and allowed Abraham to enter into the decision-making process. Indeed, that was expected in the Hebraic-biblical concept of covenant.[23]

---

[23] Some Bible teachers talk about other types of covenants such as grant and kinship covenants. Indeed, the covenant God made through Moses may be considered a grant covenant, but the covenant God made with Abraham and his descendants was a relational covenant in which God committed to work with His people. This relational aspect of covenant can also be seen in the new covenant; for example, Jesus promised that God will answer the prayers of those who abide with Him.

God of Abraham

Father-Son theology agrees with Open Theism concerning the cooperative relationships that are formed through the Hebraic-biblical covenants. In the introduction of this book, I described Open Theism as a theological perspective that recognizes God's open relationships with individuals. Father-Son theology agrees with adherents of Open Theism that God is open for the input of people, and therefore, some of the future is open. Those open relationships are established through God's covenants.

An open relationship can be seen in God's interaction with Moses. After the Hebrew people made a molten calf, God was angry enough to destroy the people, but Moses was God's covenant partner, so he had the courage to step in:

> *Then Moses entreated the Lord his God, and said, "O Lord, why does Your anger burn against Your people . . . ."*
> (Ex. 32:11)

Moses went on in the passage, giving God reasons why He should not destroy the Hebrew people (Ex. 32:12-13). Amazingly, God relented:

> *So the Lord changed His mind about the harm which He said He would do to His people.*
> (Ex. 32:14)

God listened to a human being and changed His mind! This is astounding. God is open for dialogue with His covenant partners, and He can be influenced in His decisions.

Point 25: Implications of Theology Are Far-reaching

There are many implications of the points being made here. Some of those implications will become evident as we continue developing Father-Son theology. Some implications we will not take the time to discuss, but I hope the ones relative to your life become evident as you meditate further on these subjects.

One implication of God's covenant-making nature pertains to relationships among people. If God is willing to open Himself up for human input, how much more should frail people who are prone to mistakes be open for the input of others?

Systematic Theology for the New Apostolic Reformation

The application of this truth is key in covenant-relationships such as marriage. The Hebraic-biblical understanding of covenant leads married people to conclude that they should allow their spouse to join in the decision-making processes.

This has implications on the relationship between Jesus and His Bride. Indeed, Jesus and His Bride will rule and reign together.[24]

Point 26: The Classical Concept of Covenant

The Classical view of God will not allow for covenant relationships in which God and humanity work together. Adherents will agree that God makes covenants with people, but they see a covenant as an unbreakable contract rather than a commitment to a partnership. Followers of Classical theology also see God's covenants as unidirectional in the sense that God promises to act favorably toward His covenant people. Of course, God expects His people to live righteously, but followers of Classical theology see God as unaffected and unmoved by the actions of people. Because Classical theologians believe that God is timeless outside of and within creation, they cannot logically believe in a covenant between God and humanity that allows for joint decisions.

Point 27: What Can Classical Theologians Believe in the Bible?

Followers of Classical theology reject the idea that God changed His mind as a result of Moses' dialogue with God (Ex. 32:11-14), but this means that they must also reject the idea that the dialogue between God and Moses ever took place—or if it did, then God was just pretending to listen and change His mind.

The rejection of Bible passages that talk about God changing is no small issue. Classical theologians dismiss every biblical account of God changing His mind (or experiencing emotions) by simply labeling them "anthropomorphisms" (figures of speech that explain God in human terms), but it is not that simple. Labeling a Bible passage as an anthropomorphism allows Classical theologians to dismiss all of those Bible passages, but anyone who does not follow Classical thought can

---

24 This is discussed in IX:C:524.

God of Abraham

rightfully ask, "Then what do those passages mean?" Labeling them does not remove those passages from the Bible.

Unfortunately, people have a tendency to stop thinking any deeper about a subject once they have labeled it. Let me offer a comparison to make this point. For several hundred years, scientists used the word *gravity* to refer to a force[25] that pulls objects toward a mass, but no one ever knew what gravity actually was. What causes it? Why does it exist? Because they had a name for it, most people were content, but the word *gravity* revealed nothing. They could have just as well invented some other word such as *tovity* or *fruple*. Whatever combination of letters they put together would have worked. Unfortunately, people tend to conclude that labeling something explains it, when in reality a word like *gravity* explains nothing.

Only people who think beyond such a label will ever come to a deeper understanding. In the meantime, accepting a label as an explanation often leaves people in the dark—and content while they are in the dark.

This is especially true with labels that are not familiar to common people. For example, medical doctors use the label *Asperger's syndrome* to refer to a developmental disorder that, among other things, causes individuals to become overly-focused or obsessed on a single topic. When individuals are diagnosed with Asperger's, they and their families are often relieved because they think that they finally have an explanation for what they are experiencing. In reality, the diagnosis of Asperger's syndrome offers no explanation, because, at the present time, no one knows what causes Asperger's syndrome. It is nothing more than a label. The word *Asperger* is the name of the doctor who labeled the disorder, and *syndrome* refers to a group of symptoms that seem to be associated with each other. In reality, no one will understand Asperger's until they look deeper than the label.

Every field of study has labels that are developed by people trained in that field. Those untrained in the field often accept those labels as explanations. When the untrained person comes to a technical word that is new to them, they usually stop thinking any further. They assume that people more educated in that field of study have information that further explains what that label means, but often the new word identifies the place where present understanding ends.

---

25 The present scientific understanding of gravity sees it as the effects of the space-time curvature.

Systematic Theology for the New Apostolic Reformation

That is the problem with the word *anthropomorphism*. When applied to the biblical accounts of God's interactions with this world, it refers to a figure of speech that explains God in human terms. Unfortunately, most people stop thinking there. They have been given a label for every Bible passage that shows God changing His mind or experiencing emotional change, BUT WHAT ABOUT THOSE BIBLE PASSAGES? Labeling them anthropomorphisms does not remove them from the Bible. They are still there in the pages that we say are inspired by God!

Consider when Abraham bartered with God about not destroying Sodom and Gomorrah. If we dismiss that interaction as an anthropomorphism as Classical theologians do, then logically we must also admit that the interchange never happened or God was just pretending to listen to Abraham. If that dialogue about Sodom and Gomorrah never happened, then how much of the story of Sodom and Gomorrah did happen?

What about Moses talking to God as he came down from Mount Sinai? (Ex. 32:11-14). We are told that God changed His mind. If that never happened as Classical theologians tell us, then did Moses even talk to God? Did Moses ever meet with God on Mount Sinai?

How about God listening to the people of Israel to give them a king, and in response, God anointed Saul to rule over them? Later on, Saul turned evil, and God said, *"I regret that I have made Saul king . . ."* (1 Sam. 15:11). According to Classical theology, God could not have regretted or changed His mind about Saul. So what did happen? Did God not say this? Did God not make Saul king in the first place? Is it all just a make-believe story?

Consider how Joshua prayed that the sun would stand still. We are told that "*. . . the Lord listened to the voice of a man*" (Josh. 10:14). If we dismiss this as an anthropomorphism, as Classical theologians must do, then we are saying that God never did listen to Joshua. And if God did not listen to Joshua about the sun standing still, did the sun stand still? How can we determine what is true and what is an anthropomorphism?

Consider Jonah preaching to the city of Nineveh. After the people of Nineveh repented, we are told:

> *When God saw their deeds, that they turned from their wicked way, then <u>God relented</u> concerning the calamity which He had declared He would bring upon them. And He did not do it.*
>
> (Jon. 3:10)

God of Abraham

God relented—He changed His mind. If this passage is just an anthropomorphism, as Classical theologians insist, then what part of the Book of Jonah is true? Is the entire book an anthropomorphism?

If we reject certain passages as literally true, then we must question if the related events ever took place. If we think beyond the Classical use of the label anthropomorphism, we discover that key passages of the Bible are being discarded.

Point 28: Immutable in Nature, Mutable in Emotions and Decisions

If we accept at face value any of the Bible passages that talk about God changing His mind, experiencing emotional variations, or changing in anyway, then we must reject the Classical view of God being timeless within creation.

If God experiences change then He is **mutable** (able to change). This is the position of Father-Son theology. However, when adherents of Father-Son theology say that God is mutable they are referring to Him changing in emotions and decisions, but not in nature.

God is mutable in decisions, but immutable in nature.

To see both of these attributes, consider how God changed His mind from destroying the city of Nineveh after Jonah called the citizens to repentance (Jon. 3:10). After God changed His mind, Jonah talked to God:

> . . . for I knew that You are a gracious and compassionate God, slow to anger and abundant in lovingkindness, and one who relents concerning calamity.
>
> (Jon. 4:2)

Jonah understood the nature of God. In relenting from His planned destruction, God was acting consistently with His nature, as Someone who is abundant in lovingkindness. Jonah knew that God was loving and forgiving, and therefore, Jonah thought God may change His mind about destroying Nineveh. In this case, God was mutable in His decision because He was immutable in nature.

It is reassuring to know that God never changes in nature or character. James tells us of the goodness of God and about the *"Father of lights, with whom there is no variation or shifting shadow"* (Jas. 1:17). In the Book of Malachi we read God's words:

Systematic Theology for the New Apostolic Reformation

> *For I, the Lord, do not change . . . .*
>
> (Mal. 3:6)

In both of these passages, God is reassuring His people that He remains the same in nature.

This is good news. We do not have to worry that at some point in the future God will change and become evil or unpredictable. We don't have to worry that there might be a different God hiding up in eternity. Even after a billion years, He will continue to be good, and in fact, the Ultimate Source of good. So God is immutable in nature, but mutable in His emotions and decisions.

Point 29: Classical Misunderstanding of Immutability

There is one passage in the Bible that has been used wrongly by some Classically trained Christians to teach that God never reverses His decisions. It is a verse from the Book of 1 Samuel where the prophet Samuel was rebuking King Saul. Samuel was speaking of God's position toward the king when he said:

> *Also the Glory of Israel will not lie or change His mind; for He is not a man that He should change His mind.*
>
> (1 Sam. 15:29)

Some have concluded from this statement that God never changes His mind. In the context, however, we see that Samuel had just told the king that God had rejected him. Even though King Saul cried out for mercy, Samuel was telling the king that God was not as a man who can be forced or bribed into changing His mind. The emphasis is on *how* Saul tried to change God's mind.

We can confirm this by reading six verses later (v. 35), where we see that God did change His mind, not because anyone forced Him, but because He can sovereignly change whenever He wants to change.

Point 30: God Also Changes His Attitude and Disposition

When we say God is mutable, we are not implying that He is changeable in the sense of being fickle or unstable. When we say that God is mutable,

God of Abraham

we are simply saying that God is influenced by humankind. He does, indeed, respond to humanity.

Each passage that reveals God changing is evidence that God acts in time. A very enlightening passage is Exodus 33:5:

> *For the Lord had said to Moses, "Say to the sons of Israel, 'You are an obstinate people; should I go up in your midst for one moment, I would destroy you. Now therefore, put off your ornaments from you, that I may know what I shall do with you.'"*

Christians who do not dismiss this passage as an anthropomorphism will conclude that God was very angry at His people. In fact, God told Moses to take the people on ahead, because He would kill them if He continued to be with them. (This sounds like a mother who has been with her children for too long.) Interestingly, God wanted some time to simmer down before being with His people again.

This concept of "time to simmer down" is totally incompatible with Classical theology. Therefore, adherents of Classical theology must insist that Exodus 33:5 is just a figure of speech. According to them, God never spoke these words to Moses, or if He did, then God was not telling the truth.

There are many examples in the Bible of God changing His mind over the course of time. In fact, God explained through the prophet Jeremiah:

> *At one moment I might speak concerning a nation or concerning a Kingdom to uproot, to pull down, or to destroy it; if that nation against which I have spoken turns from its evil, I will relent concerning the calamity I planned to bring on it.*
>
> (Jer. 18:7-8)

Classical Christians cannot accept this aspect of God's nature that He can relent or vary in any way. To them, this promise of God is just an anthropomorphism.

It is important to note that the changes God makes involve more than His mind and thoughts. His entire attitude toward people can also change. For example, Isaiah explained God's dealings with Israel.

> *But they rebelled
> And grieved His Holy Spirit;*

Systematic Theology for the New Apostolic Reformation

Therefore He turned Himself to become their enemy,
He fought against them.

(Is. 63:10)

God completely turned. He changed His attitude, disposition, and actions toward the people because of their rebellion. Classically-trained Christians must see this as an anthropomorphism. In contrast, Christians who see God as temporal within creation accept such biblical accounts as true. The fact that these accounts are true will have profound implications upon most of the theological points that we will be developing throughout this book.

Point 31: What We Know about the God of Abraham

Let's summarize what we have learned thus far about the nature of God:

Father-Son Theology

Cornerstone: God determined in love to have sons.
Foundational in the Nature of God:
  Creator
  Eternal (has always existed and always will exist)
  Powerful
  His Spirit Is Temporal within Creation
  Exists in a Spiritual Realm that Fills the Natural Realm
  Entered into Space and Time
  Limited Himself within Creation
  Acts from within Creation
  Relational and Social
  Personal and Responsive
  Judge
  Acts in Mercy
  Sovereign (can do whatever He wants, whenever He wants)
  Emotional
  Temporal within Creation
  Covenant-Maker
  Allows Covenantal Interactions
  Mutable in Emotions and Decisions
  Immutable in Nature

This is what the Bible reveals about God. This is who God is.

Section D
God of the Old Testament

It is time to take a broader view of God as He is revealed in the OT. We can do this by looking at the names with which God identified Himself. This is meaningful because people in Bible times chose names that revealed a person's character and nature.

In this section, we will also briefly discuss the key characteristics of holiness and jealousy, along with God's nature as a consuming fire.

Point 32: Revelation in the Name *El Shaddai*

God revealed Himself to Abraham as *El Shaddai* (Gen. 17:1), which is commonly translated as "God, the Almighty One."

The term *El* refers to God, but when God revealed Himself as *El Shaddai*, He was communicating to Abraham in a very personal way. To grasp the full meaning of this, it is important to know that Hebrew words are closely tied with the function that is being communicated. The root, *Shad*, is associated with the Hebrew word for breast, and therefore, *Shaddai* may be interpreted as "the Abundantly-Breasted One."[26] Hebrew scholars would also be comfortable interpreting *El Shaddai* as "God, the All-Sufficient One." In these names, God was revealing Himself personally to Abraham as his Provider, Shelter, Giver, Life, and all he needed.

Some Christians interpret *El Shaddai* as "God, the Omnipotent One" or, "God, the All-Powerful One," but that is not accurate. If we were to interpret El Shaddai as "God, the Omnipotent One," we would be saying something that the Hebrew words are not actually saying. The word *omnipotent* does

---
26 Some Hebrew scholars will argue that this should be the "Dual-breasted One."

Systematic Theology for the New Apostolic Reformation

not communicate too much, but rather it communicates too little. It does not convey God's heart. God was not interested in revealing that He is the "All-Powerful One." He was interested in making Himself known to Abraham—and us—as Provider, Shelter, Giver, Life, and all we need.

As we continue, I will use the word *Almighty* as a characteristic of God, but I hope you will keep in mind the relational aspect that was communicated in the Hebrew language.[27]

Point 33: Revelation in the Name *Yahweh*

God revealed Himself to Moses with a name written with four Hebrew letters that are usually transliterated to YHWH (Ex. 3:14). This name is difficult to express in English because the Hebrew language of the period was written without vowels and some of the consonants can be transliterated into more than one letter in English. Some Christians pronounce this name as Jehovah, but recent scholarship favors the pronunciation as Yahweh. God declared, *"This is My name forever"* (Ex. 2:15).

No one is able to give the exact meaning to this name, but it is often translated as "I Am Who I Am."

We can develop a sense of the meaning of this name by seeing the context in which God revealed Himself as Yahweh. Moses was just commissioned by God to go to Egypt and set the Hebrew people free. Yet, Moses was fearful to go before Pharaoh, and he was also unsure if the Hebrews would follow him. In that context God told Moses to tell the people that "I Am" sent him (Ex. 2:13-14). In saying this, God seems to be using His name as a declaration that:

> "There is no greater name."
> "You don't need to know anything more."
> "You don't need to say anything more."
> "I am God and that settles it."

Again, no one knows for certain everything entailed in the name Yahweh, but these thoughts give us a sense of what God was revealing about Himself.

---

[27] For an enlightening discussion on the difference between *almighty* and *omnipotent* see John Sanders, *The God Who Risks* (Downers Grove, IL, 1998), p. 188-194.

God of the Old Testament

Still, it would be wrong to equate the name of a person to the literal meaning of that name. Take for example the name Amos, which means "strong." When we think of a person named Amos, we may be aware of the name's meaning, but if that is all we think of then the image we have of that person will be very sterile. When we think of Amos, we should be aware of the person who bears that name.

So also the name Yahweh may be interpreted as "I Am Who I Am," but rather than thinking of the implications of this name, we should first of all think of the Person—Yahweh—and everything revealed about Him in the Bible.

Point 34: Revelation of God in Other Names

The name "Yahweh" is linked with other names in the OT. Some of the most noted names, along with their meanings, are as follows:[28]

> Yahweh Jireh (God, Our Provider) (Gen. 22:14)
> Yahweh Rapha (God, Our Healer) (Ex. 15:26)
> Yahweh Nissi (God, Our Banner) (Ex. 17:15)
> Yahweh Shalom (God, Our Peace) (Judg. 6:24)
> Yahweh Tsidkenu (God, Our Righteousness) (Jer. 33:16)
> Yahweh Rohi (God, Our Shepherd) (Ps. 23:1)
> Yahweh M'kadesh (God, Our Holiness) (Ex. 31:13)

Notice that each of these names includes the recipient of God's blessing associated with God's nature. This is how the Hebrew language works. To translate Yahweh Jireh as "God, the Provider" would be incomplete. Yahweh Jireh is a name indicating that God is the Provider of the person who speaks the name. So if you say, "Yahweh Jireh," you are saying, "Yahweh is my provider."

When God revealed Himself as Yahweh Rapha, He was not interested in revealing that He has all power to heal all disease. Of course, we may believe that God has all power to heal every disease, but this name does not say that. This name, Yahweh Rapha, means He is the Healer of the person who speaks the name.

---

28 In each of these names, Yahweh is translated as "God," but keep in mind that Yahweh is actually the name of God rather than the generic label for God.

Systematic Theology for the New Apostolic Reformation

The names of God in the Bible do not focus on how great or powerful God is. Instead, they each communicate God's love for human beings. He is not declaring how big He is. Rather, He is declaring how much He loves.

Point 35: God Is Holy

The name Yahweh M'kadesh (God, Our Holiness) deserves special emphasis. The truth that God is "our" holiness has implications on our understanding of salvation, which we will discuss in Volume VI when we study soteriology.

Now we can note that God is holy:

There is no one holy like the Lord,
Indeed, there is no one besides You.

(1 Sam. 2:2)

Who is like You among the gods, O Lord?
Who is like You, majestic in holiness.

(Ex. 15:11)

It is difficult to define the word *holy*, because God is the ultimate standard of what it means to be holy. A useful definition is "sinless purity." However, holiness is more than the absence of sin. The holiness of God stands out as the characteristic of God that is immediately evident in the sense of being breathtaking to the onlooker. The seraphim in the throne room of the Lord, cry out to one another: "*Holy, Holy, Holy, is the Lord of hosts*" (Is. 6:3 ; see also, Rev. 4:8). This declaration is offered in the sense that our Lord's holiness is so obvious and magnificent that it needs to be declared. If the angels do not shout it out, even the rocks will cry out.

We can compare this to a human-to-human interaction when a person walks into a room and finds himself suddenly standing face-to-face with a champion bodybuilder. The first thought that may come to mind is, "Huge." Or another person may unexpectedly run into a woman of extreme beauty and want to speak out, "Gorgeous!"

In a comparative way, we can say that the first thought that bursts from a person encountering God may be, "Holy!" It is such an obvious and overwhelming characteristic of God that it compels one to verbalize it.

God of the Old Testament

In the presence of God's holiness, people may also become instantly aware of their own unholiness. Adam and Eve were ashamed of their own sin when God entered the Garden of Eden. When Isaiah saw the Lord, he cried out:

> *Woe is me, for I am ruined!*
> *Because I am a man of unclean lips,*
> *And I live among a people of unclean lips;*
> *For my eyes have seen the King, the Lord of hosts.*
>
> (Is. 6:5)

Not only his own sins, but simply the fact that Isaiah lived on earth where there are unholy people made him feel unqualified to stand in the presence of the holy God. Here we see the holiness of God exposing all that is unholy.

So then, we should see God's holiness as more than the lack of sin. It is also the presence of purity, perfection, and innocence in such a measure that it strikes the onlooker with awe!

Point 36: God Is a Jealous God

God also reveals Himself as *"the Lord, whose name is Jealous"* (Ex. 34:14). The Hebrew word *Qanna*, from which *jealous* is translated, associates a zealousness and passion with God's jealousy.

God is passionately jealous for the hearts of His people, and so they are warned not to worship any other god.

> *You shall not worship them or serve them; for I, the Lord your God, am a jealous God . . . .*
>
> (Ex. 20:5)

God also zealously protects that which He considers holy. This helps us understand why Uzzah died when He touched the ark of the covenant (1 Chron. 13:10) and why blasphemy of the Holy Spirit is an unforgivable sin (Matt. 12:31-32). God *"jealously desires the Spirit . . ."* (Jas. 4:5). He protects the Spirit and those upon whom His Spirit rests. He said:

> *Do not touch My anointed ones,*
> *And do My prophets no harm.*
>
> (1 Chron. 16:22)

Systematic Theology for the New Apostolic Reformation

At times, we see God zealously protecting those He has anointed with His Spirit.

Of course, no one can explain God's actions and know fully why He does what He does, but allow me to offer a possible explanation of His jealousy for the holy things. Those things that God protects are holy in the sense that they are the intimate expressions of His own heart. God, who is perfectly holy, exposes Himself and reveals that which is normally hidden. That is what the holy things are—the exposure of God to humanity. If, therefore, a human treats the holy things in an unholy manner, it can be compared to a woman who first reveals herself to her husband on their wedding night, but rather than adore her, her husband ridicules her. It is one thing to be mocked by someone who does not know you. It is another to reveal one's innermost personhood and then be mocked by someone who should love and cherish you. Holiness comes from the invisible God revealing Himself. To reject the holy things is to reject God's intimate revelations of Himself. God is jealous of those holy things.

HOLINESS AS THE REVELATION OF GOD IN THE NATURAL REALM

Point 37: God Is Motivated According to His Nature

This is an ideal moment for the observant reader to identify and embrace God as a Person—just as He is revealed in the Bible.

God of the Old Testament

The God of the Bible has emotions, He makes covenants, He is jealous, and so forth. He is motivated by these attributes and characteristics of His nature. God is not an unfeeling robot who acts only out of sterile reason. Let me put this truth in other words. To act out of some motivation different than reason means a person will at times act unreasonably. By saying this I am not implying that God is ever irrational. No, God is always perfectly rational, but sometimes His actions are motivated by aspects of His nature other than reason.

Many Christians will not allow themselves to consider this because it touches on our most basic understanding of who God is. We want a reasonable God. We want an invisible stream of logical thoughts governing the universe. We want a Super Computer, but that is not what the Bible reveals. All of the characteristics about God that we are identifying add to our understanding about Him. They are not merely words on a page. They are descriptive of God's nature. The God of the Bible acts according to His nature. Emotions, jealousy, zeal, and love are part of who He is.

Consider Jesus. He chased the money changers out of the temple in Jerusalem (John 2:13-17). John noted that this was to fulfill a prophecy in the OT: *"Zeal for Your house will consume me"* (Ps. 69:9). Jesus did not act like an unfeeling robot. His love for His Father's house motivated Him to act. Zeal determined His actions. Jesus was jealous of the holy things, just as His Father is jealous.

Until we accept this about God, we will not understand Him. We will not understand why He killed Uzzah when Uzzah touched the ark of the covenant (1 Chron. 13). Nor will we understand why He sent His only begotten Son to die for us.

Point 38: God Is a Consuming Fire

Another prominent revelation of God in the OT is as a consuming fire. Moses warned the Hebrews not to follow after false gods: *"For the Lord your God is a consuming fire"* (Deut. 4:24). God also declared to the Hebrews that He would be a consuming fire going before them to destroy their enemies (Deut. 9:1-3). God revealed Himself as this consuming fire when He descended upon Mount Sinai; the whole mountain quaked violently, and the people were terrified (Ex. 19:16-18).

Systematic Theology for the New Apostolic Reformation

Typically this aspect of God's nature is correlated with His holiness—a holiness so pure that anything near Him that is not holy will be instantly consumed. Similarly, those who oppose God will be utterly consumed, as God can destroy anything in His path. Knowing this aspect of His nature demands that God be worshiped with reverence.

Lest we think this aspect of God's nature is limited to the OT revelation, we can note Hebrews 12:28-29, which reminds us, *"so worship God acceptably with reverence and awe, for our 'God is a consuming fire.'"* Notice that the writer of Hebrews refers to "our God." It is the NT God of Christians who is a consuming fire. This is important, because He is not only a God of love, peace, and joy. The writer of Hebrews gives clear teaching that the Mosaic religious system passed away and now believers live within the new covenant (Heb. 8-10). Yet, the God of the new covenant remains a consuming fire who must be worshiped with reverence and awe.

Point 39: What We Know about the God of the Old Testament

Up to this point in our study we have worked through the OT, picking out key revelations concerning the nature of God. Of course, other characteristics and revelations about the nature of God could be identified, but the ones that we have discussed are obvious points that form the foundation for Father-Son theology.

> Father-Son Theology
> Cornerstone: God determined in love to have sons.
> Foundational in the Nature of God:
> Creator
> Eternal (has always existed and always will exist)
> Powerful
> His Spirit Is Temporal within Creation
> Exists in a Spiritual Realm that Fills the Natural Realm
> Entered into Space and Time
> Limited Himself within Creation
> Acts from within Creation
> Relational and Social
> Personal and Responsive
> Judge
> Acts in Mercy

God of the Old Testament

Sovereign (can do whatever He wants, whenever He wants)
Emotional
Temporal within Creation
Covenant-Maker
Allows Covenantal Interactions
Mutable in Emotions and Decisions
Immutable in Nature
El Shaddai (God Almighty)
Yahweh Jireh (God, Our Provider)
Yahweh Rapha (God, Our Healer)
Yahweh Nissi (God, Our Banner)
Yahweh Shalom (God, Our Peace)
Yahweh Tsidkenu (God, Our Righteousness)
Yahweh Rohi (God, Our Shepherd)
Yahweh M'kadesh (God, Our Holiness)
Holy
Jealous
Consuming Fire

Point 40: God of the OT Is God of the NT

Before we go on in the next section to discuss God as He is revealed in the NT, it will be helpful to consider how the God of the OT is the God of the NT.

In the OT we see how Moses was terrified when God was revealed on Mount Sinai—a mountain filled with blazing fire, darkness, gloom, and a whirlwind (Heb. 12:18-21). In contrast, the NT shows us Jesus walking the streets of Jerusalem, healing the sick, teaching the masses, and ministering in love. Jesus seems very different than the God of Mount Sinai.

The writer of Hebrews contrasts the revelation of God on Mount Sinai with God as revealed on Mount Zion. He explains that Christians come to:

> *Mount Zion and to the city of the living God, the heavenly Jerusalem, and to myriads of angels, to the general assembly and to the church of the firstborn who are enrolled in heaven, and to God, the judge of all, and to the spirits of the righteous made perfect, and to Jesus, the mediator of a new covenant . . . .*
>
> (Heb. 12:22-24)

Systematic Theology for the New Apostolic Reformation

The same God was revealed on both Mount Sinai and Mount Zion, but Mount Zion is a glorious place of celebration. There fear is replaced by love and acceptance. The good news is that God's children meet God on Mount Zion, not Mount Sinai.

To see this from another perspective, compare God to a female grizzly bear. For a stranger to surprise a mother grizzly with cubs can be a terrifying experience. To a stranger, the bear is extremely dangerous. On the other hand, we can think of the mama bear through the eyes of her cubs. To them, mama is warm, soft, and tender. She protects and cares for them. It is the same bear seen from two different perspectives. In a comparative way we can say that the revelation of God on Mount Sinai and His revelation on Mount Zion are revelations of the same God seen from two different perspectives.

However, the distinction is more than different perspectives. Paul explained that when people read the OT a veils lies over their eyes (2 Cor. 3:14-15). The revelation of God in the OT is unclear. It is harder to see His forgiving and loving nature. The perfect revelation of God is in Jesus. He is the clearest picture we have of God.

Section E
God of Jesus

Let's look at the revelation of God in and through Jesus. The writer of Hebrews began his letter explaining that in OT times God spoke through *"the prophets in many portions and in many ways,* [but] *in these last days has spoken to us in His Son"* (Heb. 1:1-2). Through Jesus, God speaks to us. Let's see what Jesus reveals to us about Father-God's nature.

Point 41: Revelation of God in Jesus

Jesus is God incarnate, which means God became flesh. So when we look at Jesus we see God. Jesus told His disciples, *"He who has seen Me has seen the Father"* (John 14:9). The writer of Hebrews explained that Jesus:

> *. . . is the radiance of His* [God's] *glory and the exact representation of His* [God's] *nature.*
>
> (Heb. 1:3)

If we want to know the nature of God, we can look at the nature of Jesus. Of course, we are not talking about the physical aspects of our Lord's nature, since Jesus taught that God is spirit (John 4:24). When we look at Jesus we can learn about God's values, heart, and character.

Point 42: Revelation of God as Father

Jesus taught His disciples to pray, *"Our Father who is in heaven"* (Matt. 6:9). This was revolutionary teaching at that time in history. The Jewish people

Systematic Theology for the New Apostolic Reformation

considered the name of God too holy to ever be spoken. Yet, Jesus was instructing His disciples to speak to God in familiar terms, even in terms of God being their Father.

The concept of God being Father is central to the way in which Jesus revealed God. It is not hidden or merely suggested. It is fundamental to our understanding of who He is. In an effort to emphasize what Jesus emphasized, we must keep this image of God being Father at the forefront of our coming discussions.

Point 43: Father-God Is Forgiving

There are several characteristics that Jesus emphasized as He described God as Father.

Jesus told a parable of two sons in which a prodigal son ran off and squandered his inheritance (Luke 15:11-24). After the prodigal son spent all of the money, he returned to his father, who ran out to greet him. There are many lessons we can glean from this parable, but one clear lesson is that God is forgiving, and He is a father who will welcome His children back with open arms if they return to Him after going astray.

Point 44: Father-God Is a Generous Giver

In another passage, Jesus explained the giving nature of the Father:

> *Now suppose one of you fathers is asked by his son for a fish; he will not give him a snake instead of a fish, will he? . . . If you then, being evil, know how to give good gifts to your children, how much more will your heavenly Father give the Holy Spirit to those who ask Him?*
> (Luke 11:11-13)

Jesus explained that our heavenly Father is better than any earthly father and He will give good gifts to His children. Father-God will even give the Holy Spirit when asked. This is especially significant in view of our earlier discussion[29] concerning how God jealousy guards the Holy Spirit. The Spirit is precious to Him, yet even this He is willing to share with His children.

---

29 Discussed in I:D:35-36..

God of Jesus

Point 45: Father-God Is a Rewarder

The writer of Hebrews explains that God *"is a rewarder of those who seek Him"* (Heb. 11:6). In one sense we can say that God can't help but reward. Of course, this is overstating the concept, because God can do whatever He wants, but in another sense we can say that God can't help Himself, because it is in His nature to reward. This is comparative to how God can't help but love because it is His nature to love. Just like a grandfather wants to reward his grandchild who pleases him, God wants to reward those who seek Him.

Point 46: Father-God Is Love

God is love. The greatest revelation of this truth is in God's willingness to offer His only begotten Son on our behalf (John 3:16). God's love is so great that He will not withhold any good things from His children. This truth is confirmed by John's declarations, *"love is from God"* (1 John 4:7) and *"God is love"* (1 John 4:8). This means that God is not only a loving Being, but love *is* His nature.

Point 47: Primacy of God as Father

If we embrace the idea that the Bible is a progressive revelation of God, we will conclude that the clearest revelations that we have of God are those that we see in Jesus and in His teaching concerning God as Father. These are the most fully developed and mature revelations of God. Therefore, we must elevate in our mind the concept of God being Father.

It is helpful to see the other concepts related to God's nature as coming from His nature as a loving Father as well. For example, we saw that God is forgiving, but even a sterile organization such as a bill-collecting agency is able to forgive a debt. God is not like a bill-collecting agency. He is forgiving like the father of the prodigal is forgiving, with open arms welcoming the forgiven child into His heart.

Similarly, we can talk about God's willingness to give good gifts. God is not like Santa Claus giving toys to children. Instead, God is a Father who gives good gifts wisely—gifts that will benefit His children.

Systematic Theology for the New Apostolic Reformation

If we recognize Jesus' revelation of God as Father, then we will see all other truths about God through this revelation. For example, we first identified God as Creator, but seeing the Creator as a Father allows us to grasp His love and personal care in the creation process. Seeing God's power as the strength of a loving Father instills peace rather than fear. Similarly, we can think of God as relational and social, but seeing Him as a relational and social Father provides us with a warmer, more revealing understanding of His nature. All of the truths we have discovered about the nature of God are best understood in view of Jesus' revelation of God as Father. Therefore, in summary of the biblical view of God, we will place all that we have learned about God's nature under the overarching concept of God as Father.

> Father-Son Theology
> Cornerstone: God determined in love to have sons.
> Foundational in *God as Father*:
> > Creator
> > Eternal (has always existed and always will exist)
> > Powerful
> > His Spirit Is Temporal within Creation
> > Exists in a Spiritual Realm that Fills the Natural Realm
> > Entered into Space and Time
> > Limited Himself within Creation
> > Acts from within Creation
> > Relational and Social
> > Personal and Responsive
> > Judge
> > Acts in Mercy
> > Sovereign (can do whatever He wants, whenever He wants)
> > Emotional
> > Temporal within Creation
> > Covenant-Maker
> > Allows Covenantal Interactions
> > Mutable in Emotions and Decisions
> > Immutable in Nature
> > El Shaddai (God, Almighty)
> > Yahweh Jireh (God, Our Provider)
> > Yahweh Rapha (God, Our Healer)
> > Yahweh Nissi (God, Our Banner)
> > Yahweh Shalom (God, Our Peace)

God of Jesus

Yahweh Tsidkenu (God, Our Righteousness)
Yahweh Rohi (God, Our Shepherd)
Yahweh M'kadesh (God, Our Holiness)
Holy
Jealous
Consuming Fire
Forgiving
Generous Giver
Rewarder
*Love
*Like Jesus

*The last two truths in our list—God being love and like Jesus—deserve extra emphasis. Not only are these part of the fully developed view of Father-God, but they are fundamental to everything that we understand about His nature. These truths will serve as anchors throughout Father-Son theology because we know that all truths determined to be biblical must come into alignment with God's nature of love and His nature revealed in Jesus Christ.

There are a few other characteristics and revelations that we could list in our understanding of the nature of God, but we have identified those that are key in developing Father-Son theology throughout the rest of this book.

Volume I
The Nature of God

Section F
God of the Greek Philosophers

While the Bible writers were inspired to reveal the One true God, the surrounding people groups developed their own concepts of god(s). The reason we must discuss these gods is because much cross-pollination of cultures took place, especially in the four centuries preceding and following the birth of Jesus. Most profoundly, it was the ancient Greek philosophers with their concept of god who influenced the views of the Jews and early Christians. So here we will identify the god of the ancient Greek philosophers. Then, in Section G we will discuss how their concept of god was syncretized with Christianity.

Point 48: The Worldview of Nature-Bound People

Most ancient peoples developed their worldview closely tied to nature. As a consequence, they were ever conscious of the sky (heavens) above and the earth around them. By heavens, we are referring to the distant realm of the sun, moon, and stars, rather than earth's atmosphere. It is helpful to think of ancient people staring up into the night sky, pondering the nature of the heavens. The heavens seemed unchanging and perfect. This understanding was reinforced as early astronomers observed the stars remaining constant, seeming to follow perfect rhythmic patterns.[30] In contrast, people experienced the world around them as changing, imperfect, and harsh. This division between the heavens and earth became a fundamental division in the worldview of most ancient civilizations.

---

30 The Greco-Roman understanding of the perfection of the stars is most obvious in the writings of the mathematician/astronomer Claudius Ptolemy (c. 90 –c. 170 AD).

Systematic Theology for the New Apostolic Reformation

Volume I
The Nature of God

FOUNDATION OF THE WORLDVIEW OF ANCIENT PEOPLE GROUPS

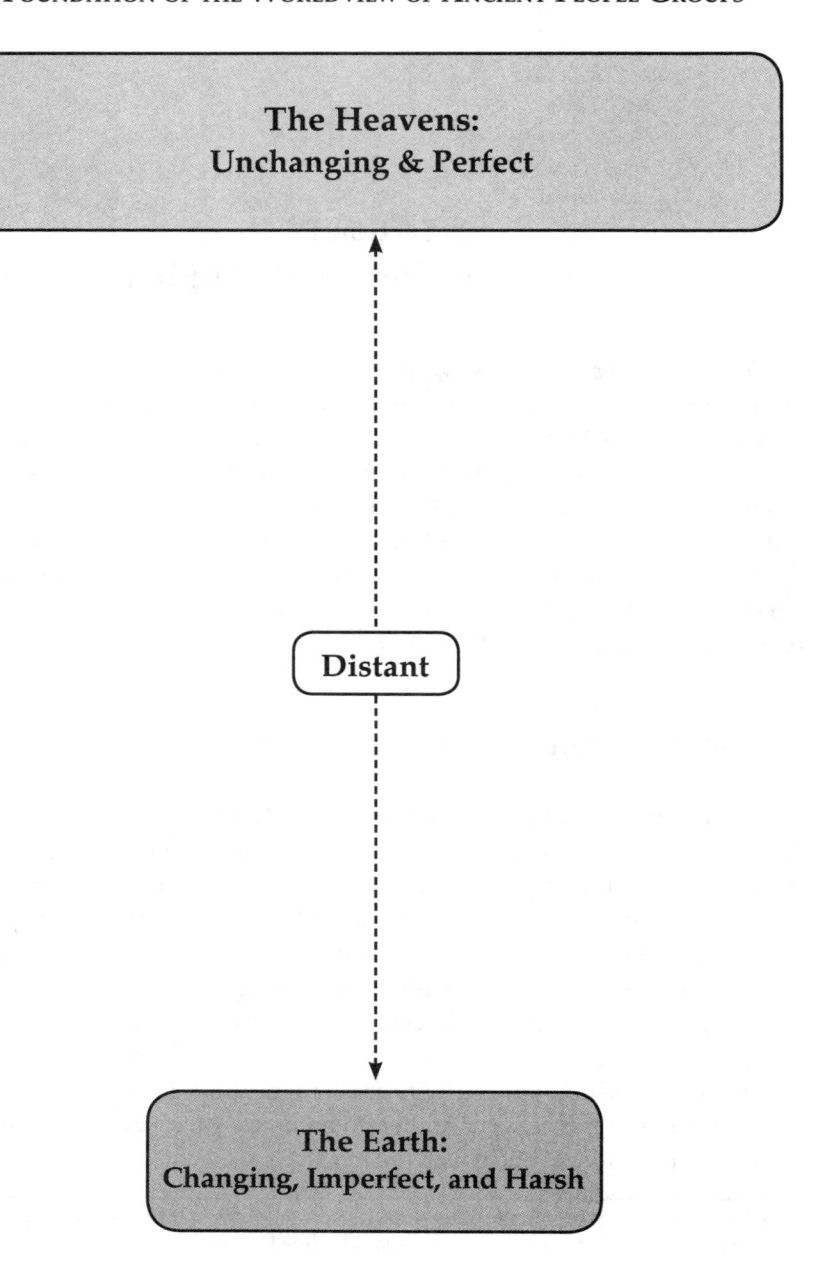

**The Heavens:
Unchanging & Perfect**

Distant

**The Earth:
Changing, Imperfect, and Harsh**

God of the Greek Philosophers

Point 49: Plato's Spiritual World of Thoughts and Ideas

The ancient Greeks had the heavens-versus-earth division at the foundation of their worldview. That was a **dualistic** worldview. Here I am using the most common definition of the word "dualistic," referring to a worldview consisting of two contrasting parts.[31] Building on that dualism, the majority of Greek people came to believe the distant heavenly realm was inhabited by many gods, such as Zeus, Hera, Apollo, and Athena. Those gods were thought to visit and influence the earth whenever they chose to do so.

The ancient Greek philosophers challenged those beliefs in many gods, especially during the period 500 to 300 years before Jesus was born. Most notably were Socrates, Plato, and Aristotle.

Socrates (c. 469–399 BC) focused on the question, "How can we know?" He used his mind to logically challenge the assumptions of the people around him. So unsettling was his questioning to the society in which he lived that government officials sentenced him to death after accusing him of leading the youth astray.

Plato (c. 427–347 BC) followed Socrates and continued to ask questions. Most significant to our discussion is the fact that Plato proposed a dualistic worldview that had no room for the ancient Greek gods. Plato envisioned a heaven that is a world of thoughts and ideals—a world of what he called "ideal forms." His ideal forms developed from his study of mathematics. In that world everything is perfect, eternal, and unchanging. He used the example of a triangle explaining that the perfect triangle exists in that spiritual realm, while every triangle in this natural world is merely a poor reflection of the perfect in the spiritual realm. Plato believed that all things in that world of ideal forms are perfect, while this natural world is temporal, imperfect, and basically unimportant. In the same way that heaven is above and beyond the earth, so Plato's world of thoughts and ideals was above and beyond this natural world.

For Plato, the world of thoughts and ideals was the real world, and it was god. Plato's god was not personal, but simply the entirety of the realm of ideal forms.

---

31 In theology, the word "dualism" is often used to refer to a doctrine that the world contains two opposing powers of good and evil. In philosophy, "dualism" often refers to a system of thought that regards a domain of reality in terms of two independent principles, especially mind and matter (Cartesian dualism). Throughout this book, dualism is used in the most common sense of consisting in two contrasting parts.

Systematic Theology for the New Apostolic Reformation

PLATO'S SPIRITUAL WORLD AS A WORLD OF THOUGHTS AND IDEALS

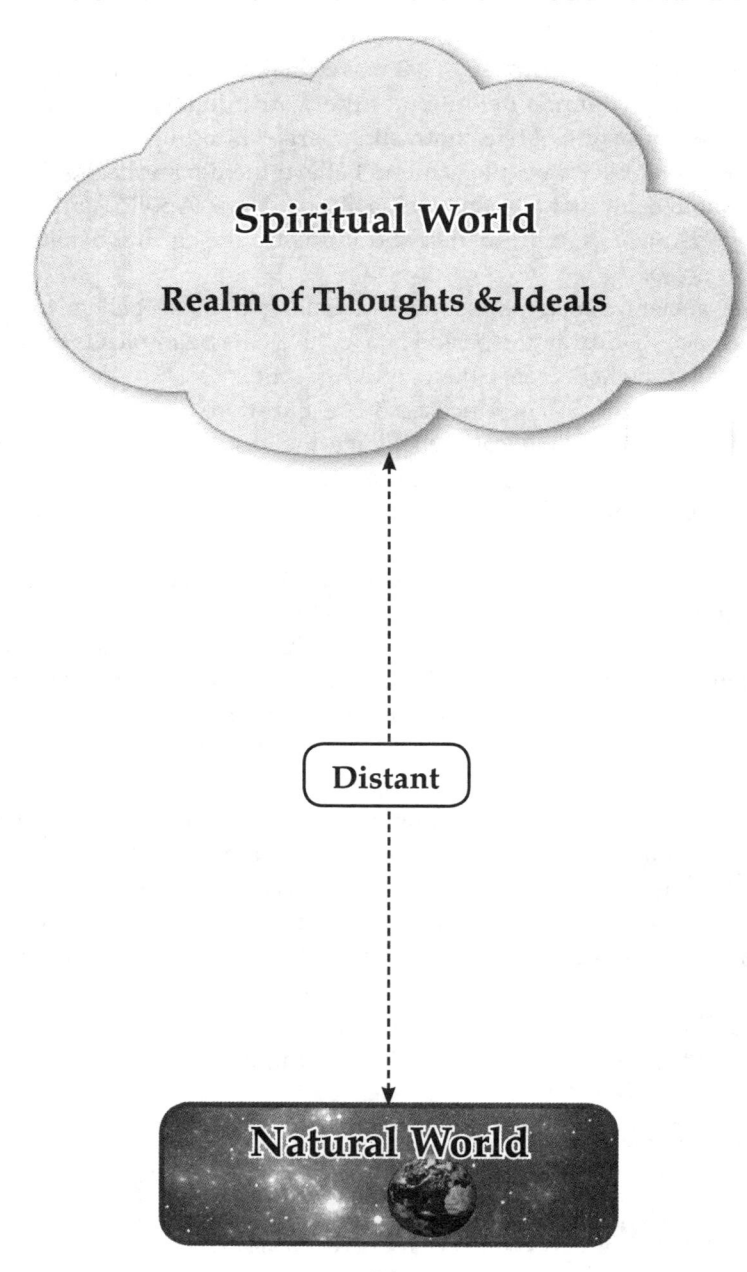

Spiritual World

Realm of Thoughts & Ideals

Distant

Natural World

God of the Greek Philosophers

Plato believed humans can access the world of ideal forms with their thoughts. As people meditate on perfect things they are actually reaching into and experiencing those ideal forms.

Point 50: The Foundation of the Ancient Hebrew Worldview

The ancient Hebrews had a very different worldview than the ancient Greeks. Since the Hebrews had the Book of Genesis as the foundation of their worldview, they recognized the God who spoke creation into existence. As discussed earlier,[32] God entered into creation. He walked and talked with Adam and Eve. Genesis 1 leads the reader to see God close to this world. Further study shows God's spiritual realm filling the natural realm.

FOUNDATION OF ANCIENT HEBRAIC-BIBLICAL THOUGHT WITH THE SPIRITUAL AND NATURAL REALMS FILLING THE SAME SPACE

This identifies the most fundamental difference between the Platonic worldview and the Hebraic-biblical worldview. The foundation of the Platonic worldview consists of two very different and separate worlds.

---

32 Discussed in I:B:7-9.

Systematic Theology for the New Apostolic Reformation

The foundation of the Hebraic-biblical worldview recognizes God's spiritual realm as very close to and even filling the same space as the natural realm.

Point 51: The Timeless Immovable Mover

Aristotle (384–322 BC), a disciple of Plato, further developed the worldview of the ancient Greek philosophers. Most importantly, he assigned the characteristic of "timelessness" to the spiritual world. This concept emerged from the contemporary philosophical idea that time is a trap in which the natural world is confined. Seeing time as a negative thing, the philosophers concluded that the distant spiritual world must not be confined to the limits of time. This concept fit well with Plato's understanding that the spiritual world is a realm of thoughts and ideals. Those thoughts and ideals were seen as unchanging, perfect, and timeless.

Once the spiritual world was seen as timeless, it was thought of as fundamentally different from the natural world. This difference cannot be overly emphasized. We can talk about oil and water being different from each other, but they still have many similar characteristics, such as both being liquid. In contrast, a timeless world has *nothing in common* with the natural world. It is infinitely beyond the natural world. Therefore, when the ancient philosophers talked of a timeless world, they were referring to a world that was totally unlike and separate from the natural world.

Aristotle also pondered the existence of a god and envisioned his god existing in the spiritual timeless world. He began to refer to this god as the **"immovable mover."** This name came from the idea that this god must have pushed everything into existence. Since the immovable mover was so powerful and magnificent that he could push everything into existence, he must be too big to be pushed by his creation. In other words, he must be immovable.

As the immovable mover was given credit for pushing creation into existence, his nature was thought of as more than thoughts and ideals. This led philosophers to think of the spiritual world as more than a mystical cloud of ideal forms. They still were dualistic and believed the spiritual world to be distant, perfect, and timeless, but now the spiritual world was thought of as more concrete—not in the sense of having physical substance, but in the sense of being a real place where the immovable mover exists.

God of the Greek Philosophers

Aristotle's Immovable Mover

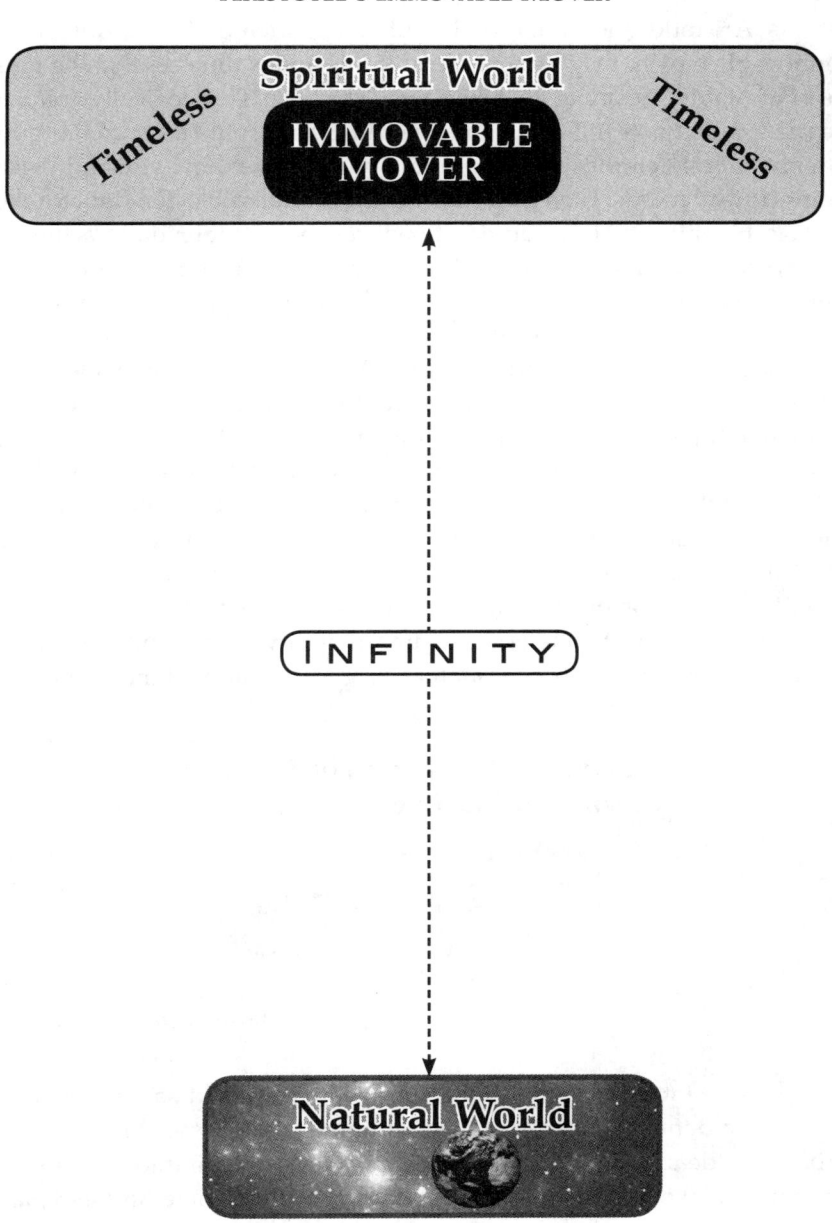

Spiritual World

Timeless — IMMOVABLE MOVER — *Timeless*

INFINITY

Natural World

Systematic Theology for the New Apostolic Reformation

Point 52: The Development of the Immovable Mover

As Aristotle and other philosophers pondered the nature of the immovable mover, they reasoned that if this god is timeless then he must be **immutable**, meaning that he never changes. This logically follows, because if this god fills all of time, nothing new could ever come to his attention. From eternity past, he would have known how you and I were going to act today. Therefore, it would be impossible for him to ever change his mind or have an emotional response to our daily activities. The word immutable also described their god because they equated the immovable mover with truth. Since truth never changes, the immovable mover could never change either.

The ancient Greek philosophers concluded that the immovable mover must be **impassible**. This refers to how this god is never passive in the sense that things can act or move upon him. A helpful way to think of this is to envision the sun and think how powerless people on earth are to vary activity on the sun. The sun is simply too big. No matter what people do, their actions do not influence solar flares or the temperature of the sun. Similarly, the philosophers saw their god as too big to be moved by his creation. He acts on everything and nothing acts upon him.

The concepts of timelessness, immutability, and impassibility are logically consistent with one another. If god fills all of time, then he is immutable and impassible.

A Logical Progression of Thought
According to the Classical View of God

God Is Timeless → God Is Immutable → God Is Impassible

The ancient Greek philosophers also saw their god as **perfect**. They went on to define "perfect" as being without lack or in need of anything. From this idea, the philosophers reasoned that if the immovable mover changed, he would change from his perfect state to something else, and hence, he would no longer be perfect. This reasoning led them back to

God of the Greek Philosophers

their conclusion that their god is immutable. It is these points that became the foundation of ancient Greek philosophical thought concerning god:

> The Immovable Mover
> Timelessness
> Immutability (Never changes)
> Impassibility (Never acted upon)
> Perfect

Out of the idea of the perfection of god developed the attributes of **omnipotence** (all-powerful), **omniscience** (all-knowing), **omnipresent** (present everywhere). Also, the philosophers concluded that their perfect god must be **self-sufficient**, meaning god is absolutely complete in himself, needing and wanting nothing.

A Logical Progression of Thought
According to the Classical View of God

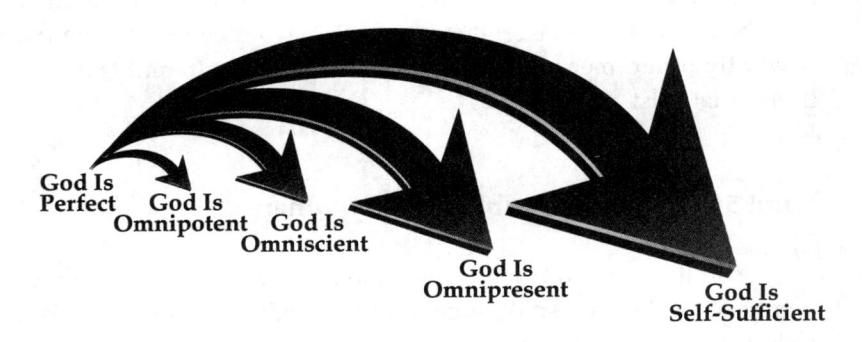

God Is Perfect → God Is Omnipotent → God Is Omniscient → God Is Omnipresent → God Is Self-Sufficient

These attributes are sometimes referred to as the **perfections of god**.[31]

> Perfections of God
> Omnipotent (All-powerful)
> Omniscient (All-knowing)
> Omnipresent (Present-everywhere)
> Self-Sufficient

---

33 Some teachers will include other attributes under the perfections of God, such as holiness and omnibenevolence (meaning, all-good), however, these aspects of perfection became more important as Christian theology developed.

Systematic Theology for the New Apostolic Reformation

Point 53: The Transcendent and Wholly Other

The timeless, perfect god of the ancient Greek philosophers became increasingly prominent among the educated throughout the Greco-Roman world. By the time Jesus was born, many intellectuals had discarded the many gods believed in by the masses and embraced the omnipotent, omniscient, omnipresent, immovable mover.

Then came Plotinus (c. 205–270), a philosopher who took the writings of Plato and reworked them into what has become known as **Neo-platonism**. Plotinus built on Plato's concept of god and referred to god as **"The One."** He taught that no human could ever see that god, but if they did it would be as gazing at the sun because truth, goodness, and beauty radiate out of The One more brilliantly than light from the sun.

Plotinus' god was so beyond the natural world that his god had absolutely nothing in common with this world. Emphasizing this, Plotinus taught that god is totally **transcendent**. By this he meant that god is completely independent of, and removed from, the material universe.

The concept of transcendence was also expressed by saying that god is **wholly other**, meaning that god is completely different from all other things that exist.

Point 54: The Unknowable, Wholly Other

A corollary to god being transcendent and wholly other is that god is totally beyond the grasp of human understanding. In other words, god is **unknowable**. Plotinus saw god as too unlike humans to ever be known. To him god was **incomprehensible**.

The unknowability and incomprehensibility of god is a logical outcome when Plotinus' glowing concept of god is imposed upon the ancient Greek dualistic worldview with the heavens being separated, distant, and totally different than the natural world. Since god belonged to a distant, timeless world, people could never know Him. God was far away. He was of a different world.

With these attributes added to those discussed earlier, we have a picture of the god that came out of Classical Greek philosophy.

God of the Greek Philosophers

"The One" of Plotinus Radiating Out His Attributes

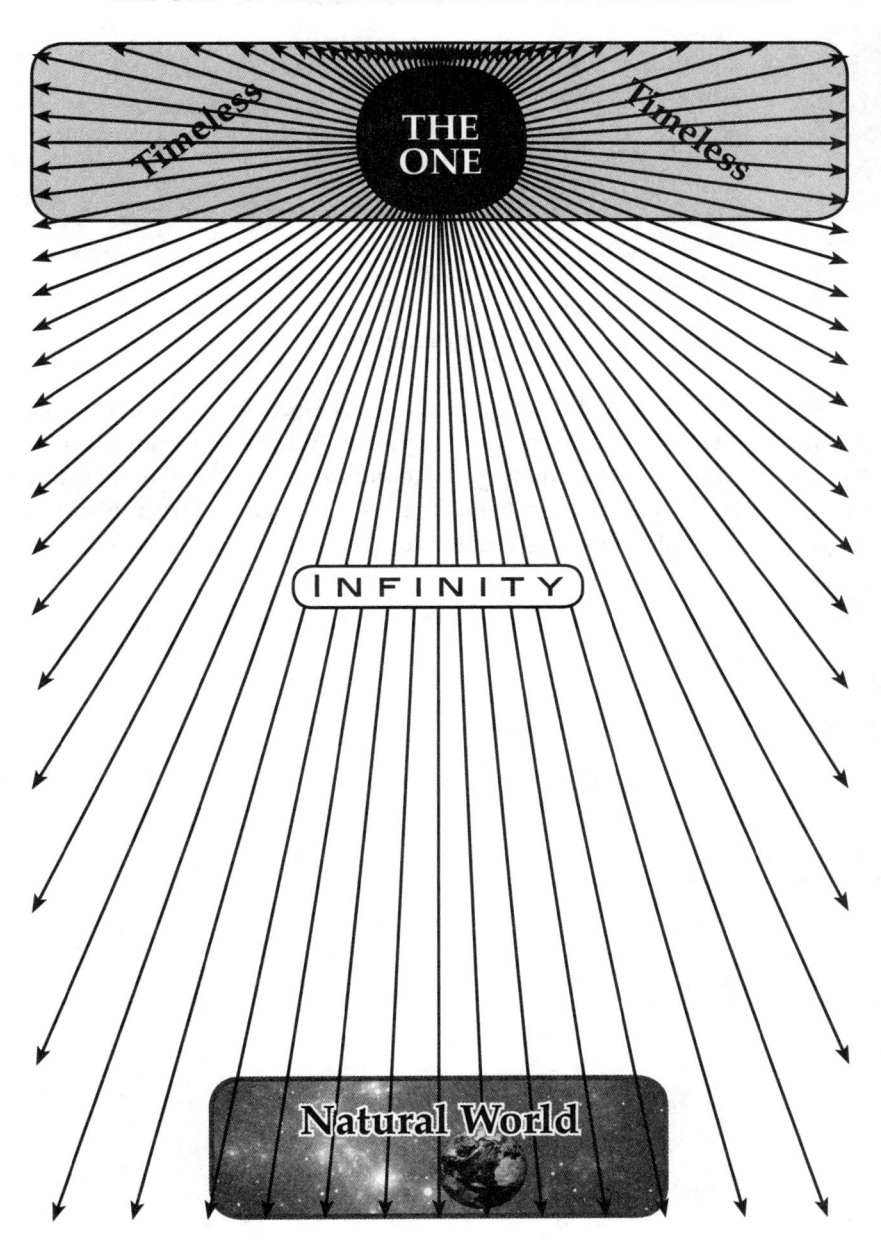

Timeless

THE ONE

Timeless

INFINITY

Natural World

Systematic Theology for the New Apostolic Reformation

<u>Ancient Greek Philosophers' Concept of God</u>
Timeless
Immutable (Never changes)
Impassible (Never acted upon)
Perfect
Omnipotent (All-powerful)
Omniscient (All-knowing)
Omnipresent (Present everywhere)
Self-Sufficient
Transcendent
Wholly Other
Unknowable and Incomprehensible

The development of this understanding of God led to a revolutionary change in Western civilization. Most importantly, it helped change society from **polytheism** (belief in many gods) to **monotheism** (belief in one God). This prepared the way for Christians to present the God of the Bible to the people throughout the Greco-Roman world.

Section G
God of Classical Theology

Modern Christians like to think their concept of God has been developed from the Bible alone, yet those studied in the field know better. What Western Christians believe today is a mixture of the Hebraic-biblical concept of God and the god who was proposed by the ancient Greek philosophers. The influence of Plato, Aristotle, Philo, and Plotinus is especially evident.

Point 55: The Hellenization of Society

During the 4th, 3rd, and 2nd centuries BC, a great purging of culture took place in the Middle East and the region around the Mediterranean Sea. Starting with Alexander the Great (356–323 BC), the Greek rulers believed that they could most effectively bring foreign people under their rule by destroying their native culture, including their art, literature, and consciousness of local history. The imposition of Greek culture became known as the **Hellenization**[34] of society.

As Greek became the primary language in the political, business, and literary world, many Jews living outside of Israel were no longer fluent in the Hebrew language.[35] Therefore, they needed a Greek translation of the OT rather than the original Hebrew used by their forefathers. For this reason, the **Septuagint** was developed during the 3rd and 2cd centuries BC.

---

34 This terminology comes from the fact that the Greek people during that period called themselves *Hellenes*, a named derived from their mythical forebear, Helen.
35 We can read in the Book of Acts about the "Hellenistic Jews" (Acts 6:1; called *Grecians* in some translations), referring to those Jews who had embraced the language, lifestyle, and culture of the surrounding Greek people.

Systematic Theology for the New Apostolic Reformation

Today when we read the Septuagint, it is easy to see how the Hebrew Bible was interpreted not only into the Greek language but also through the Greek worldview. Because the Classical Greek philosophical concept of god was of a god who cannot be seen and is unknowable, some passages in the Septuagint were deliberately changed eliminating what the translators considered anthropomorphisms of God.

For example, the original Hebrew version of Exodus 24:10 tells about the Hebrew leaders "seeing" God, but the translators of the Septuagint inserted the word "place," saying that the leaders saw the place where God was, since they did not believe anyone could see God. In the Hebrew version of Isaiah 38:11, we read about Hezekiah bemoaning the fact that he will not see the Lord any longer; the Septuagint inserts the word "salvation," hence telling us that Hezekiah will not see the salvation of the Lord. The translators of the Greek Septuagint made numerous such changes reflecting their concept of god as unseeable and unknowable.

It is important to realize that the Septuagint was the principle version of the OT used by the early Church until after the *Latin Vulgate* was completed by Jerome in 405 AD. This helps us understand how and why the early Church was influenced so strongly by the Classical Greek philosophical view of god.

Today we need to seriously consider what we want as the foundation of our concept of God. If we believe that what the original Bible-writers wrote were accurate records of God's interactions with this world, then we must question those passages that were altered from the original words.

Point 56: Syncretization of Yahweh with the Immovable Mover

During the 1st century, the teachings of the Greek philosophers were at the forefront of intellectual thought. Many Church and secular leaders wrestled with the related issues.

An influential Jewish philosopher, Philo of Alexandria (c. 20 BC–50 AD), attempted to harmonize Greek philosophy with Jewish philosophy. In that attempt, he equated the Hebrew creator-deity Yahweh with Aristotle's immovable mover. As it turned out, Philo's work influenced Christian thinkers more than his own Jewish brethren.

God of Classical Theology

Point 57: Syncretization of Greek Philosophy with Christianity

Many of the early Church fathers eagerly embraced the fundamentals of Classical Greek philosophy because the philosophers offered a foundation upon which Christianity could be easily built. Most importantly, Greek philosophy offered a belief that there must be one God rather than the multiple gods believed in by the common Greeks/Romans and that humans must have an immortal soul.

> Greek Philosophical Thoughts upon which Christianity Could Be Built
> 1. There must be one Supreme God.
> 2. Human beings have an immortal soul.

People who accepted these fundamentals of Greek philosophy could be easily presented with the God of Christianity.

Hence, Clement of Alexandria (c. 150–c. 215 AD) regarded Greek philosophy as a gift of God preparing the world for Christianity. Justin Martyr (100–c. 165 AD) admired Socrates and thought that Plato had borrowed his wisdom from Moses and the OT prophets. Origen (185–254 AD) spent much time trying to reconcile Greek philosophy with Christianity, as did other teachers.

At the other extreme were Church fathers such as Tertullian (c. 160–c. 225 AD), who saw the teachings of the Greek philosophers as little more than the foolishness and delusion of the pagan world.

During that period, Greek philosophy was on the forefront of intellectual thought. It was the worldview with which early Christian thinkers had to wrestle. To confirm this, we can note that the 33 most well-known works of the early Church fathers make at least 2,069 references to Pythagoras, Socrates, Plato, Aristotle, and Plotinus.[36] That fact is the most revealing evidence concerning how Christianity was syncretized with Greek philosophy.

Christian leaders could not offer to the people of the Roman Empire a god who was less powerful or magnificent than the god offered by the

---

36 The number in this reference was compiled by performing a series of simple, exact-word, individual name searches of the Greek thinkers in the 37 volume collection of the *Writings of the Early Church Fathers*, English Translation, contained in the *Professional Reference Edition; PC Study Bible 5* (PC Study Bible formatted electronic database © 2003, 2006 by Biblesoft, Inc.).

Systematic Theology for the New Apostolic Reformation

Greek philosophers. Hence, the starting point for discussions about God was of a timeless, perfect, transcendent Being. Many of the Church fathers set out to convince the masses that the God of the Bible and revealed in Jesus Christ is the god taught by the Greek philosophers.

Modern Classical theologians try to downplay the significance of Greek philosophical influence, but distancing our fathers from the Greek philosophers is intellectually dishonest. As mentioned, those fathers made at least 2,069 references to Pythagoras, Socrates, Plato, Aristotle, and Plotinus. With the Greek philosophers being referenced that many times, the reader can be assured that their thoughts permeated the writings of the early Church.

Point 58: Augustine's Training in Greek Philosophy

Of all the Church fathers, Augustine (354–430 AD) was the most influential in the syncretization of Greek philosophy with Christianity.

To understand Augustine's influence, it is helpful to first identify the major influences on his life. As a young man, Augustine lived a hedonistic lifestyle, although his mother tried to raise him to be a Christian. As a teenager he left the Church to follow Manichaeism, a major religion founded in Babylon, built on the belief that there are two gods, one who created everything good and another who created everything evil. After spending at least nine years (c. ages 20 to 29) studying Manichaeism, Augustine left that and became a student of Plotinus' teaching.

We already discussed Plotinus (c. 205–270 AD), who referred to god as "The One" and explained how god is above all human understanding. Further, Plotinus taught that a human seeing god is like gazing at the sun because truth, goodness, and beauty radiate out of "The One" more brilliantly than light from the sun.

This was the concept of god that Augustine held when he began investigating Christianity as a young adult.

At first, Augustine was unimpressed by what he read in the Bible, because the God revealed in Scripture did not meet his expectations. In particular, Augustine could not accept the numerous verses in the Bible that talk about God changing His mind and showing emotions. Augustine was so committed to the philosophical concept that God was timeless and immutable that he was unable to accept the Bible as true.

God of Classical Theology

Augustine Embraced "The One" of Plotinus

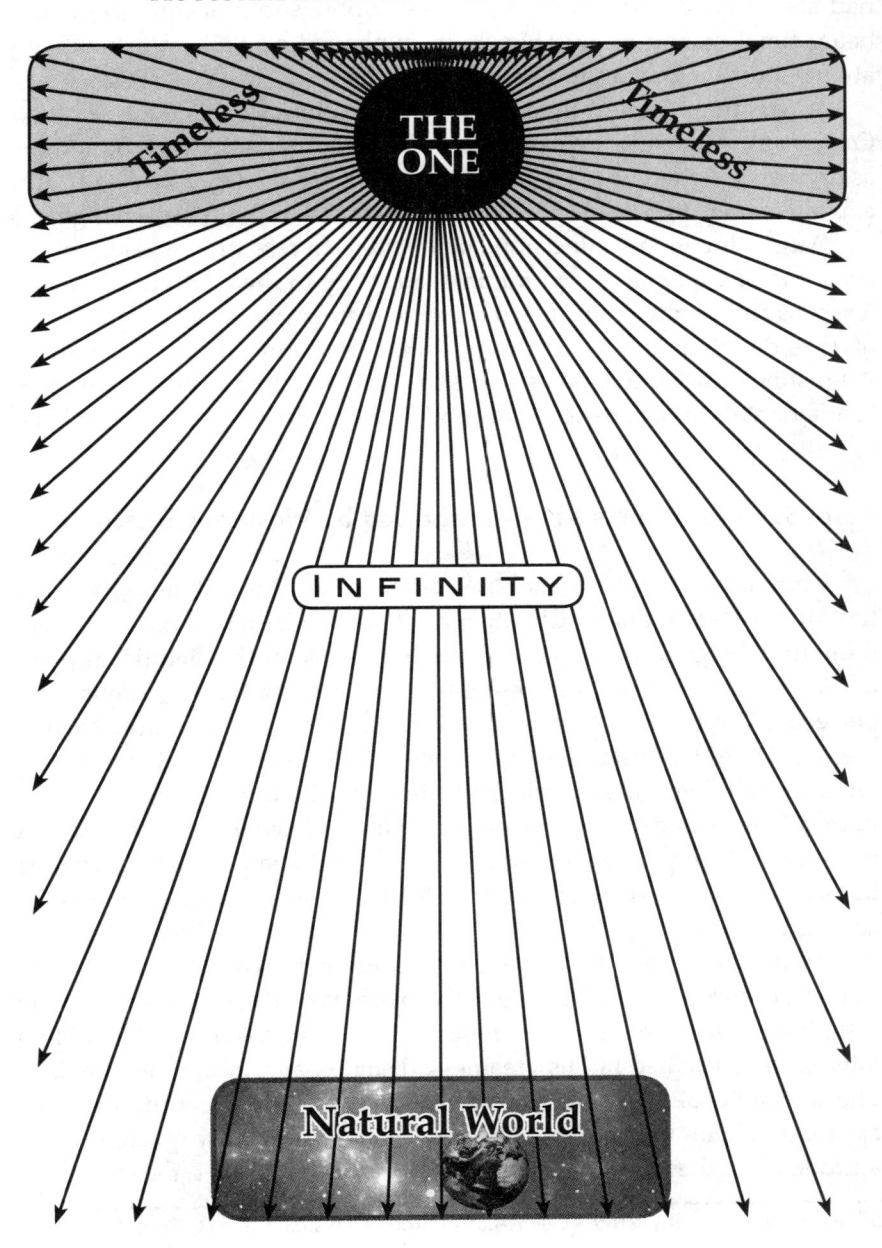

THE ONE

Timeless   Timeless

INFINITY

Natural World

Systematic Theology for the New Apostolic Reformation

Then Augustine was attracted to the ascetic lifestyle and teaching ability of Ambrose (340–397 AD), the bishop of Milan. Bishop Ambrose had also studied and embraced the Greek philosophical concept of God being timeless and immutable, so he explained all Bible verses talking about God changing as anthropomorphisms.

Augustine accepted the bishop's explanations. In his book, entitled *Confessions,* Augustine explained how he could not accept the Scriptures as divinely inspired until he heard Bishop Ambrose allegorize the OT and explain as mere figures of speech the verses that talk about God changing.[37]

Augustine made a decision. He decided to reject the literal biblical accounts of God changing and, instead, cling to the attributes of timelessness and immutability. It is difficult to over-emphasize the significance of that decision. It was a turning point in Church history. Although Augustine recognized God as a personal Being, to him God had the same fundamental characteristics as the god of the ancient Greek philosophers.

Point 59: Augustine's Views Embraced by Western Christianity

Church historians generally agree that Augustine's theology has dominated Western Christianity (Roman Catholic and Protestant thought). His great influence was partly because of the significant point in history in which he lived. Preceding the 4th century, Christians were persecuted and tens of thousands were martyred for their faith. Then in the year 313 AD, Constantine, the emperor of Rome, passed a law granting religious freedom. Soon Christianity became the official religion of the Roman Empire, and several million people flooded into the Church. The vast majority of those people were of the Greek and Roman culture. Facilitating this sudden and massive expansion of Christianity were Church leaders such as Augustine.

Augustine's concept of God can be seen in the construction of huge cathedrals during the Middle Ages. The places where people met with God were built with massive stones, reflecting the immovability of God. High lofty ceilings testified of His greatness, distance, and incomprehensibility. The unemotional and stoic concept of God can be seen in how people approached Him within those cathedrals, taking on a very quiet, reverent attitude. Since they conceived of God as being quiet and stoic, they naturally

---

[37] Augustine, *St. Augustine's Confessions I,* Loeb Classical Library, Book VI, p. 285.

God of Classical Theology

wanted to take on the same demeanor when coming into the sanctuary of God.

Point 60: Augustine as Symbolic of His Times

At this point it is helpful to think of Augustine as symbolic of his times. Of course, Augustine was a real person who lived and profoundly influenced Western civilization, however, he is symbolic in the sense that he is a historic figure who is representative of the thinking of that period. As we try to understand what theologians and philosophers were thinking in his time period, Augustine's writings are the most beneficial in this endeavor. He was brilliant, and his writings are the ones most available to us today.

However, as people looking back nearly 1,600 years, we are not necessarily thinking of an individual named Augustine. We have no personal connection with him, and if he walked into our world today, none of us could recognize him. So for our discussion here, Augustine is a historic figure who is representative of many leaders of that period.

I am taking this perspective because individuals alive today who feel a personal connection with Augustine may feel defensive when I point out Augustine's weaknesses and errors. Most of us are simply interested in understanding the development of Western thought and do not mean to criticize the person named Augustine. To us, Augustine is a symbol. He was molded by the culture around him. He took the ideas at the forefront of intellectual thought and syncretized them into Christian thought. Many other Church leaders were wrestling with the same issues. They were trying to explain Christianity in terms that made sense to them and to the educated people of their time. Hence, we can be grateful to Augustine for his contribution to Western Christianity. However, we can objectively analyze his thinking in the same way he analyzed the thinking of leaders who contributed to the thoughts of his time.

Point 61: God, the Maximally Excellent Being

Many Christian philosophers and theologians followed in the footsteps of Augustine. During the early Middle Ages, philosophy was thought of as "faith seeking understanding." The logical arguments of philosophy were

Systematic Theology for the New Apostolic Reformation

seen as supporting theology, and hence, philosophy and theology were seen as inseparable and totally compatible. With philosophy and theology married together, the Classical view of God was further developed and firmly seated in Western Christianity.

Contributing to Classical theology was the period of intellectual endeavor known as *Scholasticism* (11th–16th century). During that period, knowledge was thought to increase as thinkers built on the ideas of those who went before them. In particular, they focused on studying, rehashing, and refining the writings of great thinkers such as Aristotle, Augustine, Anselm, and Aquinas.

Anselm (c. 1033–1109 AD) was a philosopher and theologian who built on the foundation laid by Augustine. By the time Anselm came along, philosophers and theologians described God as a "maximally excellent Being." By this, they meant that God must be the best of everything. Anselm took this concept and described God as a being ". . . than which nothing greater can be conceived."[38] This description of God was used so much that it became a standard for philosophical thought. Once this became the standard, the attributes of timelessness, immutability, and impassibility, along with the perfections, were fixed in Western intellectual thought.

Then during the late Middle Ages, Aristotle's works became popular. Significant amounts of Classical Greek writings were translated and made available in Latin, the common language of the educated population throughout most of Europe. Aristotle's influence was so predominant during that period that he was often referred to as *"the* Philosopher."

Drawing heavily upon Aristotle's writings, Thomas Aquinas (1225–1274 AD) is known for battling the philosophical issues of his time. Aquinas is most remembered today for his logical arguments on the existence of God. However, it is important to know that Aquinas set out to prove the existence of the Timeless, Impassible, Immutable One. As a result, his efforts established the Classical view of God more firmly in the minds of the Western Church.

Eventually, the whole of Europe was being transformed by the founding of universities. Theology and philosophy held positions as king and queen in the kingdom of education. Students were expected to first and foremost master these subjects. The marriage of Western philosophy with theology assured the outcome of the Classical view of God.

---

38 This description was used by Anselm of Canterbury in 1078 in his *Proslogion*.

God of Classical Theology

Point 62: Reformed Theology, the Child of Classical Theology

When the Protestant Reformation erupted in the 16th century, God was portrayed by the Church as the immovable Being who was worshiped by quiet, somber people sitting in massive cathedrals. That concept of God profoundly influenced the theology of Martin Luther (1483–1546) and John Calvin (1509–1564). Luther was an Augustinian monk when he took his bold stand against the established Church. Calvin quoted Augustine in his writings more than he quoted any other person. Both Luther and Calvin held to all of the attributes of God that identify the Classical view of God. As many theologians and historians have noted, the theologies of Luther and Calvin are the children of Classical theology.

HISTORICAL INFLUENCE OF AUGUSTINE UPON LUTHER AND CALVIN

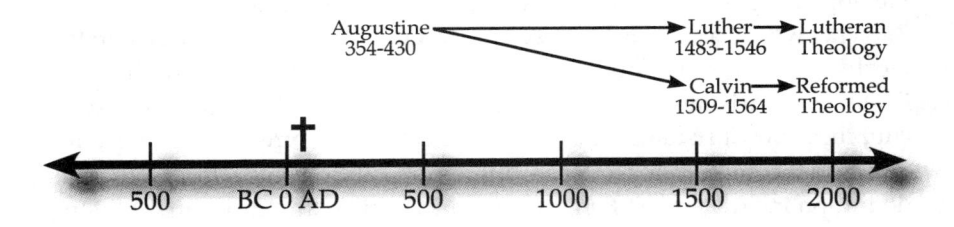

Augustine (354-430) → Luther (1483-1546) → Lutheran Theology
Augustine → Calvin (1509-1564) → Reformed Theology

Timeline: 500 BC — 0 AD — 500 — 1000 — 1500 — 2000

Point 63: Reformed Theology and Evangelical Christianity

As Calvinism developed, it became known as Reformed theology. Today the *Westminster Confession of Faith* is a document that is used by thousands of Reformed churches as their own statement of faith. This document begins its description of God as follows:

> There is but one only living and true God, who is infinite in being and perfection, a most pure spirit, invisible, without body, parts, or passions, immutable, immense, eternal, incomprehensible . . . .[39]

---

[39] Cornelius Burges, *Westminster Confession of Faith*, ed. S.W. Carruthers (Glasgow, UK: Free Presbyterian Publications, 1986), p. 6.

Systematic Theology for the New Apostolic Reformation

When the writers of this confession stated that God is eternal, they were equating this with timelessness. The writers followed the logical implications of timelessness, stating that God is also immutable and without passions, meaning that He never changes His mind or has any inner emotional experiences. When God is said to be "infinite in being and perfection," the writers were including the attributes of omnipotence, omniscience, and omnipresence. The Westminster Confession also declares that God is incomprehensible, meaning that humans cannot understand God in any way (unless God reveals Himself from His infinitely-distant, timeless world).

Today Reformed theology functions as the big brother of evangelical Christianity. In other words, teachers of Reformed theology hold a prominent position within evangelical circles, serving as an anchor, trying to keep evangelicals tethered to their historic roots (Classical theology). Evangelical Christians have been sitting at the feet of Classical/Reformed theology for years, although most evangelicals do not know it.

The word *evangelical* is used differently in different parts of the world today. In much of Europe, it refers to all Protestant churches and Protestant Christians. In the United States, evangelical refers to Protestant churches and Christians who believe the Bible is inspired, see the need for a personal commitment to Jesus, and emphasize evangelism. (Note: This definition includes most Pentecostal and Charismatic Christians[40]). Using this latter definition, we can note that evangelical Christianity has been profoundly influenced and shaped by Classical/Reformed theology.

Today some evangelicals fully embrace the teaching of John Calvin (Reformed theology). Others reject some aspects of Calvin's teachings. Most often they reject Calvin's strong emphasis on how all things are predestined by God. Unfortunately, those who reject Calvin's emphasis on predestination tend to think that they are free of Calvinism, but that is rarely the case. Reformed theology reaches into evangelical theology much deeper than that. Until Christians have rethought and made the appropriate changes to their concept of God, they have not escaped the Augustinian/Calvinistic concept of God that was profoundly influenced by Plato, Aristotle, and Plotinus. Until that concept of God is changed, it is almost impossible to change the rest of one's theology. (Of course, that is one goal of this book.)

---

[40] In popular usage of the word *evangelical* in the United States (as in Christian bookstores), Pentecostals are identified as a group separate from evangelicals.

God of Classical Theology

Point 64: Augustine's Influence on Roman Catholicism

Not only Protestantism, but all of Western Christianity is deeply rooted in Augustinian thought. The Roman Catholic Church considers Augustine a saint and preeminent doctor of the Church. Many historians have referred to Augustine as the father of Roman Catholicism. Of course, Augustine does not deserve all of the credit (or blame, depending upon your perspective) for the development of Western theology, because countless numbers of theologians and philosophers contributed to its development. However, Augustine clearly communicated the synthesis of the ancient Greek philosopher's god with the God of the Bible.

That synthesis comes down to modern times, as can be seen in the popular *Penny Catechism* of the Catholic Church. To the inquiry, "What is God?", it replies:

> God is the Supreme Spirit, Who alone exists of Himself, and is infinite in all perfections.

Although the average Roman Catholic sitting in the pew does not know it, the terminology, "Supreme Spirit, Who alone exists of Himself," originated with the discussions of the Church fathers wrestling with the thoughts of the ancient Greek philosophers. The phrase, "infinite in all perfections," reaches back to the Transcendent Being of Plato, the Immovable Mover of Aristotle, The One of Plotinus, and the maximally excellent Being of the philosophers of the Middle Ages.

Point 65: Theology of Karl Barth

One of the most influential Protestant theologians of the 20th century was Karl Barth (1886–1968), now known as the father of Neo-orthodoxy. Barth built his theology in the Classical/Reformed tradition, although he disagreed with some of Calvin's basic teachings.

Barth is especially known for having emphasized that God is wholly other, meaning God is unlike anything in the created world. Barth praised the early Church fathers who taught that God is transcendent, and he rightly associated their views with those of Plato and Plotinus:

Systematic Theology for the New Apostolic Reformation

> ... the early Church and its theology ... they spoke of ... the incomprehensibility of God, they were [not] saying anything basically different from what Plato and Plotinus could also say when they spoke about the inaccessibility of the true and supreme being and the transcendence of the knowledge of this being.[41]

Here, Barth pointed out how Classical theology is built on the same foundation of transcendence and incomprehensibility that was held by the non-Christian philosophers Plato and Plotinus.

Barth is also famous for his statement that Jesus is the only true and perfect revelation of God that we have, and therefore, all of our theology must start and finish with Jesus as He is revealed in the Bible. However, Barth did not follow his own advice, but instead he built his theology on God being timeless, immutable, transcendent, wholly other, and incomprehensible—none of which can be identified in Jesus Christ as He is revealed in the Bible.

Point 66: Modern Classical/Reformed Theologians

Classical/Reformed theologians repeat Barth's error over and over again. In their books offering a systematic theology they almost always state (usually within the prolegomenon) that the Bible is the source of truth that will be used to determine all truth. Then immediately after asserting that, authors will launch into a study on the nature of God, and in the first few pages, they will either state that God is timeless or list attributes of God that are derived from the belief that God is timeless. Where did they find that in the Bible? This leap from the Bible to the unknown is obvious in all Classical/Reformed systematic theologies.

No other field of study would tolerate such inconsistency. If someone in the field of physics, geology, chemistry, biology, medicine, sociology, geography, or astronomy tried to develop a system of thought built on such an obvious leap, colleagues would rush to point out the error lest their whole field of study be discredited.

Similar mistakes are repeated about Jesus being the foundation of truth. Theologians feel good about declaring that Jesus is the standard

---

41 Barth, *Church Dogmatics*, II/1, p. 185.

God of Classical Theology

by which all theological truth is to be determined. But then, if they are Classical or Reformed theologians, they will use the concept of timelessness as their cornerstone. Nowhere does the Bible state or imply that Jesus was timeless.

In spite of these obvious inconsistencies, most Bible colleges and seminaries in the Western world continue to teach some form of Classical/Reformed theology (usually with their own unique perspective). In order to make Classical/Reformed theology acceptable it is almost always taught alongside of Western philosophy. This union is necessary because without the philosophical idea that God is timeless, Classical/Reformed theology has no foundation on which to build. But as we have been emphasizing, timelessness is nothing more than an assumption.

Point 67: Classical Theologians Agreeing with Plotinus

The attributes that originated with the ancient Greek philosophers are logically consistent with timelessness and, therefore, are accepted by most modern Classical/Reformed theologians:

<u>Classical/Reformed Concept of God</u>
Timeless
Immutable (Never changes)
Impassible (Never acted upon)
Perfect
Omnipotent (All-powerful)
Omniscient (All-knowing)
Omnipresent (Present everywhere)
Self-Sufficient
Transcendent
Wholly Other
Unknowable and Incomprehensible

Classical/Reformed teachers do embrace other attributes and descriptions of God, such as God is like Jesus, He is love, and He is Father. Especially important in their theology are the attributes of sovereignty and holiness. Later on we will talk more in-depth about these and other attributes of God accepted by Classical/Reformed teachers. However, so far we have identified and focused on those attributes that originated

Systematic Theology for the New Apostolic Reformation

with the Classical Greek philosophers and are now accepted by Classical/Reformed teachers. All of the attributes listed above were evident in Plotinus' concept of "The One" back in the 3rd century.

Of the above list of attributes, there is one that some modern Classical/Reformed theologians are questioning or even rejecting. It is the impassibility of God. This is important enough for us to explain.

Point 68: The Modern Rejection of the Impassibility of God

As we discussed earlier, the ancient Greek philosophers concluded that God is impassible, meaning that God is active, rather than passive, because He acts on everything and nothing acts upon Him. God is too big to be moved by His creation (like the sun cannot be influenced by what humans on earth do). God does not respond to humanity or to anything He created. He is never passive in the sense that things can act or move upon Him.

This concept of God being impassible held sway over Western Christianity for about 1,500 years, from the 4th century to the early 1900s. Just in the last century, some noted theologians have taken the position that God is passible. Among these are Andrew M. Fairbairn, Karl Barth, James Cone, Robert Jenson, Eberhard Jungel, Kazoh Kitanmori, Jung Young Lee, John Macquarrie, Jurgen Moltmann, Worlfhart Pannenberg, Alan Torrance, Thomas F. Torrance, Keith Ward, Nicholas Wolterstorff, and Hans Kung. Even though these theologians and others have rejected impassibility as an attribute of God, they disagree as to the manner and extent of God's passibility.

The concept of passibility can cover a broad spectrum of God's responsiveness to humanity. Some who accept passibility think of God as very sensitive to and responsive to people on earth. At the other end of the spectrum are those who accept God's passibility but only apply it to God sharing in some fashion the experience of His Son suffering during the crucifixion. This spectrum is broad because Classical/Reformed theologians can continue to dismiss as anthropomorphisms the reports in the Bible of God responding to ordinary people. However, it is more difficult to think of Father-God being totally unfeeling toward His Son.

God of Classical Theology

THE BROAD SPECTRUM CONCERNING THE PASSIBILITY OF GOD

God Is Responsive ◄──────────────► God Suffered
to All Humanity   Only with Jesus

In most discussions on this subject, theologians talk about the end of the spectrum where God suffered with Jesus: Did God experience any sorrow, anguish, or pain as His Son suffered on the cross? If He did not, then was the death of His Son truly a sacrifice on His part? On the other hand, if God did suffer, Classical/Reformed theologians have another conflict in their systematic theology. Since they believe God is timeless and immutable, they must see the anguish which Father-God experienced as continuing throughout eternity. As explained earlier, in a timeless world, nothing ever changes.

Some Classically-trained Christians are inconsistent on this issue. They try to incorporate into their understanding the idea of God experiencing anguish during the crucifixion of Jesus, but they think of that anguish diminishing and moving into some dark recess of God's consciousness over time. But that is illogical. If God is timeless, then what He experienced at the moment of Jesus' most excruciating pain is what He experiences throughout all of eternity. If Jesus' pain was on the forefront of God's mind at the instant of Jesus' death, then it will remain on the forefront of God's mind throughout eternity's future. Plus, it was always on the forefront of God's mind throughout eternity past—never decreasing, never being placed in the back of His mind. This is the inescapable conclusion when Classical/Reformed teachers say that God experienced pain when Jesus was crucified.

Modern Classical/Reformed theologians who continue to hold to the impassibility of God accuse their colleagues of being inconsistent. Indeed, if those colleagues hold to the timelessness of God and see God's experience of Jesus' pain changing over time, then they are being inconsistent.

On the other hand, if they recognize that God experienced something during the crucifixion of Jesus, why couldn't He experience something when other humans suffer? Doesn't God love humanity? How can He be sensitive toward His Son and hard-hearted toward the rest of humanity on whose behalf He sent His Son to die?

Systematic Theology for the New Apostolic Reformation

This issue is more than God experiencing humanity's pain throughout eternity. It is whether or not God experiences anything at any time when people suffer. If He does experience anything, then it is certainly possible that the biblical accounts of God responding to people are true accounts rather than just anthropomorphisms. All Classical/Reformed theologians know that if they accept the biblical reports of God responding to people in time, then God is not timeless within creation. Rather than question their doctrine of timelessness, theologians seated in Classical/Reformed thought continue to label all such accounts as anthropomorphisms.

Theologians such as myself believe that such reasoning is foolish. If God can respond to the sufferings of Jesus, then He can respond to the sufferings of any human being. Since He can respond to people, He is not impassible. Since He is not impassible, He is not timeless—at least, not within creation.

Section H
Two Views in Conflict

We have identified the attributes assigned to God by the ancient Greek philosophers and now embraced by Classical/Reformed theologians.

<u>Classical/Reformed Theologian's Concept of God</u>
Timeless
Immutable (Never changes)
Impassible (Never acted upon) (Rejected by some)
Perfect
Omnipotent (All-powerful)
Omniscient (All-knowing)
Omnipresent (Present everywhere)
Self-Sufficient
Transcendent
Wholly Other
Incomprehensible and Unknowable

These attributes originated with non-Christians (and non-Jews) independently of the Scriptures. This is no reason to discard them, but it does give us reason to think seriously and then decide if and how these attributes correspond to the revelation of God given in the Bible and revealed through Jesus Christ.

However, challenging these attributes is not easy. They are so deeply embedded within Western Christianity that most modern Christians treat them as sacred. Christians may even feel sinister simply questioning if God does or does not possess each of these attributes. Christians want to think of God as the maximally excellent Being. They want to accredit Him with the best of everything. To do otherwise seems dishonoring.

Systematic Theology for the New Apostolic Reformation

Today someone who questions these attributes may be put to death as Socrates was for asking too many questions. Of course, I speak metaphorically, as in the death of a career, ministry, or even close personal relationships, yet one great truth that Socrates contributed to Western society is that we will never know truth unless we question everything. Only if we have been critical of our own beliefs will we ever know if what we believe is true.

Point 69: Western Communication about God Is Abstract

If we ask questions and compare the philosophically originated Greek ideas of god with the biblical revelation of God, there are several truths that immediately become evident.

First, the Bible uses very different terminology than that of Greek thought. The OT uses Hebrew words which relate one concept to another. For example, Yahweh Jireh refers to God who is the Provider of the person who speaks the name. Note that God is related to a recipient of His help.

In contrast, Western thought, which has its foundation in the ancient Greek worldview, typically communicates in *abstract* terminology. By abstract we mean that words isolate that which is being spoken of from everything else. For example, if we say that God is omnipotent, we are distinguishing God from everything that is not all powerful.

Another example would be how Western thought would be comfortable saying that God is merciful, while Hebraic-biblical thought would say, "God is merciful *to us.*" The point is that Hebraic-biblical thought tends to explain things by *relating* one concept to another.

Consider a modern rabbi who introduced the Scriptures to a classroom of children. Before they began reading, the rabbi placed a drop of honey on each of the children's copy of the Scriptures. Then he asked each child to lick the honey and know that this is what the Scriptures are like. In contrast, Western teachers will explain the Bible with abstract terms. Instead of associating the Scriptures with honey, the Western mind distinguishes it from all other books.

A Western person may describe the Scriptures with terms such as *inerrant* or *infallible*. These are abstract words. Compare this to the terminology I offered in the prolegomenon of this book, i.e., how we should take the Scriptures *seriously*. This word is not abstract because

Two Views in Conflict

anyone who takes the Scriptures seriously will have to adjust their life accordingly. In contrast, someone who believes the Bible is inerrant or infallible may choose to ignore what it says. The words *inerrant* and *infallible* fall tragically short of any human contact.

Consider how Jewish writers speak about the Scriptures. The Psalmist says, *"Your word is a lamp to my feet"* (Ps. 119:105). Notice how the Word of God is tied to its role in a person's life. Similarly, Paul wrote:

> *All Scripture is inspired by God and profitable for teaching, for reproof, for correction, for training in righteousness; so that the man of God may be adequate, equipped for every good work.*
> (2 Tim. 3:16-17)

Paul related Scriptures to God breathing on the words and to their relational function in the life of a godly person.

This pattern of communication is evident throughout Hebraic-biblical thought, which is especially significant in our discussion about God. All of the attributes assigned to God by the ancient Greek philosophers are abstract. This will become obvious as we discuss omnipotence, omniscience, and omnipresence.

Point 70: Is God Omnipotent?

Today Christians are taught that God is omnipotent (all powerful). Indeed, the power of God is an aspect of His nature which is prominent throughout Scripture. He created the universe with His spoken Word and destroyed humanity (except Noah and his family) with a flood. Obviously, God's power is tremendous!

But does the Bible ever say that God is omnipotent? Before I answer this, try to think in Hebraic-biblical terms. The God who reveals Himself in the Bible was not interested in revealing the things about Himself that the ancient Greek philosophers thought important. For example, God revealed Himself to Abraham as *El Shaddai*. As explained earlier, some teachers interpret *El Shaddai* as "God, the Omnipotent One," but that is not what this name means. God was not interested in telling Abraham that He was the Most, the Greatest, or the Best of Everything. God was making Himself known to Abraham as his "Abundant, Loving Provider and Caretaker."

Systematic Theology for the New Apostolic Reformation

Compare this to a father who happens to be the richest person in the world. He may choose to never tell his children how wealthy he is. Instead, he communicates with his children how much he cares for them and that he is able to care for them. So also, when God revealed Himself to Abraham as *El Shaddai*, He was *not* trying to tell Abraham how powerful He is. God was declaring how powerfully He loves!

The Bible was written in Hebraic thought. Unfortunately, we Western people try to make the Bible say what we with our Western minds want it to say. So then, does the Bible say that God is omnipotent? Anyone who knows Hebraic-biblical thought knows that *omnipotent* is an abstract word. It is *not* the kind of word that the original Bible used.

There is one verse in the KJV of the Bible that declares, *"Alleluia: for the Lord God omnipotent reigneth"* (Rev. 19:6). The Greek word translated as "omnipotent" here is *pantokrator*. Most Bible versions such as the NASV and NIV translate this word as *"almighty."* Indeed, this is a more accurate translation. When we see *pantokrator* used before the word *reigns*, it gives us the sense of "all-ruling." Certainly, our God governs over all His creation, but that is not exactly the same as omnipotent.

Let me make it clear that I am not stating or implying that God is not omnipotent. Maybe this is a true attribute of His nature. Personally I like to think that God is omnipotent. However, there is no Bible verse that says this. That concept came from ancient Greek philosophical thought, not the Bible. If we are claiming to develop our theology based on the Bible, then we will have to remain faithful to what the Bible actually states.

Point 71: Is God Omniscient?

Consider omniscience (all-knowing). Matthew 10:29-30 is the Bible passage most often used by Christians trained in Classical/Reformed theology to teach that God is omniscient:

> *Are not two sparrows sold for a cent? And yet not one of them will fall to the ground apart from your Father. But the very hairs of your head are all numbered.*

Obviously, God knows a lot, but does this verse tell us that God is omniscient? Not really.

Two Views in Conflict

To say that God knows the number of hairs on your head is not equivalent to omniscient. Being told that He knows the number of hairs on your head does not communicate less than being told He is omniscient. It communicates more—much more. It tells you that He knows everything about you and He cares about you. When the Bible says that no sparrow falls to the ground without God's notice, it is saying that nothing happens to you without His notice. He cares for you.

People who know the Bible understand this about the Bible. They know how the Bible communicates.

Compare this to knowing a friend and how that friend communicates. For example, if you knew me personally, you would know that I have never been a person who curses. So if someone told you, "Harold Eberle said, 'Blankety, blank, blank, blank . . .'" you would immediately suspect that you were being told something that is not true. Because you know me, you know that I do not communicate in those words. In like fashion, anyone who is well-versed in Hebraic-biblical thought knows the Bible never says God is omniscient.[42] Perhaps that is a true attribute of God, but God was not interested in declaring His own brilliance. He was and is interested in declaring that He knows what concerns us.

There is only one verse in the Bible that can be reasonably construed to teach God is omniscient, but when we look more carefully at that verse, we see that even it does not say it in the way the Western mind wants to hear it. In 1 John 3:20, we are told that *"God is greater than our heart and knows all things."* Certainly, this verse says God knows all things, but the context is about our heart. Other Bible verses also tell us that God sees into the heart of every person (Jer. 17:10 ; Acts 1:24). Such statements are relational rather than abstract. They are not saying that God is omniscient in the Western sense of being an attribute of God. Instead, 1 John 3:20 is saying that God sees into your and my heart. We cannot hide anything from Him.

Point 72: Is God Omnipresent?

What about omnipresence (present everywhere)? Christians trained in Classical/Reformed theology most often use Psalm 139:7-8 to "prove"

---

[42] There is a verse that tells us that God's knowledge is infinite (Ps. 147:4-5), but even this does not mean omniscient. To see this consider how infinity minus one million is still infinity, but it is no longer omniscient. The two words are not synonymous. We will discuss this in more depth in II:E:124-128.

Systematic Theology for the New Apostolic Reformation

that God is omnipresent:

> *Where can I go from Your Spirit?*
> *Or where can I flee from Your presence?*
> *If I ascend to heaven, You are there;*
> *If I make my bed in Sheol, behold, You are there.*

The Psalmist was praising God, acknowledging that God will never leave him and God will be wherever he is. Similarly, you and I can be reassured that God will always be with us. That is the primary message of this passage.

But does this passage say that God is omnipresent? Psalm 139:7-8 does not tell us if God is on Jupiter right now. It does not tell us if God is right now in the Lake of Fire. No, Psalm 139 does not say that God is omnipresent. Christians who use this passage to try prove that God is omnipresent are reading into the Bible what they, with their Western minds, want it to say.

There is a verse in Jeremiah that is closer to revealing God's all-pervasive presence:

> *"Can a man hide himself in hiding places*
> *So I do not see him?" declares the Lord.*
> *"Do I not fill the heavens and the earth?" declares the Lord.*
> (Jer. 23:24)

Indeed, God fills the heavens and earth.

However, we must be careful as Western-minded people not to force biblical revelation into our Western framework. If we are going to analyze Jeremiah 23:24 with critical thought, we would question whether or not "heavens and earth" includes every realm. Is hell in the heavens or earth? We can also ask, "Is God in Satan's heart?" Both of these questions open to us the possibility that God is not omnipresent in the Western sense of the word.

The first part of Jeremiah 23:24 says, *"Can a man hide himself . . . ?"* The main message is that no person can hide from God. In this context, God declared that He fills the heavens and earth. God was not making a scientific or technical statement about His existence. He was expounding on the futility of hiding from Him. It is wrong to take that type of a statement and force it into a Western thought. Maybe God is omnipresent, but Jeremiah 23:24 does not actually say that.

Two Views in Conflict

Furthermore, the next discussion point offers a serious challenge to the Western idea of God being omnipresent.

Point 73: The Omni's May Deny God's Sovereignty

The Western ideas of omniscience and omnipresence may actually be contradictory to our belief in God's sovereignty. Please think about this.

God's sovereignty means that He can do anything He wants to do whenever He wants. Yet, if we insist that God is omniscient, then we are saying that God knows everything and that He has no choice about this. Consider the possibility that God can choose to make Himself unaware of certain things. For example, in several Bible verses God says, "*I will remember their sins no more*" (Heb. 8:12). Of course, this may be a figure of speech, but it is also possible that God can sovereignly decide to remove from His own consciousness the sins He has forgiven. In other words, it is possible that a perfect God can perfectly forget. Maybe we should take His words literally.

We must similarly consider the attribute of omnipresence. Perhaps God can sovereignly choose to remove Himself from some place. For example, there may be a place so evil and corrupt that God does not want His presence to be there. This may explain what happened in the case with Sodom and Gomorrah. Before destroying the cities:

> . . . the Lord said, "The outcry of Sodom and Gomorrah is indeed great, and their sin is exceedingly grave. I will go down now, and see if they have done entirely according to its outcry, which has come to Me; and if not, I will know."
>
> (Gen. 18:20-21)

If we take this passage literally, we would have to conclude that God was somewhat aware of what was going on in Sodom and Gomorrah, but not entirely. Of course, this may be a figure of speech, i.e., an anthropomorphism, but it is also possible that a sovereign God chose to not make Himself aware of everything going on in those evil cities. It is possible that God sovereignly chose to remove Himself from that environment.

It is also possible that God does not force His presence where He is unwanted. For example, it is possible that He is not in Satan's heart. If we insist that God is omnipresent, we are saying that God is incapable of removing Himself from any aspect of His creation. If we insist that God is omniscient, then we are saying that God has to know everything, and He has no choice in the matter. Since there is no Bible verse that says God is omnipresent or omniscient, maybe we should forget those attributes and cling to His sovereignty, which the Bible does say is one of His attributes.

Point 74: Is God Immutable?

In Volume I, Sections B and C, I explained how God is immutable in nature, but mutable in decisions and emotions. This is no small issue. In fact, I will later discuss how this determines what we believe about how God interacts with this world, which profoundly influences what we believe about prayer, the atonement, the Kingdom of God, the work of the Holy Spirit, and almost every point in our systematic theology.

Therefore, it is vital that we decide if God is immutable in all things, as Classical/Reformed theology teaches, or is He immutable in nature, while still having the ability to experience emotional variation and change His mind? I have already made my position clear: God is immutable in nature, but mutable in emotions and decisions.[43]

Point 75: Is God Impassible?

Consider impassibility. We can define this as the impossibility for anything created to influence the Creator. The ancient Greek philosophers reasoned that it is impossible for the Creator to respond to things and people within creation. This attribute was closely associated with the immutability of God, re-emphasizing the fixed nature of God. If God is impassible, then He will never respond to a human being. God's emotions will never rise or fall in response to human activity.

Even a casual reading of the Bible reveals a God who is responsive to His people. He answers prayer. One of the most striking examples of this responsiveness was when Joshua asked God to cause the sun to stand still so he could defeat his enemies:

> And there was no day like that before it or after it, when <u>the Lord</u>

---

[43] Explained in I:B:20-21 and I:C:27-30.

Two Views in Conflict

listened to the voice of man; for the Lord fought for Israel.
(Josh. 10:14)

Classical/Reformed theologians must consider this and all other passages that show God responding to people as being anthropomorphisms. I do not. I believe that *"the Lord listened to the voice of a man."* Therefore, I have to reject the attribute of impassibility.

Point 76: Is God Perfect?

Classical/Reformed theologians say that God is perfect. Indeed, there is a verse in Matthew that tells us God is perfect:[44]

Therefore you are to be perfect, as your heavenly Father is perfect.
(Matt. 5:48)

However, the perfection being spoken of in this verse does not refer to omnipotence, omniscience, omnipresence, and so forth. We know this because this verse tells us that *we* should be perfect in the same way that God is perfect. Certainly we are not expected to be omnipotent, omniscient, and omnipresent. The context is talking about being loving and giving toward both good and evil people alike. In that sense, we are exhorted to be perfect as God is perfect.

The bigger point is that there is no verse in the Bible that tells us God is perfect in the Greek philosophical sense. Of course, we all want to think God is perfect in every way. Some would consider it sacrilegious to even question this attribute, but there is something to gain if we dare question it. Truths are often revealed by considering the alternatives.

For example, imagine for a moment that we were reading the Bible and we discovered that God has some characteristic that we never thought of before, some characteristic that is not in the Classical list of characteristics, some characteristic that surprises us. For example, let's say that we learn that the God of the Bible has a sense of humor. If, indeed, we discover this from the Bible, what should we do? Well, if we are attempting to develop our concept of God from the Bible, it is incumbent upon us to accept the Bible's revelation.

---

[44] The Bible also speaks of God's Law and love as perfect (Ps. 19:7 and 1 John 4:18), but neither of these equate to the Greek philosophical attributes related to perfection..

Systematic Theology for the New Apostolic Reformation

I propose to you that this is the same approach that we should have concerning all of the attributes, concepts, and names of God. We should not decide ahead of time that He is such-and-such and then go look in the Bible trying to find Him. Instead, we should embrace the God who is revealed in the Bible as He is revealed in the Bible.

Concerning perfection, the Bible reveals that God is perfect in the sense of being loving and giving to both good and evil people. Let's accept that. Let's be content with what the Bible reveals. We don't need to add our own thoughts to what the Bible clearly reveals.

Point 77: Is God Self-Sufficient?

Another attribute assigned to God by Classical/Reformed theologians is **self-sufficiency**. They claim that this idea logically follows from God being perfect. If, indeed, He is perfect in the sense that Classical/Reformed theologians hold, then He needs nothing and wants nothing. The word **aseity** is used to refer to this attribute of God. It means God is complete in Himself; nothing can be added to Him.

Of course, we like to think of God as totally secure and not dependent upon anything or anyone. Perhaps in eternity past He existed totally self-sufficient. However, God created individuals whom He could love. True love gives, but it also wants. God wants us to do good. He wants to bless us, and He delights in the prosperity of His people (Ps. 35:27). God takes pleasure in seeing us succeed. More importantly, God wants our hearts. The fact that God is jealous[45] means He experiences disappointment when His people turn away from Him.

The Classical/Reformed view of God cannot accept this idea of God experiencing disappointment or having any feelings related to us rejecting Him. That would make Him dependent upon us and no longer totally self-sufficient.

Yet the Bible does not tell us that God is self-sufficient in the sense of needing or wanting nothing. That idea came from Greek-originated philosophical thought—not the Bible. The biblical revelation shows us a God who is very much invested in His people. God not only loves His people, but He is "in love" with them. This means He has yielded

---

45 Discussed in I:D:36.

Two Views in Conflict

Himself to the dynamics which become established when one individual loves another. When God fathered humanity, and then further, when He entered into covenant relationships, He opened Himself for the dynamics of relationships. Perhaps He was, indeed, totally self-sufficient in eternity past, but the God who reveals Himself in Scripture shows Himself very much involved and responsive to His people.

This does not make God less than perfect, but it changes our understanding of perfection, i.e., vulnerability can be seen as an aspect of perfection. Consider the opposite. What would a parent be who remained detached and unfeeling toward his or her children? A perfect Father should be emotionally connected with His children.

Perhaps in eternity past God was self-sufficient, but it is possible that His vulnerability developed as He planned for His children. Of course, this cannot be reconciled with Classical/Reformed theology because adherents believe that God is timeless and, therefore, cannot plan anything or change in anyway. However, if we abandon that assumption, we can consider the possibility that God is like a parent who dreams and plans for coming children. It is possible that God opened His heart to people as He created them.

The vulnerability of God is consistent with the revelation of God in Jesus Christ. In coming into the world, Jesus emptied Himself and, hence, limited Himself. He then became vulnerable to humanity. He hurt. He made this great sacrifice in order to come to us and restore relationship with the Father. Knowing that the heart of Jesus is the heart of God, we should not be surprised that God may allow Himself to be vulnerable by loving people.

Point 78: Is God Timeless?

Consider the concept of **timelessness.** Christians following Classical/Reformed theology accredit timelessness to God so rigidly that they usually consider it foolish to question. Indeed, questioning this is a threatening proposition, because if God is not timeless, then the cornerstone of Classical/Reformed theology is nonexistent. Yet, Socrates' lesson still holds true: Unless we question every assumption, we will never know if what we believe is true.

Systematic Theology for the New Apostolic Reformation

The Bible does say God is **eternal** (*aiónios*, in Greek). As we pointed out in Section A and B, God is eternal in the sense that He has always existed and always will exist. However, Classical/Reformed theologians usually equate *eternal* with *timeless*. In reality, there is no biblical justification for equating these words.

To see evidence that *aiónios* does not mean timeless, consider how *aiónios* is used twice in Romans 16:25-26, once to refer to the past time period and second as a description of God:

> . . . *the revelation of the mystery which has been kept secret for long ages* [aiónios] *past . . . according to the commandment of the eternal* [aiónios] *God . . . .*

The first use of the word *aiónios* refers to the distant past, even the infinite past, but not timelessness. The second use of the word *aiónios* is used descriptive of God, but aside from trying to support the Classical/Reformed view of God, there is no reason to say that eternal means timeless.

Consider how the word *aiónios* is used when speaking of the life all Christians possess. For example, 1 John 5:11 tells us that God has given us eternal (*aiónios*) life, and this life is in His Son. The same life that is in Jesus is in us. Therefore, if *aiónios* means "timeless," then all Christians are timeless. Yet, even Classical/Reformed theologians will not say that Christians are timeless. Instead, we know Christians have received eternal life, and hence, they will live forever. Using the same definition of the word *eternal*, we can say God is eternal, but there is no justifiable reason for us to change its meaning in order to equate it with "timeless."

It is also worth considering the Greek word, *aión* which literally means "age." Christians trained in Classical/Reformed theology refer to the time periods before and after creation as "eternal ages" and then assume the eternal ages are timeless. Yet, there is no biblical support for that assumption. The Bible scholar Oscar Cullmann convincingly argues:

> If we wish to understand the Primitive Christian use of *aion* ("age"), we thus must free ourselves completely from all philosophical concepts of time and eternity.[46]

---

46 Oscar Cullmann, *Christ and Time* (Philadelphia: The Westminster Press: 1964), p. 48.

Two Views in Conflict

Cullmann explains how the Jews and early Christians had no concept of a timeless realm, but they thought of the future ages as unending time—which is very different than timelessness.[47]

As explained, the assumed attribute of timelessness cannot be determined from the Bible. That idea had its origin with ancient Greek philosophers. Since then, many philosophers have made the same assumption, but many others have arrived at the alternative conclusion that God is temporal. In reality, the concept of timelessness outside of creation is unknown. Since the Bible doesn't reveal it, we don't need it.

Point 79: Classical Defense of God's Timelessness?

The Bible reveals God acting in time within creation. We saw this with God's Spirit moving about earth, God talking with Adam and Eve, and God experiencing emotional variation and changing His mind. Classical theologians will agree that a literal understanding of those passages does reveal God acting in time. However, Classical theologians do not take those passages literally. They continue to argue that God is timeless outside of and within creation. There are two primary explanations that Classical theologians use to try to make their viewpoint seem reasonable.

The first is to say all of those biblical examples of God acting in time are anthropomorphisms. We have already discussed that explanation enough.

Second, they offer an illustration that God's position is comparable to a person looking through a peephole in a fence at a passing parade. Therefore, God only sees what is directly in front of Him. This illustration is supposed to explain how God can both exist outside of time and still act in time. In reality, the idea of timelessness means that God is *not* looking through a peephole. The whole argument is about whether or not God is timeless *on this side of the fence*. If He is timeless on this side of the fence, then He always sees the whole parade. On the other hand, if He can only see what is directly in front of Him, then He is temporal on this side of the fence. That supports the viewpoint of Father-Son theology (and Open Theism).

---

47 This topic is more fully discussed in III:E:172.

Systematic Theology for the New Apostolic Reformation

Point 80: Is God Transcendent and Wholly Other?

Now consider the attribute of transcendence which was attributed to God by Plotinus and is now embraced by Classical/Reformed theologians. Transcendence means God is totally independent of and absent from the material universe. Further, God is so beyond the natural world that He has absolutely nothing in common with this world. This concept (with which I strongly disagree) is also expressed by saying God is "wholly other."

Understanding this concept is key to understanding the cornerstone of Classical/Reformed theology. To understand it, envision the two worlds proposed by Classical/Reformed theology: the spiritual world and the natural world. According to them, the spiritual world is timeless and the natural world is temporal. This means, according to them, that the two worlds can never meet.

What does it mean that these two worlds can never meet?

If you have two objects such as a rock and a piece of wood you can cause them to meet simply by moving them together until they touch. If you have a dog and a cat, you can cause them to meet by enclosing them in a cage together. You can even cause imaginary things in your mind to meet. For example, you can imagine a rock and a dog in your mind and then envision the rock hitting the imaginary dog in your mind. Each of these scenarios is possible.

However, now you have a dog sitting next to you and you imagine a rock in your mind. No matter how hard you try (apart from some supernatural transformation), you can never make your imaginary rock hit the real dog sitting next to you. It is impossible. Even if you make an infinite number of attempts you will never get the imaginary rock to hit the real dog. The two will never meet.

In Classical/Reformed thought, the gap between the spiritual world and the natural world is even greater. Infinitely greater. The two worlds can *never* meet. The two worlds have *nothing* in common with each other. For this reason, we rightfully refer to the foundation of Classical/Reformed theology as a dualistic worldview. As mentioned earlier, we are using this word "dualistic" to refer to two contrasting worlds.

Two Views in Conflict

THE CLASSICAL/REFORMED TRANSCENDENT WHOLLY OTHER

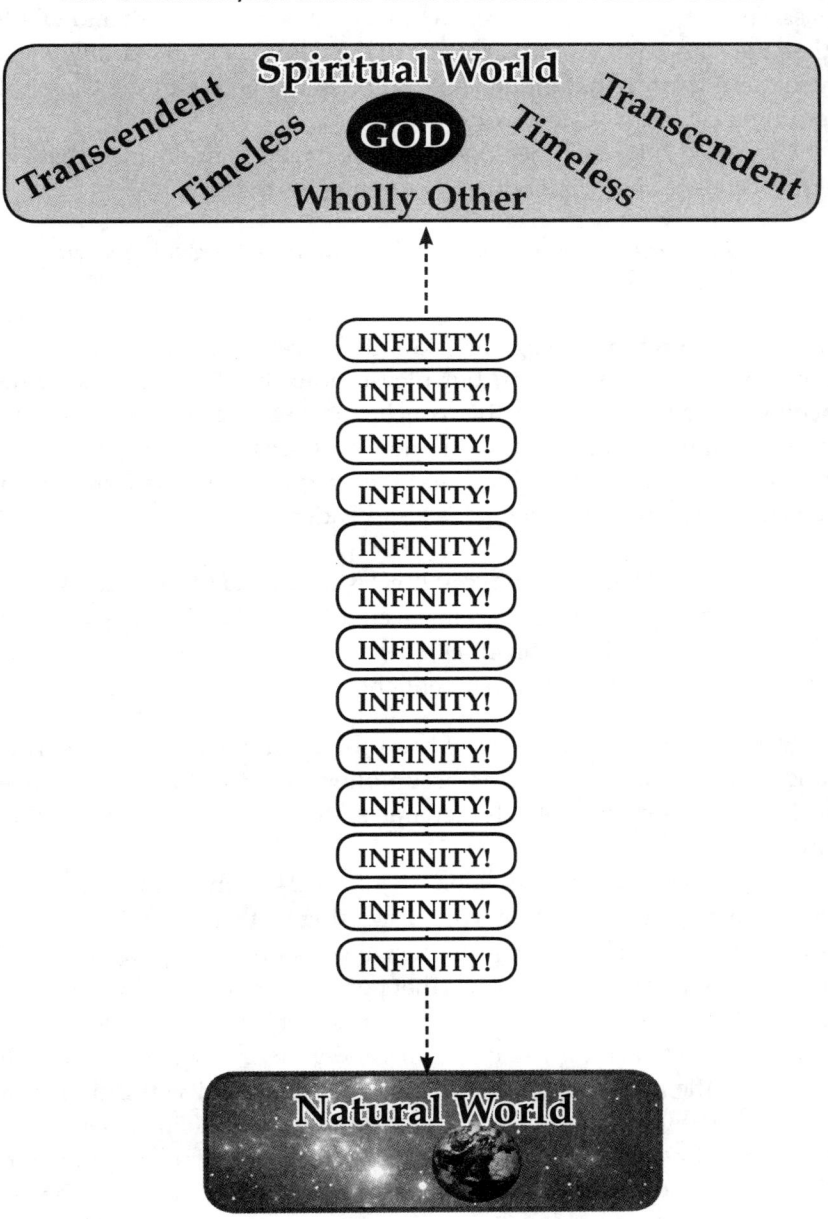

Spiritual World
GOD
Wholly Other
Transcendent *Timeless* *Transcendent* *Timeless*

INFINITY!
INFINITY!
INFINITY!
INFINITY!
INFINITY!
INFINITY!
INFINITY!
INFINITY!
INFINITY!
INFINITY!
INFINITY!
INFINITY!
INFINITY!

Natural World

Systematic Theology for the New Apostolic Reformation

In Classical/Reformed thought, not only are the two worlds infinitely separate, but God is also finitely separate from the natural world. When Classical/Reformed theologians say that God is transcendent and wholly other, they are saying there is *nothing* in the nature of God like *anything* in the natural world. That infinite separation is implied with the Classical/Reformed claim that God's world is timeless.

Classical/Reformed theologians try to defend their doctrine that God is transcendent and wholly other by quoting John 4:24:

> God is spirit, and those who worship Him must worship in spirit and truth.

Classical/Reformed theologians take this reference to "God being spirit" to mean He is transcendent, but please note that Classical/Reformed theologians are arriving at this conclusion because they have already embraced the ancient Greek worldview that sees the spiritual world as transcendent. Their assumption that the spiritual world is transcendent leads them to conclude that God is transcendent.

<u>Classical/Reformed Reasoning Concerning Transcendence</u>
1. The spiritual world is transcendent.
2. God is spirit (John 4:24).
3. Therefore, God is transcendent.

In reality, we have no biblical basis to say that the spiritual world is transcendent. That is purely an assumption based in the ancient Greek worldview, which completely separates the spiritual world from the natural world.

To see this more clearly, look at John 4:24 with fresh eyes. In the context, a Samaritan woman was discussing with Jesus what location people should worship God. Jesus answered her by saying the location is irrelevant, but what is important is that people worship God in spirit (John 4:20-24). Jesus was not telling this woman that it is impossible to worship God because He is far away in a transcendent world. Jesus was actually telling her the opposite. He was saying that she (and we) can worship God by worshiping Him in spirit so we can worship Him wherever we are. Jesus was saying the spirit realm is available. God is available. John 4:24 tells us God is spirit, and therefore, immanent (addressed in the next discussion point).

Two Views in Conflict

The Classical/Reformed idea that God is wholly other is not in the Bible. The overall message of the Bible is *not* that God is different and unreachable to humanity. The Bible actually *emphasizes how humans are like God*. Adam and Eve were created in His image and likeness. God breathed His own spirit (*ruach*, in Hebrew) into humanity (Gen. 2:7). There is something in this world that is something like God—man!

Point 81: Is God Immanent?

To be fair to Classical/Reformed thinkers, we need to point out that they typically teach God's **immanence** right alongside of God's transcendence. Immanence refers to God's all-pervading presence and power within the world. The Bible is filled with examples of God's activity within nature, with humans, and in history. There is no doubt that the immanence of God is a true characteristic of God. This concept does agree with the Scriptures.

However, God's immanence is the opposite of God's transcendence.

Here we are not using the common definition of *transcendence* which is "beyond the limits of ordinary experience" or "beyond the governance of physical laws." These are common definitions in agreement with Webster's dictionary, however, in theology *transcendence* has a different meaning. When Classical/Reformed theologians apply the word *transcendent* to the nature of God, they mean that God is "totally independent of and absent from creation." They are also saying that God is so far *beyond* that no person in this world can comprehend anything about God. To the Classical/Reformed theologian, transcendence means God is wholly other.

It is impossible for God to be absent from creation and present at the same time. It is impossible for God to be unknowable and knowable at the same time. Classical/Reformed theologians are completely aware of this contradiction in their own theology, but they rationalize the contradiction by saying that *it is a mystery* how both can be true.

They call it a "mystery." I call it absurd. A fundamental principle of logic is that two contradictory ideas cannot both be true.

Classical/Reformed theologians *need* both immanence and transcendence to be true. Certainly immanence is in the Bible, so they cannot get rid of that. However, they cannot get rid of transcendence because their entire theology is founded in a worldview where the spiritual world is separate

Systematic Theology for the New Apostolic Reformation

and distinct from the natural world. Their spiritual world is timeless, while the natural world is temporal. If Classical/Reformed theologians give up transcendence, they are giving up the distinction and separation between the two worlds. If they give up that distinction, then all of the other attributes that logically follow from timelessness disappear. For their theology to be maintained, they must hold that God is transcendent. They must hold contradictory ideas that God is both transcendent and immanent at the same time.

Some Classical/Reformed teachers try to reconcile transcendence and immanence by saying that we must "hold two truths in tension." Using this phrase, they try to explain to their students that some spiritual truths are so complex that we with our limited human understanding must at times hold two truths that contradict each other.

That is nonsense. Of course, there are some spiritual concepts that are so complex that we with our human minds cannot understand them. In that case, two spiritual concepts may *seem* to contradict each other, but this does not apply with discussions about transcendence and immanence. It is no mystery what these concepts mean. The definitions of these words are clear. The concepts are understandable to our human minds. Not only do they *seem* to contradict each other, but *they definitely do* contradict each other. It is impossible for God to be transcendent and immanent at the same time.

The Bible is very clear that God is immanent, but there is no Bible passage that can be reasonably construed to mean that God is transcendent in the Classical/Reformed sense. We already discussed the primary Bible passage that they use to teach transcendence (John 4:24), and that verse is actually teaching the opposite of what Classical/Reformed theologians are trying to make it say. Plotinus' concepts of transcendence and wholly other are not in the Bible.

Point 82: Is God Unknowable and Incomprehensible?

A corollary to the idea that God is transcendent is that He is completely unknowable and incomprehensible. Adherents of the Classical/Reformed school see God as so totally different from humanity that humans are incapable of *any* knowledge of God. They say the chasm between God and humanity is just too great. However, Classical/Reformed theologians will admit God has reached across the chasm and revealed Himself. That is humanity's only hope of any knowledge of God.

Two Views in Conflict

Classical/Reformed theologians try to support their belief in God's unknowability and incomprehensibility by quoting Isaiah 55:8-9:

"For My thoughts are not your thoughts,
Nor are your ways My ways," declares the Lord.
"For as the heavens are higher than the earth,
So are My ways higher than your ways
And My thoughts than your thoughts."

Certainly this Scripture reveals that God is magnificent and far greater than humanity, but when Christians trained in Classical/Reformed theology use these verses trying to prove that God is totally incomprehensible, they are trying to make the Hebrew Bible say what they, with their Western minds, want to hear. In the context of Isaiah 55:8-9, where God said His thoughts are higher than man's thoughts, He was calling His OT people back to Himself. Two verses earlier, God said:

Seek the Lord while He may be found;
Call upon Him while He is near.

(Is. 55:6)

God is near. He can be found. Furthermore, He wants to be known by people. Of course, there are many things about God that are too magnificent for us to fully understand, but there are also many things about Him that we can know.

For example, Paul concluded something about the nature of God simply by looking at the nature of humanity. When Paul was in Athens speaking to the Epicurean and Stoic philosophers (Acts 17:16-31), he noted that all people are children of God, and so, we know that God's nature cannot be like a man-made statue of stone or wood. This truth was understandable to Paul, and he expected the philosophers to also be able to grasp this truth.

Paul dedicated his life to explaining God to others. Paul's explanations were comprehensible to his audiences. God is not totally incomprehensible. There are many truths about God that people can understand. Plotinus was wrong. Teachers of Reformed theology are wrong. God is not wholly other.

Rather than the unknowability of God, the all-pervasive, dominant message shouting from the Holy Pages is that God is available and knowable. God walked in the Garden with Adam and Eve. He covenanted with the

Systematic Theology for the New Apostolic Reformation

Hebrews, saying, "I will be your God and you will be My people." God's *"invisible attributes, His eternal power and divine nature, have been <u>clearly seen</u>, being <u>understood</u> through what has been made . . ."* (Rom. 1:20). A day will come when *"the earth will be full of the knowledge of the Lord as the waters cover the sea"* (Is. 11:9). John wrote to his disciples, *"You know the Father"* (1 John 2:13) and *"you know Him who has been from the beginning"* (1 John 2:14). To be reconciled to God is to know Him.

Point 83: Let's Be Hebrew, Not Greek—Biblical, Not Western

Classical/Reformed theologians (with the exception of those who reject impassibility) assign to God all of the following attributes:

<u>Classical/Reformed Theology</u>
Cornerstone: God is timeless.
Foundational in the Nature of God:
    Immutable (Never changes)
    Impassible (Never acted upon)
    Perfect
    Omniscient (All-knowing)
    Omnipresent (Present everywhere)
    Omnipotent (All-powerful)
    Self-Sufficient
    Transcendent
    Immanent
    Wholly Other
    Incomprehensible and Unknowable

The only characteristic in this list that can be supported by Scripture is God's immanence. This is also the only characteristic in the list that did not originate with the ancient Greek philosophers.

Yet, Reformed theology is built on a god who has these attributes.

Some readers who have studied theology may be wondering what I am including in the label "Reformed theology." This is because Reformed theology has taken many different forms since the time of John Calvin. Different Reformed teachers have focused on various aspects of God's nature. Also, various teachers have added attributes to the nature of God that are contrary to the attributes listed above. For example, some

Two Views in Conflict

Reformed teachers have talked about God being knowable, while at the same time explaining that He is unknowable. In spite of such variations, *all* forms of Reformed theology are built on the philosophical assumptions that god is timeless, immutable, perfect, omniscient, omnipresent, omnipotent, self-sufficient, transcendent, wholly other, incomprehensible, and unknowable.

If Adam was alive today and sitting in a Reformed seminary classroom hearing about a timeless, transcendent being, he would never identify that being as the Loving Father who walked with him in the garden. If Abraham was around reading a theology book about an incomprehensible, unknowable god, he would want people to know the true God who was his Covenant-Making Provider and Caretaker. If Moses had met on Mount Sinai with an immutable, impassible being, he would never have pleaded with that being to change his mind and refrain from destroying the Hebrew people. If Jesus heard a modern theology professor talk about a self-sufficient wholly other, He would show the nail prints in His hands.

The Bible reveals God as our Healer, our Peace, our Righteousness, and our Shepherd. God is like Jesus. He is our Father. He is like honey. These are Hebraic thoughts. This is what the Bible reveals.

Volume I
The Nature of God

Section I
Building on the Biblical View of God

Now we need to decide upon which view of God we will build our theology, the Classical/Reformed view or the biblical view.

> Classical/Reformed Theology
> Cornerstone: God is timeless.
> Foundational in the Nature of God:
>   Immutable (Never changes)
>   Impassible (Never acted upon)
>   Perfect
>   Omniscient (All-knowing)
>   Omnipresent (Present everywhere)
>   Omnipotent (All-powerful)
>   Self-Sufficient
>   Transcendent
>   Immanent
>   Wholly Other
>   Incomprehensible and Unknowable
>
> Father-Son Theology
> Cornerstone: God determined in love to have sons.
> Foundational in *God as Father*:
>   Creator
>   Eternal (Has always existed and always will exist)
>   Powerful
>   His Spirit Is Temporal within Creation
>   Exists in a Spiritual Realm that Fills the Natural Realm
>   Entered into Time
>   Relational and Social

Systematic Theology for the New Apostolic Reformation

Personal and Responsive
Judge
Acts in Mercy
Sovereign (can do whatever He wants, whenever He wants)
Emotional
Temporal within Creation
Covenant-Maker
Allows Covenantal Interactions
Mutable in Emotions and Decisions
Immutable in Nature
El Shaddai (God, Almighty)
Yahweh Jireh (God, Our Provider)
Yahweh Rapha (God, Our Healer)
Yahweh Nissi (God, Our Banner)
Yahweh Shalom (God, Our Peace)
Yahweh Tsidkenu (God, Our Righteousness)
Yahweh Rohi (God, Our Shepherd)
Yahweh M'kadesh (God, Our Holiness)
Holy
Jealous
Consuming Fire
Forgiving
Generous Giver
Rewarder
Love
Like Jesus

When Christians discuss the attributes, concepts, and names related to God's nature arising from the biblical view of God, they have mixed reactions. Some will say they have always held these. Others will say the Classical view is the historic Church's view and, therefore, we should not challenge it. Still others will attempt to combine the Classical view and the biblical view.

Some of the attributes and concepts from each view may be held at the same time, while others are mutually exclusive. Some people don't mind holding opposing views at the same time, while others believe that if two views contradict each other, then at least one of those views is wrong. I hold the second. It is intellectually dishonest to hold two views that contradict each other. If we want to develop a systematic theology based on the Bible, then we will have to abandon those attributes and concepts that cannot be found in the Bible.

Building on the Biblical View of God

Point 84: Challenging Current Beliefs Is Difficult

Classically-trained Christians are unlikely to give up the Classical understanding of God without clear proof concerning how the related attributes and concepts are not found in the Bible. In the preceding section, I discussed the primary Bible verses that are typically used by Classical teachers to support the Classical understanding of God. We saw how those Bible verses do not say what Classical teachers claim that they say. In fact, the Bible does not even communicate on these subjects in the same terminology that Classical theology does.

To make this point more clear, let me challenge you to come up with any Bible verse or passage that supports any of the Classical attributes or concepts (other than immanence). Try to think of a corresponding Bible verse or passage and write it down in the right hand column below:

Classical Theology	Supporting Bible Verse
Cornerstone: God is timeless.	_____
Foundational in the Nature of God:	
Immutable (in nature, decisions, & emotions)	_____
Impassible	_____
Perfect (in the philosophical sense)	_____
Omniscient	_____
Omnipresent	_____
Omnipotent	_____
Self-Sufficient	_____
Transcendent	_____
Immanent	Acts 17:27
Wholly Other	_____
Unknowable	_____
Incomprehensible	_____

Can you write down any verses? The plain truth is that there are no Bible verses that clearly state any of the attributes and concepts listed with the Classical view of God (other than immanence). Even the idea that we are trying to find a verse to support an attribute and concept should raise a warning. "Trying to find support" is very different than reading the Bible and allowing it to reveal truths.

In Sections B, C, D, and E, we noted specific Bible verses that reveal truths about God. We did not try to find support for what we already

Systematic Theology for the New Apostolic Reformation

believed. Instead, we read through the Bible and accepted what was revealed. For this reason, it is very easy to now write down Bible verses that reveal the attributes, concepts, and names that are associated with the biblical view of God. Allow me to list one of many Bible verses that reveal each truth:

Father-Son Theology	Supporting Bible Verse
Cornerstone: God determined to have sons	Ephesians 1:4-5
Foundational in *God as Father:*	Matthew 6:9
Creator	Genesis 1:1
Eternal	Revelation 1:8
Powerful	Genesis 1:1
Holy Spirit: Temporal in Creation	Genesis 1:2
Exists in Spiritual Realm that Fills the Natural Realm	Jeremiah 23:24
Entered into Time	Jeremiah 23:24
Relational and Social	Genesis 2-3
Personal and Responsive	Genesis 4:4-5
Judge	Romans 2:5-6
Acts in Mercy	Genesis 8:21
Sovereign (Does what He wants)	1 Timothy 6:15
Emotional	Genesis 6:6
Temporal within Creation	Genesis 33:5
Covenant-Maker	Genesis 17:2
Allows Covenantal Interactions	Genesis 18:17
Mutable in Emotions and Decisions	Exodus 32:11-14
Immutable in Nature	Malachi 3:6
Motivated According to His Nature	Exodus 32:10
El Shaddai (God, Almighty)	Genesis 17:1
Yahweh Jireh (God, Our Provider)	Genesis 22:14
Yahweh Rapha (God, Our Healer)	Exodus 15:26
Yahweh Nissi (God, Our Banner)	Exodus 17:15
Yahweh Shalom (God, Our Peace)	Judges 6:24
Yahweh Tsidkenu (Our Righteousness)	Jeremiah 33:16
Yahweh Rohi (God, Our Shepherd)	Psalm 23:1
Yahweh M'kadesh (God, Our Holiness)	Exodus 31:13
Holy	1 Samuel 2:2
Jealous	Exodus 20:5
Consuming Fire	Deuteronomy 4:24
Forgiving	Luke 15:11-24
Generous Giver	Luke 11:11-13

Building on the Biblical View of God

Rewarder	Hebrews 11:6
Love	1 John 5:8
Like Jesus	Hebrews 1:3

If you are familiar with the Bible, you will be able to add other Bible verses that support every one of the attributes, concepts, and names listed above. There is no doubt that these have been derived from the Bible.

Even in the face of such evidence, it is difficult to give up long-held ideas. For over 1,500 years the Church clung to the teaching of the Greek/Egyptian astronomer Ptolemy, that the sun revolved around Earth. That geocentric understanding was seeded more deeply into Western thought by Aristotle, whose thinking dominated the intellectual and Church world during the Late Middle Ages. In the 16th century, Copernicus' work was published proving that Earth revolves around the sun. Then Galileo tried to convince the Roman Catholic leadership of the heliocentric (sun at center) world, using his telescope and mathematical calculations. Many of the Jesuit priests were scientists, and they readily embraced Galileo's conclusions. However, most of the Church leadership clung to the long-established way of thinking and refused to even look through Galileo's telescope.

Rather than a telescope, our source of truth is the Bible. I am asking you to look at the Bible. Look through that telescope.

Changing views is not only an intellectual challenge, but it can also be very emotional—too emotional for many to even consider. It is easier to remain comfortable in currently held views. It is easier to not think through the implications, but if you are willing, the rewards will be great.

Point 85: Building on the Right Foundation

Embracing the biblical view of God requires rejecting the foundation laid by the ancient Greek philosophers. This is the same battle the Church fathers of the 2nd and 3rd centuries faced. As we mentioned, Church fathers such as Clement of Alexandria regarded Greek philosophy as a gift of God preparing the world for Christianity. While at the other extreme, Church fathers such as Tertullian saw the teachings of the Greek philosophers as little more than the foolishness and delusion of the pagan world.

We do not need to choose which of the Church fathers was correct. Instead, we should look to Jesus, who is the Cornerstone of the Church. As far as we know, Jesus never referred to or quoted from the ancient Greek philosophers, even though their ideas were well-known during that period.

Modern theologians who want to link the NT writers to the ancient Greek philosophers point out how the apostle John referred to Jesus as the Word (*Logos*, in Greek) of God (John 1:1). Then those theologians explain that *logos* can refer to reason or logic similar to how Plato's god was equated with a realm of ideals or reason.

Of course, it is possible that John was borrowing a term from the Greek philosophers, but that association is very speculative. It is more likely that the apostle wrote John 1:1 after the pattern set up in Genesis 1:1, which had been around centuries before the Greek philosophers and was much more familiar to John. Genesis 1:1 tells us God spoke creation into existence. There we see that the Word of God was with God at creation and all things came into being through the Word. The similarities between John chapter 1 and Genesis chapter 1 are obvious to anyone who is not determined to link John to the Greek philosophers.

To see that John was not associating the true God with the god of the philosophers we can note that John did not say that the Christian God is like their god in timelessness, immutability, impassibility, omnipotence, omniscience, or omnipresence. Nor did John teach that God is wholly other, transcendent, or incomprehensible. Instead, John explained how the true God became flesh, walked the earth, healed the sick, died on a cross, and resurrected from the dead. Rather than borrow the Greek concept of god, John proclaimed a God who was personal, relational, caring, and close. This God was markedly different than the god of the Greek philosophers.

With similar discernment we should examine Paul's writings. When he was in Athens, he spoke to the Epicurean and Stoic philosophers (Acts 17:16-31). The only common ground he found was their altar to an "unknown God." The very fact that Paul had to refer to their "unknown God" indicates that he did not accept their understanding of God. This was in spite of the fact that Paul was highly educated and would have been well-acquainted with the god of the philosophers. Paul did not say that the Christian God is like their god in timelessness, immutability, impassibility, omnipotence, omniscience, omnipresence, or in any other way. Instead, he preached about the one God that they did not know. Paul proclaimed the one true God who will judge the world through Jesus Christ (Acts 17:30-31).

Building on the Biblical View of God

Furthermore, Paul warned believers:

> *See to it that no one takes you captive through philosophy and empty deception, according to the traditions of men . . . .*
> (Col. 2:8)

To whose philosophy do you suppose Paul was referring? At that time in history, the Greek philosophers were "the philosophers."

The plain truth is that Jesus and the apostles never referred to even one of the attributes that we have identified with the ancient Greek concept of God. Not one.

Point 86: Rejecting the Greek Philosophers

Of course, God can use non-Christians to reveal truth, but here we are endeavoring to find truth about God. In Romans chapter 1, Paul drew a correlation between sexual depravity and a person being darkened in their understanding about God (Rom. 1:18-27). The ancient Greek philosophers were known for practicing pederasty (erotic relationships between an adult male and a younger male usually in his teens). Plato is especially known for indulging his sexual attractions to boys and young men.

Yet, Augustine praised Plato for his understanding of God and wrote:

> But, among the disciples of Socrates, Plato was the one who shone with a glory which far excelled that of the others, and who not unjustly eclipsed them all.[48]

The prominent Greek philosophers would have never met Paul's qualifications as elders of a local church (1 Tim. 3:2-7). Augustine should have never allowed Plato to be his instructor concerning God, and we should not allow Plato, via Augustine, to be a teacher of the entire historic Church.

Aristotle's teachings about God should also be rejected. Historical writings do not reveal much about his sexual practices, but Jesus taught us to identify false prophets by their fruit (Matt. 7:15-20). The most known disciple of Aristotle was Alexander the Great, who referred to Aristotle as his father. Aristotle provided Alexander with the intellectual justifications for enslaving multitudes and for the massacre of all he considered

---

[48] Augustine, Translated by Marcus Dods, *The City of God* (New York: The Modern Library: 1993), VIII, 4.

Systematic Theology for the New Apostolic Reformation

barbarians, especially the Persians. Almost all of those massacres were unprovoked. Estimates range from hundreds of thousands to over a million whom Alexander and his armies murdered for no other reason than Alexander's own obsession to conquer. Europeans have chosen to herald Alexander as a hero, but in much of Asia he is referred to as the "accursed one" or "two-horned Satan." Alexander believed that he was the son of the supreme god Zeus, and later in life he demanded that he be worshiped as the "invincible god."

With similar discernment we must look at Plotinus (204–270), whom Augustine followed most closely. Plotinus made no mention of Christianity in his writings, but his closest disciple, Porphyry, wrote 15 very damaging treatises entitled, *Adversus Christianos (Against the Christians)*. In those treatises, Porphyry portrayed Plotinus as the pagan alternative to the incarnate God of Christians. Porphyry related various instances of spiritual power demonstrated by Plotinus, and Plotinus was confident that he himself was being guided by a spiritual entity he referred to as a *daimon*.[49] Plotinus' friend Eustochius was present at his death and testified that as Plotinus died a snake glided from under his bed and out through a hole in the wall and disappeared.[50]

Someone who has much to lose by rejecting Plotinus may ignore this report as irrelevant. Yet, if we had a similar report of this happening at the death of Nero, Hitler, Stalin, or any other evil leader, Bible-believing Christians would seriously consider if a snake sliding out at the instant of death was evidence of demonic influence. Of course, no one can say for sure, but it does give us reason to question even more.

Even Karl Barth conducted his life in a manner that should leave us appalled. His 35-year relationship with his secretary/mistress, Charlotte von Kirschbaum, was scandalous to say the least. When Barth's wife, Nelly, refused to give him a divorce, Barth brought Charlotte to live in their home with Nelly and their five children. In a home filled with over three decades of bitterness and a protesting wife, Barth and his mistress together developed his major work, the 13-volume systematic theology called *Church Dogmatics*. Today, the names of Barth, his wife, and his mistress are all on the same tombstone in Basel, Switzerland.

---

49 At that time in history *daimons* were thought to be either good or evil spirits, similar to ghosts or spirit guides: http://www.folklore.ee/folklore/vol9/plotinus.htm.
50 William Smith and Henry Wace, *A Dictionary of Christian Biography, Literature, Sects and Doctrines,* Vol. IV (London: John Murray, 1887), p. 420.

Building on the Biblical View of God

We must not ignore these facts. Karl Barth would never be allowed to be an elder in any local church that attempted to follow the Bible. Shouldn't we exercise a little discernment concerning whom we accept as our greatest teachers? Thoughts have consequences. This is the reason we study theology.

Let me state it clearly so there is no confusion: Those philosophers and theologians were not good people.

With questions about what inspired them, it is best to leave their teachings aside and go with what we have accepted as God-inspired, i.e., the Scriptures. We are safe with God's Word. Let this be our foundation.

Point 87: God Fills the Heavens and Earth

In setting aside the teachings of the ancient Greek philosophers, we can begin by abandoning the dualistic worldview of Plato. We must not envision God existing in a distant, timeless world that is totally unlike our world.

Instead, we must develop our worldview by reading the Bible. A direct reading of Genesis leads the reader to see God as creating the universe and entering into creation. God exists in a spiritual realm that fills the natural realm. God fills the heavens and earth.

GOD FILLS THE HEAVENS AND EARTH

Systematic Theology for the New Apostolic Reformation

Concerning God's existence before creation or outside of creation, the Bible reveals nothing. What we do know is that God is close to us within creation.

Point 88: Rejecting the Sun-like Image of God

In order to develop an accurate view of God we must also rid ourselves of the influence of Plotinus.

The idea that God is wholly other is unfounded and contrary to the biblical revelation. Rather than being totally unlike us, the Bible clearly reveals that we are created in God's image and He has placed some of His Spirit within us. In some way, we are like Him. This is the biblical revelation.

To embrace the biblical revelation we must also abandon Plotinus' false image of God as the sun radiating out light. Most Christians do not know it, but the sun-like image of God lies at the foundation of much of Western Christianity today. Yet, God commanded that we should not make for ourselves any images to represent Him. This includes *"any likeness of what is in heaven above or on the earth beneath . . ."* (Ex. 20:4). We must not think of God as the sun radiating light. I wish I could thunder from heaven, land on a mountaintop, and hand everyone this command written on stone. But I can't. Maybe someone else will. Maybe someone else already has.

With what should we replace the sun-like image?

The single most perfect image of God that we have available to us is Jesus. He is God incarnate, the exact representation of the Father. Of course, we know that God is spirit, so He has no material substance to His being. Therefore, we must not limit our understanding of God to something that we can see, such as a human figure. However, we can examine Jesus' heart and see His values, purpose, priorities, and passion. We can observe His compassion for the oppressed and His disdain for religious arrogance. We can also envision Him visiting Zaccheus, telling a paralyzed man that his sins are forgiven, and having no condemnation for a women caught in adultery. There is much we can know about Father-God by studying Jesus.

After Jesus, the single most perfect image of God that we have is Adam. This can sound almost blasphemous to Christians who have always envisioned God like the sun, radiating out His glory. Yet, the Bible reveals that Adam was made in the image and likeness of God. He is the best (aside from Jesus) model that we have revealing what God is like.

Building on the Biblical View of God

Of course, we know that God is infinitely greater than humanity.
Of course, we know that God is the Creator.
Of course, we know that God always was and always will be.
Of course, we know that Moses had to hide in the cleft of the rock just to survive while God's glory passed.
Of course, we know that God's ways are higher than humanity's ways.

Yet, none of these truths change the fact that we have an image of God right here on earth—man. The similarities between God and humanity are real. James wrote about people who bless God with their words, but *"curse men who have been made in the likeness of God"* (Jas. 3:9). James was pointing out the contradiction in such behavior. If someone loves God, then they will love humans who are created in His image. This is profound. It implies that there is enough similarity between God and humans that it is impossible to love one and hate the other.

Of course, God is unlike people in many ways. Paul explained that God *"lives in unapproachable light"* (1 Tim. 6:16). This implies that light is His abiding place, but it does not mean that light radiates out of Him.

GOD DWELLS IN LIGHT

To see this, it is helpful to think of light at creation in Genesis 1. On the first day, God created the light, but He did not create the sun, moon, and stars until the fourth day. Some Bible readers have a difficult time

Systematic Theology for the New Apostolic Reformation

conceiving of this because their minds are fixed on light radiating from a source. Yet, that fixation is unnecessary. Think of God creating light without a central location point from which to emanate. Similarly, we should think of God. The light in which God dwells does not emanate from any one point, because God does not exist at any one point. He fills all. He is. Light is. He dwells in light.

Point 89: The Knowability of God

Finally, we must embrace the God who is knowable. We must reject the philosophical reasoning that led Classical/Reformed theologians to conclude that God is unknowable and incomprehensible. Those concepts did not come from the Bible.

I am especially sensitive about this issue because of a personal experience I had which related to understanding the Trinity. When I was a child, my parents had me attend a parochial school. One day my teacher told the class a story about Augustine trying to understand the Trinity. Augustine lived in North Africa near the Mediterranean Sea. While walking the beach, Augustine saw a boy digging a hole in the sand with a sea shell. When finished digging, the boy ran to the sea, filled the shell with water, and hurried back to his hole to pour in the water. The boy continued running back and forth while Augustine watched, knowing the boy would never succeed in filling the hole with water. Augustine wrote about that incident, explaining how he himself was like the little boy, trying to do the impossible. As the boy was trying to fill the hole, Augustine was trying to understand the Trinity. Augustine resolved that he would never fully understand God.

The moral of this story has some truth: No one can fully comprehend God, but I want to tell you about the impact that story had on me as a young student. The vision of the boy and Augustine paralyzed my mind for over 40 years. As a child, I concluded that Augustine could never understand the Trinity, so I would never understand it. That message was so impactful I never attempted to study the Trinity. I served as a teacher of Christian thought and doctrine for decades, and I accepted the doctrine of the Trinity as true, but I never felt capable of understanding it. For over 40 years, I avoided any serious thought about the subject, having no hope of ever understanding it.

Building on the Biblical View of God

Eventually I escaped the curse of negative words, and today my study of the Trinity has been one of the most rewarding experiences of my life.

I am not blaming Augustine for delaying my study of the Trinity. I am explaining the profound impact upon people's minds that can result when someone they respect tells them that God is incomprehensible. It can cripple them for years.

The incomprehensibility of God is not the emphasis of Scripture. If anyone simply reads the Bible, they will learn of individuals who interacted with and knew God. The message shouting from the Holy Pages is that God is available and knowable. He meets with people. He leads people. He loves people. The "knowability" of God is the foundation of a biblical worldview.

Point 90: A Revolution in Theology for Reformation in Society

It is difficult to question the teachings of great leaders. People put them on pedestals. To challenge the foundations laid by historical figures may seem ominous, but it is necessary. Some foundations need to be shaken.

Leaders like Plato, Aristotle, Augustine, Luther, and Calvin contributed greatly to Western civilization, but today the average eighth grade student knows more than they did about astronomy, physics, anatomy, biology, chemistry, geography, microbiology, embryology, climatology, neurology, genetics, psychology, sociology, history, anthropology, zoology, archaeology, pathology, technology, ecology, and so forth. If you finished high school successfully, you know more than Plato and Calvin about every one of these subjects. So it is time to think for yourself. You are able.

Western Christianity is built on the foundation of Greek philosophical thought. It should be built on the foundation laid by the apostles and prophets, with Jesus Christ being the cornerstone.

As stated in the introduction of this book, systematic theology has always served as an anchor for the Church. Without moving the anchor, there can be no major, lasting changes within Christianity. Short-time revivals and awakenings may come and go, but reformation of society can only come through the Church if she pulls the anchor and repositions herself. It is time to pull the Church's historic anchor in Plato's dualistic worldview and the corresponding Classical view of God founded in the philosophical reasoning of the ancient Greek heathen. Now is the time to replant the anchor in the Hebraic-biblical worldview and the biblical concept of God.

Volume II
God's Involvement with this World

Our view of God determines how we understand His interactions with this world. Here we are not talking about how He created the world but how He interacts with this world and humanity since creation.

In this volume, we will primarily compare Father-Son theology to Reformed theology, rather than Classical theology. This is because the writings of John Calvin (the father of Reformed theology) are more relevant to the subjects we will be discussing. As we explained, Reformed theology is the child of Classical theology.

Also, Augustine (the historical figure most associated with Classical theology) was inconsistent in his own theology on the related issues. In his earlier writings, Augustine supported the ideas related to people having free will, e.g., *On Free Choice of the Will*. In later writings Augustine emphasized God's sovereignty to the exclusion of people having free will, e.g., *On Predestination of the Saints* and *On the Gift of Perseverance*. Because of Augustine's inconsistencies in this area, it is difficult to use his teachings as a standard.

In Section A, we will explain God's involvement with this world from the perspective of Reformed theology. Then in Section B, we will see what is revealed in the Bible about God's interactions with the world. This second perspective will be the perspective that matches the biblical view of God and Father-Son theology.

Then in Section C, we will discuss cooperative relationships between God and humanity, in which God desires to work with people to fulfill His purposes and goals in the earth.

Systematic Theology for the New Apostolic Reformation

These discussions will determine our **theodicy**, which is a theological term referring to how we explain the goodness and power of God in view of the existence of evil and suffering in the world. Theodicy will be considered in Section D.

Then in Sections E and F, we will address issues that typically surface as Christians reconsider how God is involved in this world. These issues include His knowledge and greatness.

• • •

In my diagrams portraying the worldview of Classical/Reformed thought, I will at times move the spiritual world of God closer to the natural world. I will be doing this simply to save space on the page. Please keep in mind that the Classical/Reformed understanding of God being transcendent necessitates God being infinitely separate from the natural world.

Section A
God's Involvement from the Reformed View

What are the implications of the Reformed view of God on our understanding of God's involvement with this world?

Point 91: God's Will Is Perfectly Accomplished

People who embrace the Reformed view of God tend to form in their mind an image of God radiating out His will throughout creation. Add to this the Reformed understanding concerning how God's will is perfectly accomplished. If God is omnipotent, then nothing stands in the way of His will. If God is impassible, then there is nothing outside of Himself that influences His will. Reformed theologians agree that whatever God wills is instantly and perfectly accomplished.

Point 92: God Exhaustively Controls this World

Reformed theologians also believe that God is in total and absolute control of everything. Theologians refer to this as **exhaustive control**. God determines every sparrow that falls to the ground, every spilled cup of coffee, and every baby that lives or dies.

Reformed theologians teach that God is not only in exhaustive control of all things, but He is also the sole originator of all that happens in this world. John Calvin taught that "Nothing happens except what is knowingly and willingly decreed by Him."[51] According to Reformed theology, God

---

51 Calvin, *Institutes*, I:16:3.

Systematic Theology for the New Apostolic Reformation

not only allows all things, but He is the cause of everything, including every thought and action of every person on earth.

A Logical Progression of Thought
Beginning with the Reformed View of God

Reformed View of God → **God's Will Perfectly Accomplished** → **God Is in Exhaustive Control** → **God Causes All Things**

To encapsulate this understanding of God, adherents of Reformed theology say that God is "sovereign." When they say God is sovereign, they mean God is exhaustively controlling of all things.

Reformed View:
God Is Sovereign and in Exhaustive Control

Spiritual World
GOD
SOVEREIGN
EXHAUSTIVE CONTROL
Natural World

God's Involvement from the Reformed View

Point 93: All Things Are Predestined

The inescapable conclusion of the Reformed view of God is that all things are predestined. If God is timeless, then all of His decisions were settled in eternity past. He has no future decisions to make. Therefore, His will is eternally established and predestined to happen.

According to Calvin, all good and evil that has ever happened is because God willed and predestined it to happen. John Calvin explained that even the fall of Adam and Eve was predetermined by God. These are the implications that logically follow from the Reformed understanding of God.

REFORMED VIEW:
ALL THINGS ARE PREDESTINED

Point 94: Reformed View of Irresistible Grace

The Reformed view of God also determines the Reformed understanding of grace. Many different definitions of grace have been offered throughout Church history, but most commonly Reformed thinkers define grace as "unmerited favor." According to Reformed theologians, this unmerited favor is *irresistible*, meaning people who have been given grace cannot resist doing what God gave them the grace to do.

Systematic Theology for the New Apostolic Reformation

Some teachers of Reformed theology prefer to use the label **efficacious grace**, which refers to God's grace that is perfect in accomplishing whatever God has given the grace to accomplish.

A LOGICAL PROGRESSION OF THOUGHT
BEGINNING WITH THE REFORMED VIEW OF GOD

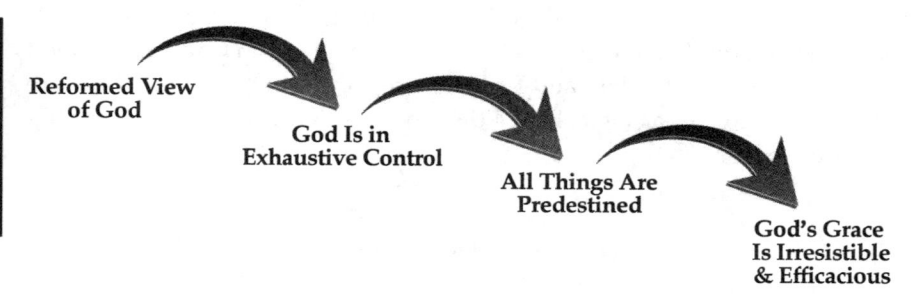

Reformed View of God → **God Is in Exhaustive Control** → **All Things Are Predestined** → **God's Grace Is Irresistible & Efficacious**

REFORMED VIEW:
GOD'S GRACE IS IRRESISTIBLE AND EFFICACIOUS

Spiritual World — **GOD**

IRRESISTIBLE & EFFICACIOUS GRACE

Natural World

In later discussions, we will see how this understanding of grace determines much about one's understanding of salvation, the atonement, and the gospel.

God's Involvement from the Reformed View

Point 95: The Strength of Classical/Reformed Theology

This is a good place to comment on the strength of both Classical and Reformed theology.

Adherents of Classical/Reformed theology have developed a system of thought consistent with God's sovereignty (as they understand sovereignty). Theologians such as Augustine, Aquinas, Anselm, Luther, and Calvin used their powers of reason to explain God's involvement with this world in ways that are consistent with their understanding that God is timeless within creation. They taught much about how humanity's will corresponds with God's predestination of all things. Classical/Reformed theologians have also tackled issues such as why there is evil in the world. Leaders such as Augustine and Calvin are honored by other theologians because of their logical integrity. Their consistency is their strength.

So when we criticize Classical/Reformed theology, we are not accusing adherents of being ignorant or illogical. On the contrary, the great theologians were brilliant. Their major errors stem from their assumptions. They start with a dualistic worldview and a concept of God based in Greek philosophical thought. They assume God is timeless within creation. They accept characteristics of the nature of God not derived from the Bible. They accept definitions of those characteristics that match Greek thought rather than Hebraic-biblical thought. The logic of the Classical/Reformed theologians is commendable, but their assumptions are wrong.

Volume II
God's Involvement

Section B
God's Involvement from the Father-Son View

Now we will look in the Bible to see what is revealed about God's involvement with this world. What we learn will be incorporated into Father-Son theology.

Notice how different this approach is to the approach in the previous section, where we discussed God's involvement with this world according to Reformed theology. In that section, we never referred to any verse in the Bible. With Reformed theology, we do not need to read the Bible, because the concept of God being timeless, impassible, immutable, omnipotent, omniscient, and omnipresent determines what is believed about how God acts. The Reformed view of God leads one to conclude that God is in exhaustive control of all things, all things are predestined, and God's grace is irresistible. Some Scriptures may be quoted to support this understanding of how God controls this world, but no Scripture is necessary to come to these conclusions.

In contrast, a student of Father-Son theology needs to read the Bible to learn how Father-God acts. We could derive some understanding by thinking about the attributes, concepts, and names of God about which we learned through our earlier study of the Bible.[52] For example, we learned that God is forgiving, so we can expect Him to forgive people. We learned that God is relational, so we can expect God to be involved in relationships. We can even think about how a human father acts and expect some similar actions from Father-God. However, our expectations would never be certain, since we would be wrong in assuming that Father-God acts exactly like a human father. We will only know for certain how God acts if we actually read the reports of God's involvement as revealed in the Bible.

---
52 I:B-E.

Systematic Theology for the New Apostolic Reformation

Point 96: Starting with a Biblical Worldview

We can begin our understanding of God's involvement with this world by embracing the foundation of a biblical worldview that we identified earlier. God entered creation and now He fills the heavens and earth. Therefore, He acts from within creation.

GOD ENTERED CREATION AND ACTS FROM WITHIN CREATION

This is in contrast to the dualistic foundation of Classical/Reformed theology that sees God acting from a distant, timeless world. To some readers this may seem like a small distinction, but it profoundly influences all areas of theology.

Point 97: God Delegated Authority to Humanity

After God created Adam and Eve, He told them:

Be fruitful and multiply, and fill the earth, and subdue it.

(Gen. 1:28)

God gave people responsibility and authority for the earth. He even instructed them to take dominion of the earth.

God's Involvement from the Father-Son View

Evidence of this delegated authority is the fact that God told Adam to name the animals. It was Adam's job. God did not tell Adam what the names were to be, but He delegated the associated responsibility.

The Psalmist divided the realms of authority, saying:

> *The heavens are the heavens of the Lord,*
> *But the earth He has given to the sons of men.*
>
> (Ps. 115:16)

Father-God wants people to govern earth.

This implies that people have the ability to govern. It implies that people have some amount of free will. However, here we are not yet ready to talk about free will. In Volume IV we will study the nature of humanity, which includes a discussion of free will—its origin, limits, and reach.

The reason people can govern this world is because it runs according to natural laws. People can apply themselves, building homes, damming rivers, cultivating crops, and managing the forest. If this world did not run according to predictable laws, it would be impossible for humanity to govern it. These natural laws are not taught in the Bible, but science has well established that this world is not chaotic or random.

Father-God commissioned Adam and Eve (and all of their descendants) to take dominion of this law-governed world. We will learn, as we continue, how God remains involved with this world, but now we can see that He has delegated some authority to humanity. Because He is a Father, He deals with humanity in a fatherly manner. He wants His children to grow up and take responsibility.

Point 98: God Is Sovereign in the Sense that He Has All Authority

Since God wants people to govern earth, He limits His own involvement. Reformed theologians strongly disagree with this because of their belief that God exhaustively controls every detail.

This corresponds with two different definitions of "sovereign." As we have discussed,[53] John Calvin understood *sovereignty* as "God controlling all things." Father-Son theology understands sovereignty to mean "God can do whatever He wants whenever He wants." There is a big difference

---

53 II:A:92.

Systematic Theology for the New Apostolic Reformation

between God controlling all things and God doing whatever He wants. This difference identifies another major distinction between Reformed theology and Father-Son theology.

DIVERGENT VIEWS ON THE SOVEREIGNTY OF GOD

Father-Son Theology	Reformed Theology
God can do whatever He wants, whenever He wants.	God is controlling all things.

In reality, the definition of *sovereign* offered by Reformed theology does not agree with the Bible. We know this because there are human kings in the Bible who are said to be sovereign (Dan. 5:18), yet we know that no human king exhaustively controlled everything within his kingdom. Knowing this, there is no justification for us to change the definition of *sovereign* when we apply it to God. Of course, God's sovereignty encompasses all that exists. He has authority over all, but having authority is not the same as controlling all things. When a person has authority, he can choose whether or not to use that authority and take control.

Therefore, the biblical understanding leads us to recognize that God can influence this world whenever He wants, anyway He wants. However, He is not controlling all things. Let's consider this further.

Point 99: God Is in Charge

God has chosen to not control all things. This is evident in many ways. For example, we are instructed to pray:

> *Your Kingdom come.*
> *Your will be done,*
> *On earth as it is in heaven.*
>
> (Matt. 6:10)

We pray for God's will to be done on earth because, at present, God's will is not being fully accomplished on earth. There are people and demons not doing God's will. There are things that grieve God's heart. There are things that happen contrary to God's will. That is why we are instructed to pray for God's will to be done on earth.

God's Involvement from the Father-Son View

A day will come in the future when every knee will bow and every tongue will confess that Jesus Christ is Lord. Then all things will be in subjection to Jesus. Then the Kingdom of God will be fully manifest. Then the will of Jesus will be perfectly done.

However, at the present time, God's will is not being perfectly carried out. There are people not doing God's will. That is the problem with this world. Many people are living in rebellion to God, and it grieves God's heart. The reason there is so much pain and suffering in this world is because God is not controlling all things.

Once this truth is realized, a person will be hesitant in using the statement, "God is in control." This phrase may be used correctly in certain situations. For example, a Christian woman who is governing her life to the best of her ability according to the will of God should have confidence that God is leading and guiding her in her daily affairs. All things will work together for good. Therefore, she can assure herself that God is in control of the specific situation with which she is dealing.

It is also correct to say, "God is in control," if by this statement we are implying that nothing lies beyond the limits of God's ability to intervene. God can control anything He wants to because He has all authority and power to do whatever He wants to do.

However, Christians trained in Reformed theology often repeat the cliché "God is in control" every time tragic events take place, such as an earthquake, storm, or death of a child. That cliché is derived from the Reformed misunderstanding of God's sovereignty.

When Reformed Christians first hear this challenge to the God-is-in-control cliché, they are often taken aback because they grew up hearing and believing without question that God is in control. Yet, that statement is not anywhere in the Bible. Furthermore, if we say that God is in control, we are saying that He is causing war, spreading diseases, and killing babies right now. If God is in exhaustive control, as Reformed theology teaches, then God is responsible for all of the evil in the world.[54]

Rather than saying, "God is in control," Christians willing to reconsider ask, "What phrase would be more appropriate and biblically accurate?" Many Christians who have thought through the related issues will say, "God has all authority," or "God is in charge." The statement, "God is in charge," affirms that God has the authority to do whatever He wants to do, but it leaves open the possibility that God is not controlling everything.

---

54 This is discussed more fully under theodicy in II:D.

Systematic Theology for the New Apostolic Reformation

Point 100: God Providentially Guides

The Bible reveals that God is working all things out with a view to the summing up of all things in Christ (Eph. 1:9-10). God is orchestrating the affairs of this world so that His ultimate will is carried out. However, steering the world's affairs toward His ultimate goals is not equivalent to controlling every detail and event that ever happens.

God's overall guidance of the world is often referred to as God's **providential guidance**. Reformed teachers sometimes use the word *providence* to refer to their all-controlling understanding of God's involvement,[55] but here we are referring to the manner in which God guides things from behind the scenes—not every detail, but the overall direction of the world's progression toward His ultimate goals.

When Christians talk about God's providential guidance they are often referring to how God can influence someone of great authority to act as He desires. For example, God stirred the heart of King Cyrus to release the Hebrew people out of slavery (Ezra 1:1-4). Proverbs 21:1 tells us:

> *The king's heart is like channels of water in the hand of the Lord;*
> *He turns it wherever He wishes.*

God can turn the heart of a king anyway He chooses, and from this verse, we can infer that God has the authority to direct any person any way He desires. However, this verse does not say that God *is* directing every decision every king makes. It simply reveals how God has the authority to direct whoever He chooses whenever He chooses.

If we insist, as Reformed teachers insist, that God determines every action of every leader, then we have to conclude that God directed Hitler to kill six million Jews. To be consistent with the Reformed understanding, we would also have to say that God made Solomon take 700 wives and 300 concubines who led his heart away from God (1 Kings 11:3). If God directs every decision of every leader, then God is the cause of great suffering in the world.

On the other hand, if we accept God's providential guidance from the view of Father-Son theology, then we will acknowledge God doing enough to guide the overall direction of the world's progression toward His ultimate goals, but not controlling every decision of every person.

---

55 Calvin used the word *providence* to refer to every event happening by God's decree.

God's Involvement from the Father-Son View

Point 101: God Can Predestine Whatever He Wants

Any Christian who takes the Bible seriously will conclude that God has predestined certain events. For example, Jesus was predestined to come into the world and die for the sins of humanity (Rev. 13:8). There are also several examples in the Bible of God predetermining what certain individuals will accomplish. For example, Jeremiah was chosen to be a prophet before he was even born (Jer. 1:5). Indeed, a sovereign God can predestine whatever He wants to predestine.

However, even though God predestined Jeremiah to be a prophet, this does not mean that God has predestined every human being to work in the career in which they find themselves. It is poor **hermeneutics** (method of understanding the Bible) to take an example of how God worked in one individual's life and assume that God works in every person's life the same way.

This is obvious as soon as we consider people who have chosen careers, such as drug dealing or prostitution, which are not according to God's will. If we embrace the Classical/Reformed view that God predestines every person into their career, then we have to accept drug dealers and prostitutes as doing God's will.

We need to reconsider how God deals with people. Just because God chose Jeremiah to be a prophet does not mean that God chose every person to be in the vocation in which they find themselves. Jeremiah was mentioned in Scripture as an individual chosen to carry out some special task that God had in mind. God's dealings with Jeremiah are not an example of how God works in everyone's life. Instead, we should see how God can uniquely choose any individual He wants whenever He wants.

God can predestine whatever He wants to predestine, but He can also choose to let things and people move without His coercion. He is sovereign, so He can do either.

Point 102: God Answers Prayer

Another way God is involved in this world is through answering prayers. When the Hebrews were in captivity in Egypt:

God heard their groaning; and God remembered His covenant with

Systematic Theology for the New Apostolic Reformation

Abraham, Isaac, and Jacob. God saw the sons of Israel and God took notice of them.

(Ex. 2:24-25)

If we take these verses seriously, we will recognize God responding to the cries of His people. Furthermore, Jesus assured His disciples, *"If you ask Me anything in My name, I will do it"* (John 14:14). God does answer prayers, especially for those who are in covenant relationship with Him.

Reformed theologians who embrace impassibility as an attribute of God and are consistent in their theology, teach that it is impossible for God to answer prayer, because God is too big to be influenced by anything He created. Reformed theologians who reject impassibility have to come to a similar conclusion but through a different progression of thought; they will say God answers the prayers of people, but He sovereignly predestined those people to pray those prayers.

Because Reformed theologians see God as immutable, they teach that prayer does not change God, but it changes the person doing the praying.

Father-Son theology agrees that people may change as they pray, but God also is able to answer prayer and change His mind.

Point 103: God Rewards

God also rewards those who diligently seek Him (Heb. 11:6). We discussed this in Volume I, Section E, where we saw God as a rewarder. Because it is in His nature to reward, He gets involved in this world by blessing those who seek Him.

Of course, this is incompatible with the teachings of Reformed theologians who accept impassibility as a characteristic of God.

Point 104: God Influences through Relationships

God also influences this world through relationships with people. As people relate to Him, they bring their lives more into alignment with His will. This can be compared to a young man who falls in love with a woman; his behavior typically changes, often in dramatic ways. Similarly, when people enter into relationship with God, their lives are brought more into

God's Involvement from the Father-Son View

alignment with God's will. As a result, God influences this world through the lives of those who love and draw near to Him.

Point 105: God Disciplines His Children

Another way in which God influences this world is by training and discipling His children to live righteously. The writer of Hebrews explained:

> *God deals with you as with sons; for what son is there whom his father does not discipline? . . . those who have been trained by it, afterwards it yields the peaceful fruit of righteousness.*
> (Heb. 12:7-11)

Point 106: God Influences via His Spirit

God also influences this world through His Spirit. An excellent example is how Paul and his companions attempted to preach in Asia, but they were *"forbidden by the Holy Spirit to speak the word in Asia"* (Acts 16:6). One aspect of the new covenant is that God puts His Spirit in His people and causes them to do His will (Ez. 36:27).[56]

God also empowers people to accomplish some tasks by putting His Spirit upon them. For example, we are told in Deuteronomy 31:3-6, that craftsmen were anointed by God to do their work with extra skill and wisdom.

When God influences via His Spirit, people typically maintain some ability to cooperate or resist the Holy Spirit. We see this freedom when prophets prophesy. Paul explained how the spirits of prophets are subject to the prophets, which means the prophets have the authority to speak God's word or not (1 Cor. 14:32). We can also see biblical evidence of people resisting what the Spirit of God is directing. Paul even warned people not to grieve the Holy Spirit (Eph. 4:30), which would only be possible if people are capable of resisting what the Spirit is directing.

So then, God can gently woo people to do His will, but He can also work more forcefully in their lives through His Spirit. Paul talked

---

[56] This is discussed in XII:E:624-625..

Systematic Theology for the New Apostolic Reformation

about how the Spirit "compelled" him to go to Jerusalem (Acts 20:22). God can work through His Spirit forcefully or gently, because He is sovereign.

Point 107: God Gives Grace that Can Be Resistible or Irresistible

God extends grace to people, however, the biblical understanding of grace is different than the Reformed theologian's understanding. As we explained,[57] Reformed teachers see God's grace as "irresistible," because their concept of God necessitates this understanding. They believe people have no choice or ability to resist doing what God gave them the grace to do.

Yet, the Bible gives us several examples that contradict the Reformed understanding of grace. For example, Paul exhorts the Corinthian Christians *"not to receive the grace of God in vain"* (2 Cor. 6:1), something which would be impossible if the Reformed understanding of grace was true. In another passage Paul and Barnabas urged their listeners to *"continue in the grace of God"* (Acts 13:43), which would be a foolish exhortation if grace was irresistible. The writer of Hebrews tells his readers not to fall short of the grace of God (Heb. 12:15), and Peter tells his listeners to be *"good stewards of the manifold grace of God"* (2 Peter 4:10), both of which show people as active participants with the grace of God.

God is able to extend His grace to individuals along with any measure of authority He chooses. Therefore, He can extend grace in a fashion that does compel a person to obey. Or He can extend grace in a less forceful manner. He can make His grace resistible or irresistible. He is God, and He is sovereign.

Point 108: God Intervenes in this World

Because God is sovereign, He can intervene in this world whenever He chooses. The Bible offers many reports of His interventions, especially in the lives of the Jews. God's interventions are evidence that He is not exhaustively controlling all things. If He was controlling all things, then He would not have to intervene.

---

57 II:A:94. Explained in more depth in VI:H:406-408.

God's Involvement from the Father-Son View

Point 109: God Influences via Angels

In Volume III, we will discuss angelology, but now we can note that God influences the affairs of this world through angels who carry out His will (Ps. 103:20).

Point 110: God Is Selectively Involved

To understand the view of Father-Son theology concerning His involvement with this world, it is helpful to compare it with Reformed theology and Deism. Reformed theology insists that God is in exhaustive control of all things. **Deism** is at the other end of the spectrum, claiming that God started the world and now is letting the world run according to natural laws without His further involvement. The view of Deism is often explained by comparing the world to a clock that God has wound up and let run on its own.

Reformed Theology ←——————————→ Deism
God   God
Exhaustively   Not
Controlling   Involved

Father-Son theology falls between these two extremes. Adherents would be comfortable saying that God is *selectively involved* with this world.[58] This understanding gives credence to the many ways God is involved with us, such as God influencing this world through answering prayers, relationships, His Spirit, giving grace, angels, and so forth.

In reality, none of these means of influence have significance in Reformed theology. If God is already controlling every thought and desire of every human being, then His answering prayers is meaningless. If God is controlling what every human being does, then any additional influence that He has in the life of the Christian through the Holy Spirit is redundant. If God is in exhaustive control of all things, then He does not need to intervene. If God is sovereign in the sense that Reformed theology dictates, then discussing how He influences this world is a frivolous dialogue. On the other hand, if God is selectively involved with this world, then the examples in the Bible of how God is involved are enlightening.

---

58 This is also the view of Open Theism.

Systematic Theology for the New Apostolic Reformation

Point 111: God Is Self-Limiting Because He Is a Father

In order to understand God's involvement from the perspective of Father-Son theology, we must recognize that God is self-limiting. Of course, He can control anything He wants to control, because He is sovereign, having the authority to do whatever He wants to do whenever He wants. However, Father-God has sovereignly decided to limit His own involvement with this world.

Why does God limit Himself? One reason is because He is a Covenant-Maker. As explained earlier, Hebraic covenants entail involving covenant partners in the decision-making process. If God was in exhaustive control and had everything predetermined, it would be impossible for people to ever influence His decisions. It would be impossible for people to enter into meaningful dialogue with God with any hope of ever changing His mind. If God was in exhaustive control of all things, it would be impossible for Him to enter into covenantal relationships.

A second reason that God may limit Himself is because He desires relationship with His children. If God existed throughout time within creation, He would know beforehand everything that His people were going to do. Therefore, it would be impossible for Him to respond to people or empathize with them. If God filled all of time, He could never experience hope or the joy of watching His children grow. Perhaps, then, God has chosen to limit Himself in time for the purpose of relationship with His children.

Third, God may limit Himself because He loves His children. Human parents often go down to the level of their children so they can relate more effectively. They drop down on one knee so their size will not intimidate younger children. Perhaps God similarly limits Himself so He can be an effective Father for His children.

Fourth, God may limit Himself because He wants His children to mature. To see this, it is helpful to think of God as *reluctant to get involved in many situations*. *Reluctance* may not be the most accurate word, because it may create a picture of God trying to decide if He should or shouldn't get involved. Such indecision should not be assigned to the character of God. However, from another perspective, *reluctance* does offer us an understanding concerning why God does what He does, because God may choose not to get involved because He wants people to grow up. He wants people to take responsibility to govern the affairs of this world. He

God's Involvement from the Father-Son View

wants people to make decisions. He wants people to fulfill the task that He initially assigned to humanity: *"Be fruitful and multiply, and fill the earth, and subdue it."* God is a Father who desires to raise sons. That is why He interacts with the world in the way He does. He acts like a Father because He is a Father.

Volume II
God's Involvement

Section C
Cooperative Relationships

God desires *cooperative relationships* with humanity. When God said to the Hebrews, "I will be your God and you will be My people," He was offering Himself in relationship to them. God loves the world and wishes all people would relate to Him as children relate to their father.

Point 112: God Works with and Through People

The understanding of cooperative relationships is shared by Father-Son theology and Open Theism. Both views recognize the significance of humanity's role in God's unfolding plans. Our prayers and actions are important. God listens. God watches. He responds.

Reformed teachers may talk about people being active participants in fulfilling God's plans, but their insistence that God is in exhaustive control negates any real participation on the part of humanity. People are merely puppets walking out a predetermined plan. People have no free will in this because God's will and grace are irresistible.[59]

In contrast, Father-Son theology and Open Theism recognize God as wanting to partner with us to help us succeed in our daily battles. He wants to give us His Spirit to inspire us to do good works. God is willing and even eager to help us:

> *For the eyes of the Lord move to and fro throughout the earth that*
> *He may strongly support those whose heart is completely His.*
> (2 Chron. 16:9)

---

59 Free will is discussed in IV:M.

Systematic Theology for the New Apostolic Reformation

God looks for people whom He can use to fulfill His will. Of course, God is sovereign so He can mechanistically carry out His predetermined will if and when He chooses. However, He has sovereignly decided to work with and through people.

Point 113: Examples of Cooperative Relationships with God

An eye-opening example of humanity's cooperative relationship with God is in the life of Esther, the Queen of Babylon. Unaware that Esther was Jewish, King Ahasuerus was deceived into believing that the Jews were rebellious and should be eliminated from his kingdom. So King Ahasuerus issued a decree that on an appointed day the Jews throughout the land would be killed (Esth. 3). Queen Esther knew that she and her people were in danger of being annihilated, but she did not know what to do to stop the actions of the king's decree. Then her uncle Mordecai spoke to her and said:

> *For if you remain silent at this time, relief and deliverance will arise for the Jews from another place and you and your father's house will perish.*
>
> (Esth. 4:14a)

As a leader of the Jews, Mordecai knew that God would rescue the Jewish people: *"Deliverance will arise!"* Mordecai knew that God would be faithful to His covenant with them. However, Mordecai also understood that Esther's involvement in this deliverance was optional. Mordecai told the queen that God would deliver, but if she did not speak up then she would be killed, and God would simply choose someone else to use.

This reveals to us a profound truth about the way God involves Himself in this world. There are things that God will do because He is faithful and He has decided to do them. However, who He uses and exactly how He works out all of His purposes and plans is negotiable in some situations. God is working out His plans, but to some degree, "the how" depends upon the cooperation of people.

For another example, we can think of Josiah the king of Israel. The prophet Elisha told the king to strike the ground with arrows but the king only struck the ground three times. This made the prophet Elisha

Cooperative Relationships

angry, because he knew that the number of times the king struck the ground determined how greatly God would help the king in war (2 Kings 13:15-19).

Consider also how Daniel was reading from the Book of Jeremiah and learned that the Hebrew people were to be in captivity for 70 years (Dan. 9:2). As Daniel read Jeremiah's prophecy, he realized that the 70-year period of captivity was over and freedom was at hand. However, Daniel did not sit around passively waiting for God to fulfill His promises. Instead, he went on a fast and sought God for the freedom and deliverance of the Hebrew people (Dan. 9:2-19). Daniel realized that he must cooperate with God for the fulfillment of what He had declared.

Consider Peter's exhortation to the early Christians:

> . . . *what sort of people ought you to be in holy conduct and godliness, looking for and hastening the coming of the day of God.*
> (2 Peter 3:11-12)

Peter understood that Christians can "hasten" the coming of the day of God by how they act and live. Of course, nothing people do will stop the day of God, however, Christians play a role in when it takes place.

Point 114: Humans Form the Future with God

One of the most theology-shaking examples of God working with humanity is from the wedding in Cana (John 2:1-11). Mary pointed out to Jesus that the wine had run out. Jesus responded to Mary, saying, *"Woman, what does that have to do with us? My hour has not yet come"* (John 2:4). Jesus knew that it was not yet according to the Father's will that He begin His public ministry. Yet, Jesus worked the miracle anyway.

In other words, the miracle happened even though it was not according to God's appointed time. This implies that God's plans were suddenly shifted, and God allowed those plans to shift according to Mary's desire.

This same truth is evident in other Bible passages. For example, after the Hebrews settled in the Promise Land, they wanted a king. Even though God did not want them to have a king, He gave them what they desired (1 Sam. 8).

This is an astounding revelation. Not only are people to cooperate with God, but God is willing to cooperate with people.

Systematic Theology for the New Apostolic Reformation

Of course, Reformed teachers cannot accept this understanding of God's relationships with people. They see God acting and people have no choice but to carry out His predetermined will. According to them, any covenants that God makes are one-way paths wherein God gives His promises and blessings, but no real mutual exchange can ever take place.

The Bible reveals that all believers have a relationship with God, and that relationship entails a relational covenant. Covenant partners make decisions together. For this reason, God allowed Abraham and Moses to influence His decisions. The same is true today. Through Jesus Christ, God's people have a covenant relationship with Him and, therefore, a relationship of cooperation.

This gives significance to the actions of each believer. The Church is essential and actually being raised to rule and reign with Jesus. God's people can work with Him to change the world and form the future with Him.

Section D
Theodicy

When we discuss God's involvement with this world, our theodicy comes to the forefront. **Theodicy** is the theological term for someone's answer to the question, "If God is good and omnipotent, why is there evil and suffering in the world?" The answer a theologian or philosopher gives to this question has historically been considered the test of his or her logical integrity.

In Volume V, we will talk about the *origin* and *nature* of evil, death, and suffering. Here we focus on why God allows evil, death, and suffering in the present world.

Point 115: Reformed Theodicy

If God is in exhaustive control as Reformed theologians claim, then He determines and orchestrates the pain and suffering you and I experience. If God is timeless, impassible, immutable, omnipotent, omniscient, and omnipresent, then He is the cause of all things. If John Calvin is right, that "Nothing happens except what is knowingly and willingly decreed by Him,"[60] then God is the One causing war and spreading diseases right now. If God has predestined from the foundations of the world everything that has ever happened and everything that will happen, then He is the One who is responsible for every baby that has ever been aborted. There is no way around this. If the Reformed concept of God is true, then God is responsible for all that happens in the world, including the bad things.

Reformed theologians are fully aware of these implications of their theology. They refer to this as "the problem of evil." Reformed theologians

---
60 Calvin, *Institutes*, I:16:3.

Systematic Theology for the New Apostolic Reformation

have never been able to form a valid theodicy that explains how there can be so much evil in the world and God can still be good. Of course, it is impossible to explain the existence of so much evil, if indeed, God is in control, as Reformed theologians claim. There is no explanation.

THE LOGICAL PROGRESSION OF THOUGHT BEGINNING WITH THE REFORMED VIEW OF GOD

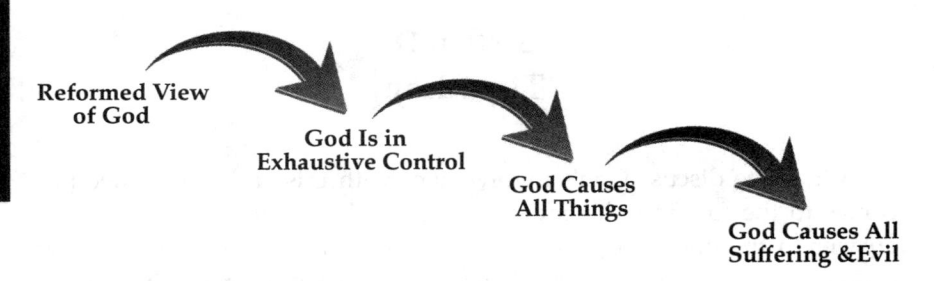

Reformed View of God → God Is in Exhaustive Control → God Causes All Things → God Causes All Suffering & Evil

Point 116: The Reformed Answer When a Baby Dies

Coming from the Reformed perspective, what can a pastor say to a mother who tragically loses her baby? He may offer condolences and give reassuring answers, such as, "God wanted the child. Or God is teaching people something. Or we simply do not understand the ways of God." However, if the pastor is logically consistent with Reformed theology, then these answers are merely intermediaries standing between the grieving mother and the timeless God who not only allows but also predestines and causes all things. According to Reformed theology, God willed and caused the death of her baby.

Holding to this understanding of God's control and predestination of all things, John Calvin wrote about the death of his own baby:

> The Lord, has certainly inflicted a severe and bitter wound in the death of our baby son.[61]

Being consistent with his theology, Calvin believed God killed his baby.

---

61 Calvin wrote this in a letter to his friend, Pierre Viret.

Theodicy

Point 117: Father-Son Theodicy

Father-Son theology offers different explanations for why there is evil, death, and suffering in this world. Rather than conclude that God is to blame, we can identify several different causes.

First, we already discussed how this world runs according to natural laws. In such a world, a tree can grow old, rot, and fall, crushing a passer-by. Rain can cause floods which destroy homes and kill people. Natural disasters happen. Diseases spread. A world that runs according to natural laws is a world where suffering happens.

Second, there are **unnatural laws** governing this world. By this, we are referring to forces that have resulted from the fall of humanity. Sin and death were released into this world. This is a harsh, cruel world where bad things happen because of sin.

An unnatural law worth noting is that all creation has been *"subjected to futility"* (Rom. 8:20). This means tragic events happen that are futile—they are meaningless—they have no positive outcome. This truth cannot be reconciled with Reformed theology. Since adherents believe God is in exhaustive control, they cannot accept any futility in creation. They often say, "Everything happens for a reason." Such trite answers are based in a profound misunderstanding of God's involvement with this world. He is not the cause of all things. Many events happen without some hidden purpose of God being fulfilled. Of course, God can turn all things toward good on behalf of those who love Him (Rom. 8:28), but for those who do not love Him, bad occurrences often have no good outcome. This is what the Bible means when it says that the world has been subjected to futility.

The third reason there is evil, death, and suffering is because God has delegated authority to people to govern this world. This implies some amount of free will on the part of humanity. In a world where people have some free will, people can hurt other people. Criminals can steal. Murderers can kill. Corrupt governments can withhold food and provisions that rightly belong to its citizens. In a world where people have authority to govern, they can govern unjustly.

Fourth, people can make mistakes. Doctors can prescribe the wrong medicine. Engineers may design buildings with flaws that will not withstand earthquakes. Parents may discipline their child for something that their child did not do. People may act based on misinformation. Mistakes are made in a world where people are not exhaustively controlled by God.

Systematic Theology for the New Apostolic Reformation

Father-Son theology recognizes these and other sources for evil, death, and suffering. For this reason. Father-Son theology has "no problem of evil." God is not responsible. What Reformed theologians are unable to answer is a non-issue for those holding to Father-Son theology. God is good and powerful, but the reason bad things happen in this world is because God has chosen not to control all things.

Point 118: Answering the Atheists

It is difficult to over emphasize the importance of this discussion.

Today, the number one argument atheists use to try to prove there is no God is this: "How can there be a God when there is so much evil in the world?" This question has been repeated millions of times, and it has undermined the faith of multitudes. Because Reformed teachers and theologians have been unable to form a valid theodicy, adherents have never been able to give a reasonable answer to the atheists.

Father-Son theology has no problem answering.

Point 119: Father-Son Theology Answers When a Baby Dies

If a newborn dies, why did it happen? According to Father-Son theology, there could be many reasons, among which are the following:

- Sudden Infant Death Syndrome
- Random selection of genes that caused a genetic disorder
- Suffocation or poisoning
- Improper nutrition or care
- An accidental fall
- The result of an infection, virus, or disease
- Errors made by medical staff
- Medical problems which we do not understand
- The activity of Satan or his demons

Any combination of the above explanations may be possible, along with an unlimited number of other explanations.

Theodicy

A pastor who holds to Father-Son theology can tell a mother who lost her child that the tragedy happened because we live in a world where terrible things happen. This is a fallen world, subject to natural laws where injustice occurs, people make mistakes, and death is an active force. Because many things happen contrary to the will of God, Father-God is grieving with the mother. Furthermore, the pastor can explain to the mother that this world has not yet been fully redeemed. Someday in the future, the Kingdom of God will fully manifest. Then *"there will no longer be any mourning, or crying, or pain . . ."* (Rev. 21:3-4). However, at the present time, the reason her baby died is because God is not controlling all things.

In the meantime, God wants His children to care for one another. He wants to be our Comforter. Father-God understands the pain in the death of a son.

Volume II
God's Involvement

Section E
Father-God's Knowledge of the World

When we talk about God's interactions with this world, it is appropriate to discuss the extent of His knowledge concerning what is actually taking place in the world. Classical/Reformed thinkers say that God is omniscient. This concept is so deeply entrenched in Western Christianity that most Christians have never considered an alternative view. Yet, the Bible never accredits omniscience to God, and the word omniscience is an abstract word foreign to Hebraic-biblical thought, i.e., the Bible never talks about God in such terms as omniscience.[62]

Point 120: What Is God's Knowledge of the Future?

Disagreements concerning God's knowledge are primarily focused on His knowledge about the future.[63] Classical/Reformed teachers believe that God knows the future perfectly. In theological terms, God has **exhaustive knowledge** of everything, including the future, according to Classical/Reformed theology.

Adherents of Father-Son theology question this.[64] Father-Son theology holds that God knows much about the future, because He created the natural laws that govern the universe. God also understands the unnatural laws (those resulting from sin).[65] He perfectly understands cause-and-effect

---

62 The abstract nature of the word *omniscience* was explained in I:H:69-71.
63 Adherents of Father-Son theology also question whether or not God can sovereignly choose to not know certain things about the present, however, discussions about the future are most relevant because they deal directly with God being timeless or temporal within creation.
64 On this, Father-Son theology is in agreement with Open Theism.
65 More about unnatural laws is offered in V:I:343..

Systematic Theology for the New Apostolic Reformation

relationships. Furthermore, God is governing the world to His ultimate end, which He has predetermined, so He knows much about what will happen. However, adherents of Father-Son theology do not believe that God knows everything about the future.

Point 121: God's Knowledge Is Tied to the Existence of the Future

Whenever we talk about God's knowledge of the future, there is an important implication that must be addressed. It is the question as to whether or not the future already exists.

Classical/Reformed teachers claim that God is timeless within creation, and therefore, He fills the past, present, and future right now. If God fills the future, then the future must already exist.

We will also come to this same conclusion if we start with the Classical/Reformed belief that all of time stands before God right now. This is more than God seeing visions of the future. If the future stands before God right now, then the future must already exist.

**A LOGICAL PROGRESSION OF THOUGHT
BEGINNING WITH THE REFORMED VIEW OF GOD**

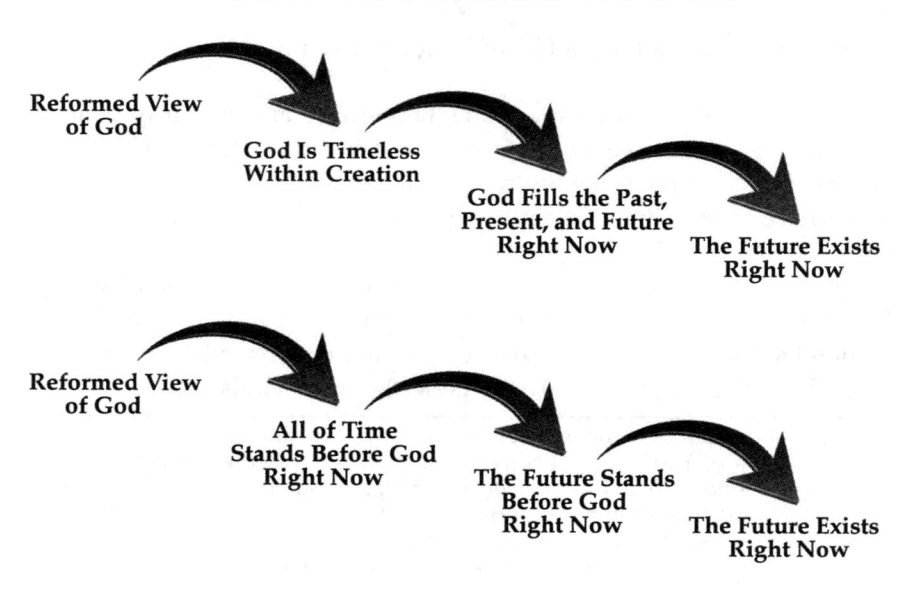

Reformed View of God → God Is Timeless Within Creation → God Fills the Past, Present, and Future Right Now → The Future Exists Right Now

Reformed View of God → All of Time Stands Before God Right Now → The Future Stands Before God Right Now → The Future Exists Right Now

Father-God's Knowledge of the World

A major problem with thinking that the future already exists is that the future cannot exist without us in it. Furthermore, according to the doctrine of God being timeless, God was watching from eternity past what you and I will be doing tomorrow. This means you and I have existed since eternity past. In fact, the doctrine of God's timelessness inside of creation necessitates that you and I have existed as long as God has existed.

A Logical Progression of Thought Beginning with the Reformed View of God

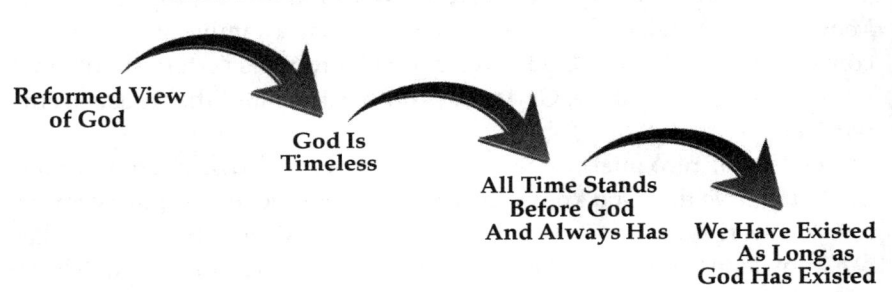

Reformed View of God → God Is Timeless → All Time Stands Before God And Always Has → We Have Existed As Long as God Has Existed

This unavoidable implication of Classical/Reformed theology is so absurd that it is worth establishing in smaller steps. Classical/Reformed thinkers hold that God fills all of time within creation and all of time stands before Him. Furthermore, they maintain that all of time has always stood before Him. According to Classical/Reformed theology, our entire life was standing before God one million years ago. And 100 billion years ago. And a zillion years ago. God was not just watching videos of us, but according to Classical/Reformed theology all of time has always existed and always stood before God. Since all of time eternally stands before God we have existed as long as God has existed according to Classical/Reformed theology.[66]

Some adherents of Classical/Reformed theology may respond, "Well, I don't believe that." Yet, if you say that God is timeless and all of time stands before God, then you are saying that you and I have existed eternally. You cannot escape this implication. It should not need to be said, but if the implication of an idea is absurd, then that idea is absurd. For me, this is another fatal blow to Classical/Reformed theology. I do not believe that I have existed as long as God has existed.

---

[66] This implication of Classical/Reformed theology is explained in more depth in III:F:165-169.

Systematic Theology for the New Apostolic Reformation

Point 122: Is Prophecy Proof of God's Foreknowledge?

If the teachers of Classical/Reformed theology are right that the future already exists, then it is possible that God knows the future exhaustively. On the other hand, if the future does not exist, it is possible that there are some things about the future that He does not know.

When debating about God's knowledge of the future, teachers like to talk about prophecy. Classical/Reformed teachers point to prophecy as proof that God knows all of the future. For example, the Prophet Agabus knew by the revelation of the Holy Spirit that a famine was about to come (Acts 11:28). Since God reveals to His prophets certain events that will happen in the future, God must know beforehand that those events will happen.

However, recognizing that God has foreknowledge of some things does not prove that God knows everything about the future. Furthermore, it is unclear whether God knows those future events because He has foreknowledge or because He has sovereignly decided to accomplish the related events.

The words of Amos are enlightening concerning how God works with prophecy in a "fore-declarative" manner.

> *Surely the Lord God does nothing*
> *Unless He reveals His secret counsel*
> *To His servants the prophets.*
>
> (Amos 3:7)

This verse tells us that God does not just tell prophets the future, but He tells prophets *what He is planning to do*. This is not merely foreknowledge, but "fore-declaration" or "fore-ordination." Please note this distinction because it influences how you understand God and prophecy. Amos 3:7 tells us prophecy is God revealing to us what He is about to do, not simply foretelling events as if He already had watched them happen.

Similarly, Isaiah records God's words that reveal how He works in the world:

> *. . . I am God, and there is no one like Me,*
> *Declaring the end from the beginning*
> *And from ancient times things which have not been done,*
> *Saying, "My purpose will be established,*

Father-God's Knowledge of the World

And I will accomplish all My good pleasure."

(Is. 46:9-10)

If we read these verses through a mindset that assumes God is timeless within creation, then we will conclude that God has perfect foreknowledge. On the other hand, if we avoid that assumption and simply embrace this passage exactly as it is written, we will note that God *declares* the end from the beginning. Declaring does not necessarily mean He has foreknowledge as if He has already seen it happen. It is just as reasonable to say that God is declaring the future because He has decided to make it happen.

Indeed, Isaiah 46:9-10 is fore-declarative, and we can verify this if we simply read the very next verse where God says:

*Truly I have spoken; truly I will bring it to pass.
I have planned it, surely I will do it.*

(Is. 46:11)

Notice God's explanation of His own words. He stated that He will bring to pass what He declares will happen.

The point is that prophecy does not prove that God has perfect foreknowledge. God explained that what He speaks through prophets is what He has decided to accomplish.[67]

Point 123: The Human Heart Is an Unknown Variable

Adherents of Father-Son theology and Open Theism question whether or not God knows all of the future. Both views say that the human heart introduces a variable in the events that will happen in the future. This means that some things about the future have not yet been determined. Since those things have not yet been determined, God cannot know those things with certainty.

Open theists are well known for taking this position on God's knowledge of the future. Unfortunately, critics of Open Theism often jump on this fact and distort the view of Open Theism to the point of absurdity. I have

---

[67] In XI:F, we discuss how God sometimes speaks through prophecy with such authority that the results are predestined, while other times God speaks through prophecy offering to His people something that they can partner with to see accomplished.

Systematic Theology for the New Apostolic Reformation

heard critics make untrue accusations, such as, "Open theists believe that God does not know anymore about the future than people do!" Such an accusation is foolish and reveals the hearts of critics who simply do not want to deal with the facts about Open Theism.

As I stated, God knows much about the future, because He created the natural laws that govern the universe. God also understands the unnatural laws. He perfectly understands cause-and-effect relationships. Furthermore, God is governing the world to His ultimate end, which He has predetermined, so Open theists believe that God knows much about what will happen in the future. However, the human heart introduces a variable.

Consider a man named Leon who lives in Detroit, Michigan. Leon is about to get in a car wreck. Most Open theists would agree that God already knows about the soon coming wreck and who will be involved in the car wreck. What an Open theist would say is the unknown is whether or not Leon will cry out to God the instant the accident occurs. The variable in the soon-coming car wreck is Leon's heart.[68]

However, Open theists do not even think of Leon's heart as totally unknown. God has watched Leon his entire life, and so, God knows it better than parents know the hearts of their own children. Even though God knows Leon's heart that well, there is always a possibility that Leon will change. He has free will. He is an individual created in the image of God with the ability to make decisions. For this reason, God continues to watch Leon's heart.

Father-Son theology agrees with Open Theism that the heart of humanity introduces an unknown variable.

The Bible reveals that God is moving through time with people and watching their hearts. Paul explained that *"God examines our hearts"* (1 Thes. 2:4). Jeremiah 17:9 reports the words of God: *"I, the LORD, search the heart, I test the mind."* Moses explained to the Hebrews how God led them in the wilderness, *"testing you, to know what was in your heart"* (Deut. 8:2).

An excellent example of this is how God tested Abraham to see if Abraham was willing to sacrifice his own son, Isaac. After Abraham prepared Isaac for the sacrifice and was about to kill him with a knife, God stopped him and said:

Do not stretch out your hand against the lad, and do nothing to

---

[68] Of course, the hearts of other people involved in the car wreck also introduce variables.

Father-God's Knowledge of the World

him; for <u>now I know</u> that you fear God, since you have not withheld your son, your only son, from Me.
(Gen. 22:12)

God said, "Now I know." If we take these words literally, we have to conclude that God did not know Abraham's heart with certainty before this test.

Every human being has a heart that is capable of good and evil,[69] Therefore, the accumulation of millions of people doing things that are not totally foreknown can result is some unknown outcomes. However, even with the variable of the human heart, God is big enough to continue guiding the world in the direction He desires. Adherents of Open Theism and Father-Son theology agree about this.

Point 124: Is God Omniscient?

Open theists and adherents of Father-Son theology may disagree on some other points concerning God's knowledge. This is a difficult topic to address because there is no written set of doctrines to which all Open theists have agreed. All adherents recognize God as in a cooperative relationship with humanity, however, Open Theism has not developed into a distinct set of doctrines.

Even though there is no agreed upon statement of faith, many Open theists say that God is omniscient even though they do not believe God knows all of the future. They can do this by redefining the word *omniscient* to mean that God "knows all that can be known." They will then go on to explain that the future does not exist, so the future cannot be known. By defining omniscience as "knowing all that can be known," Open theists can exclude information about the future and continue saying that God is omniscient. Not all Open theists have agreed to this definition of omniscience, but it has become commonly accepted by many Open theists.

To me, using the word *omniscient* in this way is disingenuous. Omniscience comes from Latin *omni* meaning " all" and *sciens* meaning "knowing." In the etymology of the word, there is no "all that can be known" in the sense of limiting omniscience to the past and present. The word *omniscience* has always been used in theology and philosophy to mean "all knowing," which includes all of the past, present, and future.

---

69 Discussed in IV:L:265-266.

Systematic Theology for the New Apostolic Reformation

For me, there is no justification for redefining a word to make it fit one's theology.[70] The plain fact is that Open theists do not believe that God is omniscient in the sense that the word has been used for hundreds of years.

Point 125: God's Knowledge Is Infinite

Father-Son theology asserts that God knows everything that the Bible says He knows. Therefore, He knows the number of hairs on our heads and every sparrow that falls to the ground (Matt. 10:29-30). God knows our thoughts (Ps. 94:11 ; 139:2) and every need that we have before we ask Him (Matt. 6:8). God's thoughts are higher than our thoughts, as the heavens are higher than the earth (Is. 55:9). God even *"counts the number of the stars"* and *"gives names to all of them."* Furthermore, *"His understanding is infinite"* (Ps. 147:4).

Father-Son theology agrees with the Bible that God's knowledge is infinite, but no where does the Bible say that God is omniscient. What is the difference?

Point 126: Is God's Knowledge Infinite or Omniscient?

Infinite knowledge is different than omniscience in several ways.

First, one came from the Bible while the other did not. The Bible accredits infinite knowledge to God. In contrast, the attribute of omniscience developed out of the ancient Greek philosopher's concept of God independently from the Bible. Biblical truths are best expressed with biblical words.

Second, infinite knowledge is different than omniscience because infinity minus one is still infinity, but omniscience minus one is no longer omniscience.

Third, God may possess infinite knowledge about the past and present, but this says nothing about the future. On the other hand, omniscience (as the word has been used historically) includes knowing all things about the past, present, and future.

---

70 Some readers may object to this statement, since I have challenged the Classical/ Reformed definition of sovereignty, but the definition I am offering for sovereignty in Father-Son theology is one in agreement with its use in Scripture. See II:B:98-99.

Father-God's Knowledge of the World

Fourth—and most importantly—Classical/Reformed theology *needs* omniscience as an attribute of God. If God's knowledge is infinite, but He is not omniscient, then all of Classical/Reformed theology crumbles. Let me explain . . .

Point 127: Classical/Reformed Theology Needs Omniscience

The characteristics assigned to God by the ancient Greek philosophers are logically consistent with one another. To show this I will make a few statements that are easy to follow:

1. If God is timeless within creation, then He is omniscient. This makes sense because *timeless* includes God being everywhere throughout time.

2. If God is sovereign (in the Classical/Reformed sense of being in exhaustive control), then He is omniscient. This makes sense because to be in control of everything necessitates knowing everything.

3. If God is omnipresent, then He is omniscient.

**A LOGICAL PROGRESSION OF THOUGHT
FROM THE CLASSICAL/REFORMED VIEW**

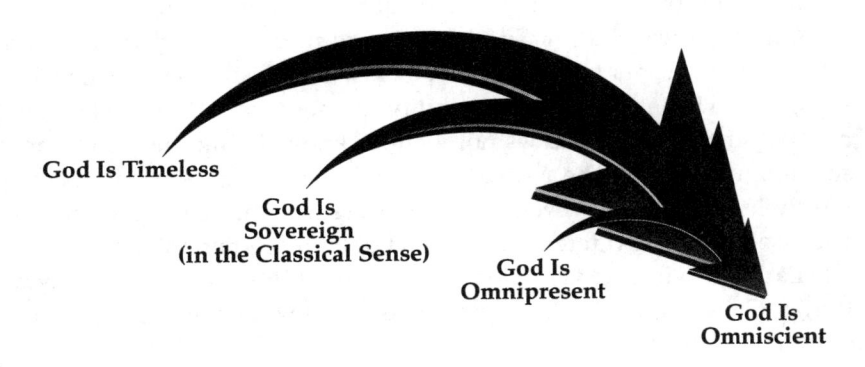

God Is Timeless

**God Is Sovereign
(in the Classical Sense)**

God Is Omnipresent

God Is Omniscient

There are many other ways that the attributes assigned to God by the ancient Greek philosophers can be tied together, but I have just made a few associations so you can see how consistent they are with one another. Together they make a nice, neat package. We can commend the philosophers

Systematic Theology for the New Apostolic Reformation

for their consistency, but this consistency also means that if we challenge any one attribute then we are challenging all of the other attributes.

So then, questioning if God is or is not omniscient challenges the whole Classical/Reformed view of God. In this sense, Classical/Reformed theology is fragile. Classical/Reformed teachers do not like to think of their system of thought as fragile, but just ask one of them to consider the possibility that God does not know everything. You will immediately see their defenses surge to the forefront. They must hold to the omniscience of God—not because they can support it with Scripture—but because their entire system of thought depends upon God being omniscient. If there is even one fact that God is not fully conscious of, then Classical/Reformed theology crumbles. For this reason, Classical/Reformed theologians cannot be satisfied with the Bible's report that God's knowledge is infinite. They must cling to the unbiblical word *omniscient*.

Point 128: Anchoring Our Theology in the Bible

It is worth looking more carefully at how God's knowledge is tied to His sovereignty.

If God is sovereign, in the sense that He is in control of all things (as Classical/Reformed theologians say), then He *must* be omniscient. To exhaustively control all things necessitates knowing all things.

On the other hand, if God is sovereign in the sense that He can do whatever He wants to do whenever He wants (as Father-Son theology says), then He has the sovereign ability to know what He wants to know and not know what He does not want to know. Using this definition of sovereign, we can still be assured that God's knowledge is infinite, because the Bible says so. However, we cannot assume that God is omniscient because He may sovereignly decide to not know certain things.

Earlier,[71] we discussed God's sovereign ability to not know certain things. Consider again, God's comments about Sodom and Gomorrah:

> . . . the Lord said, "The outcry of Sodom and Gomorrah is indeed great, and their sin is exceedingly grave. I will go down now, and see if they have done entirely according to its outcry, which has come to Me; and if not, I will know."
>
> (Gen. 18:20-21)

---

[71] I:H:73

Father-God's Knowledge of the World

If we take this passage literally, we will conclude that God was somewhat aware of what was going on in Sodom and Gomorrah, but not entirely. It is possible that a sovereign God chose to make Himself unaware of everything going on in those evil cities.

Another interesting example of this is when God was discussing with Jeremiah the evils that Israel had been committing.

> *Then the Lord said to me in the days of Josiah the king, "Have you seen what faithless Israel did? . . . I thought, 'After she has done all these things she will return to Me'; but she did not return . . . ."*
> (Jer. 3:6-7)

If we take these words of God literally, then we must conclude that God expected the people of Israel to repent, but they did not. This surprised God! This means God did not have complete foreknowledge concerning what the people of Israel were doing.

Another example is when God accused the people of Judah of doing things *. . . which I had not commanded them nor had it entered My mind that they should do this abomination . . ."* (Jer. 32:35). This is tragic, yet profound. God was surprised that people could contrive of such evil.

Classical/Reformed thinkers must say that God's statements in each of these verses (Gen. 18:20-21 ; Jer. 3:6-7 ; Jer. 32:35) were not true. Instead of saying that God lied or pretended, they will call these verses anthropomorphisms. In contrast, Father-Son theology sees God having the sovereign ability to not know certain things. Therefore, it is possible that God was telling the truth in these passages.

Notice how the Classical/Reformed definition of *sovereign* (controlling all) is consistent with the Classical/Reformed understanding of God's knowledge (omniscience). So also the biblical definition of *sovereign* (does what He wants) is consistent with the biblical description of God's knowledge (infinite).

Definition of Sovereign		God's Knowledge
In Control ⟶	consistent with ⟶	Omniscient
Does What He Wants ⟶	consistent with ⟶	Infinite

We could continue making such associations with the other attributes assigned to God by the Bible versus the Greek philosophers. The point is that the attributes are all tied together.

Systematic Theology for the New Apostolic Reformation

Since the attributes of God are tied together, a discussion concerning whether or not God is omniscient is no small issue. Classical/Reformed theology *needs* omniscience. Father-Son theology does not. However, this is more than simply discarding the unnecessary. To reject omniscience is a fatal blow to Classical/Reformed theology, because tied to it are several other attributes that the Greek philosophers assigned to their immovable mover. To reject omniscience as an attribute of God is to reject the Greek philosopher's god. It is to reject the nice, consistent package of Classical/Reformed theology.

It is time to embrace the biblical truth that God's knowledge is infinite. It is time to reject the unbiblical concept that God is omniscient. It is time to pull the anchor of our systematic theology out of Greek philosophy and let it crumble. We need to plant our systematic theology in the Bible.

Section F
Father-God Is Bigger and Greater

When Christians seriously consider God's interactions with this world, they have to reconsider the uncertainties of life that arise. This is true because the Classical/Reformed view of God offers a God who is timeless, omnipotent, omniscient, and omnipresent, leading one to believe that God is in exhaustive control of all things. In some ways it is reassuring to think that God is in control.

In contrast, Father-Son theology sees this world running according to natural laws established by God and unnatural laws resulting from humanity's sin. People were given authority over earth, so they can exercise their free will and even rebel against God. Of course, God can influence this world in many ways, but Father-Son theology maintains that God is not in exhaustive control. This can be very unsettling, because it means that we live in an unsure world.

Point 129: God Takes Risks but Makes No Mistakes

If God allows people to exercise their own free will, then He is taking risks. Indeed, we see that God took a risk simply by creating humanity with some degree of free will. As a result, the wickedness of humanity became great in the days of Noah and the *". . . Lord was sorry that He had made man . . ."* (Gen. 6:6). Another example of God taking a risk is when He anointed Saul king over Israel. Certainly God knew that it was possible for Saul to turn evil. When Saul did, God regretted that He had made Saul king (1 Sam. 15:11).

According to the Reformed view of God, examples such as these are figures of speech. If God is timeless within creation, then it is impossible

Systematic Theology for the New Apostolic Reformation

for God to take a risk, because a timeless God would know every outcome before His actions that initiated that outcome. If, however, we accept these Bible passages literally, then we have to reject the idea that God is timeless within creation.

Point 130: God Makes No Mistakes

If God takes risks, can He make a mistake? If He truly grieved about choosing Saul, did He make a mistake in choosing him?

To answer this, think of parents who take a risk by allowing their teenager to drive the family car. That teenager may have an accident, and later the parents may regret the decision they made to let their teenager drive the car. However, that does not mean they made a mistake. When people are given freedom, there is always a risk that they will make a bad choice. However, it is not always a mistake to take a risk and give people a choice.

Similarly, God takes risks, but He never makes mistakes.

Point 131: The God of Father-Son Theology Is Bigger

The idea of God taking risks places us in an uncertain world. This can be too scary for some people to accept. They would rather cling to the Classical/Reformed view of God with its understanding that God is in total, absolute control.

However, now we have a different perspective. Father-Son theology reveals God taking risks and people having free will, but this does not mean things are out of control. As we have been studying, God can intervene whenever He wants. He is very involved through relationships, the Holy Spirit, angels, and so forth. He is watching over the affairs of His children. He is providentially guiding the affairs of this world to the ultimate fulfillment of His goals.

From the perspective of Father-Son theology, God is confidently working out His will in the earth. He can even give people some measure of free will and still keep all things on track. He is great enough to deal with all situations that may arise. In this sense, the God of Father-Son theology is bigger and greater than the God of Classical/Reformed theology.

Volume III
The Nature of Creation

Our understanding of the nature of God should correspond with our understanding of the nature of all He created. So here we will study creation and see that correspondence.

As we discuss the nature of creation, we will focus on the questions, "Who?" "What?" and "Why?" These questions are the focus of theology. In contrast, science attempts to answer the questions, "How?" "What?" and "When?" This does not mean theology and science have nothing to say to each other. On the contrary, what is discovered in one field should agree with the other. Therefore, we will note some correlations between theology and science.

This volume is divided into the following sections.

- Section A: The Who and What of Creation
- Section B: The Why of Creation
- Section C: Natural Theology
- Section D: Spiritual Aspects of Creation
- Section E: Angelology
- Section F: Creation and Time
- Section G: Theology and Science

Of course, humanity is a part of God's creation, but we will address that subject in Volume IV.

Volume III
Nature of Creation

Section A
The Who and What of Creation

This section focuses on **cosmology**, which refers to one's understanding of the origin and development of the world. We will discuss who created the world and what is included in the word *creation*. We will discover the answers to these questions from the view of Classical/Reformed theology and Father-Son theology, contrasting the two and explaining why Father-Son theology is more biblically accurate and closer to reality.

Point 132: Who Created?

Genesis 1:1 tells us that *God* created the heavens and earth. John, the Gospel writer, tells us that Jesus was Co-creator with God:

> *All things came into being through Him, and apart from Him nothing came into being that has come into being.*
> (John 1:3)

Genesis 1:2 gives us more information about "the Who" of creation:

> *Now the earth was formless and empty, darkness was over the surface of the deep, and the Spirit of God was hovering over the waters.*

From this we know that the Spirit of God was also involved with creation. Classical/Reformed theology and Father-Son theology agree that the three Persons of the Trinity were involved in creation.

Systematic Theology for the New Apostolic Reformation

Point 133: What Is Creation?

When we say, "creation," to what are we referring? Both Classical/Reformed theology and Father-Son theology can answer this by referring to Genesis 1:1 where we are told that God created the heavens and earth. However, adherents of each view form in their minds different images of the heavens and earth.

As we explained, Classical/Reformed theology has at its foundation a dualistic cosmology similar to what the ancient Greek philosophers held. Adherents envision a spiritual, timeless world infinitely separated from and totally unlike the natural world. Building on that dualistic worldview, Classical/Reformed teachers think of God reaching out of His timeless world and creating a world distant and separate from Himself.

CLASSICAL/REFORMED UNDERSTANDING OF CREATION

Spiritual, Timeless World of God

↑
INFINITY
↓

Creation

The Who and What of Creation

In I:B, we discussed the view of Father-Son theology and saw the spiritual realm filling the same space as the natural realm, however, we diagrammed the spiritual realm hidden behind the natural realm.

NATURAL CREATION SUPERIMPOSED UPON THE SPIRITUAL REALM

We also explained that there is no separation between the spiritual and natural realms, so it is best to envision the two realms in one package.

SPIRITUAL AND NATURAL REALMS WITHIN ONE WORLD

Systematic Theology for the New Apostolic Reformation

This identifies a fundamental difference between the cosmology of Classical/Reformed theology and the cosmology of Father-Son theology. In the dualistic cosmology of Classical/Reformed theology, there are *two worlds* separated by a huge chasm. In Father-Son theology, there is *one world with two inseparable realms*: the spiritual realm and the natural realm.

Notice that we use the word *realms* rather than *worlds* when referring to the cosmology of Father-Son theology. The Bible shows God only creating one world, but there are spiritual and natural realms within that one world.

In both Classical/Reformed thought and Father-Son theology, each of their cosmologies form the foundation of their worldviews. The dualistic cosmology of Classical/Reformed thought yields a dualistic worldview. The cosmology of Father-Son theology is the foundation for a biblical worldview.

Point 134: Understanding the First, Second, and Third Heavens

Differences between the cosmology of Classical/Reformed theology and Father-Son theology become more evident when we talk about the first heaven, second heaven, and third heaven.

Classical/Reformed and Father-Son teachers agree that the third heaven is the throne room of God. This corresponds with Paul's description of when he was taken into the third heaven:

> *I know a man in Christ who fourteen years ago—whether in the body I do not know, or out of the body I do not know, God knows— such a man was caught up to the third heaven.*
> (2 Cor. 12:2)

Seeing the third heaven as the throne room of God, Classical/Reformed teachers equate the third heaven with their timeless, distant world of God. When Classical/Reformed teachers try to fit the first and second heaven into their dualistic cosmology, they have only one other place to put them—in the natural world. So they usually equate the first heaven with the atmosphere of Earth (including the clouds) and the second heaven with outer space (including the sun, moon, and stars). Therefore, the first and second heavens are both part of God's natural, physical creation.

The Who and What of Creation

CLASSICAL/REFORMED VIEW OF THE FIRST, SECOND, AND THIRD HEAVENS

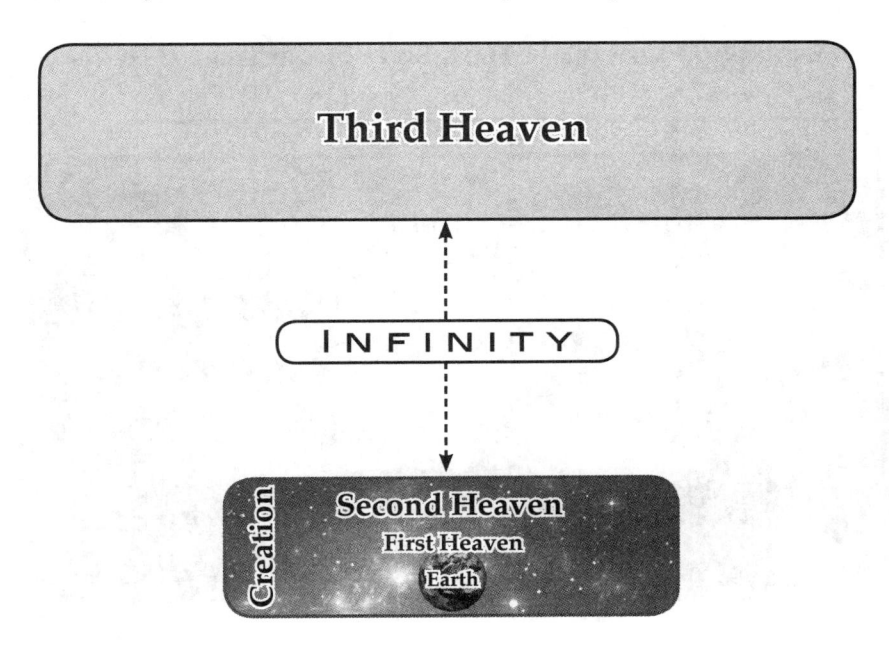

[Diagram: A large box labeled "Third Heaven" at the top, connected by a double-headed arrow labeled "INFINITY" to a smaller box below containing "Second Heaven," "First Heaven," and "Earth," with "Creation" labeled vertically along the side.]

To see how different the Father-Son view is from the Classical/Reformed view, we must first abandon the dualism of Western philosophy. The very fact that the Bible speaks of three heavens leads us to believe that it is, at the very least, a three-part world rather than two worlds separated by a huge chasm.

Father-Son theology agrees with Classical/Reformed theology that the third heaven is the realm in which God dwells, however, it disagrees on where that third heaven exists. As we have been explaining, God entered into creation and now exists in a spiritual realm that fills the natural realm. God is not far away in a distant, timeless world. He fills the heavens and earth. It is possible that God exists in some timeless realm outside of creation, but the only truth we can learn from Scripture is that God exists in the third heaven, which is part of His creation.

Father-Son theology recognizes the second heaven as a spiritual realm between the third heaven and the natural realm. It is where most spiritual dynamics occur, including where angels and demons interact.

Systematic Theology for the New Apostolic Reformation

The first heaven is everything in the natural realm beyond earth, including the atmosphere, clouds, sun, moon, and stars.

FATHER-SON VIEW OF THE FIRST, SECOND, AND THIRD HEAVENS

God created a world with three realms:

Third Heaven: the spiritual realm (within creation) where God dwells

Second Heaven: the spiritual realm (within creation) between the third heaven and the natural realm; the realm where most spiritual dynamics occur, including where angels and demons interact

First Heaven: the natural realm (within creation) beyond earth, including the atmosphere, clouds, sun, and stars

It is vital that we know that the third heaven is within creation. Contrary to what Classical/Reformed theology insists, the third heaven cannot be a timeless realm, because the Bible clearly reveals events taking place and things changing in the throne room of God. As we pointed out earlier, Jesus ascended into heaven and sat down at the right hand of God. Then

The Who and What of Creation

the Father said to the Son, *"Sit at My right hand, until I make Your enemies a footstool for Your feet"* (Acts 2:34-35). There could be no "until" in a timeless world. In a timeless world, there can be no before and after.

In the Bible, we can read about many other events taking place in the throne room of God. For example, Daniel got to see into the throne room and watch the Ancient of Days transferring authority to the Son of Man (Dan. 7:13-14). The apostle John watched Jesus in the throne room undo the seals upon a scroll (Rev. 6). In Revelation 6:10, we read about the saints in heaven crying out to the Lord, asking how long He will *"refrain from judging and avenging"* their blood. These reports make no sense without the passing of time. For this reason, we see the third heaven as part of creation.

Of course, someone may categorize the accounts of people seeing into God's throne room as anthropomorphisms or visions that have no basis in reality, but that forces a person to reject many key passages in the Bible. Anyone who takes the Bible seriously would have a difficult time concluding that God's throne room exists in a timeless world.

Most importantly, Genesis 1:1 clearly tells us that God created the "heavens" so the heavens must be part of creation.

Finally in our cosmology, it is necessary to see that the three realms fill the same space. They fit together in one package.

First, Second, and Third Heavens within One World

Third Heaven
Second Heaven
First Heaven
Atmosphere and Outer Space

Systematic Theology for the New Apostolic Reformation

Creation may not be exactly like this. The third and second heavens may be other dimensions, such as fourth, fifth, or greater dimensions. They may also be realms that make no sense to human understanding. However, seeing the three realms within creation fits what is revealed in the Bible.

Point 135: Understanding the Second Heaven

There are many passages in the Bible that do not make sense without a second heaven—that is, a spiritual realm existing between the third heaven and the natural realm. For example, Jacob saw a stairway upon which angels ascended and descended (Gen. 28:11-12). That stairway was only seen by Jacob in a dream, so it must not have existed in the natural realm. The stairway also ascended into the throne room where God dwells (Gen. 28:12-13). So in this account, we can identify the natural realm, the throne room of God, and a realm spanning between those two realms. That in-between realm is what we call the second heaven.

Consider Paul's words:

> *For by Him all things were created, both in the heavens and on earth, visible and invisible, whether thrones or dominions or rulers or authorities . . . .*
>
> (Col. 1:16)

We are told that these thrones, dominions, rulers, and authorities are created, so they must exist within creation. But they are invisible, so they must not exist in the natural realm. Because there are both good and evil authorities they must not all exist in the throne room of God.

The Classical/Reformed worldview has no place to put these invisible thrones, dominions, rulers, and authorities. Adherents will occasionally talk about angels and demons, but the location of their existence is left vague. Adherents cannot fit the invisible thrones, dominions, rulers, and authorities into the uncreated, timeless world of God. Nor can they can they put them into the physical world. Followers of Classical/Reformed theology have no explanation because their worldview is built on a dualistic cosmology

Father-Son theology has no problem locating the invisible thrones, dominions, rulers, and authorities, because it is not bound to the dualism of Western philosophy. It recognizes the second heaven as part of creation.

The Who and What of Creation

Point 136: Spiritual Energies and Forces in the Second Heaven

The Bible-writers built on a cosmology that had a spiritual realm where angels and demons interact, but they also understood that in the same realm there are spiritual energies and forces. Those spiritual energies and forces must exist in the spiritual realm, yet they are sometimes associated with physical items.

For example, Paul's handkerchiefs were carried to sick people so that they could be healed (Acts 19:12), and Elisha's bones held enough power to bring a dead man to life (2 Kings 13:21). The Bible indicates that things in our created world may have spiritual energy associated with them:

> *For everything created by God is good, and nothing is to be rejected if it is received with gratitude; for it is sanctified by means of the word of God and prayer.*
> (1 Tim. 4:4-5)

Sanctified means to be made holy, which reveals to us that literal physical things can be changed from unholy to holy by Christians praying and speaking the Word of God over those things. We could also talk about physical items and places being desecrated or made unholy (e.g., Lev. 18:24-25 ; Num. 35:34).

Those spiritual energies cannot be put in the natural world, because they are spiritual. Nor can they be put in the distant, spiritual, timeless world of Classical/Reformed theology, because they are associated with physical things. The cosmology of Father/Son theology has no problem with this, because it recognizes the second heavens as a spiritual realm that fills the same space as the natural realm.

It is worth inserting a caution here: Some Christians have taken the related teaching about the existence of these spiritual energies and gone to extremes, assigning spiritual values to everything around them. Such thinking tends to make them overly spirit-conscious, even superstitious. However, examples of the ridiculous give us no justification for rejecting that which is true. A biblical cosmology recognizes a spiritual realm between God's realm and the natural world.

Systematic Theology for the New Apostolic Reformation

Point 137: Significance of a Second Heaven to Non-Western People

It is important that we recognize the second heaven when we are developing a systematic theology that will be understandable to the masses of humanity who live outside of Westernized society. Most of the non-Western world is very conscious of an invisible, spiritual realm that is very close to and integrated with our natural realm. The billion plus people in India are influenced by the Hindu and Buddhist worldviews and are, therefore, ever aware of spiritual forces determined by karma and other spiritual dynamics. Most of the billion plus people in China are ever conscious of *ch'i*, which to them is the basic stuff of the cosmos, which is thought of as matter-energy or vital force; to most Chinese people, *ch'i* permeates all things that exist in the natural realm. Add the people living in third world countries who commonly believe in spiritual energies and forces surrounding them. Similarly, most primitive tribal people think of many physical things as charged with energy, whether we are speaking of a mountain, tree, or bird. In reality, a large percentage of humanity holds to a worldview that acknowledges a spiritual realm that is close to and associated with the natural realm.

It is when people are brought under the influence of Western thought, primarily through Western education, that their worldview changes to a dualistic worldview that minimizes or totally denies the existence of a spiritual realm that is closely associated with the natural world. In this area, the cosmology of uneducated third world people groups is more biblical than the cosmology of educated Western people.

This is one major reason why Westernized people have a difficult time believing in the miraculous and supernatural. The dualistic worldview of Classical/Reformed theology has nothing connecting the natural world with the distant, timeless world of God. As people are indoctrinated into that dualistic worldview, God is moved farther away, and the natural world around us is sterilized in the sense of being void of spiritual influences.

Dualism is also one of many reasons why people in the far Eastern part of this world have a difficult time fully embracing the type of Christianity offered by Western Christians. In fact, some key Christian leaders in the East have worked hard to stop Western Christians from teaching their people. They don't want Western Christianity.[72]

---

[72] For an excellent discussion of this see: Hwa Yung, *Mangoes or Bananas?* (Oxford, UK: Regnum Books International, 2014).

The Who and What of Creation

Point 138: Association of the First, Second, and Third Heavens

Many Bible passages lead the reader to conclude that the three heavens and the natural realm must be closely associated and integrated into one another. For example, Jesus cast demons out of people. We understand those demons are spiritual beings, so they did not exist in the physical realm. Yet, they were associated with the physical bodies of human beings. In other words, the demons were *right there* located in human bodies.

This association between the spiritual and the physical is equally evident in the example of Jesus casting a group of demons into a herd of pigs (Matt. 8:30-32). If we take this biblical testimony seriously, we must see those demons as actually moving from one physical location to another.

THE SPIRITUAL AND NATURAL REALMS ARE INTEGRATED

Such correlations between the spiritual and physical realms can be seen in other biblical examples, as well. For example, Elisha's servant saw the spiritual fiery chariots and those chariots were located on the natural mountain tops (2 Kings 6:17). When Jacob saw a stairway upon which angels ascended and descended, he placed a pillar in that place to mark the physical location corresponding to the spiritual vantage point (Gen. 28:10-22).

Systematic Theology for the New Apostolic Reformation

We can identify similar correlations between the third heaven where God dwells and creation where people dwell. We know that God fills creation, but there are also times when God revealed Himself at physical locations such as on Mount Sinai and in the temple in Jerusalem. Consider also how Christians are temples for God's Spirit to indwell and they are seated with Christ in heavenly places. This reveals a close association between God who dwells in the third heaven with the physical bodies of Christians, which exist in the natural realm.

CHRISTIANS ARE JOINED TO GOD

As we study these truths from the Bible, we form a picture in our minds of three realms closely associated and integrated into one another.

This way of thinking is foreign to Classical/Reformed theology. Adherents do make accommodations for biblical examples of spiritual entities having contact with natural entities. For example, when they read about the angel of God talking to Abraham, they do envision a spiritual messenger from God manifesting in the natural world. When they read about demons being cast into a herd of pigs, they may think of spiritual beings actually inhabiting physical animals. However, those associations between the spiritual and physical are allowed only in the sense of momentary accommodations to the biblical evidence. As soon as discussion of those

The Who and What of Creation

spiritual entities is complete, the mind trained in Classical/Reformed theology returns to its dualistic foundation that sees a spiritual world as distant and separate from the natural world. In the development of their theology, adherents of Classical/Reformed theology cannot escape the dualism of Western philosophical thought.

Point 139: Spiritual and Natural Realms Influence One Another

The Bible reveals the spiritual and natural realms as integrated. What is changed in one realm influences what exists in another realm.

For example, David played music so an evil spirit would leave King Saul (1 Sam. 16:23). This means that what David did in the natural realm (made music) changed what was happening in the spiritual realm.

For another example, consider Paul's exhortation that a husband and wife should not abstain from sexual relations for too long so that Satan will not tempt them (1 Cor. 7:5). In other words, having a healthy sex life can defuse the devil's temptations to have an affair or be unfaithful.

We can also think of examples where changes in the spiritual realm affect the natural realm. For example, Jesus cast demons out of certain people, and they were physically healed. He also rebuked storms, and the authority of His words caused those storms to be still. In Acts 14:23, we read about an angel that struck Herod, and as a result, Herod fell down dead.

This truth concerning the spiritual and natural realms being integrated applies to innumerable areas. For example, a young man experiencing sexually-perverted thoughts may free himself from those thoughts by going to play basketball. A teenage girl may find herself giving in to the constant temptations of the devil until someone cares and becomes involved with her life.

An example on a larger scale is what happens in war. Many times in history, soldiers have burned communities and wandered the streets, killing thousands and raping without restraint. Christians who believe in the activity of demons would consider the possibility that hordes of demons may have been involved in stirring hate and violence. If, indeed, demons do get involved in such evil events, think of the change that occurs when a war ends. Let's say a large, organized army comes into the region and subdues the violence. Then in a short time, communities are restored,

Systematic Theology for the New Apostolic Reformation

schools open, and people begin rebuilding their lives. The demons that once were active no longer have the ability to stir people toward such evil behavior. In such circumstances, God uses a natural force, such as an army, to subdue demons.

This principle is key in understanding many biblical passages. When God had His OT people go to war, they knew those wars were both spiritual and natural. Often, when people take authority over the natural realm they are also taking authority over the spiritual realm related to that area.

The fact that the spiritual and natural realms are integrated and influence each other has far-reaching implications. A prayer warrior may, indeed, be subduing demons. So also may a medical doctor who is helping people get free of physical illnesses. Or a school teacher preparing students for the future. Or a businessperson who is helping families physically and spiritually by creating employment for people. All human activities are physical and spiritual.

Such correlations between the physical and spiritual realms are not as easy to see with the Classical/Reformed worldview that portrays the spiritual world as distant and disconnected from the natural world. It is the worldview of Father-Son theology that brings many related truths to light.

Point 140: More Problems With the Classical/Reformed View

More problems with the dualistic worldview of Classical/Reformed theology become evident when we talk about spiritual beings moving back and forth from the natural realm to the spiritual realm. According to Classical/Reformed theology, the third heaven is the timeless, spiritual world of God. Using this model for a moment, envision an angel (which Classical/Reformed teachers understand is created and, therefore, not timeless) going into the world of God (which Classical/Reformed teachers claim is timeless). What happens to that angel?

When a time-bound angel moves into a timeless world (if that is possible), it steps into a world where the past, present, and future will be opened before that angel. But *timeless* by definition means nothing ever changes in that realm. It is impossible in such a timeless world for one moment to be followed by another. It is impossible for an angel to be in the timeless world one moment and not a moment later.

The Who and What of Creation

Yet, reports in the Bible reveal events happening in the spiritual realm in which one moment is followed by another. Consider the angel Gabriel who carries messages from the throne room of God to individuals on earth. Consider Paul who was taken into the third heaven. Consider when Satan went into the throne room of God in the days of Job. If, indeed, God's throne room is timeless, then it is logically impossible for Gabriel, Paul, and Satan to enter and then leave that world.

Classical/Reformed View:
Angels Moving from Earth to Heaven and Back Again

Timeless, Uncreated World
Third Heaven

ANGELS

Second Heaven
First Heaven
Earth

Creation

Systematic Theology for the New Apostolic Reformation

Father-Son theology does not have this problem since it recognizes the second and third heavens as part of creation and, therefore, governed by time. In Father-Son theology there is nothing illogical about beings moving between the natural realm and the heavens.

FATHER-SON VIEW:
ANGELS MOVING FROM EARTH TO HEAVEN AND BACK AGAIN

Point 141: Time and Space Do Exist in the Spiritual Realm

This is a good place to correct the cliché parroted by millions: "There is no time or space in the world of the spirit."

If there was no time, nothing could ever change in the spiritual realm. Yet, we have mentioned several events requiring time changes that the Bible tells us took place in the spiritual realm. Most importantly, Jesus sat down at the right hand of Father-God in the third heaven. Corresponding to that, Father-God is making every enemy a footstool for the feet of Jesus. Those changes would be impossible if the spiritual realm where Jesus' enemies exist was timeless.

Similarly, we can talk about space. If there was no space then there would be no space limitations in the spiritual realm. Therefore, it would be impossible to restrict spiritual beings such as Satan to the Lake of Fire. If there was no space in the spiritual realm, then everything would be

The Who and What of Creation

mixed together in the sense of existing as one. If there was no space, then angels and demons would exist within each other and neither angels nor demons could move around. Furthermore, if there was no space or time in the spiritual world, then everything existing in the spiritual realm—including Satan—would be omnipresent.

Space is a good thing. It makes it possible for spiritual entities to be at different locations and to move around.

Time is also a good thing. It makes it so all events that have ever happened or will ever happen don't take place simultaneously.

Point 142: A Biblical Worldview Necessary to Understand the Bible

The third heaven is created, and it is governed by time. God has entered into time. This means that the Bible's reports of God's interactions with humanity are not from a timeless dimension. Those reports are not anthropomorphisms. They actually took place. They are real. God was not pretending to have emotions or change His mind. God was able to listen to His covenant partner Moses and change His mind in response to Moses' prayer. Furthermore, many changes have taken place in God's throne room.

GOD INTERACTS WITH THE NATURAL WORLD FROM THE THIRD HEAVEN

Systematic Theology for the New Apostolic Reformation

The cosmology that fits the biblical revelation is that which portrays the three heavens as filling the same space. Then we see God acting from within creation.

Point 143: The Throne Room of God Is Governed by Time

Embracing this view of the three heavens is necessary to understand the nature and ongoing ministry of Jesus.

Jesus is God incarnate. He became flesh. Jesus did not abandon His human nature after He died, resurrected, and ascended. Jesus was glorified, but He still has a body. Being incarnate, Jesus now sits on a throne in heaven. Jesus was given all authority over heaven and earth, and He now governs the created world from the throne room. All of these activities require the passing of time.

Remember Stephen who saw into heaven as he was being stoned to death: *"he gazed intently into heaven and saw the glory of God and Jesus standing at the right hand of God"* (Acts 7:55). If the throne room of God was timeless, it would be impossible for Jesus to be sitting one moment and standing the next. The Bible shows us many things changing in the throne room of God, so the throne room talked about in the Bible is definitely governed by time.

Section B
The Why of Creation

Why did God create the world? Let's see . . .

Point 144: Why Creation According to Classical/Reformed Theology?

Classical/Reformed theology sees God as "self-sufficient," needing nothing and wanting nothing. This means that God is complete in Himself. Therefore, creation cannot offer anything to God. He does whatever He wants to do, but it does not benefit Him in any way. For this reason, Classical/Reformed theologians have concluded that everything God does is simply a revelation of Himself. It is "for His own glory" or "for the manifestation of His glory." God is the Giver, and He receives nothing.

According to Classical/Reformed theology, there is no higher purpose than God's own glory. This is why God does what He does. This purpose is repeated often in writings based on the Classical/Reformed view of God. For example, the Westminster Confession of Faith says:

> It pleased God the Father, Son, and Holy Ghost, <u>for the manifestation of the glory</u> of his eternal power, wisdom, and goodness, in the beginning, to create or make of nothing the world . . . .

When the Westminster Confession of Faith states that "it pleased God" to create, this does *not* mean that creation pleased God, for nothing outside of God can please Him according to Classical/Reformed theology. The Westminster Confession is expressing the Classical/Reformed view by

Systematic Theology for the New Apostolic Reformation

saying that "it pleased God" in the sense that God wanted to create, so He did.

CLASSICAL/REFORMED UNDERSTANDING THAT GOD DOES EVERYTHING FOR HIS OWN GLORY

[Diagram: Rays emanating from "GOD" in the Spiritual World outward, labeled "FOR HIS OWN GLORY," toward the Natural World.]

Christians trained in Classical/Reformed theology like to support their view of God doing all things for His own glory by referring to Scriptures that talk about creation revealing God's glory. For example, Psalm 19:1 says:

> *The heavens are telling of the glory of God;*
> *And their expanse is declaring the work of His hands.*

Indeed, creation reveals the greatness and glory of God.

Point 145: For His Own Glory?

Creation does reveal God's glory, but it does not necessarily follow from this that God's *purpose* for His creation is to reveal His glory. Consider how a carpenter might build a beautiful house. That house reveals how skilled the carpenter is, but he did not necessarily build that house to reveal his

The Why of Creation

own skills. His true purpose may have been to provide someone with a home, to make a financial profit, or some other goal. Similarly, God's creation reveals His glory, but it does not logically follow from this that this was His only purpose or even His primary purpose for creation.

The concept of God doing all for His own glory is simply a philosophical concept consistent with a timeless, immutable, impassible, self-sufficient God. Father-Son theology rejects that philosophical construct so it is free to read the Bible and find other reasons for creation.

Point 146: Why Creation According to Father-Son Theology?

The Bible tells us that God determined to have sons. Creation fits into this overall plan and purpose. His actions came forth from His love. Creation came from His love. Because He loves, He created. This is the primary reason He created.

Paul offered more insight about the purpose of creation. He wrote about Jesus as Co-creator: *"all things have been created through Him and for Him"* (Col. 1:16). According to this statement, all things were created *for Jesus*. Creation is God's gift to the Son. A gift is an expression of the heart. Creation is an expression of God's love. Of course, God the Father and God the Son were Co-creators, but it is worth noting that creation was a love gift for the Son.

Seeing creation as God's love gift allows us to see why the universe is so big and majestic. God gave a wonderful gift to the Son.

This explanation is inconsistent with Classical/Reformed theology. The doctrine of self-sufficiency demands that nothing can be added to God (or to Jesus). There is no gift that can please God. There is nothing that can benefit God in any way. Yet, the Bible is clear that all things were created for Jesus.

Furthermore, there is something within creation that is particularly captivating to the heart of God the Father and God the Son—humanity. As we have been emphasizing throughout this book, God wanted children. God wanted children for Himself and a Bride for His Son.

It is not possible to diagram what it would look like to have creation coming forth from God's love, but building upon the biblical foundation that sees the spiritual and natural realms as near and fully integrated, we must see all of creation as revealing God's nature and, in particular,

Systematic Theology for the New Apostolic Reformation

His love. Of course, God's creation reveals His glory, but the reason God created is because He loves. Furthermore, love is written all over creation.

Creation Came Out of God's Love, and Now It Reveals God's Love

Section C
Natural Theology

Creation reveals the nature of the Creator. Paul explained:

> *For since the creation of the world His invisible attributes, His eternal power and divine nature, have been clearly seen, being understood through what has been made* . . . .
> (Rom. 1:20)

God left His imprint upon all He created. Because God's glory is evident in all of creation, Paul explained that no one has an excuse before God (Rom. 1:20). God's existence and nature are obvious.

Point 147: Rejection of Natural Theology

During the enlightenment of the late 17th and 18th centuries, many leaders in philosophy and theology rejected the Bible as a reliable source of truth, but attempted to develop proof of God's existence and an understanding of God's nature from what He created. The related studies became known as **natural theology**. Supporters of natural theology often referred to Paul's explanation that creation reveals God's *"invisible attributes, His eternal power and divine nature"* (Rom. 1:20).

However, certain influential philosophers and theologians began to question and then reject natural theology in the late 19th and early 20th centuries. Karl Barth (1886–1968) is one theologian in the Classical/Reformed tradition known for rejecting natural theology. Barth explained that Paul's words in Romans 1:20 are only true for someone who has already received revelation of God's existence.

Systematic Theology for the New Apostolic Reformation

Barth was wrong. Anyone who reads Paul's words in Romans 1:20-32 can see that Paul was actually writing about non-believers who had given themselves over to sin. Paul was making the argument that even sinners have no excuse, because God has made Himself known through creation to everyone.

Barth's misguided rejection of natural theology goes back to his theological framework that God exists in a distant, timeless world. Like Plotinus, Barth saw God as the transcendent wholly other.[73] Barth believed that God is totally unknowable, and therefore, the only means by which people can know God is through God's sovereign revelation of Himself.

Today, the philosophical idea concerning the unknowability of God permeates Western institutions of higher learning. It has also seized many theologians—Protestant and Roman Catholic. It is tragic how many modern theologians have embraced a worldview that leads them to conclude that creation does not provide evidence of God's existence and nature. They have arrived at a conclusion that is diametrically opposed to Paul's conclusion. It should not need to be said, but a worldview that leads to an unbiblical conclusion is an unbiblical worldview.

Point 148: The Philosophical Black Hole

Rejecting the truth that God has revealed Himself in creation does not come easily. Students at our secular universities are typically taken on the historical path of philosophical thought beginning with Socrates' questioning and Plato's dualistic worldview. Then the thoughts of "great" philosophers are traced which continue to distance God from humanity. Throughout this process, students are led to think that those brilliant philosophical minds were actually trying to understand God. Yet, the road traveled ends with a distant, unknowable God.[74]

A large percentage of students coming out of our Western universities have been knowingly or unknowingly taken through this indoctrination process. The end result is a mind trained to see God's existence as unprovable and Him as totally out of reach to the rational mind.

Teachers who have guided their students down this philosophical path have provided themselves and their disciples with a rationalization

---

73 This was discussed in I:G:65.
74 For a more complete discussion of this process, see my book entitled, *Christianity Unshackled*.

Natural Theology

for sin. In their minds, God has failed to prove His existence. In a world without God, right and wrong cannot be determined with certainty. All things are relative according to the teacher and student who deny the existence of God.

Once people have been indoctrinated in Western philosophical thought, they are very unlikely to pursue God. They may try to understand theology and gain an intellectual grasp of related issues, but it is unlikely that they will ever attempt to seek God so as to know Him. The worldview that has been imposed upon their minds becomes a black hole from which they can neither escape nor see God.

Yet, a child can look upon the stars and know that the Creator of those stars is magnificent. But if that child grows up and is sent through the Western educational system with its dualistic worldview and historical philosophical path, that child is likely to emerge as an adult convinced that God's existence is unprovable and His nature is unknowable.

Point 149: The Blind Lead the Blind

It is difficult to overemphasize how destructive the rejection of natural theology has been. Students who have been taken down the historical path of Western philosophical thought come out the other end concluding that there is no proof for God's existence. When they can "see" as the Western philosophers "see," they become blind to the obvious proof of God's existence.

Teachers and students are moved down that path toward blindness even quicker when they get involved in sexual sins. Paul explained the correlation between people engaged in sexual perversions and being darkened in their understanding of God (Rom. 1:21-27). Paul also associated that darkening with their futile speculations that lead them to profess to be wise, while they become fools (Rom. 1:21-22).

Those who are considered wise in the eyes of the world are least able to grasp the truths of God. Jesus praised God, saying:

> *I praise You, Father, Lord of heaven and earth, that You have hidden these things from the wise and intelligent and have revealed them to infants.*
>
> (Matt. 11:25)

Systematic Theology for the New Apostolic Reformation

Today, the blindness of many leaders has resulted from their journey down the historical Western philosophical path. They concluded that they can see (as other intelligentsia of the Western world) once they came to believe that there is no proof of God's existence. In the meantime, creation continues to declare the existence of God and His invisible attributes. God's divine nature is being declared every second of every day by all of creation. It is *"clearly seen"* (Rom. 1:20), except by teachers and disciples of those who are clearly blind.

Section D
Spiritual Aspects of Creation

Creation has many spiritual aspects. There are invisible beings, such as angels, which we will discuss in Section E. Here we will discuss spiritual things that are associated with physical things.

Point 150: Creation Reveals God's Glory

Inherent within creation is glory. Paul explained:

> *There is one glory of the sun, and another glory of the moon, and another glory of the stars; for star differs from star in glory.*
> (1 Cor. 15:41)

People are able to experience different aspects of God's glory revealed in creation. They can stare up at the stars and soon be overwhelmed by the grandeur. They can sit quietly in a forest and become fixated on the resilience of plant life, the industriousness of animal life, and the glory of the interconnectedness of the whole environment. They can also sit before an aquarium and sense the nature of God reflected in the water-world. God's glory is evident in all of creation, and anyone with eyes to see will behold it.

A good way to think of this glory is to envision the words that God spoke at creation now reverberating throughout time. When we hear the sound of an instrument, we recognize the instrument that produced it. So also we can behold the glory of creation and sense the nature of the One who spoke all things into existence.

Systematic Theology for the New Apostolic Reformation

Point 151: The Force of Life

In creation we can observe a force of life. It causes plants and animals to move in positive directions. Living organisms are busy securing and reorganizing millions of molecules into unique and intricate patterns necessary for energy, growth, and reproduction. The force of life causes trees to sink their roots into the soil and branches to lift toward heaven. It causes the fox to hunt for food and provide for its pups. It moves the goat on the mountaintop and the spider on a tree branch to spin its web. Life is busy.

Science can answer questions about what grows and how fast it grows, but only theology can tell us *why* things grow and *who* is responsible. In Genesis 1, God said, *"Let the earth bring forth . . . ."* With this declaration, plant and animal life came forth. When God speaks, there is power in His words, and His words continue producing until they have accomplished all God sent those words out to accomplish (Is. 55:11). As a result of God's spoken words, plants and animals came alive, and they are still living and reproducing today.

Life is a power that overcomes death. In time, death overcomes life, but life has the power to reproduce, hence conquering death by passing life on from one generation to another.

Point 152: The Soul of Animals

Some animals have a spiritual side to their existence that is called a "soul." Before we point out the nature of the animal soul, it is important to distinguish it from the human soul. In Genesis 1 and 2, we see that God created people distinct from animals by releasing His own breath into them. Adam and Eve were created in the image of God, while animals were not.

Yet, the Hebrew word *nephesh* is used to refer to some invisible aspect of animal life. The word *nephesh* is sometimes translated as "soul" and other times as "life." The New American Standard Version of Genesis 1:20 says:

> *Then God said, "Let the waters teem with swarms of living* [nephesh] *creatures, and let birds fly above the earth in the open expanse of the heavens."*

Spiritual Aspects of Creation

Similarly, in verse 24:

> *Then God said, "Let the earth bring forth living* [nephesh] *creatures after their kind . . . ."*

Christian teachers disagree about what this animal life (soul) actually is, and those arguments continue because the Bible does not shed much light on the subject. Several OT verses associate the *nephesh* with the blood of the animal. For example, Leviticus. 17:11 says, *"the life [nephesh] of the flesh is in the blood . . . ."* Of course, this *nephesh* may refer simply to the living nature of the animal, but the rest of Leviticus 17:11 assigns value to the *nephesh* that implies it is more than just life. God's people are told to never eat the blood of animals, or they will be cut off from among the Hebrews. God gave added value to the blood of animals saying:

> *I have given it to you on the altar to make atonement for your souls; for it is the blood by reason of the life [nephesh] that makes atonement.*
>
> (Lev. 17:11)

The fact that God instructed the Hebrews to take care with the blood and to use animal blood in making atonement for themselves implies that there is something more to it than just the fluid that flows through the animals' arteries and veins.

Again, we can note that the Bible does not provide enough information for anyone to make firm assertions about the nature of the *nephesh* of animals. However, a reasonable association can be made between animals having a *nephesh* and animals that have oxygenated blood flowing through their veins. Many Christian teachers say that warm-blooded animals have some type of soul that identifies them as of a higher order than creatures (such as bugs, snakes, fish, and lizards) which are not warm-blooded. Some Christian teachers say that those animals that possess this type of *nephesh* (soul) are able to bond and form relationships. This includes relationships with humans. Of course, pet-lovers enjoy hearing this and even think of their pet as able to develop deep relationships. However, all of the related questions must be discussed from the perspective of conjecture and experience, rather than the Bible, since God's Word reveals little on this subject.

Systematic Theology for the New Apostolic Reformation

Point 153: Will There Be Animals in Heaven?

It is possible that animals have souls, but we have no biblical evidence that their souls will allow them to live forever.

However, animals were part of God's original design in creation. He declared that they are good. Furthermore, the Bible talks about a time when this creation will be redeemed, and some verses imply that animals will be part of that redeemed creation. For example, Isaiah prophesied:

> *The wolf also shall dwell with the lamb, and the leopard shall lie down with the kid; and the calf and the young lion and the fatling together; and a little child shall lead them.*
>
> (Is. 11:6)

Many Christian teachers understand verses such as this as figures of speech and, therefore, do not believe animals will actually be in the redeemed earth or heaven. However, there are other reasons to believe that animals will be present.

Creation was subjected to futility as a result of humanity's sin, so now all of creation is groaning for the revealing of the sons of God to set creation free (Rom. 8:19-21). At that future time, when God fully reveals all that He has done for His children, He may give His people authority over this earth in the sense that they will even have authority over death. Indeed, if they do, they may have the authority to raise their lost pets to life. This may seem impossible because of the decay processes acting upon the physical bodies of the dead, however, the same could be said for the human body which God will raise. Of course, no one knows for certain, but pet lovers have reason to hope that they may be able to see their lost pets again.

Section E
Angelology

Angelology refers to the study of angels. The word *angel* in Greek is *aggelos*. This Greek word is literally translated as "messenger." *Aggelos* is used in a few Bible passages to refer to human messengers (e.g., Mark 1:2 ; Luke 9:22), but most often it refers to spiritual beings that are heavenly messengers. It is these heavenly messengers that we will be discussing here.

As almost all other subjects in theology, our understanding of angels is profoundly influenced by our cosmology. The dualism of Western civilization leads Christians to think of angels as primarily far away in a distant heaven and only visiting earth on special occasions. In contrast, the Hebraic-biblical cosmology sees the heavens as close by and fully integrated into the natural realm, and therefore, angels are all around us, involved and interactive with the natural realm.

Point 154: Origin of Angels

God is given credit for creating the angels. The psalmist wrote:

Praise Him, all His angels;
Praise Him, all His hosts . . .
For He commanded and they were created.

(Ps. 148:2-5)

We do not know how many angels God created, but the Scriptures mention myriads of angels (Heb. 12:22). Genesis 2:1 tells us:

Systematic Theology for the New Apostolic Reformation

Thus the heavens and the earth were completed, and all their hosts.

This verse and its context lead us to conclude that God completed His creation by the sixth day of creation, including the creation of the hosts in heaven.

However, the word *hosts* may include more than what we typically think of when we envision angels. Ezekiel 1:5-14 and Revelation 4:6-8 tell us about the **living creatures** around God's throne. Individuals in the Bible who saw these living creatures were overwhelmed with awe. Each creature had the face of a lion, an ox, an eagle, and a man. Whether or not we call these heavenly beings angels, depends upon our definition of *angel*. In the Bible, they are never referred to as angels, so here we will use the word *angel* in the narrower sense, excluding the living creatures and other hosts of heaven about which we know little to nothing.

Point 155: The Nature of Angels

Angels are spiritual beings referred to as "ministering spirits" (Heb. 1:14). They are **incorporeal**, meaning they have no physical bodies, but some angels take on bodily form so as to appear as humans (Heb. 13:2). Some people have been allowed to see angels in their spiritual, incorporeal state (e.g., Num. 22:31 ; Luke 2:13). Sometimes angels appear clothed in shining light (Matt. 28:3).

Some angels are very powerful. The Psalmist refers to them as "mighty ones" (Ps. 103:20), as does Paul (2 Thes. 1:7). Angels have emotions. For example, they experience joy when a sinner repents (Luke 15:10). Angels appear to be intelligent, but not all-knowing. Jesus referred to the angels not knowing when His future coming will be (Matt. 24:36). Peter referred to angels longing to understand truths about salvation (1 Peter 1:12). Angels are immortal. We know this because Jesus compared people who rise from the dead with angels that cannot die anymore (Luke 20:36).

Jesus also revealed how angels do not marry (Mark 12:25). Some teachers take this to mean that angels are nonsexual or asexual, but that concept does not necessarily follow from our Lord's statement that they do not marry. Some angels appear in Scripture as men (Gen. 18:2), but we simply do not know if angels have gender.

Angelology

Point 156: The Role of Angels

The Psalmist describes angels as those who carry out the words and commands of God (Ps. 103:20). They are reported appearing at significant moments in history, such as the birth of Jesus (Luke 2:13), His resurrection (Matt. 28:2-6), and His ascension (Acts 1:10). Indeed, they seem to be servants of God who see that God's will is carried out.

The writer of Hebrews also says:

> *Are they not all ministering spirits, sent out to render service for the sake of those who will inherit salvation?*
> (Heb. 1:14)

Here we learn how angels serve humanity, especially those who are Christians.

Specific angels seem to have specific tasks to which they are assigned. For example, Michael is called an "archangel," which means chief or ruling angel (Jude 9). We see Michael mentioned as a ruler over other angels as they war against the enemies of God (Rev. 12:7). Warring seems to be a major role that Michael plays as he battles with Satan and his demons. Michael is the only angel called an archangel, but Daniel 10:13 refers to him as *"one of the chief angels,"* so there must be more.

Gabriel is an angel whom we see delivering messages from God to humans (e.g., Dan. 9:21 ; Luke 1:19). When Gabriel appeared to Zacharias, he stated that he stands in the very presence of God (Luke 1:19).

Several times in the Bible we read about "the angel of the Lord" or "the angel of God." This phrase is used to refer to a particular angel that seems to be indistinguishable from the Lord Himself. The angel of the Lord appeared to Moses in a burning bush. As we read about that appearance, we see how Moses understood that angel to be God Himself (Ex. 3:2-6). Hagar had a similar experience when the angel of the Lord appeared to her. Hagar referred to that angel as God (Gen. 16:7-13). Theologians refer to such manifestations of God so humans can see Him as **theophanies.** With some theophanies, God manifested as an angel.

We also read about the **cherubim** who seem to play a role as guardians. It was a cherub that was given the task of guarding the path to the tree of life (Gen. 3:24). God instructed the Hebrews to carve two cherubim in gold and place one at each end of the mercy seat above the ark of the covenant

Systematic Theology for the New Apostolic Reformation

(Ex. 25:18-22). In more than one Bible passage, God is said to be enthroned upon the cherubim (e.g., 1 Sam. 4:4 ; Ps. 80:1).

Then we have **seraphim,** which are only mentioned in Isaiah 6:2-7. There we see that they continually worship the Lord. As such, many Bible teachers say that seraphim are angels created simply to worship God, but it is presumptuous to arrive at that conclusion from only one reference in the Bible.

Jesus mentioned children having angels that have direct access to God:

> *See that you do not despise one of these little ones, for I say to you, that their angels in heaven continually behold the face of My Father who is in heaven.*
>
> (Matt. 18:10)

This passage has been used by some teachers to say that everyone, especially each child, has a "guardian angel" watching over them in their daily affairs. It is nice to think that guardian angels watch over every person, but these words of Jesus do not offer enough evidence to state this as fact.

Point 157: Angels Having Free Will and Able to Turn Bad

Angels are revealed as having free will, able to make moral decisions. Paul explained how angels will one day be judged (1 Cor. 6:3), and for there to be a basis on which they will be judged, they must have some amount of free will. Some angels have made decisions contrary to the will of God, and some have become so bad that God already cast them into hell (2 Pet. 2:4). Jude referred to angels who *"abandoned their proper abode,"* and so, God placed them in eternal bonds waiting for a future judgment day (Jude 6).

A common understanding among Christians is that angels who turned against God became demons. That idea may be true, but it cannot be proven with Scriptures (nor can it be disproved). The two passages mentioned above reveal that some angels sinned, but those rebellious angels are never referred to as demons. Nor do we have any other Scriptures that clearly talk about angels becoming demons. We will discuss this topic in V:D, where we talk about the origin of Satan and demons.

Section F
Creation and Time

Now we will study creation and time. To give this the attention it deserves, we must first reconsider our Western cosmology. We can only have a biblical understanding of time if we build on a biblical cosmology. With a biblical cosmology we can also examine the present scientific understanding of time. In particular, we will look at how time is relative.

Point 158: Mythology Forms the Foundation of Cosmology

Every major culture has its own mythology that profoundly influences its cosmology. That cosmology determines its understanding of time.

$$\text{Mythology} \xrightarrow{\text{Determines}} \text{Cosmology} \xrightarrow{\text{Determines}} \text{Understanding of Time}$$

In this context, I am using the word *mythology* to refer to a set of stories that were developed to help a people group understand how the world came to be as it is.

Of course, people want to believe that the stories belonging to their own group's mythology are founded in truth. Indeed, as a Bible-believing Christian, I am convinced that the book of Genesis was given to humanity by God. However, in the next few pages, I will use the word *mythology* to refer to stories forming the foundation of various cultures, including our Christian culture. Please be open to my association of Genesis with mythology. Again, let me say that I have accepted our mythology as the truth. However, in this context, I will refer to Genesis as mythology so I can explain how mythology lays the foundation of cosmology.

Systematic Theology for the New Apostolic Reformation

Point 159: The Foundation for Ancient Greek Mythology

Lying at the foundation of Western civilization is the mythology of both the ancient Greeks and Hebrews. Of course, various people groups within Western civilization have their own mythology; for example, most Europeans cherish stories about the ancestors who are uniquely theirs. However, the mythology of the ancient Greeks and Hebrews are overwhelmingly the most influential in forming the foundational thoughts of Western civilization.

Yet, the mythologies of the ancient Greeks and Hebrews are vastly different from one another. While the ancient Hebrews had a written record given to them by God, the ancient Greeks had no such divine revelation. Like most ancient people, the ancient Greeks lived closely tied to nature. As a result, they were ever conscious of the natural rhythms of life. The sun rises and sets each day, the moon repeats its pattern each month, and the seasons of each year reoccur. People are born, they live, and they die. Everything happens over and over again. This led the ancient Greeks to think of all things as trapped in endless cycles.

THE ANCIENT GREEKS BELIEVED EVERYTHING IN THE
NATURAL WORLD IS TRAPPED IN CYCLIC TIME

The ancient Greeks even believed that kingdoms come and go. One would rise up, only to be overthrown by another, which would someday be overthrown by another. This fatalistic understanding of time was the foundation for why the ancient Greek philosophers saw time as a trap. Not only does everything repeat, but everything grows old under the pressure of time. Time was seen as destructive and partly evil.[75]

The ancient Greeks were also ever conscious of the sky above and the earth around them. This division between the sky (heavens) and earth became a fundamental division in their worldview. As we have discussed, this became the foundation for a dualistic worldview.

---
75 For an enlightening discussion of this see: Thorleif Boman, *Hebrew Thought Compared with Greek* (New York: W.W. Norton & Company, 1970), p. 128.

Creation and Time

THE FOUNDATION OF ANCIENT GREEK MYTHOLOGY

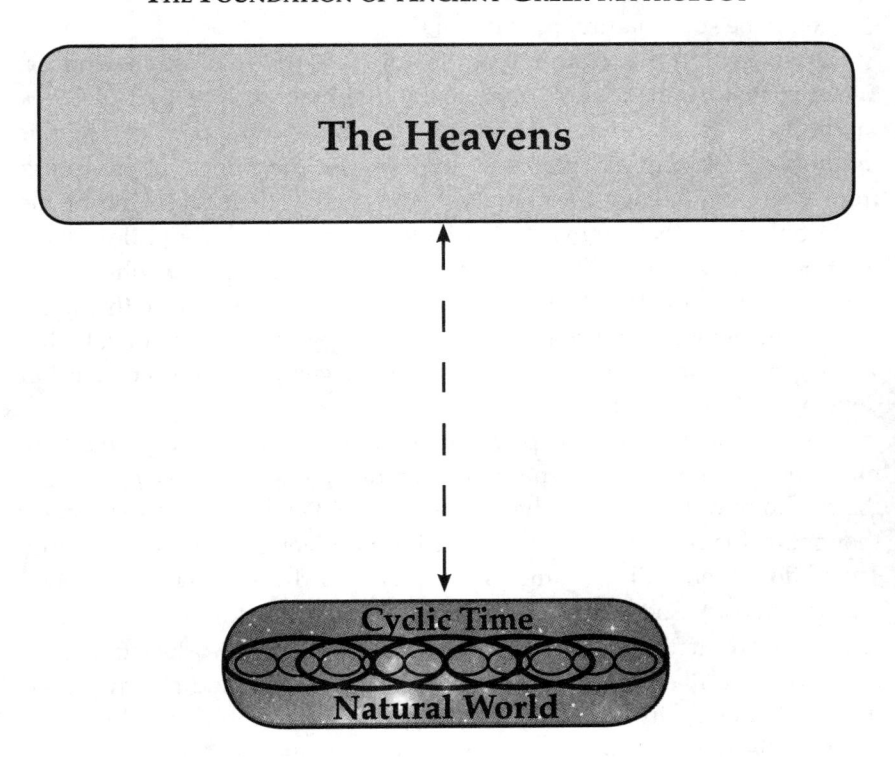

The Heavens

Cyclic Time
Natural World

Point 160: The Development of Ancient Greek Mythology

Today, we can study the mythology of the Greeks by reading ancient Greek literature, some of the oldest being Homer's epic poems, the *Iliad* and *Odyssey*. In addition to ancient writings, there are many artifacts, including statues and paintings, revealing the mythological stories of the people. Prominent in Greek mythology were their gods, Zeus, Apollo, Athena, Poseidon, and Hermes, among others.

Mythology was at the heart of everyday life in ancient Greece (similar to how the Bible is today at the heart of many Christians' lives). The writings of Homer were at the center of education. Every student was required to master the intricacies of the *Iliad* and *Odyssey*. People enjoyed tracing

Systematic Theology for the New Apostolic Reformation

their own family lineage back to a mythological hero or god. The Greeks used myth to explain history and the world around them, including what seemed to be supernatural phenomena.

It was within that culture that the ancient Greek philosophers arose. Socrates, Plato, and Aristotle were real individuals and are part of Greek mythology, just as Adam, Abraham, and Moses are part of Hebraic mythology. Western people tend to separate the Greek philosophers from Greek mythology. They make heroes out of them, thinking of the philosophers as the original free thinkers. In reality, those philosophers built on the thoughts of those who preceded them. The philosophers were simply trying to explain the world in the way that made sense to them, just as thinkers before them tried. They were not separate from the developing worldview of the ancient Greek people. They were part of it and further developed the Greek story.

As the ancient Greek philosophers moved from polytheism to monotheism, they built on the same cosmology that had developed from the mythology of their forefathers. They still held at the foundation of their thoughts a dualistic cosmology with cyclic time governing the natural world. The philosophers still saw time as a trap and partly evil, so they reasoned that the perfect God whom they were imagining must not be limited to time. Instead, there must be another world, a spiritual world where time does not exist. Plato called that timeless world *eternity*, and he envisioned that world of eternity as infinitely separated from the natural world.

Note the fundamental beliefs lying at the foundation of Plato's cosmology.

> Foundation of Plato's Cosmology
> 1. There are two worlds (dualism).
> 2. Time is destructive and partly evil.
> 3. God's world is timeless.

It is important to realize that the ancient Greek philosophers never claimed to have encountered God in the way the leading figures of the Bible did. The foundation of the philosopher's thoughts came from ancient Greek mythology, and they built on that foundation. The three fundamental beliefs listed above are nothing but assumptions. Tragically, they are in conflict with the revelation of the words inspired by God in Genesis. This will become clear as we continue in this section.

Creation and Time

Point 161: Other Cultures Have Different Foundations

We have identified some of the fundamental thoughts lying at the foundation of the ancient Greek culture. Other cultures have different foundations. For example, Manichaeism taught there are two divine beings (gods), one responsible for everything good and another responsible for everything evil.[76] In contrast, the ancient Chinese believed that everything in existence is balanced between two opposing forces called Yin and Yang.

For a worldview that seems very strange to us today we can consider a primitive tribe which divided all things into two categories: sharp objects and soft objects. With this as the foundation of their thought patterns, they placed sharp rocks in the same category as animals with sharp spines. Because that tribe thought in terms of sharp versus soft objects, it had no category for animals. In their minds the porcupine was more like a sharp rock than it was like a dog. A soft section of grass was more like a furry rabbit than it was like a tree. Since some animals fit in the sharp category and others in the soft category, the people were unable to form a category for all animals. What is an animal? What is a plant? These questions were difficult to answer given their worldview. Further, it was difficult for the tribe to learn another language with entirely different categories.

Every people group has organized their concepts and language into specific categories and patterns. Those patterns became established through the culture's mythology and evolved over the course of hundreds or thousands of years. The categories that lie at the foundation of thought and language become so ingrained into people's culture that they cannot understand the world apart from them. Those patterns form the framework through which people view the world.

We need to realize that our own culture has formed categories and patterns that form our worldview. However, as a Christian, I am convinced that the most accurate worldview must be developed from the Bible.

Point 162: The Foundation of Western Christian Thought

Christians in the Western world assume their worldview came from the Bible, but elements of ancient Greek cosmology lie at the foundation

---

76 Discussed in V:A:275.

Systematic Theology for the New Apostolic Reformation

of the Western Christian worldview. That worldview forms a framework into which Western people put all new information, even information that is gleaned from the Bible.

To better understand this, consider the Dewey Decimal System, a system developed for librarians to classify books according to subjects and authors. Envision a new library just beginning to stock books on the shelves. Each new book is placed where the Dewey Decimal System dictates. Every culture has a system of thought like the Dewey Decimal System. It is the framework they use to categorize and store new thoughts.

At the foundation of Western culture is a Platonic cosmology with two worlds: the timeless world of God and the natural world. Let me show you how that affects the way you understand the Bible. Genesis 1:1 says:

In the beginning God created the heavens and the earth.

When you envision creation as it is described here, what picture comes to your mind? Most Western Christians will be unable to form a precise vision of what God looks like, but they will envision a blurred, glowing form floating in another world and then speaking creation into existence.

Now think critically of that vision. Why do most Western people envision God as a blurred, glowing form? Why do most see Him in a world separate from creation? Before creation did God need a world in which to exist? Did God need space to exist? Was there any space before creation? Genesis does not answer these questions but our assumptions provide answers that are not in the text.

Perhaps there are other ways to understand Genesis 1:1. Perhaps *creation exists within God*. We know that God fills creation, so there is no part of creation that extends outside of God. I am not saying that creation is God. I am simply offering another interpretation that fits the Genesis account but does not fit with Platonic cosmology.

Here is another possibility. Many scientists today accept the Big Bang theory with its understanding that the universe began as a singularity, i.e., an infinitesimally small, infinitely dense spot that no one understands. According to that theory, nothing existed outside of that singularity—no space, no matter, nothing. Now add God into that cosmology. Rather than envisioning God outside of that singularity, consider the possibility that He filled it just as He fills the universe today. Perhaps God filled the only space that existed—the singularity.

Creation and Time

With that understanding, the next question is, "Did God exist anywhere else?" Of course, no one knows. There is no biblical, philosophical, or scientific evidence that God existed in some other world.

Next consider the philosophical assumption that God's world is timeless. Where did that idea come from? Many Christians read the progression of the days of creation in Genesis chapter 1 and conclude that time began with day one. Think critically about that. Perhaps there is another way to understand the progression of days. For example, what if God stepped into our world today and started creating something? What if He arrived on our doorstep and began six more days of creation? Would those six days indicate the beginning of time? Of course, not.

In the same way, we don't know if time began in Genesis 1:1. The passing of days does not create time; it merely measures time in 24-hour increments.[77] Compare this to a watchmaker who made a watch. The instant the watch began to tick did not mark the beginning of time anymore than day one of creation did.

So why do Western Christians envision a timeless world before creation? Because they have assumptions from the ancient Greek cosmology lying at the foundation of their worldview.

Point 163: Building on the Scriptures Alone

How can we form a biblical cosmology free of the ancient Greek assumptions? It may be impossible to be totally free of our culture's assumptions, but we can make a serious attempt at it. We will have to focus on reading each word of the Bible, determine the meaning of each word precisely, and then add one idea upon another as carefully as we are able. We will have to try very hard not to let our present system of thought recategorize any of the biblical information that we are reading.

Try that. Focus on Genesis 1:1:

In the beginning God created the heavens and the earth.

Does this verse tell us that God has another world in which He exists? Does it tell us that God's world is timeless? No.

---

77 Of course, there is the possibility that a day consisted of a different time increment at creation, but that does not change the point that the passing of days merely measured time, not created time.

Systematic Theology for the New Apostolic Reformation

I propose that if we read the Bible without the assumptions of Greek philosophy at the foundation of our worldview, we will come up with the cosmology that I offered at the beginning of Volume I. God created the heavens and the earth. The heavens are part of creation. What exists outside of creation? No one knows.

THE COSMOLOGY DEVELOPED FROM THE BIBLE

Point 164: The Early Church Building on the Greek Foundation

As we have said many times, the ancient Greek philosophers had a dualistic worldview at the foundation of their thoughts. They also saw the natural world trapped in cyclic time.

In contrast, Jewish and early Christian thought was strongly founded in linear time.[78] The foundation of their thoughts was firmly planted in the book of Genesis which revealed God creating the world with one day following another, and one generation begetting another generation in

---

78 The Hebrews had an element of cyclic time, especially evident in how they celebrated annual feasts in which they saw themselves as tied to their forefathers throughout time.

Creation and Time

similar succession. The first five books of the OT provided the Hebrews with the written records of their history, including escaping slavery in Egypt, traveling through the wilderness, and settling in the Promised Land. God also gave the Jews promises that could only be fulfilled in the future. These written records, studied intently by the Jews, aligned their thoughts to a linear progression of time.

During the first three centuries of the Christian Church, people of the Jewish, Christian, and Greco-Roman worlds intermingled more than any previous time. As a result, the Greco-Roman belief in cyclic time ruling over the natural world diminished. Of course, the Jews and the early Christians were not the only people causing this change, but they played a significant role in shifting thoughts from cyclic time to linear time, at least with respect to how time governs the natural world.

THE NATURAL WORLD GOVERNED BY LINEAR TIME

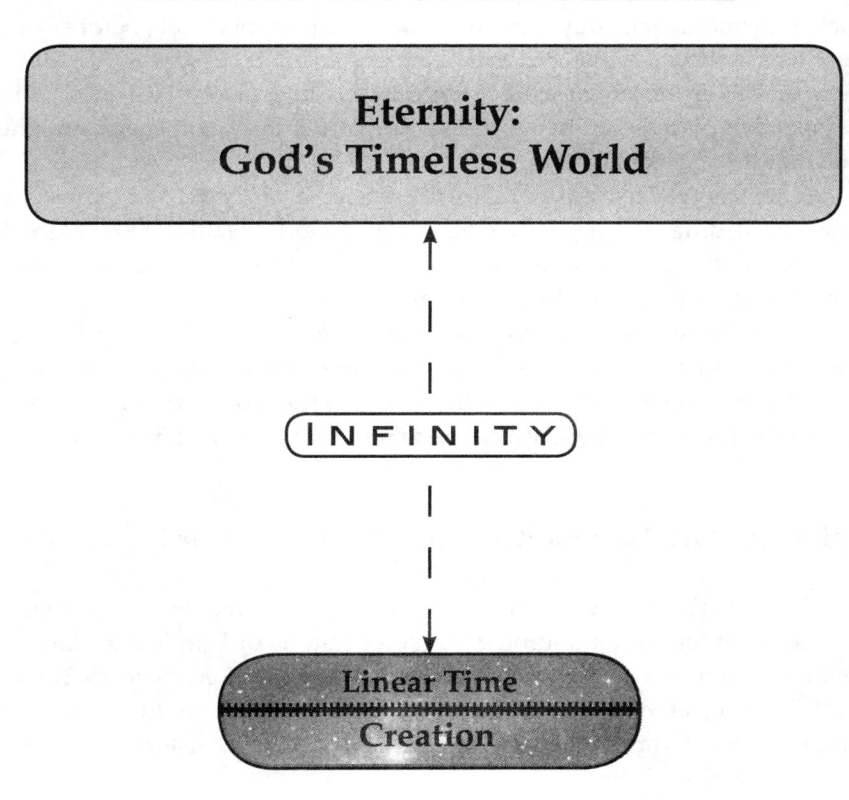

**Eternity:
God's Timeless World**

↑
|
|
(I N F I N I T Y)
|
|
↓

**Linear Time
Creation**

Systematic Theology for the New Apostolic Reformation

After the first apostles died, most of the subsequent Church fathers were Greeks or Romans, if not by birth, at least by education and cultural rearing. By the end of third century, most had abandoned their understanding of cyclic time in the natural world, but they continued to think that the spiritual world of God is timeless.

Point 165: Augustine's Eternal Now

By the time Augustine came along in the 4th century, his family had been Roman from a legal standpoint for at least 100 years. Being raised and educated in Roman Africa, Augustine thought like a Roman. Hence, he built his theology on the Greco-Roman foundation.

Concerning time, Augustine added to the philosopher's understanding by teaching that God exists in the "eternal now." By this, Augustine meant that every moment throughout all of time stands immediately before God: He exists in the year 3,000 BC, and in the present, and in the year AD 3,000. God sees every moment as if it were happening before His eyes. This perspective placed God in a timeless world, and it saw time as a straight line that stood before God.

A helpful way to think of this is to envision a yardstick that represents time. According to Augustine's teaching of God existing in the eternal now, the entire yardstick of time stands before God so He can see all of time. Furthermore, God always sees all of time.

As we have discussed, Augustinian thought has dominated Roman Catholic and Protestant theology for most of Church history even to this day. His teaching about God existing in the eternal now is the cornerstone upon which Western theology has been building for over 1,500 years.

Point 166: Karl Barth Built on God's Existence in the Eternal Now

Among Protestants, Reformed theologians have been especially consistent in logically building on the cornerstone of God being timeless and existing in the eternal now. Within the Classical/Reformed tradition, Karl Barth (1886–1968) followed what many people would consider a natural progression of thought and explained God's existence from the Reformed point of view:

Creation and Time

As the eternal One He is present personally at every point of our time. As the eternal One it is He who surrounds our time and rules it with all that it contains.[79]

This vision of a timeless world enveloping creation and time is the cornerstone of Classical and Reformed theology.

CLASSICAL/REFORMED CORNERSTONE: TIMELESS WORLD WRAPPED AROUND CREATION[80]

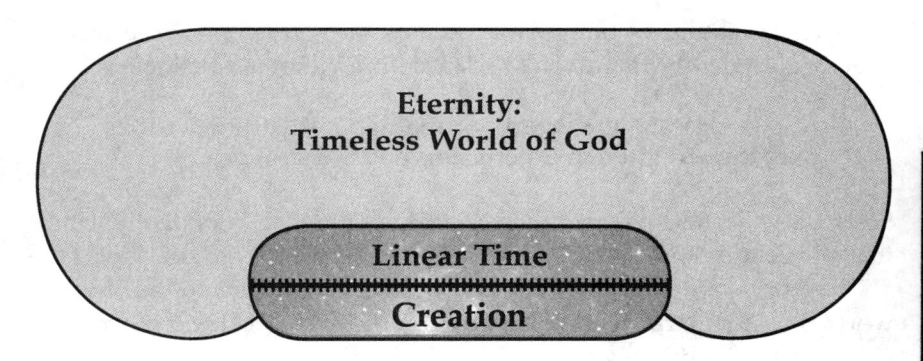

Eternity: Timeless World of God

Linear Time

Creation

Even though most people who have been educated in the Western world hold to this understanding of eternity and time, it is unbiblical, unscientific, and absurd. Let me show you . . . .

Point 167: The Limits of Science in Understanding Time

The cosmology of a timeless world enveloping a time-governed world lies at the foundation of all of Western civilization—even Western science. This is difficult for most people trained in science to accept because scientists like to think that all of their knowledge has been derived from the scientific method (the accumulation of knowledge through observation of the physical world). Yet, the Western philosophical cosmology undergirds Western science.

Too see this, consider how scientists, particularly physicists, assert that

---
79 Barth, *Church Dogmatics*, II:1.
80 A three-dimensional view would show eternity completely surrounding and enveloping a capsule of creation and time.

Systematic Theology for the New Apostolic Reformation

time began when mass came into existence. This assertion corresponds with a correlation physicists have identified between time and mass. When Western scientists identify this correlation between time and mass, they form in their minds and the minds of their students a cosmology in which the natural world is governed by time and outside of the natural world there is no time. Furthermore, they envision a timeless world enveloping the natural world. In other words, they form the fundamental cosmology of Plato—or more specifically, the cosmology of Plato as modified by Augustine.

To see that this cosmology was built on the mythology of the ancient Greeks, consider the definition of science from Webster's dictionary:

> Knowledge about or study of the natural world based on facts learned through experiments and observation.

Scientists will whole-heartedly agree with this definition, confidently stating that all scientific knowledge is the result of studying the physical world.

In other words, *science* is the tool we have to understand the physical world. In a comparative way, we can say that *reading* is the tool we have to understand what is written in a book. For another comparison we can say that auto mechanics have *diagnostic computers* to help them understand what is going on inside of an automobile engine. Each of these tools allows people to gain understanding, yet each tool is also limited. Reading is a tool that *only* allows people to gain information concerning what is written. The mechanics' diagnostic computer *only* provides information about automobiles. So also, science *only* allows scientists to gain information about the physical world.

Since science only provides information about the physical world, any ideas concerning what exits outside of the physical world cannot be derived from science.

Why then do most scientists (and most people in the Western world) have a cosmology in which there exists a timeless world outside of the physical world? Because Western thought is built on Plato's philosophical assumptions. There is no scientific evidence that time does not exist outside of the physical world. The only thing science can tell us is that, within the universe, there is a correlation between time and mass. True science—free of Platonic assumptions—tells us nothing about what exists outside of the physical world. Let me repeat: It tells us nothing.

238

Creation and Time

The well-known scientist, Carl Sagan, was able to escape Plato's assumptions about a timeless world, as can be seen in his famous statement, "The cosmos is all that is or was or ever will be." Please do not misunderstand what I am saying here. I am not agreeing with Sagan that the cosmos is all that exists. However, I am pointing out that Sagan was one of the first scientists to have been faithful to the scientific method. He decided to believe what science has been able to reveal, and nothing else. Science—by definition—cannot not tell us anything about what exists outside of the physical world.

In other words, anyone who tells you that time does not exist outside of the physical world is speaking nonsense.

Point 168: The Fundamental Errors of Western Cosmology

All of Western civilization is built on the fundamental assumptions of the ancient Greek cosmology. Most modern people do not even know what those assumptions are, but their thoughts rest on that foundation.

<u>Foundation of Ancient Greek Cosmology</u>
1. There are two worlds (dualism).
2. Time is destructive and partly evil.
3. God's world is timeless.

Equally fundamental to this cosmology is Augustine's addition of God existing in the eternal now. Then add on what Karl Barth said about "the eternal One . . . who surrounds our time and rules it with all that it contains."[81]

Anyone who thinks deeply about this Western cosmology will realize that it is not only based on assumptions, but it is absurd. To see the absurdity, first notice that Karl Barth moved God's timeless world close to the natural, time-governed world. In other words, he closed the gap of infinity that Plato envisioned between the two worlds. Then Barth envisioned God's timeless world as enveloping the natural world, in the sense of existing before, during, and after the natural world. The problem with this is that a timeless world, by definition, cannot exist before, during, or after anything. By definition, a timeless world has nothing to do with time and it cannot be correlated with any sequence of events.

---

81 Barth, *Church Dogmatics*, II:1.

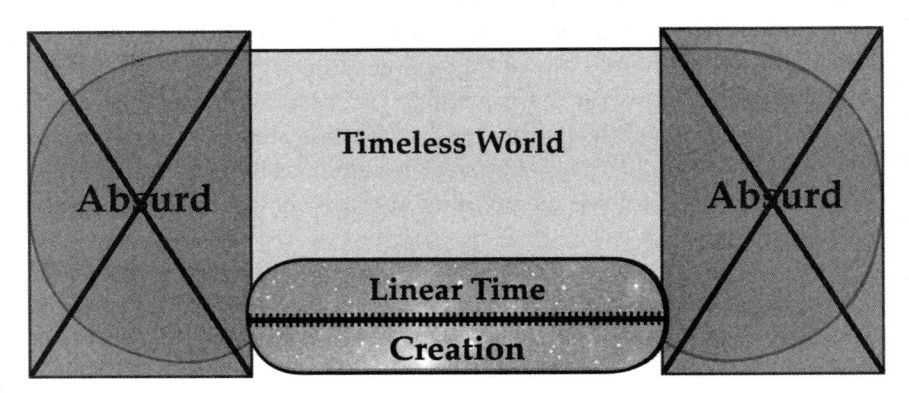

Systematic Theology for the New Apostolic Reformation

THE ABSURDITY OF CLASSICAL WESTERN COSMOLOGY[82]

Timeless World

Absurd — *Absurd*

Linear Time

Creation

To help readers understand this, let me refer back to an illustration I offered earlier.[83] I asked you to consider two objects such as a rock and a piece of wood that you can move together so they touch one another. Next, consider a dog and a cat that you can put in a cage together so they meet. You can even cause imaginary things in your mind to meet. For example, you can imagine a rock and a dog, and then envision the rock hitting the imaginary dog. Each of those scenarios is possible. However, if you have a real dog sitting next to you and an imaginary rock in your mind, you cannot make the imaginary rock hit the real dog. It is impossible. Even if you make an infinite number of attempts, you will never get the imaginary rock to hit the real dog. The two will never meet.

Karl Barth brought the timeless world of God next to the time-governed natural world. By definition, a timeless world and a temporal world cannot be brought together. So long as Plato held the two worlds as infinitely separate, his cosmology was logically consistent, but as soon as Barth brought the two worlds together, he violated the very definition of what timeless means.

Barth confused a *timeless world* with a *world that transcends time.*[84] These are very different from one another. A world that transcends time

---

82 Although this diagram does not show it, even the idea that a timeless world exists simultaneously alongside of natural world is absurd.
83 I:H:80.
84 In this paragraph, I am using the common scientific definition of transcend (beyond the natural laws), rather than the definition used in theology that God is wholly other. This difference explained in I:H:81.

Creation and Time

may indeed reach across time and envelop the natural world, as Barth proposed. A world that transcends time may also exist before and after the natural world. But a world that is timeless cannot envelop a natural time-governed world, because it cannot exist before or after anything.

If Barth or anyone else, wanted to develop a concept of God based on God transcending time,[85] I would enjoy being a part of that discussion, but Classical/Reformed theology does not do that. Theologians like Barth claim that God's world is timeless, but then they go on to describe God as transcending time. They are trying to hold contrary ideas simultaneously, but that is a product of their theology. They need God to be timeless, so they imagine Him in a timeless world. They also need God's world to transcend time, so they try to make the transition from timelessness to transcending time without the students of their teachings noticing.

Anyone who thinks logically will realize that Barth's portrayal of a timeless world enveloping a time-governed world is absurd.

Point 169: False Assumptions Lead to Wrong Conclusions

False assumptions lead to wrong conclusions. This is evident when we follow a logical progression of thought beginning with Augustine's idea of God existing in the eternal now. If God exists in a timeless world and all of time stands before God right now, as Augustine taught, then all of time must exist right now. In other words, if time is as a yardstick and the whole yardstick stands before God, then the past, present, and future exist right now. Furthermore, the past, present, and future will always stand before God. This was Augustine's view, a view upon which Classical/Reformed theology is built.

This leads to problems. If the past, present, and future always stand before God, then the evil in the world will exist forever. The evil that existed before Jesus died on the cross will stand before God forever. If, indeed, the whole yardstick is forever before God, then evil will never decrease from God's perspective. It will be constantly before God forever.

This places in question some of our most basic understandings of how Jesus came to undo the evil that is in the world. It denies the possibility of a final judgment day when evil will be cast away from the presence

---

[85] In this paragraph, I am using the common scientific definition of transcend (beyond the natural laws), rather than the definition used in theology that God is wholly other. This difference is explained in I:H:81.

Systematic Theology for the New Apostolic Reformation

of God. If we believe Augustine or the Classical/Reformed view of God, then it logically follows that evil has always existed and will exist forever, never decreasing, never changing from God's perspective.[86]

Another implication of Augustine's idea of the eternal now has to do with our own existence. Augustine built his theology on the idea that the future already exists, but the future cannot exist without us in it. We are part of the future. Therefore, if the future has always existed as Augustine's theology demands, they you and I have always existed. If, in eternity past, God was watching what we are doing today, then we have existed since eternity past. According to Augustine's doctrine of eternal now, we have existed as long as God has existed.[87]

Some readers may react and say, "Well, I don't believe that!" Yet, that is the inescapable implication of Augustine's assumption that God exists in the eternal now. For me, this is another death blow to Classical/Reformed theology. I have not existed as long as God has existed.

Point 170: Eliminate Plato's Assumptions

So where did Classical/Reformed theology go wrong? It built on Plato's three assumptions listed earlier:

1. There are two worlds (dualism).
2. Time is destructive and partly evil.
3. God's world is timeless.

Let's dare question these assumptions.

First, are there two worlds? Plato assumed that God lives in another world that pre-existed creation. Is that true? Science tells us nothing about whether or not that world exists. The only thing we know from the Bible is that God fills creation. He exists within our world. I propose that we only accept what the Bible or true science has revealed to us. Let's get rid of as many assumptions as possible. The truth is that we don't know if there are two worlds.

---

86 For an in-depth discussion of this see William Lane Craig's comments in: Gregory E. Ganssle, *God and Time* (Downers Grove, IL: Inter Varsity Press, 2001), 66-67.
87 Another absurdity of this view is the implication that we existed before we were created.

Creation and Time

Next, consider Plato's assumption that time is destructive and partly evil. That assumption is contrary to biblical truth. God created a world that is governed by time, and He declared that this world is very good (Gen. 1:31). God's evaluation of the world being good included time.

Time is good. It is the only thing that keeps all events from happening simultaneously—and continually. The passing of time solves the problems that we discussed earlier. Only because time passes can evil someday be expelled from the presence of God. Time guarantees that mistakes made in the past will not exist forever. Time is not a trap. The progression of time is actually the way to escape the trap of evil. The passing of time is good.

This truth is vital. Some readers may want to pass it off as an insignificant point, but the very reason Plato envisioned a world where time does not exist is because he assumed time is evil. Plato's assumption was wrong. Time is good.

Finally, consider the third assumption of Plato's cosmology: God's world is timeless. Today, philosophers and theologians argue about whether the world outside of creation is timeless or temporal, but do you see how foolish such arguments are? We don't even know if such a world exists. If we can't even determine if such a world exists, why should we argue about whether or not that world is timeless? If we can't determine if such a world exists, why should we build a theology upon a cosmology that assumes its existence? Let's build on what we do know rather than what we don't know.

Point 171: Time Is Good

Since time is good, let's consider another possibility for God's existence.

What I am about to propose is simply for your consideration. It should not be considered biblical or scientific fact. The reason I am proposing it is because I am still trying to help readers who continue clinging to the philosophical assumption that God is timeless. Sometimes it is easier to let go of an idea if other possibilities are considered.

So consider this. Time is good. If all good things are part of God's nature, perhaps time is part of His nature.

Then perhaps God is not the one who is timeless. Maybe Satan is timeless. After all, in a timeless world nothing ever changes. Since nothing ever changes, timelessness is a trap. If Satan is timeless then he will exist in his corrupt, wicked, tormented state forever. In contrast,

Systematic Theology for the New Apostolic Reformation

God may be temporal, which actually gives Him great advantages over Satan. A temporal God who exists in a different world can escape evil someday. A temporal God can someday exist in a world where evil does not exist. A temporal God can leave the past in the past.[88] Again, I don't propose this as fact, but as another possibility—a real possibility.

Father-Son theology is open to such possibilities but, for Father-Son theology to stand, the only essential position concerning time is that *God is temporal within creation*. The Bible reveals Him as temporal, changing His mind, experiencing emotional variation, and moving through time with us. That is the cosmology on which Father-Son theology stands. It is built on what we do know from the Bible.

Point 172: The Early Jewish and Christian Concept of Time

Before the Hellenization of Jewish society,[89] we have no historical record of the Jewish people believing in an age when time does not exist. The early Jews did not separate eternity from time. The landmark book on this subject is Oscar Cullmann's, *Christ and Time*. Cullmann explained how the Jews and the early Christians understood that time

> . . . *is unlimited in both the backwards and the forward direction, and hence is, "eternity."*[90]

They saw eternity as unending time, not the absence of time. The early Jews and Christians believed that before creation, time extended into the infinite past. They also saw time going into the infinite future.

THE EARLY JEWISH AND CHRISTIAN UNDERSTANDING OF TIME

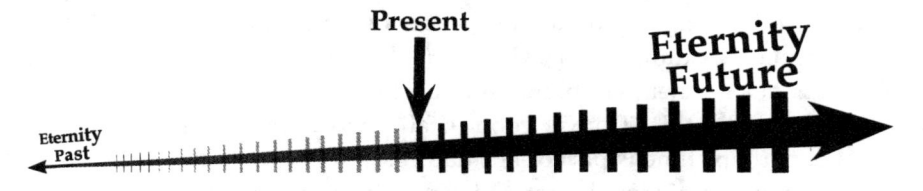

---

88 In III:F:169, we discussed how it is impossible for a timeless God to ever escape the presence of evil.
89 Explained in I:G:55.
90 Oscar Cullmann, *Christ and Time* (Philadelphia: The Westminster Press: 1964), p. 48.

Creation and Time

If we develop our cosmology directly from the Bible we will arrive at the same understanding of time as the early Jews and Christians. In other words, if we believe the Bible and read it without the dualistic cosmology of Plato, along with Plato's concept of eternity being timeless, we will conclude that eternity is time continuing into the past and future forever.

To see this, let's read Genesis 1:1 again, but we must read it, as discussed earlier, focusing on the precise words and determining not to let our preprogrammed system of thought recategorize any of the biblical information that we are accepting as inspired by God:

In the beginning God created the heavens and the earth.

If we are Bereans,[91] we will see the heavens and the earth coming into existence in the beginning. The heavens and the earth did not exist before Genesis 1:1.

Already we have identified a fact that is incompatible with Classical/Reformed theology. Their doctrine of God existing in the eternal now is only true if creation has always stood before God and, therefore, has always existed.

If we continue reading Genesis chapter 1, we will see God creating during six days. If we read carefully without recategorizing any information into Plato's or Augustine's categories, we will conclude that day two did not exist until after day one and day three did not exist until after day two. Both of these conclusions are incompatible with Classical/Reformed cosmology. The doctrine of God existing in the eternal now necessitates that all days always existed, i.e., the whole yardstick of time has always existed. Therefore, according to Classical/Reformed theology, no single day came into existence before any other day.

If you develop your cosmology only from reading the Bible, without first having within your mind Plato or Augustine's categories, you will conclude that tomorrow does not exist yet. You will conclude that the future does not yet exist. You will conclude that the doctrine of eternal now is wrong. If you actually read the Bible and form your cosmology while reading it, you will develop a cosmology exactly like the cosmology of the early Jews and Christians.

---

91 This refers to the group mentioned in Acts 17:10-11, who were diligent to search the Scriptures to see if what they were hearing was true.

Systematic Theology for the New Apostolic Reformation

Point 173: Time Existed *Before* Creation

The cosmology of the early Jews and Christians is further revealed when we read Bible passages referring to events that took place before creation. For example, Ephesians 1:4 tells us that God *"chose us in Him before the foundations of the world."* If everything outside of creation was timeless, then God could not have made a decision *before* creation. This is simple, but profound. "Timeless," by definition, means it cannot be associated with "before" or "after" anything. Therefore, if God made a decision before creation, then time was already in existence.

A careful reading of the Bible also leads us to conclude that the Lamb's Book of Life was written before creation. Further, Jesus was slain before the foundation of the world (Rev. 13:8). The obvious point is that the cosmology of the Bible writers was firmly seated in an understanding of time as existing before creation.

Concerning eternity future, we do not have a lot revealed in the Bible, but think about Jesus as He appeared to His disciples after His death and resurrection. After He received His glorified body, He still existed in time. While He talked and ate with His disciples, He acted in time. If we will receive a body like His, then our resurrected bodies will also be in time. Further, if we accept Revelation chapters 21 and 22, as descriptions of the world in eternity future,[92] we will also conclude that eternity is time going into the future forever. This is true because Revelation 21 and 22 reveal many events happening in time.

Let me state the obvious again: The Bible writers held to a cosmology that saw time as existing before and after creation.

Even in the face of such biblical evidence, some Western Christians will continue to fight for their Platonic cosmology. I have learned that it does not matter how much evidence is presented to some people. They will continue believing what they believe simply because they have always believed.

Yet for anyone seeking the truth, it becomes obvious that the cosmology of Classical/Reformed thought did not come from the Bible. Furthermore, the cosmology of Classical/Reformed thought contradicts both the biblical and scientific evidence. Of course, a lot is at stake here, because if one gives up Platonic cosmology, Classical/Reformed theology crumbles. But then, whatever is built on a false foundation always crumbles in time.

---

[92] This understanding does not hold for Bible teachers who see Revelation 21 and 22 as metaphorical.

Creation and Time

Point 174: The World Exists in the Present

A biblical cosmology leads one to conclude that the world exists in the present. This means the world does not move through time, but time moves through the world.[93] To see this, think of time as a wind that blows from the future into the present and then into the past. The present remains stationery, but time moves like the wind. This is the view of creation and time we develop from a direct reading of the Bible.

In order to illustrate this understanding of time and creation, I will use the diagram that we have already developed of creation with the spiritual and natural world filling the same space. I will rotate that diagram out from the flat page, and then I will add a timeline coming out perpendicular to the diagram that represents creation existing in the present.

THE WORLD EXISTS IN THE PRESENT

With this biblical cosmology, envision God who fills creation. His spiritual realm fills the same space as the natural realm. Creation contains the heavens and earth. What exists outside of creation? No one knows.

---

93 Some teachers who have thought through these issues are more comfortable saying time acts upon the world.

Systematic Theology for the New Apostolic Reformation

Point 175: Scientific Evidence Concerning Time Being Relative

Before we complete this study of creation and time, it will be beneficial to consider the scientific fact that time is relative. Physicists have concluded and demonstrated that time slows down as one approaches the speed of light. If we develop the technology to allow an astronaut to travel at or near the speed of light, that astronaut could travel away from Earth to some distant galaxy and then return to find that the people on Earth have aged more than he has. The astronaut will not have aged as much as the people he comes back to meet on Earth, but he will still exist in the same present moment as the people on Earth exist. They will be able to talk to each other. They will be able to touch each other and eat together. The astronaut and the people on Earth always stayed in the present, but time passed them at different speeds relative to each other.

Think again of time as the wind coming from the future and moving into the present. Creation does not move, but time moves. Time can move at different rates just like the wind can blow at different speeds.

THE MOVEMENT OF TIME AT DIFFERENT RATES

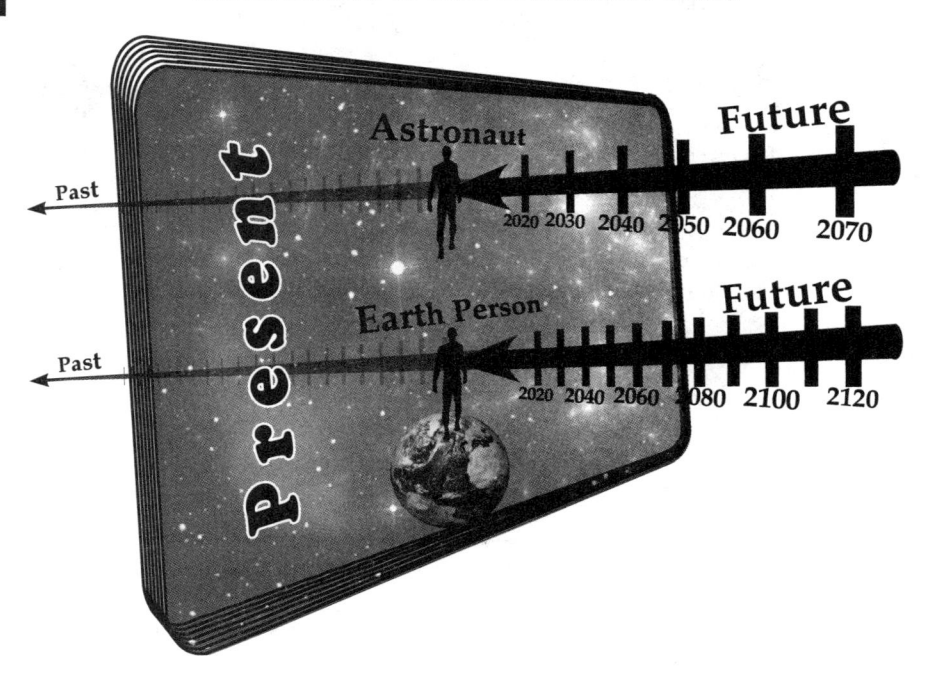

Creation and Time

For verification on this, consider what physicists have named "gravitational time dilation." This refers to how the passing of time is affected by gravitation fields.[94] Not only does time slow down as one approaches the speed of light, but time is also influenced by large masses with strong gravitational fields. The farther away from a center of gravity one is, the slower time passes (relative to places closer to centers of gravity). For this reason, astronauts returning from missions on the International Space Station will have aged slightly less than they would have had they remained on Earth. This has been scientifically verified.

The relevant fact for our discussion is that when the astronauts arrive back on Earth, they are still in the same present moment as the people on Earth. The astronauts did not move into a different time period. They aged less compared with people on Earth, but they stayed in the same present as the people on Earth exist.

Point 176: Time Is Relative, But the Future Does Not Exist

To grasp the view of time being presented here, imagine yourself sitting on one end of a couch and your friend sitting on the other end of the couch. Now think of time passing your friend much faster than it is passing you. Of course, this is impossible, because you are both equidistant from the center of gravity, and neither of you are traveling near the speed of light. However, just imagine that time is passing your friend faster than it is passing you. If this could really happen, you would be able to watch your friend age right before your eyes. When you age one day, he may age an entire year. When you age 20 days, he may age 20 years. If you can grasp that happening, then you can understand how time is relative, even though you and your friend stay in the present together.

This explanation corresponds with current scientific discovery and with biblical evidence. At the forefront of scientific investigation in this field are scientists working with particle accelerators, i.e., machines using electromagnetic fields to propel charged particles. Scientists have succeeded in accelerating particles almost to the speed of light, but none of those particles have been observed disappearing in the sense of moving into another time period. Even though time may pass some particles at a different speed compared with other particles, all particles stay in the present.

---

94 https://en.wikipedia.org/wiki/Gravitational_time_dilation

Systematic Theology for the New Apostolic Reformation

This corresponds with what we see in the Bible. For example, God answered Joshua's prayer for the sun to stand still. God may have changed the speed at which time was acting upon the sun and planets, but the important point is that everyone and everything involved stayed in the same present as Joshua. Similarly, when Aaron's rod budded, God may have changed the speed at which time acted upon the rod but the rod stayed in the present with Aaron (Num. 17:1-8).

Time is relative, but the Bible and present scientific investigation reveal that the present is all that exists.[95]

Point 177: Modern Mythology Reveals the Same Truths

Unfortunately, Western civilization is founded on Plato's cosmology as modified by Augustine, rather than a cosmology derived from the Bible or science. Tragically, ancient Greek mythology continues to determine the thoughts of millions. As a result, most modern people in the Western world believe that the past still exists and the future already exists.

This modern Western belief is reinforced by modern mythology. For example, there are several famous movies, such as *Back to the Future* and *The Terminator*, that are built on Plato and Augustine's cosmology. When movies show characters traveling through time, they are assuming that the past still exists and the future already exists. Such movies function as our modern mythology fixing the fundamental thought patterns of society.

In reality, there is no scientific or biblical evidence that the past still exists or that the future already exists.

This truth is vital in theology because Classical/Reformed theology needs the past and future to exist eternally. In other words, Classical/Reformed theology lives or dies based on whether or not an unbiblical and unscientific cosmology is true or not.

In contrast, Father-Son theology does not need God to be timeless. With Father-Son theology, God's existence outside of creation is a non-issue. The only point about God and time that is necessary for Father-Son theology to be true is that God is temporal within creation. Indeed, that is what the Bible reveals with every verse that shows God acting in time—which is every verse that shows God acting.

---

[95] Some discoveries in quantum mechanics have led physicists to suspect that the future may exist a tiny fraction of a second before the present but this is still being researched and it is does not change the implications of this discussion.

Section G
Theology and Science

In this section on the nature of creation, I will discuss some of the conflicts that have arisen between theology and science. The most challenging issues are those related to the age of Earth and the theory of evolution. Current studies in quantum mechanics are also opening a new world of questions.

The Bible is not a science book, but nor was it written by ignorant, prescientific people. While many of the people outside of Israel believed that the world was supported on the back of a tortoise, Job praised God who *"hangs the earth on nothing"* (Job 26:7). Isaiah declared how God *"sits above the circle of the earth"* (Is. 40:22), and the Hebrew word for circle in this verse is accurately translated as "sphere." Recognizing that the Bible was not written as a science book, but still believing in the reliability of the Book, we can confidently study it and science side-by-side.

I will avoid being dogmatic on these issues, because I have too much at risk. I don't want you to disagree with me on issues of the origins of life and then reject the theological issues that I believe are more important. My personal positions on some issues are not as important as the overall purpose of this book, which is to present God as Father.

Point 178: Conflicts between Theology and Science

Secular scientists commonly assert that the universe is about 13.7 billion years old and Earth is about 4.5 billion years old. The theory of evolution teaches that life started as non-living compounds developed into simple organisms that evolved over the course of millions of years into more complex life forms, including humans.

Systematic Theology for the New Apostolic Reformation

In contrast, a literal interpretation of the Bible leads one to conclude that the six days of creation occurred 6,000 to 10,000 years ago. These dates are determined by studying Genesis 5 and 11, which give us the genealogies from Adam and Abraham. Historians generally agree about the period of Abraham's life, so it is easy to start from there and work backwards to calculate when Adam lived. The discrepancy between the 6,000 and 10,000 dates results from uncertainty about the Hebrew word for "son" which can also mean "grandson" or even refer to someone further down the lineage.

We must also consider the theory of evolution, because Genesis 1 tells us about all of life being created in six days rather than evolving over the course of millions of years. One of the main objections Christians have to evolution is its dependency upon natural selection leading to the survival of the fittest. That process requires the death of the less fit. Yet, many Christians have a theological position which negates any death before Adam sinned. In Volume V, Section B, we will discuss how the death of plants and animals (but not people) was part of God's original design, so we do not have to reject the theory of evolution on that basis. However, there are other topics worth considering.

To simplify our communication, let me clarify the scientific understanding of the word *theory* as used in the *theory of evolution*. People untrained in science typically use this word to refer to a *possible explanation*. However, scientists use the word differently. To them, *theory* refers to a system of thought that explains how things work. This is also how the word *theory* is used in *music theory* or *economic theory*. To a scientist, the theory of evolution is not merely a possible explanation. It is a system of thought that explains how life came to exist as it does today.

I point this out because definitions of relevant terms are important when people trained in different fields are trying to communicate with each other. Sometimes disagreements happen because we have different definitions of words.

Point 179: Various Views of Origins

Christians who tenaciously hold to a literal understanding of the Bible concerning creation are called **creationists**. They believe that the world was created in six literal days, approximately 6,000 years ago. At the other

Theology and Science

end of the spectrum (but still Christian) are **theistic evolutionists** who do not interpret Genesis 1 literally but claim that God used evolution to bring life, including humanity, into existence.

For many years, I rigidly held to and taught the creationist's position. I embraced Genesis 1 as historically and scientifically accurate. I also earned my undergraduate degree in wildlife management. For several years, I used that training to present the beliefs of creationism to churches and Christian audiences. I also did some presentations at secular universities, even to some antagonistic groups. I was effective in communicating the creationist's view. I say this to let you know that I am well-acquainted with creationism, but today I am not a strict creationist. Please let me explain.

There are several ways in which Christians try to reconcile their belief in the Bible with some of the teachings of evolution and an apparently 4.5 billion year old Earth.

The first way is referred to as the **gap theory**, which says that there was a gap of unknown duration sometime between the first and third verses of Genesis 1. Adherents develop this theory by first quoting Genesis 1:1-2:

> *In the beginning God created the heavens and the earth. The earth was formless and void . . . .*
>
> (Gen. 1:1-2)

Then they will point out that the word translated as "was" can also be translated as "became." Hence, this passage can be translated as:

> *In the beginning God created the heavens and the earth. The earth <u>became</u> formless and void . . . .*
>
> (Gen. 1:1-2)

With this translation, the reader may understand that God created Earth at some point in the distant past (even 4.5 billions years ago), but some tragic incident occurred and Earth "became" formless and void. Using this line of reasoning, proponents of the gap theory explain that all of the events of evolution, evidenced by the fossil record, occurred during the gap between "the beginning" and the time when Earth became formless and void. Then proponents suggest that the six days of creation were actually God's acts of *recreating* things that had been destroyed.

Systematic Theology for the New Apostolic Reformation

Another view of how both Genesis 1 and the theory of evolution can be reconciled is called the **day-age theory**. This view sees each of the six days of creation as representing a long period of time. Proponents like to support their view by quoting Peter:

> ... with the Lord one day is like a thousand years, and a thousand years like one day.
>
> (2 Peter 3:8)

Proponents of the day-age theory also point out that the Hebrew word *yom*, which is translated in Genesis 1 as "day," does not necessarily refer to a literal 24-hour long period. It is used in other Bible passages (e.g., Hosea 6:2 ; Zech. 14:7) to refer to a period of time.

The day-age theory is a reasonable explanation, but the argument concerning the Hebrew word, *yom*, referring to a long period of time is not a good argument. This is because Exodus 20:11 uses the Hebrew word, *yamim*, which does refer to a literal day 24 hours in length:

> For in six days the Lord made the heavens and the earth . . . .

Other explanations have been offered by various Christian leaders in an effort to reconcile the biblical account with the claims of modern science, but the gap theory and the day-age theory are the most common.

Point 180: Theistic Evolution

Christians who hold to theistic evolution have more confidence in modern science. In trying to reconcile science with the Bible they reason that God used evolution to bring all living things into existence.

Creationists tend to become defensive when theistic evolutionists present their view. Their greatest concern is that the credibility of the Bible is being undermined. Creationists reason that if someone rejects a literal interpretation of Genesis 1, then they may as well reject the accuracy of the entire Bible, including the NT accounts of Jesus' life, death, and resurrection.

Theistic evolutionists will typically respond by pointing out that the Bible is not one book, but a library containing books of many different

Theology and Science

genres, written by different authors to different groups of people in different time periods. One book in the Bible can be written from one perspective while another book can be written from an entirely different perspective. For example, the Song of Solomon may have been written as a Hebraic love poem, while Luke wrote his Gospel from a biographical-historical perspective. Therefore, it is reasonable to accept the poetic nature of the Song of Solomon and still recognize Luke's writing as an accurate record concerning the life of Jesus.

Following this line of thought, theistic evolutionists can logically hold that the Gospel of Matthew is historically accurate, while at the same time read chapter 1 of Genesis as a poem.

Personally, I have a difficult time thinking of Genesis 1 as a poem. The label "poem" implies a freedom in communication that I don't see in Genesis 1. John Lennox, PhD., offers what I consider a more reasonable perspective. Dr. Lennox is a Christian scholar known for debating atheists concerning the existence of God. When discussing creation, he asks the listeners to envision a pan of water boiling on the stove.[96] Then he asks, "Why is the water boiling?" A scientist may answer by saying that heat from the stove is being transmitted through the metal pan and into the water molecules. Those molecules are caused to vibrate so rapidly that they escape the surface tension of the water, breaking free, then flying off as a gas. Dr. Lennox then offers another explanation for why the water is boiling: "Because I am preparing to have a cup of tea."

Notice that both answers may be true and literally accurate. However, the answers are coming from two entirely differently contexts. In a comparative way we can look at Genesis 1. It was never meant to be a scientific explanation for creation. Genesis 1 was not written to modern people. If it had been written with scientific and historical accuracy (with information about evolution and a 4.5 billion year old earth), no person who lived before the last 200 years would have understood it. The author of the Book of Genesis wrote to people who lived in his lifetime. He wrote Genesis so they would understand it.

We must see Genesis 1 in context. Yet, we can still accept it as truth. If we do this, there are several truths being clearly communicated. I consider these nonnegotiables.

---

[96] I am putting Dr. Lennox's explanation in my own words, but the meaning is the same.

Systematic Theology for the New Apostolic Reformation

Point 181: Nonnegotiable Truths about Origins

As we read Genesis 1, there are several truths that stand out.

1. God created the heavens and Earth.
2. God created all living things, and He blessed them.
3. People are a unique creation of God—created in His image.
4. God delegated to humanity the responsibility to care for Earth.

It seems to me that these are nonnegotiables that all Christians who take the Bible seriously should agree upon concerning the origin of the world.

I do not offer these as the only truths. Indeed, Genesis 1 communicates innumerable truths that preachers have been expounding upon for generations. I see the points listed above as the minimum amount of information that every Christian should take from Genesis 1.

In addition to the nonnegotiables mentioned above, there is another truth evident through both the Bible and science. This has to do with the "force of life." Earlier[97] we discussed God's declaration: *"Let the earth bring forth . . . ."* With this declaration plant and animal life came forth. It was the power of God's words that released the force of life that resulted in plants and animals still being alive today and continuing to reproduce.

It is worth asking if the force of life is great enough to cause plants and animals to change and adapt to their environment. And, if so, can living creatures pass those changes on to their offspring? In other words, can plants and animals evolve?

The force of life has allowed plants and animals to survive many years. Through those years, numerous changes have taken place in the environment. Many plants and animals have gone through dramatic environmental changes and came out the other side not only surviving but thriving. Fossil evidence does reveal changes that have occurred in both the plant and animal kingdoms.

However, a literal interpretation of Genesis 1 leads us to recognize some limitations on how much change is allowed. We can read how God blessed the animals and declared that they must reproduce after their own kind:

> *God created the great sea monsters and every living creature that moves, with which the waters swarmed <u>after their kind</u>, and every*

---

[97] III:D:151,

Theology and Science

winged bird <u>after its kind</u>; and God saw that it was good . . . Then God said, "Let the earth bring forth living creatures <u>after their</u> <u>kind</u>: cattle and creeping things and beasts of the earth <u>after their</u> <u>kind</u>"; and it was so. God made the beasts of the earth <u>after their</u> <u>kind</u>, and the cattle <u>after their kind</u>, and everything that creeps on the ground <u>after its kind</u> . . . .
(Gen. 1:21-25)

God decreed that animals are to reproduce after their own kind, and He gave us some idea of what He meant by "own kind." He placed the animals that swarm together in the waters as belonging to one kind. He placed all of the birds in one group of kind. He placed the cattle in a group of kind. The other beasts of the field in a group of kind, and the animals that creep on the ground as another kind. If we take God's words literally, we will conclude that animals belonging within one kind will not evolve into another kind. This means the offspring of swarming fish will always be fish. Birds will always be birds. Cows will always be cows, and bugs will always be bugs.

However, the Bible leaves room for animals within the grouping of one kind to change and adapt into other animals within their own kind. Birds may evolve into other types of birds. Bugs evolve into other bugs. The Bible leaves open the possibility for one type of fish to adapt to its environment over the course of many years and then pass those characteristics on to its offspring which will also be fish.

I point this out, but not to insist that this is the only reasonable understanding of Genesis 1. There are millions of devout Christians who hold to the gap theory, the day-age theory, or theistic evolution. Many have reconciled in their own minds the theory of evolution with the Bible. Their views are worth everyone's respect. However, we are discussing how even a literal understanding of Genesis 1 allows for evolution within kinds. Therefore, even creationists should accept the idea of adaptations within kinds.

Some Christians prefer to call such changes "adaptations," so as not to give any credence to evolution. In reality, there is no difference between the mechanism of adaption described here and the mechanism of evolution. The only difference in the adaptations described here is that evolution is seen as limited within the biblical grouping of kind.

Systematic Theology for the New Apostolic Reformation

Such limited evolution is sometimes referred to as **micro-evolution**, in contrast to **macro-evolution**. The later refers to all plants and animals evolving from non-living compounds. Micro-evolution is commonly accepted by creationists but usually in a very limited sense, such as a bird's beak increasing in length. I am including a change in beak size in micro-evolution, but also including the ability of one bird species to evolve into another species of bird. This is within the Genesis grouping of kind.

Point 182: A Theory of Biological Development

Rather than totally rejecting the concept of evolution, Bible-believing Christians should, at the very least, note the God-given ability of plants and animals to adapt to their environment and change within their own kind. This leads Christians to accept evolution as "a theory of biological development," while still questioning evolution as "a theory of origins."

It should be questioned as a theory of origins because no one has ever observed non-living compounds develop into simple organisms. Science, by definition, is the accumulation of knowledge through observation. No one has observed what the theory of evolution maintains is true concerning the origin of life. Therefore, it is unscientific to accept evolution as a theory of origins.

The theory of evolution as a theory of origins should also be questioned because there remain too many unanswered questions. For example, huge gaps remain in the fossil record. Paleontologists have studied hundreds of thousands of fossils, yet the intermediate forms necessary for one kind of animal to evolve into another kind are scant at best.

Another big question not answered by the theory of evolution has to do with the Cambrian explosion, which refers to how almost every phyla (major grouping) of plants and animals appear suddenly in the rock strata called the Cambrian. This is difficult to reconcile with the theory of evolution, which claims that all of life started as non-living compounds and developed into simple organisms that evolved over the course of millions of years into more complex life forms. Every honest paleontologist will admit that the absence of life forms before the period forming the Cambrian rock strata is a mystery to them.[98]

---

98 Charles Darwin acknowledged this as a serious argument against his own theory of evolution.

Theology and Science

A fourth question that evolutionists are unable to answer has to do with the development of complex biological processes, which I will discuss next.

For now I can say that a reasonable person is only going to embrace the theory of evolution, if it is a reasonable theory. Indeed, it is reasonable as a theory of biological development, but as a theory of origins, it takes too much blind faith to believe.

Point 183: The Development of Complex Biological Processes

Even as a theory of biological development, evolution fails to explain the diversity and complexity in the plants and animals that we see in the world around us.

Too see this, consider how atheistic evolutionists maintain that all advancements in the plant and animal world result from chance mutations followed by natural selection. Chance mutations are explained as totally random changes that happen in the genetic code of living things. Secular evolutionists then explain that natural selection, i.e., survival of the fittest, allows for the beneficial mutations to continue and, therefore, be passed on to offspring.

That explanation is inadequate to explain the complexity of life. Michael J. Behe, in his book, *Darwin's Black Box*, identifies this insurmountable obstacle to evolution. Behe explains how many features of plant and animal life are only functional in their fully developed state. To see this, consider a mouse trap consisting of a bottom plate, spring, trigger, and rod that snaps closed upon an approaching mouse. If any one of the pieces were missing, the entire mouse trap would be useless. Comparatively, we can note that there are thousands—even millions—of biological processes in the plant and animal world that depend upon multiple factors. The intermediate stages that would have been necessary for the development of those factors would have offered no survival benefit. In the struggle for survival of the fittest, there would have been pressure for those unfinished adaptations to be discarded. Hence, we see natural selection working against the development of complex organisms.[99]

---

99 Michael J. Behe, *Darwin's Black Box* (New York, NY: Touchstone, 1996).

Systematic Theology for the New Apostolic Reformation

Point 184: Intelligent Design and the Force of Life

Christians who acknowledge some amount of evolution but also agree that chance mutations and natural selection are inadequate in explaining the development of complex organisms offer two alternative explanations.

The first is called **Intelligent Design**. This refers to the understanding that the complexity of living things is evidence that an Intelligent Designer has been and is involved with the development of life. Advocates of Intelligent Design have attempted to have this view presented in secular schools as an alternative view to the atheistic version of the theory of evolution. Of course, atheistic scientists have opposed any teaching of Intelligent Design, labeling it a masked version of creationism.

In this case, atheists are building on shifting sand. They start their system of thought with the assumption that there is no God. That is, of course, an assumption because no one can prove that there is no God. Any scientist without the atheistic assumption of there being no God would come to believe in an Intelligent Designer. Paul made this point when he wrote that all of creation is revealing God's "... *invisible attributes, His eternal power and divine nature* ..." (Rom. 1:20). Obviously, Paul agreed with Intelligent Design.

Still, there is an alternative view with equal validity. As we explained, Bible-believing Christians should recognize the force of life. In Genesis chapter 1, we read that God blessed all living things, commanding them to be fruitful and multiply. God created and released a force that moves living things in the direction of survival and advancement. Because this force exists, living things will do whatever it takes to fulfill God's command. It is evident that the force of life is great enough to allow living things to exist as a closed system within which the force of life works against entropy—which is no small feat.

Notice how this explanation differs from Intelligent Design. The force of life entails the release of God's blessings at creation. In contrast, Intelligent Design envisions God's ongoing involvement as living things develop. Both of these views deserve serious consideration. It seems to me that both are reasonable since we see in the Bible that God was involved with the rest of creation and throughout history.

The acknowledgment of an Intelligent Designer and/or the force of life radically changes our view of evolution. In particular, evolution as a

260

Theology and Science

theory of biological development is *evidence for the existence of God*. This can be quite surprising to Christians who have always looked at the theory of evolution as the enemy of Christianity. In reality, Bible-believing Christians should commend scientists (and Darwin) for identifying the force that pushes living things to advance. Secular scientists cannot adequately explain why this force of life exists. In contrast, Bible-believing Christians can. God spoke. He is the Source of life, plus He remains involved with the process of evolution.

Point 185: We Don't Need All of the Answers

Atheistic evolution as a theory of origins falls short. No one has ever observed it. There are too many gaps. There are too many unanswered questions. It is unscientific to accept as fact what has not been verified through observation. Every honest, unbiased person who is studied in the field will admit that there is not enough scientific evidence to accept evolution as a theory of origins.

Someone who is true to the scientific method is okay with that. Not knowing is okay. One thousand years ago people did not know what we know today. One thousand years in the future (if the world continues as it is) humanity will know much more than we know now. In fact, to those future inhabitants of Earth, our thinking may seem very simplistic and, in some areas, blatantly wrong.

Those who have a long-term view do not need all the answers today. Also, those who are true to the scientific method, i.e., that conclusions are based on observable facts, do not need all the answers today. True scientists understand that knowledge is constantly increasing. Tomorrow we will discover truths that we do not know today.

Because of this perspective, true scientists do not prop up their beliefs with untested theories. So then, we do not need evolution as a theory of origins. Someone may respond by saying, "Evolution is the only explanation that we have!" True science does not accept "the only explanation that we have." True science waits until the evidence is sufficient to arrive at a verifiable explanation.

While scientists continue looking for scientifically derived answers, Christians know that the Bible is a source of divinely inspired truth. The Bible reveals that God created humanity in His image. It also tells us that all of creation came into existence because God spoke.

Systematic Theology for the New Apostolic Reformation

Point 186: Back to the Hebraic-biblical Cosmology

The truth that God spoke creation into existence has profound implications in the field of quantum physics. The world of quantum physics is so new and mind-boggling that no one yet grasps the implications. One truth that is clear is that the dualistic worldview of Western civilization will not work in explaining the new discoveries in quantum physics.

The scientific revolution of the 16th and 17th centuries was built on the dualistic cosmology of Plato and Aristotle. At that time, Newtonian physics brought great understanding and revolutionized Western civilization. Once people embraced the truth that the world runs according to natural laws, they eagerly applied their mental abilities to understand the natural world and then master it accordingly.

However, in recent years quantum physicists have been telling us that the world does not function according to Newtonian physics at the quantum level (subatomic level, less than 100 nanometers long). There is an entirely different set of laws that governs creation at that level.

What is now being discovered fits more with the Hebraic-biblical cosmology than the dualistic cosmology of Western civilization. Only time will tell, but Christians who are studied in the field have a whole new respect for the Hebraic-biblical cosmology that sees the spiritual and natural realms as totally integrated.

Volume IV
The Nature of Humanity

If our systematic theology is logically consistent, our understanding of God's nature will correspond with our understanding of human nature. In the development of Father-Son theology, we have had to change our view of God away from that of Classical/Reformed theology. Therefore, we should also expect to change our view of human nature away from that of Classical/Reformed theology.

In this volume, we will make this change.

In Section A, we will briefly discuss the Classical/Reformed view of human nature, then go on in Sections B through M to see what the Bible reveals about human nature. We will divide this discussion concerning the biblical view of human nature into the following sections.

> Section B: How People Are Like God
> Section C: The Original Blessing
> Section D: Separated from God?
> Section E: The Original Sin
> Section F: Rethinking Original Sin
> Section G: Born Sinful and Condemned?
> Section H: How Bad Are People?
> Section I: The Pelagian Controversy
> Section J: The Triune Nature
> Section K: The Soul of a Person
> Section L: The Heart of a Person
> Section M: The Will of a Person

Systematic Theology for the New Apostolic Reformation

We will see human nature in a more positive light than Classical/Reformed theology teaches. Since I will be presenting a more positive view of human nature, I must be very careful to communicate accurately. When people are hearing new ideas or are being challenged in what they presently believe, they often mishear what is being communicated. Therefore, I ask you to read as carefully as I am trying to write.

I did not always hold the more positive view of human nature that I am about to explain. For over 20 years of ministry, I believed and taught that non-Christians are totally depraved (explained in Section A) and unable to do anything good. During those early years of ministry, I simply repeated the teachings of those who trained me. I had never considered any other view about the nature of humanity, because I was told that only liberal Christians believed that non-Christians are capable of doing any good. I certainly did not want to be liberal, since I was also trained to think of liberals as the bad guys who had gone astray by abandoning their foundation in the Bible. But I kept coming across Bible verses that did not correspond with the negative view that I had been taught about the nature of humanity.

One of the verses that kept taunting me was Luke where Jesus was speaking to His disciples and encouraging them to love their enemies. In that passage, He said:

Even sinners love those who love them.
(Luke 6:32)

When we examine these words of Jesus carefully, we find that the word, *love*, is translated from the Greek word, *agape*, which we usually associate with a very giving, sacrificial love. I had been taught that non-Christians are incapable of doing any good. Yet, Jesus said sinners *agape love* those who love them.

If this was the only verse in the Bible accrediting positive characteristics to unbelievers, I probably would have been able reason it away and continue holding to the negative view of humanity that I had been taught. But there are many similar verses, some of which I will show you in the pages that follow.

Determined to seek out and find the truth, I committed to serious study of the Scriptures and the historical development of the Classical/Reformed understanding of human nature. What I learned shook a pillar

The Nature of Humanity

in my theology. Because I believe the Scriptures are inspired by God, and therefore, serve as the final standard for doctrinal truth, I could no longer teach what I had been taught.

Then I had to make a decision as to whether or not I should make my new convictions known. It was inevitable that if I spoke out some other Bible teachers would rise up to challenge me and such challenges can get ugly. Worst of all are people who throw out accusations based on what they have heard secondhand, rather than based on their own examination concerning what I have written. I welcome all who will look at this subject with me seriously. In the process of our learning together I will take my stand with Luther when he said:

> Unless I am convinced by the testimony of the Holy Scriptures or by evident reason—for I can believe neither pope nor councils alone, as it is clear that they have erred repeatedly and contradicted themselves—I consider myself convicted by the testimony of Holy Scripture, which is my basis; my conscience is captive to the Word of God. Thus I cannot and will not recant, because acting against one's conscience is neither safe nor sound. God help me. Amen.[100]

As I present my convictions concerning the nature of humanity, some readers may wrongly think that I am teaching Pelagianism, which we will explain in Section I. Let me confidently assure you that I believe and teach that every human being is a sinner and every person is totally dependent upon the grace of God for salvation. However, I will show you how people are not as bad as Classical/Reformed theology teaches.

---

[100] This is from Heiko Oberman's English rendering of Luther's sermon: *Luther: Man Between God and the Devil* (English edition Yale, 1989).

Volume IV
Nature of Humanity

Section A
Classical/Reformed View of Humanity

As already explained, the foundation of Classical/Reformed theology is the ancient Greek philosophical dualism that separates a timeless, spiritual world from a temporal, natural world. Adding to this, Augustine had a strong dualistic perspective, separating light from dark, good from evil.[101] Like other Classical theologians, Augustine believed in a God who is timeless outside of and within creation. This foundation oriented his understanding of human nature down a predetermined path. Let me explain.

Point 187: The Infinite Difference between God and Humanity

If the spiritual world is timeless, then God exists in a realm that people cannot comprehend. If God is transcendent and wholly other, then *He is nothing like people*. According to Classical/Reformed theology, God is infinitely unlike people. Classical/Reformed theologians sometimes refer to this as the "otherness" of God.

Adherents of Reformed theology sometimes talk about people being less than microscopic worms in comparison with God. They say people have *no intrinsic value*. Man is dust. However, according to Reformed theology, people do have *extrinsic value*, because God has sovereignly decided to value humanity. In other words, we have value because and only because God assigns value to us by choosing to value us.

This view of humanity can develop from a reasonable progression of thought beginning with the dualistic worldview that sees God as existing in an infinitely distant, timeless, perfect world.

---

101 This is discussed in V:A-B.

Systematic Theology for the New Apostolic Reformation

THE GAP OF INFINITY BETWEEN GOD AND HUMANITY

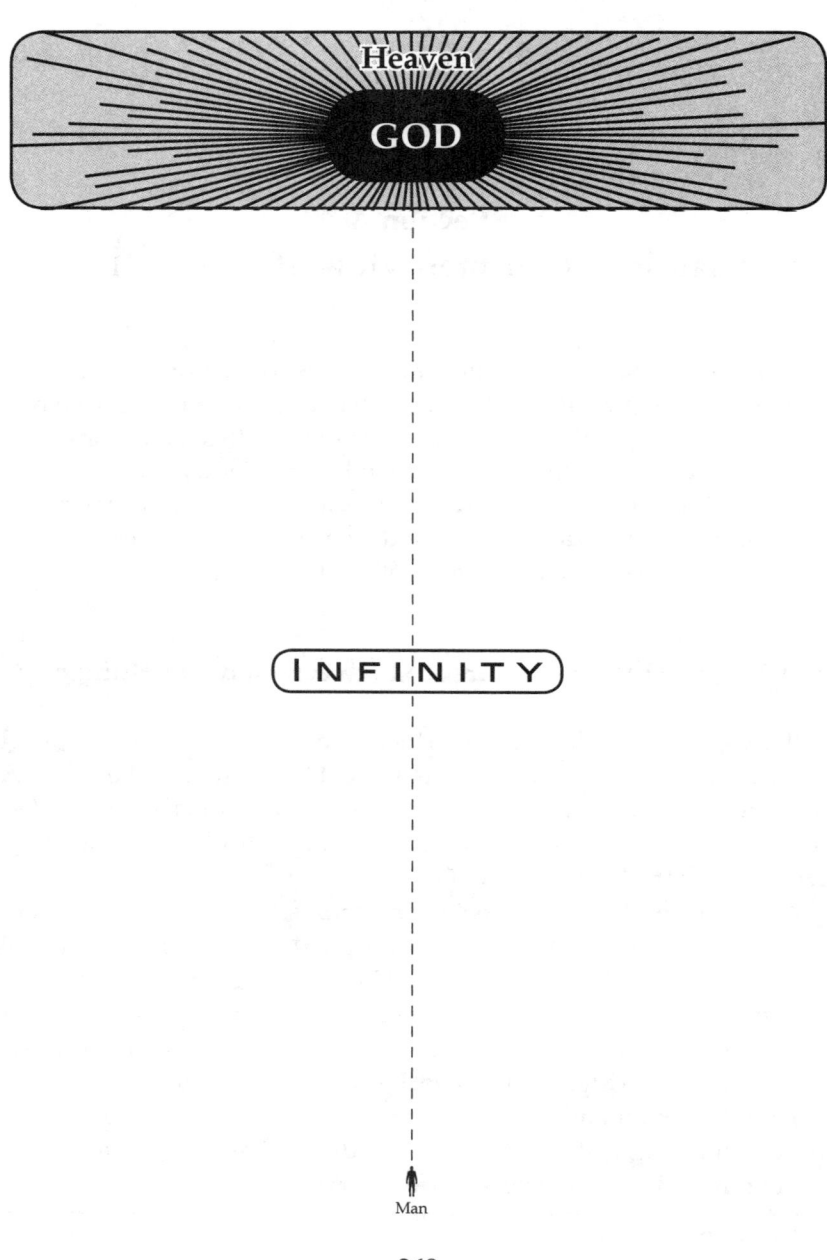

Heaven

GOD

INFINITY

Man

Volume IV
Nature of Humanity

Classical/Reformed View of Humanity

Point 188: People Are Unlike God Because of Sin

Followers of Reformed theology will admit that God created Adam and Eve in His image, however, the sin of Adam was so horrific that it wreaked havoc on that image. John Calvin was inconsistent in his teaching concerning this. In one place, Calvin wrote that "the heavenly image was obliterated" in Adam because of the fall.[102] In another place, Calvin wrote that "God's image was not totally annihilated and destroyed in him, yet it was so corrupted that whatever remains is frightful deformity."[103] Either way, people are infinitely unlike God according to John Calvin.

Point 189: God's Holiness Separates Him from People

The distance between God and humanity that is perceived by Classical/Reformed thinkers is fixed more firmly in their minds with their understanding of God's holiness.

To see this, consider how followers of Classical/Reformed theology associate God's holiness with the God who exists in a distant, timeless, perfect world. The popular Reformed theologian, R. C. Sproul, wrote of God's holiness as follows:

> When the Bible calls God holy it means primarily that God is transcendentally separate. He is so far above and beyond us that He seems almost totally foreign to us. To be holy is to be "other," to be different in a special way.[104]

Earlier we defined holiness as God's sinless purity. Classical/Reformed teachers will agree with this definition, but they add to that by associating His holiness with the attributes that originated with the ancient Greek philosophers. As seen in the quotation above, adherents of Classical/Reformed theology typically equate God's holiness with His transcendence. Some adherents define holiness as "the essence of His otherness." Still others associate God's holiness with His incomprehensibility. Karl Barth associated God's holiness with His "aloofness."[105]

---

102 Calvin: *Institutes*, II:1:5.
103 Calvin: *Institutes*, I:15:4
104 R. C. Sproul, *The Holiness of God* (Wheaton, IL: Tyndale House Publishers, Inc., 1985), p. 55.
105 Barth, *Church Dogmatics*, II/1, p. 361.

Systematic Theology for the New Apostolic Reformation

The Classical/Reformed Understanding of God's Holiness

Holiness
Transcendence
Otherness
GOD
Incomprehensibility
Aloofness

INFINITY

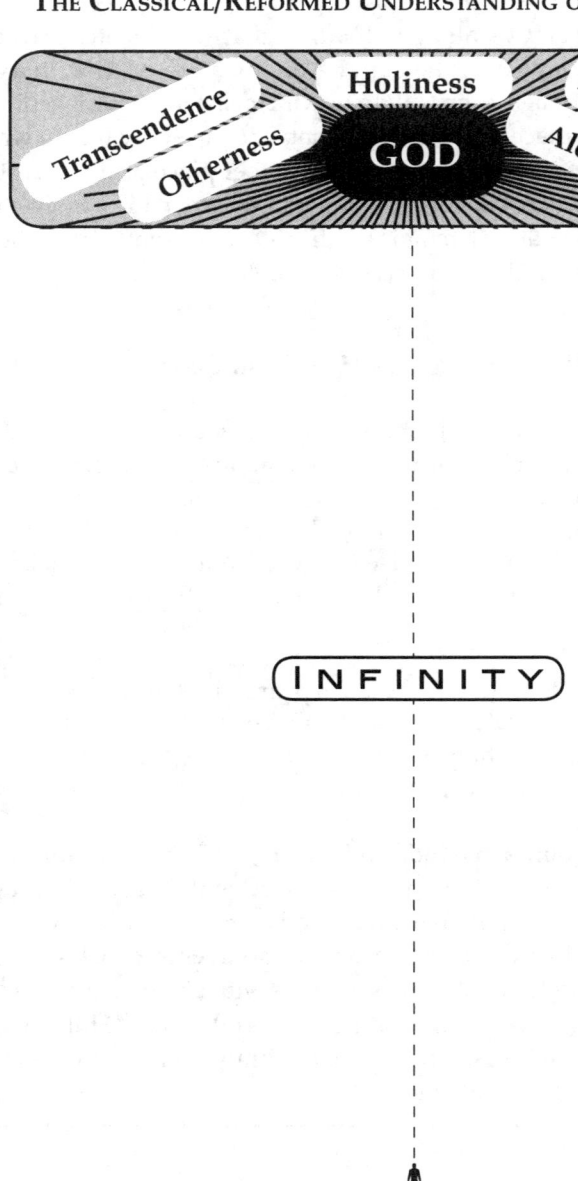

Man

Volume IV
Nature of Humanity

Classical/Reformed View of Humanity

Point 190: God Separates Himself from Sin

According to Classical/Reformed theology, the separation between God and humanity exists because God's nature is holy. However, that separation also exists because God's holiness demands that He separate Himself from sin.

To support this understanding, Reformed Christians often quote the KJV of Habakkuk 1:13:

> *Thou art of purer eyes than to behold evil, and canst not look on iniquity . . . :*

The idea that God cannot look at sin has been used to support the idea that God separates Himself from sinners.

Isaiah 59:2 is also used to support this doctrine:

> *But your iniquities have made a separation between you and your God,*
> *And your sins have hidden His face from you so that He does not hear.*

This amplifies the concept of God being far away from sinful humanity.

Point 191: Eternal Separation as a Result of Adam's Sin

According to Classical/Reformed thought, the sin of Adam by itself was enough to create an infinite separation between God and Adam, along with all of Adam's descendants. To support this doctrine, a specific progression of thought is used which goes as follows.

God warned Adam about not eating of the tree of the knowledge of good and evil, saying, *"in the day that you eat from it you will surely die"* (Gen. 2:17). Adam did not die physically that day, so teachers who follow Reformed theology explain this to mean that Adam died spiritually. Spiritual death is understood to be separation from the life of God. Reformed teachers also say Adam's sin was passed into all of his descendants through a sinful nature, and therefore, all of humanity is estranged from God until they are reconciled to God through Jesus Christ.[106]

---

[106] Augustine laid out this pattern of thought in several places, including: *The City of God*, 13:2, 12-14.

Systematic Theology for the New Apostolic Reformation

The Classical/Reformed Understanding:
Adam's Sin Totally Separates God and Humanity

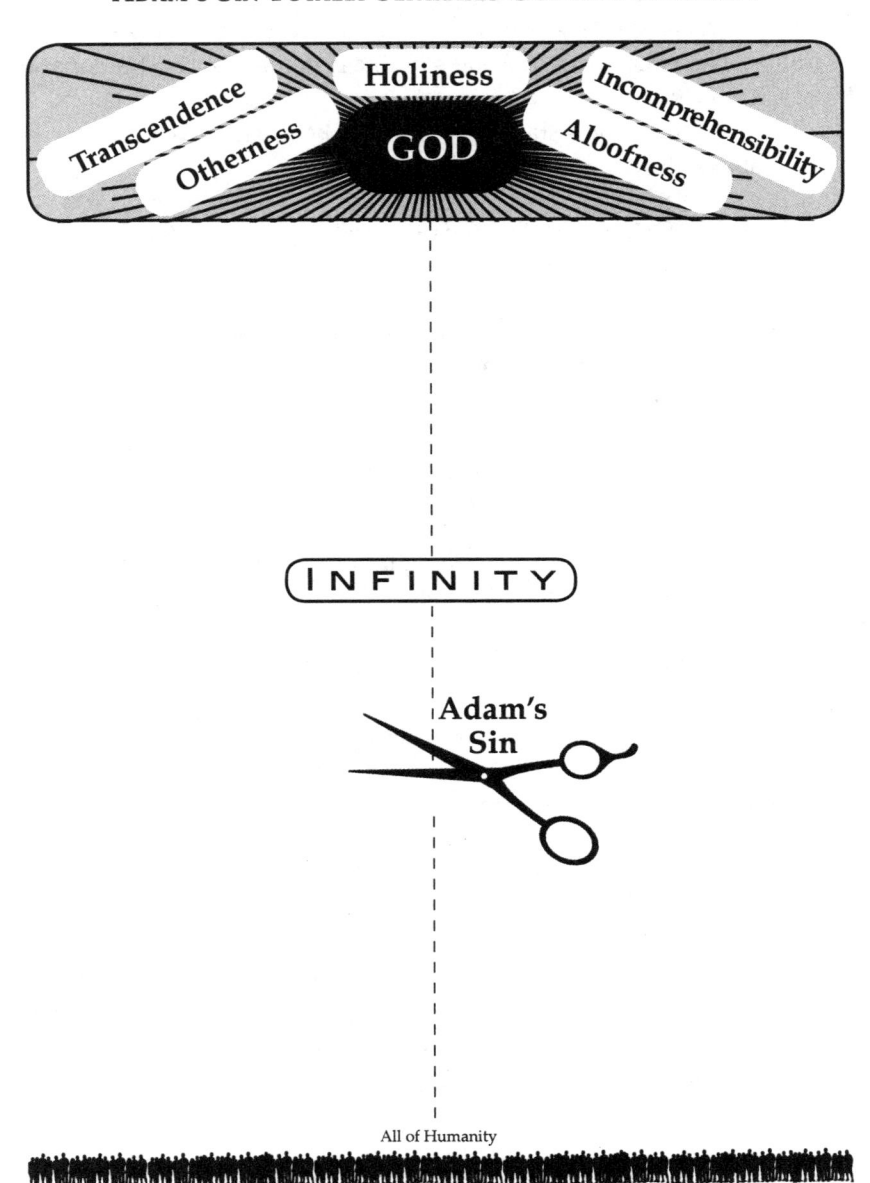

GOD — Holiness, Transcendence, Otherness, Incomprehensibility, Aloofness

INFINITY

Adam's Sin

All of Humanity

Classical/Reformed View of Humanity

<u>The Classical/Reformed Progression of Thought about
Humanity's Eternal Separation from God</u>
1. God told Adam he would die the day he ate the forbidden fruit (Gen. 2:17).
2. Adam did not die physically, so he must have died spiritually.
3. Spiritual death means eternal separation from God.
4. Adam's sin and eternal separation apply to all of Adam's descendants.

According to Classical/Reformed theology, the gap between a holy God and sinful humanity is infinite. Taking their lead from Classical/Reformed theology, modern evangelical teachers often communicate this doctrine with a diagram in which God is shown to be on one side of a cliff and humanity is seen on another cliff with a huge chasm separating the two. Jesus is seen as the only bridge that can span the infinite chasm between God and humanity.

CLASSICAL/REFORMED UNDERSTANDING THAT
THERE IS A HUGE (INFINITE) CHASM BETWEEN GOD AND HUMANITY

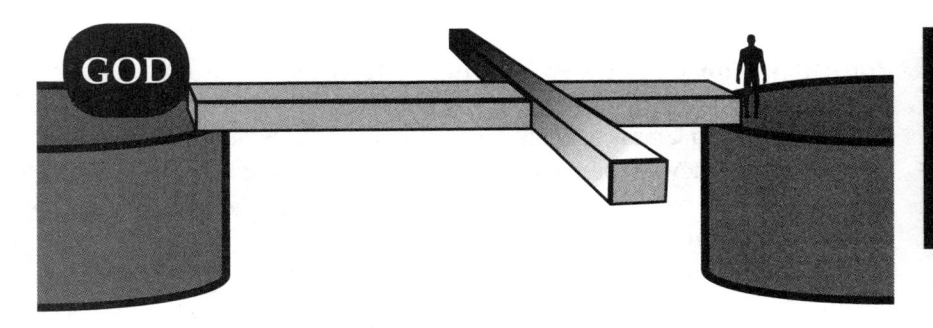

(In the sections to follow this one, we will see what is wrong with this understanding of God and humanity.)

Point 192: Augustine and Calvin Say Babies Are Born Evil

According to Classical/Reformed thinkers, even babies come into this world totally alienated from God and corrupted by Adam's sin. That sin is called original sin. They believe that Adam's sin released a moral corruption

Systematic Theology for the New Apostolic Reformation

so devastating that all humans are born with a nature to sin. That sinful nature is also referred to as inherited depravity.

Augustine wrote:

> ... each man, being derived from a condemned stock, is first of all born of Adam evil and carnal.[107]

Augustine saw all people as starting out evil to the core of their being—not because of anything they did but because they were born as descendants of Adam.

Following in Augustine's theological footsteps, John Calvin held a similar view, explaining how children come into this world:

> ... their whole nature is a seed of sin; hence, it can be only hateful and abhorrent to God.[108]

Although modern Classical/Reformed theologians may not be as negative as Augustine and Calvin were, they all believe babies are born with a nature to sin.

Point 193: Non-Christians Are Totally Depraved

According to Classical theology, not only are babies born evil but all people (before they become Christians) are evil to the core of their being. Following in the path of Classical theology, Reformed theologians use the descriptive terminology *totally depraved*.

The terminology, **totally depraved**, is used today by different leaders in different ways. Those who follow the teachings of John Calvin use this terminology most frequently. Concerning the nature of humanity, adherents of Reformed theology define total depravity as "a sinfulness which pervades all areas of life or the totality of human existence."[109] When applied to the subject of salvation, total depravity refers to a person being completely unable to seek God, choose God, or even want God. However, when the terminology is used as a general description of humanity, it

---

107 Augustine, *The City of God*, 15:1.
108 Calvin, *Institutes*, II:1:8.
109 This belief is one the five canons of the Calvinistic Synod of Dort (1618–1619) and is part of the acronym TULIP, which is used to identify the five pillars of Calvinism.

Classical/Reformed View of Humanity

includes the idea that nothing any non-Christian does is good; even that which appears to be good, such as going to Church, praying, and giving to the poor, is done out of evil motives. Therefore, every action, thought, and deed coming from non-Christians (apart from God's intervening grace) is evil in God's eyes.

Promoting the most negative definition of total depravity, John Calvin wrote:

> . . . all human works, if judged according to their own worth, are nothing but filth and defilement. And what is commonly reckoned righteousness is before God sheer iniquity.[110]

The *Westminster Confession of Faith* expresses the negative view of Reformed theology when it explains that all good works done by non-Christians are sinful:

> . . . because they proceed not from a heart purified by faith; nor are done in a right manner, according to the Word; nor to a right end, the glory of God, they are therefore sinful, and cannot please God . . . .[111]

Adherents of Reformed theology agree that all good works done by non-Christians (apart from God's intervening grace) are sinful. However, adherents typically change their definition of total depravity when called upon to defend it. They will then slip back to "a sinfulness which pervades all areas of life or the totality of human existence." This definition is vague, implying that sinfulness merely has its influence upon all areas. This is not nearly so hard to defend as Calvin's understanding that "all human works . . . are nothing but filth and defilement."

---

110 Calvin, *Institutes*, III:12:4.
111 *Westminster Confession of Faith,* from the original manuscript written by Cornelius Burges in 1646, chapter XVI, point 7.

Volume IV
Nature of Humanity

Section B
How People Are Like God

Now we will begin studying the nature of humanity from the view of Father-Son theology. First, we will see that the Bible emphasizes how people are like God, while Classical/Reformed theology emphasizes how people are unlike God.

Point 194: Start with a Biblical Worldview

In order to approach this subject with a fresh perspective—a biblical perspective—we need to abandon the Greek philosophical cosmology that lies at the foundation of Western civilization. We must abandon the dualism of Plato. We must not envision a timeless, spiritual world infinitely separated from the natural world. That cosmology predisposes our concept of humanity to be infinitely distant from and different than God. Instead, we must embrace the biblical cosmology that recognizes God who fills creation and is very close to humanity.

Second, we must abandon Plotinus' concept of God being wholly other. That idea is wrong. Man cannot be created in the image of God and, at the same time, God be wholly other.

Third, we must abandon Plotinus' concept of God being like the sun shining in a timeless dimension. That also predisposes our concept of God to be extremely different than humans. Unfortunately, many Christians are unwilling to let that sun-like image go because they sense that if they release that image then they will have nothing on which to anchor their understanding of God. With no anchor, their image of God may be swayed too easily. When we talk about how humanity and God are similar, they

Systematic Theology for the New Apostolic Reformation

may find their concept of God is becoming too human-like. Yet, if we are going to approach this subject free of the ancient Greek philosopher's cosmology, then we will have to take that risk.

Envision God filling the heavens and earth. He is very close to every human being. This is the biblical revelation.

Start with the Biblical Cosmology

Point 195: Created in God's Image

Genesis 1:27 tells us:

> *God created man in His own image, in the image of God He created him; male and female He created them.*
>
> (Gen. 1:27)

This is where the Bible starts developing an understanding of human nature, so this is where we should start our understanding, i.e., both male and female were created by God and in the image of God.

Let me point out again that this is not where Classical/Reformed theology starts. It starts with a vision of God's world being infinitely different and separated from the world of humanity.

How People Are Like God

If we start where the Bible starts, we will see God as very close to creation and that He created Adam and Eve in His image. Genesis 5:1 adds to our understanding:

> *In the day when God created man, He made him in the likeness of God.*

The most fundamental aspect of human nature as revealed in the Bible is that people are made in the image and likeness of God.

Even after the fall, Adam and Eve still existed in the image and likeness of God. In fact, all of humanity remains in His image and likeness. Several Bible passages affirm this. For example, after Noah's flood, God gave a warning that no person is ever to kill another person because all people are made in the image of God:

> *Whoever sheds man's blood,*
> *By man his blood shall be shed,*
> *For in the image of God*
> *He made man.*
>
> (Gen. 9:6)

The significance of humans being created in the image of God is made clear by the context of this passage. God sanctioned the killing of animals, but not the killing of humans, because people are made in His image. This distinction between animals and people would be meaningless if humans no longer existed in the image of God. Because people are created in God's image, it is a terrible thing to take the life of another human being.

The apostle Paul explained that even after the fall, every person *"is the image and glory of God"* (1 Cor. 11:7).

Contrast this truth with the emphasis of Reformed theology. They so emphasize the fall of humanity that they minimize any likeness to God's nature remaining in humanity. As mentioned earlier, John Calvin vacillated in his writings concerning this. Sometimes he would refer to minor remnants of the image of God in people, but other times he would say that God's "image was obliterated"[112] because of the fall. Calvin was wrong. Even after the fall, humans remain as image-bearers of God.

Of course, there are areas in which God is very different than people. He always existed, having no beginning. His knowledge is infinite while

---

112 Calvin, *Institutes*, II:1:5.

Systematic Theology for the New Apostolic Reformation

ours is finite. We humans have all fallen short of His glory. In these and many other ways, God is much greater than we are, and yet, we are still created and exist in His image.

Point 196: Created in His Glory

Humanity was created not only in the image of God, but also in His glory (1 Cor. 11:7). In the Bible, glory is correlated with a presence that demands respect and creates awe in the observer. Glory was often associated with authority, especially the authority that abides upon a king or other ruler. The Psalmist made this correlation when he praised God, saying:

> *Yet You have made him a little lower than God,*
> *And You crown him with glory and majesty!*
>
> (Ps. 8:5)

It was well after the fall that the Psalmist made this declaration that God crowned humanity *with glory and majesty*. In other words, glory is a sustained aspect of humanity's nature.

Of course, humanity's glory is not as great as God's glory, but it still exists. Romans 3:23 tells us that we all *"fall short of the glory of God."* John Calvin misquoted this verse and taught, "All sinned and *lack* the glory of God."[113][114] John Calvin was wrong. People still have glory in their nature.

Point 197: All People Are Created as Children of God

Not only are we created in the image and glory of God, but the Bible also tells us that *we are* children of God. This is not only referring to Christians. The Bible refers to all people as children of God. Of course, we know that Christians hold a unique relationship as children of God (John 1:12), and we will explain later how that relationship is unique. For now, we need to affirm what the Bible reveals about Adam and all of his descendants being children of God.

---

113 Calvin, *Institutes*, III:14:17.
114 Many modern Reformed theologians disagree with Calvin on this, reaffirming their understanding of the dignity of humanity.

How People Are Like God

When Paul talked with the philosophers and other leaders in Athens, he referred to the words of their poets, that all people are God's children (Acts 17:28). Paul went on to argue:

> *Being then the children of God, we ought not to think that the Divine Nature is like gold or silver or stone, an image formed by the art and thought of man.*
>
> (Acts 17:29)

Paul was saying that since people are children of God, we can conclude certain things about the nature of God. In particular, Paul was arguing that God is more like humanity than a man-made statue. The foundation of Paul's argument was that *all people are children of God*.

To confirm this, look at the genealogy from Jesus back to Adam recorded in Luke 3:23-38:

> *Jesus Himself was about thirty years of age, being, as was supposed, the son of Joseph, the son of Eli, the son of Matthat, the son of Levi, . . . the son of Enosh, the son of Seth, the son of Adam, the son of God.*

Notice that Adam is referred to as *"the son of God."* Then the same word "son" is used as the link from generation to generation.

This truth must correspond with God's original intention. Before He created the world, God determined to have sons (Eph. 1:4-5). Therefore, we should not think of Adam and Eve as creatures totally unlike Him. God did not create strange animals so He could some day change those animals into His sons. God created people as His children.

Point 198: A Challenge to Continue

At this point, some of my readers may want to disassociate themselves from me. Their theology is so firmly built on the wickedness of humanity that they cannot allow their view to be challenged. I understand that concern. It is difficult to have foundational beliefs shaken. We Christians like to think we base our doctrines on the Bible, but we all have selective hearing. We consciously and unconsciously hear what agrees with what we already believe.

Systematic Theology for the New Apostolic Reformation

In addition, we all want to belong. Different denominations and streams of Christianity have their own unique perspectives. For a person within one group to abandon that group's unique, deep-seated doctrines may mean risking rejection by those whom that person has fellowshipped with for years. It is always easier to remain the same, keep it safe, ride the wave. It's easier to be in agreement with those around you. Furthermore, our desires to belong to a certain group influence what we allow ourselves to hear and believe. Loyalty to any one group *requires a commitment to not think seriously about certain topics contrary to that group's deep-seated beliefs.* To belong always requires some compromise.

So, I understand if you cannot reconsider your present view of human nature. We know that everyone sins, but I am presenting a more positive view than many Christian groups can accept. If you are a truth-seeker willing to pay the price of change, let me show you what the Bible actually says.

Point 199: All People Are Fathered by God

The link between God's nature and human nature is undeniable when we study the account of Adam's creation in Genesis 2. There we see God personally involved with forming Adam from the dust of the ground. God breathed His own breath into Adam. The significance of God's breath must not be minimized. God put something of Himself in Adam.

That which was released into Adam is in every living human being. Later,[115] we will discuss how the breath that God released into Adam is passed from generation to generation. The spiritual breath that brought Adam to life allows every human being to be alive. Proof that every human being has God's breath within them is in Job 34:14-15:

> *If He should determine to do so,*
> *If He should gather to Himself His spirit and His breath,*
> *All flesh would perish together,*
> *And man would return to dust.*

According to this verse, some of God's spiritual substance is within every person, Christians and non-Christians.

---

115 IV:J:255.

How People Are Like God

The writer of Hebrews tells us that God is the *"Father of spirits"* (Heb. 12:9).[116] Not only did God create man in His image, but in some way, God fathered humanity. Paul referred to God as the *"Father, from whom every family in heaven and on earth derives its name"* (Eph. 3:15). By saying God fathered humanity, I am not implying any type of sexual interaction, but indeed, we are recognizing that God released something of Himself into humanity that made human life possible.

In trying to explain how God and humanity are alike, Christians have often used the comparison of God being like the ocean and a person being like one molecule of water. Perhaps a more appropriate comparison would be that the ocean puts one of its own molecules into a human being. Of course, this comparison falls short. Unlike the ocean, God is a Person. He is also infinite in many ways. Yet, the "so wonderful that it is difficult to grasp" biblical truth is that the infinite God put something of Himself in Adam and that something has been passed into all of Adam's descendants.

God is the Father of all humanity. God is not "wholly other." People are created in the image of God, and some of His nature is actually in each person. Each person is a child of God.

This truth raises important questions about the difference between Christians and non-Christians. We know the Bible clearly teaches about a unique relationship Christians have as children of God. So then, in what sense are all people children of God, and in what sense are Christians children of God? We will answer that in Volume VI, when we study soteriology. For now we need to embrace the biblical truth that all people are children of God, in the sense that God fathered Adam and Adam is our forefather.

Point 200: People Are Valuable

When you think of the nature of humanity, what is the first thing that comes to your mind? Sinner? Of course, all people sin, but more fundamental to human nature is the fact that all people are created in the image of God. God created people as "very good" (Gen. 1:31). People are creative, social, funny, smart, industrious, artistic, and so on. God did a good job in what He created. We are grand creatures—crowned with glory and majesty (Ps. 8:5).

---

116 More than once in the OT God is described as the *"God of the spirits of all flesh"* (e.g., Numb. 16:22 ; 27:16).

Systematic Theology for the New Apostolic Reformation

Contrary to what Reformed theology teaches, people have intrinsic value. Adherents of Reformed theology emphasize how Adam was created out of dirt, but that picture of dirt is not the complete picture. An artist can take dirt, make clay, and fashion a work of art. The Greatest Artist did just that when He created Adam. Then He breathed His own spirit into Adam.

Therefore, every person is of inestimable value. All people deserve to be respected, and the overriding dynamic in relationships should be the desire to help everyone live and be treated as children of God. Everyone should value their neighbors as worth more than earthly treasures. Husbands and wives should cherish their spouses as image-bearers of God. Children should be recognized as gifts of the Creator. This Judeo-Christian ethic of the dignity of humanity lies at the foundation of human rights. If all people are created in the image of God, then all people deserve to be treated with respect.

Point 201: What Do People Deserve?

What do people deserve?

A Christian who is consistent with Classical/Reformed theology will answer that people are dust, sinners, deserving of nothing; all people deserve to be cast into hell, and it is only the grace of God that spares anyone from eternal damnation. Augustine believed that every person, including newborn infants, deserve to be condemned to hell. He wrote:

> . . . *man, being of his own will corrupted, and justly condemned, begat corrupted and condemned children.*[117]

When Augustine said, "justly condemned," he was referring to people deserving eternal torment in hell. Notice that Augustine was applying this to newborns! Augustine taught that babies deserve eternal damnation, not because of any sin they have committed, but because they are born as descendants of Adam.

When we talk about what people deserve, we need to consider more than their eternal destiny. What they deserve while on earth is just as revealing.

---

117 Augustine: *The City of God*, 13:14.

How People Are Like God

John Calvin vehemently disagreed with the theology of his contemporary Michael Servetus. When Servetus was sentenced to be burned at the stake as a heretic, Calvin arranged that green wood be used so he would burn slowly and more painfully.[118] Calvin did not act or think as cruelly as he did simply because of the culture in which he lived. His actions were the logical outworking of his belief system. He and Augustine both believed that all non-Christians are evil, deserving of eternal conscious torment.

I do not mean to imply that Christians today who follow the teaching of Augustine or Calvin would be so cruel. Many of the historic ideas of Classical/Reformed theology have been rethought and restructured. Even if some modern Christians believe that all people deserve to be cast into hell, they may live their daily lives by a different standard. I have found modern followers of Reformed theology to be some of the most warm and loving people on earth. However, that warmth is not consistent with their own theology. One day they will say that people are dust, sinners, deserving of hell, but then the next day they may give money to drill wells for those sinners in Africa. They may talk Sunday at church about how every baby comes into this world totally depraved, but then love their "totally depraved" children all week long. They do not live consistent with what they say they believe.

Someone who lives consistent with Father-Son theology will treat all people with respect and dignity. Even those who have committed vile sins deserve respect—because they are created in the image, likeness, and glory of God.

---

118 On the following website you can find a list of quotations from Calvin expressing his understanding that heretics should be painfully put to death: http://socrates58.blogspot.com/2009/05/john-calvins-advocacy-of-capital.html.

Volume IV
Nature of Humanity

Section C
The Original Blessing

After God created Adam and Eve, He blessed them. That was the **original blessing**. The original blessing is more fundamental to human nature than the original sin.

This may sound heretical to followers of Reformed theology, because they rarely, if ever, recognize the original blessing. Furthermore, their entire theology is built around original sin. We will discuss original sin in Sections E and F, but here let's discuss the profound impact God's original blessing has had on humanity and how it continues to this day.

Point 202: God Spoke a Blessing

Immediately after creating Adam and Eve:

> God <u>blessed</u> them; and God said to them, "Be fruitful and multiply, and fill the earth, and subdue it . . . ."
>
> (Gen. 1:28)

This is more than a commission or command. The word *blessing* in this verse comes from the Hebrew word *way-bā-rek*. This Hebrew word implies a creative act.

The same Hebrew word is used in Genesis 1:22, when God blessed the animals swarming in the seas and the birds of the air:

> God <u>blessed</u> them, saying, "Be fruitful and multiply, and fill the waters in the seas, and let birds multiply on the earth."

Systematic Theology for the New Apostolic Reformation

With these words, God was not commissioning the sea animals and birds to be fruitful in the sense of instructing them what to do. God was blessing them in the sense of releasing His power to cause the sea animals and birds to be fruitful, multiply, and fill.

God's words carry creative power. When He speaks, His words continue to produce until they have accomplished all that God intended (Is. 55:11). When God said, "Let the earth bring forth vegetation," He released a force that causes plants to go on reproducing throughout the duration of this world. Because God has spoken His blessing, plants and animals are still living and reproducing today.

So also, God's words over Adam and Eve activated a force pushing humanity to act in the direction of multiplying and filling the earth. However, God's blessing over Adam and Eve was different than His blessing over the animals. God added the word *subdue*. This activated an additional force within humanity.

This positive force to subdue is in each and every descendant of Adam and Eve. It motivates and inspires individuals to advance in their personal life. They want to make progress. It is frustrating for people to be in the same conditions year after year. The same force is at work in society as a whole. Civilization is advancing. We are not stuck where we were 1,000 years ago. We have advanced year by year and will continue to do so.

Envision this positive force to subdue as a wave originating with the voice of God at creation and from that time forward moving ahead with time. Riding the crest of this wave are people who are motivated to subdue all realms of creation and solve the problems facing humanity, e.g., pioneers, inventors, innovators, and researchers. At the front of this wave are those who advance society, like political leaders pointing the way, songwriters expressing the hearts of people, authors writing books, and artists inspiring change. Think of those people who are driven from within to explore new territories, engineer technological advancements, and discover medical breakthroughs. What motivates those people, often at great personal sacrifice? It is God's blessing. It is the force of God's spoken word at creation. It is the blessing of God made manifest.

Point 203: Progress Is a Gift from God

God released into humanity a force to subdue this world. This force includes a drive to solve the problems that face us all.

The Original Blessing

This is one way in which humans are different than animals. Animals do not advance year after year in their understanding of and use of the world. They are basically in the same place that they were 1,000 years ago. Animals may advance in their ability to multiply and fill the earth, but not in their creativity to subdue and steward this world.

Because humanity has been blessed, society will advance. It is as if there is a divine timeline upon which humanity moves in the direction of advancement. For this reason "the fullness of times" arrives when some new invention or breakthrough must happen. It may come through enduring labor and research or as a flash of insight, a dream, or a eureka moment. Repeatedly throughout history, leaders have experienced a burst of insight and energy at the most appropriate moments. If one inventor has a new idea but does not act upon it, some other inventor will act upon a similar idea. If one researcher does not experience a needed breakthrough, some other person in the related field will. Because of God's original blessing, civilization is predestined to advance.

This does not mean every advancement is good. People may use their innovative ideas and entrepreneurial skills to promote evil ends. Some advancements such as nuclear power may be used for good or evil. Yet, if we realize that God is the source of the blessing to advance, we must recognize that progress is part of God's plan. In other words, progress is, generally speaking, good.

Point 204: God's Blessing Is More Powerful than Humanity's Sin

Progress is inevitable because of the original blessing. Humanity has experienced many setbacks, but civilization marches forward. In the future we will continue overcoming the problems that face us. It is only a matter of time until we cure cancer and AIDS. If we run out of petroleum fuel, we will come up with another source of energy. If other resources disappear, we will find alternatives. Our grandchildren will see technological advancements that are beyond our comprehension. Solutions will come because God has spoken: *"be fruitful, multiply, fill, and subdue it."* Nothing can stop the power of God's spoken blessing.

Of course, new problems will arise. This is in part because of the sin that is in the world, but humanity's sin is not powerful enough to stop the power of God's spoken blessing. Wars may come and destroy, but resto-

Systematic Theology for the New Apostolic Reformation

ration will follow. New diseases may develop, but medical breakthroughs will continue.

The original blessing is more powerful than sin, and it will continue until humanity has succeeded at filling and subduing the earth. Some of that subduing may not happen until after the return of Jesus to earth. However, it will happen. God's word to subdue will continue to produce until it is fulfilled.

Point 205: God's Blessing Is Added to Human Nature

It is important to add God's blessing to our understanding of human nature. His blessing is upon all people, including sinners.

In the preceding section, we discussed how people are created in the image, likeness, and glory of God. We also saw how all people are children of God. Those are the most fundamental aspects of human nature. Now we can add to our understanding by saying that people are blessed by God. As a result, people are creative, inventive, industrious, adventurous, and motivated problem solvers. They have everything in their nature necessary to take dominion of this world. This is another aspect of human nature revealed to us in the Bible.

This view that we are developing is very different than the Reformed view which emphasizes that people are first and foremost sinners. Many Reformed teachers will say that people are created in the image and glory of God, but it is so overshadowed by their emphasis on the sinfulness of humanity that it is functionally moved way down the list in their understanding of human nature. Once Reformed teachers establish their idea of sinner, they think of people as enslaved to Satan. Then they conclude that people are cursed because of sin. They read about the consequences of sin and think of humanity with a dark cloud over each and every person.

DIVERGENT VIEWS ON THE NATURE OF HUMANITY

Father-Son Theology	Reformed Theology
1. Created in the image, likeness, and glory of God	1. Sinner
2. Children of God	2. Enslaved to Satan
3. Blessed by God	3. Cursed

The Original Blessing

Of course, Father-Son theology recognizes that everyone sins and there are negative consequences to sin, but here we are prioritizing. If we develop our view of humanity as the Bible reveals it, we will first see the positive side of human nature. Now that we have established the most fundamental aspects of human nature, we can go on to study sin and its effects upon humanity.

Volume IV
Nature of Humanity

Section D
Separated from God?

Classical/Reformed and Father-Son theology agree that there is a break in the relationship between God and humanity, but their understandings of that break are very different from one another.

Point 206: Start with a Biblical Worldview

To understand the view of Father-Son theology, we must start with the biblical cosmology that sees God filling creation. Since God fills creation, it is impossible for Him to be distant.

GOD IS VERY CLOSE TO EVERY HUMAN BEING

Systematic Theology for the New Apostolic Reformation

Paul explained that God *"is not far from each one of us"* (Acts 17:27). In the context of this statement, Paul was talking about Christians and non-Christians. The Psalmist revealed a similar truth:

> *Where can I go from Your Spirit?*
> *Or where can I flee from Your presence?*
> *If I ascend to heaven, You are there;*
> *If I make my bed in Sheol, behold, You are there.*
>
> (Ps. 139:7-8)

No one can escape God. God remains close to all people:

> *"Can a man hide himself in hiding places*
> *So I do not see him?" declares the Lord.*
> *"Do I not fill the heavens and the earth?" declares the Lord.*
>
> (Jer. 23:24)

Once we abandon the dualistic cosmology of Classical/Reformed thought and then embrace the Hebraic-biblical cosmology, we cannot accept any separation between God and humanity having to do with distance. So what is the separation?

Point 207: A Profound Misunderstanding of God's Holiness

As we explained in Section A, Reformed theology associates God's holiness with the ancient Greek philosophically derived attributes of timelessness, otherness, transcendence, and incomprehensibility. Karl Barth even associated God's holiness with His aloofness.[119] Those philosophically derived attributes are about as foreign to God's holiness as can possibly be imagined. *There is nothing in the nature of God that makes Him separate Himself from sin or sinful people.* Please let me prove this.

We defined holiness as sinless purity. This definition has *no* implications of a holy God being transcendent or aloof. In fact, our ultimate example of a holy person is Jesus Christ. He is our Standard. He is the One who gives us a clear revelation of what holiness and godliness is. Jesus was perfectly holy, yet He walked the streets of Jerusalem talking and eating with sinners.

---

119 Barth, *Church Dogmatics*, II/1, p. 361.

Separated from God?

The Jewish religious leaders had a difficult time understanding this. When the religious leaders complained about Jesus associating with sinners, Jesus responded by telling them a parable of a man who had left 99 sheep to seek after one that was lost (Luke 15:1-7). Jesus said this parable to explain His actions and the heart of His Father.

On another occasion, Jesus was visiting the home of a Pharisee when a woman with a sinful past came into the house, poured perfume on Jesus' feet, and kept wiping His feet with her hair. The Pharisee was disgusted with the woman and reasoned that Jesus would never let such a sinful woman touch Him if He truly was a prophet from God (Luke 7:36-50). Jesus had a different understanding of holiness than the Jewish religious leader. Jesus was holy, but His holiness caused Him to reach out to sinners.

The Pharisees thought they could only remain holy by refusing to eat with sinners, touch lepers, or talk to Samaritans. That thinking was reinforced by misunderstandings of some of the religious practices established by Moses. For example, the people were warned not to touch unclean things such as carcasses, lest they become unclean (Lev. 11:24). Today we know that those Mosaic laws served as physical precautions that helped stop the spread of diseases.

When Jesus came, He explained that holiness has nothing to do with contacting physical things:

> *Listen to Me, all of you, and understand: there is nothing outside of the man which can defile him . . . .*
> (Mark 7:14-15)

Jesus went on to explain that only what is in the heart of people can defile them (Mark 7:17-23).

This truth is key. Holiness is something of the heart. God's heart is perfectly holy. For this reason, He is not afraid to have contact with the unholy. His holiness is not contaminated by the presence of sinners. Jesus taught that a holy individual is *not* made unholy by coming in contact with unholy things. On the contrary, unholy things become holy by having contact with holy things. Paul explained this, saying that the believer who is married to an unbeliever sanctifies the unbeliever (1 Cor. 7:14). Light overcomes darkness, not the other way around.

To understand God's holiness, we should associate it with His love rather than aloofness. God's holiness/love moves Him to reach out to sinners, to pursue them, and to be close to them. He goes after sinners like a shepherd goes after lost sheep. God's holiness is like Jesus' holiness.

GOD'S HOLINESS CAUSES HIM TO DRAW CLOSE TO PEOPLE

This truth has been discovered by countless sinners in the world. Many people who were lost in sin discovered God chasing them no matter where their sins carried them. Untold numbers of people have encountered God when they were intoxicated or high on drugs. Many prison chaplains have discovered God manifesting His presence most powerfully in prison where desperate criminals gather to hear about God. This is because God is unaffected by the sins of humanity. He is sovereign, and He reveals Himself wherever He wants whenever He wants, regardless of the condition of people's souls. Let me repeat: *There is nothing in the nature of God that causes Him to separate from sin or sinful people.*

Point 208: God *Can* Look at Sin

There is no huge chasm between God and humanity, even though this is one of the pillars of Reformed theology. In order to support their belief, Christians trained in Reformed thought like to quote the KJV of Habakkuk 1:13:

Separated from God?

Thou art of purer eyes than to behold evil, and canst not look on iniquity:

Reformed teachers use this verse and claim that God is so holy that He has to separate Himself from that which is unholy. In reality, the KJV translates this verse poorly. The NASV conveys the meaning more accurately, saying:

> *Your eyes are too pure to <u>approve of evil</u>,*
> *And You can not look on wickedness <u>with favor</u>.*

Here we see the true meaning: God does not look at wickedness with *"approval"* or *"favor."* Think about this. God cannot approve of sin, but there is no Bible passage that says or implies that God cannot look at sin. In fact, Proverbs 15:3 tells us:

> *The eyes of the Lord are in every place,*
> *<u>Watching the evil</u> and the good.*

God has no problem looking at sin. He looks at it continually.

Point 209: Biblical Support for the Huge Chasm Doctrine?

Reformed thinkers also try to defend their "huge chasm" doctrine by quoting Isaiah 59:2:

> *But your iniquities have made a separation between you and your God,*
> *And your sins have hidden His face from you so that He does not hear.*

Using this verse, adherents of Reformed theology say Adam's sin created a huge chasm between God and all of Adam's descendants.

A closer look at the context of Isaiah 59:2 reveals that Isaiah was talking about his own people, the Jews. He was describing their condition at a specific time in history. The Jews had been disobedient for so many years that God was no longer protecting them from their enemies. Isaiah was explaining to the Jews why God had allowed them to be exiled from the Promised Land.

Indeed, there is a point at which God may withdraw His blessings from people, but God did not abandon His OT people. One verse earlier, Isaiah reassured the Jewish people:

Systematic Theology for the New Apostolic Reformation

Behold, the Lord's hand is not so short
That it cannot save;
Nor is His ear so dull
That it cannot hear.

(Is. 59:1)

In this verse, Isaiah told the Jews that God would still hear their prayers if they simply asked for help. Isaiah assured the Jews that God was still within reach.

In the context of Isaiah 59, God promised that He would continue working with them, send a Redeemer, forgive their sins, and establish a new covenant with them (Is. 59:16-21).

Once readers identify the context of Isaiah 59:2, they immediately see how wrong it is to use this verse the way followers of Reformed theology teach it. This verse does *not* say that all people are alienated from God because of Adam's sin. *It never refers to Adam's sin. It never refers to Adam.* It is referring to the sins of the Jews at a particular time in history. Their own sins separated them from God, but even that separation was not "eternal separation from God." One verse earlier, God reassured the people that He was right there. He was within arm's reach. He could still hear their prayers. God promised that He was willing to respond to their prayers at any moment they would turn to Him.

Contrary to what Reformed theology claims, Isaiah 59:1-2 is not saying that there is a huge separation between God and all of humanity because of Adam's sin.

Point 210: Inconsistencies in the Huge Chasm Doctrine

Once Christians step back and look objectively at the Classical/Reformed huge chasm doctrine, logical inconsistencies become evident. Remember that Classical/Reformed theologians traditionally accept impassibility as an attribute of God.[120] Impassibility means that God acts and is never influenced by what humans do. Yet, at the same time, followers of Augustine and Calvin claim that Adam and Eve's sin caused God to separate Himself from humanity. That is illogical. God cannot be impassible and at the same time influenced by humanity's sin.

---

120 Discussed in I:F:52 and I:G:68.

Separated from God?

If we reject the doctrine of impassibility, we do not have this problem. God can and does respond to what people do. However, we are questioning if God distanced Himself from humanity because of Adam and Eve's sin. The answer is no, but this deserves more investigation.

Point 211: Classical/Reformed Misunderstanding

In order to understand the relationship between non-Christians and God, we need to further dismantle the Classical/Reformed progression of thought concerning the effects of Adam's sin:

The Classical/Reformed Progression of Thought about
Humanity's Eternal Separation from God
1. God told Adam he would die the day he ate the forbidden fruit (Gen. 2:17).
2. Adam did not die physically, so he must have died spiritually.
3. Spiritual death means eternal separation from God.
4. Adam's sin and eternal separation apply to all of Adam's descendants.

In reality, these statements do not logically follow one another, and there is at least one serious error in each of these points.

Consider point number one. God warned Adam and Eve that in the day they ate of the forbidden fruit, *"you shall surely die"* (Gen. 2:17). These words are wrongly translated from the original Hebrew OT. In Hebrew, this verse uses the imperfect form of the verb (you shall die) with the infinitive absolute form of the same verb (dying).[121] Hence the phrase *"you shall surely die"* can be literally translated as *"dying you shall die."* Or as the respected OT Bible scholar, John Walton said, "'you shall surely die' could be better translated 'you will be doomed to die, sentenced to death.'"[122] Notice the ongoing nature of this death followed by the finality of death. Similar terminology is used in Numbers 26:65, where God said that a generation of the Hebrew people would die in the wilderness. Dying they died, but they died over the course of 40 years.

---

121 For a scholarly study on this see: Bruce K. Waltke and M. O'Conner, *An Introduction to Biblical Hebrew Syntax* (Winona Lake: Eisenbrauns, 1990).
122 Kevin P. Emmert, "The Lost World of Adam and Eve," *Christianity Today*, March 2015, p. 44. William A. Henry, III, "Journalism Under Fire," Time, December 12, 1983, 76.

Systematic Theology for the New Apostolic Reformation

The point is that Adam and Eve *did not die* in the sense of an immediate, final event taking place on that day. Instead, they began experiencing death, and that experience ended in death.

Mistranslation of Genesis 2:17
1. God told Adam he would die.

Correct Translation of Genesis 2:17
1. God told Adam, *"Dying you will die,"* or *"You will be sentenced to death."*

This changes everything.

What actually happened when Adam and Eve ate of the forbidden fruit is that they began dying on that very day. That "dying" was an on-going experience of the consequences of sin, which many teachers refer to as *corruption*. The on-going corruption resulting from Adam's sin includes shame, guilt, hopelessness, loneliness, sickness, fear, anxiety, broken relationships, lack of vision, purposelessness, sadness, deception, self-hatred, and so forth. This ongoing corruption can be thought of as a road of death carrying every person toward death and ending in death. This is what God literally warned Adam would happen the day he ate of the forbidden fruit.

To understand the nature of this death, it is helpful to think of the opposite, which is the life that we obtain through Jesus Christ. When people become Christians, they step onto a path of life. They begin experiencing the life of God, because new life is breathed into their hearts, and Jesus came so that believers may experience life and life abundantly (John 10:10). That life includes freedom from shame and guilt, along with the addition of hope, strength, love, companionship, acceptance, vision, purpose, joy, and so forth. The Christian life is to be an ongoing experience of being transformed from glory to glory. That road of life ends in the totality of life, when each Christian sees Jesus and is completely conformed to His image.

As the Christian's time on earth is meant to be a road of life, so the sinner's time on earth is a road of death, ending in the totality of death. Therefore, we should not think of Adam and Eve as dying on the day they ate of the forbidden fruit. Instead, they were sentenced to death and they began dying that day. Adam and Eve stepped onto a road leading to ultimate death. This is what Genesis 2:17 says!

Separated from God?

THE PATH OF DEATH OR LIFE

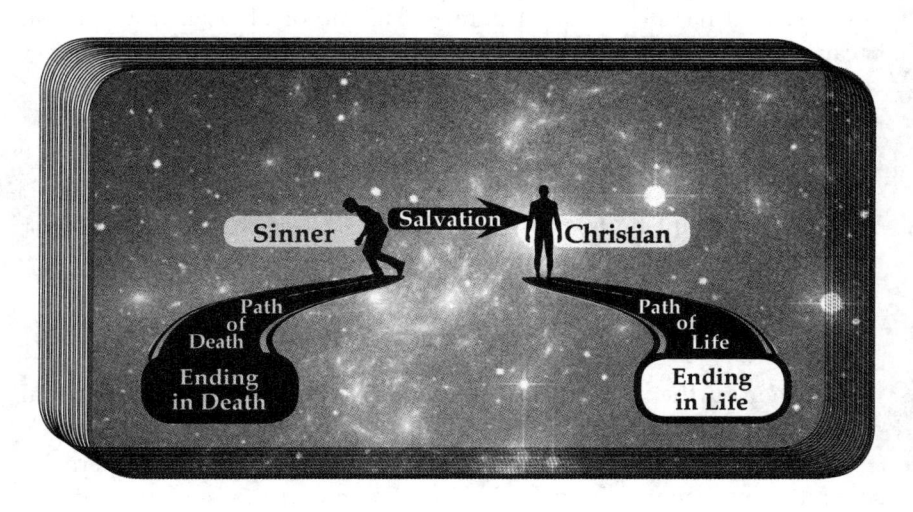

Point 212: Did Adam Die Spiritually?

Once we correct point number 1 in the Classical/Reformed progression of thought concerning the separation between non-Christians and God, then we must change point number 2 if we want to stay logically consistent:

<u>Classical/Reformed Error</u>
2. Adam did not die physically, so he must have died spiritually.

<u>Corrected Understanding</u>
2. Adam did not die physically or spiritually on that day.

The false idea that Adam and Eve died spiritually on the day they sinned has been repeated so many millions of times that followers of that view have a difficult time reconsidering. Yet, Job 34:14-15 tells us:

> *If He should determine to do so,*
> *If He should gather to Himself His spirit and His breath,*
> *All flesh would perish together,*
> *And man would return to dust.*

Systematic Theology for the New Apostolic Reformation

According to this passage, if God withdrew His Spirit and breath from any human being, that person would die physically and turn to dust. The point is: God has not totally separated His life or Himself from people because of Adam's sin. That Classical/Reformed doctrine is not true.

Point 213: Eternally Separated or Alienated God?

Consider point number 3 in the Classical/Reformed progression of thought concerning the separation between non-Christians and God:

3. Spiritual death means eternal separation from God.

John Calvin further defined this Reformed idea by saying that spiritual death means "alienation from God."[123]

The biblical evidence does not reveal that Adam and Eve were eternally separated or alienated from God. After Adam and Eve sinned, God still filled the heavens and earth. Adam and Eve went and hid, but God did not distance Himself from them. Of course, something changed in their relationship with God (which we will explain), but the biblical evidence does not show us a God who was eternally separated or alienated from Adam and Eve.

Anyone wanting to think more deeply about the related issues will ask, "How did Classical/Reformed thinkers come up with this idea of spiritual death resulting from Adam's sin?" Remember that we already saw how there is no biblical basis to say that Adam died spiritually on the day he ate of the forbidden tree. But even if he did, what was the basis on which Classical/Reformed theologians defined spiritual death as eternal separation from God?

Their understanding of spiritual death is a philosophical construct that developed from a dualistic cosmology. As we have explained, leaders such as Plato, Plotinus, and Augustine embraced an image of God who is totally other and infinitely distant from humanity. Of course, Classical/Reformed teachers say that God reached across the distance, but if that link between God and humanity is severed, then the chasm separating God from humanity is infinite—or so Classical/Reformed thinkers say.

---

[123] Calvin, *Institutes*, I:15:4.

Separated from God?

THE CLASSICAL/REFORMED UNDERSTANDING:
ADAM'S SIN TOTALLY SEPARATES GOD AND HUMANITY

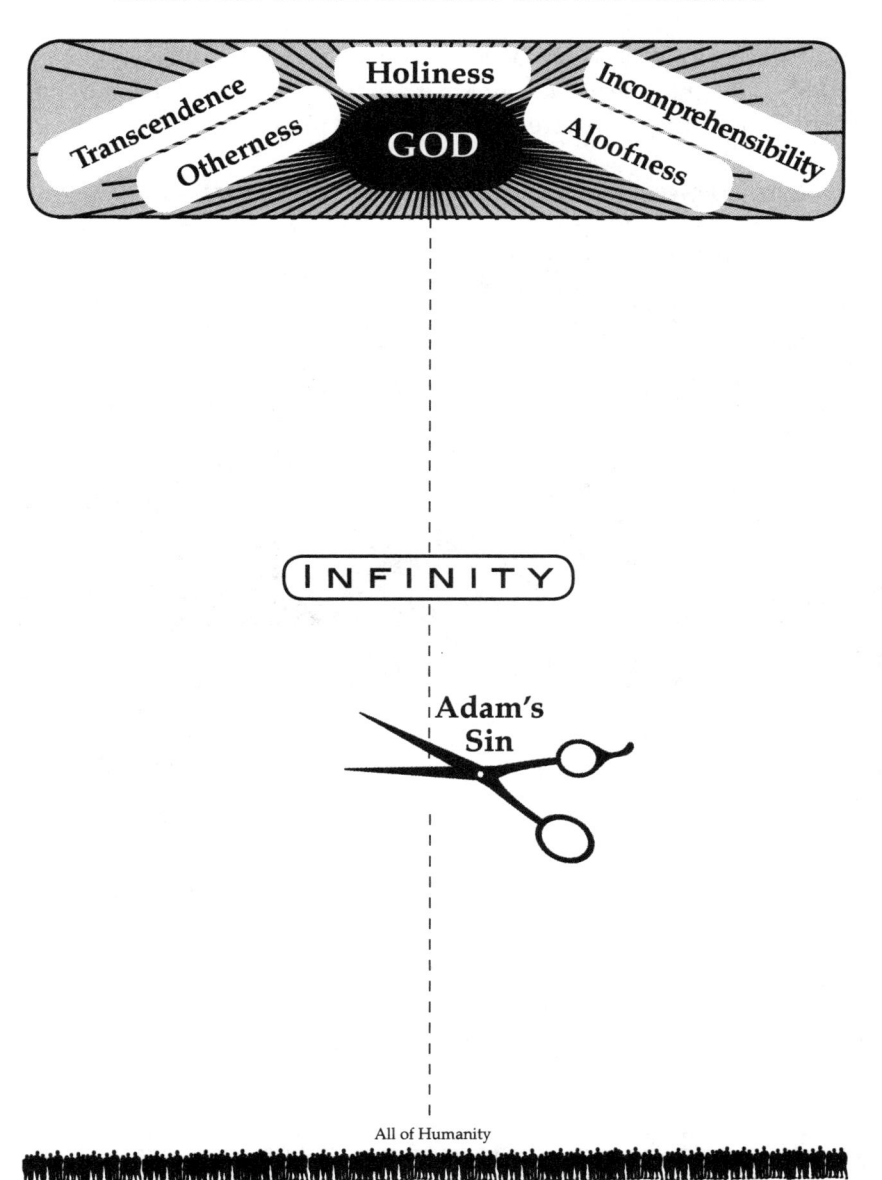

- Transcendence
- Otherness
- Holiness
- Incomprehensibility
- Aloofness

GOD

INFINITY

Adam's Sin

All of Humanity

Systematic Theology for the New Apostolic Reformation

If we are going to develop our theology independently of the Western dualistic foundation, we will conclude that God is very close to every human being (Acts 17:27). The only point at which eternal separation or alienation from God could happen is on judgment day, when God may say, "Depart from Me." Eternal separation and alienation from God is an entirely different state of existence that can only happen in the Lake of Fire which is also called hell. (We will discuss hell in IX:D).

Eternal Separation Can Only Happen on Judgment Day[124]

Until the final judgment day, God remains at work within the life of every sinner. God is shining His love, letting the sun and rain come upon the righteous and unrighteous (Matt. 5:45). God is not the kind of God who abandons humanity or severs people from His love before they have been judged. In fact, God *loves* sinners.

---

124 This diagram shows hell outside of creation, but we actually do not know if hell is within or outside of creation. Genesis 1:1 tells us the God created the heavens and the earth, but that does not reveal anything about hell.

Separated from God?

Let me state it clearly: It is impossible for God to be eternally separated from any living human being. They would not be alive if God separated Himself. This is what the Bible teaches (Job 34:14-15).

Point 214: Abandoning the Huge Chasm Doctrine

Christians under the influence of Classical/Reformed theology have bought into the huge chasm doctrine. They have had corresponding misinterpretations of three Bible verses (Gen. 2:17, Hab. 1:13, and Is. 59:2) drilled into their minds. We have seen how these three Bible verses do not teach the huge chasm doctrine. Followers of Classical/Reformed theology assume that there are other verses that teach the same concept. In reality, *there are no other verses* (except, perhaps, Romans 5:12 which we will discuss in Sections E and F). If there were other relevant verses, Classical/Reformed teachers would use them. Reformed theology is wrong. Humanity is not eternally separated from God because of Adam's sin.

Consider Cornelius in the NT. He was not a Christian (nor a Jew). Acts 10:14 tells us that Cornelius' prayers ascended to God. From this testimony it is reasonable to think that God answers the prayers of non-Christians. In reality, every prayer that God answered during OT times was prayed by a descendant of Adam who was not saved. Yes, God hears and answers the prayers of non-Christians. In fact, there are millions of people in the world today, whom we would not consider Christians, but who will testify to some time in their lives when God answered their prayers. This is true, because God loves sinners.[125]

The huge-chasm doctrine is unbiblical. Yet, it is popular today partly because it serves evangelists well in their presentation of the gospel. It offers a clear picture of people being separated from God, which then allows evangelists to give the solution which is Jesus Christ. Yet, the usefulness of a doctrine does not make it biblical. The huge chasm doctrine cannot be developed from a direct reading of the Bible. So if we are going to build a systematic theology based on the Bible, then we will have to leave that doctrine out.

Please do not misunderstand what I am explaining here. Sin *has* caused a break in the relationship between God and humanity. Furthermore, all

---

[125] We know that sin can hinder a person's prayers from being answered, but it is not Adam's sin that hinders their prayers. It is their own sins (1 Pet. 3:12).

Systematic Theology for the New Apostolic Reformation

people need to be reconciled to God, and Jesus is the only Mediator. However, the God to whom we must be reconciled is very close.

It is also important to know that the break in the relationship is primarily on the part of humanity, not God. Let me explain.

Point 215: Shame Created a Separation!

When Adam and Eve ate of the tree of the knowledge of good and evil, the most significant consequence was that they came to know good and evil. This is exactly what God said changed: *"Behold, the man has become like one of Us, knowing good and evil"* (Gen. 3:22). Genesis 3:7 tells us, *"Then the eyes of both of them were opened . . . ."* Because they knew good and evil, they knew that God was good and that they had sinned.

Knowing the difference between God and them, they became ashamed: *"they knew that they were naked"* (Gen. 3:7). In Genesis 3:8, we read:

> *They heard the sound of the Lord God walking in the garden in the cool of the day, and the man and his wife hid themselves from the presence of the Lord . . . .*

Adam and Eve were ashamed so they tried to distance themselves from God.

God did not distance Himself from Adam and Eve. He did the opposite. He pursued them. Because Adam and Eve were ashamed, God made garments for them to cover themselves (Gen. 3:21). The garments were not for God's benefit. They were for Adam and Eve to feel less ashamed.

Before Adam and Eve ate of the tree of the knowledge of good and evil, they could not see the difference (in relation to holiness) between themselves and God. Before they sinned, they were unashamed to be in the presence of God. They causally and freely talked with God, but once they ate of that tree they could see what goodness is, and they could see that they did not measure up. So *"the man and his wife hid themselves from the presence of the Lord God"* (Gen. 3:8). Shame caused them to try to separate themselves from God.

Separated from God?

SEPARATION RESULTING FROM SHAME

At the end of Genesis 3, we read about God putting Adam and Eve out of the garden so they would not eat of the tree of life, but God did not abandon Adam and Eve. The first verse in Genesis 4, shows us Eve giving birth to a son *"with the help of the Lord."* Throughout chapter 4, God interacts with Cain and Abel. There is no evidence of God distancing Himself from Adam's descendants. In fact, a central theme of the OT is God's relationship with people. He declared to the Hebrews, "I will be Your God and you will be My people." God did not abandon humanity because of Adam's sin. There was no chasm of infinity created between God and humanity. The separation that we see in the Bible was on the part of people who hid in shame in the presence of God.

Point 216: Guilt/Law Versus Shame/Relationship

Embracing this understanding that shame plays the major role in the separation between God and humanity is difficult for Christians trained in Western society to grasp. This is partly because of a Western cultural bias. Let me explain.

Systematic Theology for the New Apostolic Reformation

Western civilization is known as a guilt/law culture, while Eastern civilization is known as a shame/relationship culture. Guilt is typically thought of as an emotion resulting from actions of wrongdoing or violation of some law. Hence, guilt is associated with law. In contrast, shame is a feeling of loss of right standing in the eyes of oneself or significant others. Hence, shame is associated with relationships and, in particular, those relationships involving others whose opinions are valued. With guilt, one's actions are determined to be wrong. With shame, one's self-image is brought into question.[126]

Although guilt and shame are usually considered negative emotions, cultural anthropologists who study this subject say that no society could maintain order without them. Guilt and shame shape behavior, because people act so as to avoid these emotions.

Every culture incorporates guilt and shame to some degree, but Western civilization is more deeply grounded in guilt/law, while Eastern civilization is more deeply grounded in shame/relationship.

Because we Western Christians are Western, we tend to read the Bible through the guilt/law lens. We like to think that we take the Bible and believe it as it is written, but all of us have cultural biases. Hence, we Western Christians tend to force our theological thinking into the guilt/law construct. We talk much about humanity's problem being sin, and when we think about sin we see it as law-breaking behavior. With our cultural orientation, it is natural for Western Christians to focus on sin, guilt, and law.

In contrast, Christians raised in the Eastern and Middle Eastern parts of this world tend to read the Bible through the shame/relationship lens. Of course, Western Christians may choose to ignore this difference and simply decide that their way of thinking is the correct way, but that is a mistake. The Middle Eastern way of thinking about shame/relationship is more closely associated with the culture of the Bible than the Western way of thinking about guilt/law is. Furthermore, the shame/relationship way of thinking actually dominates a larger percentage of the world's population today than the Western way of thinking. Because of this, Christians in Eastern parts of the world read the same Bible we read, but they often come to different conclusions than we do.

---

126 Further teaching on this can be found in: Jackson Wu, *Saving God's Face* (Pasadena, CA: WCIU Press, 2012) and Bruce K. Waltke and M. O'Conner, *An Introduction to Biblical Hebrew Syntax* (Winona Lake: Eisenbrauns, 1990).

Separated from God?

The answer is not to abandon our Western way thinking. No one is capable of abandoning the cultural biases in which they have been raised. However, we can allow ourselves to be suspicious of our own traditions and then listen to the thoughts of others whose culture is different. This is what I now ask you to do. Since most of my readers are Westerners, please consider looking at humanity's problem through the lens of our brothers and sisters who live in the Eastern and Middle Eastern parts of the world.

Point 217: A Legal Relationship Versus Family Relationship

If we read the Bible through the shame/relationship lens rather than the guilt/law lens, we will conclude that the break in the relationship between God and humanity is more the result of shame than guilt.

Let me make this clear by telling you about an experience in my own family. As a teenager, our youngest son reached out to a younger boy from a troubled home. For several years our son mentored the younger boy, whom I will call Micah. In some ways Micah became part of our family, often staying at our home several days each week, and then in his own home with his mother the rest of the week. After our son grew up, he moved away, but Micah continued being part of our family.

One day my wife and I were out of town, so Micah had no supervision. While we were gone, Micah and a friend of his stole my pickup truck. They were much too young to drive, so the local police quickly spotted and captured them. A judge ordered Micah to spend a short time in a juvenile detention center. After he served his time, the legal system no longer held anything against him. Micah paid his debt and was justified in the eyes of the law. So far this illustration reveals the incident through the lens of guilt/law.

Now consider this same incident through the eyes of one grounded in a culture of shame/relationship. The real drama in this story did not involve Micah's law-breaking behavior, guilt, the judge, or the penalty. The most life-transforming dynamics took place between Micah and me. I had become like a father to him. He stole my pickup. He knew he disappointed me, and he was filled with shame. The suffering he experienced in the detention center had little to do with confinement. It was more about his feelings of shame while in there. When Micah was released, I wanted the relationship restored, but he was too ashamed to be in my presence.

Systematic Theology for the New Apostolic Reformation

Compare Micah's relationship with the judge to his relationship with me. The judge was very objective, simply enforcing the law. The judge had no real relationship with Micah, and Micah's act of stealing my pickup did not change their relationship with each other in any significant way. However, the relationship Micah had with me was dramatically changed—not because I was angry at him, but because Micah was too ashamed to see me.

The point is that Western civilization is a guilt/law culture. Hence, we Westerners read the Bible through that lens. Whenever there is misbehavior we focus on the guilt resulting from violating a law. In contrast, whenever there is misbehavior in a shame/relationship culture, the people involved focus on the damage to the relationships and the resulting shame in the life of the offender.

Point 218: God Is a Father

This discussion ties into the overall theme of this book. How do we understand God? Is He a Judge having a sterile relationship with the law standing between Him and humanity, or is He a Father wanting face-to-face relationship? This distinction is seen in the Bible as God was revealed on Mount Sinai as a Judge who gave the Law, but in the NT, Jesus revealed God as a Father. Of course, God is both a Judge and Father, but the Father image is that which Jesus revealed to us so we must give it precedence.[127]

In Volume V, *Evil, Sin, and Suffering*, and Volume VI, *Soteriology*, we will have much to discuss concerning how God acts as both a Judge and a Father. For now, I ask you not to limit your thinking to the Western guilt/law lens. Shame was the predominant element that separated Adam and Eve from God. Shame also plays the predominant role in separating people from God today. Hence, the separation between humanity and God is primarily on humanity's side, not God's.

Point 219: Not Wanting Sins Exposed Creates a Separation!

Jesus talked about another element separating people from God. It is related to shame, but more focused on people wanting to keep their sins

---

127 This precedence to God as Father was explained in I:E:47.

Separated from God?

hidden. Jesus said:

> . . . men loved the darkness rather than the Light, for their deeds were evil. For everyone who does evil hates the Light, and does not come to the Light for fear that his deeds will be exposed.
> (John 3:19-20)

People do not want their evil deeds exposed so they distance themselves from God. Of course, no one can literally distance themselves, but people deceive themselves into thinking that they have hidden from God.

We see this with the Hebrews shunning the presence of God as He manifested on Mount Sinai (Ex. 20:18-19). God's light and glory was so grand that it exposed darkness. Even Isaiah had a difficult time beholding the light and glory revealed from the Lord in His throne room (Is. 6:1-7).

Notice that in these cases it was not God who distanced Himself. God actually desired to reveal Himself to the Hebrews and Isaiah. They were sinners but God did not pull away from them because of His holiness. It was they who pulled away from God.

Point 220: Wanting to Continue in Sin Creates Separation

In the Scripture passage last quoted (John 3:19-20), Jesus pointed out how people avoid the light lest their sins be exposed. He also revealed how they shun the light because they want to continue in sin. They simply do not want to obey God so they try to stay away from Him.

We can see this in the story of Jonah as he fled from the presence of the Lord. Jonah did not want to preach to the city of Nineveh so he ran from God (Jonah 1:1-3). So also today people turn away from God because of their unwillingness to obey. They cannot serve two masters. Their heart cannot be turned toward God and toward sin. Therefore, those who desire to continue in sin choose to turn away from God.

So we have identified three reasons people try to distance themselves from God:

1. Shame
2. Don't want their sins exposed
3. Want to continue in sin

Systematic Theology for the New Apostolic Reformation

The most important point is that each of these reasons point to people separating themselves from God, not the other way around.

Separation Results from Shame, the Avoidance of Exposure to Light, and the Desire to Sin

Notice that we discovered each of these reasons as we read specific Bible passages. They did not develop out of a philosophical/theological construct. The plain truth is that there are no Scriptures showing us God separating Himself from people (other than in hell).

Point 221: The Nature of Father-God

Finally, concerning this topic of separation, reconsider your concept of God. He is a Father.

In the illustration concerning Micah stealing my pickup, I explained how shame caused him to avoid me. He also had a wrong concept of me. Micah thought I would be angry at him. He did not know that I had a father-heart toward him. I was disappointed but my heart toward him did not change.

God is more of a loving Father than any human father can be. He so loved the world that He gave His only begotten Son. When people sin,

Separated from God?

He may become angry at the sin because of the destruction it brings to humanity and relationships, but Father-God does not separate Himself. He is a Big Boy. He is unmoved. There is nothing in the nature of God that makes Him distance Himself from that which is unholy. Father-God is like Jesus. He pursues sinners. If possible, God would let an adulteress wash His feet with her hair. It would not bother Him, because nothing from outside can defile Him. In fact, He would love an adulteress washing His feet. That is the kind of God He is.

Volume IV
Nature of Humanity

Section E
The Original Sin

Classical/Reformed theology identifies Adam's sin as a catastrophic "fall." It is where humanity went wrong and became alienated from God. It is the turning point where all of Adam's descendants plunged into evil and destruction. According to Classical/Reformed theology, all of humanity is eternally alienated from God and totally depraved because of Adam's sin. In contrast, Father-Son theology recognizes the fall and sees that Adam's sin has influenced all of humanity, however, we need to look more carefully at what that influence is.

Point 222: The Origin of Original Sin

In the writings of the Church fathers, the earliest reference to original sin is from Irenaeus, the bishop of Lyons, in his famous work, *Against Heresies* (c. 180 AD). This is important to note because it reveals how the 1st century Church had no doctrine of original sin.[128] Later, Cyprian (c. 208–258), the bishop of Carthage, taught that the stain of original sin could only be removed through water baptism. It was Augustine who formalized these doctrines in the 5th century.

Augustine believed that Adam's sin released a moral corruption so devastating that every child deserves to be condemned. He wrote:

> ... man ... begat corrupted and condemned children.[129]

---
128 Some readers may object to this statement because they interpret Paul's words in Romans 5:12 as teaching original sin, but later in this section, we will show how wrong that interpretation is.
129 Augustine: *The City of God,* 13:14.

Systematic Theology for the New Apostolic Reformation

In Augustine's mind, every baby is born radically selfish, totally subject to human passions and desires.

These beliefs came to the forefront of Christian thought as Augustine engaged in intellectual battles with a British monk named Pelagius (c. 354–c. 420). Taking the opposing view, Pelagius taught that infants are born innocent, and as they grow, they develop the ability to choose good or evil. He argued that people are created in God's image and are morally free.

Augustine's and Pelagius' views became so divisive that supporters of both views rioted in the streets of Rome in 417 AD. Two years earlier, two councils of bishops in Palestine declared Pelagius and his views as orthodox. However, two opposing councils of African bishops, under the direction of Augustine, condemned Pelagius' teachings. Soon afterward, Pope Innocent sided with Augustine. When the pope died, his successor, Pope Zosimus, first declared Pelagius' teachings orthodox, but later reversed his decision. The battle continued for more than ten years, with Pelagius' devout follower, Julian of Eclanum, taking over after the death of Pelagius.[130]

Augustine ultimately won the battle in the eyes of the Roman Catholic Church, but Church leaders did not fully embrace Augustine's teachings. Pope Gregory softened Augustine's negative view by saying that people inherit Adam's sin, but not his guilt.

Having described the view of Roman Catholicism (the largest denomination in the world), it is also worth mentioning the view of the Orthodox Church (the second largest denomination). Orthodox teachers prefer to use the term *ancestral sin* rather than *original sin* to avoid the Roman Catholic belief that Adam's sin is passed on to the generations to follow. Orthodox teachers will say that neither Adam's sin nor his guilt are passed on to humanity. What happens as a result of Adam's sin is that all of humanity suffers the consequences of sin, which is death and corruption (not sin or guilt).

There has been much discussion and disagreement throughout Church history concerning the nature of humanity, but Augustine's negative view has most profoundly influenced Roman Catholicism and Protestant Christianity.

---

130 Elaine Pagels, *Adam, Eve, and the Serpent* (New York, NY: Vintage Books, 1988), p. 129-132.

The Original Sin

Point 223: Augustine's Errors Concerning Original Sin

Today as we analyze Augustine's reasoning, it is easy to identify his major errors concerning original sin.

Even though I will point out those errors, do not assume that I am agreeing with Augustine's opponent, Pelagius. Today we have very few of Pelagius' writings, because they were mostly destroyed or simply disappeared.[131] What we know of Pelagius today primarily comes from the surviving writings of his opponents. It is difficult to sort out truth from error when only one side of an argument is available. Pelagius was accused of teaching that people could be good enough to get to heaven without the redemptive work of Jesus Christ. If Pelagius taught this, he was wrong. Jesus is the only mediator between God and humanity. No one will get to heaven apart from Jesus Christ. However, we do not even know if Pelagius taught contrary to this or if it was just the accusations of his opponents.[132] It seems clear that Pelagius taught that babies are born innocent, unstained by Adam's sin. However, this does not necessarily mean that he was teaching that people can get to heaven apart from Jesus.

We do have the writings of Augustine, and he is the one who most profoundly influenced Western Christianity. As we look at Augustine's understanding of human nature, there are two glaring errors that immediately become evident.

Point 224: Conceived in Sin?

First, Augustine held a very negative view of sexual relations, even in marriage. He reasoned that the passion and lust that arise during intercourse are beyond the control of the individual and, therefore, evil. Augustine believed that the passions involved with the sexual act are the avenue through which sin is passed from generation to generation.[133]

---

131 In recent years some writings accredited to Pelagius have been found, most significantly, his commentary on Romans.
132 Pelagius denied this in some of his personal letters.
133 One of several places Augustine laid out this pattern of thought is, *The City of God*, 14:16-26. The Council of Trent (1545–63) gave the official stamp to the idea that original sin was transferred from parent to child by propagation, i.e., the sexual act that lead to conception.

Systematic Theology for the New Apostolic Reformation

Augustine tried to support his doctrine using Psalm 51:5:

Behold, I was brought forth in iniquity,
And in sin my mother conceived me.

Using this verse, Augustine taught that every human being is conceived in sin because their conception was a sinful act involving uncontrollable passions between the parents.

In reality, sexual intimacy is a wonderful gift of God meant to be experienced and enjoyed in marriage. Furthermore, Augustine's idea that sexual passion is the avenue through which Adam's sin is passed generation to generation seems foolish today. Foolish because of our modern medical practice of in vitro fertilization, which is the process by which egg cells are fertilized by sperm outside the body. If Augustine was correct, then babies resulting from in vitro fertilization, which involves no sexual passion, would be born without original sin. No reasonable Bible teacher today would accept this implication of Augustine's teaching.

We also should reject Augustine's misunderstanding of Psalm 51, because David's words, *"in sin my mother conceived me,"* actually apply to David's mother. She was in sin at his conception. To see this, substitute some other words for "in sin." For example, "in shame my mother conceived me" or "in joy my mother conceived me." If we read either of these statements, we immediately know that the shame or joy point to the experience of David's mother. "In sin" is an adverbial phrase qualifying the verb, not the object. They point to David's mother, not David.

To understand this it is helpful to know that later rabbis taught that David was conceived in an adulterous act.[134] David's father was Jesse, but the Bible reveals nothing about David's mother—neither name nor origin. This is significant because family lineages—especially of the kingly line—were of key importance in Hebrew thinking of the time.

The idea of David as an illegitimate child is supported by an incident we read about in 1 Samuel 16:1-13. God told the prophet Samuel to go to the town of Bethlehem to anoint one of Jesse's sons to be the next king. When Jesse was asked to bring his sons to Samuel, Jesse did not even bring David. Further, David held the role of shepherd boy. This was considered the lowest family position. As a boy assigned to care for the sheep, it was

---

[134] *Ellicott's Commentary on the Whole Bible* (Grand Rapids, MI: Zondervan, 1981) Vol. IV, p. 161; see also, Arthur Penrhyn Stanley, *The History of the Jewish Church* (New York: Scribner, Armstrong, and Co, 1878) Vol. II, Lecture XXII, p. 50-51, note.

The Original Sin

very unlikely that David would ever have a chance to receive an education or be raised to a position of stature. He was the rejected son.

David's position made him the fitting type of Christ, who also lived under the accusation of being illegitimate, since people knew that Mary had conceived before being married.

These facts lead us to believe that David was an illegitimate son, but it is impossible to *prove* that Jesse committed adultery. Yet, from another perspective, we can prove that David was illegitimate. The Law of Moses barred those of illegitimate birth—even unto the tenth generation—from entering into the assembly of God:

> *A bastard shall not enter into the congregation of the LORD; even to his tenth generation shall he not enter into the congregation of the LORD.*
>
> (Deut. 23:2 KJV)

David was a ninth generation descendant of Perez, the bastard son of Judah and Tamar. Further disqualifying David was the fact that Ruth, David's great-grandmother was a Moabite convert. This disqualified him from entering into the assembly of God because the same law of exclusion applied to Moabites (Deut. 23:3). These facts may seem insignificant to modern Western people who live in a society where illegitimate births are common, but for Hebrew society, purity of Hebrew lineage was of upmost importance—especially for kings.

In light of these historical facts, consider David's words, *"in sin my mother conceived me"* (Ps. 51:5). If people approach this verse with the presupposition that people are totally evil, they could read into David's words that everyone is a sinner from conception. However, if they read David's words from the actual position in which David found himself, they will come to an entirely different conclusion.

Psalm 51 is a record of David's response after being confronted by the prophet Nathan concerning the sins he committed, namely adultery with Bathsheba and the murder of Bathsheba's husband (2 Sam. 12:1-15). Throughout Psalm 51, David was crying out to God in repentance. His heart was gushing out the bitter cry of a man crushed by guilt. In that cry, David declared how unworthy he was; he was not born of royalty, but was actually an illegitimate son, not deserving to be among God's covenant people.

Systematic Theology for the New Apostolic Reformation

Many Christians have not been taught this truth about David. Proponents of the traditional doctrine of original sin do not like it to be known because it undermines their doctrine of people being born evil. In reality, Psalm 51:5 reveals nothing about the condition of all humanity. The verse is talking about David's conception. Once we understand this, we can see how wrong it is to take David's statement and apply it to every human being throughout all of time. David was conceived in sin. There is nothing in this verse to lead the reader to believe that you and I are conceived in sin. Therefore, it is wrong to use Psalm 51:5 as a description of every person's nature.

Point 225: Augustine's Errors Concerning Romans 5:12

The second—and most significant—error in Augustine's understanding of human nature becomes evident as we learn about the Latin translation of the NT which Augustine used. When the Greek NT was translated into Latin, mistakes were made. Most importantly for the topic we are discussing, Augustine had a mistranslation of Romans 5:12.

The modern NASV accurately translates Romans 5:12 as follows:

> *Therefore, just as through one man sin entered into the world, and death through sin, and so death spread to all men, <u>because all sinned</u>.*

Notice the last phrase says, *"because all sinned."* This leads us to believe that death spread to all of humanity because each person sins.

Augustine's Latin translation did not say, "because all sinned" but rather *"in quo omnes peccaverunt."* This means "in whom all have sinned." From his mistranslation of Romans 5:12, Augustine concluded that *all of humanity was in Adam* when he sinned. Augustine wrote:

> But even the infants, not personally in their own life, but according to the common origin of the human race, have all broken God's covenant in that one <u>in whom all have sinned</u>.[135]

There is a profound difference between "because all sinned" and "in whom all sinned." The first tells us that each and every person sins, and hence, suffers the consequences of sin. The second tells us that all human

---

135 Augustine, *The City of God*, 16:27.

The Original Sin

beings suffer the consequences of sin because they were in Adam when he sinned.

Today we know that Augustine had an inferior translation of the Bible. His Latin translation of Romans 5:12 was wrong. We did *not* all sin in Adam. At this point, our entire understanding of human nature changes. It would be dishonest to continue teaching Augustine's conclusion when we know he arrived at that conclusion based on misinformation.

Point 226: The Absurdity of Augustine's Reasoning

Augustine's misunderstanding of Romans 5:12 is so deeply seated in many branches of Western Christianity that today it is difficult to challenge successfully. Perhaps if you see how illogical Augustine's reasoning was you will be able to think independently of it.

Augustine taught that all of Adam's descendants were in Adam when he sinned. From this, Augustine reasoned that the sin and death that Adam and Eve experienced were passed into their descendants, "for nothing else could be born of them than that which they themselves had been."[136] If Augustine was right in this pattern of thought, then the same would apply to people today and their descendants. Parents could only pass on to their descendants "that which they themselves had been." Consider what this would mean.

A fundamental truth of the gospel is that Christians are forgiven and spiritually alive (Rom. 8:10). So then, if two Christians have a child, is that child born with Adam's sin? According to Augustine's reasoning, parents could only pass on "that which they themselves had been." If all of Adam's descendants were in Adam when he sinned, then all of the descendants of Christian parents were in those parents when they came alive in Christ.

Do not misunderstand what I am saying. I am *not* saying that some babies are born spiritually dead while others are born spiritually alive. I am merely pointing out the absurdity of Augustine's reasoning. If sin and death are passed inherently into the nature of one's descendants, then Adam's sin and death could not be passed through a generation that has been forgiven, cleansed, and made a new creature in Christ. The only reasonable conclusion is that sin and death are *not* passed like an inheritance between generations.

---

136 Augustine: *The City of God*, 13:3.

Systematic Theology for the New Apostolic Reformation

Point 227: Various Views on Original Sin

Augustine's reasoning about original sin is losing acceptance on many fronts. One front is with those Christians who have embraced the theory of evolution. I already stated my view that Bible-believing Christians should accept the theory of evolution as a theory of biological development, but be critical of it as a theory of origins.[137] Yet, many Christians are more comfortable than I am with accepting the theory as an explanation concerning the origins of all plants and animals. If they are going to be consistent with the theory as taught by evolutionists today, then they must reject the doctrine of original sin. This is true because the theory of evolution sees mutations occurring in individuals, but evolution happening in communities. Therefore, according to evolutionists, the human race was never just one person or even a couple. According to the theory of evolution, Adam had to have been surrounded by a large population, and hence, he was just one contributor to the gene pool. The implications of this negate the doctrine that Adam's sin was passed into all of humanity.

However, most Christians who have rejected Augustine's reasoning do it on theological grounds. All evangelicals endeavor to develop their doctrines from the Bible, but we can identify among them the entire spectrum of views concerning original sin and the nature of humanity. Some churches hold to Augustine's negative view while other denominations do not even believe in original sin. Among these denominations are The Christian Church, The Church of Christ,[138] the Seventh-day Adventists, and many of the churches in the Anabaptist tradition.

The best known leader who rejected the doctrine of original sin is Charles Finney (1792–1875). Finney openly expressed his disbelief in original sin, along with its implications of inherited depravity. In *Finney's Systematic Theology*, he wrote the following concerning the doctrine of inherited depravity:

> It is a relic of heathen philosophy, and was foisted in among the doctrines of Christianity by Augustine, as everyone will know who takes the trouble to examine for himself.[139]

---

137 III:G:181-184.
138 Members of The Church of Christ do not like their association of churches to be called a denomination, nor do they claim to all have one standard set of doctrines, but the rejection of the doctrine of original sin is very common among them.
139 Charles Finney, *Finney's Systematic Theology*, compiled and edited by Dennis Carroll, Bill Nicely, and L. G. Parkhurst, Jr. (Minneapolis, MN: Bethany House Publishers, 1994), pp. 261-263.

The Original Sin

Finney was the president of Oberlin College and the most prominent preacher of the Second Great Awakening in the United States.

I am not suggesting that we should completely discard the doctrine of original sin. I am just asking you to reconsider *how the sin of Adam influences Adam's descendants.*

Volume IV
Nature of Humanity

Section F
Rethinking Original Sin

It is time to rethink what influence Adam's sin has had on the world.

Point 228: Sin Came into the World

Our understanding of the influence of Adam's sin pivots on our interpretation of Romans 5:12:

> *Therefore, just as through one man sin entered into the world, and death through sin, and so death spread to all men, because all sinned.*
>
> (Rom. 5:12)

Augustine interpreted this verse to mean that sin and death came into the inherited nature of humanity.

Consider an alternative understanding. In Romans 5:12, notice where sin went as a result of Adam's sin. We are told that *"sin entered into the world."* The word *world* has been translated from the Greek word *kosmos*. This Greek word can refer to humanity, but it can also refer to creation, the earth, or corrupt society. Most often it is translated as "world," referring to creation.

In Romans 5:12, *kosmos* must be referring to creation because three chapters later, Paul explained that *"creation was subjected to futility"* (Rom. 8:20). Paul also talked about a day when *"creation itself also will be set free from its slavery to corruption"* (Rom. 8:21). So then, we see Paul's understanding that sin influenced all of creation, not just Adam's descendants. This implies that Adam's sin came into all of the world in the sense of creation.

Systematic Theology for the New Apostolic Reformation

Sin and Death Came into the World

Please give this understanding a chance. Not only is it more in keeping with Paul's understanding throughout the Book of Romans, but it also leads us to conclusions that correspond better with several other Bible passages.

Point 229: Sin as Outside of Humanity

Consider what God said to Cain, the immediate descendant of Adam and Eve:

> *And if you do not do well, sin is crouching at the door; and its desire is for you, but you must master it.*
>
> (Gen. 4:7)

Notice that God did not say, "Sin is inside of you because your parents have sinned." God warned Cain that sin was *"crouching at the door"*; that is, sin was outside of him waiting to come into his life.

Rethinking Original Sin

Point 230: The Power of Sin and Death

Think of sin like a corrupting force that permeates creation. Sin has its own power to seek out and destroy. Paul wrote, *"for sin . . . deceived me, and through it killed me"* (Rom. 7:11). Sin is not a passive entity. It is actively working to corrupt humanity.

In Romans 5:12, Paul explained that death came through sin. Now sin and death are active and powerful. Paul took this further, explaining that ever since Adam sinned, sin and death have *"reigned"*:

"death reigned"	(Rom. 5:14)
"death reigned"	(Rom. 5:17)
"sin reigned in death."	(Rom. 5:21)

No one escapes the influence of sin and death. Paul referred to the *"law of sin and death"* (Rom. 8:2). This law is comparable to the law of gravity: inescapable and all-inclusive. Everyone will sin. Everyone will die.

BECAUSE OF ADAM'S SIN, SIN AND DEATH REIGN OVER HUMANITY

As the Orthodox Church has taught for over 1,500 years, all of humanity experiences corruption because of Adam's sin. Corruption includes all of the consequences of sin, including shame, guilt, fear,

Systematic Theology for the New Apostolic Reformation

hopelessness, loneliness, sickness, anxiety, broken relationships, lack of vision, purposelessness, sadness, deception, self-hatred, and so forth. This corruption is at work upon every human being.

Point 231: How People Are "Made Sinners"

This understanding, that sin and death came into the world (*kosmos*), rather than into the inherited nature of humanity, has vast implications in our theology. For example, consider Romans 5:19:

> *For as through the one man's disobedience the many were made sinners, even so through the obedience of the One the many will be made righteous.*

Christians who follow Augustine's understanding that Adam's sin released sin into the inherited nature of humanity interpret this verse to mean that all people are made sinners because they inherited a sin nature from Adam.

In contrast, Christians who understand Romans 5:12 to mean that sin came into creation conclude that all people are made sinners because sin reigns over humanity. Hence, people are *"made sinners"* because sin is an active power corrupting and ruling over everyone.

Point 232: How Does Sin Enter a Person?

If sin came into the world as into creation, how does sin get inside of people? James explained:

> *But each one is tempted when he is carried away and enticed by his own lust. Then when lust has conceived, it gives birth to sin ....*
> (Jas. 1:14-15)

Notice the progression:

1. A person is tempted when carried away by lust.
2. Lust conceives.
3. Sin is birthed.

Rethinking Original Sin

"Lust conceives." This offers us the image of a woman conceiving a baby within her womb. Of course, a mother contributes the egg in the conception of a baby, but it is wrong to call the egg a baby until that which is outside of her enters into her and joins with the egg. So also, every individual has desires within them, but those desires are not sin. Only when a person is carried away by desires does lust conceive. Only when desires draw within a person the sin that is in the world is sin conceived.

After sin is conceived, it is then born and becomes active, bringing forth death. Like a virus that multiplies and destroys its host, so also sin actively works in people, corrupting them.

So then, we see that sin came into the world when Adam sinned. It is conceived in people when they open their hearts to sin. Therefore, people are not conceived in sin, but sin is conceived in them. People are not born in sin, but sin is born in them.

Point 233: The Sin Nature Is Developed

What does this understanding mean concerning the "sin nature."

Perhaps the Bible passage that is most condemning of human nature is Ephesians 2:1-3:

> *And you were dead in your trespasses and sins, in which you formerly walked according to the course of this world, according to the prince of the power of the air, of the spirit that is now working in the sons of disobedience. Among them we too all formerly lived in the lusts of our flesh, indulging the desires of the flesh and of the mind, and were by nature children of wrath, even as the rest.*

"Children of wrath?" Indeed, people have a sin nature. Father-Son theology and Classical/Reformed theology agree that people have a sin nature.

But how do people get a sin nature?

Classical/Reformed theology teaches that every person inherits a sin nature from Adam. But if that is true, then every person would inherit the same evil nature. They would all be equally evil.

An alternative understanding is that people *develop* a sin nature. Indeed, a careful look at Ephesians 2:1-3 reveals that people become sinful by walking:

Systematic Theology for the New Apostolic Reformation

> "... *according to the course of this world,*"
> "... *according to the prince of power of the air,*"
> ... according to "*the spirit that is now working in the sons of disobedience.*"

In Ephesians 2:1-3, Paul never says or implies that sinfulness results from Adam's sin. *Adam is never even mentioned in the passage.* Paul talks about people living in the lust of their flesh and indulging the desires of the flesh. This agrees with James' explanation that sin is conceived in people when they are carried away by their lust. As people give themselves over to sin, they increasingly develop evil desires and consistent habits of sinning. Plus, the sin in the world rules over and corrupts their nature. That is how they develop a sinful nature.

This is the only understanding that makes sense once we see how Paul uses the term *sin nature*. In Galatians 2:15, Paul said to Peter:

> *We are Jews by nature and not sinners from among the Gentiles.*

Paul claimed that the Jews are *not sinners by nature*. If we maintain that Paul was speaking of "inherited nature," then from this verse we have to conclude that the Jews inherited a sinless nature from their fore parents while non-Jews inherited a sinful nature from their fore parents. This conclusion is unavoidable if we assume that Paul is referring to inherited nature.

The alternative explanation (which I hold) is that Paul was speaking of "developed nature." With this understanding, we can see from this verse (Gal. 2:15) that the Jews raised their children in a godly environment, and therefore, those children were not sinners by nature. At the same time, the sinners in Paul's day raised their children in an ungodly environment, and as a consequence, they developed a sinful nature.

This truth is also evident in Romans 11:16-24, where Paul compared the Jewish people with the root of an olive tree and the Gentiles who believed in Jesus with branches that have been grafted into the root. Paul said, "*the root is holy*" (v. 16), and he referred to the Jews as "*a cultivated olive tree*" (v. 24). In contrast, Paul described the Gentiles saying they are "*by nature a wild olive tree*" (Rom. 11:24). Notice that these differences between Jews and Gentiles refer to their differing "natures." If we assume Paul is speaking of inherited natures then we have to conclude that the Jews inherited a

Rethinking Original Sin

holy nature while the Gentiles inherited a wild nature. In contrast, if we understand that Paul is speaking of developed nature, then we can see how the Jews developed a more holy nature as they raised their families in the Jewish traditions and heritage that God gave them. Indeed, that is the context of Romans 11.

Paul was not talking about a nature that Jews or Gentiles inherited from Adam. No where in Romans 11 is Adam mentioned. If Paul was talking about inherited nature, then the Jews and Gentiles would have the same evil inherited nature. But they don't according to Paul. The only logical conclusion is that Paul understood the sin nature to be developed and influenced by the environment of each person.

Point 234: Generational Curses and Sins?

Sin and death came into the *kosmos* (creation). It only comes into the nature of humanity as individuals open their heart through lust.

Some Christians have a difficult time accepting this truth, because they have fixed in their mind a certain understanding of Exodus 20:5, which says:

> . . . *for I, the LORD your God, am a jealous God, visiting the iniquity of the fathers on the children, on the third and the fourth generations of those who hate Me.*
>
> (Ex. 20:5)

Christians often use this verse to teach that children may be born with a nature to sin corresponding to the sins of their parents and grandparents.

Yet, careful examination leads us to a different understanding. God said He would "visit" the iniquity of fathers "upon" the children. God did *not* say that He would instill the parents' iniquities *within* their children.

God also said that He would visit the iniquity only upon *"those who hate Me."* This means that sin is *not* passed automatically from parent to child. God said that He would allow the iniquity of parents to be visited upon the children only if, during their lifetime, they become antagonistic toward Him. So, indeed, the sins of parents can influence their descendants, but Exodus 20:5 does not say that the sins of parents are automatically instilled within the inherited nature of their children.

Systematic Theology for the New Apostolic Reformation

It is worth reading the whole thought expressed in Exodus 20:5-6:

> . . . *for I, the LORD your God, am a jealous God, visiting the iniquity of the fathers on the children, on the third and the fourth generations of those who hate Me, but showing lovingkindness to thousands, to those who love Me and keep My commandments.*
>
> (Ex. 20:5-6)

The primary message here is not about sin being passed from parent to descendants. Instead, this is God's declaration from Mount Sinai concerning who He is. And what do we learn about God? He is jealous. Furthermore, He is the kind of God who allows the iniquity of the parents to go to the third and fourth generations. More significantly, however, is the fact that He extends His lovingkindness to thousands of generations. These verses reassure us that sin will *not* be passed on to ten, twenty, thirty, or more generations (or all the way from Adam to the present). Only God's love will go that far.

Even though sins are not passed into the inherited nature of children, we can identify certain negative characteristics that seem to be shared by parents and children. For example, some people are born with a weakness for alcoholism, while others may have temper problems similar to those of their parents. It seems evident that human weaknesses and desires can be passed on into the inherited nature of humanity. However, weaknesses and desires are not sin. James told us that people are tempted when they are carried away by their own lusts. It is not the desires or the temptations which are sin. Even Jesus was tempted, yet without sin. Therefore, it would be more accurate to refer to these weaknesses as *generational weaknesses*, rather than *generational sins*.

Because of generational weaknesses, some people are more likely to yield to certain temptations to sin. We are all vulnerable, but those with strong generational weaknesses are even more vulnerable. They are more likely to succumb to specific sins which are in the world. But this is not necessarily all bad. People with stronger desires toward negative things may have an advantage in that they may become more quickly aware of their own need for a Savior.

Section G
Born Sinful and Condemned?

Classical/Reformed theology teaches that Adam's sin released a moral corruption into the nature of humanity that is so destructive that every baby comes into this world totally depraved, sinful, alienated from God, and deserving of condemnation to hell.

In contrast, I am teaching that this world is fallen because of Adam's sin, and as a result, sin and death reign. Babies come into this fallen world, innocent, but weak and vulnerable. Furthermore, all things—including babies—are subject to futility and corruption.

Point 235: Changing Views Is a Challenge

Christians often listen to their teachers expound upon certain doctrines, thinking that those doctrines are taught throughout the whole Bible. In reality, the verses that teachers use to form a certain doctrine are the foundation for the best arguments that they have. There are no verses that could make their point better; otherwise they would have chosen those verses.

Concerning the doctrine of babies coming into this world with an evil inherited nature, Psalm 51:5 (*"in sin my mother conceived me"*) is their best shot. Romans 5:12 (*"sin entered into the world"*) is also used, but we saw in Section E how this verse has been mistranslated and misinterpreted to teach that babies are born evil.

What actually seats specific doctrines in people's minds are often clichés which do not even come from the Bible. For example, many Christians have seated in their mind an argument that has been repeated millions of times:

Systematic Theology for the New Apostolic Reformation

Proof that a child is evil is the fact that no one has to teach a toddler to stomp his foot and say, 'No!'" In reality, this worn-out argument falls apart upon any serious examination. If a toddler stomping his foot in defiance of mom means that the child is evil, then the opposite must also be true. If that same toddler smiles and says "yes" to the mother, does this mean the toddler is good? If bad behavior means the toddler is bad, then good behavior means the toddler is good.

The fact is that each and every child is capable of good or bad behavior.

Point 236: Embracing Jesus' View of Children

Consider again, Classical/Reformed theology's negative view of human nature. Augustine wrote:

> . . . each man, being derived from a condemned stock, is first of all born of Adam evil and carnal.[140]

John Calvin held a similar view, explaining how children come into this world:

> . . . their whole nature is a seed of sin; hence, it can be only hateful and abhorrent to God.[141]

When we read the words of Jesus, we hear a view of children that is very different than Augustine's or Calvin's. Jesus said:

> *Yes; have you never read, "Out of the mouth of infants and nursing babes Thou hast prepared praise for Thyself"?*
> (Matt. 21:16b)

> *Let the children alone, and do not hinder them from coming to Me; for the Kingdom of heaven belongs to such as these.*
> (Matt. 19:14b)

Obviously, Jesus had a different view of infants than John Calvin, who taught that infants "can only be hateful and abhorrent to God."[142]

---

[140] Augustine, *The City of God*, 15:1.
[141] Calvin, *Institutes*, II:1:8.
[142] Calvin, *Institutes*, II:1:8.

Born Sinful and Condemned?

So we must decide upon whose views we will build. Many Christians do not want to be shown where their heroes' thoughts disagree with Jesus' thoughts, because then they will have to make a decision. They must admit that their favorite leaders may have been wrong. Yet, that is the cost of change. That is the cost of learning truth.

Point 237: Children Are Connected to God

Jesus talked about a divine connection that children have with God. Matthew records His words:

> *See that you do not despise one of these little ones, for I say to you, that their angels in heaven continually behold the face of My Father who is in heaven.*
>
> (Matt. 18:10)

According to Jesus, our attitude toward children should be influenced by an awareness of how their angels stand openly before God.

This truth is incompatible with Classical/Reformed theology. Adherents teach that because of Adam's sin, he and all of his descendants are alienated from God. In contrast, Jesus warned His disciples to be careful how they treated children because there is some unique and precious connection between the angels associated with each one of them and the presence of God. So it is appropriate to ask, "When people look into the face of a newborn, are they aware of the child's angel which looks in the face of God or do they see a baby who is 'evil and carnal' as Augustine taught?"[143]

Point 238: Where Do Dead Babies Go When They Die?

If Augustine was right that everyone is conceived in sin and comes into the world separated from God, then every baby that dies goes to hell. Augustine knew this was the implication of his understanding of original sin, but he got around it by saying that the sin of Adam can be removed from babies through water baptism. Following Augustine's theology, the Roman Catholic Church began water baptizing infants in the 5th century as the only way to spare children from eternal damnation.

---

143 Augustine, *The City of God*, 15:1.

Systematic Theology for the New Apostolic Reformation

In the 14th century, the Roman Catholic Church added the possibility that unbaptized babies who die may go to a neutral place called **limbo**. In that eternal resting place, unbaptized babies will neither experience the presence of God nor suffer the pain of eternal torment in hell.[144]

I propose to you that we don't have to put our hearts at ease by imagining a place called limbo. Nor do we need to implement the practice of water baptizing infants. Instead, we should get rid of the unbiblical idea that babies are born separated from and condemned by God.

These issues become especially important when we have to face the death of a child. All of us want to believe that children go to heaven when they die. However, if a Christian is going to stay consistent with the doctrine that all people are conceived in sin (Augustine's misinterpretation of Ps. 51:5) and all people were in Adam when he sinned (Augustine's mistranslation of Rom. 5:12), they have to follow through to the inescapable conclusion that all babies go to hell if they die.[145]

Yet, many Christian teachers are not consistent with their own beliefs. A minister may teach on Sunday morning that every human being is born in sin and alienated from God, but before the week is over, she will have to perform a funeral for an infant, at which time she may tell everyone that the child is in heaven. When a leader does this, she contradicts her own teaching. Either babies are alienated from God and, hence, go to hell or else they go into the presence of God if they die. I believe the second is true.[146]

---

[144] The doctrine of limbo is currently being reconsidered by Roman Catholic theologians. In 1992, Pope John Paul II had limbo removed from the Catholic catechism. In April 2007, Pope Benedict XVI approved the findings of a report by a Vatican advisory body, which found grounds that the souls of unbaptized children would go to heaven, thus revising traditional Catholic teaching on limbo.

[145] These issues become even more significant when we consider the millions of babies who are aborted each year.

[146] I believe the vast majority of babies that die go to heaven, but I must leave open the possibility that some do not go to heaven because Psalms 58:3 tells us about some who are evil even in the womb.

Section H
How Good or Bad Are People?

I am offering a more positive view of human nature than Classical/Reformed theology teaches. Still, the Bible is very clear that everyone sins. I want to make this point very clear because many Christians are defensive about their belief in the total depravity of humanity. Plus, there is a dualistic tendency at the root of Classical/Reformed theology. Such dualism channels people's thoughts down one of two paths: either people are totally depraved or they are good. I am not teaching either extreme. There is an entire spectrum between these extremes, and people appear everywhere along that spectrum.

Two Extremes Concerning the Nature of Humanity

Totally Depraved ◄||||||||||||||||||||||||||||||||?||||||||||||||||||||||||||||||► Good

Let me clearly state again that everyone sins and everyone needs a Savior, who is Jesus Christ. However, we are now asking the question, "How good or bad are people?"

Point 239: Is Man's Heart Deceitful or Good?

Classical/Reformed teachers interpret key Bible verses through a very negative lens. For example, Jeremiah 17:9 (KJV) tells us:

> *The heart is deceitful above all things, and desperately wicked: who can know it?*

Systematic Theology for the New Apostolic Reformation

Adherents of Reformed theology often quote this verse and emphasize how every person's heart is desperately wicked.

In reality, this is an example of poor hermeneutics (way of interpreting the Bible). To see how wrong it is, all we have to do is read the context of Jeremiah 17:9. In verses 5 to 9, Jeremiah is a making a contrast between people with evil hearts and those with good hearts. In verses 5 and 6, Jeremiah talks about people with evil hearts:

> *Thus says the Lord,*
> *"Cursed is the man who trusts in mankind*
> *And makes flesh his strength,*
> *And whose heart turns away from the Lord.*
> *For he will be like a bush in the desert . . . ."*

Then in verses 7 and 8, Jeremiah talks about people with good hearts:

> *Blessed is the man who trusts in the Lord*
> *And whose trust is in the Lord.*
> *For he will be like a tree planted by the water . . . .*

Once we see that Jeremiah is making this comparison between people with evil hearts and those with good hearts, we see how wrong it is to take verse 9 out of context and declare that every person has a desperately wicked heart.

For further confirmation, consider this. When Jeremiah said the heart of man is "deceitful," do not interpret this word to mean "totally evil." Instead, think how easily people can deceive themselves. For example, a person who is committing a sin can easily rationalize that sin. As the Bible says, *"All the ways of a man are clean in his own sight . . ."* (Prov. 16:2). The heart is deceitful in the sense that any one of us can justify our own actions to ourselves. That is the message of Jeremiah 17:9.

In the very next verse God says:

> *I, the LORD, search the heart, I test the mind,*
> *Even to give to each man according to his ways, according to the results of his deeds.*

(Jer. 17:10)

Do you see what is being addressed here? People can deceive themselves, but God can see the truth.

How Good or Bad Are People?

The tragic point for our discussion here is how some Christians today would claim for all people—including themselves—a totally evil heart. They isolate Jeremiah 17:9, misinterpret it, and remain fixed there. As a consequence, they despise their own heart. In reality, they may be one of the blessed ones whose heart *"trusts in the Lord"* as described by Jeremiah in the previous two verses.

Point 240: People Are Not All Bad

Consider what Jesus said when He first saw Nathanael:

Behold, an Israelite indeed, in whom there is no deceit.

(John 2:47)

Nathanael was not a Christian, yet Jesus recognized that there was no deceit in his heart.

This leads us to conclude that some non-Christians have some positive qualities in their hearts. This does not mean their hearts are good in the sense of perfection. This does not mean they will get to heaven apart from Jesus. It simply means that not every non-Christian is totally depraved.

Consider how Jesus recognized both evil and good people in the world. In Matthew 5:45, He spoke of God, who *"causes His sun to rise on the evil and the good . . . ."* Jesus was not speaking in terms of non-Christians versus Christians. He was speaking of the whole of humanity—people who had not even heard the gospel yet.

Jesus referred to good people in Matthew 12:35:

The good man out of his good treasure brings forth what is good . . . .

According to Jesus, some people have a good heart:

. . . these are the ones who have heard the word in an honest and good heart . . . .

(Luke 8:15)

Blessed are the gentle . . . the merciful . . . the pure in heart . . . the peacemakers . . . .

(Matt. 5:5-9)

Systematic Theology for the New Apostolic Reformation

Yes, Jesus believed some people have an honest, good, and/or pure heart.

By acknowledging our Lord's positive comments about other people, I am not saying that these people are good in the sense of perfection. The adjective *good*, as used in the NT, is most commonly translated from the Greek word *agathos*. *Agathos* can mean good in the sense of perfection, or it can be used in a less strict but still very positive way.

For example, it was used in the sense of perfection when a certain man came to Jesus and called Him "Good Teacher." Jesus answered:

> *Why do you call Me good? No one is good except God alone.*
> (Mark 10:18)

Jesus answered the man, as if to say, "Only God is good and you call Me good; do you realize who I am?" In this context, the word *good* is being used in the sense of perfection. The only human who met that standard is Jesus Christ.

We can also see the word *good* (*agathos* in Greek) being used in other passages in a less strict sense. For example, Luke 23:50 describes Joseph:

> *And behold, a man named Joseph, who was a member of the Council, <u>a good and righteous man</u>* . . . .

The Bible is not contradicting itself when it says in one verse that no one is good, and then in other verses points out certain individuals who are, indeed, good. Rather, the word *good* can be used in different ways.

Even today we use the word *good* in various ways. Someone may say to their dog, "good dog," but they do not mean their dog is perfect. Similarly, in Bible times, people referred to some people as good, realizing that this does not necessarily mean perfection.

With this understanding, we can see how our Lord Jesus referred to good people. Jesus did not think in dualistic terms. He did not fit people into one extreme or the other. He was capable of seeing people as they are.

The significant point for our discussion is how our Lord used this descriptive term, *agathos*, independently of any Christian experience. He referred to certain non-Christians as good.

How Good or Bad Are People?

Point 241: Differing Levels of Righteousness

Similarly, the words *righteous* and *righteousness* are used in the Bible in the sense of perfection or in a less strict but still positive way.

We know that the perfect righteousness of Jesus is required for anyone to get to heaven. No one but Jesus has that righteousness and those who are accredited with His righteousness by grace through faith.

However, several individuals in the Bible are said to be righteous even though they were not Christians. For example, Luke tells us about a priest named Zacharias and his wife, Elizabeth:

> *They were both <u>righteous in the sight of God</u>, walking blamelessly in all the commandments and requirements of the Lord.*
> (Luke 1:6)

Of course, Zacharias and Elizabeth were not as righteous as Jesus. Nor were they righteous enough to get to heaven apart from Jesus Christ. But they were righteous in the sense of keeping the laws and requirements of the Lord.

In Matthew 5:20, Jesus talks about different levels of righteousness:

> *For I say to you that unless your righteousness surpasses that of the scribes and Pharisees, you will not enter the kingdom of heaven.*

Notice that Jesus referred to:

1. your righteousness
2. the righteousness of the scribes and Pharisees
3. a righteousness greater than the scribes and Pharisees

Jesus acknowledged that the scribes and Pharisees had some righteousness, but He also stated that it would require greater righteousness to enter into heaven.

Once we see how the word *righteousness* can be used in these different ways, we can understand Paul's words when He wrote, "There is none righteous, not even one" (Rom. 3:10). In the sense of perfect righteousness, no one can match that. Everyone falls short except Jesus Christ.

However, some people do have some righteousness. Their own righteousness will not get them to heaven, but non-Christians can do some things right.

Systematic Theology for the New Apostolic Reformation

Point 242: Are All of Our Righteous Deeds Despised by God?

John Calvin did not believe that non-Christians can do anything right on their own initiative:

> ... all human works, if judged according to their own worth, are nothing but filth and defilement. And what is commonly reckoned righteousness is before God sheer iniquity.[147]

Followers of John Calvin often try to support this idea by quoting the KJV of Isaiah 64:6:

> *But we are all as an unclean thing, and all our righteousnesses are as filthy rags* . . . .
>
> (Is. 64:6 KJV)

From this verse, followers of Reformed theology teach that everything the natural person does—even that which appears righteous—is as filthy rags in God's eyes. In other words, God hates whatever non-Christians do to try to please Him.

In reality, people who use Isaiah 64:6 to try to support the negative view of Reformed theology are taking the verse out of context. Anyone who reads the context of Isaiah 64:6 will learn that Isaiah was *not* referring to all of humanity. When Isaiah said, *"we are all as an unclean thing,"* he was referring to his own people, the Jews. Isaiah was speaking about the condition of the Jews during the time they were exiled out of the Promised Land.

To see this, we can note that the KJV of Isaiah 64:6 does not translate the verb tense correctly. The NASV says it accurately:

> *For all of us <u>have become</u> like one who is unclean,*
> *And all our righteous deeds are like a filthy garment* . . . .
>
> (Is. 64:6)

When we read this verse with the proper verb tense—*have become*—then we realize that the Jews were not always rejected by God. They had come to a point in their rebellion against God where, indeed, God did turn His favor away from them. God was no longer accepting their righteous deeds.

---

[147] Calvin, *Institutes*, III:12:4.

How Good or Bad Are People?

But just a few years earlier, the Jews were in God's favor. God instructed them how to make offerings, and those offerings were a soothing aroma to Him. At those times, God was pleased with His OT people.

To confirm this understanding of Isaiah 64:6, all we have to do is read the preceding verse, which tells us how God responds readily and willingly to people who do righteous deeds:

> *You meet him who rejoices in doing righteousness.*
> (Is. 64:5)

Seeing this verse, we must conclude that verse 6 is neither condemning nor rejecting every non-Christian's acts of righteousness. They are not always *"filthy rags"* in God's eyes.

In fact, God loves it when a mother cares for her child. He takes pleasure in a man who pays his bills. He blesses a nation that implements just laws. God does not hate every non-Christian's righteous deeds.

Unfortunately, teachers of Reformed theology often quote the KJV of Isaiah 64:6 alone and then declare that everyone's righteous deeds are despised by God. But to separate verse 6 from verse 5 and then apply it to all people in every generation is another example of poor hermeneutics.

Point 243: The War within a Person between Good and Evil

To teach their doctrine that all non-Christians are totally depraved, followers of Reformed theology misinterpret other Bible verses as well. A favorite verse of theirs is Romans 7:18, where Paul wrote, *"For I know that nothing good dwells in me . . . ."*

In reality, the context of this verse reveals something very different than what the Reformed teachers are implying. Paul's next words are *"that is, in my flesh."* We must include these words, because Paul was teaching that there was nothing good in the flesh part of his nature. The flesh part is the corrupted part. By definition, there is nothing good in the corrupted part of one's nature, but in the context of Romans 7, Paul was talking about the war going on between the good part of a person's nature and the bad part. If there was no good part, then there would be no war with the bad part.

Systematic Theology for the New Apostolic Reformation

Everyone has good and bad within them. There must be something good, because every person is created in the image of God. If humanity had been created in the image of Satan, then every person would be bad to the core of their being, but they are not because the image of God is the foundation of human existence.

Point 244: Spanning the Spectrum of Good to Evil

In the introduction to this volume, I referred to our Lord's words in Luke 6:32. Jesus was speaking to His disciples and encouraging them to love their enemies. In that passage, He said:

Even sinners love those who love them.

The word, *love,* in this verse has been translated from the Greek word, *agape.* So then, we must conclude that sinners have *agape love* for people who love them.

Followers of Reformed theology often say it is impossible for non-Christians to have true love for anyone. They quote 1 John 4:19, which says, "We love, because He first loved us." They reason from this verse that only Christians can love because only Christians have experienced God's love. In reality, 1 John 4:19 is talking about how God's love will grow in us and cause us to encompass our brothers and sisters in Christ. Indeed, we should embrace this truth. However, to say that non-Christians are incapable of love is simply wrong. Jesus said that everyone *agape loves* their own.

Think about this. God created humanity. Since He is love and we are created in His image, there must be some residue of love in everyone of us. Indeed there is, according to Jesus.

All of this is not to deny the existence of evil people. Indeed, there are some very bad people in the world. Psalm 58:3 says:

The wicked are estranged from the womb;
These who speak lies go astray from birth.

Psychologists tell us of some individuals who are sociopaths (also diagnosed as antisocial personality disorder). Although psychologists have varying views on what this means, many will point out that there

How Good or Bad Are People?

are some sociopaths who seem to be estranged from everyone, in the sense that they cannot bond with any other human being, even their parents. Some sociopaths can and do hurt others without experiencing any feelings of shame or guilt.

At the other end of the spectrum, we can identify individuals in the Bible who seem to be good (but not perfect) from birth. Luke explained that John the Baptist was *"filled with the Holy Spirit while yet in his mother's womb"* (Luke 1:15).

So we can identify in the Bible people spread across the spectrum, some who are very bad and some who are good (but not perfect).

PEOPLE SPREAD ACROSS THE SPECTRUM

Depraved ⟵||||||||||||||||||||||||||||||||||||||||||||||||||||||||||||||||||||||||||||||||⟶ Good

In seeing people across the spectrum, I do not mean to be judgmental toward any one person. No one knows the heart of another person. No one can determine with certainty why a specific person acts the way that person does. There are many influences acting upon each human being, and God wants us to look with compassion upon all people.

Volume IV
Nature of Humanity

Section I
The Pelagian Controversy

The topics we are discussing are so foundational to Christian theology that it is necessary to address a few points concerning the orthodox Christian faith. I am offering a more positive view of human nature than Classical/Reformed theology does, so I need to address the relevant issues. Christians trained in Classical/Reformed theology will not seriously consider this more positive view of humanity unless I explain how this view is not **Pelagian**.

Point 245: Understanding Pelagianism

Earlier I mentioned how Augustine engaged in intellectual debates with a British monk named Pelagius. Pelagius taught that infants are born innocent, and as they grow, they develop the ability to choose good or evil. Certain aspects of Pelagius' teaching were condemned by the Church in the 5th century. As a result, Christians who follow Augustine or Calvin's teachings tend to label any positive view of humanity as *Pelagian*. In their mind, this term, *Pelagian,* is equivalent to *heretic.*

Many of the modern arguments about Pelagianism center around the definition of the word *Pelagian*. When used in a very general sense, it simply refers to a positive view of human nature. To see this, consider the historical influence of Pelagius on his own countrymen. Being British, Pelagius strongly influenced the British isles, including Celtic Christianity. That influence is evident even today, leading Karl Barth to accuse the modern British of being "hopelessly Pelagian." With this accusation, Barth was accusing the British of holding to a positive view of humanity.

Systematic Theology for the New Apostolic Reformation

As Christian teachers become more focused in their discussions about Pelagianism, they identify more specifically what it is about Pelagius' teachings that they believe is heretical. Those who are careful students read the rulings of the Church councils which addressed the teachings of Pelagius.

The Church Council of Diospolis in 415 AD actually ruled that Pelagius himself was orthodox. It was only certain teachings of his that were condemned. The Council of Carthage in 418 AD passed 19 canons, 7 of which had implications on the teachings of Pelagius concerning the nature of humanity. Canons numbered 6, 7, and 8 of the Council of Carthage condemn anyone teaching that a person can live without sin. Canons numbered 3.2, 4, and 5 condemn anyone teaching that a person can live righteously without the empowering of God's grace.

Father-Son theology agrees with the rulings of these canons. As we discussed, *sin and death rule over humanity*. Furthermore, *sin and death have a corrupting influence upon every person*. Therefore, no one can live without sin, and no one can live righteously without the empowering of God's grace.

SIN AND DEATH REIGN OVER HUMANITY

Of course, this explanation will not satisfy adherents of Reformed theology. They want to hear me say that people cannot live righteously

The Pelagian Controversy

because people are totally depraved. In contrast, I am saying that they cannot live righteously, *because sin rules over humanity and everyone is subject to corruption.* So then, I am not saying what Reformed teachers want me to say, but I am still in agreement with all (except one) of the rulings of the Church councils of 415 and 418.

The only canon with which I disagree is number 2:

> If any man says that new-born children need not be baptized, or that they should indeed be baptized for the remission of sins, but that they have in them no original sin inherited from Adam which must be washed away in the bath of regeneration, so that in their ease the formula of baptism "for the remission of sins" must not be taken literally, but figuratively, let him be anathema; because, according to Romans 5:12, the sin of Adam (*in quo omnes peccaverunt*) has passed upon all.[148]

The view that I am presenting disagrees with this canon, but then most non-liturgical churches around the world also disagree with this canon, because *the main focus of this canon is a justification for the water baptism of infants.* So if we are going to condemn someone based on this canon, then we must condemn, as Pelagian, all Christians and Christian denominations that do not practice infant baptism.

Point 246: Pelagianism according to Popular Usage Today

In reality, the definition of Pelagianism that is most often used today has little to do with the Church councils. Most people who accuse others of being Pelagian have never read the rulings of the Church councils, but the label *Pelagian* has been around and used so much by adherents of total depravity that its definition has been remolded to refer to the belief that humans are capable of choosing good without God's aid. Some even use the label Pelagian to refer to the belief that humans have the ability to live a sinless life and, hence, earn salvation by their own efforts.

This is what many teachers today think of when they hear the word *Pelagian*. In reality, Pelagius denied that he taught these ideas, and if he were alive today, he would be deeply grieved about the doctrines that are

---

[148] Notice that the entire argument here is based on the mistranslation of Romans 5:12 made in the Latin Vulgate (*in quo omnes peccaverunt*).

Systematic Theology for the New Apostolic Reformation

being associated with his name. Unfortunately, we have to deal with the definitions that people have embraced.

Point 247: Father-Son Theology Is Not Pelagian

So let's answer the key question, "Is the view of humanity being presented with Father-Son theology Pelagian?" The answer depends on one's definition of Pelagian.

If someone is casually and informally using the word Pelagian to talk about any positive view of humanity, then, yes, Father-Son theology is Pelagian, but that definition of Pelagian is not accurate from a theological perspective.

If someone is evaluating Father-Son theology while actually reading the rulings of the Church councils, then no, Father-Son theology does not teach that a person can live righteously without the empowering of God's grace. Nor does Father-Son theology teach that anyone can get to heaven apart from the work accomplished through our Savior Jesus Christ. On the other hand, Father-Son theology does disagree with the one cannon that says all babies must be water baptized for the remission of sins.

Let me state my view clearly. No human being is capable of living a sin-free life. The only hope of salvation is by grace through faith. No human being can be good enough to earn their salvation by their own efforts. However, I am teaching that people are able to choose to do some good. "Some good" will never earn anyone salvation.

Point 248: The Semi-Pelagian Debate

Semi-Pelagian is another label often placed upon any positive view of human nature. In the mind of the accusers, semi-Pelagian is thought to be less severe than Pelagian but still as seriously in error. More specifically and accurately, the semi-Pelagian view is the view that recognizes humanity's nature as corrupted by Adam's sin, but each person still has enough goodness to be able to turn to God and ask Him for help. In contrast, biblical Christianity acknowledges that God and God alone must initiate the salvation process. God must turn the heart of each person toward Himself.

The Pelagian Controversy

For most modern Christians, the related debates are unknown, but for devout followers of Reformed theology, the issues raise heated controversies lying at the very foundation of what the gospel actually means. This is because followers of Reformed theology see people as so totally corrupt that no one is even able to turn to God and ask for God's help.

In reality, the action of turning toward God does not have to be a positive step requiring any goodness on the part of the individual. To see this, consider the homeless beggar who is being offered a piece of bread. The beggar's action of taking the bread need not be out of any goodness in his own nature. In fact, he may take the bread out of pure selfishness. So too, the initial action when a non-Christian receives what God is offering through Jesus Christ does not require any goodness on the part of the non-Christian. The non-Christian may be motivated by fear of hell or simply the logical conclusion that salvation is a good deal. Even a sinner can recognize a good deal.

Yet, this explanation does not satisfy followers of Reformed theology, because their rejection of semi-Pelagianism goes deeper than humanity's ability or inability to turn toward God. The real reason they must reject semi-Pelagianism is because of their concept of God as being in total control of and having predestined all things. Because they believe God is in exhaustive control of all things, they cannot logically accept humanity even turning toward God without God being the cause of that turning.

A Logical Progression of Thought
Beginning with the Reformed View of God

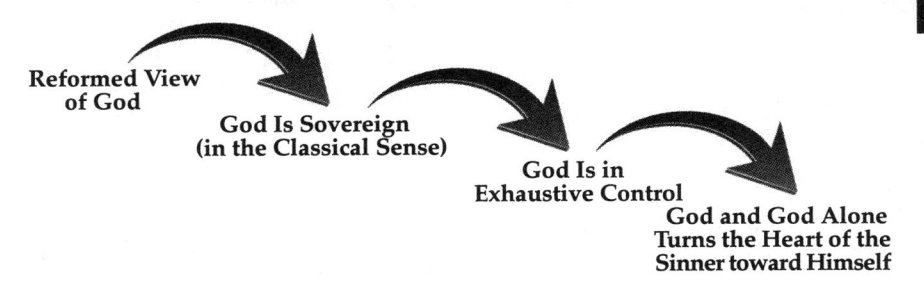

Reformed View of God → **God Is Sovereign (in the Classical Sense)** → **God Is in Exhaustive Control** → **God and God Alone Turns the Heart of the Sinner toward Himself**

Point 249: The Repulsive Implications of Reformed Theology

Adherents of Classical/Reformed theology emphasize humanity's total dependence upon God for salvation. Of course, total dependency

Systematic Theology for the New Apostolic Reformation

upon God is good. No one can be saved apart from the grace of God. We are helpless to save ourselves.

However, Classical/Reformed teachers have a significant misunderstanding concerning grace. Their understanding of God being timeless, immutable, impassible, omnipotent, sovereign, and in exhaustive control of all things leads them to see grace as efficacious and irresistible.[149] Efficacious means 100 percent effective, so if God gives grace to someone to be saved, then they will be saved. They also see grace as irresistible, so people are incapable of resisting whatever purpose God gave the grace to accomplish. Therefore, if God gives grace to someone to be saved, then they will be saved. Furthermore, in the minds of Reformed thinkers, grace is only grace if God does all of the work and people add nothing.[150]

That understanding of grace leads one to conclude that God determines who will be saved by giving grace to them. It also means God determines who will go to hell by not extending His grace to people. This is the inescapable conclusion of Reformed theology, and it is called **double predestination**, meaning every person is predestined to heaven or predestined to hell.

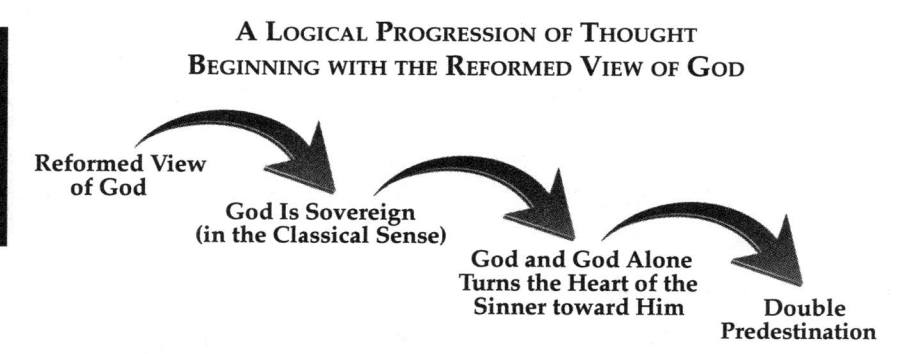

A LOGICAL PROGRESSION OF THOUGHT
BEGINNING WITH THE REFORMED VIEW OF GOD

Reformed View of God → God Is Sovereign (in the Classical Sense) → God and God Alone Turns the Heart of the Sinner toward Him → Double Predestination

If we continue following a logical progression of thought concerning who will be saved, we will arrive at some conclusions that are difficult for most Christians to swallow. If God is sovereign as Classical/Reformed teachers understand sovereignty, then God's decisions concerning salvation are based on absolutely nothing a person does, but solely on

---
149 Explained in II:A:94.
150 This is discussed in more depth in VI:H.

The Pelagian Controversy

His sovereign will. This means that God *wills* to send some people to hell. In fact, Christians who think like Augustine or Calvin believe God will torment the vast majority of humanity in hell forever—not because of what they have done, but because He wants to torment them.

A Logical Progression of Thought
Beginning with the Reformed View of God

Reformed View of God → Double Predestination Based Only on God's Sovereign Will → God Wants to Send Most People to Hell → God Wants to Torment Most People Forever

Point 250: The God of the Bible Is Not the God of Reformed Theology

I find the doctrine of double predestination abhorrent and contrary to the nature of God as revealed in Scripture. It is abhorrent because it accredits Father-God with the most heinous actions. We identify as evil men like Hitler who ordered the death of millions of people. We consider sociopaths who torture others as the most vile humans who have ever lived. Yet, the God of Reformed theology *wants* and *chooses* to send the majority of humanity to eternal conscious torment.

Reformed teachers often divert the conversation away from this implication of their theology by saying God is good to save even one human being. Adherents may also try to make God seem less cruel by saying humans deserve hell, and God is only acting in justice. Yet, no explanation can disguise the God of Augustine and Calvin who sovereignly sends billions of people to experience the most excruciating pain forever and ever—not because of their sin and not because they deserve it, but because God wants to torture them.

The God of Reformed theology is contrary to the God revealed in Scripture. The Bible makes it clear that God does *not* want to send billions of people to hell. Peter explained that God is:

353

Systematic Theology for the New Apostolic Reformation

... not wishing for any to perish but for all to come to repentance.

(2 Peter 3:9)

Paul described God:

... who desires all men to be saved and to come to the knowledge of the truth.

(1 Tim. 2:4)

Peter and Paul's words are diametrically opposed to the view of Reformed theology. God does not want to send people to hell.

Point 251: Father-Son Theology Is Not Semi-Pelagian

Where did Reformed teachers go wrong? We know that any logical progression of thought that leads to a false conclusion is based on false assumptions. Reformed theology is built on the ancient Greek philosopher's assumptions that God is timeless, immutable, impassible, omnipotent, sovereign, and in exhaustive control of all things. Those false assumptions lead adherents to conclude that grace as efficacious and irresistible. That conclusion is unavoidable, but it is wrong. Let me explain.

It is clear in Scripture that God initiates the salvation process. Jesus said, *"No one can come to Me unless the Father who sent Me draws him"* (John 6:44). God must extend grace to people before they can turn toward God for salvation.

However, God's initial action of extending grace is understood differently by different Bible teachers. If Reformed teachers are correct in saying that grace is irresistible and efficacious, then when God gives grace to be saved, the recipients of that grace have no choice but to be saved. On the other hand, if God's grace is resistible, then people can choose whether or not to cooperate with the grace that is given to them.

I believe the latter is the biblical view. God and God alone must initiate the salvation process by giving grace to people, but this does not mean God is forcing the recipients to be saved. The recipients must play a role in responding to God.[151]

---

[151] This view is called *synergism* in contrast to *monergism*. Both views are discussed in VI:H.

The Pelagian Controversy

A helpful analogy to understand this is to think of a limousine showing up at your front door and the driver invites you to get in the limo so he can take you to meet someone important. In a comparative way, God may extend grace to you with an invitation to come and meet Him. Of course, this analogy would be more accurate if the driver of the limo actually offered to pick you up in his arms and literally carry you out to the vehicle. That way the driver is doing all of the work and all you are doing is allowing it to happen. Of course, you can also refuse the offer.

Father-Son theology recognizes that people have free will. They can refuse salvation. Grace is resistible. God desires all people to be saved (1 Tim. 2:4), but not all people will be saved. The reason is because God does not force people to be saved.

Notice that this view sees God always initiating the salvation process but people may reject the grace that God gives. Since Father-Son theology sees God always initiating, it is not semi-Pelagian.

We could say much more about this subject, but our discussion is now turning more toward salvation, so we will leave further discussion about this to Volume VI, *Soteriology*.

Volume IV
Nature of Humanity

Section J
The Triune Nature

There is more to the nature of humanity than just a state of sinfulness or separation from God. The Bible has much to reveal. Here we will examine human nature in the sense of consisting of a spirit, soul, and body.

Point 252: The Tri-Part View of Human Nature

As we have explained, Classical/Reformed theology has been married to Western philosophy which gave birth to a dualistic worldview. With a worldview consisting of two parts, i.e., a spiritual world and a natural world, it was easy to think of a person's nature as consisting of two parts, i.e., a spiritual part (the soul) and a natural part (the body). This view of a person's nature as a two-part being is called the **dichotomous view,** and it has dominated Western thought since Plato's thoughts were syncretized with early Christianity.

In reality, the Bible reveals people as three-part beings. We can see this in the creation of Adam:

> *And the Lord God formed man of the dust of the ground, and breathed into his nostrils the breath of life; and man became a living soul.*
>
> (Gen. 2:7 KJV)

In this verse, the Hebrew word for "breath" is *ruach*, which can also be translated as "spirit." Recognizing this, we can identify three parts to Adam's being: spirit, soul, and body. The spirit came from God, the body

Systematic Theology for the New Apostolic Reformation

was formed from the earth, and the soul was the created element that came into existence when the spirit of God had contact with the physical body. This three-part view is called the **trichotomous view**.

GOD BREATHED INTO THE BODY OF ADAM

Just as the dichotomous view corresponds with Plato's dualistic cosmology, the trichotomous view corresponds with the biblical cosmology. With the biblical cosmology, we can see that Adam's body existed in the natural realm. Adam's spirit originated with the breath that came from God who dwells in the third heaven.

THE TRICHOTOMOUS VIEW FITS THE BIBLICAL WORLDVIEW

The Triune Nature

Paul identified this three-part nature in all people:

> *Now may the God of peace Himself sanctify you entirely; and may your <u>spirit</u> and <u>soul</u> and <u>body</u> be preserved complete, without blame at the coming of our Lord Jesus Christ.*
> (1 Thess. 5:23)

We need to see the three parts of a person's nature as joined together. We can separate them for discussion purposes. Also, we can separate them when we talk about their origins, the spirit coming from God, the body coming from the earth, and the soul being the created element. However, we should not see the three parts functioning independently. What happens in one part influences what happens in the other two parts. A person exists as a fully integrated unit—spirit, soul, and body.

Point 253: The Structure of the Soul and Spirit

To further develop our understanding of human nature, let's form an image of what the soul and spirit actually look like.

If we could see the soul separated from the physical body, we would see how the soul is structured as the human body. There are several reasons to believe this.

We can see the structure and shape of the soul as we study Bible passages that describe the human soul after it has left the body due to death. In 1 Samuel 28:8-19, we read the story of how King Saul had a medium conjure up the prophet Samuel from the dead. This was an evil exercise forbidden by God, but note from this Bible account how the prophet Samuel appeared in the recognizable form of an old man (v. 13-14). We can also see the "recognizable soul" in Luke 16:19-31, where our Lord spoke about Lazarus and a rich man who had died. In this passage, Jesus referred to the finger of Lazarus and the tongue of the rich man, even though their physical bodies were decaying in the grave. Lazarus and the rich man were able to recognize each other.[152] We can conclude from such accounts that if we were able to see the soul with our natural eyes, it would appear as the body, having arms, legs, head, and facial features.

---

152 Some Christians understand the story of the rich man and Lazarus as a parable referring to how the Jewish religious leaders had been living in luxury. So for them, the explanation provided here carries no merit.

Systematic Theology for the New Apostolic Reformation

We can also see this as the Bible associates the soul with the blood. This is seen in several Bible passages, although some translators interpret the Hebrew word *nephesh* as "life," rather than "soul."

> *For the life* [soul] *of the flesh is in the blood . . . .*
> (Lev. 17:11)
>
> *Only you shall not eat flesh with its life* [soul], *that is, its blood.*
> (Gen. 9:4)
>
> *Only be sure not to eat the blood, for the blood is the life* [soul], *and you shall not eat the life* [soul] *with the flesh.*
> (Deut. 12:23)

As the blood saturates every part of a person's physical body, the soul does also. This means that the soul is shaped like the body that it fills.

In contrast, we should not think of the spirit in any shape or size. It originated with God's breath. As such, it cannot be defined in terms of shape or size. It is helpful to think of the spirit as the "spark of life." It is the divine energy that caused Adam to come alive. Although there is no way to accurately picture the spirit, I will diagram it as a spark of energy.[153]

THE SPIRIT, SOUL, AND BODY SUPERIMPOSED UPON ONE ANOTHER

---

153 For a fuller discussion of this, see: my book entitled, *The Spiritual, Mystical and Supernatural*.

The Triune Nature

Point 254: The Spirit, Soul, and Body, as One Package

The spirit, soul, and body are totally integrated, filling the same space. The spirit and soul are so intertwined that in many ways they are one.

To see this we must build on the Hebraic-biblical worldview that sees the spiritual and natural realms as fully integrated. The spiritual realm is not some distant world and totally unlike the natural realm. As we explained, there is a spiritual realm (second heaven) that fills the same space as the natural realm. Once we see the spiritual and natural realms filling the same space, then we can envision the soul and body existing in the same space. The soul of a person does not exist in a distant spiritual world. Rather it is *right there* where the physical body is located.

It is helpful to think of the body as the physical expression of the soul. It is also helpful to think of the soul as the invisible expression of the body.

We should also think of the spirit as existing in the same space as the soul and body. If we understand that the spiritual and natural realms are fully integrated, it is easy to see the spirit and soul fully integrated with the physical body. They are not separate but are "one package."[154]

The Scripture does not make it clear if the spirit of a person exists in the third heaven or the second heaven. God may have released His breath from the third heaven into the second heaven so a person's spirit may exist in the second heaven with the soul. On the other hand, Paul writes that *"the one who joins himself to the Lord is one spirit with Him"* (1 Cor. 6:17). In that case, the Christian's spirit may be entirely in the third heaven, existing as one with the Holy Spirit. That would explain how the Christian's spirit may be positioned with Christ in heavenly places (Eph. 2:6),[155] however, the Bible does not give us enough information to be conclusive on this.

Point 255: The Breath of God in all Humanity

We saw that God's breath brought Adam's soul into existence and his body to life, but it is worth seeing this same function of God's breath in every human being. Job 34:14-15 tells us:

---

[154] Although Plato saw the body and soul as in separate packages, Aristotle saw them as one.
[155] For a fuller discussion of this, see: my book entitled, *The Spiritual, Mystical and Supernatural*, chap. 18.

Systematic Theology for the New Apostolic Reformation

If He [God] should determine to do so,
If He should gather to Himself His spirit and His breath,
All flesh would perish together,
And man would return to dust.

This reveals that God's breath is in every living human being and sustains the life of every person (Christian and non-Christian).

God released His breath into Adam, but how does His breath actually get into all other human beings? The spiritual substance of life originated with the breath of God, and it is passed on through the generational lines. Even today, the spirit which sustains life in a newborn baby originated with that first breath released into Adam.

Consider the power in that first breath. Compare it with God's other creative acts, such as when He spoke plant life into existence. In God's spoken words, *"Let the earth sprout vegetation"* (Gen. 1:11), there was enough power to give life to all plants for the duration of this world. In a corresponding way, there was enough power in the divine breath released into Adam to give life to all the generations which would follow him. God is the Originator, the Source, the starting point for all of life. As the writer of Hebrews tells us, God is the *"Father of spirits"* (Heb. 12:9). The spiritual substance which God released into Adam became the substance of life that has continued to energize all of humanity.

THE BREATH OF GOD RELEASED INTO ALL HUMANITY

The Triune Nature

It is important to recognize that God began the entire human race *through* Adam. The apostle Paul explained this:

> He Himself gives to all people life and breath and all things; and <u>He made from one man</u> every nation of mankind to live on all the face of the earth....
> (Acts 17:25-26)

At this point some Christians have a misconception. They imagine God releasing or creating spiritual life in the womb of a mother each time there is conception or at some point during the gestation period. That is a common misunderstanding, and we need to establish the fact here that the spirit-substance of life itself is passed through the generational lines.

Evidence of this truth can be seen when we study the account concerning Abraham and Levi in Hebrews 7:9-10. There we are told that when Abraham brought his offering to God, Levi was *"in the loins"* of Abraham. Levi was not born until four generations later, but notice his location when Abraham was alive. The Bible tells us that he was in the loins of his great-great-grandfather. When Levi was conceived, he did not come down to earth from heaven and then enter the womb of his mother. The spiritual substance was resident in his forefather.

This does not mean Levi fully existed before his conception, but the spiritual substance existed within Abraham. Levi's soul—the created element—would not have come into existence until the spiritual substance came in contact with the physical substance in the womb of his mother. Both the genetic code and the spirit (or what we call the "spark of life") are passed through the generational lines.

When does human life begin? Notice what King David said as he praised God:

> For You formed my inward parts;
> You wove me in my mother's womb.
> (Ps. 139:13)

The soul of a person comes into existence simultaneously as the body is formed within the womb of the mother.[156]

---

[156] Some Bible teachers hold to the traducian theory, which says the soul is transferred from parents to offspring through procreation. In contrast, I am explaining that the spirit and DNA are passed from parents to offspring, then the soul is created.

Systematic Theology for the New Apostolic Reformation

We can summarize this by saying that all human beings depend upon the breath of God to sustain their lives. That breath originated from the first breath released into Adam. Through Adam, God fathered all of humanity. The breath is passed through the generational lines just as the genetic code is. When the spirit and the genetic code are activated within the womb of the mother, a new soul comes into existence.

The only exception to this was the birth of Jesus. He was born of the Holy Spirit as the Spirit came upon the virgin Mary (Luke 1:26-35). He descended directly from heaven as the Word became flesh (John 1:14 ; 6:46-51 ; 8:23, 42). Jesus was the *"only begotten Son"* of God (John 3:16). In contrast, all the rest of humanity has been born of Adam.

Section K
The Soul of a Person

In the preceding section, we explained how the soul would appear as the physical body if we could see it with our natural eyes. Now let's see of what the soul consists.

Point 256: The Common View of Western Christianity

Seeing the spiritual world as separate and distinct from the natural world, it was easy for Plato to envision the soul as separate and totally different than the physical body. Plato also saw the natural world as inferior, temporary, and insignificant compared with the eternal spiritual world. In line with that way of thinking, Plato saw the physical body as a temporary container for the soul, which he considered the real person.[157]

Seeing the soul as the real person, Plato taught that the soul is composed of the rational (mind), the appetitive (base desires), and the spirited (higher desires). By defining the soul in this way, he was assigning to the soul what he considered all of the core functions of a human being.

Profoundly influenced by Plato's view, Western Christians typically think of the soul as united to the body, but still a distinct entity from the body. They also say that the soul of a person consists of the mind, will, and emotions.[158] This understanding of the soul resulted from various Church leaders refining Plato's understanding over the course of many years.

---

157 Aristotle and Aquinas are known for being less dualistic than Plato on this issue and, therefore, seeing the soul and body as more of a unit than Plato did.
158 Calvin typically spoke of the soul as consisting of two parts, the intellect and will (e.g., *Institutes*, I:15:7).

Systematic Theology for the New Apostolic Reformation

In reality, the soul is not the mind, will, and emotions. We already saw the biblical view with the soul structured and shaped as the body. What the body has, the soul has. The body has a head, feet, heart, lungs, and so forth, so the soul has a head, feet, heart, lungs, and so forth. As we explained, the body is the physical expression of the soul. Likewise, the soul is the invisible expression of the body.

Again, the soul is *not* the mind, will, and emotions. That Platonic view of human nature is so deeply seated in Western Christianity that I will have to offer clear evidence before Western Christians will reconsider. So let's look carefully at the mind, will, and emotions, so that we may see how they *do not* define soul.

Point 257: The Mind of a Person

We can identify thought processes occurring on all three levels of a person's being.

Within the physical body, each person has a physical brain that processes information, makes decisions, and sends millions of electrical impulses coursing through the nervous system throughout each day. Millions of thoughts are processed every hour at the physical level.

However, people must be able to process information independently of their physical bodies, because we see in the Bible people who have died and separated from their physical bodies, but are still able to think. For example, we mentioned Samuel who had been called up from the dead. Samuel communicated with the living people present there, even though he had no physical body (1 Sam. 28:8-19). We can also think of the great cloud of witnesses who have died yet remain watching over us (Heb. 12:1).

We can also identify thought processes at the level of the spirit of a person. The apostle Paul posed the question:

> *For who among men knows the thoughts of a man except the spirit of the man which is in him?*
>
> (1 Cor. 2:11a)

The obvious answer to this question is, "No one." It is the spirit within people that illuminates their being and reveals thoughts. It is helpful to see the spirit as a light shining within people, illuminating their mind.

The Soul of a Person

The point is that thought processes occur throughout one's entire being: spirit, soul, and body.

THOUGHT PROCESSES INVOLVE A PERSON'S ENTIRE BEING

Point 258: The Emotions of a Person

Next consider emotions. In the Bible we can see verses that attribute emotions to both the soul and the spirit. For example:

> Psalm 42:11 tells us of emotional turmoil within the soul
> 1 Kings 21:5 speaks of sadness of spirit
> Luke 1:47 tells us of joy coming from a person's spirit
> Psalm 94:19 ; 103:1-2 speak of joy within the soul
> John 13:21 tells us that Jesus was troubled in spirit
> Matthew 26:38 tells us Jesus was grieved in His soul

From these and many other verses in both the OT and NT, we have to conclude that emotions should not be assigned to the soul only.

Furthermore, we know the physical body plays a role in emotions. Various physiological changes and biochemical reactions are evident whenever emotions rise or fall. Medical technicians can measure the related changes in bodily functions. This feature of a person's emotional

Systematic Theology for the New Apostolic Reformation

existence in the physical body is even more interesting when we consider certain physical stimuli. For example, when depressant drugs are injected into the bloodstream of individuals, their entire being is affected. There are other drugs that can cause the sexual passions to be aroused. Electrical impulses on certain parts of the nervous system can trigger many different emotional responses.

EMOTIONS EXIST THROUGHOUT A PERSON'S ENTIRE BEING

Once we see that emotions and thought processes involve the whole person—spirit, soul, and body—we see how wrong it is to think of them as compartmentalized in the soul.

Point 259: The Will of a Person

It is also incorrect to compartmentalize the will of a person to the soul. To see where a person's will is located, we must abandon the Western mindset that equates the soul with the mind, will, and emotions. Certainly the soul is involved with the will, but the will of each person permeates the person's entire being.

Consider the control of your breathing. You are capable of making a conscious decision to stop breathing. In that case, your spirit/soul,

The Soul of a Person

to some degree, is ruling over the natural governing processes of your body. However, you cannot hold your breath indefinitely. In just a short time, you will lose consciousness, and your physical body will overrule your inner being. So, we see that your conscious mind has some degree of authority over your body, but your physical body has some degree of control over your conscious decisions.

The truth is that many things about your life are decided at the level of your body, and you do not have the willpower in your spirit/soul to overpower them. This is true of many physical desires and needs, some of which you are not even conscious.

THE WILL INVOLVES A PERSON'S ENTIRE BEING

Decisions made within the body go beyond physical functions. Paul explained that the body is actually involved in moral decisions and that the body may have within it the desire to sin:

> *For I joyfully concur with the law of God in the inner man, but I see a different law in the members of my body, waging war against the law of my mind and making me a prisoner of the law of sin which is in my members.*
>
> (Rom. 7:22-23)

Systematic Theology for the New Apostolic Reformation

Notice that the will is located in both the inner man and outer man. In the experience Paul described in these verses, the will of the body was greater than the will of the inner man. We must conclude from this that the will of a person to sin or not to sin is located in part within the physical body.

So we see the will is associated with the entire person, as are the emotions and thought processes.

Point 260: What Is the Soul?

What does all of this mean? Contrary to what Western Christianity has taught, the soul is *not* the mind, will, and emotions. That way of thinking developed from Platonic thought, not the Bible.

Because this is a new concept to many Western Christians, it is worth repeating. The body is the physical expression of the soul, and the soul is the invisible expression of the body. What the body has, the soul has. What the soul has, the body has. This does not mean that the soul has physical substance like the body has, but it does mean that the soul has arms and legs because the body has arm and legs. The soul has a heart and lungs because the body has a heart and lungs. Think about it. This is the biblical revelation free of Platonic thought.

THE THREE-PART NATURE OF HUMANITY

Spirit   Soul   Body

Section L
The Heart of a Person

The heart deserves extra attention because of its central role in human life. Let's investigate.

Point 261: The Location of the Heart

To understand the location of the heart, it is important to keep in mind the lesson we learned in the previous section: A person functions as a unit. If we over compartmentalize human nature into the spirit, soul, and body, we will try to locate the heart in only one of those compartments. In reality, the heart of a person exists on all three levels of a person's being.

THE HEART IS THE CORE OF A PERSON'S BEING

Spirit   Soul   Body

In the body, we have a physical organ pumping blood that we call the heart. However, we must see the heart as existing throughout the core of a person's being. The Greek word for heart, *kardia,* also means

Systematic Theology for the New Apostolic Reformation

the core or the center. In our everyday conversation, we can talk about the heart of an issue or the core of a specific item, such as the core of an apple. It is in this sense that we can also talk about the heart of a person being at the deepest center. At the center of a person's body is the heart; at the center of a person's soul is the heart; and at the core of a person's spirit is the heart.

Earlier, we saw how a person's emotions, thought processes, and will, involve the entire person. Now we see how the heart also exists throughout one's being.

THE HEART EXISTS THROUGHOUT A PERSON'S BEING

Point 262: The Central Role of the Heart

According to Hebraic-biblical thought, the heart is the most central part of a person's being, governing a person's entire life. Proverbs 4:23 tells us:

> *Watch over your heart with all diligence,*
> *For from it flow the springs of life.*

The heart is the fountainhead of a person's life. Just as blood flows from the physical heart, so *"the springs of life"* flow from the heart of a person's

The Heart of a Person

spirit/soul. Just as the physical heart draws in oxygen through the lungs and food from the stomach, the invisible heart draws in good through holy desires and evil through lusts. That which is received grows and flows outward. The heart, then, is the core of a person's being, while at the same time serving as the fountainhead of life.[159]

THE HEART IS THE FOUNTAINHEAD OF ONE'S BEING

Spirit/Soul/Body

People in the Western world tend to think that the mind (brain and intellect) governs a person's life. This way of thinking reaches back to the Western foundation in ancient Greek philosophy. Plato and his followers thought of the spiritual world as the world of thoughts and ideas. According to Plato, people access that world through their own thoughts. Because that world was also considered the world of truth and God, the mind was exalted as the connection point to truth and God.

Because Westerners consider the mind (brain and intellect) as the control center, they spend many years training the minds of children in school. At the same time, the heart is typically seen as untrainable and uncontrollable, wanting what it wants. Little to no time is invested in training children how to watch over their heart, let alone to watch over it *"with all diligence"* (Prov. 4:23).

---

[159] For more teaching on this and other subjects related to the tri-part nature of humanity, see my book entitled, *The Spiritual, Mystical and Supernatural*.

Systematic Theology for the New Apostolic Reformation

Yet, in the modern world, more people end in disaster by failure of the heart than failure of the mind. This is true on the physical, relational, and spiritual level. The weak heart will fail when trials come. The untrained heart is easily lured away. Relationships are destroyed. Priorities are confused, and lives end in ruin because the heart is allowed to go anywhere without restraint.

The heart is also a vital factor in determining achievement and success. An athlete needs determination more than intelligence. A businesswoman with heart will find answers to the problems facing her. A politician will stay on course if she is fully committed. A couple will overcome sexual temptation outside of their relationship if they rule over their hearts. Parents will stay connected to their children if they resist being lured away by other heart attachments such as materialism and greed. Friends will stay friends if they have the fortitude of heart to forgive each other.

The heart is the seat of desires (Matt. 5:28), faith (Rom. 10:10), and purpose (Acts 11:23 ; 2 Cor. 9:7). For this reason, God watches the hearts of people. In fact, He is more interested in what is in their hearts than what is in their heads.

Point 263: The Heart Governs the Mind

The heart actually governs the mind (including the brain and intellect). A good way to see this is to consider how people can easily learn things that interest them. When students love a subject, they will quickly learn about the related topics. All people search out, find, and incorporate into their thinking ideas that reinforce what they want to believe in their hearts. Those ideas do not even have to be true. For example, people who are critical in their hearts of some other individuals will form related thoughts that are distorted to align with the judgments they have already made. Desires seated in the heart of a person orient that person's thoughts down corresponding pathways.

Consider how the heart governs thoughts in the life of a person who does not want to believe in God in contrast to a person who does want to believe in God. Let's take the example of Nathan and Conrad. Both were raised in Church and both had experiences in their younger years that they each considered were from God. However, as Nathan and Conrad grew up and went off to attend a university, they began asking questions

The Heart of a Person

about God. Deep in his heart, Nathan did not want to continue following God, so he asked himself, "Is it possible that my earlier experiences can be entirely explained as psychological phenomenon?" In contrast, Conrad did want to follow God, so he asked himself, "Is it possible that my earlier experiences actually were from God?" Both Nathan and Conrad answered their questions in the affirmative, which is a reasonable answer in each of their cases.

Notice that Nathan's question was formed according to his desire to not believe in God. In contrast, Conrad's question was formed according to his desire to believe in God.

Nathan and Conrad continued to ask more questions. Nathan went on to ask himself, "Since my earlier experiences may have been entirely psychological, do I have any evidence that God exists?" At the same time, Conrad asked himself, "Since my earlier experiences may have been truly of God, do I have evidence that God exists?" Nathan concludes that he has no evidence of God's existence while Conrad concludes that he may have proof of God's existence. Notice that each of their conclusions are aligned with what was already in their hearts.

Nathan and Conrad then asked themselves if they have any basis for morality. Nathan reasoned that God has given him no proof of His existence, and therefore, he has no basis for determining right from wrong. In contrast, Conrad reasoned that God may have proven His existence, and therefore, he should govern his life according to God's will. As a result, Nathan lives his life with no moral compass, while Conrad attempts to live his life according to what he understands as God's will.

Of course, Nathan and Conrad had to ask and answer dozens of related questions for themselves, but the simplified progression of thought that we have described reveals how the heart steers the development of a person's thought processes. The questions that we each ask ourselves are directed down paths that we want to follow. We each subconsciously engineer questions that will lead us where we want to go. Every person develops a system of thought that supports what they truly desire.

For this reason, the questions people ask are more revealing of their hearts than the answers they give. Sincere answers may come from a logical, unbiased mind, *but sincere questions always come from a biased heart.*

The system of thought each person develops is formed not only by their own questions but also by the people around them. Parents, teachers, and friends offer the questions and answers with which they have wrestled.

Systematic Theology for the New Apostolic Reformation

Everyone likes to think of themselves as logical, but in reality, all people form their questions in alignment with their desires. For this reason, the heart, not the mind, controls the course of each person's life.

Point 264: Historical Untethering of the Mind from the Heart

The truth that the heart controls the mind is in direct opposition to much of Western philosophy, which has identified the mind (brain and intellect) as the control center of a person's being.

In the 13th century, Thomas Aquinas (c. 1225–1274) taught that the heart of man is fallen but the mind is able to arrive at truth. Leaders ran with Aquinas' conclusion, placing trust in their minds, which gave a launching pad for the Scientific Revolution of the 16th century. Aquinas never meant that reason should be separated from faith, but his teachings were used by those who desired to untether themselves and society from religion.

The Enlightenment followed the Scientific Revolution, leading to modern education, which are both grounded in the assumption that the mind can lead to truth and eventually provide the answers to humanity's problems. Indeed, many positive developments came forth once people began to confidently use their reasoning powers to solve problems. Great advancements resulted from the philosophical idea that the mind is trustworthy. However, the severing of the mind from faith also guided Western civilization down some darkened paths.

In reality, confidence in the mind is only justified when the heart is anchored in Jesus. When God sent His Son into the world, He planted a standard, which is an anchor for all truth. When Jesus declared that He is the way, truth, and life (John 14:6), He was revealing Himself as the anchor for the human heart and, therefore, for all logical, unbiased thought.

Point 265: Good or Evil Coming from the Heart

The heart not only governs the mind, but it also produces life or death. Jesus explained that the mouth speaks out of that which fills the heart. James further explained that the mouth is like a fountain, able to release fresh or bitter waters (Jas. 3:10-11). As the fountain of a person's being, the heart can produce good or evil (Luke 6:45).

The Heart of a Person

Jesus testified that a person can bring forth good, saying, "*The good man out of the good treasure of his heart brings forth what is good*" (Luke 6:45). An excellent example of good coming from an individual is from the passage we discussed earlier, where Jesus said, "*even sinners love those who love them*" (Luke 6:32).

This truth, that good can come out of the heart of a person, has profound implications, but before we consider the implications, recognize how evil can also come from the human heart. Jesus said:

> *For out of the heart come evil thoughts, murders, adulteries, fornications, thefts, false witness, slanders.*
> (Matt. 15:19)

The heart of humanity is the source of these evils.

The people of Judah engaged in abominable actions when they had their children dedicated to the false god, Molech. God accused them of doing things "*. . . which I had not commanded them nor had it entered My mind that they should do this abomination . . .*" (Jer. 32:35). This is tragic, yet profound. People came up with evil ideas and actions.

James stated that God cannot be the source of evil or of temptation (1:13), but temptation is the result of someone being carried away by *their own lusts* (1:14). This passage is especially revealing because it is in the context of explaining the source of evil. This means that God was not and is not the source evil in the world. The human heart has the ability to originate evil desires and thoughts.

Point 266: The Creative Ability of the Human Heart

Being created in the image of God, people have the creative ability to be the source of their own desires and thoughts—good or evil.

By saying that people have creative ability, we are not saying that people can bring physical things into existence out of nothing. The Bible tells us that God created the heavens and earth (Gen. 1:1), and all things came into being through Jesus (Col. 1:16). However, we can say that people are creative in the sense that they can initiate desires and thoughts. Desires and thoughts are not *things* in the sense of having material substance. However, in another sense they are *things* because they exist. Using this

Systematic Theology for the New Apostolic Reformation

definition of *things,* we can say that human beings who are created in the image of God can bring things into existence that were not in existence.

The fact that people can initiate desires and thoughts in their own hearts has profound implications. People are not just robots being moved about by the predetermined plan of God.

Another implication reflects back on our understanding of God's nature. Consider how God searches the hearts of people, watching to see what will proceed out of their hearts. He even tests people to see what is in their hearts (Gen. 22:12 ; Deut. 8:2 ; 1 Chron. 28:9). We also know that:

> *And there is no creature hidden from His sight, but all things are open and laid bare to the eyes of Him with whom we have to do.*
> (Heb. 4:13)

This leads to a question. If right now God is able to see everything that is in a person's heart, why does He keep watching and testing to see what will come out of the heart? The only way we can explain this is to say that new things can arise in a person's heart. Things that were not there one moment may arise later.

This brings us back around to a major issue that we have been addressing throughout this book. If God was timeless, it would make no sense for Him to keep watching to see what was going to come out of the hearts of people. Nor would He ever have to test people to see what is in their hearts. On the other hand, if He is moving through time with humanity, then it does make sense that He continues watching and testing the hearts of humanity. So then, our understanding of the human heart corresponds with our understanding of God's nature.

Section M
The Will of a Person

To conclude our study on the nature of humanity, here we will discuss free will. In particular, we will identify the extent and reach of a person's free will.

Point 267: Exhaustive Control versus Free Will

The subject of this section is inseparable from our understanding of God's sovereignty. As we discussed, the Classical/Reformed understanding that God is timeless, immutable, impassible, omnipotent, omniscient, and omnipresent logically leads one to conclude that God is in exhaustive control of all things. If God is in exhaustive control, then people are puppets being moved around by the sovereign, irresistible will of God.

Some Classical/Reformed theologians claim to be **compatibilists**, meaning that they hold to the view that God's exhaustive control and human free will are both true at the same time. I believe the compatibilist's arguments are absurd. The Classical/Reformed understanding of God's exhaustive control does not mean that God merely knows what people will decide, but that He predestined before creation every decision that every person will make. Therefore, compatibilists who hold to the Classical/Reformed understanding of God are trying to hold to two mutually exclusive ideas. Because I hold to this position, I would be called an **incompatibilist**. I maintain that any person consistent with the Classical/Reformed view of God must conclude that people have no free will.

Systematic Theology for the New Apostolic Reformation

IF GOD IS IN CONTROL, PEOPLE HAVE NO FREE WILL

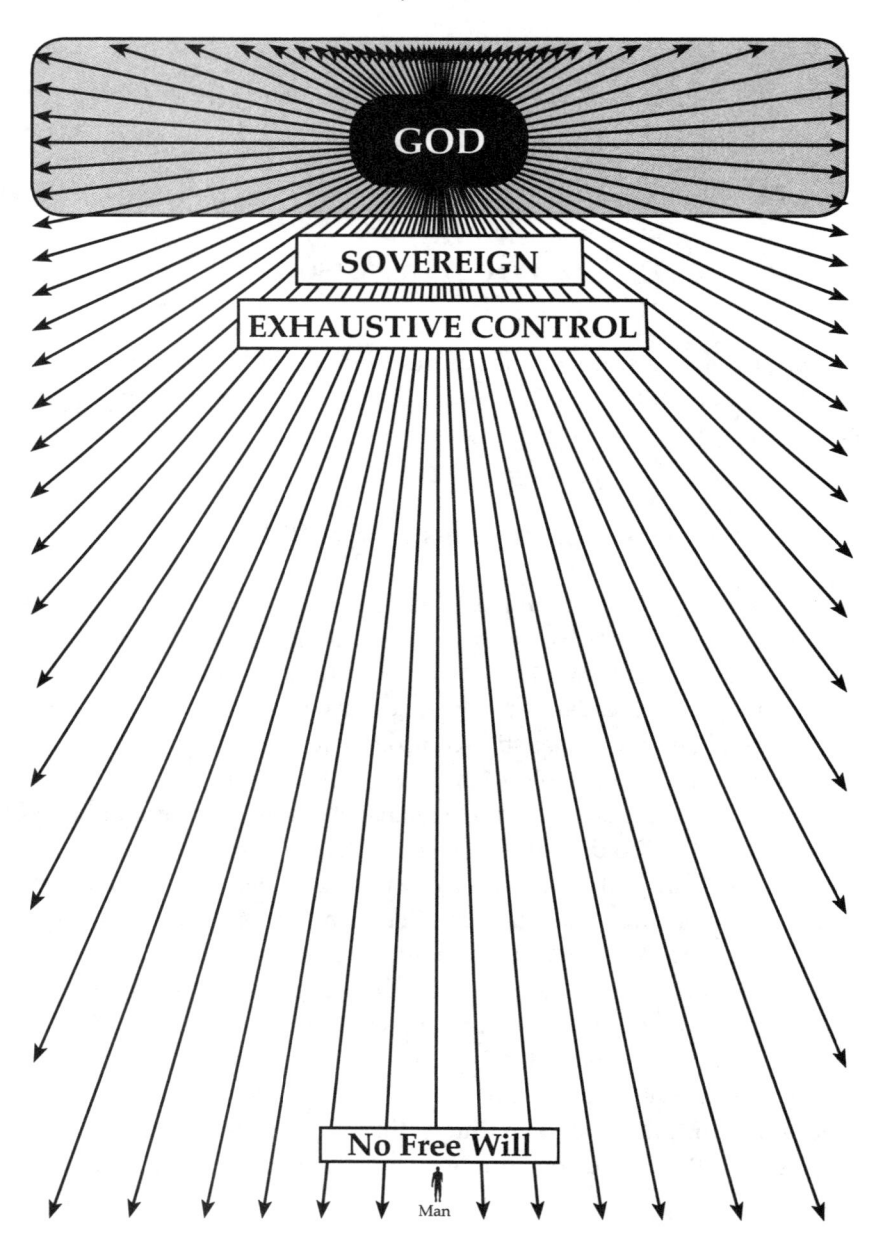

GOD

SOVEREIGN

EXHAUSTIVE CONTROL

No Free Will

Man

The Will of a Person

Martin Luther was consistent in his theology on these issues and wrote a book entitled, *Bondage of the Will*. In that book, Luther declared that free will "is a downright lie."[160]

John Calvin taught that people have free will, but only in the sense that they are free to sin. Calvin did not believe people have free will in the sense that they can choose between good and evil on their own (called **libertarian freedom**). In one passage, Calvin suggested the possibility that Adam may have had some free will (libertarian freedom) before the fall, but then Calvin went on to argue that even the fall of Adam was predestined by God. In reality, that view makes God the author of sin.

Augustine did not like to think of God as the author of sin, so he taught that Adam was created with a free will. In his book, *On Free Choice of the Will*, Augustine defended the existence of free will, but in other writings he denied the existence of free will and supported God's determination of all things.

Other Classical/Reformed theologians have been inconsistent on this issue as well, but all Classical/Reformed theologians agree that non-Christians are incapable of contributing anything to the salvation experience, and therefore, people have no free will to turn to God in order to be saved. This idea has a profound impact upon our understanding of salvation, which we study in Volume VI, *Soteriology*.

Point 268: Exhaustive Control versus Free Will

According to Father-Son theology, God is not in exhaustive control of all things. God deals with humanity much as a father deals with his children. Because God is sovereign, He controls what He wants to control and He delegates what He wants to delegate. When He delegates something to His children, He wants them to accept responsibility.

Even when God chooses not to control a situation, this does not mean that people are totally free to do what they choose. There are many forces acting upon each person. Sin rules over humanity, and sin is a force acting upon all people. Everyone is also influenced by their upbringing, past experiences, the people around them, circumstances, and many other

---

160 Martin Luther, *The Bondage of the Will* translated by Henry Cole (Grand Rapids, MI: Baker Book House,1976), p. 17.

Systematic Theology for the New Apostolic Reformation

factors. So when we say that people have free will, we are not saying they are free to act independently of all outside influences. We are simply saying that Father-God does allow people to make some decisions freely in the sense of free of His control.

Point 269: God Works Uniquely with Each Person

Followers of Reformed theology like to quote Proverbs 17:1, which tells us that the heart of the king is in the hand of the Lord. From this verse they conclude that God controls the heart of every king and, by implication, every human being.[161] But just because God *can* steer any king's heart does not mean that He is. If God is controlling every decision every king makes, then we have serious problems, because it means that God has caused some kings and leaders to torture and slaughter millions of people. Again, Reformed theology makes God the author of much evil.

Those trained in Reformed theology like to talk about God hardening Pharaoh's heart (Rom. 9:17) as an example of how God is in exhaustive control of every human being. Indeed, God intervened in history and sovereignly chose to make Pharaoh refuse to let the Hebrew people go free. However, this does not mean that God also predetermined the thousands of other decisions that Pharaoh made during his lifetime. Nor does it mean that God preordained every decision of the two million Hebrews who were enslaved under Pharaoh.

It does not follow logically that how God works in one person's life is how He works in every person's life. The Lord sovereignly seized the heart of Pharaoh, but God pursued Jonah until Jonah finally submitted. Our Lord intervened in the life of Saul/Paul, striking him with a flash of light (Acts 9:3-4), but God does not strike every person with lightening.

Most people seem to be wooed gently by the Holy Spirit. The love of God leads them to repentance, and they respond to God in a step-by-step fashion. The Bible reveals varying amounts of God's influence, guidance, and control being exercised in the lives of different individuals. This means that we cannot take one example of how God works and conclude that that is how God works in every person's life.

Again, we see that God is sovereign, doing whatever He wants whenever He wants.

---

161 Calvin makes this argument several times, e.g., *Institutes*, II:4:7.

The Will of a Person

Point 270: The Death of Each Person

One area that we can apply our understanding of free will to is in the determination of when a person will die. According to Classical/Reformed theology, the day, hour, and second of every person's death has been predestined from before this world was created. This means more than God knowing when each person is going to die. Classical/Reformed theology teaches that God decided when each person will die, and He is orchestrating all necessary circumstances to make it happen.

To support this understanding, followers of Reformed theology like to quote David's words when he wrote:

> *Your eyes have seen my unformed substance;*
> *And in Your book were all written*
> *The days that were ordained for me,*
> *When as yet there was not one of them.*
>
> (Ps. 139:16)

Using this verse, adherents of Reformed theology teach that the exact days of every person's life are preset from the foundations of the world, and no one can change the date he or she is appointed to die.

In reality, David was talking about his own life in Psalm 139:16. It is wrong to take a Bible verse in which David was talking about his own life and apply it to every human being. God may have raised David for a specific purpose at a specific time in history in order to accomplish His predetermined plan. However, that gives us no basis to say that the life of every human being is so tightly orchestrated.

Of course, God can take a life whenever He chooses, but most people do play a role in determining how long they live. What they eat, how recklessly they drive their automobiles, and what types of risks they take in life do influence how long they live on earth. Within the limits set by God, people do play a role in how long they will live.

Some people even die prematurely, that is, before God wanted them to die, as in the case of a suicide or murder. Of course, God could have stopped their premature death—He has the authority and power to do so—but He is not controlling everything, so people sometimes die outside of His intended will. To some extent, our own lives are in our own hands.

Systematic Theology for the New Apostolic Reformation

Point 271: The Birth of Each Person

Let's apply these truths to the subject of when each person is born. Christians consistent with Classical/Reformed theology must say that the day and second of every person's birth was determined before this world was created. Furthermore, God's exhaustive control goes to the minutest detail, even the choice of which egg and which sperm come together at fertilization.

However, if someone is going to be consistent with that view, then they must also believe that God preordained every baby born with a genetic defect. They must conclude that God chose and desired the deformities, mutations, and resulting suffering that occurs.

Furthermore, if God predetermined the instant every person is born, then He is responsible for the millions of miscarriages in which babies are born too young to live. He is also responsible for the millions of abortions each year. If, indeed, God preordains the birth of every baby, then God also preordains the rape and incest that results in some conceptions. Not only does God allow it, but according to Classical/Reformed theology, God orchestrates all events, desires, and thoughts to make those rapes and incestuous acts happen.

The implications of Classical/Reformed theology are just as disturbing when we talk about the days of Noah when the sons of God were having relations with the daughters of men (Gen. 6:4). Although there is much disagreement as to who the sons of God are in this passage, there is no question that God disapproved of their actions. Yet, if we are going to be consistent with Classical/Reformed theology, then we have to conclude that God willed and ordained those sexual relations and the resulting births. Yet, at the same time, we must recognize God's disapproval of what happened, leading to His destruction of the world.

What is the alternative understanding? God is not controlling the decisions of everyone. He allows some things to happen independently of His control.

This means that to some extent procreation is in the hands of humanity. Of course, God can intervene whenever He chooses. He can choose a specific egg to join with a specific sperm. However, He can also choose to let things run according to natural laws. To some extent, people can choose how many children they want. God may decide to open or close a certain womb. He may decide to give a certain family responsibility to

The Will of a Person

raise a child called for a specific purpose, but God may also let a father and mother decide if they want another child.

This truth has profound implications. If God allows even one child to come into this world that He did not preordain, then the entire course of history may change. For example, in the days of Noah, when the sons of God were having relations with the daughters of men, the world was going in a direction that God did not want it to go. Of course, God intervened in Noah's day, but that does not mean He intervenes every time the world goes contrary to His will. The truth is that God gives people some amount of free will in procreation That means this world has many variables resulting from human freedom.

As we explained earlier, the God of Father-Son theology is big enough to handle every possible outcome of free-will decisions. In this sense, the God of Father-Son theology is greater than the God of Reformed theology.[162]

Point 272: The Life-Choices People Make

Let's apply the truths we are learning to individuals' life-callings and to what they will accomplish on earth.

According to Classical/Reformed theology, God decided before this world was created what each person will accomplish while alive. To support their view, they often quote Jeremiah 1:5, where we are told that God chose Jeremiah to be a prophet before he was even born. However, it is wrong to refer to God's dealings with Jeremiah and conclude that God deals in every person's life with such control. Consider the possibility that God's dealings with Jeremiah were pointed out to reveal how exceptional Jeremiah was. Even though God chose to use Jeremiah as a prophet, this does not necessarily mean that God is directing the career decisions of all seven billion people on earth today.

Not all people do what God wants them to do. In fact, Jesus talked about *"the Pharisees and the lawyers* [who] *rejected God's purpose for themselves . . ."* (Luke 7:30). In the context, Jesus was talking about the Jewish leaders not receiving John the Baptist whom God sent to them. In contrast, Acts 13:36 tells us that David *"served the purpose of God in his own generation . . . ."* From these examples, we know that some people do fulfill what God put them on the earth to do, while others do not.

---

162 II:F..

Systematic Theology for the New Apostolic Reformation

If we see God dealing with humanity as a father deals with his children, we will see God allowing His children to make many decisions on their own. Father-God may appoint a specific person to fulfill a certain career, while allowing other people to choose their own careers.

We can apply this same principle to one person choosing a partner for marriage. Christians consistent with Classical/Reformed theology have to find that one person whom God has appointed as their mate. In contrast, Father-Son theology agrees that in some cases God may arrange one specific individual to marry another, but He does not always exercise such tight control. Just like natural parents, God wants His children to choose a spouse who will meet their needs and be faithful. However, God does not always prearrange every marriage. Therefore, single people do not need to find that one person on earth whom God has appointed for them to marry. Instead, they should ask for God's guidance but use their own good judgment to find a suitable mate. Then that mate becomes the right person by their commitment to him or her.

Seeing God's involvement in the world this way helps us understand the many failures that people make. If people have some amount of free will, then we can understand why so many marriages fail. On the other hand, if we are consistent with Classical/Reformed theology, then we have to conclude that God predestined some people to get married and divorced several times. Similarly, we have to conclude that God made many people make terrible lifestyle decisions, including God making drug dealers and prostitutes choose their lifestyles. The plain truth is that God does not control every person. He allows people to make choices, even when that means they will make some bad choices.

Point 273: God Working with Humanity

The concept of God working directly in one person's life but not as directly in another person's can be difficult to grasp when heard for the first time. However, it is much more understandable when we think of God governing the earth to achieve His overall goals rather than God controlling every detail of every person's life. For example, God must have orchestrated the events leading up to the death of Jesus, but He did not need to orchestrate all the events leading up to some local fisherman catching one extra fish that day. Catching that extra fish probably would not have dramatically impacted the course of history.

The Will of a Person

Consider the words of Jesus when He spoke to His brethren about going to Judea:

My time is not yet here, but your time is always opportune.
(John 7:6b)

From this we can infer that the timing of our Lord's entrance into Judea was being orchestrated to fit into the overall plan of God. In contrast, the phrase, *"your time is always opportune"* implies that the timing for the others to enter Judea was not so significant or tightly orchestrated.

This reveals to us a profound truth about the way God relates to the world. There are some things that He carefully orchestrates and other events that He does not control with such second-by-second precision. God is selectively involved with this world, doing whatever He wants to do. He can let people exercise their own free will in some situations, while intervening and controlling them in other situations.

It is best to understand humanity's free will from the perspective of God being a Father. Any good father is going to allow his children to make some decisions, but get involved with the affairs of his children whenever it is necessary. In similar fashion, Father-God watches over the affairs of His children, intervening when He needs to intervene and delegating responsibility when it is important for the growth of His children. Father-God acts like a father, because He is a Father.

Point 274: Why Do People Have Free Will?

Why did God even give humanity free will?

Augustine answered this by saying, "God gave us free choice in order to enable us to act rightly."[163] Augustine explained that a just God could only reward good behavior if humans freely behaved in ways that deserve to be rewarded. However, the consequence of giving humans free will is that people are free to choose evil, which deserves to be punished.

This explanation has been reworked by countless theologians and philosophers, but a very common explanation among Christians today is that God gave humanity free will because He wants people to freely choose to love Him. True love cannot be forced, but must be a choice.

---

163 Augustine, *On Free Choice of the Will*, Thomas Williams, trans. (Indianapolis: Hackett Publishing Co., 1993), Book II, 18.

Systematic Theology for the New Apostolic Reformation

These answers have some validity to them, however, to gain a more accurate understanding we have to change the question. Do not ask, "Why did God give humanity free will?" Instead, we must ask, "Why do people have free will?" To see this distinction, think of a horse. Why does a horse have legs? Did the parents of that horse give him legs? In one sense we can say, "Yes, the parents gave him legs." But we can also say that the horse has legs because it is made in the image of its parents. It has legs because its parents have legs. In a comparative way we can say that people have free will because they are created in the image of God.

Of course, some teachers do not want to think about this topic in these terms, because it brings our understanding of God's nature and human nature closer together. Because a foundational doctrine to their theology is how humans are nothing but insignificant worms, they try to minimize similarities between God and humanity. Father-Son theology does not have this problem. We admit that God is infinitely greater than humanity and we all fall short of God's glory, yet we are still created in His image. That is the real reason that we have free will.

Volume V
Evil, Sin, and Suffering

Why is there evil, sin, and suffering?

In order to answer this question from a fresh perspective, we will have to dismantle what already has a hold on our minds. This is necessary, because Western philosophy/theology has programmed Western people to think along certain lines. We must separate our thinking from those thought patterns long enough to gain objectivity. We will identify those thought patterns in Section A.

Then in Sections B through H, we will discuss the various sources of pain, sickness, and suffering in this world. Those sections will be divided into the following subjects:

- Section B: The Best World in Which to Raise Sons
- Section C: God's Role in Causing Pain and Suffering
- Section D: Satan's Role and Origin
- Section E: Humanity as a Source of Evil
- Section F: Sin as Something People Do
- Section G: Transgressions and Iniquities
- Section H: Outside Influences of Sin and Evil

Finally in Section I, I will summarize by explaining why there is pain, sickness, and death in the world.

Volume V
Evil, Sin, & Suffering

Section A

Classical View of Evil, Suffering, and Death

Classical reasoning concerning the origin of evil has two foundational progressions of thought that lead to two compatible propositions:

<u>First Progression of Thought</u>
1. If God created evil, then He would be evil.
2. Since God is good, He did not create evil.

<u>Second Progression of Thought</u>
1. God created all things, but He did not create evil.
2. Therefore, evil must not be a "thing."
3. If evil is not a thing, it must be the absence of good.

Before we consider alternative views, it will be helpful to consider how these progressions of thought became rooted in Western civilization.

Point 275: Augustine's Cosmology

When addressing these subjects, Classical theologians/philosophers draw much upon the writings of Augustine. Therefore, a basic understanding of his thoughts concerning evil is helpful.

As mentioned earlier,[164] Augustine was a follower of **Manichaeism** for at least nine years before becoming a Christian. At its height during the 4th century, Manichaeism was one of the most widespread religions in the world. It was the main rival to Christianity in the competition to replace classical paganism during the first five centuries AD.

---
164 I:G:58.

Systematic Theology for the New Apostolic Reformation

Manichaeism was founded on a dualistic cosmology that sees the world resulting from two contrasting and opposing forces. Manichaeism taught that there are two divine beings/gods, i.e., one responsible for everything good and another responsible for everything evil. Manichaeism presented the spiritual world as a world of light—good in every way—and the material world as a world of darkness—evil in every way. This dualistic cosmology considered all pain, sickness, and death as evil.

DUALISM OF MANICHAEISM

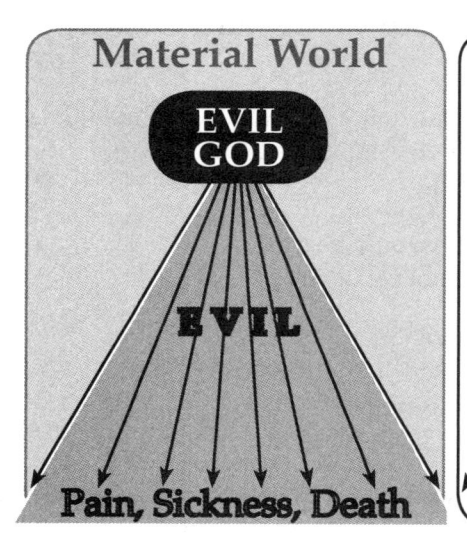

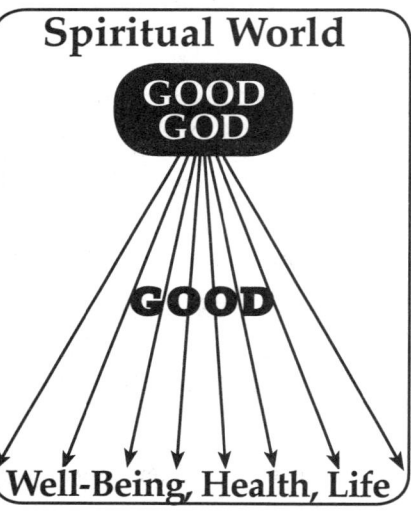

Material World — EVIL GOD — EVIL — Pain, Sickness, Death

Spiritual World — GOOD GOD — GOOD — Well-Being, Health, Life

After Augustine became a Christian, a major theme of his writings was the rethinking of his earlier Manichaeism. He abandoned the view of two gods and saw the Christian God as the Creator of all. Augustine also became less dogmatic concerning the goodness of the spiritual world and evilness of the material world (although some of that dualism remained ingrained in his philosophical reasoning).

Although Augustine came to believe in one God, he built his cosmology upon the ancient Greek philosopher's concept of God existing in a distant, separate spiritual world. Having been a student of Plotinus' teaching, Augustine also embraced Plotinus' concept of God being like the sun, with all of His attributes radiating out of Him.

Classical View of Evil, Suffering, and Death

Most important for our discussion is that Augustine taught that only good can come from God. He reasoned that if God created evil things, then He would be evil. Augustine summarized his view of creation, writing, "a good God made it good."[165]

AUGUSTINE'S TEACHING THAT ONLY GOOD COMES FROM GOD

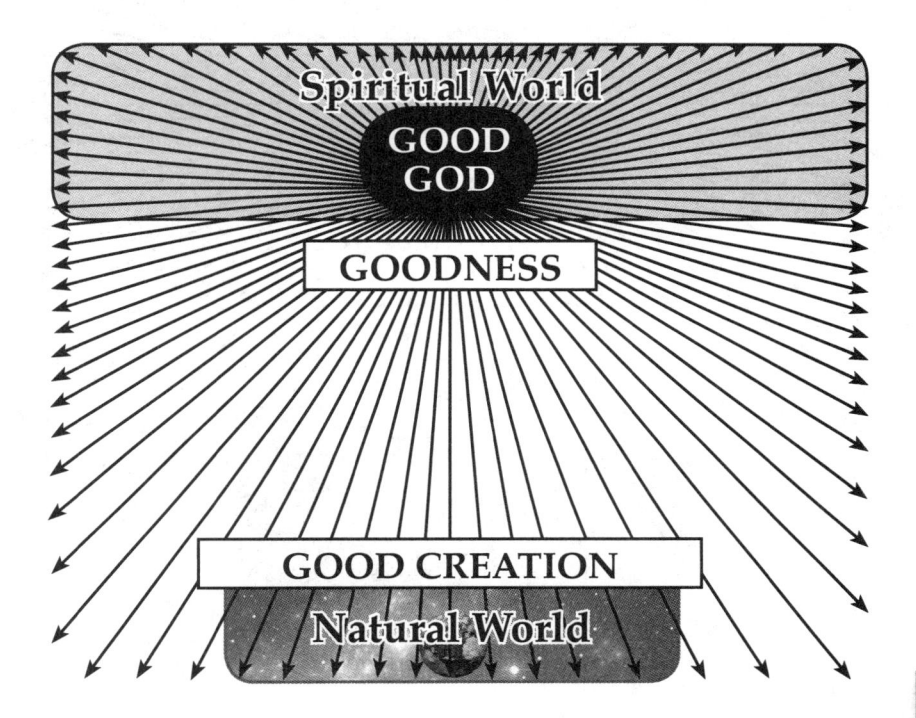

Point 276: Augustine's Thoughts on the Origin of Evil

Once Augustine concluded that God created every *thing* good, he reasoned that evil must not be a *thing*.[166] He explained that evil is the "bending of the will away from . . . God."[167] Evil is the absence of good. Sickness is the absence of health. Death is the absence of life. A thief is evil because he lacks honesty. Everything is created good by God, but it

---

165 Augustine, *City of God*, 11:23.
166 Augustine, *Confessions*, 7:12. Also, explained in his *Enchiridion*.
167 Augustine, *Confessions*, 7:16. Also, explained in his *Enchiridion*.

becomes evil when it is altered from its original good nature. To Augustine, "the loss of good has received the name 'evil.'"[168]

AUGUSTINE'S TEACHING THAT EVIL IS THE BENDING OF GOD'S WILL

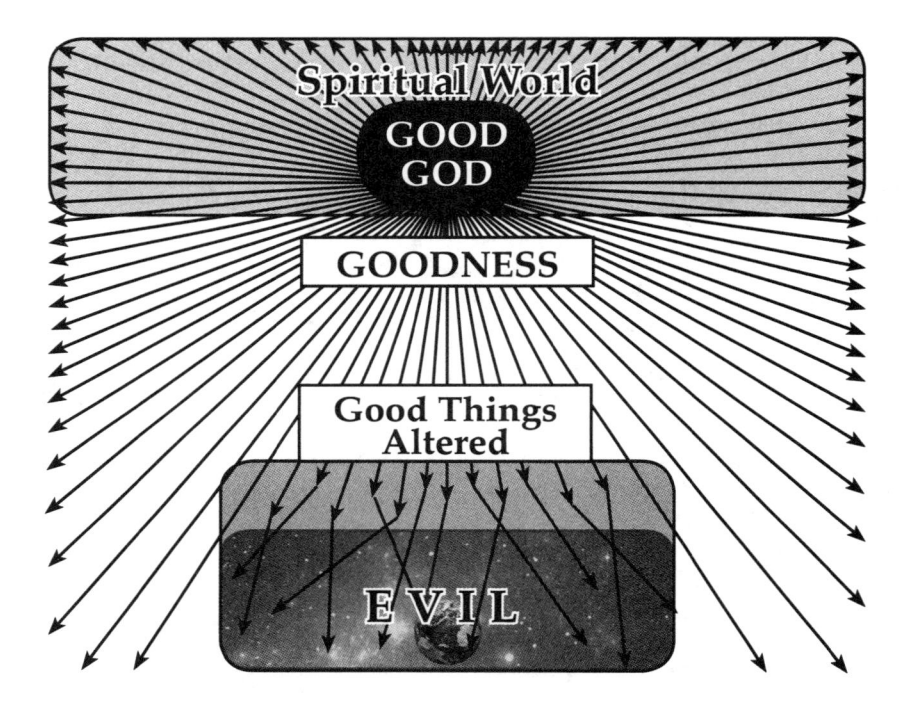

[Diagram: Rays emanating from "Spiritual World / GOOD GOD" downward through "GOODNESS," then "Good Things Altered," then to "EVIL."]

By explaining the existence of evil in this fashion, Augustine could acknowledge the existence of evil without blaming God for creating evil.[169] This way of explaining the existence of evil as the absence of good was taken directly from Plato—not the Bible, as we will see.

Point 277: Countless Implications

Many of the points being made have implications beyond those that

---

168 Augustine, *City of God*, 11:9. Also, explained in his *Enchiridion*.
169 In reality, Augustine's explanation does not remove any blame from God, because Augustine still taught that God is in exhaustive control of all things—even the bending of His own will.

Classical View of Evil, Suffering, and Death

we have the space or time to discuss. For example, Augustine's understanding of good versus evil has played a foundational role in the ethics of Western civilization.

To see this consider the ethics related to birth control. Because the Roman Catholic Church has clung to the fundamentals of Augustinian thought throughout most of its history, Catholic leaders have determined that using most forms of birth control are wrong. To follow their logic, think of Augustine's starting point that good is whatever comes out of God; evil is to bend or alter the will of God. Roman Catholic thinkers have determined that God's original purpose for sexual relations is procreation. Since birth control frustrates the purpose of procreation, then it is evil—according to ethics founded in Augustinian thought.[170]

Protestants are also profoundly influenced by Augustinian thought, but most divert when it comes to issues related to birth control. Yet, Augustinian philosophical thought influences Western thought on many other ethical issues, such as homosexuality. When people argue that homosexuality is genetic, i.e., the way God made them, and therefore good, they are building on the Augustinian/Platonic foundation.[171]

Much of the modern environmental movement is founded in Augustinian ethics. Hence, adherents see that everything is good in its natural state. Many environmental advocates think of evil as anything that interferes with that which is natural. In reality, that way of thinking is unbiblical because God placed humanity on the earth to take dominion, in the sense of stewarding and making it better. People are supposed to intervene in that which is natural. They are suppose to manage it.

There are countless other ethical issues that could be addressed here, but this is not a book on ethics. The only error that we have space to correct here is Augustine's foundational idea concerning ethics. What is right versus wrong should be determined by looking forward, not backwards. It is not origin that determines how people should use what God created. What is important is the outcome of behavior, i.e., you will know them by their fruits. Also, we must look to the future when all of humanity will be judged according to their deeds. Ultimately, these are the only relevant bases for ethics.[172]

---

170 The Roman Catholic Church does allow for natural family planning.
171 This is not meant to be an argument for or against homosexuality. It is simply to help the reader identify Augustinian/Platonic thought.
172 We have some understanding concerning that future judgment by studying judgments that God has already made.

Systematic Theology for the New Apostolic Reformation

Point 278: Augustine's Thoughts on Satan

Augustine applied his understanding of the origin of evil to his understanding of the origin of Satan. Since he believed that a good God can only create good things, Augustine reasoned that God must have created Satan good, but Satan rebelled against God and became evil. Augustine explained this by teaching that Satan was once a good angel in heaven named Lucifer, but Lucifer became filled with pride and turned against God.[173] Then Satan became opposed to God in every way, determined to set up his own kingdom in direct opposition to God.

AUGUSTINE'S TEACHING THAT SATAN WAS ONCE A GOOD ANGEL WHO FELL

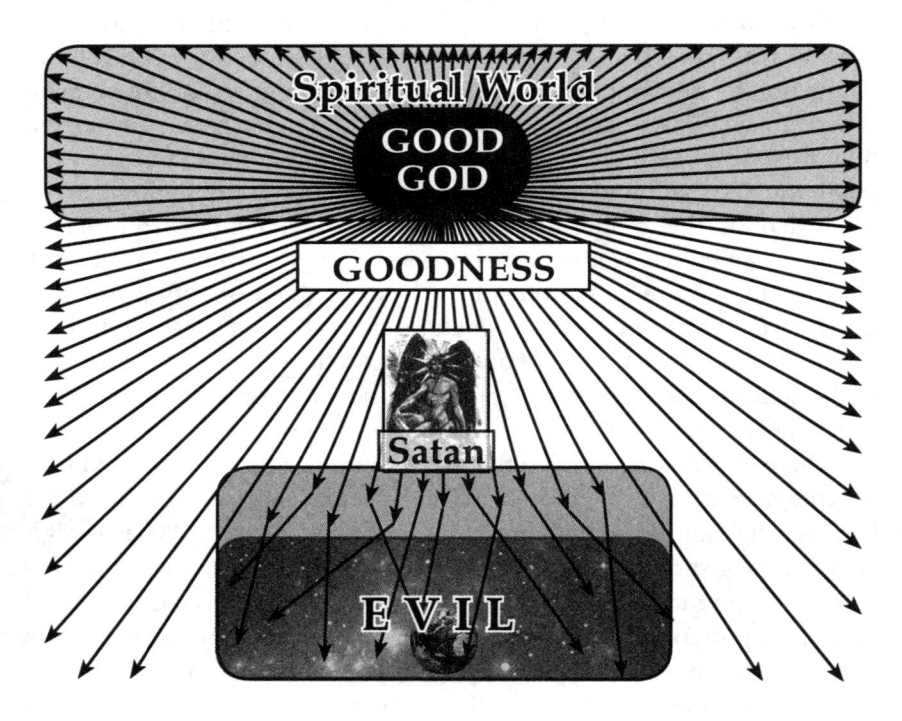

Theologians such as Anselm (c. 1033–1109) and Aquinas (1225–1274) further developed Augustine's teaching that Lucifer was created good but became evil. They also wrote about the angels who followed Satan

---

173 Augustine, *City of God*, book 11.

Classical View of Evil, Suffering, and Death

in his rebellion against God. In time, this understanding of Satan and his demons became dominant in Western Christianity.

It is important to see how this reasoning is dualistic. Of course, it is not dualistic in the sense of Manichaeism; it does not envision two gods, one responsible for evil and the other responsible for good. Yet, it is dualistic in the sense of categorizing everything that comes from God as good and everything that has been distorted as evil.

Point 279: Augustine's Thoughts on Humanity Becoming Evil

Augustine applied similar philosophical reasoning to Adam's origin. Augustine reasoned that God created Adam good, but Adam rebelled against God and became evil. More specifically, Adam rebelled against God and submitted to Satan. As a result of his submission to Satan, Adam became a doorway for Satan's evil to enter into this world. This understanding of how evil originated became commonly accepted in Western Christianity.

Many Christians have assumed that these explanations are straight from the Bible. Therefore, it may be difficult for them to see how Augustine and other early thinkers gave us their philosophical interpretations of the Bible rather than what the Bible actually teaches. I am asking you to reconsider. I am asking you to read the Bible with me and see what it actually says.

Volume V
Evil, Sin, & Suffering

Section B
The Best World in Which to Raise Sons

Here we will contrast Augustine's philosophical reasoning about the origin of pain, sickness, and death with what the Bible actually says.

Point 280: Original Condition of the Garden of Eden

Augustine reasoned that only good can come from a good God, and he saw good as that which results in well-being, health, joy, and life for humanity. Therefore, Augustine taught that God originally created the Garden of Eden as the perfect place for well-being, health, joy, and life. Augustine described the original Garden of Eden as a place of bliss—Paradise itself.[174]

Western Christianity then, being influenced by Augustinian thought, began to envision Adam and Eve casually strolling down smooth pathways surrounded by beautiful flowers and luscious fruit-bearing trees. Christians typically think of the Garden in its original condition as good in the sense that there was no death or suffering. No animals killed each other. There were no thorns or thistles. Adam and Eve strolled around the garden, talking with God and loving each other. This view of the Garden of Eden has been reinforced by countless paintings throughout Church history in which artists restated Augustine's view pictorially. Everything in the Garden is seen as good in the sense of no harm ever being done, while peace and joy reigned.

I will describe that Augustinian rendition of the Garden as good, in the sense of everything being "warm and fuzzy."

---
174 One of several places Augustine discussed this was in his book, *City of God*, 15:1.

Systematic Theology for the New Apostolic Reformation

According to the Bible, the Garden of Eden was not like that. Right from the start God told Adam and Eve that they would have to *"subdue"* everything (Gen. 1:28). He put them in the Garden *"to cultivate and keep it"* (Gen. 2:15). This was before the fall. This means plants did not grow in straight rows by themselves. Adam and Eve had to work six days each week subduing the earth, in the sense of stewarding and caring for it. This leads us to believe that God created the Garden in a needy condition. It needed humanity to tend it.

Even more needy was the world outside of the Garden. Adam and Eve were told to multiply, fill the earth, and subdue it. They were to make a garden out of the whole earth or at least bring order to it. This would have taken millions of descendants. The world needed people to cultivate and improve it.

The point is that earth was not originally created good in the sense of being well-groomed and finished. It was not all warm and fuzzy. Augustine's philosophical reasoning distorted his view. He was unable to accept what the Bible clearly reveals about the Garden.

This warrants more investigation.

Point 281: Death in the Garden of Eden?

Was there anything dangerous in the Garden before the fall? Yes. God placed the tree of the knowledge of good and evil in the Garden. That tree was dangerous. If Adam and Eve ate of it, they would be sentenced to death and begin to experience death.[175] God placed that tree there.

Were there any other things associated with death in the Garden before Adam and Eve sinned? Our answer depends upon whose death we are talking about. Paul tells us in Romans 5:12 that death spread to humanity because all people sin::

> *Therefore, just as through one man sin entered into the world, and death through sin, and so <u>death spread to all men</u>, because all sinned—*

Many Christians infer from this that Adam and Eve were not originally subject to death. But Romans 5:12 tells us nothing about plant and animal life. This verse specifically says that death came to all *men* because of sin.

---

175 Discussed in IV:D:211.

The Best World in Which to Raise Sons

What about the plants and animals? Were they subject to death before the fall? Yes, we can identify death at several different levels.

First, God told Adam and Eve to eat from the plants (Gen. 1:29). It is impossible to eat a plant without killing the part you eat. Every cell wall is broken down before it is absorbed in the human digestive system. So, in God's original design, we recognize one form of death in existence prior to the sin of Adam and Eve.

It was not only plants that experienced death in the Garden. Consider the fact that plants are covered with bacteria and other microscopic organisms. Thousands, even millions, of those organisms are consumed each time a plant is eaten. Most of those microscopic organisms die within the human digestive system.

Think about the fur, hair, and feathers that grow from the skin on certain animals. The root of every hair and feather is made of living cells. Those cells die as they emerge from the skin. If there was no death in creation, then every hair that fell from Eve's beautiful locks would still be lying on the ground alive. Obviously, death was part of the original creation.

Now consider large animals. Picture an elephant walking through the Garden of Eden. Is it possible for an elephant to walk very far without stepping on and crushing a few insects? I doubt it.

Consider how rapidly rabbits reproduce. If rabbits are allowed to reproduce unhindered, with none of them dying, every square foot of earth's surface will be covered by a living rabbit in less than 30 years.

Beetles are even more prolific. If they reproduce unhindered, the entire earth will be covered with a layer of beetles in less than a year.

How did God originally create this world? Plants and animals were not created to be immortal. Death was in His original design. This did not include the death of humans. People may have been created to have dominion over all things on earth, including death. However, after Adam sinned, the power of death overcame and spread to all of humanity. However, even before Adam's sin, the cycles of life and death were part of God's original creation.

Point 282: Could Death Have Come from God?

Christians influenced by Augustinian philosophical thought can only envision good—warm and fuzzy things—being created by a good God.

Systematic Theology for the New Apostolic Reformation

Therefore, they have a difficult time reconciling their view of God with the truth that God created the cycles of life and death in creation. They typically explain that death is the result of Satan corrupting the good things God created. Later we will talk about Satan and his role, but now we need to give more proof of the fact that death was part of God's original plan.

Consider the words of God to Job. God declared that He created the lion to hunt and kill her prey (Job 38:39), the wild ox to be untamable (Job 39:5-12), the ostrich to treat her young cruelly (Job 39:16), the eagle to spy out food from afar while the young suck blood (Job 39:26-30), and Leviathan with teeth that terrify (Job 41:14). Yes, the Bible tells us God created fearsome animals that kill and eat one another.

Similarly, the Psalmist praised God who created all things, including:

> *The young lions roar after their prey*
> *And seek their food from God . . .*
> *And Leviathan, which You have formed . . . .*
>
> (Ps. 104:21-26)

Make no mistake. God created the lion to hunt and Leviathan which terrifies.

Point 283: A Source of Pain and Suffering

The death of plants and animals was a part of God's original design in creation, but was there pain and suffering? Consider what God said to Eve:

> *I will greatly multiply*
> *Your pain in child birth*
>
> (Gen. 3:16)

Pain got worse because of the fall, but notice that some pain was already involved with childbearing before the fall.

Pain is not entirely bad. Some physical pain is necessary for survival. For example, if Adam walked through the Garden and a tree branch poked him in the eye, the resulting pain made it clear to him that he needed to pull away from that tree branch. God instilled the ability to feel pain.

We can also recognize pain in the animal kingdom if we accept God's words to Job that He created the lion to hunt and kill her prey (Job 38:39),

The Best World in Which to Raise Sons

the eagle to spy out food from afar (Job 39:26-30), and so forth. The world was good in its original condition, but not in the sense of it being pain-free.

Point 284: Creation Fulfills Father-God's Purpose

We know that God created the world good, but in what way was it created good? To answer this, it is helpful to step back and identify again God's purpose for creation. It was a gift to the Son.[176] Humanity was part of that gift, but God intended to accomplish something with humanity. Paul explained:

> [God] *made from one man every nation of mankind to live on all the face of the earth . . . that they would seek God, if perhaps they might grope for Him and find Him . . . .*
> (Acts 17:26-27)

God wants people to seek Him. In fact, God even sees value in people groping for Him, if that's what it takes for them to find Him. Indeed, finding Him is one of God's primary goals for humanity.

To accomplish this goal, God placed us in a world in which we need help. It is not a pain-free world. It is a big world, an unfinished world, a world that needs to be managed. We cannot be successful here without God. This world is good, but it needs us and God working together to manage it. God created the world that way.

I have a woodworking shop. When my youngest son still lived at home, we would occasionally go out into the shop and work on projects. Sometimes my son asked for my advice. I enjoyed that. The shop was the perfect environment for us to build a relationship. However, there were many sharp tools in the shop. It was easy to get injured there. The shop was dangerous, but it was also good.

In similar fashion, the world is good, but it is not a big pillow upon which people are to spend their lives sleeping and casually eating. It needs to be managed. People need to work. They can only be successful with God's assistance. They need God. This world is the perfect environment to fulfill God's purpose—to lead people into a relationship with Him. In this way the world is good.

---

176 Explained in III:B:146.

Systematic Theology for the New Apostolic Reformation

Point 285: God's Puzzle that We Are Commissioned to Fix

I am challenging Augustine's dualism. He was wrong that only warm and fuzzy things come from God.[177]

A helpful analogy to understand this challenge is to compare Augustine's philosophical understanding of creation to a big puzzle with every piece in its proper position so as to create a beautiful, complete picture. Because Augustine envisioned this perfect puzzle as God's original design, anyone who removed or changed a piece of the puzzle would be altering God's design and, therefore, doing evil.

In contrast, the understanding that we develop from a direct reading of the Bible can be compared to a puzzle with many pieces that are not in their appropriate places. God created the world that way. Then He put humanity in the Earth to put those puzzle pieces where they belong. He intended and commissioned people to make this world a better place. This means that changing God's original design is not evil. Of course, people can sin and put the puzzle pieces where God does not want the pieces to be, but God originally put Adam and Eve in the Garden to make it a better place and then to bring order to the whole world outside of the Garden.

Point 286: Father-God's Purpose to Raise Sons

We can understand how God designed the natural world if we see Him as a loving Father. Our Father wants us to mature. We cannot mature in a world where everything is perfectly in order and finished. God placed us in a world that needs to be managed. It needs us and God working together to make it a better place.

This world is also a place where bad stuff happens. It is not all warm and fuzzy. God placed us in a world where pain and suffering are real. The truth is that people cannot mature without some pain and suffering. There are several Bible passages that talk about the positive results produced in people because of suffering. For example, Paul wrote:

> . . . tribulation brings about perseverance; and perseverance, proven character; and proven character, hope.
>
> (Rom. 5:3-4)

---

[177] Augustine was inconsistent in this, with some of his writings acknowledging pain and suffering coming from God.

The Best World in Which to Raise Sons

Even Jesus learned through His suffering (Heb. 5:8). Evidently, suffering is a part of maturing.

I know this is contrary to the teaching of some leaders. They teach that life will be easy if we simply live as God wants us to live. It is true that a life of obedience is filled with love, peace, and joy. However, God did not put us in a world without pain or suffering. This world is beautiful, but it can be dangerous. The oceans shout of the magnificence of our Creator, yet they also beat against the cliff's base, eventually causing it to crumble, burying all in its path, including living creatures. The rain causes crops to grow, but it can also flood the homes of ground squirrels where those furry little creatures drown. The wind can blow and carry seeds to fertile ground, but it can also dislodge a bird's nest from a tree, resulting in the death of young chicks. Earthquakes happen. Volcanoes kill people.

This is the world God created. It is a world where bad stuff sometimes happens, a world where we need God, a world that we need to subdue, a world where we can mature. This world is a place where we can learn how to love and care for one another. God put us in a world that is the perfect environment to fulfill His purpose, which is to raise sons.

Volume V
Evil, Sin, & Suffering

Section C
God's Role in Causing Pain and Suffering

We have seen how God created the perfect world to raise sons, and that world can result in human pain and suffering. Now we can consider God's ongoing involvement in this world. In Volume II, *God's Involvement in this World*, we saw how God is selectively involved and how some pain and suffering happen because God is not controlling all things. Now we are focusing on God's actions that may result in pain and suffering.

Point 287: God's Good Judgments

Christians seem to gravitate toward one of two extremes. Some focus on God's wrath, and see God as very intolerant, waiting to crush any disobedience. At the other extreme are Christians who focus on the love of God to the exclusion of *any* judgment coming from Him.

In order to understand God's ongoing judgment in this world, we must see Him as a Judge, but not according to the Western understanding. Earlier we discussed how Western people tend to think of a judge as someone who sits at the front of a courtroom and declares people as guilty or innocent. The Hebraic understanding of a judge was very different. Think of the judges who are talked about in the Book of Judges. God raised up each of those judges to deliver the oppressed, correct injustice, and set things straight. It is in that sense that God is a Judge.

So when God brought destruction with Noah's flood, it was for the purpose of setting things straight. Humanity had gotten so far off course that correction was required.

Systematic Theology for the New Apostolic Reformation

So also, God sent an angel to kill the firstborn male in every household of the Egyptians so that Pharaoh would let the Hebrews go free. By taking this action, God was setting the oppressed Hebrews free and fulfilling His will for the Hebrews.

All of God's judgments are right and good, however, they can result in human pain and suffering.

GOD'S GOOD ACTIONS MAY RESULT IN SOME PAIN AND SUFFERING

With this understanding, we can study the Book of Revelation. There we see God rendering judgments as a King taking authority over His domain. Each decree of the King is to overthrow evil powers and put everything under the feet of Jesus. Throughout the Book of Revelation we see the kingdoms of this world becoming the Kingdom of our God.

So we can note again that only good comes from a good God, but His good judgments can result in some pain and suffering.

Point 288: Challenging Dualism

What we are challenging is a dualistic way of thinking about good and evil. Here we are using the term *dualistic* to refer to the thinking that associates all of God's actions with what people consider good such as

God's Role in Causing Pain and Suffering

well-being, health, joy, and life (or warm and fuzzy things). At the same time, dualistic thinking associates everything that causes pain, sickness, and death as evil.

Augustine was a dualist in this sense. He offered the foundation of his worldview in Book 11 of the *City of God*, where he explained that God created the light but not the darkness. Then Augustine associated the good angels with the light and the angels that rebelled against God with darkness. That foundation was taken directly from Manichaeism—not the Bible.

Consider what the Bible says. God declared in Isaiah 45:6-7:

> *I am the Lord, and there is no other,*
> *The One forming light and creating darkness,*
> *Causing well-being and creating calamity;*
> *I am the Lord who does all these.*

God created darkness. He created calamity.

Augustine was wrong.

Point 289: God Can Do Whatever He Wants

Our good God is capable of doing some good things that result in pain, suffering, and death. It was God who destroyed Sodom and Gomorrah. God told the Hebrews that if they did not serve Him, then He would send enemies against them *"in hunger, in thirst, in nakedness, and in the lack of all things; and He will put an iron yoke on your neck until He has destroyed you"* (Deut. 28:48). When David sinned, *"the Lord sent a pestilence upon Israel from the morning until the appointed time"* (2 Sam. 24:15).

Some Christians are so dualistic concerning good and evil that they cannot accept any of these examples in the Bible of God being the source of pain and suffering. Their dualistic worldview keeps them from believing what the Bible reveals. Yes, God is good, but not in the sense that He is limited and, therefore, only able take warm and fuzzy actions. He is sovereign. He can do anything He wants to do whenever He wants.

Consider 1 Samuel 2:6:

> *The Lord kills and makes alive;*
> *He brings down to Sheol and raises up.*

Systematic Theology for the New Apostolic Reformation

Psalm 104:29 also talks about how God gives life and takes it away:

> *You take away their spirit, they expire*
> *And return to their dust.*

This does not mean that God is responsible for all the tragedy that we see in the world. This does not mean the disease and pain that you and I experience are from God. It simply means that God is sovereign, and *He can* be a source of pain and suffering when He selectively chooses to be.

Point 290: Father-God Is the NT Judge

Lest anyone think that God was only a Judge in the OT times, it is worth mentioning some examples from the Book of Acts in which God's actions resulted in pain and suffering for people.

Most Christians are familiar with the story Ananias and Sapphira who lied to the Holy Spirit and, as a result, died (Acts 5:1-10). If that was the only example in Acts, we may be able to explain it away, but Acts 12:21-23 tells us about Herod allowing people to worship him as a god:

> *And immediately an <u>angel of the Lord struck him</u> because he did not give God the glory, and he was eaten by worms and died.*
> (Acts 12:23)

Similarly, when a magician named Elymas opposed Paul, Paul said:

> *"Now, behold, the <u>hand of the Lord is upon you, and you will be blind</u> and not see the sun for a time." And immediately a mist and a darkness fell upon him . . . .*
> (Acts 13:11)

So here we have three examples from the Book Acts. Let every fact be confirmed by the mouth of two or three witnesses.

Christians who cannot incorporate these three examples of God being the direct cause of pain, suffering, and death, have fallen into dualistic philosophical reasoning. That dualistic reasoning can distort their understanding of the entire Bible.

God's Role in Causing Pain and Suffering

Point 291: Rest Assured that God Is Good

Having shown that God can be a source of pain and suffering, it is important to remind everyone that *God does not want to inflict pain and suffering upon His people.* This is especially important to emphasize because many Christians have worked long and hard to learn that God loves them. Those Christians who are insecure in their relationship with Father-God don't need me to tell them that God sometimes causes pain and suffering.

We should separate in our minds what God *can* do and what He *will* do. He can cause pain and suffering, but that is not in His heart for those He loves. Christians can be reassured that Father-God wants the best for His children.

In the prolegomenon of this book, I compared God to a human father who has several children. This father loves and dotes over his children. At the same time, this father is a soldier in the army. This father never talks to his children about his work as a soldier, and they have never seen him on the battlefield. The only father they know is the one who loves them, provides for them, and tucks them into bed at night. In a comparative way, we can say that God is love. We wish all people knew Him this way. However, it is unbiblical and foolish to say that Father-God is incapable of causing pain.

Point 292: Mentally Prepared for Battle

The truth that God can be a source of pain and suffering is especially difficult for Christians who have been trained in the current **healing movement**, which is a branch of Christianity in which Christians are taught to believe God for physical healing. Teachers in that movement often say that God is never the source of pain, sickness, or death. They teach this because they do not want Christians to passively accept pain and sickness. They want Christians to use their faith and resist these evils. Such resistance is good.

It is difficult to overcome anything evil unless you identify it as evil. For this reason, soldiers at war typically see their enemies as evil. They do not allow themselves to think of their enemies as individuals with spouses and children. To think of their enemies as real people with normal lives

Systematic Theology for the New Apostolic Reformation

would undermine their determination to defeat their enemies. In similar fashion, people who are fighting with sickness need to think of their sickness as their enemy. Any thoughts to the contrary would undermine their determination and faith. More importantly, to think that God may have caused their illness would completely obliterate their faith for healing.

For this reason, Christian ministers who teach about God's healing power typically teach that God *never* causes sickness. They often quote John 10:10, where Jesus said:

> *The thief comes only to steal and kill and destroy; I came that they may have life, and have it abundantly.*

This verse can be used to promote a dualistic way of thinking in which Satan is seen as the one who steals, kills, and destroys, while Jesus only does good things associated with life, health, blessings, and happiness.

Indeed, identifying the enemy allows the combatants to focus energy to defeat the enemy. A teacher who simplifies the battle by telling everyone that their enemy is evil can help the listeners focus and win the battle. Comparatively, a general in the army can rally his troops by talking about the evil scum whom they are about to defeat.

Yet, in reality, the enemies are not always evil scum. Nor is Satan the author of all sickness and pain. Reconsider John 10:10. The "thief" that Jesus talks about in this verse is not Satan. The context never mentions Satan, but it identifies the thief as a person who comes into the sheepfold and leads the sheep astray. Jesus was actually talking about religious leaders who lead in directions where the True Shepherd is not leading them. Once we read the whole passage, we see how wrong it is to take John 10:10 out of its context and use it to teach a dualistic doctrine that Satan does all bad things (in the sense of pain and suffering), while God does all good things (in the sense of well-being and happiness).

Point 293: Abandon Dualistic Reasoning, and Think Deeper

Once we reject dualistic thinking about good and evil, it becomes clear that we should not accredit all warm and fuzzy things to God and all pain and suffering to Satan. That does not leave us in confusion. It simply requires us to think deeper about the related subject.

God's Role in Causing Pain and Suffering

When a person is suffering we should not mechanistically apply the dualistic formula. Instead, we should look to the heart of Father-God. We know that He is capable of causing pain and suffering, however, our knowledge of Him reveals to us how loving He is. Father-God does not want to cause suffering in the lives of His children. We can rest our faith in His love. That is where our faith should be founded. Faith should not rest on a dualistic doctrine. Instead, it must rest in the Person who loves us.

The person who is sick can be reassured that God is Yahweh Rapha (Lord Our Healer). Father-God wants His children to resist sickness and obtain whatever help is available. He wants to heal. God is for us, not against us.

Volume V
Evil, Sin, & Suffering

Section D
Satan's Origin and Role

Now it will be helpful to consider the role and origin of Satan (and demons). Like so many other theological subjects, this one has been profoundly influenced by Western philosophy and its inherent dualism. If we read the Bible without the biases of Western philosophical reasoning and dualism, we will arrive at very different conclusions than Classical/Reformed theology does concerning Satan's role and origin in the world.

Point 294: Satan's Role in Evil

We saw how God created a world where pain, sickness, and death are real. Satan is an enemy of humanity, and his activity in the world has increased pain, sickness, and death. This can be seen in the life of Job. Satan smote Job with painful boils (Job 2:7). Then Satan killed Job's sons, daughters, servants, and animals (Job 1:13-19). Pain, sickness, and death were in the world, but Satan was able to use these against Job.

We can also read about Jesus casting demons out of individuals, and as a result, they were physically (Matt. 9:33) and psychologically (Mark 5:1-20) healed. Even today, demons are wandering the earth seeking someone to devour. They can cause pain, sickness, and death.

Of course, in the modern world many teachers deny the presence and activity of Satan and demons. They try to explain the pain and suffering that was once accredited to demons as psychological and physiological problems. Indeed, much suffering is the result of psychological and physiological problems. However, anyone who takes the Bible seriously will also recognize Satan and demons as real beings, created by God, yet capable of causing great pain and suffering.

Systematic Theology for the New Apostolic Reformation

Point 295: Satan as a Fallen Angel

Let's consider Satan's origin.

Augustine reasoned that God is good, so only good (warm and fuzzy things) comes from Him. Therefore, according to Augustine's philosophical reasoning, God must have originally created Satan good, but Satan rebelled and became bad.[178]

Christian teachers who have embraced Augustine's reasoning typically say that Satan was originally created by God to be the angel who led worship in heaven. At that time, Satan, who was called Lucifer, became filled with pride and turned against God. When Lucifer rebelled, he convinced one-third of all the angels to rebel with him. This led to Satan and his minions becoming evil. According to this view, Satan and the demons are trying to set up a kingdom that is diametrically opposed to God.

Augustine's Teaching that Satan Was Once a Good Angel Who Fell

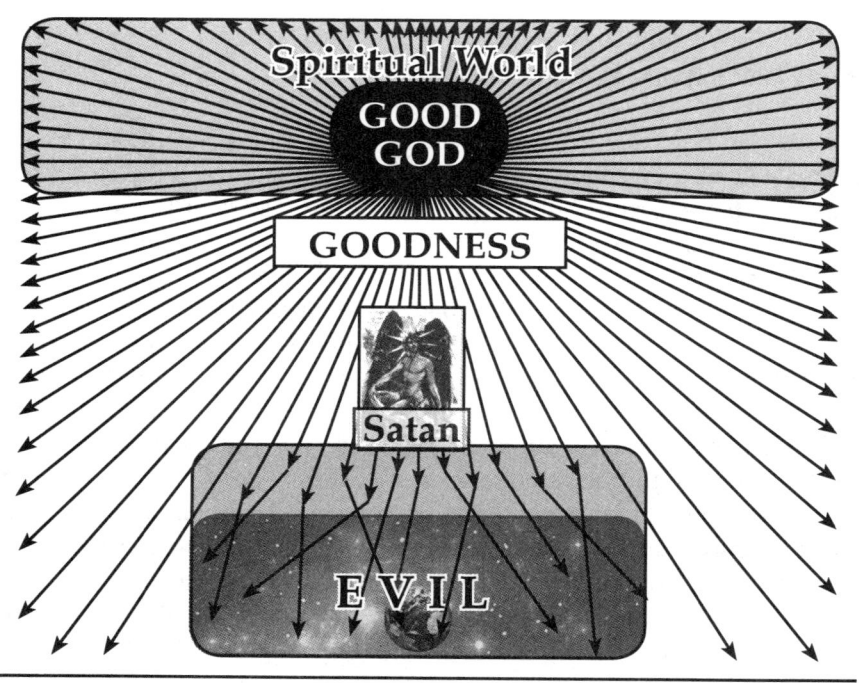

---

178 Augustine, *City of God*, book 11.

Satan's Origin and Role

Many Christians have incorporated this understanding of Satan as a fallen angel so deeply into their theology that they cannot bear to have it challenged, but this "fallen angel" doctrine did not originate from Scripture. It developed as a philosophical explanation for the origin of Satan and evil. Then certain Bible passages were used to support it—four Bible passages to be exact. Let me show you.

Point 296: "Lucifer" Falling in Isaiah 14?

The Bible passage most used to teach that Satan was once an angel that rebelled against God is the KJV of Isaiah 14:12:

> *How art thou fallen from heaven, O Lucifer, son of the morning! how art thou cut down to the ground, which didst weaken the nations!*

Those who believe that Satan was once the supreme worship angel in heaven say that the name *Lucifer* refers to Satan. Then they take this passage to teach the doctrine that Satan had *"fallen from heaven."*

In reality, the name *Lucifer* was not in the original Hebrew manuscripts of this Bible passage. The historical origin of this name Lucifer is vague, but our earliest records show us that the Church fathers Tertullian (c. 160–220 AD)[179] and Origen (185–251 AD)[180] began associating Lucifer with Satan. However, it was not until the 5th century that Lucifer began to be used as a proper name for Satan. This was primarily the result of Jerome (347–420 AD) inserting the name in the *Vulgate*, his Latin translation of the Bible. When the KJV was produced, the translators carried over this name—not from the original manuscripts but from the Latin Vulgate.

In Isaiah 14:12, there is a Hebrew word, *helel*, which is accurately translated "son of the morning" or "morning star." However, there is no justifiable reason to equate this with Lucifer or Satan. Therefore, most modern translations—Protestant and Roman Catholic—do not include Lucifer in this verse.

Knowing that Lucifer is not mentioned in Isaiah 14, many great thinkers throughout Church history, including Martin Luther and John Calvin, attempted to break the unfounded teaching that Isaiah 14 was

---

[179] *Contra Marrionem*, v. 11, 17.
[180] *Ezekiel Opera*, iii. 356.

Systematic Theology for the New Apostolic Reformation

talking about Satan. Concerning the reference to Lucifer in Isaiah 14, Luther wrote, "This is not said of the angel who once was thrown out of heaven but of the king of Babylon, and it is figurative language."[181] Concerning the same passage, John Calvin wrote, "The exposition of this passage, which some have given, as if it referred to Satan, has arisen from ignorance; for the context plainly shows that these statements must be understood in reference to the king of the Babylonians."[182]

As Luther and Calvin noted, Isaiah 14 is literally talking about the king of Babylon who was alive at the time Isaiah wrote the passage. It is understandable that some modern Bible teachers use Isaiah 14 as a possible allegory to talk about Satan. However, to say that Isaiah 14 definitely refers to Satan is unfounded.

Point 297: "Lucifer" Falling in Ezekiel 28?

A second Bible passage often used by those who believe that Satan was once the worship angel in heaven is Ezekiel 28. The key verses are 14 and 15:

> *You were the anointed cherub who covers,*
> *And I placed you there.*
> *You were on the holy mountain of God;*
> *You walked in the midst of the stones of fire.*
> *You were blameless in your ways*
> *From the day you were created*
> *Until unrighteousness was found in you.*

Christians take the phrase, *"the anointed cherub,"* and from this conclude that Satan was the angel who led worship.

In reality, Ezekiel 28 is clearly addressed to the king of Tyre: "*Son of man, take up a lamentation over the king of Tyre . . .*" (Ez. 28:11). This king was a literal human being who lived at the time of Ezekiel. In verse 2, the king is clearly told, "*Yet you are a man and not God,*" then again in verse 9, "*Though you are man and not God.*" He is called a man, and never an angel or a demon.

---

181 *Luther's Works*, vol. 16, p. 140.
182 *Commentary on Isaiah*, vol. 1, p. 442.

Satan's Origin and Role

In order to understand the phrase, "*the anointed cherub,*" we must recognize the context. Ezekiel 28 is a taunt toward the king of Tyre. Compare this taunt to a modern-day saying, such as, "So you think you are God's gift to humanity." Indeed, this fits the context in which the king of Tyre was being addressed.

Once we see this, we can consider the possibility that Ezekiel 28 is allegorically referring to Satan, but it is shaky ground to build a doctrine based solely on allegory.

Point 298: When Did "Lucifer" Fall?

There are two other Bible passages that are used to prop up the "Satan once being the worship angel in heaven" doctrine, but they are also shaky props at best.

Luke 10:18 tells us about Jesus speaking to his disciples:

> *And He said to them, "I was watching Satan fall from heaven like lightning."*

Any quick reading of the context of this verse shows that the disciples had just returned from preaching and casting demons out of people. In that context, it does not make sense that Jesus was referring to seeing Satan fall from heaven thousands or millions of years earlier. A straight reading of this passage leads us to understand that Jesus was seeing Satan losing his authority right at that time, as the disciples were out preaching and casting demons out of people. Therefore, it is poor hermeneutics to use Luke 10:18 to support a doctrine that Satan fell from heaven before Adam and Eve sinned in the Garden.

The only other Bible passage that teachers have to teach that Satan once was the worship angel in heaven is Revelation 12:7-9:

> *And there was war in heaven, Michael and his angels waging war with the dragon . . . And the great dragon was thrown down, the serpent of old who is called the devil and Satan, who deceives the whole world; he was thrown down to the earth, and his angels were thrown down with him.*

Systematic Theology for the New Apostolic Reformation

Most Bible teachers understand that the apostle John wrote the Book of Revelation, and John was reporting events that would take place in his future (sometime after the death and resurrection of Jesus). Therefore, Revelation 12 was not talking about events that took place thousands or millions of years before Jesus died and resurrected.

When we take the timing into account, we come to a very different understanding of Revelation 12. Satan was once god of this world (2 Cor. 4:4). When Jesus died and resurrected, He *"disarmed the rulers and authorities"* (Col. 2:15). The ruler of this world was judged (John 16:11). Indeed, Satan fell from his position of authority over this world when Jesus sat down on His throne in heaven approximately 2,000 years ago. The fall being talked about in Revelation 12 is that which happened after the death and resurrection of Jesus.[183] Therefore, it is wrong to use this passage to teach that Satan fell before Adam and Eve fell.

Point 299: Is It True or Is It Unfounded Tradition?

As Christians endeavoring to build on the biblical revelation, we need to recognize the lack of biblical support for the idea that Satan was once the worship angel who was thrown out of heaven.

That doctrine was developed to solve a philosophical dilemma. It was unknown to the early Church. *As far as we know, the first apostles had never heard of that doctrine.*

The doctrine developed through the centuries and brings us to modern times when Christians have been handed a philosophical explanation that is accepted by many as fact. Perhaps there is *some* truth in it. However, we should not naively embrace that which cannot be found in Scripture.

We also have reason to question the doctrine because it is troubling to conceive of Satan becoming filled with pride while he was the angel leading worship in heaven. Is it possible for any being to stand in the very manifest presence of God and there to become filled with pride and evil? The way Isaiah describes the presence of God in Isaiah 6:1-7, it sounds impossible to even have a negative thought while in the midst of God's manifest glory.

---

183 For a fuller explanation of this fall of Satan and his kingdom see my book entitled, *Victorious Eschatology*.

Satan's Origin and Role

There are other reasons to doubt that Satan was ever the worship angel in heaven, but I will just give you one more. According to that doctrine, Satan had to have been cast out of heaven before Adam and Eve listened to him in the Garden of Eden. Yet, there are several examples in the Bible of Satan having access to the throne room of God long after the Garden of Eden incident. For example, in Job's day, Satan went right into the throne room (Job 1:6). Also, we read how Satan accuses the brethren day and night before the throne of God (Rev. 12:10). It does not sound like Satan had been thrown out of heaven.

Point 300: Satan's Origin Is Unknown

If Satan was not the angel who once led worship in heaven, then who was or is he? And from where did he come?

We know that God created all things, including Satan (Col. 1:16), but we do not know any more than that. Everything else about Satan's origin is pure conjecture. If we are going to stay true to what the Bible reveals, then we must teach only that which can be found in the Bible.

Perhaps Satan never was a good angel. Jesus spoke of the devil saying:

> *He was a murderer from the beginning, and does not stand in the truth because there is no truth in him. Whenever he speaks a lie, he speaks from his own nature, for he is a liar and the father of lies.*
>
> (John 8:44)

Notice that Jesus refers to the devil having a nature to lie and says he was a murderer from the beginning. John wrote:

> *. . . the devil has sinned from the beginning.*
>
> (1 John 3:8)

We cannot conclusively develop a doctrine about Satan's origin from these passages, but it sounds like Satan was a liar from the beginning, rather than the angel that led worship in heaven from the beginning.

It is possible that God created Satan as a deceiver and liar. Remember, He created the hawk to hunt and kill prey (Job 38:39). He

Systematic Theology for the New Apostolic Reformation

could have created Satan as a being to oppose humanity. God could have created Satan anyway He wanted to create him. As God said through Isaiah, *"I am the Lord, and there is no other, The One forming light and creating darkness"* (Is. 45:6-7). God is capable of creating anything He wants to create. If He so chose to do so, He could have created Satan as a liar from the beginning.

Paul expounded upon the sovereignty of God, writing:

> *Or does not the potter have a right over the clay, to make from the same lump one vessel for honorable use and another for common use?*
> (Rom. 9:21)

I am not saying that God created evil. I am not saying that God is the cause of all suffering and pain. I am simply saying that God can do whatever He wants to do.

So what is the origin of Satan? No one knows. The Bible does not tell us. This should not surprise us, because the Bible is not about Satan. It is about God and His relationship with humanity.

Point 301: The Origin of Demons Is Unknown

How did demons come into existence? Many Christian teachers will say that demons are the angels that followed Satan when he rebelled against God. There are other possible explanations.

Some teachers have developed their understanding from an ancient Jewish religious work called, *The Book of Enoch*. In that book there is a passage that takes some truths from Genesis 6:1-4, where we are told about the sons of God having relations with the daughters of men and about the Nephilim who were in the world at that time. *The Book of Enoch* expounds upon that discussion, saying that the Nephilim were killed in Noah's flood, but the spirits of the Nephilim became the demons that have been on earth ever since that time.

In reality, it would not be wise to put much credence in *The Book of Enoch*. Almost all scholars say it is a **pseudepigraph**, meaning that it was not written by the Enoch of the OT, who was the great-grandfather of Noah. According to the genealogy recorded in Genesis 5, that Enoch died several hundred years before Noah's flood. In ancient Jewish society, there

Satan's Origin and Role

were hundreds and possibly thousands of men with the name Enoch. Furthermore, the content and style of the book lead scholars to believe that it was probably written no earlier than the 3rd century BC.

The Book of Enoch was considered non-canonical by the Jews. It was also rejected by mainstream Christianity.[184] It should also be doubted because it does not make sense that God would send a flood in Noah's day to purge the earth of evil and in that flood destroy the Nephilim, but leave their evil spirits in the earth.

If we stay with the biblical revelation, we have to say that the origin of demons is unknown. God chose not to reveal this. They may be fallen angels, but it is also possible that demons were created as completely different spiritual creatures than angels. We simply do not know. The Bible does not tell us.

Point 302: The Foundation for Father-Son Theology

Why would we want to question the idea that Satan was once the worship angel in heaven?

1. It lacks biblical support.
2. It gives Satan too much credit. We do not know if he ever held the position of leading worship in heaven.
3. It leads to a subtle, yet profound, change in one's theology.

To see this change, consider how Genesis 1 starts with God creating the heavens and earth. The Bible does not start with a report of Satan being a good angel in heaven who fell. It starts with God, creation, and then Adam and Eve being created in the image of God.

Starting our theology where the Bible starts, i.e., Genesis 1, gives us a biblical foundation for our theology. In contrast, starting a theology on something that supposedly happened before Adam and Eve were created leaves us "with a supposedly true" foundation. When Christians begin their worldview with a story about Satan being a good angel who fell, their entire worldview builds on that foundation. Hence, they tend to develop a dualistic worldview and theology, concluding that the world is about a war going on between God and Satan.

---

184 The Ethiopian Orthodox Tewahedo Church and Eritrean Orthodox Tewahedo Church have accepted the *Book of Enoch* as canonical.

Systematic Theology for the New Apostolic Reformation

Beginning with Satan's Fall Leads to a Dualistic Worldview with a War Between God and Satan

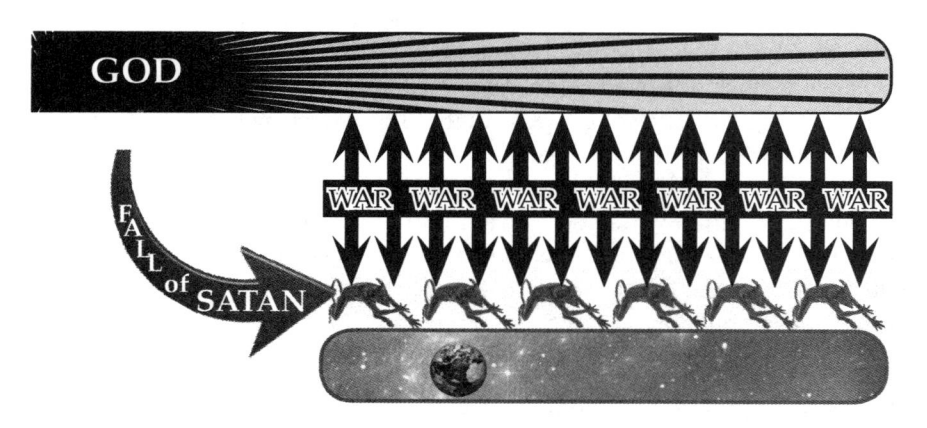

In contrast, if we start where the Bible starts, we learn about God creating a world and then Adam and Eve. This foundation leads us to develop a worldview and theology based on God and what He is doing with people. *The world is not about a war between God and Satan. It is about God raising sons.*

Point 303: Satan Is Not at War with God

Pitting Satan against God in war is a huge distortion of the biblical revelation. If God wanted to get rid of Satan and his demons, He could do it by simply speaking a word. In Revelation 12:7-9, we see that Michael and his angels dethroned Satan. Notice that Satan was pitted against Michael, not God, and even in that fight, Michael won.

Sometimes Christians envision Satan pitted against Jesus which is also a distortion. Of course, Satan tempted Jesus in the wilderness, but Jesus overcame Satan. More importantly, Jesus conquered Satan through His death and resurrection. Then God raised Jesus up *"far above all rule and authority and power and dominion"* (Eph. 1:21). To emphasize this, let me say that Satan and Jesus should not even be mentioned together in the same sentence. Of course, this is an overstatement, but Satan should be aligned counter to Michael, not Jesus.

Satan's Origin and Role

Point 304: The Role and Purpose of Satan

The fact that God does not eliminate Satan implies that He has a purpose for Satan's existence. What could that purpose be? Well, if we embrace the overriding purpose of God to raise sons, then we can see how Satan and his demons play a role in helping God fulfill that goal. God leaves Satan and his demons on earth so God's people will learn to be overcomers. Satan and his demons are obstacles for God's children to conquer.

This fits with the nature of Satan. The word *satan* actually is not even a proper name in the Bible. It is a generic term meaning "adversary," "opponent," or "rival."

God has placed in the earth an adversary for His children to overcome. We can compare this to a body-builder who has to lift weights to increase his muscle size. So too, people need something to press against to mature. That pressure is provided by the adversary and his demons. However, we should not think of that pressure as a war. God already won the war, and the adversary knows he is defeated. He also knows that he only has a limited time left. The only fight that remains is a series of battles between Satan and God's people. We must fight against the enemy's devices (Eph. 6:12). Those are the battles necessary to help us mature.

**A BIBLICAL WORLDVIEW WITH GOD RAISING SONS:
THE ONLY BATTLES ARE BETWEEN SATAN AND PEOPLE**

Systematic Theology for the New Apostolic Reformation

Of course, the battles we face will never be too difficult for us. God limits Satan's activity. God has also given us the armor necessary to resist the enemy (Eph. 6:13). He has given us the shield of faith with which we *"will be able to extinguish all the flaming arrows of the evil one"* (v. 16). When we resist him, the adversary will flee from us (Jas. 4:7).

The battle between God's children and Satan can be compared to the Hebrew people as they took possession of the Promised Land. God could have wiped out the Canaanites and allowed the Hebrews to simply walk victoriously into the Promised Land. Instead, God required the Hebrews to fight for every inch of the land that was already promised. In like fashion, God's people must conquer. They have an adversary. God is using Satan and his minions to develop and mature His people.

Point 305: Satan Opposes God's People, Not God Directly

The understanding of Satan presented here sees Satan and his demons being adversarial to God's people. Opposition to God's people is different than opposition to God. This distinction is important.

When the Hebrews fought to take the Promised Land, the Canaanites were adversaries to the Hebrews. The Canaanites were not trying to conquer God. God was never threatened by the Canaanites. There was no war between God and the Canaanites.

Likewise, we can see that Satan is not directing his energy against God. To see this, think of Satan's kingdom on earth. That earthly kingdom is insignificant compared to God's Kingdom, which includes the whole universe. Earth is less than a speck of dust compared to the universe. Satan's kingdom is no threat to God.

Why is this important? Because we are noting again how the world is not about a war between God and Satan. The idea that Satan was once the worship angel in heaven leads people to imagine Satan in a high place of influence. It also leads them to believe that Satan is diametrically opposed to God. Adherents tend to think that Satan is trying to set up a kingdom in direct opposition to God or even to overthrow God's Kingdom. That understanding of Satan's work does not correspond with what we see in the Bible.

For example, in Job 1:6-12, we read about Satan asking God's permission to attack Job. The discussion between Satan and God does not sound like a

Satan's Origin and Role

discussion between two arch enemies. God had total authority over Satan, and Satan could not touch Job without God's permission. Obviously, God is on a much higher level of authority than Satan.

Satan is oriented toward attacking God's people, not God. Satan is the accuser *of the brethren*, roaming the earth seeking someone to devour. In Revelation 12, we read about a time when Satan went off to make war with those *"who keep the commandments of God and hold to the testimony of Jesus"* (12:17). Satan was trying to deceive the nations of the earth. All of these passages show us that Satan is oriented against God's people.

Satan's battle with God's people is serious, but the battle against God is insignificant. In fact, there is no biblical evidence that such a battle against God even exists or ever has existed.

Point 306: The Structure of Satan's Domain

Bible teachers often point out that God gave Adam and Eve authority over the earth (Gen. 1:28), but when they submitted to Satan, in some way they gave their authority to Satan. Satan then continued to deceive the descendants of Adam and Eve, and through the process of deception, Satan became god of this world. There is no biblical proof that this is how Satan gained authority over this world, but it is a reasonable explanation.

As Satan gained authority over the earth, he organized some sort of kingdom, which has various levels of authority. As Paul wrote:

> *For our struggle is not against flesh and blood, but against the rulers, against the powers, against the world forces of this darkness, against the spiritual forces of wickedness in the heavenly places.*
> (Eph. 6:12)

There have been hundreds of books written with various explanations of how these levels of authority relate to the earth and to each other within Satan's realm of authority. Many prayer warriors and intercessors (Christians called to a life of praying for others) have developed their own unique understanding of Satan's realm. Most often they talk about:

1. the rulers ("principalities" in the KJV) having authority over cities or similar sized areas

Systematic Theology for the New Apostolic Reformation

    2. powers as demons trying to work through the human powers that influence larger numbers of people through such avenues as media, music, education, and entertainment[185]

    3. world forces that influence major regions of the world

    4. spiritual forces that rule the earth from positions of authority over the whole earth

All of these levels of authority are seen as under Satan's authority. Indeed, intercessors may have discovered some of these ideas through their experiences as they battle in prayer against our spiritual enemies.

However, any Bible teacher who is honest will admit that very little is revealed in the Bible concerning these subjects. The verse quoted above (Eph. 6:12) is the only verse in the Bible that refers to four levels of authority in Satan's realm. Colossians 2:15 mentions rulers and authorities, but aside from these two references we have no biblical revelation concerning how Satan's realm is set up.

This does not mean that Satan's realm or activity is insignificant. It is real. It is a threat, and Christians must put on the full armor of God to stand against it. Battles are going on. However, we simply do not have much biblical evidence concerning what Satan's realm is like or how it operates.

This lack of biblical information does not leave us in the dark. On the contrary, it pushes us into the light. It redirects our lives toward God. As we draw near to Him, evil flees. As we live as God guides us, our enemies are defeated by His power.

Of course, there may be times when believers need to face and defeat a specific spiritual enemy. As Jesus cast demons out of individuals, so also His followers may. Also, there may be times when Christians (especially intercessors) spend extended time in prayer, resulting in the defeat of spiritual entities. We can read about this in Daniel chapter 10, where Daniel was praying on earth, while a battle was taking place in the spiritual dimension (vv. 12-13). Daniel did not need to know what was going on in the spiritual realm. He just continued to pray and seek God while the battle was raging. So also, while God's people do what He guides them to do, spiritual enemies will be defeated.

---

185 This does not mean that media, music, education, and so forth are evil. We are simply pointing out how powers may try to influence and work through these human means of influence.

Satan's Origin and Role

The main point here is that Christians do not need to orient their lives toward fighting Satan and demons. The Christian life is meant to be oriented toward God and His Kingdom.

Point 307: The Defeat of Satan's Kingdom

The most important truth to know about Satan's domain is that it has been defeated. Satan himself was judged (John 12:31 ; 16:11). When Jesus ascended into heaven, He was raised above all rule and authority. As Jesus triumphed, He defeated Satan:

> *When He had disarmed the rulers and authorities, He made a public display of them, having triumphed over them through Him.*
> (Col. 2:15)

Two thousand years ago when Jesus sat down on His throne, He was given all authority over heaven and earth. Too many Christians think that Satan is still god of this world, but in reality, his kingdom has been conquered.

To see this more clearly, consider the fact that the term *kingdom of Satan* or *Satan's kingdom* is used in only one context in the Bible. When Jesus was casting a demon out of a certain man, some Pharisees accused Him of casting out demons by the authority of Beelzebub, the ruler of demons (Matt. 12:24). Jesus responded by saying,

> *Any kingdom divided against itself is laid waste; and any city or house divided against itself will not stand. If Satan casts out Satan, he is divided against himself; how then will <u>his kingdom</u> stand?*
> (Matt. 12:25-26)

This is the only context in which "his kingdom," that is, Satan's kingdom, is referred to in the Bible (although this conversation is also recorded in Mark 3:23-27 and Luke 11:17-18). Notice that in this context Jesus was declaring the fall of Satan's kingdom. Our Lord went on to say:

> *But if I cast out demons by the Spirit of God, then the kingdom of God has come upon you. Or how can anyone enter the strong man's house and carry off his property, unless he first binds the strong man? And then he will plunder his house.*
> (Matt. 12:28-29)

Systematic Theology for the New Apostolic Reformation

Two thousand years ago, One stronger than Satan came and defeated him. Ever since that day Satan's realm has been crumbling. What remains is for his house to be plundered.

In another passage, the apostle Paul explained that when people commit their lives to Jesus, they are transferred from the domain, realm, or authority (*exousias,* in Greek) of darkness and brought into the Kingdom of Jesus (Col. 1:13 ; see also, Acts 26:18). Hence, we can appropriately call Satan's region of influence a domain, realm, and region of authority, but to call it a kingdom is to give him too much credit. Satan is still active, and his demons are busy here on earth, but he no longer has a kingdom. For this reason, we are taught to pray to God, *"For Yours is the kingdom and the power and the glory forever"* (Matt. 6:13). There is only one kingdom now, and it is the Kingdom of God.

Point 308: Satan's Role in Evil

It is important to recognize that the activity of Satan and demons cannot all be categorized as countering the will of God or serving the will of God. We noted that God allows demons in the world as an opposition to God's people. In that sense, demons do serve a purpose for God. So also, when God sent evil spirits, such as in the case of Saul (1 Sam. 18:10), God accomplished His will through evil spirits.

However, there are other examples in the Bible where demons are definitely working against God's will. For example, the fact that Jesus cast demons out of people implies that He was stopping those demons from doing things that He did not want them doing. Jesus explained His ministry of casting out demons was proof that the Kingdom of God had arrived and was here to defeat Satan (Luke 11:17-22).

Of course, this understanding of Satan's activity cannot be reconciled with Classical/Reformed theology, which sees God as in exhaustive control of all things. According to that view, God orchestrates and accomplishes His perfect, unalterable will through Satan and demons. According to that view, all pain, sickness, and death that is brought about by evil spirits is the will of God.

In contrast, Father-Son theology sees that God has total authority, but He has sovereignly decided not to control all things. Therefore, there are many tragic events that take place that grieve His heart. People suffer

Satan's Origin and Role

outside of His will. God may put limits on Satan and demons as He did in Job's life (Job 1:10), but they continue to deceive and hurt people. A day will come when every enemy bows. Then Satan and all demons will be removed from the earth. But until then, Satan and demons will continue doing things that result in pain and suffering.

Volume V
Evil, Sin, & Suffering

Section E
Humanity as a Source of Evil

Now we can consider what role people play in bringing and causing evil in the world. We will break this study into three sections. In this section we will explain sin and evil as a "thing." In Section F we will see sin as something people do. Then in Section G we will discuss sin as it is related to transgressions and iniquities.

Point 309: Sin as a Thing

Earlier,[186] we discussed the capability of the human heart to bring forth good or evil. In Matthew 15:19, we read Jesus' words:

> *For out of the heart come evil thoughts, murders, adulteries, fornications, thefts, false witness, slanders.*

James gave a more specific teaching on how people are a source of evil in the sense that they can bring forth sin:

> *But each one is tempted when he is carried away and enticed by his own lust. Then when lust has conceived, it gives birth to sin . . . .*
> (Jas. 1:14-15)

Desires turn into lust. Then lust conceives. Then sin is given birth. This process reveals something actually being born.

---

186 IV:L:265.

Systematic Theology for the New Apostolic Reformation

As we accept the biblical evidence that sin comes into the world through the human heart, we will see sin as a thing, in the sense of being a real entity.

SIN COMES FROM THE HEARTS OF PEOPLE

Other Bible verses confirm that sin is a thing. Paul explained that sin came into the world as a result of Adam's disobedience (Rom. 5:12). For something to be in a location (the world), when it previously was not in that location, implies that it is a thing. John also talked about sin as if it is associated with a location:

> *You know that He appeared in order to take away sins; and in Him there is no sin.*
>
> (1 John 3:5)

Paul also explained that sin reigns over humanity. He wrote that sin was at work in the members of his body (Rom. 7:20-23) and *"sin came alive"* when he was under the Law (v. 9). Paul said *"sin . . . deceived me, and through it* [the commandment] *killed me"* (v. 11). Consider also what God said to Cain: *"sin is crouching at the door"* (Gen. 4:7). Of course, we could dismiss all of these references as mere figures of speech, but even as figures of speech they are accrediting characteristics to sin as if it is a real entity.

Humanity as a Source of Evil

Point 310: Metaphors for Sin

Paul said that sin reigns over humanity, so metaphorically we can say that sin is an oppressive king. Paul wrote that sin was at work in the members of his body, so we can say that sin is an active, corrupting force. Paul wrote about sin being alive in him, so we can say that sin is a parasite. Because Paul said *"sin deceived me and through it killed me,"* we can say that sin is a deceiver and a killer. Because God described sin as *"crouching at the door,"* we can say sin is an invisible predator ready to attack.

These metaphors of sin bring images to mind of some entity that looms in dark places ready to destroy bystanders. We know that sin cannot be seen or touched like a physical item. So perhaps we should think of sin as an evil thought or desire. Or perhaps a force or energy. None of these can be seen, yet they exist as real things.

SIN REIGNS OVER HUMANITY

It is helpful to think of sin as a virus. Viruses are not actually alive in the normal sense of having the ability to reproduce on their own. Viruses are composed of a single strand of genetic material encased within a protein capsule. That genetic material contains information similar to a thought, an idea, or a way of thinking. That genetic material must enter

Systematic Theology for the New Apostolic Reformation

into a living plant or animal cell and combine with the genetic material within the cell's nucleus. The cell becomes the host, and then the genetic material of the virus is replicated. Typically, the virus damages the cell and then is released back out into the world.

Using this image of a virus we can metaphorically say sin was released into the world because of Adam's disobedience, but sin becomes alive as it enters into a person. That sin is incorporated into the thoughts and desires of the individual. Then it is multiplied and released back into the world where it influences other people, weakening and eventually destroying them. It is contagious!

Point 311: A Biblical Worldview that Has Room for Sin

To comprehend the nature of sin, it is helpful to embrace the biblical concept of creation existing as three realms filling the same space. With this in mind, we can envision sin existing in the second heaven (the spiritual realm that fills the same space as the natural realm).[187]

This understanding is helpful because it is difficult to conceive of sin as an invisible entity that actually exists if we cling to a dualistic worldview. If all we can conceive of is a natural world and a distant spiritual world, then there is really no place to fit spiritual forces or energies closely associated to humanity. So again, we see the importance of embracing a biblical worldview to understand biblical concepts.

Point 312: Pain and Sickness Are Things

Recall Augustine's progression of thought concerning evil not being a real thing:

1. God created all things, but He did not create evil.
2. Therefore, evil must not be a "thing."
3. If evil is not a thing, it must be the absence of good.

Following this progression, Augustine concluded that evil is not a thing, but it must be the bending of the will of God. Then Augustine associated pain, suffering, and sickness with evil.

---
187 This was explained in III:A:134-139..

Humanity as a Source of Evil

In reality, sin, pain, and sickness are real "things." Anyone who experiences pain knows that pain is a thing. We may not be able to see it with our eyes, but it is real. When carpenters hit their fingers with a hammer, thousands of electrical impulses send signals to the brain. Pain is more than the absence of good feelings. So also, sickness is more than the absence of health. Think of the following examples:

> 1. Malaria is a serious disease. To remove health from people does not make them have malaria. Malaria is something in addition to the absence of health.
>
> 2. Caleb is mute. Caleb cannot communicate, so he has the inability to communicate truth. However, the absence of truth telling does not make Caleb a liar.
>
> 3. Terri has cancer. Somewhere in her body there are cells growing out of control. Doctors can surgically remove some of those growths. Cancer is real.

Each of these examples reveal how pain and disease are more than the absence of good. They are real things.[188]

Augustine's philosophical reasoning is wrong. As we have stated before, if the conclusion of a progression of thought is wrong, then that progression of thought is wrong.

Point 313: Adam as the Source of Sin

We must also question Augustine's reasoning because it leaves no place for people being the "source" of evil. According to Augustine, people may take what God has created and bend it toward evil, however, humans cannot actually be the source of evil. Yet, our Lord clearly said that *"evil thoughts, murders, adulteries, fornications, thefts, false witness, slanders"* come from the hearts of people (Matt. 15:19). James described the origin of sin without mentioning the bending of God's will, but rather revealing the lusts of humanity as the source.[189]

If we embrace the truth that people can be the source of evil, it reveals another possible explanation for how sin first came into the world. Paul

---

188 It is still debatable if death is a thing or simply the absence of life.
189 This is discussed in IV:F:232.

Systematic Theology for the New Apostolic Reformation

explained that sin came into the world through Adam (Rom. 5:12), but how do we envision that sin actually coming into the world?

Most Western Christians form a picture in their minds of good coming from God, then Satan bent (or distorted) that good. After that, Satan tempted Adam and Eve so that Adam and Eve would be the channels (not the source) through whom Satan's evil would come into the world.

If we reject this philosophical reasoning, we can reconsider this issue. Jesus said evil thoughts can come out of the hearts of people. Therefore, it is possible that the first sin originated in the hearts of Adam and Eve. Of course, Genesis 2 shows us that Satan was involved, tempting Adam and Eve, so Satan fed the desires that turned to lust within them. But it is still possible that Adam and Eve's hearts were the point of origination. This is not presented as the only explanation, but just another possibility that is incompatible with Augustine's philosophical reasoning, but compatible with the Bible.

Section F
Sin as Something People Do

We have studied sin as a real entity. Now we can discuss sin as something people do. Our understanding of this sin is determined by our understanding of the nature of God and the nature of humanity.

Point 314: The Legal Understanding of Sin

Reformed teachers define sin as *missing the mark* or as *law-breaking behavior*. We will discuss the definition of *missing the mark* shortly, but first consider *law-breaking behavior*. This definition corresponds to the Reformed concept of God being a judge. John Calvin was especially influenced by his training as a lawyer before becoming a minister. Consequently, it was natural for Calvin to understand God in terms of a judge sitting in a courtroom. His resulting *legal* understanding of sin and salvation has been recognized by countless theologians and historians.

Expressing the Reformed view, the *Westminster Shorter Catechism* defines sin as:

> ... any want of conformity unto, or transgression of, the law of God.

Those who see sin as law-breaking behavior often quote 1 John 3:4:

> *Everyone who practices sin also practices lawlessness; and sin is lawlessness.*

Systematic Theology for the New Apostolic Reformation

The understanding of sin as *law-breaking behavior* makes sense if we envision Judge-God sitting in His courtroom and all of humanity appearing before Him to give an account for what they have done.

Point 315: Law-Breaking Behavior Plus Total Depravity

Reformed theologians define sin as "law-breaking behavior," but this does not tell us much unless we go on to explain what they mean by law-breaking behavior. As we delve deeper, we discover that their understanding of sin includes every action, thought, and deed coming from people (apart from the grace of God).

Remember that Reformed teachers believe that humans are totally depraved. As I explained,[190] this terminology is used differently at different times. Today, when teachers of Reformed theology want to defend total depravity, they usually define it as "a sinfulness that pervades all areas of life or the totality of human existence."[191] This definition is vague, implying that sinfulness merely has its influence upon all areas.

In contrast, John Calvin's understanding of human behavior is much more straightforward and condemning. Calvin wrote:

> . . . all human works, if judged according to their own worth, are nothing but filth and defilement. And what is commonly reckoned righteousness is before God sheer iniquity.[192]

The *Westminster Confession of Faith* expresses the view of Reformed theology when it explains that all works done by non-Christians are sinful:

> . . . because they proceed not from an heart purified by faith; nor are done in a right manner, according to the Word; nor to a right end, the glory of God, they are therefore sinful, and cannot please God . . . .[193]

---

190 IV:A:193.
191 This belief was one the five canons of the Calvinistic Synod of Dort (1618–1619) and is part of the acronym TULIP, which is used to identify the five pillars of Calvinism.
192 Calvin, *Institutes*, III:12:4.
193 *Westminster Confession of Faith,* from the original manuscript written by Cornelius Burges in 1646, Point XVI:VII.

Sin as Something People Do

According to Reformed theology, all non-Christians have a heart that is *"desperately wicked"* (Jer. 17:9 KJV), and as a consequence, every action, thought, and deed (apart from God's intervention) is sin.

Point 316: Bending of the Will of God

The Reformed understanding of sin is profoundly influenced by Augustine's philosophical reasoning. Augustine envisioned God's will radiating out like rays from the sun, perfectly straight, unbending, and never wavering. Building on that vision, Augustine defined evil as the "bending of the will away from . . . God."[194] If we see God's will as perfectly straight, any bending, to any degree, is sin. Every line is either straight or bent; there is no middle ground. Since no one can perform the will of God perfectly, everyone sins continually.

REFORMED VIEW THAT SIN IS BENDING THE WILL OF GOD

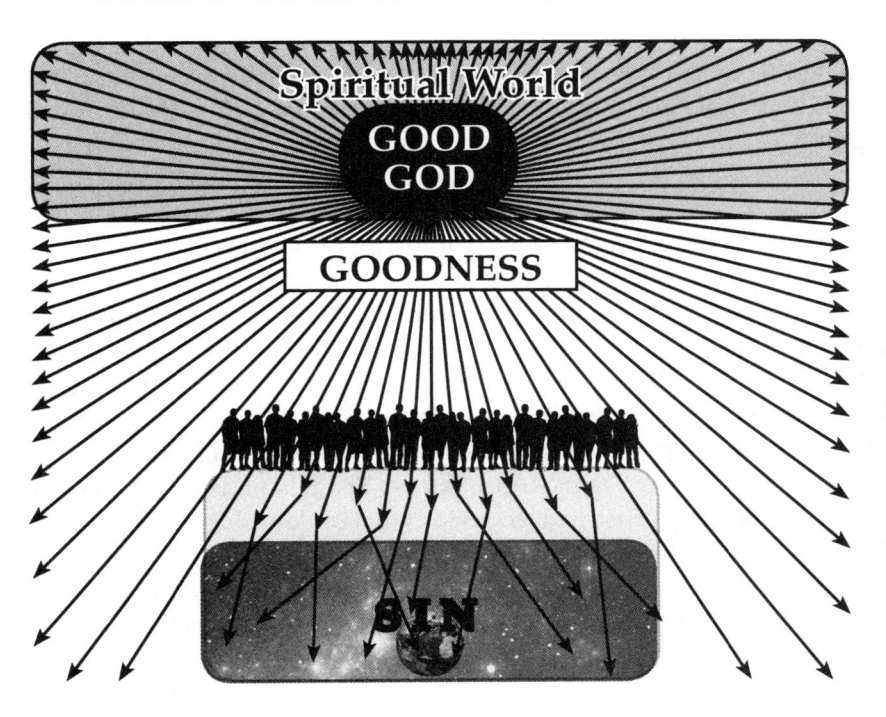

---

194 Augustine, *Confessions*, 7:16.

Systematic Theology for the New Apostolic Reformation

Point 317: Missing the Mark

Reformed thinkers build on their all-condemning view of human nature by pointing out that the word *sin* in the NT is usually translated from the Greek word *hamartia*. This Greek word literally means "missing the mark." With this in mind, a person may envision a sinner as someone who misses the bullseye on a target—a bullseye that is very small. In fact, adherents of Reformed theology see the bullseye as the perfection that has been established by Jesus' perfect life. This understanding leads one to believe that everything not perfectly aligned to God's will is sin. Therefore, it is impossible to hit the bullseye (unless God intervenes and gives grace).

Many Reformed teachers further emphasize the all-pervasiveness of sin by quoting James 2:10:

> *For whoever keeps the whole law and yet stumbles in one point, he has become guilty of all.*

Using this verse, adherents of total depravity say everyone stumbles in some aspect of God's Law, and therefore, everyone is totally and equally guilty.

Point 318: There Are No Rays Shooting Out of God

The Reformed view of sin we just explained is seriously distorted. In order to come to a better understanding of sin, we must first abandon the underlying influence of Western philosophy with its foundation in a dualistic worldview. Then we must remove from the foundation of our thoughts the image of God radiating out His attributes like rays from the sun—an image that began with Plotinus. There is no Bible passage that can be reasonably construed to arrive at that philosophical image of God.

Because Augustine was a student of Plotinus' teachings, it was natural for him to envision God's will radiating out of Him. Augustine saw the rays of God's will as perfectly straight, unbending, and never wavering. Hence, it was easy for Augustine to think of sin as the "bending of the will away from ... God."[195]

---

195 Augustine, *Confessions*, 7:16.

Sin as Something People Do

In reality, God's will does not radiate out of Him. God fills all, and therefore, there is no distance between Him and creation. There is no place for His will to radiate. There are no perfectly straight lines radiating out of God.

GOD FILLS THE HEAVENS AND EARTH

If we want to develop a biblical understanding of sin, we must build on a biblical worldview. We must abandon the dualism of Western thought and the image of God radiating out His will. Those errors force our understanding of good and evil into an unrealistic and unbiblical construct. Once we abandon the related images, then Augustine's reasoning about sin makes no sense. Sin has nothing to do with the bending of the will away from God. That concept did not come from the Bible.

Point 319: People Are Capable of Good and Evil

To further develop a biblical understanding of sin, we must also reject the Reformed idea that people are totally depraved. We already discussed the nature of humanity and presented a more positive view than

Systematic Theology for the New Apostolic Reformation

Reformed theology offers. We do not need to repeat that discussion but simply refer readers back to Volume IV, *The Nature of Humanity*. Not every action, thought, and deed coming from non-Christians is a sin. My favorite verse that proves this is Luke 6:32, where Jesus told His disciples that even sinners *agape* love their own. Of course, everyone sins, but not every action, thought, and deed coming from non-Christians is law-breaking behavior. As we explained in Volume IV, people are capable of good and evil.

Consider George, who starts his day by getting out of bed, taking a shower, getting dressed, and then sitting down for breakfast. There are dozens of decisions he must make just to arrive that far in his daily routine. Are those decisions good or evil? Taking a shower for example: Is this a totally depraved action?

Christians trained under Reformed theology will judge George's taking a shower as rooted in sinful selfishness, perhaps to feel good about himself or to impress people so he can further his own evil goals throughout the day. In contrast, Christians with a more positive view of human nature will see George taking his shower as something that is probably according to God's will. In fact, George's natural desires to clean up, get dressed, and eat breakfast are basically God-instilled, good desires.

Christians with a positive view will admit that on some days George may have corrupted or perverted motives, even in his morning routine. For example, even though George is married, he may put on cologne one morning in hopes of impressing some woman at his place of work. George may make several decisions during his morning routine that are influenced by more evil goals. However, such negative decisions are seen as departures from the normal actions of his day. The majority of his decisions are simply decisions, not necessarily sin, i.e., law-breaking behavior.

George also makes some good decisions. He stops to tell his children that he loves them. He gives his mother a telephone call and wishes her a blessed day. Before George drives off to work, he helps his neighbor catch his runaway dog. George is not breaking any of God's laws in these actions. God does not have laws dictating every move throughout George's day. George is capable of both good and bad.

Point 320: What Is Sin in the Life of Non-Christians?

So what is sin? Just as 1 John 3:4 says, *"sin is lawlessness."*

Sin as Something People Do

However, God is not a Judge enforcing laws that have been written in stone. Jesus revealed this when the Jewish religious leaders accused Him and His disciples of breaking the Sabbath law. Jesus said to them:

> *Have you not read what David did when he became hungry, he and his companions, how he entered the house of God, and they ate the consecrated bread, which was not lawful for him to eat nor for those with him, but for the priests alone? Or have you not read in the Law, that on the Sabbath the priests in the temple break the Sabbath and are innocent?"*
>
> (Matt. 12:3-5)

Notice that David and the priests broke the law but they were *"innocent."*

If people only know God as He was revealed on Mount Sinai, then they may think of Him as the Uncompromising Judge. On the other hand, if they embrace the revelation of God given by Jesus, they will understand that God is merciful. He is a Father.

In Romans 9, Paul quoted the words that God said to Moses:

> *I will have mercy on whom I have mercy, and I will have compassion on whom I have compassion.*
>
> (Rom. 9:15)

In the context of this verse, Paul argued that God is so high in authority, that He can do whatever He wants. Because He is sovereign, God can have mercy and still be just at the same time.[196]

God's mercy can be seen in how He does not label law-breaking behavior as sin unless there is consciousness of law. Paul explained that *"where there is no law, there also is no violation"* (Rom. 4:15). Jesus shared the same truth to the Jewish religious leaders saying, *"If you were blind, you would have no sin"* (John 9:41). In the context, Jesus was telling the Jews that if they did not understand what they were doing, then their behavior would not be sin. This is God's view of all humanity. For this reason, a two-year-old girl may act defiantly toward her mother, but that behavior is not judged as sin. In His sovereignty, God acts in mercy toward those who do not know right from wrong.

God's sovereignty can also be seen in how He acts in mercy towards people who show mercy to others. Jesus explained:

---

[196] This was discussed in I:B :16-17.

Systematic Theology for the New Apostolic Reformation

> *For in the way you judge, you will be judged; and by your standard of measure, it will be measured to you*
>
> (Matt. 7:2)

God is merciful to the merciful. James expressed the same truth:

> *For judgment will be merciless to one who has shown no mercy; mercy triumphs over judgment.*
>
> (Jas. 2:13)

God's sovereignty means He can be easier on some people, dependent upon their judgment toward others.

God's judgment of sin is unique to each and every person. Compare this to how parents deal with each of their children differently. What they expect from one child is different than what they expect from another child. A loving and wise parent takes all things into account, including age, gender, mental acuteness, experience, personality traits, attitudes, maturity, circumstances, outside influences, and so forth. Of course, God is far more aware of each person's situation than natural parents are of their children. Therefore, what God considers sin in one person's life may not be sin in another person's.

This vagueness in defining sin can be frustrating to people who want to know where the boundaries of the law begin and end, but that frustration reveals that they are thinking of God as a Judge in a courtroom enforcing laws. God is not like that. The God who was revealed on Mount Sinai seems to be that unwavering Judge, but Jesus revealed the nature of God to us more clearly. God is full of compassion. He is a Father. As stated earlier, our concept of God influences our understanding of sin. This is most evident in the life of the Christian, as we will discuss next.

Point 321: God Is a Father, Not a Judge, toward His Children

Discussions concerning sin must take a major shift when talking about the relationship between Father-God and His children.[197] John explained:

---

[197] Here I am speaking about born again Christians. I must make this point because earlier I explained that God is the Father of all humanity. The distinction between all of humanity and born again Christians is made more clearly in VI:D:383-384.

Sin as Something People Do

He who ... believes Him who sent Me ... does not come into judgment.
(John 5:24)

He who believes in Him is not judged.

(John 3:18)

When people come to faith in Jesus, their relationship with God changes. God welcomes them into His family and deals with them as His children.

GOD RELATES TO HIS CHILDREN AS A FATHER

Spiritual Realm
Natural Realm
Father-God

In several ways Jesus revealed to us how we should look to God as our Father. One of those ways was with the parable of the prodigal son (Luke 15:11-32). After the prodigal son had squandered his inheritance, satisfying his lustful desires, he returned home. When the father saw his son returning home, he ran out to greet him. The father did not make his son pay for his sins. He did not take him to court and have him judged as a criminal. The father embraced his son and welcomed him back into his good favor.

In the story of the prodigal son, we also read about a second son who had not rebelled (at least outwardly) toward the father. That faithful son thought their father was being unfair to welcome the prodigal son home so easily. The faithful son wanted his rebellious brother to pay for his evil

447

Systematic Theology for the New Apostolic Reformation

behavior, but the father was so full of love for his prodigal son that he forgave his son and treated him as if he had not done anything wrong.

Jesus told us this parable to explain how God acts as a Father toward His children. A father does not deal with his children as a judge deals with criminals. Envision a judge sitting in a courtroom as various criminals are brought before him to be sentenced to pay penalties for their crimes. Then one day the judge's own son is brought into the courtroom because he has broken a law. What will the judge do? If he has a father's heart for his son, he will do everything necessary to take his son out of the courtroom and deal with him in his own personal office.

Point 322: What Is Sin for the Child of God?

Accepting God as Father changes our understanding about sin. To see this, we must remove ourselves from the courtroom and see ourselves in the family environment. Parents dealing with their children do not think in terms of law-breaking or law-keeping behavior.

In normal daily routines, parents watch over their children, wanting them to enjoy life while they attempt to keep their children safe from harm. They want their children to get along and even love one another. If a certain child misbehaves and treats another child harshly, the parents are likely to step in and discipline or redirect that child's behavior, but parents are not likely to label every action of their children as sin or not sin. To parents, most wrong actions of their children are *misbehavior,* rather than *law-breaking behavior.*

If you are a parent with a teenage daughter, how do you look at your daughter when she misbehaves? You will not immediately label her a sinner or criminal. You love your daughter and you see the whole course of her life. You remember first holding her as a baby after coming home from the hospital. You remember when she took her first steps and her first day of school. You helped her learn how to ride a bicycle, and you cheered at the sidelines when she participated in sports. You helped your daughter with her school work, and you tucked her into bed each night. You know your daughter as fun-loving, outgoing, intelligent, thoughtful, energetic, and caring of others. She has a personality, and she is much more than a criminal. She is the daughter you love.

Sin as Something People Do

God is a Father. He does not see His children through the eyes of the law. He sees their entire life, their successes and failures, laughter and tears. Father-God knows everything that has made His children who they are. He knows how they will be fully transformed into the image of His Son. Therefore, He will never see His children as criminals.

Children of God will sin, but when they do, God does not stop being their Father and suddenly step back into His role as Judge. If His children misbehave, He will not take them into the courtroom. As Jesus said, believers will not be judged (John 3:18). Our Lord explained that they will never *"come into judgment"* (John 5:24). Their misbehavior may grieve Father-God's heart. God may intervene and discipline them, but He will not respond to His children like a courtroom judge. He will always act like a father, because He is their Father.

Point 323: Rethinking Missing the Mark

While thinking of God as a Father, reconsider the etymology of the Greek word, *hamartia*, which literally means "missing the mark." When followers of Reformed theology think of this missing of the mark, they see the bullseye on a target as the perfect righteousness of Jesus.

It is true that the perfect righteousness of Jesus is required for salvation, but it doesn't come from *our* behavior. When we study soteriology in Volume VI, we will see how the righteousness of Jesus is accredited to all who believe in Jesus. No one will get to heaven without the perfect righteousness of Jesus being accredited to them.

But God does not expect His children to hit the bullseye of being perfect like Jesus. If we could be perfect, then we would not have needed Jesus to come. God knows people are weak and prone to mistakes. When God stated that Job *"was blameless, upright, fearing God and turning away from evil"* (Job 1:1), He was not using the standard of perfection established by the life of Jesus. Job could have never met that standard. Obviously, God was not requiring Job to be perfect in that way.

Now envision someone shooting a rifle at the bullseye on a target. If the bullseye is the perfection of Jesus, then that bullseye is so small that it is impossible to hit. But missing the bullseye is not a criminal offense. It is the information needed to adjust the sights on the rifle. If the shooter misses the bullseye several times, it is an indication that he needs to do more adjustment and practice.

Systematic Theology for the New Apostolic Reformation

Father-God doesn't think of missing the bullseye as criminal behavior. Of course, God demands the perfect righteousness of Jesus for salvation, but once a person has been welcomed into His family, God is a Father to them. He is pleased whenever His children try to be like Jesus. God is proud of them when they even come close to the bullseye. *In fact, Father-God is delighted that His children have a desire to hit the bullseye.*

Point 324: Live and Be Judged by the Law of Liberty

Consider how Reformed teachers emphasize the all-pervasiveness of sin by quoting James 2:10:

> *For whoever keeps the whole law and yet stumbles in one point, he has become guilty of all.*

Using this verse, many (not all) Reformed teachers say that everyone stumbles in some aspect of God's Law, and therefore, everyone is equally and totally guilty.

In reality, James was explaining to his readers that if they live by the Mosaic law, then they will be judged by the Mosaic law. The answer is not to try to keep the Mosaic law perfectly (which is impossible), but rather to live by a different law—the law of liberty:

> *So speak and so act as those who are to be judged by the law of liberty*
> (Jas. 2:12)

If people live by the law of liberty, then they will be judged by the law of liberty.

James' explanation of living by the Mosaic law versus the law of liberty may be compared to a father who is cautioning his non-athletic son not to try to become a professional football player. The father is concerned for his son, knowing that his son can never succeed as a professional football player. The father tells his son that he will have to be one of the best athletes in the world to succeed and that it is impossible for his non-athletic son to ever be that good. So, lovingly, the father advises his son to pursue a more appropriate career. In a comparative fashion, James is advising us to stop trying to keep the Mosaic law and start living by the law of liberty.

Sin as Something People Do

This understanding of James 2:10 is very different than that of Reformed theology. James was not saying that everyone is equally and totally guilty. He was saying that it is impossible to keep the Mosaic law so do not even try. Father-God does not want to judge us by the Mosaic law. He does not want to see us fail. He does not want to declare that we are guilty of all.

God wants us to live by the law of liberty, which is not a courtroom type of law but a law based on mercy:

> *So speak and so act as those who are to be judged by the law of liberty. For judgment will be merciless to one who has shown no mercy; mercy triumphs over judgment.*
> (Jas. 2:12-13)

Mercy is better. It is a better standard. It is the standard by which Father-God wants to judge His people.

Point 325: God Wants a Father-Son Relationship With You

God does not want a Law-Giver/law-obeyer relationship with humanity. He wants a Father-son relationship.

Of course, this does not negate all laws. Paul explained that laws are still necessary and should be enforced in the lives of serious sinners:

> *. . . realizing the fact that law is not made for a righteous person, but for those who are lawless and rebellious, for the ungodly and sinners, for the unholy and profane . . . .*
> (1 Tim. 1:9-10)

The laws made for sinners include God's laws and all of the laws governing a civil society. They are necessary for society to maintain peace and order. However, living by laws is not God's highest. He wants people to live by a different standard. Paul understood this. He wrote:

> *All things are lawful for me, but not all things are profitable.*
> (1 Cor. 6:12)

Since all things were lawful for Paul, it was impossible for him to break

Systematic Theology for the New Apostolic Reformation

the law. He had no law-breaking behavior because God was his Father, not his Judge. As Jesus said, whoever *"believes in Him is not judged"* (John 3:18 ; 5:24).

Of course, Paul understood that he still sinned, but his sins were no longer tied with law-breaking behavior. Paul understood that the decisions he was to make during his life were to be governed by what is profitable, meaning, "What is the best thing to do?"

This is how a father wants his children to govern their lives. He does not want his children thinking, "How far can I go before breaking any laws?" A father hopes his children never have to think about the outer boundaries. Instead, he wants his children to grow up, take responsibility for their actions, and make wise decisions. He hopes his children will govern their lives thinking, "What is the best action to take? What would my father want me to do? How can I please him?" So also, Father-God wants all of His children to live this way.

Point 326: Father-God Wants to Talk to You about Your Heart

Once the Law-Giver/law-obeyer relationship is abandoned, we can see God's will for our lives differently. As a Father, God is interested in characteristics like integrity, forgiveness, patience, humility, and love. He is interested in our hearts.

With this in mind, consider Jesus' Sermon on the Mount. Jesus made several statements that start out with, *"You have heard that it was said . . ."* (Matt. 5:27). Jesus then went on to give His audience (and us) a different, more perfect way to think. For example, Jesus said:

> *You have heard that it was said, "You shall not commit adultery"; but I say to you that everyone who looks at a woman with lust for her has already committed adultery with her in his heart.*
> (Matt. 5:27-28)

A Christian who has been trained to think of God as a Judge in a courtroom may read these words of Jesus and conclude that the commandment, "Thou shalt not commit adultery" was replaced by an even harder to keep commandment—in fact, one that is impossible to keep. In that Christian's mind, Jesus has upped God's requirements.

Sin as Something People Do

That is the wrong way to understand the Sermon on the Mount. This is the sermon in which Jesus tells us to call God *"Father"* (Matt. 6:9). This is the sermon in which Jesus tells us how to be *"sons of our Father in heaven"* (Matt. 5:45). This is the sermon in which Jesus tells us what to do to *"be called sons of God"* (Matt. 5:9). Jesus is trying to get us out of the Law-Giver/law-breaker relationship and into the Father/son relationship.

Jesus was not making the law more strict. Instead, He was revealing the heart of His Father toward His children. In Matthew 5:27-28, we see how Father-God wants to talk to His children about where lust starts—in their hearts. He wants to mentor them. Father-God wants to help His children know how they can avoid committing adultery by dealing with their hearts.

Consider when Jesus said:

> *Again, you have heard that the ancients were told, "You shall not make false vows, but shall fulfill your vows to the Lord." But I say to you, make no oath at all . . . But let your statement be, "Yes, yes" or "No, no"; anything beyond these is of evil.*
> (Matt. 5:33-37)

To understand this, remove the whole sin-versus-obedience construct out of your mind. Let God be your Father for a moment, and read the Sermon on the Mount as your Father in heaven wanting to talk to you about your heart. Rather than forbidding you to make vows, see our Lord's words as the counsel of your Father to be a person of integrity. Be a person who does what you say. Let your yes be yes. When you say you are going to do something, do it.

Compare this to a modern situation in which a father is teaching his son how to drive a car. The father may exhort his son to stay under the posted speed limit, but that is not the father's greatest interest. A good father wants his son to be careful, respectful, and considerate. If the son gets caught by the police for speeding, the judge will make a decision based on whether or not the boy broke the law. In contrast, the father will be disappointed with his son for not being careful, respectful, and considerate.

Look at one more example from Jesus' Sermon on the Mount. Jesus said:

> *You have heard that it was said, "You shall love your neighbor and hate your enemy." But I say to you, love your enemies and pray for*

> those who persecute you, <u>so that you may be sons of your Father</u> who is in heaven.
>
> (Matt. 5:43-45)

Jesus is not making the commandments more difficult. He is setting aside the commandments and talking to people about their hearts. He does not want people living by commandments. He wants them to live like *"sons of your Father in heaven."*

Of course, this does not replace the standard of perfection demanded for salvation. In the Sermon on the Mount, Jesus also said:

> For I say to you that unless your righteousness surpasses that of the scribes and Pharisees, you will not enter the kingdom of heaven.
>
> (Matt. 5:20)

The perfection of Jesus is necessary for salvation. That can only be attained through faith in Jesus. However, that perfection is accredited to God's children. Once they become children of God, Father-God wants them to set aside the whole Law-Giver/law-obeyer relationship.

When you read the Sermon on the Mount, hear the heart of a Father. See no judgment in His eyes. See Father-God with eyes that want to help you be a better person:

> Blessed are the gentle, for they shall inherit the earth.
> Blessed are those who hunger and thirst for righteousness, for they
>   shall be satisfied.
> Blessed are the merciful, for they shall receive mercy.
> Blessed are the pure in heart, for they shall see God.
> Blessed are the peacemakers, for <u>they shall be called sons of God</u>.
>
> (Matt. 5:5-9)

These are the words of your Father.

Point 327: Freedom to Make Decisions

A father wants his children to grow up, take responsibility, and make right decisions. In order to do that, he must give his children some freedom to make decisions. In order to make wise decisions, children must have

Sin as Something People Do

some level of confidence that their father will not punish them for the slightest errors they make.

Reformed theology does not facilitate that development, because adherents see obedience to God as hitting a small bullseye on a target. For them, obedience to God is difficult since people must obey each and every command of God exactly as instructed. They must live like slaves walking a tightrope, with no slips allowed. They must hit the mark every time.

In contrast, Father-God wants His children to live like children rather than slaves. He wants His children to walk in His ways, but walking in His ways is like walking down a highway rather than on a tightrope. There is a ditch on both sides of the highway. If God's children get into the ditch, He will discipline them, but while they are on the highway of life they have freedom to make decisions. Most decisions have nothing to do with sin. They have nothing to do with law-breaking behavior. They are simply decisions. Father-God will even allow His children to make mistakes without the slightest bit of condemnation on His part.

This truth is difficult for some people to grasp, but it is worth wrestling through. Too many Christians have been trained to think of God's will like the bullseye on the target. Hence, in their minds, they never meet God's expectations. They think they are sinning with every action, thought, and deed. They live in more bondage than most non-Christians. The unfortunate truth is that many non-Christians have a healthier image of God than the uptight Christians who live under the bullseye paradigm!

God is not demanding His children to hit the bullseye. He has already accredited believers with the prefect righteousness of Jesus. He knows His children are weak and imperfect. God is a good and merciful Father. He gives His children a lot of leeway.

Point 328: Live in Freedom

Teachers who believe in total depravity want our definition of *sin* to be as broad as possible. That way they can support their belief that people sin continually in action, thought, and deed. One way they keep their definition of sin broad is by quoting the last few words of Romans 14:23: *"whatever is not from faith is sin."* When these words are quoted alone, a listener may conclude that the vast majority of our actions are not motivated by faith, and therefore, the vast majority of our actions are sin.

Systematic Theology for the New Apostolic Reformation

In reality, the context of Romans 14:23 talks about Christians having freedom to eat what they want to eat. In verse 22, Paul wrote:

> *The faith which you have, have as your own conviction before God. Happy is he who does not condemn himself in what he approves.*

This reveals the context in which we should have faith. If Christians have faith to eat anything, they should not feel condemned in enjoying whatever food is put before them. In this light, we see that phrase, *"whatever is not from faith,"* was never meant to be Paul's attempt at including as much as possible in his definition of sin. Quite to the contrary, Paul was encouraging Christians to have faith, and hence, live in freedom and refuse to feel like sinners when doing things they have the faith to do.

Point 329: God Will be a Judge to Those Who Reject His Son

God wants to be a Father to all of humanity. His arms are open. He wants all people to believe in Jesus, so they may pass out of judgment and into a Father-child relationship.

Unfortunately, many refuse His invitation. They will not accept Him as their Father. Therefore, God will act as their Judge. John explained:

> *He who believes in Him [Jesus] is not judged; he who does not believe has been judged already . . . he who does not obey the Son will not see life, but <u>the wrath of God abides on him</u>.*
>
> (John 3:18, 36)

As the writer of Hebrews explained, *"It is a terrifying thing to fall into the hands of the living God"* (Heb. 10:13). God does not want to deal with anyone through the Judge-criminal relationship. However, He will if they do not accept Jesus.

That we will study in Volume VI, *Soteriology*.

Section G
Transgressions and Iniquities

The Bible refers to sins, transgressions, and iniquities:

Then I acknowledged my sin to you and did not cover up my iniquity. I said, "I will confess my transgressions to the Lord."
(Ps. 32:5)

What is the difference and why is it important?[198]

Point 330: Understanding the Differences

Some verses in the Bible seem to group the words *sins, transgressions,* and *iniquities* together as if they are synonyms. Indeed, all three can be placed in the same group and labeled *sin*. However, there are other verses that use each of these words in a narrow sense, focusing in on their distinctives.

Sin literally means missing the mark.

Transgression is sin, but it is more serious, implying that the transgressor has deliberately crossed a boundary or intentionally disobeyed a known rule.

Iniquity is even worse. It literally means bend, twist, or distort. Iniquity is sin, but it includes the lasting, corrupting impact of sin upon the soul of an individual. Serious iniquity may be called wickedness, and it is sometimes translated as wickedness in various versions of the Bible. Iniquities are so consuming that they may be identified with the lifestyle of the offender.

---

[198] The seed thoughts for the discussion in this section came from a teaching by Apostle Fernando Guillen.

Systematic Theology for the New Apostolic Reformation

To see these differences, consider that people who get intoxicated may sin. People who get intoxicated and drive drunk are transgressing the law. People who repeatedly get intoxicated may develop addictions resulting in iniquity in their hearts. That iniquity would include all of the lusts and thought processes they have developed to rationalize their alcoholism.

Point 331: Iniquities May Impact Generations

All three: *sins*, *transgressions*, and *iniquities*, can be forgiven by God (Ex. 34:7). However, the consequences of each are different.

Transgressions involve some type of violation, therefore, amends must be made to correct the resulting consequences.

Iniquities are more serious, resulting in the corruption of the offender's soul. Such corruption may influence succeeding generations. Exodus 20:5, tells us:

> . . . *for I, the LORD your God, am a jealous God, visiting the <u>iniquity</u> of the fathers on the children, on the third and the fourth generations of those who hate Me.*
>
> (Ex. 20:5)

Notice that iniquities—not sin or transgressions—may influence three or four generations.

Point 332: Atonement for Sins, Transgressions, and Iniquities

The seriousness of sins, transgressions, and iniquities can be seen in how they were to be dealt with under the Mosaic religious system.

Sin offerings could be made at any time, but they were for the atoning of sins that were committed unintentionally (Num. 15:27-28).

Transgressions and iniquities could only be atoned for once a year on the Day of Atonement. On that day, the high priest took two male goats: the first one he offered to God as a sin offering; the second goat was considered the scapegoat, the one upon which the high priest laid his hands to transmit the transgressions and iniquities of the people:

Transgressions and Iniquities

Then Aaron shall lay both of his hands on the head of the live goat, and confess over it all the iniquities of the sons of Israel and all their transgressions in regard to all their sins . . . The goat shall bear on itself all their iniquities to a solitary land; and he shall release the goat in the wilderness.

(Lev. 16:21-22)

Sins were simply forgiven, while transgressions and iniquities had to be removed.[199] To understand this, it is helpful to compare transgressions and iniquities with sicknesses and diseases that can be transmitted to the scapegoat and then carried away.

This helps us understand the sacrifice Jesus made. Our sins were forgiven through the new covenant, but Isaiah 53 tells us that our transgressions and iniquities were placed upon Jesus:

But He was pierced through for our transgressions,
He was crushed for our iniquities.

(Is. 53:5)

But the Lord has caused the iniquity of us all
To fall on Him.

(Is. 53:6)

That He was cut off out of the land of the living
For the transgressions of my people, to whom the stroke was due?

(Is. 53:8)

My Servant, will justify the many,
As He will bear their iniquities.

(Is. 53:11)

We will discuss the atonement of sins, transgressions, and iniquities more when we study soteriology in Volume VI, but it is worth noting here that transgressions and iniquities are definitely treated as "things" in the sense that they can be transmitted from one place (the sinner) to another (Jesus). Again, Augustine was wrong in defining evil as the absence of good. Transgressions and iniquities are real things.

---

199 For this reason, some people feel like something has been lifted off of them when their transgressions and iniquities are removed.

Volume V
Evil, Sin, & Suffering

Section H
Outside Influences of Sin and Evil

Now let's consider outside influences that act upon people causing them to sin and, hence, increase the suffering and pain in this world.

Point 333: Sin Causes More Sin

A powerful entity that influences people to sin is sin itself.

This understanding of how sin influences humanity only makes sense if we accept that sin and evil can be real entities. People are capable of releasing negative forces, energies, or thoughts into the world. As a consequence, sin and evil can exist like a force or dark cloud—created by, but independent of, humanity.

This understanding is incompatible with Augustine's philosophical reasoning that leads to the conclusion that sin and evil are not things.

In reality, sin and evil must be able to exist independently of humanity in some fashion. We saw how sin came into the world because of Adam's disobedience, and now sin rules over humanity. As Paul wrote, sin was at work in the members of his body (Rom. 7:20-23) and *"sin . . . deceived me, and through it killed me"* (Rom. 7:11). Sin has a corrupting influence upon all of creation—humanity included. Every one of these descriptions of the activity of sin assume that sin is a real thing.

Because sin and evil are real, they influence people. People are vulnerable and weak. They cannot resist all sin. From time to time, every person yields to the power of sin. So then, we must recognize sin as a power that influences people to sin.

Systematic Theology for the New Apostolic Reformation

Point 334: The Role of Satan in Sin

Satan and demons also play a role in causing people to sin. They are capable of influencing people's thoughts through temptations. Satan's temptations are most effective when they match the desires of a person.

To see this connection between temptations and a person's desires, consider how Satan tempted Jesus in the wilderness. Satan tempted Jesus to command stones to become bread, which matched our Lord's desire for food after 40 days of fasting. When Satan offered Jesus all of the kingdoms of this world, he was offering Jesus something that matched His goal of establishing a kingdom.

Similarly, we can read Paul's warnings that a husband and wife should not abstain from sexual intimacy for too long *"so that Satan will not tempt you"* (1 Cor. 7:5). Satan and his demons find access to the hearts of people by offering the things they desire. Then, as James said, people are carried away by their lusts, lusts conceive, and sin is given birth.

People may be carried away by lust for power, riches, fame, food, drugs, alcohol, love, sex, companionship, acceptance, and so forth. Any human desire may be nurtured and fed by the enemy of people's souls.

Of course, we should not categorize all sin as caused by Satan and his demons. Desires may start within people. People do not need Satan to give them evil ideas. They can come up with their own. However, in some cases Satan is at work. No one knows how much of the evil in the world is the result of Satan's work and how much is the result of humans by themselves being carried away by their own lusts, but putting too much blame on Satan can cause people to be irresponsible. It is helpful to think of demons as houseflies trying to get access to a person's open wounds so they can feast on exposed flesh (Interestingly, "Beelzebub" is known as "Lord of the Flies"). If there was no wound, the flies would have no access point. In a comparative way, we can say that people who have their hearts filled with the Spirit and love of God offer demons no access point. Then there is no wound. This truth is evident in the life of Jesus, who said that Satan *"has nothing in Me"* (John 14:30).

Point 335: The Law Arouses Sin

Paul wrote about another entity that influences sin in people, explaining that the sinful passions within him *"were aroused by the Law"* (Rom. 7:5). In

Outside Influences of Sin and Evil

the context, Paul was talking about the Jewish Laws that came through Moses. He was careful to point out that the Law did not cause him to sin. Rather, he sinned because of his own passions, but *"sin came alive"* when he was under the Law (Rom. 7:9).

This principle applies not only when people try to live by the Laws of Moses, but whenever they live legalistically, their own sin tendencies may be aroused, making it more difficult to live as God desires.

Point 336: The Role of Chemicals in Sin

For many people, the greatest evils they deal with involve their own or their loved ones' addictions to alcohol or drugs. We can understand how these chemicals trigger sin as we study James' explanation that desires turn to lust and people are carried away by those lusts. Drugs and alcohol can play a major role in triggering powerful desires and lusts within people. Addicts may steal from neighbors, friends, and even family members. They may tell lies and do whatever is necessary to get access to the desired drugs or alcohol.

There are also people with chemical imbalances that result in cravings to steal, speed, start fires, commit adultery, self-mutilate, torture, and even kill others. Many people behave in ways that are totally out of character with their natural selves when they are experiencing some depletion of certain chemicals, especially neurotransmitters. Many of those people can be transformed into kind, law-abiding citizens when they receive the correct medical treatment.

The fact that chemicals can reduce or increase sin reveals an intimate interaction between the physical and spiritual realms.

Point 337: Physical/Emotional Strength Versus Exhaustion

Another factor influencing sin is the physical and emotional condition of people. For example, a mother who has reached her limits in dealing with her children may act irrationally and totally out of character. She may even hurt her children in ways that she would never think of under normal conditions.

Systematic Theology for the New Apostolic Reformation

Soldiers at war may experience battle fatigue to such an extent that they act out of pure survival instincts without any concern for others.

Reformed teachers who believe in the total depravity of humanity often point to people in such states of utter physical and emotional exhaustion, then state, "You never know the true nature of people until all of the facade is stripped away through exhaustion." Such thinking is profoundly distorted! The true nature of a mother is not the person who hurts her children when she is exhausted. Her true nature is that loving person who cares for her children when she is physically and emotionally healthy. That is how God made her. When she is exhausted, then she is not herself.

Even human judges know enough to take into account people's physical and emotion conditions when judging behavior. How much more is our merciful God aware of people's conditions.

Point 338: Corporate Evil Leading to Sin

The thoughts of other people are another influence for sin. As people talk and share their negative ideas, others listening may agree with those ideas and, hence, align their own hearts to the desires of the speakers. Bad thoughts and desires spread from one person to another. As Paul wrote, *"Bad company corrupts good morals"* (1 Cor. 15:33). Evil is like leaven in a piece of dough (1 Cor. 5:6-8). It grows like seeds in soil (Matt. 13:38-39).

Evil thoughts and ideas can be shared among a large group of people. For example, the crowds at the trial of Jesus were stirred to demand His crucifixion. Many people in that crowd probably had no desires of their own to see Jesus crucified. The energy of the masses can sweep in unsuspecting bystanders. The mob mentality is capable of seducing large numbers of people.

Even small numbers of people are able to release great forces of evil into the world when those people are in unity. Then evil exists like a dark cloud ready to overwhelm larger groups. This may result in a shared consciousness. Of course, each person must orient his or her heart accordingly to access that shared consciousness, but sin and evil are available as forces existing in the spiritual realm waiting to influence those who are impressionable. Large masses of people, such as a certain political party or an entire nation (such as Nazi Germany), may be swayed according to a shared consciousness.

Outside Influences of Sin and Evil

We all like to think of ourselves as independent thinkers, able to make our own decisions, but all people are followers in many areas of their lives. No one is able to excel in all areas, so we have to depend upon others. For example, an athlete may be the best in her sport, but she needs someone to help her speak effectively in public. A singer may reach heights of fame but have to learn how to be a good father. A computer expert may be world recognized for her technical skills but needs to belong to a certain political party to know what to think about issues related to government. We are all followers. For this reason, we can be carried along by the people we have come to depend upon. We have to trust people in some areas but that leaves us vulnerable to sharing in the sins of those who lead us.

For this reason, Jesus gave strong warning to those who lead innocent ones to stumble (Matt. 18:6).

Point 339: Corporate Evil Consuming a Leader

When people are bonded together in heart, they begin to share similar thoughts, resulting in a shared consciousness. Then one or more leaders may rise and become spokespersons for the shared ideas. When a spokesperson speaks, all those whose hearts are oriented accordingly will sense an agreement in their own minds and hearts. As a unit, a group may walk farther and farther into evil. Satan may also get involved, inspiring thoughts and desires in the midst of that group.

The leader is especially vulnerable. The spokesperson becomes a hero to the people. The adoration of the masses can seduce a leader to have grandiose ideas. As an actor can lose himself in his role, so also a leader may take on a different personality as he is consumed in the expectations and hopes of the people who are admiring him. Many leaders have listened to the praise of their fans and have become enamored with themselves. The resulting sin that is nurtured may seize the hearts of leaders and their followers.[200]

This can even happen in the Church environment. Paul warned that people elevated too quickly may *"become conceited and fall into the condemnation incurred by the devil"* (1 Tim. 3:7).

---

200 The theologian, Paul Tillich (1886–1965) wrote in-depth on this form of evil.

Systematic Theology for the New Apostolic Reformation

Point 340: Sin Reigns in Death

When individuals determine their own identity by other people's judgments, they are susceptible to conform to those judgments. This is not only true with the praise and adoration of others, but also with negative judgments. Therefore, a child growing up in an environment of condemnation may believe what he is being told and act out on those beliefs. A woman who has decided she is worthless may act in ways that reinforce that belief.

Paul explained that sin reigns in death (Rom. 5:21). Many truths can be drawn from this verse, but when we understand death as shame, guilt, condemnation, self-hatred, and so forth, we can see how people convinced of their own wickedness will discover sin reigning as a king over them. They will not have the strength to resist sin. The power of sin will be too great.

For this reason, we can be assured that the man drunk at the bar every night is not having positive thoughts going through his mind. The woman who is driven to drug addiction is in part motivated by her self-hatred. The teenage boy who has developed a reputation as a troublemaker will have to overcome the forces of other people's opinions in order to change his life. No one lives on an island. We are all products of the beliefs of those around us.

Section I
Why Is There Pain, Suffering, and Death?

Let's put together what we have learned thus far, so we can develop a holistic picture concerning the causes of pain, suffering, and death in the world.

Point 341: God Is Not Controlling All Things

In Volume II, entitled *God's Involvement with this World*, we discussed some subjects related to the ongoing existence of pain, suffering, and death. Most importantly, we explained how God has total authority in the world, but He has sovereignly decided not to control all things. That discussion led us to Father-Son theodicy, revealing that bad things happen because God is not controlling all things.

Of course, this conclusion is incompatible with Classical/Reformed theology because adherents believe God is timeless, omnipotent, and sovereign in the sense of being in exhaustive control of all things. Since they believe God is in exhaustive control, they must also conclude that God is the cause of all things, including all pain, suffering, and death.

In contrast, Father-Son theology teaches that many things happen contrary to God's will. That's why we pray, "Thy Kingdom come, Thy will be done on earth . . . ." A day will come in the future, when the Kingdom of God fully manifests on earth. Then all things will be in submission to King Jesus. Then there will be no more pain or suffering, but until that day, pain and suffering exist because God is not controlling all things.

Systematic Theology for the New Apostolic Reformation

Point 342: Natural Laws Govern this World

In Section B of this volume, we discussed how God created this world as the perfect environment to raise sons. As such, this world is not a soft pillow on which humans are to spend their days casually relaxing. It is a world that needs to be subdued and managed. It is a world where people need God. Father-God has placed humanity in the perfect environment where they can be tested, care for one another, and learn how to love. God created a world where people must work hard, accept responsibility, and mature.

Furthermore, this world runs according to natural laws. Because it runs according to natural laws, there are certain inherent dangers and trials. The same gravity that holds people on earth can cause them to fall and hurt themselves. The shifting tectonic plates result in earthquakes in which people die. In a world that runs according to natural laws much natural pain and suffering happen.

Point 343: Unnatural Laws Also Govern this World

There are also *unnatural* laws governing this world. These are the forces released as a result of humanity's sin. Once sin was released into the *kosmos*, creation no longer responded to the authority of humanity in the way God originally designed. Weeds grew out of control. People had to work harder—by the sweat of their brows. Diseases and death became more powerful. Pain increased. The world became more difficult to manage. As a consequence of sin, the world today is more cruel and harsh than originally created.

One of the most significant unnatural laws is that *"creation was subjected to futility"* (Rom. 8:20). *Futility* means fruitlessness, pointlessness, uselessness, vanity, and ineffectiveness. Creation lost its purposeful and guided nature. As a result, many things happen in this world that do not have a positive outcome. Just like there is a law of gravity, there is also a law of futility. Creation is subject to this futility. Creation is under this curse. Therefore, bad things, i.e., meaningless things, happen.

This truth cannot be reconciled with Reformed theology. Since adherents believe God is in exhaustive control, they cannot accept any futility in creation. They often express this belief saying, "Everything that

Why Is There Pain, Suffering, and Death?

happens, happens for a reason." Adherents must rationalize that even if no immediate positive purpose can be identified, God must have some hidden purpose for everything that happens.

A Logical Progression of Thought
Beginning with the Reformed View of God

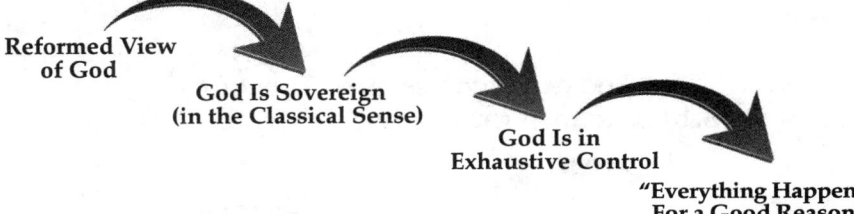

Reformed View of God → **God Is Sovereign (in the Classical Sense)** → **God Is in Exhaustive Control** → **"Everything Happens For a Good Reason"**

In contrast, Christians who have embraced the idea that God is not controlling all things may conclude that not all things have a positive outcome. Some deaths happen from which no one benefited. Some people are lonely and no one is benefiting from their loneliness. Some people have been tortured, and their suffering was futile, accomplishing no good. Because this world is subjected to futility, there is much pain, sickness, and death in the world.

Of course, God can turn all suffering into good on behalf of those who love Him. Christians have God's promise that He is working in all things for the good for those who love Him (Rom. 8:28). However, for those who do not love God, many things do not work for good. Tragic events have tragic results. Many things that happen in this world benefit no one.

Think of a small fawn in a remote region of the wilderness where no human being will ever visit. One day that fawn, out of curiosity, approached a porcupine and that porcupine succeeded in lodging a quill in the eye of the fawn. For the rest of its life, that fawn will live in pain. According to Reformed theology, God made that happen and He has some positive reason for making that fawn suffer. According to Reformed theology, this reasoning must apply not only to that fawn, but to millions of animals that suffer with diseases, parasites, broken limbs, genetic defects, wounds, and torment by other animals. God not only allows that suffering, but He causes it and He has caused it to billions of animals.

Systematic Theology for the New Apostolic Reformation

For followers of Reformed theology, this pattern of thought also applies to everything that happens to people. If a child is born with a genetic defeat, God caused it. Every time someone dies a painful death, it was for some good reason.

In contrast, Father-Son theology recognizes that this world runs according to natural and unnatural laws. Many things happen contrary to God's will. This world is subject to futility and, therefore, many things have no positive outcome.

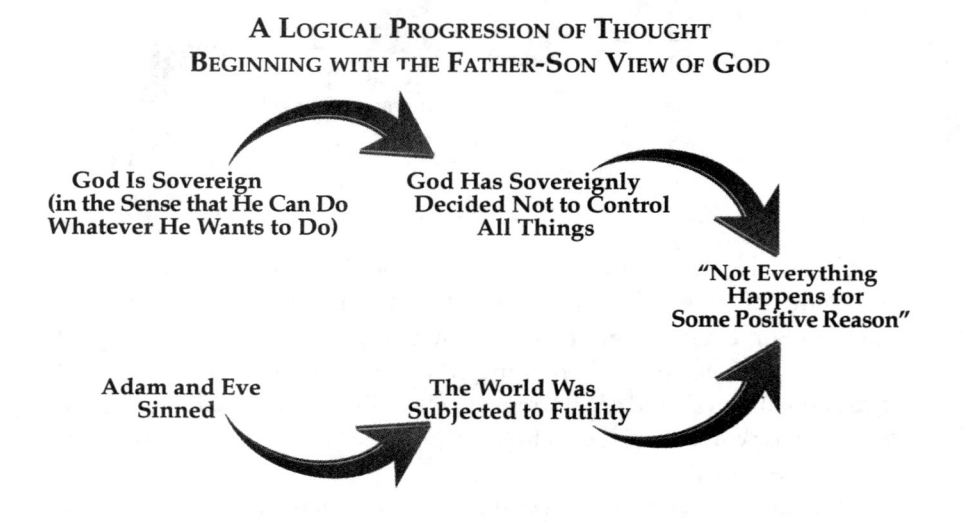

A Logical Progression of Thought Beginning with the Father-Son View of God

- God Is Sovereign (in the Sense that He Can Do Whatever He Wants to Do)
- God Has Sovereignly Decided Not to Control All Things
- "Not Everything Happens for Some Positive Reason"
- Adam and Eve Sinned
- The World Was Subjected to Futility

Point 344: Human Free Will Results in Suffering in the World

According to Father-Son theology, another reason there is pain, suffering, and death is because God has delegated authority to people to govern this world. This implies some amount of free will on the part of humanity. In a world where people have some free will, people can make mistakes. They can also willingly hurt others. Criminals can steal. Murderers can kill. Corrupt governments can withhold food and provisions that rightly belong to its citizens.

Even more devastating can be the evil that envelops an entire group of people. Together they may cause war, oppress others, and neglect to help those who lack the basic essentials of life. People can be the source of much pain and suffering, individually or as a group.

Why Is There Pain, Suffering, and Death?

Of course, according to Reformed theology, God wills all the resulting pain and suffering. He is the One who caused Hitler to kill millions of handicapped children, homosexuals, and Jews. According to Reformed theology, God has a good reason for causing every war and disease.

Point 345: God May Be the Cause of Pain and Suffering

In Section B of this volume, we discussed some cases in which God was the cause of pain, suffering, and death. The OT and NT clearly show us incidents when God acted as a judge and suffering resulted. Therefore, Father-Son theology recognizes the possibility that God may be the cause of some suffering today. However, God does not cause all pain and suffering. Furthermore, Christians should not be afraid of Father-God inflicting pain upon them. He is a loving Father. It is not God's heart to hurt His people.

Point 346: Satan and Demons Are a Cause of Pain and Suffering

Add to all these other causes of suffering, the activity of Satan and demons. Anyone who takes the Bible seriously will conclude that demons may be involved in causing suffering. Jesus told Peter that Satan demanded to sift him like wheat, which gives us a picture of Satan planning destruction in Peter's life. The Bible is clear that Satan wanders the earth seeking someone to devour. Great pain and suffering is the result of Satan's work in this world.

Of course, Reformed theology sees all of Satan's activity as controlled by God, and therefore, God is the cause of all that Satan does.

In contrast, Father-Son theology sees that God created Satan to be an adversary to humanity and Satan has a free will. Within the limits set by God, Satan chooses on his own free will upon whom he will inflict pain and suffering. In some cases, God may use demons for His purposes, but most activities of demons are not orchestrated by God. According to Father-Son theology, Satan and demons have a nature to oppose the success of people, and as a consequence, they cause much destruction.

Systematic Theology for the New Apostolic Reformation

Point 347: Many Factors for All Pain, Sickness, and Suffering

When we consider all of these sources of pain, sickness, and suffering, we have a complete picture. Too many people try to oversimplify questions and answers about the source of suffering. They want to point to one specific cause of the suffering that they experience. Rarely is it that simple.

Of course, it is simple for those who adhere to Reformed theology. For them there is only one cause—God. He causes it all. But for someone who embraces Father-God, there are many causes of suffering.

Consider Andy, who got brutally mugged one evening after wandering into a dangerous neighborhood. Whose fault was it? Of course, the mugger was the person directly responsible. However, Andy was partly responsible for being in that dangerous area. That mugger's parents may be partly responsible because of the cruel environment in which they raised him. The mugger's whole neighborhood may be responsible because it may be a breeding ground for violence. Society may be responsible for not providing the mugger with an education and opportunities to do something productive with his life. The city workers may be partly responsible because the street lights were not shining in that dark neighborhood. The police may be partly responsible because they neglected to patrol that area that evening. Satan and his demons may be partly responsible because of their activity in stirring discontent and hatred in the mugger and neighborhood. The hot weather may be partly responsible, because it influenced the mugger to be in an especially bad mood. The law of gravity is partly responsible because it pulled Andy to the ground where he hit his head on concrete. God is also responsible because He created Andy and the world in which Andy lives. Adam and Eve are responsible because they ate the forbidden fruit.

We could easily come up with many other causes for Andy's mugging, but the point is that nothing happens in a vacuum. There are *always* many factors leading to all pain, sickness, and suffering.

An interesting analogy is of the energy dynamics that take place when space engineers use a gravitational slingshot[201] to accelerate a spacecraft as it moves into outer space. Engineers direct the spacecraft to fly nearby a planet and the gravitational field of that planet draws the spacecraft closer, accelerating it to greater speeds. Then as the spacecraft circles the planet, it breaks free of the gravitational field and flies off into outer space.

---

201 Also called "gravity assist maneuver" or "swing-by."

Why Is There Pain, Suffering, and Death?

In the process, the spacecraft changes direction and accelerates to much higher speeds.

GRAVITATIONAL SLINGSHOT USED TO ACCELERATE A SPACECRAFT

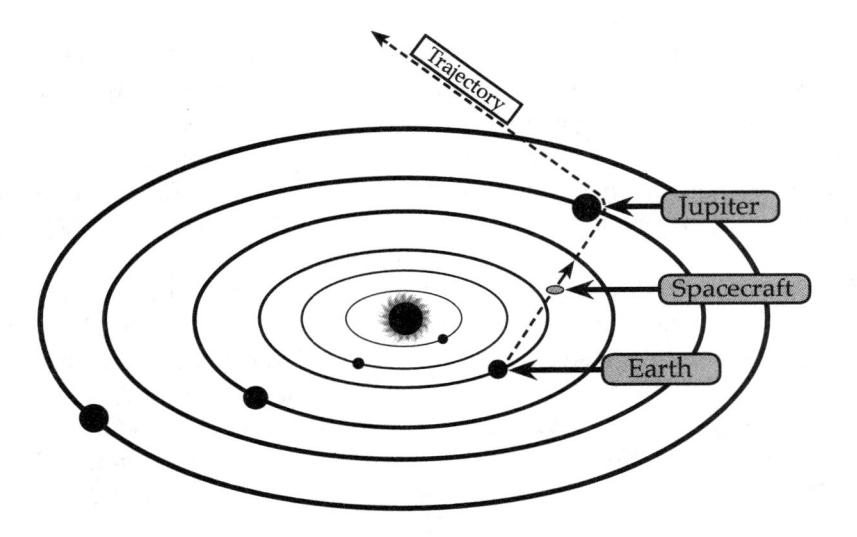

An observer may ask, "Where did the spacecraft obtain the energy necessary to accelerate to greater speeds?" As first glance, it may seem that the spacecraft gained energy by the pull of the gravitational field of the planet and by the motion of that planet. Indeed, that conclusion would be correct but not complete because it is impossible to change the energy of one planet without influencing all of the other planets and everything else in the solar system. When one object moves, all objects move. Some of those movements may be so small that they cannot even be measured, but they do move. This is true because the solar system is a system, with everything influenced by everything else. Where does the energy come from that allows the spacecraft to accelerate? From the system.

Likewise, we can talk about the bad things that happen in our world. What causes them? Everything. Our world is a system. As Jesus said, "*In the world you will have tribulation . . .*" (John 16:33). Why do bad things happen? Because we live in the world.

Systematic Theology for the New Apostolic Reformation

Point 348: The Answer Is in Our Relationship with Father-God

I do not want to end this discussion simply by blaming the world for all of our problems. In one sense that is the single best answer, but in another sense it leaves people hanging. This is because people usually want to identify the source of their problems so they can find a solution. Indeed, there will come a final solution when Jesus returns, transforms our mortal bodies, eliminates evil, and creates the new heavens and earth. Then there will be no more pain and suffering (Rev. 21:4). However, in the present time people want answers as to how they can fix their present problems. Therefore, they want to know the direct cause of each problem.

Even when looking for a direct cause, there is rarely only one. Consider Job. Satan was the direct cause of much pain, but Satan had God's permission and perhaps even God's encouragement (Job 1:8-12). Yet, even Job was directly responsible to some degree. We can see this in the last chapter of Job where Job finally understood what God wanted to reveal to him. If Job had learned the lesson sooner, Job's suffering may have ended sooner.

In Job's case his problems could have been directly stopped at several points. If Satan stopped, Job's problems would have stopped. If God decided to end it, Job's problems would have ended. If Job had immediately learned what he was suppose to learn, his problems would have been over.

People can spend their entire lives trying to solve their problems but the solution corresponding to Father-Son theology always begins with understanding God as a Father and ourselves as sons of God. Father-God does not want His children to suffer. He is for us, not against us. Therefore, our beginning point is knowing God and, hence, knowing His heart.

From there the solution is in our relationship with Him. He desires our heart. He wants us to turn to Him and trust Him. When our heart is right, our actions will be right.

Right actions lead to right solutions. Paul praised God saying:

> But thanks be to God, who <u>always leads us in triumph</u> in Christ, and manifests through us the sweet aroma of the knowledge of Him in every place.
>
> (2 Cor. 2:14)

When our heart is connected with God's heart, He will lead us in the direction of victory. The path to victory may be a path with many lessons

Why Is There Pain, Suffering, and Death?

along its course. That path may be longer than we expected. And the victory may not look like we expected, but we will triumph.

Not understanding this, Christians tend to oscillate between one of two errors. Some Christians become victims, passively accepting problems, concluding that God wants them to suffer. At the other extreme are Christians who believe that believers should never experience problems or trials. Therefore, they conclude something is seriously wrong with them if and when they encounter problems that are not quickly resolved.

Again, it comes back to our relationship with God. He is a Father who wants to help us. Even when the answer does not come as we expect, He is still a Father. He is always very near.

Volume V
Evil, Sin, & Suffering

Volume VI
Soteriology

Soteriology is the study of salvation.

In systematic theology, it is customary to have soteriology follow a study on the nature of humanity and the nature of sin, because salvation is God's answer to humanity's problem. People need saving.

However salvation needs to be placed in the context of God's overall plan for humanity. In Volume I, Section A, we identified God's plan from before this world was created. He wanted sons (Eph. 1:4). Evangelical theology tends to miss this. Instead, adherents tend to develop their worldview starting with the fall of humanity. As a consequence, they see the rest of the Bible as God's solution to that fall. DeVern Fromke points out this error in his insightful book entitled, *Ultimate Intention*:

> It is often made to seem that man appeared on the stage of time just so he could be saved. Thus, it seems man becomes important in God's purpose only in his Fall. Consequently, God's chief work is seen as redemptive.[202]

Rather than the fall of humanity, we need to start at Father-God's heart for humanity. We need to start at His original intention. This places the redemption plan of God in its proper place. The plan of redemption is not the central feature of God's plan nor of the Bible. "Redemption is not the end, but only a recovery program. It is but a parenthesis incorporated into the main theme."[203] Because people sinned, God made a way to reconcile

---
202 Fromke, DeVern, *Ultimate Intention* (Shoals, IN: Sure Foundation, 1963), p. 20.
203 Fromke, *Ultimate Intention*, p. 25.

Systematic Theology for the New Apostolic Reformation

them to Himself. But that is not the finished product. Father-God will have sons for Himself, a Bride for His Son, and a Temple for His Spirit.[204]

With this in mind, we will study salvation.

From what do people need to be saved? This is the question we will answer in Section A. Then in the rest of this volume, we will investigate what salvation entails and how it is accomplished. We will study:

Section B: The Covenantal View of the Atonement
Section C: Benefits of the New Covenant
Section D: Becoming Children of God
Section E: What Is the Gospel?
Section F: What Is the Proper Response to the Gospel?
Section G: What Is Necessary for Salvation?
Section H: *Sola Gratia* (Salvation by Grace Alone)
Section I: *Sola Fide* (Salvation through Faith Alone)

We will discover that our concept of God determines what we understand about His activity in salvation. Classical/Reformed theology emphasizes God's role as a Judge who must punish sin, while Father-Son theology emphasizes God's role as a Loving Father who forgives sin.

As you read this volume, it will be helpful to keep in mind an earlier discussion we had concerning Western civilization as a sin/guilt culture. Whether we Western people realize it or not, we read the Bible through our cultural bias. Our thoughts naturally gravitate toward seeing sin as law-breaking behavior and, therefore, we see sinners as guilty in the legal sense.[205]

The Bible was not written from the Western worldview. It was written from a relational perspective rather than a legal perspective. For Western people to understand the Bible in its historical context we need to be suspicious of our own cultural traditions. When studying salvation, we must think in terms of relationship rather than law.

---

[204] A similar perspective is offered in: C. Baxter Kruger, *God Is For Us* (Jackson, MS: Perichoresis Press, 2000), p. 1-27.
[205] Explained in IV:D:216-218.

478

Section A
Saved from What?

Before we determine how salvation is accomplished, it is helpful to determine from what people need to be saved.

Point 349: The Reformed View: Saved from God's Wrath

Reformed teachers focus on God as a Judge. For them, God is not a Judge in the Hebraic-biblical sense of being a person of authority who has determined to set the oppressed free and make things straight.[206] According to Reformed teachers, God is a Judge in the Western legal sense of a judge sitting in a courtroom determining who is guilty and then demanding justice to be satisfied. This understanding corresponds with Calvin's training as a lawyer before becoming a minister. He saw humanity's sin as law-breaking behavior and all people as guilty. Therefore, justice must be satisfied. The penalty must be paid.

Calvin portrayed God as a legal Judge, but that Judge was not detached as a modern judge who simply passes sentences in accordance with the law. According to Calvin, God is a Judge who is extremely angry at sin. In His anger, God will personally inflict the just penalty due to law-breakers. In other words, Calvin saw Judge-God as the Torturer who administers all punishments. Using this descriptive word "Torturer" does not overstate the Reformed view of God. In fact, there are no words that can fully instill within the reader the full terror that Reformed thinkers associate with God and His wrath.

---

206 The judges in the Book of Judges reveal the Hebraic-biblical understanding. This is discussed in I:B:15.

Systematic Theology for the New Apostolic Reformation

THE WRATH OF GOD UPON HUMANITY

Saved from What?

God is a consuming fire. This is at the forefront of Reformed thought. So also is God's judgment of sin as described in Romans 1:18:

> For the wrath of God is revealed from heaven against all ungodliness and unrighteousness of men who suppress the truth in unrighteousness....

According to Reformed theology, God's wrath pours forth from Him continually, throughout eternity. Because Reformed teachers believe God is timeless, they cannot logically believe that God's wrath ever changes. It will be constant and unchanging throughout eternity future, and it has been constant and unchanging throughout eternity past.

By portraying God with wrath pouring out of His nature, I do not mean to imply that this is the totality of His nature. Reformed teachers also believe that love and other attributes pour forth from God. However, here we are focusing on what threatens humanity. From what do people need to be saved?

According to Reformed theology people need to be saved from the wrath of God. Reformed teachers will also say that people need to be saved from hell, but that too is the administration of God's wrath. Teachers of Reformed theology may include other elements in salvation, but those other elements are dwarfed in significance when compared to the Reformed understanding that people most need to be saved from the Judge and Torturer.

Point 350: Does Jesus Save People from God?

The Reformed view of God, His wrath, and the salvation offered through Jesus Christ leads to a troubling question: "Does Jesus save humanity from God?" Anyone who is logically consistent with Reformed theology will have to answer yes.

In the last few years, an increasing number of public figures have been asking and answering this question. Of course, followers of Reformed theology do not like others putting the Reformed view in this light, but the question is out of the box and it will not go back in. According to Reformed theology people need to be saved from God.

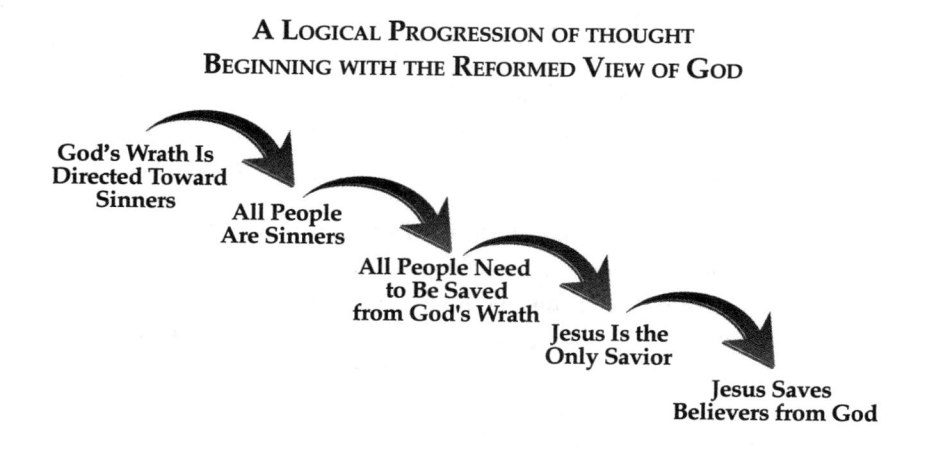

Systematic Theology for the New Apostolic Reformation

A LOGICAL PROGRESSION OF THOUGHT
BEGINNING WITH THE REFORMED VIEW OF GOD

- God's Wrath Is Directed Toward Sinners
- All People Are Sinners
- All People Need to Be Saved from God's Wrath
- Jesus Is the Only Savior
- Jesus Saves Believers from God

Point 351: The Father-Son View of God as Judge

Father-Son theology does not lead to the troubling conclusion that Reformed theology does. This is true because it does not build on the wrath of God. Of course, Father-Son theology acknowledges that God is a Judge and *"the wrath of God is revealed from heaven against all ungodliness and unrighteousness of men . . ."* (Rom. 1:8). However, there are several ways in which Father-Son theology offers a different perspective.

First, God is not timeless within creation. Therefore, God does not pour forth wrath continually throughout eternity. He is capable of directing wrath when and wherever He chooses. He can even turn it on and off.

Second, Father-Son theology sees God as a judge in the Hebraic-biblical sense of One who delivers the oppressed and sets things straight.[207] God is not the kind of judge who identifies law-breaking behavior and then inflicts just punishments. For example, when God judged Sodom and Gomorrah He did not select evil individuals and then inflict pain upon them. Rather His judgment was the result of His desire to stop the propagation of sin. Similarly, when God judged humanity in the days of Noah, it was motivated by His desire to redirect the course of civilization. The Hebraic-biblical view of God as a judge is more like a Western physician than it is like a Western judge in a courtroom. God is the Great Physician of humanity intervening when necessary to heal from sickness.

---

207 Also explained in I:B:15.

Saved from What?

Father-Son theology also associates God's nature as a Judge with His nature as a Covenant-Maker. As a Covenant-Maker, God obligates Himself to protect His covenant people. In the OT, if God had not defended His covenant people, He would have been unrighteous because righteousness entails, among other actions, the keeping of one's covenants.[208] Hence, God acted as a Deliverer repeatedly setting His covenant people free of oppression by their enemies.

The image of God as a Judge must also be *subject* to His nature as a Loving Father. We studied this in Volume I, when we identified the view of Father-Son theology which sees God's nature as a Loving Father overarching all of the attributes of God.[209] As a Loving Father, God experiences righteousness indignation. This is true because sin wreaks havoc upon humanity and God does not want to see the people He loves suffer. Hence, His indignation and wrath are a product of His love.

Followers of Reformed theology may verbally agree with this reason for God's wrath, however, they do not see God's wrath as a product of His love in the way that I am explaining here. Followers of Reformed theology see God's wrath as a characteristic of His nature as much as His love is a characteristic of His nature. That is another one of their fundamental errors. To understand what I am saying, think of love being removed from God's nature. If that was possible and if we did it, Reformed thinkers would still see God's wrath toward sin as a characteristic of God's nature. In contrast, Father-Son theology sees God's wrath as a product of His love.[210] Therefore, if we subtracted love from God's nature, we would at the same time subtract His wrath because the only wrath God experiences is that which is stirred by His love.

Point 352: The Father-Son View: Saved from Three Things

Now to identify from what people need to be saved according to Father-Son theology, think of God, first and foremost, as a Loving Father. He is a Father who looks down upon the world and sees the people He loves estranged from Him. So what is on Father-God's heart and mind?

---

[208] Explained in I:C:23.
[209] Explained in I:E:47.
[210] We established this truth when we explained how God's nature can only be understood if we subject all of His attributes and characteristics to His nature as a Loving Father; I:E:47.

Systematic Theology for the New Apostolic Reformation

Compare God to loving parents who had a teenage daughter run away from home. When the parents realized their daughter ran away, their first reaction was not anger at their daughter for sinning. Because they love their daughter, their first and foremost desire was to have their daughter safe at home. They wanted their relationship with their daughter restored, and they were concerned that their daughter would be hurt or even die while out in the world.

God is a good Parent. When He looks at the world, wrath over sin is not what consumes Him. Love does.

FATHER-GOD LOVES HUMANITY

This is what Jesus communicated with the story of the prodigal son. When the father saw his prodigal son returning home, he ran out to greet him. The father did not take his son to court and have him judged as a criminal. The father expressed no anger. He embraced his son and welcomed him into his arms.

It is worth noting again how important Jesus' revelation of God is. Jesus declared that He is the only One who has seen the Father (John 1:18 ; 6:46). Therefore, no one has a more accurate view of God. Jesus and Jesus alone is able to reveal to us who God really is. Therefore, we will only have an accurate understanding of Father-God if and when we see the revelation that Jesus offered as trumping all other revelations of God's nature. Above

Saved from What?

all else, Jesus revealed God as a Father who so loved the world that He gave His only begotten Son that whosoever believes in Him will be saved.

Seeing God as a Loving Father determines our understanding of salvation. Think again of the parents who had a daughter run away from home. Those parents first wanted their relationship with their daughter restored, and second, they wanted their daughter safe. Father-God has a similar heart. When He looks at humanity, His first thought is not "sinners!" God loves humanity. Captivating His heart is a longing for the relationship with humanity to be restored. Because of sin, the relationship between God and humanity has been broken. God wants the relationship reconciled.

Number two, God wants people to be safe. He wants to save them from the consequences of sin, which we have been referring to as death. In this context, death includes all of the consequences of sin including shame, guilt, self-hatred, hopelessness, loneliness, sickness, fear, anxiety, broken relationships, lack of vision, purposelessness, sadness, deception, and so forth.[211] This is the death from which God wanted to spare Adam and Eve. This is the death from which God wants to save all of humanity.

The third most important thing that people need to be saved from is the world. In Volume V, *Evil, Sin, and Suffering*, we studied the evil and suffering that is in the world. We saw how it results from natural and unnatural laws. Suffering also results from humanity's sin, Satan, and demons. In addition, sin and death reign in this world. The combination of all these results in the entire world system being dark and dangerous.[212] Father-God wants to save people from this dark world.

FROM WHAT MUST PEOPLE BE SAVED?

Reformed Theology	Father-Son Theology
Wrath of God	1. Broken Relationship
	2. Death (Consequences of Sin)
	3. The World

Point 353: Father-Son View: Saved from Wrath

So what about the wrath of God? Father-Son theology acknowledges God's wrath, but its perspective is different than that of Reformed theology.

---

[211] Explained in IV:D:211.
[212] Explained in V:I:247.

Systematic Theology for the New Apostolic Reformation

First of all, God's wrath is not an immediate threat. Because God is temporal within creation, He is able to hold His wrath in check. He is able to be patient (2 Peter 3:7-9). God has not yet "turned on" His wrath for the final judgment.

To see this consider again Paul's warning that *"the wrath of God is revealed from heaven against all ungodliness and unrighteousness of men . . ."* (Rom. 1:18). Certainly this is a terrifying thought, but Paul was not describing wrath that constantly and continually pours forth from God as Reformed theology leads one to believe. Paul was talking about a future judgment day when God's wrath literally will be revealed from heaven. In the context of Paul's warning, he went on to talk about how sinful people are *"storing up wrath"* for themselves:

> *But because of your stubbornness and unrepentant heart you are <u>storing up wrath</u> for yourself in the day of wrath and revelation of the righteous judgment of God . . . .*
>
> (Rom. 2:5)

Indeed, a judgment day is coming when God's wrath will be revealed from heaven, but at the present time He is withholding His judgment.

Jesus explained that *"the wrath of God abides"* on unbelievers (John 3:36). Wrath is real, but it is "abiding" in the sense of being held in check for a future day of judgment. Paul explained that *on that future day*, believers shall *"be saved from God's wrath"* (Rom. 5:9).

So the present threat for humanity is not God's wrath. What negative things people are experiencing right now are estrangement from God, death (i.e., consequences of sin), and the darkness of this world. People need to be rescued now. And God is offering a Savior, Jesus Christ. How salvation is accomplished is what we will explain in the two sections that follow.

We will learn that God wants to save people from estrangement, death, and the world, but as He does this He brings them into His family, making them children of God. One of the benefits of being children of God is that they will escape the future judgment. Jesus explained:

> *He who . . . believes Him who sent Me . . . does not come into judgment.*
>
> (John 5:24)

Saved from What?

And again:

He who believes in Him is not judged.
(John 3:18)

When people come to faith in Jesus, their relationship with God changes. God welcomes them into His family and deals with believers as His children. As a result, they will never experience the wrath of God.

Notice that salvation from God's wrath is a by-product of His action to save humanity from estrangement, death, and the world.

From What Must People Be Saved?

Reformed Theology	Father-Son Theology
Wrath of God	1. Broken Relationship
	2. Death (Consequences of Sin)
	3. The World

By-product
↓
Salvation from
God's Wrath

The point is that freedom from wrath is not the focus of salvation. It is the result. Please let me show you . . .

Volume VI
Soteriology

Section B
The Covenantal View of the Atonement

The word, **atonement,** refers to reparation for sin. The Hebrew word translated as atonement, literally means, "to cover over." From the NT perspective, atonement focuses on how people are made one with God through Jesus Christ. A study of the atonement also answers the important question, "Why did Jesus die on the cross?"

We will briefly describe the major views of the atonement and how they developed historically, but then we will narrow our focus to the penal substitutionary view (which is the view of Reformed theology) and the covenantal view (which is the view of Father-Son theology).

Point 354: The Christus Victor View of the Atonement

Throughout Church history, leaders have offered various explanations concerning how atonement was accomplished through Jesus and His death.

During the early Church period, leaders combined several aspects of Jesus' death into a united picture. Most prominently, they talked about humanity being held captive by Satan and God giving the life of Jesus as a ransom to set humanity free. They also focused on Jesus' death and resurrection, resulting in the devil being defeated and Jesus emerging victorious. This view was taught consistently by nearly all of the Church fathers including Augustine. It was, in fact, the dominant view in Christianity for the first 1,000 years.[213]

---

213 This view is still the predominant view of the Eastern Orthodox Church.

Systematic Theology for the New Apostolic Reformation

This view of the atonement may be referred to as the **classical view of the atonement**, but today it is more commonly known as the **Christus Victor view**. This second label was popularized by Bishop Gustaf Aulén (1879–1977), who attempted to revive the old classical view, as can be seen in his book, *Christus Victor: An Historical Study of the Three Main Types of the Idea of Atonement*. Bishop Aulén emphasized how God, in Christ, intervened in the world to stand up to Satan and the forces of materialism, violence, and oppression.

Point 355: The Satisfaction View of the Atonement

During the 11th century, a theologian, named Anselm (c. 1033–1109) rejected the classical view of the atonement. In particular, he challenged the idea of God giving the life of Jesus as a ransom to set humanity free. Anselm reasoned that God should not have to pay anything to Satan for humanity.

Anselm offered an alternative view known as the **satisfaction theory** of the atonement. To understand this theory, think of the world in which Anselm lived where lords governed over various regions of Europe throughout the Middle Ages. Of upmost importance to the lords was their honor. If anyone offended their honor, lords were expected to punish the offender. With this understanding, Anselm reasoned that humanity had violated God's honor by sinning. Therefore, humanity owes a great debt to God. Since no human can pay this debt, God became man and satisfied the debt for us.

Anselm's view of the atonement gradually became the predominant view during the Late Middle Ages, replacing not only the classical idea of ransom but also the classical view of Jesus conquering Satan. Adherents still believed that Jesus conquered Satan, but it was no longer seen as a central feature of the atonement.

Point 356: The Penal Substitutionary View of the Atonement[214]

During the Protestant Reformation, several leaders further developed Anselm's satisfaction theory. John Calvin was at the forefront of the

---

[214] Between the satisfaction theory and the penal substitutionary view, Peter Abelard (1079–1142) proposed the **subjective view** of the atonement, which emphasized how the death of Jesus revealed perfect love as an example for us to follow.

The Covenantal View of the Atonement

related discussions, but as explained earlier, Calvin thought in legal terms, being trained as a lawyer (also because he lived in the Western guilt/law culture[215]). In line with this, Calvin envisioned *God as a Judge who must punish sin*. Calvin concluded that Jesus was our substitute, taking on the punishment that was legally due to us, the law breakers.[216]

This view became known as the **penal substitutionary view** or simply the **substitutionary view**. *Penal* refers to the punishment necessary to pay the penalty for our sins. *Substitutionary* refers to Jesus taking on the punishment in our place.

The progression of thought for penal substitution goes as follows:

1. God is just.
2. Therefore, God must punish sin.
3. Jesus took on the just punishment for us.

Add to this progression the Reformed idea that God is angry at sin. His wrath is directed toward sin and the sinner. Jesus placed Himself between the sinner and the wrath of God. Then Jesus paid for sins by taking on the wrath of God.[217]

According to the penal substitutionary view, God's wrath continues to be directed toward all who do not believe in Jesus. That wrath is upon non-Christians today, and it will be fully released upon them on judgment day.

This view leads us to think of Jesus as a wall between Christians and the just wrath of God. The modern popular Reformed theologian, R. C. Sproul, is known for saying that "Jesus is our asbestos suit against the white-hot wrath of God against sinners." This penal substitutionary view has been championed by Reformed theologians, and it is most prominent in evangelical thinking today.[218]

---

215 Explained in IV:D:316-317.
216 Although Calvin is most often associated with the penal substitutionary view, theologians give Charles Hodge (1797-1878) credit for fully developing this view.
217 Some Reformed teachers prefer to say, "God poured out His wrath against sin on the person of Jesus Christ." Although this reveals God's wrath as against sin, it results with the same outcome that God's wrath came upon Jesus.
218 Another view is called the governmental view or the moral governmental view, taught by Hugo Grotius (1583–1645). This view sees Jesus taking on the punishment for sin, but more as a general revelation of how angry God is about humanity's sin, rather than as the actual acceptance of the punishment due to humanity.

Systematic Theology for the New Apostolic Reformation

THE PENAL SUBSTITUTIONARY VIEW OF THE ATONEMENT:
JESUS TOOK ON THE WRATH OF GOD

The Covenantal View of the Atonement

In the following discussions, we will see how the penal substitutionary view leads to serious errors in one's understanding of Father-God, Jesus, and the atonement.

Point 357: The Covenantal View of the Atonement

If one thinks in relational terms, rather than legal terms, then another explanation of the atonement comes into focus. It is the **covenantal view of the atonement**, which I believe is the most biblically accurate view.

Through the OT prophets, God declared that He was going to establish a new covenant. The first promise of that covenant was to forgive sins and iniquity.[219] Jeremiah expressed the words of God:

> But this is the covenant which I will make . . . I will forgive their iniquity, and their sin I will remember no more.
> (Jer. 31:33-34)

The writer of Hebrews talked about this new and better covenant (Heb. 8:6), repeating God's promise to forgive sins: *"For I will forgive their wickedness and will remember their sins no more"* (Heb. 8:12).

This new covenant was established through the shedding of Jesus' blood. One of several places this is evident is in the explanation that Jesus gave to His disciples at the last supper. He said, *"This cup is the new covenant in My blood . . ."* (1 Cor. 11:25). The shedding of Jesus' blood was the means by which the new covenant was established.

Point 358: Father-God Is Sovereign

In order to accept the covenantal view of the atonement, the most important truth to embrace is that *God can forgive sins*. This may sound simplistic at first, but the concept of forgiveness is incompatible with the Reformed view. The Reformed view of the atonement (which is the penal substitutionary view) states that God is just and, therefore, *He must punish sin*. The idea that God must punish sin is mutually exclusive to the idea that God can forgive sin.

---

219 The difference between sins and iniquity is explained in V:G.

Systematic Theology for the New Apostolic Reformation

To see the distinction between punishing sin and forgiving sin, consider this. Let's say you owe a large amount of money to the bank, an amount that you cannot pay, but you have a wealthy brother who went to the bank and paid the amount you owed. After the debt was paid off, would it be right for the bank officials to come to you and say, "We forgive that debt"? No. If the debt was paid, it doesn't need to be forgiven. On the other hand, if a debt is forgiven, it doesn't need to be paid.

The penal substitutionary view starts by saying, "God is just, and therefore, He must punish sin." The idea that God *must* push sin, negates Him forgiving sin. According to Reformed theology, the penalty must be paid.

In contrast, Father-Son theology with the covenantal view sees God forgiving sins. This view starts by saying *God is sovereign*. Because God is sovereign, He can do whatever He wants to do whenever He wants—this includes forgiving sins. The fact that God forgives sin does not mean that God is unjust. Because He is sovereign, He can forgive whomever and whenever He wants and still be just. This is Paul's main point in Romans 9:14-15:

> *There is no injustice with God, is there? May it never be! For He says to Moses, "I will have mercy on whom I have mercy, and I will have compassion on whom I have compassion."*

In the context of this passage, Paul was arguing that the authority to forgive is an aspect of God's sovereignty. God can show mercy to whomever He wants and still be just.

God does not "have to" punish sin. Calvin was wrong. Father-God can forgive sins.

This truth is revealed beautifully in the story of the paralyzed man meeting Jesus. When the man was lowered through the roof, Jesus said, *"Your sins are forgiven."* The simplicity with which Jesus forgave sins is astounding. Jesus did not demand any price to be paid. He simply spoke the words, and the man's sins were forgiven. The scribes who were listening considered Jesus' words as blasphemy, so Jesus spoke to them:

> *Which is easier, to say, "Your sins have been forgiven you," or to say, "Get up and walk"?*
>
> (Luke 5:23)

The Covenantal View of the Atonement

Then Jesus said to the religious leaders:

> *But, so that you may know that the Son of Man has authority on earth to forgive sins,—He said to the paralytic—"I say to you, get up, and pick up your stretcher and go home."*
>
> (Luke 5:24)

Jesus had authority to forgive sins, and He demonstrated His authority by healing the paralyzed man.

Father-God can forgive sins like Jesus forgave sins. *There is nothing in the nature of God that dictates that He must punish sin.* The God who tells us to forgive one another can forgive us.

Point 359: The Covenantal Progression of Thought

Once we determine that God is sovereign and, therefore, able to forgive sins, we can free ourselves of the Reformed idea that "God must punish sin." Therefore, we can free ourselves of the idea that Father-God had to take out His wrath on Jesus. That cruel image of God taking out His wrath on the Son developed out of a legal and philosophical concept of God. It is a philosophical construct based in a misunderstanding of God's nature.

Now we can build a logical progression of thought corresponding to the covenantal view of the atonement.

1. God is sovereign.
2. Therefore, God can forgive sin.
3. God established His forgiveness by making a new covenant.

Notice that each of these points are biblical. Anyone who knows the Bible can think of verses that clearly teach these points.[220]

Point 360: What Killed Jesus?

If we embrace the covenantal understanding of the atonement, we will want an answer to the question, "What killed Jesus?" This question comes

---

[220] This is in contrast to the Reformed assumption, "God must punish sin," which cannot be found in the Bible.

to the forefront because we have discarded the Reformed idea that God's wrath killed Jesus. Now we must consider an alternative explanation.

God established a new covenant. The Hebraic understanding of covenant entails two parties joining their lives. The covenant means that what one person owns the other person owns. This is similar to a modern marriage in which two people share all possessions. If a woman has a million dollar debt before she gets married, her husband will have a million dollar debt after they get married.

When Jesus became our covenant partner, our sins, transgressions, and iniquities became His. Peter explained that *"He Himself bore our sins in His body on the cross"* (1 Peter 2:24). Isaiah wrote that *"the Lord has caused the iniquity of us all to fall on Him"* (Is. 53:6).

Jesus not only took on our sins, but He received upon Himself the consequences of our sins.

The *consequences of sin* are different than the *punishment for sin*. To see this, think of a young man who takes within his body a large amount of illegal drugs. The *consequences* may be addiction, physical illness, hallucinations, and even death. In contrast, the *punishment* for taking those illegal drugs may be imposed by a judge who sentences the drug user to prison.

Again, the consequences of sin are different than punishment for sin. Consequences are the natural outworking of one's actions. Punishment is something inflicted by a higher authority.

This point is so important I will offer another comparison. Go back to our example of a man marrying a woman with a million dollar debt. As a consequence of taking on that debt, the husband will have to pay the million dollars. However, there will be no punishment inflicted upon the husband for taking on that debt. The husband did nothing wrong. No one will come beat him up or throw him in prison for taking on that debt.

The Bible tells us Jesus took on our sins, but there is no verse that says or implies that Jesus took on God's punishment for our sins (and remember that if God forgave our sin, there would be no punishment for our sins).

When Jesus took on the sins of humanity, He received upon Himself the consequence of the sins of humanity. Therefore, He had to die, because *"the wages of sin is death"* (Rom. 6:23). When we talk about these wages (in Greek, *opsonion*[221]), we are referring to the natural outworking of sin,

---

[221] The only other places this Greek word is used are in Luke 3:14 and 2 Corinthians 11:8, which refer to financial remuneration.

The Covenantal View of the Atonement

including shame, guilt, self-hatred, and so forth. The wages of sin include all of these consequences, and they always end in death (Rom. 6:23).

Just like the man who took a large amount of drugs died, so also Jesus took the sins of humanity upon Himself and then died. Following this line of thought, we can say, "Our sins killed Jesus."

Point 361: The Wrath of God Was Not Put upon Jesus

God did *not* take out His wrath on Jesus.

In saying this, I am not denying the wrath of God. There are many verses in the Bible that talk about God's wrath against sin. There is a coming day of judgment, when God's wrath will be revealed from heaven, and *"the wrath of God abides on"* those who do not obey Jesus (John 3:36). I am *not* asking you to deny the wrath of God, but I am asking you to consider the biblical evidence that God did not take His wrath against sin out on Jesus. Father-God did not add to the pain that Jesus suffered on the cross.

Supporters of the penal substitutionary view like to use portions of Isaiah 53 to argue that God took out His wrath on Jesus. In particular, Isaiah 53:5, which says:

> *But He was pierced through for our transgressions,*
> *He was crushed for our iniquities;*
> *The chastening for our well-being fell upon Him . . . .*

Indeed, this verse tells us that Jesus was crushed for our iniquities, but the next verse tells us:

> *But the Lord has caused the iniquity of us all*
> *To fall on Him.* (Is. 53:6b)

Notice that what crushed Jesus was not the wrath of God. Instead, Jesus was crushed by *our iniquities*.

Similarly, Isaiah 53:10 says:

> *But the Lord was pleased*
> *To crush Him, putting Him to grief . . . .*

Systematic Theology for the New Apostolic Reformation

Proponents of the penal substitutionary view see in this verse God taking His wrath out on Jesus, but the next verse tells us:

> *My Servant, will justify the many,*
> *As He will bear their iniquities.*
>
> (Is. 53: 11)

Father-God took the iniquities of humanity and placed them upon Jesus. Then our iniquities crushed Jesus.

So we see two different explanations for the death of Jesus. The penal substitutionary view leads Christians to believe that *God's wrath killed Jesus*. The covenantal view reveals that *our sins killed Jesus*. This distinction is an accurate way to distinguish between the two views. If Christians who understand theology say, "Our sins killed Jesus," then they have rejected the penal substitutionary view of the atonement.

Point 362: Rethinking the Atonement

For Christians who have never heard the covenantal view of the atonement, it takes some rethinking. Those who are trained in the penal substitutionary view have to reinterpret certain Bible passages, such as Hebrews 9:22:

> . . . *without shedding of blood there is no forgiveness.*

This is a favorite verse of Christians trained in the penal substitutionary view. They envision God taking out His wrath against sin on Jesus and the resulting bloodshed as necessary to pay the penalty for the sins of humanity.

In reality, the context of Hebrews 9:22 says nothing about Jesus paying for sins. Nowhere in the context is the wrath of God even mentioned. However, the word *covenant* is mentioned six times between verses 15-22. The passage is about the establishing of the new covenant. Verse 16 tells us:

> *For where a covenant is, there must of necessity be the death of the one who made it.*

The Covenantal View of the Atonement

The context of this passage explains how a covenant was established through the shedding of our Lord's blood and enacted through His death.

The new covenant assures us that God forgives our sins. No one has to pay for sins that have been forgiven. Jesus did not pay for our sins. There was no wrath of God placed upon Jesus.

It is important to note that both the covenantal view and the penal substitutionary view of the atonement say that Christians have been saved from the wrath of God. However, the penal substitutionary view leads one to believe that Christians are saved from the wrath of God because Jesus is a wall between them and the wrath of God. In contrast, the covenantal view leads one to believe that Christians are saved from the wrath because they have been forgiven.

Point 363: Old Testament Sacrificial System

To embrace the covenantal view of the atonement, we need to rethink the Jewish sacrificial system in the OT times.

First, think of the Passover Lamb that was slaughtered just before the Hebrew people were released from captivity in Egypt. This is especially significant because Jesus died on Passover night. At the first Passover, the Hebrews were told to place the blood of the lamb on the doorpost of their homes. Did that blood pay for their sins? No. Did the Hebrews take their wrath out on the lamb? No. Please think about this. The blood on the doorpost signified that the residents of each home were God's covenant people. Seeing the blood, the death angel passed by each home without bringing destruction. This accurately foreshadows the covenantal view of the atonement, not the penal substitutionary view.

Next, consider the laws of offerings laid out in Leviticus 1-6. Repeatedly those offerings were described as a *"soothing aroma to the Lord"* (e.g., Lev. 1:9, 13, 12). The offerings were not animals to be tortured on behalf of an angry God. They were propitiations (discussed next), which are gifts that pleased God so He would overlook their sins. Many times in Leviticus we are told that through those offerings the sins of the people would be atoned for and the people's sins would be forgiven: *"So the priest shall make atonement for them, and they will be forgiven"* (Lev. 4:20 ; see also, 4:26, 31, 35 ; 5:10, 13, 16, 18). Numerous Scriptures tell us that God forgives sins, but there is not one verse in the Bible mentioning payment for sins through sacrifices.

Systematic Theology for the New Apostolic Reformation

Think of the Day of Atonement when the Jewish high priest atoned for the sins, transgressions, and iniquities of the people (Lev. 16). Two goats were brought to the high priest. From this we can infer that one goat was not enough to foreshadow what would be accomplished through Jesus' atonement. One goat was offered up to God as a soothing aroma. The other goat was brought to the high priest, who laid his hands on the head of the goat, representing how the transgressions and iniquities of the people were transmitted to the goat. This foreshadows how the transgressions and iniquities of humanity were placed upon Jesus. However, it is important to note that after the transgressions and iniquities were placed upon the goat, the goat was not tortured or beaten up. No one took their wrath out on the goat. The goat was released into the wilderness. The goat took on the people's transgressions and iniquities but did not take on the penalty for those transgressions and iniquities.

Point 364: Jesus Is the Propitiation for Us

First John 2:2 tells us that Jesus was *"the propitiation for our sins"* (see also 1 John 4:10 ; Rom. 3:25 ; Heb. 2:17). What is a propitiation?

Christians trained in the penal substitutionary view of the atonement envision Jesus fulfilling this role of propitiation by taking on the wrath of God.

To see the function of a propitiation more accurately, consider an example of a propitiation from ancient times. On various occasions a king would become angry with the citizens of some city, so the king would come with his armies to destroy that city. If the leaders of the city realized that they had no chance of survival, they may have assembled a gift of gold and silver and then carried that gift out to the angry king. If the king accepted the gift and his anger subsided, then the gift served as a propitiation. As a result, the king would change his mind and do no harm to the city. The king would not take his anger out on the city or on the gift. He would simply accept the gift and leave without punishing anyone.

For a modern example of a propitiation, we can think of a husband who has offended his wife. If the wife beats him with a frying pan then she is satisfying her anger. On the other hand, if the husband brings her flowers, those flowers will serve as a propitiation if her anger subsides and she forgives him.

The Covenantal View of the Atonement

God sent His own Son to be the propitiation for our sins. His own Gift caused His anger to turn away from us so that we could be forgiven and reconciled to Him. Jesus appeased the Father. The fact that a propitiation is to serve as an appeasement rather than satisfaction of anger is most obvious when we simply consider the definition of the word *propitiation*. It literally means "appeasement," not "satisfaction." By definition, a propitiation is a gift or action which appeases the anger of someone.

Point 365: The Reformed Rejection of the Covenantal View

Adherents of Reformed theology cannot accept the truth of a propitiation being an appeasement, because they cannot logically accept the idea that God can be appeased. They do not believe God can change His mind. If God is timeless, then it would be impossible for Him to be angry about sin at one time and then forgive sin at another time. To admit that God changed His mind about sin is to reject their doctrine of God's immutability and, therefore, their doctrine of God being timeless within creation.

Remember how Moses interceded for the Hebrew people when God became angry and almost destroyed them (Ex. 32:9-14)? Moses reasoned with God and we are told:

> *So the Lord changed His mind about the harm which He said He would do to His people.*
> (Ex. 32:14)

Moses interceded and God listened, deciding not to punish the Hebrews. God did not take out His anger on Moses. Because of His covenant relationship with Moses, God listened and *"the Lord changed His mind"* (Ex. 32:14).

Classical/Reformed thinkers cannot accept this because they have assumed God is timeless within creation. They have already decided that the biblical records of God changing His mind are anthropomorphisms not to be taken literally. They cannot logically believe that God could change His mind about anything—especially judgment of sin. Hence, they conclude that Moses did not change God's mind. Nor could Jesus have changed Father-God's mind, according to the Classical/Reformed

Systematic Theology for the New Apostolic Reformation

view of God. Their assumption of God being timeless within creation disallows Classical/Reformed teachers from accepting a propitiation as an appeasement.

Adherents of Classical/Reformed theology sometimes ridicule the idea that God would have to be "appeased." They sometimes compare appeasement to how primitive people had to appease their many gods by offering sacrifices. Adherents of penal substitution try to portray such appeasement as primitive and barbaric. In reality, it is the penal substitutionary view that is barbaric. The idea that God had to take His anger out on someone (through torture and death) is not only primitive but something we would expect from a very immature and/or mentally deranged person.

In contrast, the acceptance of an appeasement can be seen as a work of dignity. A woman who accepts her husband's flowers as a peace offering may do it as a woman of grace. A king who accepts a gift of gold and decides not to punish a city leaves as victor having revealed his sovereignty and mercy. The concept of appeasement is even more glorious when we recognize that God provided His own propitiation. No one outside of Himself had to appease Him. He was able to change His own mind. He was able to forgive. In fact, that is what the cross represents: the truth that God does not require any outside appeasement. He took care of that Himself and forgave.

Point 366: Implications of Our View of the Atonement

Another problem with the penal substitutionary view has to do with double predestination. Let me explain.

If, indeed, Jesus took on the wrath of God as the penal substitutionary view claims, it is worth asking, "How much wrath did Jesus take on?" "Did Jesus take on *all* of the wrath of God for all of humanity's sin?" If Jesus did, then He already paid the penalty for all of humanity. If that is true, then there is no more penalty left to be paid. If there is no more penalty to be paid, then everyone's sins are taken care of and there can be no basis for judgment in the future. In other words, if Jesus paid the penalty for all of humanity's sins past, present, and future, then all of humanity is already saved from the wrath of God.

The Covenantal View of the Atonement

The only other logical understanding of the penal substitutionary view is that Jesus only took on the wrath of God on behalf of the elect. Indeed, this is one of the five points of Calvinism asserted in the acronym TULIP, with the "L" standing for **limited atonement**.[222] According to Reformed theology, Jesus only died on behalf of those who are going to be saved.

But if Jesus only died on behalf of those who are going to be saved, then those for whom Jesus died are predestined to go to heaven, and those for whom Jesus did not die are predestined to hell. This is called **double-predestination**.

Calvin taught that this double predestination was set from eternity past. God decided ahead of time for whom Jesus would die. This decision of God was not made on the basis of His foreknowledge of who would eventually believe in Jesus. According to Calvin, God sovereignly predestined some people to heaven and everyone else to hell:[223]

> For all are not created in equal condition; rather, eternal life is foreordained for some, eternal damnation for others.[224]

It is difficult for most Christians to accept this idea that God predestined some people to heaven and others to hell, but double-predestination is the only logical outcome of the penal substitutionary view of the atonement. (It is also the only logical outcome of the idea that God is timeless within creation.)

The Reformed Progression of Thought

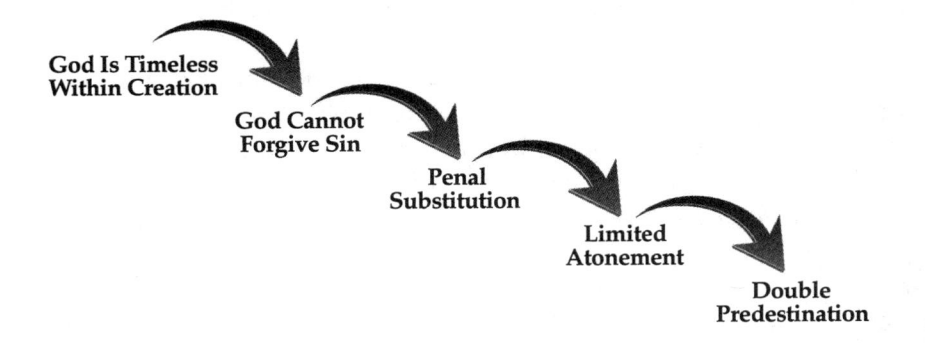

God Is Timeless Within Creation → **God Cannot Forgive Sin** → **Penal Substitution** → **Limited Atonement** → **Double Predestination**

---

222 Some teachers like to place this in a more positive light by calling it "particular atonement," implying that Jesus died on behalf of the elect.
223 Calvin discussed this several times, including: *Institutes* III,:21.
224 Calvin's *Institutes* III:21:5.

Systematic Theology for the New Apostolic Reformation

The covenantal view of the atonement does not have this problem of double-predestination. A logical progression of thought starts with God being temporal within creation, and therefore, He can change His mind, including forgiving sin. God established His forgiveness through the new covenant. In that new covenant, God made provision for the sins of all humanity. In fact, Jesus *"is the propitiation for our sins; and not for ours only, but also for those of the whole world"* (1 John 2:2). Even though God has made it possible for all to be saved, salvation is only given to those who enter into the new covenant by believing in Jesus (John 3:36):

THE FATHER-SON PROGRESSION OF THOUGHT

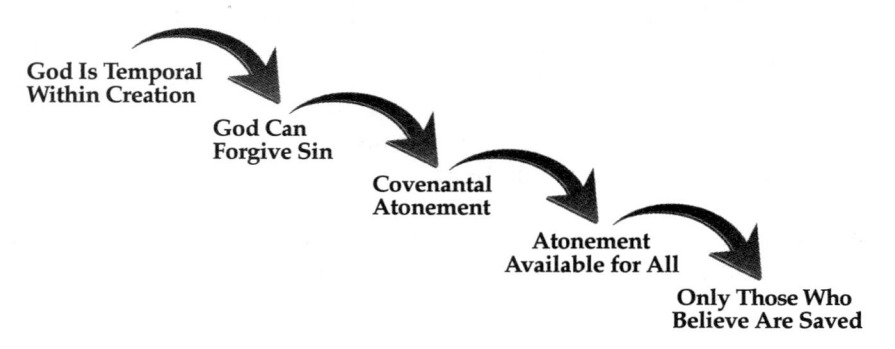

- God Is Temporal Within Creation
- God Can Forgive Sin
- Covenantal Atonement
- Atonement Available for All
- Only Those Who Believe Are Saved

Point 367: Jesus Is the Open Door between Us and a Forgiving God

Accepting the covenantal explanation of the atonement changes our understanding of Jesus and Father-God. Jesus is not a wall between us and an angry God. He is the open door between us and a forgiving God.

Furthermore, our forgiving God does not have a wall separating Himself from His people. People can walk through the open door that Jesus is offering (Heb. 4:16). Also, Father-God moves through the open door to come into the lives of His people. Better yet, Father-God joyfully steps into the lives of all those who enter into the new covenant. He moves onto "this side of the cross" and dwells with His people while they are alive on earth.[225]

---

[225] The penal substitutionary view also leads one to believe that God will dwell with His people, but only after they have been purged of all sin and gone to heaven.

The Covenantal View of the Atonement

Jesus as the Open Door between Us and a Forgiving Father

Point 368: Father-God Did Not Separate from the Son

Another implication of the covenantal view of the atonement in contrast to the penal substitutionary view has to do with the relationship between Father-God and Jesus Christ as Jesus died on the cross.

Earlier,[226] we discussed the Classical/Reformed misunderstanding that God must separate Himself from sin and sinners because of His holiness. This misunderstanding has led many followers of Reformed theology to envision Father-God separating Himself from Jesus as Jesus became sin for us on the cross. Adherents quote Matthew 27:46, where Jesus was hanging on the cross and cried out, *"My God, My God, Why have You forsaken Me?"* Quoting these words, they explain that God had to turn away from His Son as He became sin, because God cannot look at sin.

The idea that Father-God separated Himself from Jesus is incompatible with the doctrine of the Trinity. Father-God and Jesus are one. They are of the same substance. It is impossible for there to be any separation. In addition, Paul clearly told us that *"God was in Christ reconciling the world to Himself"* (2 Cor. 5:19).

---

226 IV:D:207-214.

Systematic Theology for the New Apostolic Reformation

Seeing these truths, we need to reconsider the words that Jesus cried out on the cross: *"My God, My God, Why have You forsaken Me?"*[227] These are the first words of Psalm 22. This is important to know because Jewish people of that period often quoted the first words of a Psalm to bring the entire Psalm to the mind of the listeners. This is similar to how people in modern times will sing the first few words of a song, and the listeners will recall the entire song.

When Jesus quoted Psalm 22:1, every faithful Jewish person listening would have thought of the entire Psalm, and that particular Psalm is the Messianic prophecy about Messiah's death. Psalm 22:16-18 says:

> *They pierced my hands and my feet . . .*
> *They divide my garments among them,*
> *And for my clothing they cast lots.*

There is no mistaking that this is talking about Jesus' death.

If we read a little bit further in Psalm 22, we find an eye-opening truth:

> *For He has not despised nor abhorred the affliction of the afflicted;*
> <u>*Nor has He hidden His face from him;*</u>
> *But when he cried to Him for help, He heard.*
>
> (Ps. 22:24)

The very Psalm that Jesus quoted while on the cross tells us that *Father-God did not hide His face from the Messiah.* It also tells us that when the Messiah cried out, Father-God heard Him.

Not all Reformed thinkers believe that the Father separated Himself from the Son, but those who do will not easily give up on that idea because it fits well with their entire concept of the Father taking His wrath out on the Son. It also fits with their understanding that a holy God cannot look at sin.

Earlier,[228] we discussed how God's holiness does not cause Him to separate from sin or sinners. Our ultimate example of a holy person is Jesus Christ. He is the One who gives us a clear revelation of what holiness is. Holiness is inseparable from love. Jesus was perfectly holy, and His holiness caused Him to reach out to sinners. We do not need to repeat our earlier discussion about this, other than to recall Jesus' explanation that nothing outside of a person can defile a person (Mark 7:14-15). Holiness is

---

[227] Some scholars in Aramaic will say that the original words can be accurately translated as "My God, My God, this is My destiny."
[228] IV:D:207-214.

The Covenantal View of the Atonement

something of the heart. God's heart is perfectly holy. For this reason, He is not afraid to have contact with the unholy. His holiness is not contaminated by the presence of sin or sinners. As explained earlier, *there is nothing in the nature of God that causes Him to separate from sin or sinful people.*

Point 369: A Timeless God Must Do What He Does Forever

The implications of the covenantal view are worth shouting in joy about, especially in comparison to the alternative view of penal substitution. Remember that the penal substitutionary view sees God unleashing all of His wrath toward sin on Jesus. But Reformed theologians also believe that God is timeless and, therefore, incapable of change. Do you see what this means? It means that according to Reformed theology, God must direct all of His wrath at Jesus forever. It was not just during the evening that Jesus hung on the cross. If, indeed, God is timeless, and He directed His wrath toward Jesus at one time, then He directed His wrath toward Jesus throughout eternity past and He will do it throughout eternity future. If we remain consistent with the Reformed view of God and believe the penal substitutionary view of atonement, then when we get to heaven, we should expect to see God still directing His full wrath toward Jesus. That will never change according to Reformed theology.

For me, this is another nail in the coffin for Reformed theology and their doctrine of God's timelessness within creation.

Point 370: New Covenant at the Forefront of Christian Thought

The covenantal view of the atonement brings the new covenant to the forefront of Christian thought. In contrast, the penal substitutionary view keeps the cross and death of Jesus at the forefront. This is worth noting.

Prophets such as Isaiah, Jeremiah, and Ezekiel foretold the days when God would make a new covenant and through that covenant God would forgive sins. It is difficult to overemphasize the new covenant. It was the hope set before the OT people of God. The new covenant signified another chance. It was the turning point in history when God would begin to deal with humanity in a different manner. He promised to forgive their sins, give them a new heart and spirit, and then put His Spirit within them,

Systematic Theology for the New Apostolic Reformation

causing them to walk in His ways (Ez. 36:26-27). The new covenant marked a much greater event than the first covenant made with Abraham or the giving of the Law through Moses.

Of course, the death of Jesus was a turning point in history, but the covenantal view of the atonement focuses more on the purpose of our Lord's death rather than on the death itself. His death was the means through which the new covenant was established and enacted. Consider again the words of Jesus at the last supper: *"This cup is the new covenant in My blood..."* (1 Cor. 11:25). Jesus was announcing the establishment of the new covenant.

In line with this realization, many church leaders around the world are removing the cross that once was located at the front and center of their sanctuaries. This change sometimes reflects the change in their understanding of the atonement. Those who accept the covenantal view of the atonement do not see the cross as the focal point of Christianity. This does not mean they remove the cross from their buildings. Rather the cross is moved somewhere where it reflects their beliefs more accurately. For example, some church leaders move the cross to a side wall in their sanctuaries. Even better, some churches have a cross positioned on or near the entry door to the sanctuary. This represents how all people must go through the cross to come into right relationship with God. However, once Christians are in the sanctuary, their attention should not be on the cross. It should be on the living Jesus who rose from the dead and now reigns from heaven.

This change may seem too radical for Christians who all their lives worshiped beneath the cross. Having lived through previous church transitions, I can tell you how hard it was for some Christians to get rid of the church organ and hymn books. Others had to battle when the pastor stopped wearing a three-piece suit. Still others threw a fit when the young people came on the stage with guitars and drums.

Of course, not all changes are good, but changing the location of the cross actually should not be so difficult. In reality, crosses never hung at the front center of church sanctuaries for the first thousand years of Church history. It was after Anselm's (c. 1033–1109) satisfaction theory was developed that church leaders began placing crosses in prominent positions. So when modern church leaders move the cross, they are actually coming more into alignment with the faith of the early Church.

Section C
Salvation via the Life of Jesus

We discussed the element of soteriology referred to as the atonement. We focused on two views: the penal substitutionary view which is the view of Reformed theology and the covenantal view which is the view of Father-Son theology. Now let's consider how these two views lead to different understandings of salvation.

Point 371: Salvation According to Reformed Theology

Reformed theology is built around the problems of humanity's sin and God's wrath against sin. The penal substitutionary view offers its answer to these problems. According to that view, God took His wrath out on Jesus and, as a result, the penalty for the sins of believers has been paid. A legal transaction was made. Therefore, believers have been declared justified in God's eyes. With this problem-and-answer scenario, Reformed thinkers see salvation happening at the cross, when Jesus paid the penalty by His suffering and death.

Followers of Reformed theology do believe that God has done more for believers than simply take care of sins. They will say God works regeneration, adoption, and sanctification in the life of believers, along with other benefits. However, escape from the wrath of God is by far the most significant aspect of salvation. According to Reformed theology, those additional works are typically seen as working out the salvation that happened at the cross.

Systematic Theology for the New Apostolic Reformation

Point 372: The Life of Jesus Saves Believers

Father-Son theology with the covenantal view of the atonement also leads one to conclude that believers have been saved from the wrath of God, however, adherents will say believers have been saved from the wrath of God because they have been forgiven.

In addition to forgiveness, the covenantal view changes the emphasis of salvation. To see this, consider Paul's words in Romans 5:10:

> *For if while we were enemies we were <u>reconciled to God through the death of His Son</u>, much more, having been reconciled, we shall be <u>saved by His life</u>.*

Notice how the death of Jesus accomplished one thing and His life something else. What did Paul say? The death of Jesus reconciles believers to God (comp. Col. 1:22). In contrast, the life of Jesus *saves* believers.

Death of Jesus ⟶ Reconciles Believers to God
Life of Jesus ⟶ Saves Believers

This truth is profound. Let's state it more boldly:

1. Believers *are not* saved by the death of Jesus.
2. Believers *are* saved by the life of Jesus.

This truth, clearly stated in Romans 5:10, is incompatible with Reformed theology and the penal substitutionary view of the atonement. In fact, it makes no sense to a person who holds to the penal substitutionary view. That view sees salvation happening at the death of Jesus because Reformed theology sees the most important aspect of salvation as salvation from the wrath of God. The penal substitutionary view sees Jesus paying the penalty for sins, and therefore, Christians are saved as Jesus was taking on that punishment and dying.

But in Romans 5:10, Paul clearly stated that salvation is the result of the *life* of Jesus and not the *death* of Jesus. Please follow this carefully because it changes how one understands salvation. Let me show you several elements of salvation, all of which happen as a result of the life of Jesus.

Salvation via the Life Jesus

Point 373: The Life of Jesus Is Poured into the Heart of Believers

According to Father-Son theology, one aspect of salvation is regeneration. Although believers are joined to Jesus at the cross via the new covenant, regeneration does not happen at the cross. After Jesus ascended into heaven, He became a life-giving Spirit (1 Cor. 15:45). His life is poured into the heart of every believer (Gal. 4:6). They are regenerated which is also referred to as the experience of being born again. That is when people are born into the family of God and become children of God.

Notice when and where believers get born again. It is not as a result of the death of Jesus. It does not happen at the cross. The born again experience is the result of Jesus' Spirit coming into believers. The Spirit flows from the throne of God. It is the Spirit that makes Christians alive. Hence, the life (not the death) of Jesus saves believers.

Compare this work of Jesus to a man who ran into a burning house to rescue some children. In the process, the heroic man got severely burned. After he got the children out of the burning house he gave each of the children mouth-to-mouth resuscitation. The breath of that man brought them back to life. In an analogous way, Jesus suffered and died for us. Because of His death, believers are reconciled to God and joined to Jesus. But believers are not saved at the cross any more than those children were saved by that man getting burned. They escaped death because the man pulled them out of the burning house, and they have life because he breathed life into each of them.

Point 374: Believers Get His Righteousness

Another element of salvation coming from the *life* of Jesus is righteousness. Once believers are covenanted with Jesus, they get what Jesus has. One thing Jesus has is righteousness, and believers get it!

> He made Him who knew no sin to be sin on our behalf, so that we might become the righteousness of God in Him.
> (2 Cor. 5:21)

Jesus' righteousness is given to all who are in covenant relationship with Him.

In order to understand this, we need to define righteousness.

Systematic Theology for the New Apostolic Reformation

Point 375: Reformed View: Believers Are Declared Righteousness

A common definition of *righteousness* among followers of Reformed theology is "right standing with God." This definition corresponds to their legal understanding of salvation. The terminology "right standing" brings to mind a person in a courtroom, standing before a judge and that judge has declared the individual as justified in the eyes of the law.

The terms *justified* and *righteous* are tied together in Reformed theology. Adherents believe that Jesus took on the punishment that was due to Christians, and then Christians are *declared justified*. With the penal substitutionary view of the atonement, justification is a *legal transaction*. Adherents of Reformed theology are comfortable saying justification "is not something wrought in man but something declared of man."[229]

Some Bible teachers have tried to soften the rigid, legal perspective of Reformed theology, by redefining righteousness as "right relationship with God." Indeed, this definition brings in a more relational understanding of salvation.

However, both of these definitions fall short because they both present righteousness as something *accomplished for believers* rather than something actually *given to believers*. The truth that righteousness is actually given to believers is huge, yet missed by followers of Reformed theology. Their penal substitutionary view of the atonement only allows for righteousness to be declared. Also, their emphasis on the evilness of all people—including Christians—causes them to downplay any righteousness that may or may not be given to believers.

Reformed teachers try to support their belief that righteousness is only declared and not given by referring to Romans 4 where several times Paul explained that righteousness was imputed to Abraham as a result of his faith (KJV). Then those Reformed teachers will explain that "imputed," as used in Romans 4, means "reckoned" or "accredited," but not "given." Following this line of reasoning, students of Reformed theology are taught that the righteousness of Jesus has been "accredited" to the account of believers, but no real impartation of righteousness takes place.

---

[229] Henry Theissen, *Lectures in Systematic Theology* (Grand Rapids: Errdmans, 1979), p 275.

Salvation via the Life Jesus

Point 376: Father-Son Theology: Believers Are Given Righteousness

It is true what Reformed teachers say about Romans 4 only talking about righteousness being "accredited" and not given, but that chapter is speaking about Abraham (with one reference to David). In the OT times, no one was *given* righteousness because Jesus had not yet died and made cleansing of sin possible. It was after the new covenant was established that believers became temples for the Holy Spirit to indwell. As a result of the new covenant, NT believers are not only accredited with righteousness, but they are actually given the righteousness of Jesus.

Several NT verses tell us about the righteousness of Jesus that is given to believers. In 2 Corinthians 5:21 (quoted above in point 374), Paul talked about the great exchange, through which our sins became Jesus' sins and His righteousness became ours; if one is true so also is the other. In Romans 5:17, Paul exhorted believers to receive *"the gift of righteousness."* In Romans 14:17, Paul explained that those who walk in the Kingdom of God will experience righteousness. We can also talk about the provisions of the new covenant. God gives believers a new spirit. The believer's *"spirit is alive because of righteousness"* (Rom. 8:10). The Spirit of Christ enters into the heart of the believer (Gal. 4:6). That Spirit is righteous.

Believers receive the righteousness of Jesus but this does not mean that they are perfectly and completely righteous the instant they become born again. Christians do sin from time to time, but something has been imparted from God into their heart and that something is perfectly righteous. They are born of incorruptible seed (1 Peter 1:23), i.e., a seed that has no unrighteousness in it.

Once we recognize that righteousness is given to believers, we can develop a definition that corresponds to this truth. It is helpful to see the correspondence of the sins of believers being transmitted to Jesus with Jesus' righteousness being transmitted to believers. That is a literal exchange. Sin is not something merely declared of man. Nor is righteousness something merely declared of man. Sinfulness is a state of being. So also righteousness is a state of being.

Jesus was righteous. His righteousness was not the result of Him fulfilling the Law and living the perfect life. Instead, He was righteous, and therefore, He fulfilled the Law and lived the perfect life.

A person who is righteous acts right. John wrote, *"Little children, make sure no one deceives you; the one who practices righteousness is righteous"*

Systematic Theology for the New Apostolic Reformation

(1 John 3:7). To put this in other words, we can say that a righteous person practices righteousness. Or in other words, a righteous person acts rightly. The point is that righteousness is *a characteristic or a quality of life that leads one to act rightly*. Put in more simple terms, righteousness is the right stuff.

Jesus had the right stuff that caused Him to act right. His righteousness is given to believers. That righteousness is planted within the believer's heart and spirit. That righteousness is growing like seeds in soil, and it will produce a harvest of right actions.

Again, we can point out that this does not mean that every believer is perfectly or completely righteous. John wrote how we all sin (1 John 1:9), but *"If we confess our sins, He is faithful and righteous to forgive us our sins and to cleanse us from all unrighteousness"* (1 John 1:9). Our state of being righteous varies, but believers always possess within them the perfect righteousness of Jesus.

Having received the righteousness of Jesus, believers come into "right standing with God" and into "right relationship with God," but these are the results of receiving righteousness rather than the definition of righteousness.

COVENANTAL VIEW OF THE ATONEMENT

Covenant Benefit	Results
Given Righteousness	→ Right Standing with God
	→ Right Relationship with God

Point 377: Righteousness Is the Answer to the Problem of Shame

The impartation of righteousness solves a major problem that separates God from humanity. In IV:D, we saw the fallacy in the Reformed view that God's holiness dictates that He must separate Himself from sinners. Instead, we saw that the primary separation between God and humanity is on the part of humanity, not God. People know good and evil; they know that God is perfectly good and holy, while they are not. As a consequence, people try to distance themselves from God. They hide in shame. They try to hide from God because they do not want their evil deeds exposed. Some also separate themselves because want to continue in sin.

Salvation via the Life Jesus

However, the problem of shame is solved when believers realize their sins are forgiven and they have the righteousness of Jesus. As a result, they can boldly approach God and confidently talk to Him. Christians can reject sin consciousness and become focused on the righteousness of Jesus that is now theirs. Hence, believers have been saved from the shame resulting from sin.

Point 378: Believers Benefit from all that Jesus Accomplished

Consider other ways in which the life, rather than the death, of Jesus saves. Believers are joined to Jesus because of the new covenant established at the death of Jesus, but once they are joined to Jesus believers benefit from all Jesus accomplished. When Jesus overcame death, all believers overcame death. When Jesus came out of the grave, He also conquered Satan, which means believers have conquered Satan. As Jesus was raised above all rule and authority, believers were raised with Him and seated with Him in heavenly places.

Consider Paul's explanation:

> *When you were dead in your transgressions . . . <u>He made you alive together with Him</u> . . . .*
>
> (Col. 2:13)

Not only were believers made alive, but as Jesus ascended into heaven, God:

> *. . . <u>raised us up with Him</u>, and seated us with Him in the heavenly places in Christ Jesus.*
>
> (Eph. 2:6)

Notice the different works accomplished through the death, resurrection, and ascension of Jesus. Through His death believers are joined to Jesus. Through His resurrection, ascension, and enthronement believers are raised and seated in heavenly places with Him.

This view is very different from the penal substitutionary view. That view does not accurately reveal how the resurrection, ascension, and enthronement of Jesus benefit believers. Of course, adherents of the penal substitutionary view believe the resurrection, ascension, and

Systematic Theology for the New Apostolic Reformation

enthronement took place, but they miss their significance in the salvation of believers. Adherents of the penal substitutionary view tend to think of the resurrection as *proof* that Jesus is the Son of God; it was the stamp of authentication that the death of Jesus was valid. They think of the ascension and enthronement as the Father's rewards to the Son for having suffered the crucifixion. However, followers of Reformed theology rarely see the significance of the resurrection, ascension, and enthronement in accomplishing an aspect of salvation for believers.

Jesus did more than die for humanity. He established a new covenant. All who believe in Him are joined to Him through that covenant. Because they are joined to Jesus, they benefit from all He did.

Compare this to a long line of train cars being linked to a train engine. When that engine starts to move, all of the cars are pulled along. Similarly, when Jesus came out of the grave, believers were pulled out of death with Him. When Jesus ascended, believers were raised with Him. Jesus "brought all believers on board" through His death. Then He carried them along as He resurrected, ascended, and sat down on His throne.

It is into the throne room of God that our Covenant-Partner has ascended. Since He has conquered, all believers have conquered. Believers get to follow in the wake of the Lord's triumph.

Point 379: Placed on a Path Leading to Full Transformation

The life of Jesus is released into the heart of the believer. From that moment forward, Jesus continues to pour out the Holy Spirit on behalf of believers. Through the Holy Spirit, Jesus leads them in His ways. He allows them to experience His life, and indeed, Jesus came that people may experience life and life more abundantly (John 10:10). Their lives are placed on a path of life.

Jesus explained:

> *I tell you the truth, whoever hears my word and believes him who sent me has eternal life and will not be condemned; <u>he has crossed over from death to life</u>.*
>
> (John 5:24)

This is the answer to the sentence of death that was placed upon Adam

Salvation via the Life Jesus

and all of his descendants.[230] Believers are moved from a path of death and placed on a path of light and life. Once they have stepped onto that path, nothing can stop the full manifestation of that which has been established in the resurrection, ascension, and enthronement of Jesus. Believers are being transformed from glory to glory (2 Cor. 3:18), and they are predestined to be conformed to the image of Jesus (Rom. 8:29-30).

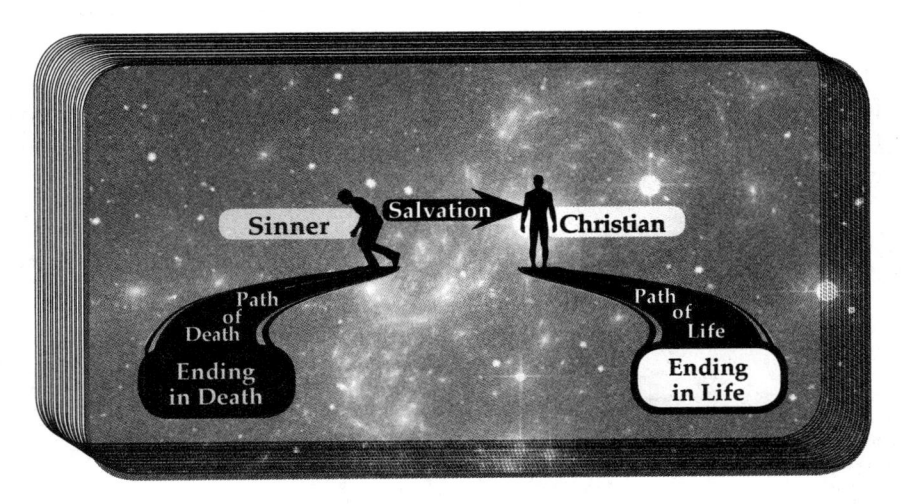

TRANSFERRED FROM THE PATH OF DEATH TO THE PATH OF LIFE

Envision the path of life as a moving walkway carrying every believer toward a destiny. A day will become when everyone who sees Jesus will be like Him, because they will see Him just as He is (I John 3:2).

This is a holistic understanding of salvation. Christians are reconciled to God through a new covenant. They are joined to Jesus and, therefore, share in His life. They are also placed on a new path—a path that leads to their complete transformation into the image of Jesus.

Now place this understanding into its proper position within the theme of this book. God is a Father who wants sons who are holy and blameless before Him (Eph. 1:4). Salvation accomplishes this.

---

230 Discussed in IV:D:211.

Systematic Theology for the New Apostolic Reformation

Point 380: Saved from Darkness and Satan

There is still one more important aspect of salvation accomplished through the life of Jesus. Paul explained:

> *For He rescued* [saved] *us from the domain of darkness, and transferred us to the kingdom of His beloved Son.*
> (Col. 1:13)

We needed saving from this evil world. Jesus accomplished that when He brought us into a Kingdom where He reigns. In that Kingdom sin, death, and Satan do not reign. The instant someone believes in Jesus they become citizens of God's Kingdom. They are transferred from darkness into the Kingdom as they are joined to Jesus who ascended into heaven.

SAVED FROM THE REALM OF DARKNESS INTO GOD'S KINGDOM

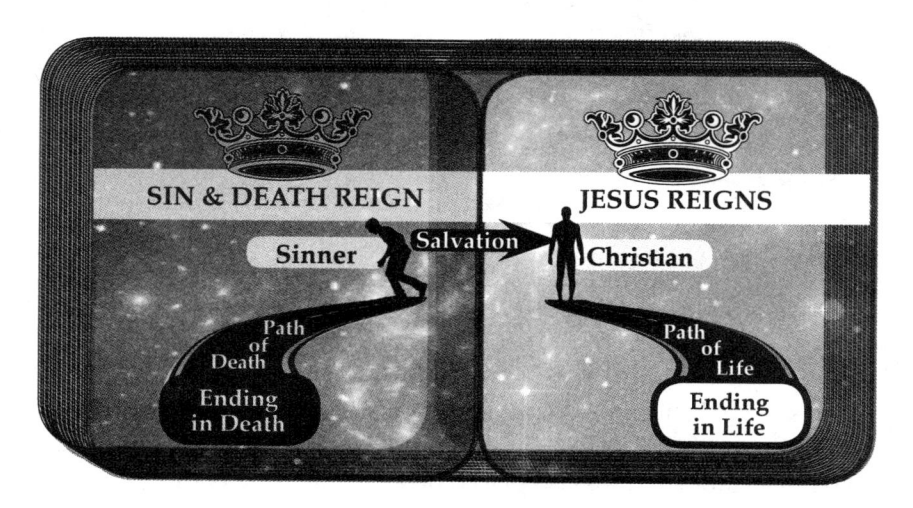

The Kingdom over which Jesus reigns is a Kingdom of light and love. It is Kingdom of relationship with the King and the Kingdom's citizens. It is a Kingdom that will endure forever.

Salvation via the Life Jesus

Point 381: Salvation Is the Answer to Humanity's Problems

Reconsider a question we asked earlier: "From what do people need to be saved?"

According to Reformed theology people need to be saved from the wrath of God. Therefore, they are saved at the death of Jesus when He paid the penalty for sins.

According to Reformed Theology

Christians Are Saved from:	Salvation Happens Because:
Wrath of God	Jesus' Suffered & Died

In contrast, Father-Son theology sees that people first need to be saved from the broken relationship between themselves and God. The answer is the new covenant. Through the new covenant believers are forgiven and given the righteousness of Jesus. They also are given the Holy Spirit. There is no greater reconciliation of the relationship between God and believers than the indwelling of God's Spirit.

Second, people need to be saved from death. The answer to death is life. Believers can walk in the abundant life available to them through Jesus.

Third, people need to be saved from the world. The answer is transference into the Kingdom of God.

According to Father-Son Theology

Christians Are Saved from:	Salvation Happens Because
1. Broken Relationship	1. New Covenant
2. Death	2. Life of Jesus
3. World	3. Transferred to God's Kingdom

Salvation for adherents of Father-Son theology includes the entirety of people becoming Christians and being transformed into the image of Jesus. Therefore, the salvation process begins when a person enters into the new covenant relationship. However, salvation continues until the believer becomes like Jesus when they see Him face to face. Hence, the NT explains that Christians are saved (Eph. 2:8-9), they are being saved (2 Cor. 2:15), and they will be saved (1 Peter 1:5 ; Eph. 1:14). Salvation includes the whole package—beginning to end.

Systematic Theology for the New Apostolic Reformation

Of course, believers are also saved from the wrath of God. However, that salvation actually will happen in the future on judgment day. As Paul wrote, *"Much more then, having now been justified by His blood, <u>we shall be saved from the wrath of God</u> through Him"* (Rom. 5:9).

Point 382: The Covenantal View with Christus Victor Worldview

This Father-Son understanding of salvation clarifies a topic that I left unfinished earlier. When we were discussing the different views of the atonement, I stated that the early Church fathers taught that Jesus was a ransom paid for us, and Jesus conquered Satan in His death and resurrection. That is the Christus Victor view.

Anselm made a valid point when he challenged the idea that God paid a ransom for us and He paid that ransom to Satan.[231] God should not have to pay anything to Satan. Yet, the Bible clearly says Jesus was the ransom that set us free (Matt. 20:28 ; 1 Tim. 2:6). So rather than think of God paying something to Satan, we can simply think of the ransom as the price needed to free us.

But the ransom view is not enough. Jesus also triumphed over Satan, disarming the rulers and authorities, destroying the powers that hold people in sin, undoing the works of the enemy, freeing humanity, and establishing a new Kingdom over which He reigns. This is more than an understanding of the atonement. *It is a worldview encompassing what Jesus did through His death, resurrection, ascension, enthronement, and ongoing ministry through the Holy Spirit.* For this reason, it is misleading to think of Christus Victor as merely a view of the atonement. It is the foundation of a victorious worldview.

This is where the covenantal view of the atonement enters. It includes the idea that Jesus was the price needed, but it rejects the penal substitutionary idea that God took out His wrath on Jesus. The covenantal view of the atonement fits well with the Christus Victor worldview. Of course, during the 1,000 years when the Christus Victor view was dominant, our forefathers associated various ideas with Christus Victor, and I do not mean to give credence to all they said, but the fundamental idea that Jesus triumphed over Satan is foundational to the worldview of the Bible. The covenantal view of the atonement, along with the Christus Victor worldview,

---

231 Explained in VI:B:355.

Salvation via the Life Jesus

give us a broader picture of salvation. Not only are believers saved from sin and judgment, but they are saved from this evil world where Satan once ruled. Believers are brought into a new Kingdom where Jesus is victorious!

In addition to these benefits of salvation, believers become children of God. This is important enough to focus on in the next section.

Volume VI
Soteriology

Section D
Becoming Children of God

The life of Jesus is imparted into the heart of every believer. That instant they become children of God. This deserves a closer look.

Point 383: Becoming Children of God

Earlier,[232] we noted how the Bible refers to all people—Christians and non-Christians—as children of God. Paul referred to all of humanity, saying, *"Being then the children of God . . ."* (Acts 17:29). So in what sense are Christians children of God, and in what sense are all people children of God?

Jesus referred to two births when He talked with Nicodemus:

> *That which is born of the flesh is flesh, and that which is born of the Spirit is spirit. Do not be amazed that I said to you, "You must be born again."*
>
> (John 3:6-7)

Both births—the natural and spiritual—have their source in God. He is the author of all life. He is the *"Father of spirits"* (Heb. 12:9).[233] God fathered Adam by breathing life into him, and all of humanity has been fathered by Adam. The breath that was released into Adam was the force of life that quickened every human being.[234] Therefore, God is the Father of all humanity.

---

232 IV:B:197-199.
233 More than once in the OT God is described as the *"God of the spirits of all flesh"* (e.g., Numb. 16:22 ; 27:16).
234 In IV:J:255, we discussed how the breath of God is passed through generational lines.

Systematic Theology for the New Apostolic Reformation

However, humanity was sentenced to death. As explained earlier,[235] when Adam and Eve sinned they began moving down a pathway of death on which they would continually experience the consequences of sins and ultimately die. Every person is dying and needs to be born again.

So God *"gave His only begotten Son, that whoever believes in Him shall not perish . . ."* (John 3:16). When people open their heart to Jesus by believing in Him, God breathes new life into them. They are born *again*. They are born a second time. The life of God that is released into believers becomes a well of water springing up to eternal life. The life of God is released into each and every person who believes in Jesus.

As a result of the second birth, believers enter into God's eternal family and become His children.

> *But as many as received Him, to them He gave the right to become children of God, even to those who believe in His name.*
> (John 1:12)

The life that is released into believers provides them with eternal life:

> *And the testimony is this, that God has given us eternal life, and this life is in His Son. He who has the Son has the life; he who does not have the Son of God does not have the life.*
> (1 John 5:11-12)

Christians have life that non-Christians do not have. That life is the same divine life that is in Jesus Christ (see also John 11:26).

Point 384: Jesus as the Only Begotten Son

At this point it is worth noting the difference between Jesus as the Son of God and believers in Jesus being sons of God. John 3:16 tells us that Jesus is the *"only begotten Son."* We can understand this when we envision the very substance of God coming into the womb of the virgin Mary. Seeing the substance of God literally becoming man allows us to see the unique manifestation of God as man in Jesus.

In contrast, the Spirit of God is released into people when they believe in Jesus. At that point they are born again. The injection of new life allows them to be born a second time and become children of God.

---

235 IV:D:211.

Becoming Children of God

To see this distinction, we can say that in Jesus the substance of God took on the nature of man. In the born again Christian, the substance of God is released into the nature of man. This truth is explained beautifully in Hebrews 1 and 2. The writer explained that Jesus is not ashamed to call believers His brothers, because He and they have the same Father (Heb. 2:11 ; cf. 2 Pet. 1:4).

Point 385: Historical Context for Understanding the Second Birth

The truth of being born a second time was especially attractive within the culture of Bible days. Historians estimate that in ancient Rome the average life expectancy for men was about 22 and, for women, 20 years. Of course, there were many older people, but life expectancy was askew because a large percentage of children died at or shortly after birth. Historians estimate that within the Roman Empire, one-third of all children died naturally before their first birthday. Natural life was fleeting. People were ever conscious of impending death.

This consciousness of death was amplified because ancient Roman people considered a family of three children as the ideal size. With the father of each family holding total and absolute control over each family member, family size was often limited via infanticide.[236] Any child with any deformity or weakness was typically discarded, and girls were often tossed out simply because girls were less valued. Rather than feed extra mouths, a father often abandoned unwanted children to die of exposure. The father's absolute authority also extended to a right to use his children as payment or collateral for debts. He could simply sell his children into slavery or servitude.

These facts caused people of that period to hold relationships with small children in a very tentative fashion. Even today in some cultures where infant mortality is very high, parents refrain from naming their children until they have reached a certain age. That hesitancy to fully acknowledge children is common in cultures where poverty and disease prevail.

Of course, assurance of life is critical to all people, but during Bible times people were much more aware of the fleetingness of life. The thought of a second birth with assurance of eternal life was as promising as a fountain of youth.

---

236 Jews historically valued human life and did not allow infanticide, but the natural death rate was still very high.

Systematic Theology for the New Apostolic Reformation

Point 386: Adoption Accompanied with Inheritances

It is also helpful to understand the practice of adoption in Bible times. In the cruel environment of the Roman empire, families often adopted children to reinforce interfamily ties and political alliances. Many adoptions also took place as a means to direct where property would be passed through inheritances.

Paul was most likely drawing on the Roman practice of adoption when he wrote to the Christians living in Rome:

> . . . *you have received a spirit of adoption as sons . . . The Spirit Himself testifies with our spirit that we are children of God, and if children, heirs also, heirs of God and fellow heirs with Christ . . . .*
> (Rom. 8:16-17)

Here Paul says the Holy Spirit is the witness to our adoption as children of God. This corresponds with the Roman practice of adoption in which a third party was required to witness any adoption to make it legal.

Point 387: Children Being Recognized as Mature Sons

We have identified three aspects of becoming God's sons: receiving God's life, adoption, and granting of the inheritance. In Galatians 4:5-7, Paul refers to all three aspects:

> . . . *that we might receive the <u>adoption</u> as sons. Because you are sons, God has sent forth the <u>Spirit of His Son into our hearts</u>, crying, "Abba! Father!" Therefore you are no longer a slave, but a son; and if a son, then an <u>heir</u> through God.*

Many cultures of the NT period practiced some rite of passage in which a child was recognized as having full rights as an adult family member. In Jewish culture, the transition was identified by the father publicly declaring something over the son, such as, "In you I am well pleased." Roman people often held ceremonies when sons were given authority to represent their father in all matters of business or politics. Such recognition was often symbolized by the father placing a ring upon the finger of his son.

Becoming Children of God

This brings light to the story of the returning prodigal son. Upon seeing his son, the father welcomed him in and placed a ring upon his finger, giving him full rights as a mature son.

In those cultures, it was one thing to be a child in the family and another to be a mature son. The distinction was much greater than it is in modern culture. Understanding this historical setting helps us better see the significance of God granting people status as sons of God.

Point 388: Sonship as the Fulfillment of the New Covenant

Key to understanding sonship is seeing it as the fulfillment of the new covenant. Of course, God promised that He would remember our sins no more, but He also promised to give us a new heart and spirit. He promised to put His Spirit within us, causing us to walk in His ways. These are the identification marks of a true son. A true son wants what his father wants. A true son acts the way his father acts. A true son has his father's heart and spirit.

We can see this on the negative side, when Jesus told the religious leaders that they were doing the works of their father the devil (John 8:44). Sons have the spirit of their father and are motivated to do the deeds of their father.

The new covenant assures us that God is writing His desires upon our heart. He is at work within us causing us *"to will and to work for His good pleasure"* (Phil. 2:13). Furthermore, God places His Spirit within us, and His Spirit is helping us act as our Father desires us to act.

This is in contrast to the Mosaic covenant which allowed the Hebrews to be faithful *servants of God*. It is one thing to be servants of God and another thing to be *sons* of God. The new covenant could only be fulfilled by making God's people His own sons, with a heart after His and a spirit that is His own Spirit. Hence, we see how the new covenant entails sonship for all who believe in Jesus.

Everything has been accomplished to make believers God's mature sons. Believers have *"the first fruits of the Spirit"* (Rom. 8:23), and now they are being transformed from glory to glory (2 Cor. 3:18). They are *"predestined to become conformed to"* His image (Rom. 8:29). God has done everything necessary to assure the fulfillment of His desire to have sons who are holy and blameless before Him (Jude 1:24-25).

Volume VI
Soteriology

Section E
What Is the Gospel?

Soteriology requires us to re-examine the gospel. The penal substitutionary view of the atonement leads us to the "gospel of salvation." The covenantal view of the atonement, along with the Christus Victor worldview, leads us to the "gospel of the Kingdom." Let me explain . . .

Point 389: The Gospel of Salvation

If you ask evangelical Christians, "What is the gospel?" most of them will answer something like this:

> Jesus died for our sins, and if we accept Him as Savior, we will be saved and go to heaven when we die.

This is certainly good news.

It is good news in keeping with the truth that all people sin and need a Savior. This message corresponds to the Reformed view of God and the penal substitutionary view of the atonement. In particular, it is founded in the idea that people need to be saved, first and foremost, from the wrath of God.

Of course, it is good news that believers will not experience the wrath of God, but upon further consideration, we learn that this gospel is a very limited understanding of salvation. This limited understanding is often called **the gospel of salvation.**

Systematic Theology for the New Apostolic Reformation

Point 390: The Gospel of the Kingdom

In contrast to the gospel of salvation is the **gospel of the Kingdom**. The gospel of the Kingdom is what we see Jesus and His disciples preaching. Jesus declared:

> *The time is fulfilled, and the Kingdom of God is at hand; repent and believe the gospel.*
>
> (Mark 1:15)

> *Jesus traveled about from one town and village to another, proclaiming the good news of the Kingdom of God.*
>
> (Luke 8:1 NIV)

The message of the Kingdom is what Jesus sent out His disciples to preach (Matt. 10:7 ; Luke 9:2). This is also the message that Paul preached:

> *And he stayed two full years . . . <u>preaching the kingdom of God</u> and teaching concerning the Lord Jesus Christ with all openness, unhindered.*
>
> (Acts 28:30-31)

The Kingdom of God is best understood in the context of the whole Bible. In the Book of Genesis, God promised that He would send someone who would crush Satan's head (Gen. 3:15). Later, God promised to King David that one of his descendants would build a Kingdom that would endure forever (1 Chron. 17:11-14). Isaiah prophesied of a child who would grow to sit on the throne of David and rule forever (Is. 9:6-7). Similar promises are given in numerous passages of the OT.

So when the NT leaders announced, "The Kingdom of God is at hand," they were referring to the fulfillment of God's OT promises. God sent a Savior into the world. That Savior came to conquer Satan and establish a Kingdom.

When Jesus and the apostles announced that the Kingdom of God was "at hand," they meant that it was available or within reach. In a modern grocery store, we might ask the clerk if a certain item is in stock. "In stock" is synonymous with "at hand." The good news that Jesus and the apostles preached is that the Kingdom of God is now available and within reach.

What Is the Gospel?

In other words, Jesus is King. Believers can now live under His reign. Believers can be part of His Kingdom, and they can experience His Kingdom today. This is not referring to when people die and go to heaven. The Kingdom of God is here, and believers can experience it while they are alive on this earth. Two thousand years ago, Jesus was given all authority over heaven and earth. He has been sitting on His throne, and now He reigns. This is the gospel of the Kingdom.

Point 391: In the Death, Resurrection, Ascension, and Enthronement

There are important differences between the gospel of salvation and the gospel of the Kingdom.

One of the differences is their foundation in the work of Jesus. The gospel of salvation is founded in the death of Jesus, while the gospel of the Kingdom expands the foundation into the death, resurrection, ascension, and enthronement of Jesus.

This does not mean that Christians who only know the gospel of salvation deny the resurrection, ascension, and enthronement of Jesus. Of course, they believe these events happened, but they tend to think of them as secondary to the death of Jesus. According to the gospel of salvation, the resurrection, ascension, and enthronement point back to the death of Jesus. The death is overwhelmingly seen as the most significant event and accomplishment of Jesus.

In a fuller way, Christians who teach the gospel of the Kingdom see the death, resurrection, ascension, and enthronement of Jesus as each being foundational and essential for establishing the Kingdom of God:

1. Through His death, Jesus enacted the new covenant.
2. When He resurrected, He conquered death.
3. As He ascended, He was raised above all authority.
4. When He was enthroned, He became King.

If any of these accomplishments had been left undone, the gospel of the Kingdom would not be the gospel. It is not enough to realize that the cross is empty. We must understand what Jesus accomplished beyond the grave.[237]

---

[237] For further study of the gospel of salvation versus the gospel of the Kingdom, see my book entitled, *Thy Kingdom Come*.

Systematic Theology for the New Apostolic Reformation

Point 392: The Availability of the Holy Spirit

In addition to the death, resurrection, ascension, and enthronement, the gospel of the Kingdom includes the good news that the Holy Spirit is now available to believers. When Jesus sat down on His throne, He received the Holy Spirit from the Father. Jesus is now pouring out that Spirit 24 hours a day, seven days a week. All who have their hearts open to Him are receiving that flow of life.

For this reason, Jesus explained,

> *He who believes in Me, as the Scripture said, "From his innermost being will flow rivers of living water."*
>
> (John 7:38)

The Spirit of God is flowing from heaven and into the hearts of all who believe in Jesus. That Spirit flows within the believer like rivers of living water.

The Holy Spirit is not separate from the gospel of the Kingdom but intrinsic to the message. When Paul wrote that the Kingdom consists of righteousness, peace, and joy, he associated these benefits with the Holy Spirit (Rom. 14:17). This is because living in God's Kingdom is inseparable from living in the Holy Spirit.[238]

---

[238] This is explained more completely in XII:C:456-457.

Section F

What Is the Proper Response to the Gospel?

In the preceding section, we explained the difference between the gospel of salvation and the gospel of the Kingdom. Now let's identify the proper response from people who hear each version of the gospel.

Point 393: The Reformed Path to Salvation

Teachers of Reformed theology champion the gospel of salvation. In line with that gospel, they teach that in order to be saved people must realize that they are sinners, turn their hearts toward God, and accept Jesus as Savior. This is considered *the* path to salvation.

<u>The Path to Salvation</u>
1. Realize one's own sinfulness
2. Turn one's heart to God
3. Accept Jesus as Savior

For the most part, evangelical Christians today accept this as the path to salvation. They typically encourage non-Christians to say what has become known as "The Sinner's Prayer." In that prayer, there is no formula of specific words, but non-Christians are expected to acknowledge their sinfulness, ask God to forgive them, and then accept Jesus as their personal Savior. The Sinner's Prayer is repeated by over a million people[239] in churches around the world every Sunday.

---

239 These are not all first time believers.

Systematic Theology for the New Apostolic Reformation

Point 394: The Kingdom Path to Salvation

If Christians embrace the gospel of the Kingdom as the gospel, then they will identify the path to salvation differently. To see this, consider how our Lord preached: *"Repent, for the kingdom of heaven is at hand"* (Matt. 4:17). The response expected from the person who hears this gospel is to "repent."

When modern Christians hear this word, *repent*, they often envision a person feeling sorry for their sins, but that is reading the Bible through the overly sin-conscious mind of evangelical Christianity. The word *repent* (*metanoeo* in Greek) actually means "turn." Turning may include turning away from sin, but that is not the primary focus. In the context of the gospel of the Kingdom, *repent* refers to a person turning in a way that brings their life into conformity with the Kingdom of God.

This understanding would have been much more tangible in the culture of Bible times. Kings often went out with their armies to conquer various people groups. When a new king was victorious, people were expected to surrender and acknowledge the new king. The people would often be allowed rights as citizens of the new kingdom, so long as they swore allegiance to the new king.

In a comparative fashion, Jesus is Lord, and He reigns over the Kingdom of God. Any person who hears this message and acknowledges the Lordship of Jesus Christ is welcomed into the Kingdom of God.

Point 395: Confessing Jesus as Lord

The acknowledgment of Jesus as Lord is what Paul said is necessary for salvation:

> . . . *if you <u>confess with your mouth Jesus as Lord</u>, and believe in your heart that God raised Him from the dead, you will be saved.*
> (Rom. 10:9)

Notice Paul's wording. He did not say, "Accept Jesus as your Savior," like evangelicals do today. He said, "Confess Jesus as Lord." There is a significant difference.

What Is the Proper Response to the Gospel?

According to Paul, two things are required of people to be saved:

> The Path to Salvation
> 1. Confess Jesus as Lord.
> 2. Believe God raised Jesus from the dead.

Confessing Jesus as Lord is an acknowledgment that Jesus reigns. It is consistent with the gospel of the Kingdom. It is also significant that Paul wrote about the resurrection, which is proof that Jesus overcame death. He conquered all!

Point 396: Accepting All Who Believe in Jesus

What is required for salvation? Acceptance of Jesus as Savior or confession of Jesus as Lord?

There is no Bible verse that offers "The Sinner's Prayer." Nor is there any Bible verse that tells us that we must accept Jesus as Savior. Those responses are the logical outcomes of reading the Bible through the worldview of Reformed theology, which is focused on humanity's problem of sin and God's wrath against sin. With those as the focal points of Reformed theology, Jesus' ministry *as Savior* is the central feature of history. Therefore, according to Reformed theology, accepting Jesus as Savior is the logical response on the part of humanity.

In contrast, if we accept the gospel of the Kingdom as the more biblical gospel, then the logical response is for a person to acknowledge that Jesus is Lord and to repent, i.e., bring one's life into conformity with the Kingdom of God. When people acknowledge Jesus as King of the Kingdom, they are saved and become citizens of God's Kingdom.

Having said this, we need to point out that God will not turn any one away who comes to Him with a contrite heart. Anyone who truly makes a heart commitment to Jesus via praying The Sinner's Prayer or confessing Jesus as Lord will be saved. God looks at the heart. We can recognize that a confession of Jesus as Lord is the most biblical response to the gospel, however, God is a gracious God. He will accept anyone who believes in Jesus. This truth is critical, so we will establish it in the next section.

Volume VI
Soteriology

Section G
What Is Necessary for Salvation?

We have identified the proper response to the gospel of the Kingdom as repenting. We also examined Paul's explanation that people must believe in their heart that God raised Jesus from the dead and confess Jesus as Lord.

Even though we have identified these as the proper responses to the gospel, we must not limit our understanding to these responses. The Bible talks very clearly about *simply believing in Jesus.*

> *For God so loved the world, that He gave His only begotten Son, that <u>whoever believes in Him</u> shall not perish, but have eternal life.*
> (John 3:16)

Faith in Jesus is required for salvation. Nothing more, nothing less.

Point 397: Belief Is of the Heart

When we speak of *believing,* we are referring to a function of the heart. The apostle Paul explained: *"for with the heart a person believes . . ."* (Rom. 10:10). This word, *believe,* can cover a broad spectrum. It is much like love, which is also a function of the heart. A person may claim to love a spouse or child, but that is not the same as loving chocolate. Comparatively, we can say that some people believe in God, but what does this mean? Even demons believe in God. In what sense does a person need to believe in Jesus in order to be saved?

Systematic Theology for the New Apostolic Reformation

As we answer this question, we will see how the verb *believe* corresponds with the nouns *belief* and *faith*. We will be using these nouns interchangeably to refer to the conviction forming within the heart when a person believes.

To identify the faith that is necessary for a person to be saved, teachers often refer to **saving faith**. Let's identify what saving faith entails.

Point 398: Biblical Examples of Belief in Jesus

Consider Zaccheus, the tax collector who brought Jesus into his home. Zaccheus repented, saying that he would give away half of his possessions and give four times as much back to anyone whom he had defrauded (Luke 19:8). Jesus responded, saying:

> *Today salvation has come to this house, because he, too, is a son of Abraham.*
> (Luke 19:9)

Jesus declared that Zaccheus was saved, but at that time, Zaccheus did not know that Jesus was going to die for his sins, resurrect from the dead, or sit down at the right hand of Father-God. Zaccheus simply believed in Jesus.

Zaccheus' faith led to a dramatic lifestyle change, but it was not his change in lifestyle that saved him. It was his faith in Jesus. Zaccheus did not accept Jesus as Savior. Nor do we read about him confessing Jesus as Lord. He simply believed, and he was saved.

What I am pointing out is that people do not need to believe in any certain accomplishment of Jesus to be saved. They do not need to understand why Jesus died on the cross. They do not need to understand that Jesus is Lord. Of course, we want all people to know these truths, but that information is not necessary for salvation.

It is belief in a Person—Jesus—that is required for salvation.

Consider Mary, the sinful woman who poured perfume on the feet of Jesus and wiped His feet with her hair. Jesus said to her, *"Your faith has saved you"* (Luke 7:50). At that time, Mary did not know Jesus was going to die for her sins. She simply believed in Jesus.

Think about the man born blind whom Jesus healed. Later on Jesus met up with the man and said, *"Do you believe in the Son of man?"* (John

What Is Necessary for Salvation?

9:35). The previously blind man responded by asking, *"Who is He, Lord, that I may believe in Him?"* (John 9:36). After Jesus declared His identity, the man believed and worshiped Jesus (John 9:38). This man came to believe in Jesus because of the miracle he experienced.

Consider the centurion who asked Jesus to heal his paralyzed servant. Jesus agreed to come and heal the servant, but the centurion told Jesus that He did not need to come to his home, but *"just say the word, and my servant will be healed"* (Matt. 8:8). Jesus responded, explaining that He had not found such great faith with anyone in Israel and that many with such faith will sit at the table with Abraham, Isaac, and Jacob in the Kingdom of heaven (Matt. 8:10-11).

If we take such passages seriously, we must conclude that salvation is not based on believing in a certain accomplishment of Jesus. It is based on believing in *Him*. The Mediator between God and man is not an action that Jesus did. The Mediator is a Person (I Tim. 2:5). Jesus is the path to salvation. The Bible is very clear about this. Jesus said:

> *I am the way, and the truth, and the life; no one comes to the Father but through Me.*
>
> (John 14:6)

The path is a Person. Faith in that Person is what is necessary for salvation.

Point 399: The Gospel Peter Preached

We want everyone to come to believe in all that Jesus did for us, but when people first come to Jesus, they may come to know Him as Savior, Healer, Miracle Worker, the Son of God, the Messiah, Lord, King, or many other ways. How they know Jesus is not the issue. What is important is that they believe in Him.

Consider what Peter preached on Pentecost Day (Acts 2:17-36). Peter mentioned that Jesus died on the cross (Acts 2:23), but he never explained *why* Jesus died on the cross. The heart of Peter's message was that Jesus had worked miracles (Acts 2:22), risen from the dead (Acts 2:24-32), was sitting at the right hand of God (Acts 2:33-35), and was now pouring out the Holy Spirit (Acts 2:33). To this message, 3,000 souls responded and were saved.

Systematic Theology for the New Apostolic Reformation

When Peter shared the gospel with Cornelius and his household, Peter never mentioned anything about Jesus being the Savior (Acts 10:36-48). Instead, Peter explained:

- that Jesus is Lord of all (v. 36)
- how God anointed Jesus with the Holy Spirit and power (v. 38)
- how Jesus went about doing good (v. 38)
- how Jesus healed those who were oppressed of the devil (v. 38)
- that He was put to death on a cross (v. 39)
- that God raised Jesus from the dead (v. 40)
- how Jesus revealed Himself after His resurrection (v. 41)
- how Jesus has been appointed by God as the Judge of all (v. 42)
- that all of the prophets foretold of Him (v. 43)
- that whoever believes in Him will receive forgiveness of sins (v. 43)

Peter's focus was not on any specific accomplishment of Jesus. Peter was helping the listeners believe in the Person, Jesus Christ.

Point 400: The Gospel Paul Preached

Consider Paul's conversion experience (Acts 9:1-19). He was violently opposed to Christianity until Jesus appeared to him in a blinding light. Paul instantly became a believer in the resurrected Jesus. At that time, he did not understand why Jesus died for his sins. Paul later came to understand that Jesus is Savior, but Paul believed in Jesus the instant Jesus revealed Himself.

After Paul had his conversion experience, *"he began to proclaim Jesus in the synagogues, saying, 'He is the Son of God'"* (Acts 9:20).

Believing that *Jesus is the Son of God* is the conversion point in the lives of many Muslims. I know one Muslim man who was converted to Jesus as a result of Jesus appearing to him in a dream. In that dream, Jesus did not explain why He died on the cross. Instead, He simply revealed Himself, and the man who was previously Muslim bowed before Jesus and believed in Him. The Muslim did not accept Jesus as Savior. Instead, he was instantly convinced that Jesus was the Son of God. It was not until later that he came to understand why Jesus died on the cross.

What Is Necessary for Salvation?

Now please do not misunderstand what I am saying. Every person who has accepted or ever will accept Jesus as Savior is saved. However, accepting Jesus as Savior is only one way in which people express their belief in Jesus. Confessing Him as Lord is another way. To be saved, all a person needs to do is believe in Jesus. It is their simple faith in Him that avails them of salvation.

Point 401: With the Heart a Person Believes

Think again of Mary, the woman who poured perfume on the feet of Jesus (Luke 7:37-50). She was not saved by her act of pouring oil upon Jesus. She loved Jesus. She believed in Jesus. So she was saved.

What do we see in common with Mary and the other examples of people having saving faith? Their lives changed. They acted according to their faith in Jesus. Indeed, it is a biblical truth that whatever is in the heart of a person flows outward. It changes a person's speech and behavior—it changes everything.

Therefore, "saving faith" can be identified as the type of faith that changes a person's life and behavior. Indeed, James explained, *"faith by itself, if it is not accompanied by action, is dead"* (Jas. 2:17). James offered further explanation that living faith will always be revealed by actions.

This does not mean that anyone's actions will save them. Faith and faith alone is required, however, saving faith does produce actions in line with that which is believed.

Point 402: All Who Believe in Jesus Are Saved

Saving faith in the Person—Jesus Christ—is all that is necessary for salvation.

Still, the idea that knowledge of the cross is not necessary for salvation is disturbing to many modern Christians. They have been indoctrinated into a certain modus operandi. They think everyone must come to Jesus in the same way they did. They think people must acknowledge their sinfulness, turn to God, and then accept Jesus as their personal Savior. They think the way to God is through a formula that their Christian community has adopted as the only path to God.

Systematic Theology for the New Apostolic Reformation

In reality, there is no formula to God. There is only a Person—a Mediator. Whoever believes in Him will be saved.

Compare this to a young girl who believes in her father. She may never know how much her father sacrificed to raise and provide for her, but she still trusts, honors, and loves her father. Of course, the father will accept his daughter's love. Their relationship is not based on the daughter's understanding of all her father did. The relationship exists because their hearts are open to one another.

All who believe in Jesus will be saved. The benefits of what Jesus accomplished on the cross will be given to all who believe in Him. Not only will the benefits of the cross be given to them, but also the benefits of His resurrection, ascension, and enthronement will be given. Even if they do not know what those benefits are, they are given to all who have become children of God.

Point 403: Emma Is a Child of God

Consider Emma, who all her life went to church, worshiped God, and trusted Jesus in her daily life. Emma did not know theology, but her faith in Jesus caused her to emulate His life. She never understood exactly why Jesus died on the cross, but she always wanted to love others like Jesus loved her.

When Emma died, Jesus said to her, "Enter into the eternal joy of My Father." Emma responded to Jesus, "I don't know if I lived good enough to get into heaven." Jesus said to her:

> ... *I was hungry, and you gave Me something to eat; I was thirsty, and you gave Me something to drink; I was a stranger, and you invited Me in; naked, and you clothed Me* ....
> (Matt. 25:35-36)

Then Emma said to Jesus:

> *Lord, when did [I] we see You hungry, and feed You, or thirsty, and give You something to drink? And when did [I] we see You a stranger, and invite You in, or naked, and clothe You?*
> (Matt. 25:37-39)

What Is Necessary for Salvation?

Jesus responded:

> *Truly I say to you, to the extent that you did it to one of these brothers of Mine, even the least of them, you did it to Me.*
> (Matt. 25:40)

Emma was taken into a place of eternal happiness with Father-God, because she too was a child of God.

Volume VI
Soteriology

Section H
Sola Gratia

The Bible is clear: We are saved by God's grace. But what does this mean?

We need to discuss the relationship between God's role in the salvation experience and humanity's role. The reason we must have this discussion is because the related issues were central in the Protestant Reformation. The leaders of the Reformation saw the Roman Catholic Church as teaching a works oriented religion in which people were being taught that they had to earn their salvation. At the forefront of the related debates were Martin Luther and John Calvin. They were adamant that salvation was by grace alone (in Latin, ***sola gratia***). In their emphasis on grace, they declared that salvation requires no work on the part of the individual. It is totally and completely a free gift of God.

Point 404: The Litmus Test

Let's follow the logical progression of Reformed thought to see how *sola gratia* is an essential doctrine for that theological viewpoint.

If God is timeless, omnipotent, and sovereign in the sense that Reformed theology dictates, then every human being is predestined to heaven or hell by God's sovereign choice, regardless of their good or bad behavior. If God is just and immutable in the sense that He cannot change His mind, and therefore, He must punish sin, then the penal substitutionary view of the atonement is a reasonable explanation of the atonement. If the penal substitutionary view of the atonement is true, then the gospel of salvation is the gospel.

Systematic Theology for the New Apostolic Reformation

If the gospel of salvation is *the* gospel, then in order to be saved people must realize that they are sinners, turn their hearts toward God, and accept Jesus as Savior. According to Reformed theology, this is the path to salvation.

<u>The Path to Salvation</u>
1. Realize one's own sinfulness
2. Turn one's heart to God
3. Accept Jesus as Savior

If people are totally depraved, as Reformed theology teaches, then people are unable to contribute any good to the salvation process. Each of the steps listed above must be accomplished by God. He, and He alone, must convict each person of sin. He must work in the heart of the person to turn that person's heart toward Himself. God must cause the person to accept Jesus as Savior. God's grace to accomplish each of these steps must be efficacious (effective in producing the desired results). The individual must be totally passive in each step of this process.

This understanding of God as the sole factor in the salvation process is called **monergism**.[240] *Mon* (for *mono*) refers to "one," and *ergi* refers to "work." So *monergism* refers to God being the only one who works in the salvation of any individual.

The alternative view is called **synergism**. *Syn* refers to "together," so *synergism* refers to God and the individual working together in the salvation process.[241]

Monergism follows logically from the doctrine of God's predestination of all things. It is also the only logical conclusion from a theology that holds to the total depravity of humanity.[242] Hence, monergism has been considered the litmus test as to whether a person is true to the Reformed view of God and humanity.

---

240 Monergism versus synergism marks a historical doctrinal distinction between Calvinism and Arminianism, with Arminianism agreeing with synergism.
241 Critics of Roman Catholicism often accuse Catholics of synergism, even though the Roman Catholic Church affirmed *sola gratia* in the year 529 in the Council of Orange and in the Council of Trent in the mid 16th century.
242 An exception to this is the case in which turning toward God is seen as a neutral or even selfish act as explained in IV:I:248.

Sola Gratia

A LOGICAL PROGRESSION OF THOUGHT
BEGINNING WITH THE REFORMED VIEW OF GOD AND HUMANITY

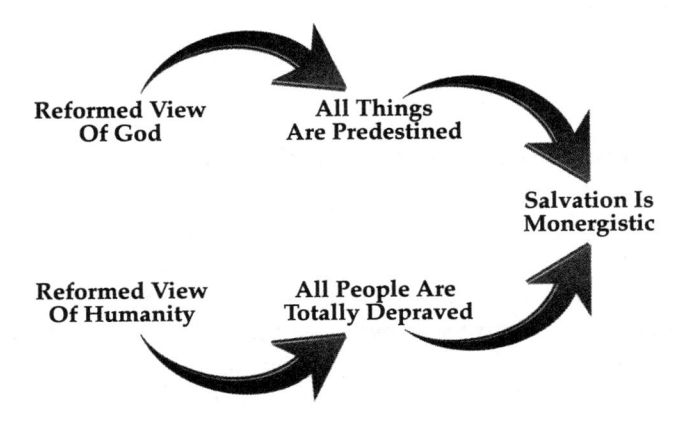

```
Reformed View          All Things
   Of God          Are Predestined

                                        Salvation Is
                                        Monergistic

Reformed View        All People Are
 Of Humanity         Totally Depraved
```

Point 405: Monergism Requires Passivity

Adherents of Reformed theology spend much time discussing how the salvation process requires no *ergi* on the part of individuals. Step one—the realization of one's sinfulness—is not discussed very much, because evangelical Christians generally agree that the Holy Spirit is the One who convicts people of sin.[243] That part of the salvation process is easily assigned to God. However, steps two and three are seen as the critical issues to see if someone's understanding of salvation passes the Reformed litmus test.

Looking carefully at step two, adherents of Reformed theology want to see that no human effort is involved in people "turning their hearts to God." Any preachers who state or imply that human effort is involved in turning one's heart will be labeled as false teachers by those who are true to the Reformed tradition. According to Reformed theology, people are totally depraved, unable to do anything good, and therefore, God must act upon the heart of the individual and turn the heart toward Himself.

Concerning step three, adherents of Reformed theology want to see that no human effort is involved in a person "accepting Jesus as Savior." Any preachers who state or imply human effort is involved in accepting

---

[243] This role of the Holy Spirit is challenged in XI:B:560-563.

Systematic Theology for the New Apostolic Reformation

Jesus will also be labeled as false teachers by those who are true to the Reformed tradition. According to Reformed theology, people are totally depraved, unable to even accept Jesus as Savior. Therefore, people must be totally passive in this step of salvation.

Passivity on the part of humanity is the mark of monergism.

Point 406: Manipulated Definitions of Grace

Before we look critically at the Reformed doctrine of monergism, we need to solidify our definition of *grace*.

In the NT, the word grace is usually translated from the Greek word *charis*. This Greek word can also be translated as "gift." The two words, grace and gift, are associated with each other in many Bible passages,[244] and many more Bible passages talk from the perspective that grace is a gift.

The most commonly used definition of grace is "unmerited favor." In the next few pages I will offer a more biblically accurate understanding of grace, but at this point let me challenge the definition of "unmerited favor," and say that it is a weak, inaccurate, and theologically biased definition of grace.

When we think seriously about the word "favor" we can see that it is weak. *Favor* can mean something as simple as a smile or an act of kindness. In reality, being saved cost God much more than a simple favor. We were saved by God sending His Son into the world, giving His life on the cross, resurrecting Him from the dead, ascending Him above all rule and authority, and then giving us access to His divine nature and pouring His Spirit into us. Once we grasp this, we can see why *favor* does not say enough.

"Favor" is also inaccurate because it loses the sense in which grace is a gift. When God saves a person by grace, He is literally giving the recipient something. In contrast, favor implies that God is acting kindly on behalf of an individual, but no impartation from God to the individual is implied with the word "favor."[245]

Too see this more clearly, recall an earlier distinction made between the penal substitutionary view of the atonement versus the covenantal view. Teachers of the penal substitutionary view see salvation as a legal

---

[244] For example, Rom. 3:24 ; 5:15 ; 12:3 ; 12:6 ; Eph.2:8 ; 3:7 ; 4:7 ; I Pet. 4:10.
[245] Reformed theologians do believe that something is imparted from God to the believer, but that is seen as separate from salvation.

Sola Gratia

transaction. According to them, justification "is not something wrought in man but something declared of man."[246] If, indeed, this is true as Reformed teachers say, then the definition of grace as a favor is acceptable.

However, if the covenantal view of the atonement is true, then salvation is more than a declaration. It is more than a legal transaction. If the covenantal view of the atonement is true, then salvation results from God making a covenant with all who believe in Jesus. That covenant assures Christians that they have their sins forgiven and they are given a new heart and spirit. With that heart and spirit, the righteousness of Jesus is literally imparted into the believer. Therefore, grace is a gift, not just a favor.

Now consider the word "unmerited" as used in "unmerited favor." This word is also inaccurate. Of course, our salvation is unmerited, but that fact is not actually implied in the literal definition of the word *grace*. When Christian teachers add the adjective "unmerited," they are implying that the recipient of the grace is passive. In reality, what the recipient of the grace does is irrelevant to the definition of *grace*. Compare this to one individual giving another a gift and saying, "Here is your unmerited gift." The word "unmerited" is unnecessary. A gift is a gift whether or not it is unmerited. Similarly, the Greek word *charis* can be translated as *grace,* but the adjective *unmerited* is not included in the literal meaning.

Compare this to someone's explanation that *grace* is God's "irresistible favor." We discussed earlier[247] how Reformed theologians understand grace as irresistible, so adherents of Reformed theology would have no problem with this definition. In fact, a person who reads the Bible through the lens of Reformed theology will naturally assume that all grace is irresistible. Yet, *irresistible* is not implied in the word *grace*.

Consider another inaccurate definition of grace. Strong's Bible Concordance (#5463) offers (among other definitions) the following definition for grace: "the divine influence upon the heart, and its reflection in the life." This definition reveals the Reformed bias of those who developed this definition. Reformed theology necessitates that God—and not man—turns the heart of each person toward Himself. Therefore, defining *grace* as "the divine influence upon the heart..." locks in their doctrine of monergism, but it does not provide the true definition of *grace*.

---

246 Henry Theissen, *Lectures in Systematic Theology* (Grand Rapids: Errdmans, 1979), p 271.
247 II:A:94.

Systematic Theology for the New Apostolic Reformation

This reveals a problem common in theology. Definitions of words are sometimes developed from a certain theological perspective. We see this with the definition "unmerited favor." This definition reinforces a specific theological viewpoint. Adding the word *unmerited* leads one to conclude that the recipient is passive. In other words, adding the word, *unmerited*, props up the doctrine of monoergism.

Now please do not misunderstand what I am saying. We know that no one can earn salvation. Nor does anyone deserve it. It is unmerited. However, the adjective "unmerited" simply is not stated or implied with the Greek word *charis*. So what is grace?

Point 407: Grace Is Active

As mentioned, the word grace has been translated from the Greek word *charis*. This word is closely associated with a gift, but if we translate *charis* as a gift, we are not saying enough. *Charis* is a gift but it is not like a child's birthday present, e.g., a bicycle or toy. The word *charis* (grace) refers to a gift that actively benefits the recipient.

To see this, consider Hebrews 13:9, which says:

> . . . *it is good for the heart to be <u>strengthened by grace</u>.*

Notice the active nature of grace, in the sense that grace strengthens the recipient. In Acts 20:32, we read:

> *And now I commend you to God and to the word of His grace, which is able to <u>build you up</u> . . . .*

Here grace is associated with building people up.

Luke agrees:

> *And God's <u>grace was so powerfully at work</u> in them all that there were no needy persons among them.*
> (Act 4:33-34 NIV)

God's grace "works." It produces something. In this passage we see how grace can cause the recipients to act as God wants them to act.

Sola Gratia

This active nature of grace is evident not only with God's grace but also in the grace given by one person to another. Paul told the Christians:

> *Let no unwholesome word proceed from your mouth, but only such a word as is <u>good for edification</u> according to the need of the moment, so that it will <u>give grace</u> to those who hear.*
>
> (Eph. 4:29)

Paul referred to words that "give grace," and by this, he was talking about words that edify, encourage, and strengthen the hearer. Such words of grace are a gift in the sense that the giver is orienting his heart toward the recipient and imparting strength.

This reveals the fundamental nature of grace. It is a gift that gives. Grace is a gift through which the recipient receives some positive impartation. That impartation motivates, strengthens, and even transforms the recipient.

Allow me to offer a few metaphors. Grace is an energy drink activating the recipient. God's grace is the most healthy food a person can ever eat—food that is so healthy that when a person consumes it, his body begins to heal immediately. Grace is a group of stem cells flowing through a person's blood stream and soon to be planted wherever Christ needs to grow in that person. Grace is the hand of God directing a person's steps and molding that person's character. Grace is a stick of dynamite, able to move mountains.

Paul gives us a confirming description of grace:

> *And God is able to make all grace abound to you, so that always having all sufficiency in everything, you may have an abundance for every good deed;*
>
> (2 Cor. 9:8)

Notice that God's grace results in having all sufficiency, or in other words, everything a person needs in order to accomplish what God wants that person to do.

Grace is a gift, and it has an effect.

Paul talked in similar terminology when he prayed for the thorn in his flesh to be removed. God did not remove the thorn, but said to Paul:

Systematic Theology for the New Apostolic Reformation

My grace is sufficient for you, for power is perfected in weakness.
(2 Cor. 12:9)

God's grace provided Paul with everything he needed to live victoriously even though his thorn was not removed. In fact, God's grace resulted in the perfecting of power in Paul's life.

The well-known author, James Ryle, offers a well-thought-out definition of grace:

> Grace is the empowering presence of God enabling you to be who God created you to be, and to do what God has called you to do—right where you are.[248]

This definition is not perfect,[249] but it allows us to see grace as a gift (the empowering presence of God), and we can see the effects of grace (enabling the recipient).

Point 408: God's Grace Is Resistible or Irresistible

James Ryle's definition is not acceptable to Christians who are faithful to Reformed theology, because Ryle's definition refers to grace "enabling" people which implies that God is merely giving people enough strength, rather than actually compelling people to be what God created them to be. So Christians consistent with Reformed theology will reject Ryle's definition. They want a definition that reveals God's grace as efficacious. Adherents of Reformed theology see God doing *all* of the work (monergism) and people being totally passive.

In reality, God can give His grace with any amount of authority and force that He chooses. At times, He may give efficacious grace that compels a person to do what He desires. At other times, God may give grace that enables individuals without compelling them. He can give grace that is resistible or grace that is irresistible.

An example of His irresistible grace is how God sovereignly chose Jeremiah to be a prophet before Jeremiah was even born (Jer. 1:5). An example of God giving resistible grace is when the writer of Hebrews told

---

[248] http://www.identitynetwork.net/apps/articles/default.asp?articleid=71830
[249] Most importantly, it does not allow for grace that can be given by one person to another person as in Eph. 4:29.

Sola Gratia

his readers not to fall short of the grace of God (Heb. 12:15). For another example of resistible grace, we can read Paul's exhortation to the Corinthian Christians "*not to receive the grace of God in vain*" (2 Cor. 6:1). Then again Paul wrote to Timothy saying, "*You therefore, my son, be strong in the grace that is in Christ Jesus*" (2 Tim. 2:1).

Notice in these last three verses, the word grace is used right along exhortations for people to use their own energy in accomplishing God's will. Indeed, when Father-God gives grace that empowers without forcing people, the recipients are responsible to exert their own energy. They are required to take action and mature.

This is how Paul understood grace working in his own life:

> *But by the grace of God I am what I am, and His grace toward me did not prove vain; but I labored even more than all of them, yet not I, but the grace of God with me.*
> (1 Cor. 15:10)

Paul labored. If he had not labored, the grace that God gave him would have proven vain.

What I am showing here is that God can give grace that compels or grace that enables without compelling a person. In other words, some acts of God's grace are monergistic and others are synergistic.

So let's compare the two understandings of grace that we have developed thus far:

Reformed Theology	Father-Son Theology
unmerited favor	impartation that builds, helps, motivates, strengthens, transforms, etc.
irresistible	resistible or irresistible
efficacious	compels or enables without compelling

Point 409: Grace Is an Impartation that Empowers

To further develop our understanding of grace, i.e., the aspect of God's *impartation*, rather than just His favor, it is worth another look. Consider this in reference to salvation.

Systematic Theology for the New Apostolic Reformation

When evangelical Christians are taught the unmerited favor definition of grace along with the penal substitutionary view of the atonement, they tend to think of God's grace as His "free pass" so Christians do not have to experience God's wrath. This develops as a natural flow of thought, since the wrath of God is the focus of salvation according to the penal substitutionary view. The explanation of salvation as a "free pass," corresponds with grace being an act of God's kindness or unmerited favor. It also corresponds with seeing salvation as a legal transaction with God as a Judge who decreed that Jesus paid the penalty for the sins of Christians.

But salvation is more than a legal transaction. The grace that is given to believers for salvation entails an impartation from God to the individual. This is evident when we join the impartation definition of grace with the covenantal view of the atonement. As explained earlier, a covenant was established and enacted at the death of Jesus. The life of Jesus is joined to believers. Believers get what Jesus has. When individuals are born again, the breath of God is released into their hearts (Gal. 4:6). That breath brings believers to life (Rom. 8:10). Once they are alive, the course of their lives are changed. From the day God's breath is released into their hearts, they begin being transformed. That process will continue, from glory to glory, until they are completely conformed to the image of Christ (2 Cor. 3:18).

We can also explain the salvation experience by referring to Peter's words:

> ... *for you have been born again not of seed which is perishable but imperishable, that is, through the living and enduring word of God.*
> (1 Peter 1:23)

The seed that is planted within the hearts of believers is alive—imperishable. It will produce after its own kind. Christ will be formed in the life of the recipients. Once they have been impregnated with God's seed, they are predestined to be conformed to the image of His Son (Rom. 8:29).

Jesus spoke several times about the seeds that are planted in the hearts of people. Those seeds will grow in the hearts of those who are like good soil. The seeds will grow to maturity, yielding a harvest.

The point here is that salvation is not just an act of kindness on God's part. It is more than unmerited favor. God's grace entails an impartation from Him. Something actually moves from God and into the heart of the believer. That which is imparted transforms the life of the believer.

Sola Gratia

For this reason, I will modify James Ryle's definition a little and say that grace is ***an impartation that empowers the recipient.*** Notice that this definition is accurate even when talking about the grace that one person gives to another. As Paul wrote, people should speak words that give grace in the sense of edifying, encouraging, and strengthening the hearer (Eph. 4:29). When talking about God's grace we can say it is His impartation that empowers the recipients to be all God created them to be.

Point 410: The Foundation of Our Understanding of Grace

This is a good place to tie our present discussion back into the overall theme of this book. The Reformed understanding that all acts of God's grace are monergistic reaches all the way back to the assumptions of Plato and Aristotle. If God is timeless, immutable, sovereign, and omnipotent in the way Augustine taught, then God is in exhaustive control of all things. If God is in control, then grace is unmerited, irresistible, and efficacious. If that is what grace truly is, then salvation is monergistic

THE REFORMED PROGRESSION OF THOUGHT

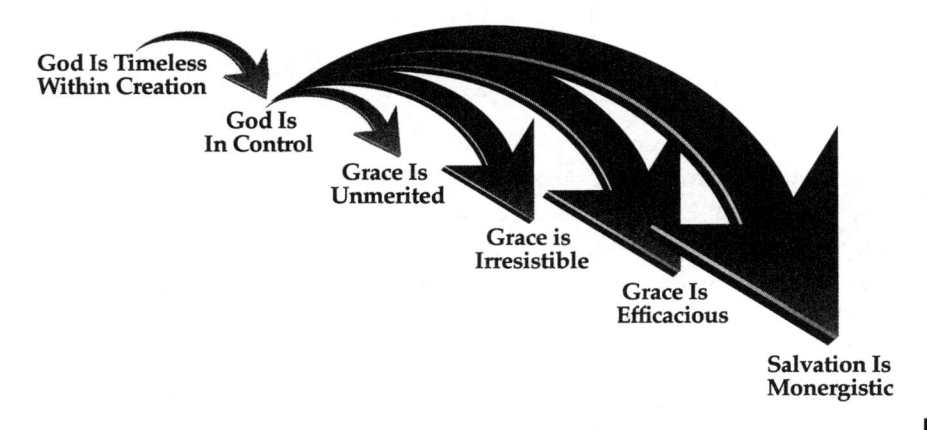

God Is Timeless Within Creation → **God Is In Control** → **Grace Is Unmerited** → **Grace is Irresistible** → **Grace Is Efficacious** → **Salvation Is Monergistic**

Notice that the Reformed belief that God's grace is always monergistic comes from a theological and philosophical progression of thought. In contrast, the understanding that I am offering to you has been derived from reading specific examples in Scripture, such as the verses mentioned above.

Systematic Theology for the New Apostolic Reformation

The good news is that the description of grace derived from reading the Bible corresponds with seeing God as a Father. As a good Father, God at times intervenes in the lives of people forcefully bringing forth His desired end. At other times, Father-God gives grace that encourages, strengthens, and/or empowers people without compelling them. A major reason God acts in a monergistic fashion at times is because He is a loving Father who wants to spare His people from things that are too big for them to handle. A major reason God acts in a synergistic fashion at other times is because He is a loving Father who wants His children to cooperate with Him and mature as His sons.

Point 411: Monergistic or Synergistic Salvation

Now let's consider a couple of examples in Scripture in which God is shown exercising great force in the salvation of individuals.

Paul was violently antagonistic toward Christians until he was on the road to Damascus and a light from heaven struck him (Acts 9:1-9). Concerning Paul, the Lord said to Ananias:

> . . . *he is a chosen instrument of Mine, to bear My name before the Gentiles and kings and sons of Israel . . .*
> (Acts 9:15)

God sovereignly chose Paul to be a light to the Gentiles (Acts 13:47).

Another example of God exerting force in the life of an individual is John the Baptist. Luke tells us that John was *"filled with the Holy Spirit while yet in his mother's womb"* (Luke 1:15). This raises the question concerning how much of a will does an unborn baby have? And how could John have heard the gospel before being born? Some teachers will argue that John still was not saved, but the fact remains that John the Baptist was sovereignly chosen by God before he was even conceived (Luke 1:13-17). These examples of John the Baptist and Paul reveal God sovereignly choosing individuals to fulfill His purposes.

In Romans 9, Paul explained that if God sovereignly decides to do something, no one can resist His will. Paul compared God to a potter who has full authority over a lump of clay. The potter has the right to make one lump of clay into a *"vessel for honorable use and another for common use"*

Sola Gratia

(Rom. 9:21). God is even able to make *"some vessels of wrath prepared for destruction"* (Rom. 9:22). Anyone who takes the Bible seriously will have to agree that God can work monergistically whenever He wants.

However, seeing that God *can* work monergistically does not mean that He always does. God's sovereignty means He can work anyway He wants whenever He wants. He can work monergistically or synergistically.

In most people's lives, we see God working *with* individuals to bring them to salvation. *"The kindness of God leads"* (not forces) them to repentance (Rom. 2:4). People need to hear the gospel being preached to them and then respond (discussed fully in the section that follows).

Point 412: Separating Grace from Works

We know that salvation is given by grace rather than works. The passage most often used to teach this truth is Ephesians 2:8-9:

> *For by grace you have been saved through faith; and that not of yourselves, it is the gift of God; not as a result of works, so that no one may boast.*

If we take the Bible seriously, we will agree with Paul that salvation is a free gift of God.

However, when Paul was saying that salvation is given independently of any human works, we must understand his statement in the historical context in which he made it. Paul was dealing with specific issues of his day. He was teaching people who were submerged in Jewish culture. Paul was primarily teaching about how no one can be saved by keeping the Jewish religious laws and ordinances. He was arguing about the issues that were at the forefront in his day.

We can reasonably extend Paul's teaching to say that no works any person does are great enough to earn their salvation. However, it is questionable to take Paul's teaching to the extreme that Reformed teachers do. It is one thing to say that people are saved through no works of their own; it is another to examine every person to see if there is or isn't a minuscule amount of work (*ergi*) used in their own salvation.

Let's consider this . . . .

Systematic Theology for the New Apostolic Reformation

Point 413: The Reformed Understanding of Works

Followers of Reformed theology are determined to separate grace from works. The farther they can separate grace and works, the better they can make their point that salvation is monergistic. Reformed teachers are so adamant about separating grace from works that they often teach that anyone who tries to add any work to accomplish their own salvation is not truly trusting God. Therefore, anyone who tries to work for their own salvation in any way will not be saved.

In order to explain this viewpoint let me offer an analogy. A major sports event was being featured in a city and everyone within that city was mailed a free ticket. There was great excitement among the citizens before the big day. Much of the excitement was about how the event was free. Some people could not believe that such a grand event would actually be free. People talked about how no one gets anything for free. Some people decided that it must be a spoof, so on the day of the big event, they did not even bother going. They did not want to be disappointed. When the day of the big event arrived, everyone who showed up with their ticket was allowed free entrance and had a wonderful experience.

So far this illustration corresponds well with how salvation is a free gift of God.

Now consider this same illustration, but this time security guards are positioned at the entrance of the arena. The guards are told that everyone must have their free ticket, but they should be denied entrance if they seem too eager to get inside. So when the masses of people lined up outside the gates, the security guards carefully combed through the crowds. Anyone who seemed too eager was turned away. Anyone who tried to push his way to the front was forced to leave. Anyone who tried to give the attendant any money along with the free ticket was told that they would not be allowed to attend the event. The only people who were allowed entrance were those who seemed totally passive while they waited outside of the gate.

This example illustrates the Reformed understanding of salvation being given only to those who are passive. Adherents of that view see that God and God alone is the One who saves. According to Reformed theology, any people who try to add any energy toward their own salvation are not truly trusting in Jesus as their Savior and, therefore, will not be saved.

Sola Gratia

Point 414: Is God's Grace Limited or Abundant?

The illustration of people being turned away from a free sports event reveals the determination teachers of Reformed theology have to defend monergism. However, it fails to expose the Reformed understanding that God is very selective concerning who He invites to the event. According to Classical/Reformed theology, God will only invite a select group of people to heaven. To those select people, God will give His grace for salvation. According to Classical/Reformed theology, God's grace is irresistible and efficacious and, therefore, 100 percent effective. There is a one to one ratio. Every person who is given God's unmerited favor for salvation will be saved.

In contrast, Father-Son theology understands that God has the authority to give grace with any amount of authority He desires, making His grace resistible sometimes and irresistible at other times. Father-Son theology also recognizes that God's grace is abundant and all pervasive. We need to add this important characteristic to our understanding of God's grace.

Reformed Theology	Father-Son Theology
unmerited favor	impartation that builds, helps, motivates, strengthens, transforms, etc.
irresistible	resistible or irresistible
efficacious	compels or enables without compelling
limited	**abundant and all pervasive**

Point 415: God's Grace Is Abundant and All Pervasive

There are many ways in which God gives His abundant grace. First, it is evident in creation, as the Psalms declare beautifully:

The heavens are telling of the glory of God;
And their expanse is declaring the work of His hands.
(Ps. 19:1).

. . . the earth is full of his unfailing love.
(Ps. 33:5)

Systematic Theology for the New Apostolic Reformation

The Lord is good to all,
And His mercies are over all His works.

(Ps. 145:9)

Creation is actively revealing the Creator, and the grace of creation is being administered abundantly 24 hours of every day to all of humanity. God also gives His grace to each and every individual:

. . . for He causes His sun to rise on the evil and the good, and sends rain on the righteous and the unrighteous.

(Matt. 5:45)

. . . for He Himself is kind to ungrateful and evil men.

(Luke 6:35)

. . . He Himself gives to all people life and breath and all things.

(Acts 17:25)

Every blessing that anyone experiences is a result of God's grace because He is the ultimate source of all good (Jas. 1:17).

Followers of Reformed theology will agree that God's grace is abundantly given to all of humanity, however, their theology dictates that God only gives grace for salvation to a select group of people. Therefore, they divide God's grace into different categories. Augustine called the grace given to all of humanity "common grace." Reformed teachers usually call grace given to the elect for salvation "saving grace."

Adherents of Reformed theology must make this distinction between common grace and saving grace for their theology to make sense. They must see common grace given to all because the Bible clearly reveals that God gives grace to all. However, their definition of grace demands that grace is efficacious, so they must say that common grace was never meant by God to aid in salvation. Furthermore, according to Reformed theology, common grace can have absolutely no effect in causing people to turn toward God. Hence, they have to identify a different type of grace, i.e., saving grace, that is efficacious for salvation.

In reality, the Bible makes no distinction between common grace and saving grace. Furthermore, the Reformed distinction between common grace and saving grace does not agree with Scripture.

Sola Gratia

To see this consider how God has made Himself known through creation. Paul explained:

> *For since the creation of the world His invisible attributes, His eternal power and divine nature, have been clearly seen, being understood through what has been made . . . .*
> (Rom. 1:20)

If the grace that is revealed through creation is common, and therefore, ineffectual in drawing people to God as adherents of Reformed theology must insist, then the next few words that Paul wrote would make no sense:

> *. . . so that they are without excuse.*
> (Rom. 1:20)

Paul was making the argument that because God has made Himself known through creation to all people, no one has an excuse to disbelieve in Him or to continue living in sin. In other words, Paul's understanding of the grace revealed through creation is enough for any and every person to know God and respond to Him.

This same truth is revealed when we talk about God's love and kindness. Paul testified of the *"riches of His kindness and tolerance and patience,"* and then Paul went on to say that *"the kindness of God leads you to repentance"* (Rom. 2:4). Here Paul does not have to specify what type of grace leads people to repentance. He simply declares that God's kindness directs people toward God, and we know that God is kind to everyone (Luke 6:35).

The truth is that neither Paul nor any other Bible writer found it helpful to distinguish between common grace and saving grace.

Consider Paul's explanation of God's self-revelation in Acts 14:16-17:

> *In the generations gone by He permitted all the nations to go their own ways; and yet He did not leave Himself without witness, in that He did good and gave you rains from heaven and fruitful seasons, satisfying your hearts with food and gladness.*
> (Acts 14:16-17)

Here Paul wrote of generations gone by, i.e., those who lived before Jesus came and before the Bible was written. God gave witness of Himself to

Systematic Theology for the New Apostolic Reformation

people by:

1. doing good for them
2. giving them rains and fruitful seasons
3. satisfying people's hearts with food and gladness

According to Paul these three things are blessings from God and witnesses of His existence. In other words, before the Bible was written and before Jesus came into the world, God was already giving witness of Himself to every human being. This too was by His grace.

The grace of God is abundant. His blessings are new every morning (Lam. 3:23). His love is pouring out upon the world.

Of course, many people do not recognize the grace that is all around them. Many recognize, but reject, it. In spite of their rejection, God continues to pour out His grace and love upon the world. That grace and love is revealing the nature of God and directing all people toward the Lover.

Point 416: God's Abundant Grace through Jesus

All grace reveals God's nature. All grace tugs on the hearts of humanity to acknowledge and worship the Giver of that grace. Yet, the greatest revelation of God's grace comes into the world through Jesus.

The apostle John wrote:

> *There was the true Light which, coming into the world, enlightens every man.*
> (John 1:9)

Even though the Light is evident to every human being, John explained how many people, including most of the Jews (John 1:11), did not receive the Light. The point is that God gives Light to each and every person, yet, they choose to reject or receive that Light.

God's grace includes everything necessary for the salvation of all people:

> *For the grace of God has appeared, bringing salvation to all men.*
> (Titus 2:11)

John explained this, writing that Jesus:

Sola Gratia

> *. . . is the propitiation for our sins; and not for ours only, but also for those of the whole world.*
>
> (1 John 2:2)

This means that God has already acted in grace to the extent that He has done everything necessary for the salvation of all of humanity—each and every person.

Paul explained that

> *He* [God] *has given proof of this to everyone by raising him* [Jesus] *from the dead.*
>
> (Act 17:31)

In the context, Paul was declaring how the proof of Jesus' resurrection means *"all people everywhere should repent"* (v. 30). Notice how Paul understood the resurrection to be the proof necessary for all of humanity to repent—not just a few people who are given saving grace.

In addition to the death and resurrection of His Son, God is now pouring out the Holy Spirit upon all flesh. On Pentecost day, Peter explained that the words of the prophet Joel were being fulfilled starting on that very day. God spoke through Joel saying:

> *I will pour forth of My Spirit on all mankind.*
>
> (Acts 2:17)

"All" means "all." The Holy Spirit is at work convicting all people and pointing them to Jesus (John 16:8-10).[250]

God's grace is sufficient for every human being.

Notice how different this understanding of God's grace is compared with that of Reformed theology. Adherents of that view envision God reaching down from heaven and giving a select group of people His saving grace. In contrast, the view I am presenting sees God flooding the world with His goodness. Grace is all around us. Proof of His existence is everywhere. God desires all people to be saved (1 Tim. 2:4), and salvation is a free gift available to all.

The only thing necessary on humanity's part is to believe, which we will examine in the section that follows.

---

250 This work of the Holy Spirit is discussed in IX:B:560-563.

Volume VI
Soteriology

Section I
Sola Fide

We receive God's grace through faith. Faith, and faith alone (in Latin, *sola fide*), is the avenue through which we obtain His grace.

Point 417: What Is Faith?

Paul explained *"with the heart a person believes"* (Rom. 10:10). So we know that belief is a function of the heart. Hebrews 11:1 tells us that *"faith is the assurance of things hoped for, the conviction of things not seen."* So one way we can explain faith is by saying it is the assurance or conviction in the heart of a person when that person believes.

Point 418: Faith Is Created by Proof

What creates faith in the heart of a person? Or in other words, what creates conviction in the heart?

Many Christians have been taught that faith entails a blind leap into the unknown truths of God. Later, we will see that that understanding is seriously flawed and developed as a result of building on the cosmology of the ancient Greek philosophers.

Now we can develop a biblical understanding, by seeing faith as *a response in heart following convincing evidence.*

For example, after Jesus resurrected, He appeared to His apostles and proved to them that He was alive. The apostles were instantly made

Systematic Theology for the New Apostolic Reformation

believers. So in that case, *seeing* Jesus alive was the convincing evidence that resulted in faith.

When Jesus first appeared to His apostles after His resurrection, Thomas was not with them. Later Jesus appeared to Thomas and said to him:

> *Reach here with your finger, and see My hands; and reach here your hand and put it into My side; and do not be unbelieving, but believing.*
>
> (John 20:27)

Jesus gave Thomas proof that He had risen from the dead. Thomas saw the proof and responded, saying, *"My Lord and my God!"* (John 20:28).

Notice that in these examples, people were provided convincing evidence, i.e., proof, that Jesus had risen from the dead. Perhaps they could have hardened their hearts and refused to believe, but that refusal would have taken much energy (*ergi*) on their part. In these examples of Jesus' apostles, it did not require energy to believe, because in the face of proof, belief is the natural outcome.

Faith Is the Change in Heart Resulting from Evidence and Proof

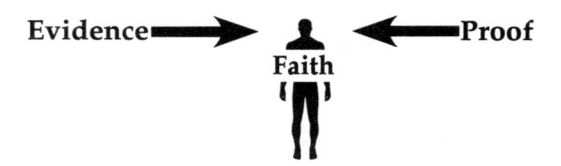

Evidence ⟶ Faith ⟵ Proof

Jesus also talked about many people believing in Him as a result of seeing the miracles He performed. In those cases, the sight of miracles resulted in faith. Again we see convincing evidence, i.e., proof, resulted in faith.

Point 419: Faith Comes by Revelation

Faith can also result from a God-given revelation. For example, when Jesus asked His disciples, "Who do people say that I am?" Peter declared, "You are the Christ, the Son of the living God." Jesus answered saying:

Sola Fide

> *Blessed are you, Simon Barjona, because flesh and blood did not reveal this to you, but My Father who is in heaven.*
> (Matt. 16:15-17)

In this case, God revealed to Peter who Jesus was. Peter did not have to exercise energy to have faith. Peter's faith was simply the unavoidable, automatic response to the revelation.

Think of how Jesus revealed Himself to Paul in a blinding light (Acts 9:3-6). Paul heard Jesus' voice. In the face of that proof, Paul's heart changed. He believed.

From these examples, we can see that a revelation from God can result in faith. In such cases, it requires no human energy to believe. In the face of such evidence, it would require human energy to resist believing.

Point 420: Faith Comes by Hearing and Reading

Faith also comes as a result of *hearing about Jesus*.

John wrote about a Samaritan woman who told many people about how Jesus had spoken to her of things that only a prophet could know. Then the people came to hear from Jesus for themselves:

> *Many more <u>believed because of His word</u>; and they were saying to the woman, "It is no longer <u>because of what you said that we believe</u>, for we have heard for ourselves and know that this One is indeed the Savior of the world."*
> (John 4:41-42)

Some people believed because of what the woman had said, and others believed in Jesus after hearing His own words for themselves.

Paul explained:

> *So faith comes from hearing, and hearing by the word of Christ.*[251]
> (Rom. 10:17)

Again, faith is not the result of energy within a person being exercised. Faith is the natural response to hearing a trustworthy testimony.

---

[251] What is the "word of Christ"? Reading or hearing the Bible can result in faith, but faith can also arise from the "word of Christ" in the sense of testimonies concerning Jesus Christ. This can be seen in the examples given here.

Systematic Theology for the New Apostolic Reformation

Words that create faith do not have to be spoken. John explained how he wrote down many of the miracles of Jesus, *"so that you may believe that Jesus is the Christ, the Son of God"* (John 20:31). Indeed, many people come to believe in Jesus as a result of reading what other people have written about Him.

Point 421: People Hear, Seeds Grow

Some of Jesus' parables also reveal how faith results from hearing. Jesus explained how the sower casts his seed into the soil. The seeds in this parable refer to the Word of God. The soil is the heart of a person. If the soil is hard or rocky, the seeds will not produce a crop, but Jesus said:

> *And the one on whom seed was sown on the good soil, this is the man who hears the word and understands it; who indeed bears fruit and brings forth, some a hundredfold, some sixty, and some thirty."*
> (Matt. 13:23)

Notice that the power for growth is in the seed. That seed produces. The only role of humanity is to hear. Hearing takes no energy. A child can hear. It is the hard-hearted person who must exert energy to resist after hearing convincing evidence.

Point 422: Faith as Acceptance of Religious Ideas

Faith, as it is being explained here, is radically different than the predominant understanding of faith in the Western modern world. To see this, let's trace the development of thought concerning faith.

As we have stated many times, Plato separated the spiritual world from the natural world. Plato also saw human thought as the avenue through which people access the spiritual world. Building on that foundation, Augustine came to think of faith as the result of an individual embracing certain truths of the spiritual world. As a Christian, Augustine identified those truths as the truths pertaining to God and Jesus Christ.

Sola Fide

FOUNDATION OF AUGUSTINE'S WORLDVIEW

Spiritual World

Realm of Thoughts & Ideas

Faith

Natural World

Corresponding to this way of thinking, Church fathers attempted to offer to people the truths that were necessary for people to embrace in order to be Christians. Hence, the development of the early creeds. Of course, the creeds served other functions, such as uniting Christendom around a set of doctrines, but the creeds also became accepted as the truths that people need to believe in order to be Christian.

This way of thinking dominated Western Christianity during the Middle Ages. As a consequence, Church leaders emphasized the importance of defending the Church's creeds and teachings. Much effort was directed toward ridding the Church of heretics. Leaders thought

Systematic Theology for the New Apostolic Reformation

coercion was appropriate at times to get people to embrace the Church's doctrines. Everyone who accepted the creeds of the Church was considered Christian—regardless of their lifestyle. Faith is what was required, and it was faith in the Church's teachings.

Modern critics of Christianity and of religion in general sometimes talk as if faith is the result of ignorant people blindly accepting what religious leaders tell them. There is some validity to that criticism if we are talking about people in the Middle Ages. However, people in the Western world gradually shifted their understanding of faith beginning during the scientific revolution of the 16th century.

Point 423: Faith According to the Modern Western Worldview

In the Late Middle Ages (c. 1300-1500), leaders across Europe began to focus more on the natural world. This was, in part, because the writings of Aristotle became available in Latin, the most common language of the educated in Europe. Those writings emphasized the natural world and how it can be known through the five human senses and our experiences with the natural world. Thomas Aquinas taught that the human heart is fallen because of sin, but the human mind is able to arrive at truth. This created new confidence in people to study and understand the physical world around them. Leaders came to believe that the natural world can be understood through their five senses, their experiences within the natural world, and their reasoning ability.

Among the many consequences of this new way of thinking was the gradual shift in the Western understanding of faith. In particular, faith became associated with the spiritual world, while sensory perception, experience, and reason became associated with the natural world.

Some philosophers and theologians tried to keep faith and reason together, saying *philosophy* is "faith seeking reason." They tried to explain faith and reason as supporting each other. However, in the Western mind faith became increasingly assigned to the spiritual world while reason was assigned to the natural world.

This separation became definitive during the scientific revolution of the 16th century. Leaders concluded that only the information that is obtained through sensory perception, experience, and reason can be truly known. Everything else—including faith—was placed in a category of the unknown.

Sola Fide

THE WESTERN WORLDVIEW SEPARATES FAITH FROM REASON

Spiritual World
Realm of the Unknown = Realm of Faith

Knowledge

Reasoning
Experience
Senses

Faith

Natural World

Today when people make this separation between faith and knowledge in their minds, they can no longer see faith as the natural outcome of proof. Instead, they think of faith as disconnected from proof. As a result, faith is seen as a mystical quality that some people have and others don't. Or people think of faith as a supernatural endowment (or a dose of gullibility) in the mind of the believer.[252] This understanding of faith has profoundly influenced most people who have been trained in secular Western universities.

---

252 For a fuller explanation of the development of this Western misunderstanding of faith, see my book entitled, *Christianity Unshackled*.

Systematic Theology for the New Apostolic Reformation

Point 424: Christianity Is Founded on Fact and Proof

The Western philosophical understanding of faith as a mystical endowment destroys the foundation upon which Christianity is built.

Christianity is built on the *fact* that God became man, walked the earth, and rose from the dead. Paul had no confusion in his mind concerning this:

> ... God is now declaring to men that all people everywhere should repent, because He has fixed a day in which He will judge the world ... having <u>furnished proof</u> to all men by raising Him from the dead.
> (Acts 17:30-31)

Notice Paul's understanding that God furnished "proof" of the coming judgment. Paul declared that the resurrection of Jesus from the grave was sufficient proof for all of humanity to know that the world will be judged.

Paul also explained that creation is proof of God's existence (Rom. 1:19-20).

Christianity is built on facts and proof of those facts.

Those who embrace the Western philosophical understanding of faith have to reject this. Beginning with Plato's dualism, they take followers down their twisted philosophical progression of thought and leave them concluding that faith has no basis in fact. They leave their followers thinking of faith as a mystical leap for which there is no rational basis.

Once any group of people have convinced themselves that faith in God and/or Jesus has no rational basis, they can further build their system of thought on that foundation. They can then create their own exclusive group in which they can reassure each other that no one knows if God exists or if Jesus was truly from God. They can also can exclude from their own group anyone who claims to possess knowledge about God or Jesus. Anyone who has ideas contrary to the ideas of the group can be dismissed as ignorant and unworthy of consideration.

Telling each other that God has refused to prove His existence, they convince themselves and their followers that no one can be justifiably held accountable for their actions. By concluding that faith is irrational, they can justify in their own minds all sinful behavior and live according to the lusts of their flesh. Seated at the foundation of a perverted lifestyle is often a perverted definition of faith.

Sola Fide

Point 425: Faith as a Blind Leap

Unfortunately, many Christians in the Western world have embraced the Western philosophical separation of faith from reason. As a consequence, they hold to the Western philosophical understanding of faith rather than the biblical understanding.

The Western philosophical understanding can be seen clearly in the writings of many philosophers and theologians. For example, Soren Kierkegaard (1813–1855) argued that faith is always irrational. He gave the example of how God asked Abraham to kill his own son, and from this he argued that God requires us to hold beliefs that are ridiculous. Kierkegaard is known for explaining faith as a blind leap, that is a leap into something for which a person has no rational or experiential justification.

Karl Barth is also known for totally separating faith from reason. He held to **fideism** meaning he taught that there is no evidence or reason that can lead to faith. Or, in other words, there are no proofs that can provide a rational foundation for faith. But again, we note that Barth built his system of thought on the cosmology of the ancient Greek philosophers.[253]

Modern Christians who hold to the Western philosophical understanding of faith often quote the KJV of Hebrews 11:1, to support their view:

> *Now faith is the substance of things hoped for, the evidence of things not seen.*

By focusing on the last phrase, *"things not seen,"* they can support their view of faith, saying that faith is to accept ideas that are not seen in the sense of not being rational or resulting from experiential proof.

This Western philosophical understanding of faith leads one to believe that faith is a mystical endowment with no basis in experience, reason, or logic. Believing is understood as a blind step into the unknown.

Point 426: The Biblical Understanding of Faith

The Bible offers us a very different understanding of faith. Recall how the ancient Hebraic-biblical worldview sees the spiritual and natural realms as totally interdependent within the one world that God created. With no separation between the spiritual and natural realms, the Hebrews

---

[253] This was explained in I:G:65.

Systematic Theology for the New Apostolic Reformation

did not separate faith from reason. They saw faith as *a response in heart following the natural outworking (the reasonable outworking) of proof, revelation, seeing, hearing, or reading.*

The Biblical Understanding:
Faith Is the Change in Heart Resulting from Evidence and Reason

[Diagram: Evidence → Reason ← Proof, with Faith below, figure standing on Earth against a starry background]

With this biblical understanding of faith, look again at the KJV of Hebrews 11:1:

> Now faith is the substance of things hoped for, the evidence of things not seen.

Note that faith is of the things not seen, but before saying that, the author clearly stated that faith is *"the evidence"* and *"the substance."* Faith is not a blind leap. Nor is faith some mystical gift that irrational people possess. It is evidence. When the evidence is accepted, faith is created in the heart.

Reconsider Soren Kierkegaard, who taught that Abraham took a blind leap when he was about to kill his own son. In reality, Kierkegaard missed the primary lesson in Abraham offering his son to God. Abraham was not being irrational or blindly obedient. The most obvious message of the Abrahamic story is that Abraham knew God. Abraham had walked with God for many years, and he knew that he could trust God. The writer of

Sola Fide

Hebrews explained that before Abraham killed his son, he knew *"that God is able to raise people even from the dead* (Heb. 11:19). When Abraham traveled to Mount Moriah to sacrifice his son, Abraham boldly told his servants that he and his son would go and worship together and then return together (Gen. 22:5). Before preparing his son for the sacrifice, Abraham confidently stated, *"God will provide for Himself the lamb for the burnt offering . . ."* (Gen. 22:8). Abraham knew that God would intervene. Therefore, Abraham was not taking a blind leap of faith. He was acting based on his knowledge of God. The results were not yet seen ahead of time, but *Abraham had years of convincing evidence* that led him to believe God.

Point 427: Our Role in Producing Faith in Others

Our understanding of faith determines what we see as our role in producing faith in other people.

Those who think of faith as an irrational blind leap do not think they can play any role in helping others have faith. This fits well with the Reformed view of God that sees God as in total control. He alone decides who will be saved and who will go to hell. With that understanding of God, no human being can influence any other human being in the salvation process. Hence, Reformed thinkers have no problem seeing faith as something in which people play no role in developing.

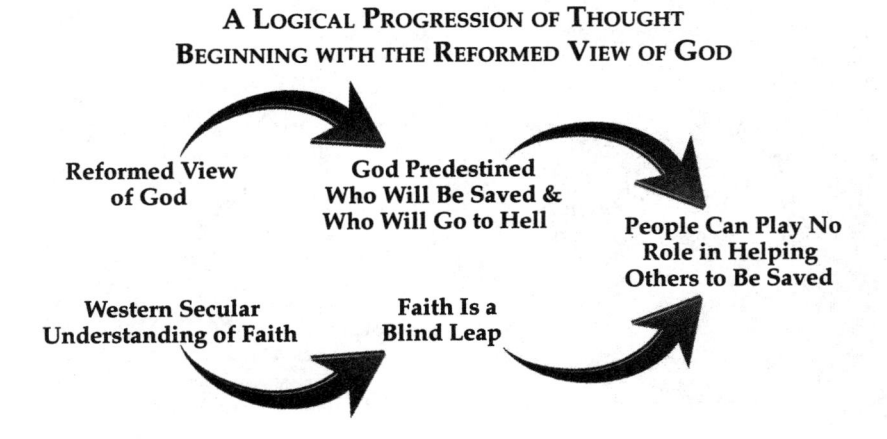

**A LOGICAL PROGRESSION OF THOUGHT
BEGINNING WITH THE REFORMED VIEW OF GOD**

Reformed View of God → God Predestined Who Will Be Saved & Who Will Go to Hell → People Can Play No Role in Helping Others to Be Saved

Western Secular Understanding of Faith → Faith Is a Blind Leap →

Systematic Theology for the New Apostolic Reformation

In contrast, the biblical view of faith is *a response in heart following the natural outworking (the reasonable outworking) of proof, revelation, seeing, hearing, or reading.* This being true, one person can play a significant role in the salvation of another person. This does not mean one person can save another person. Of course, God alone saves. However, the Bible is very clear about the role that Christians can play in leading others to Jesus.

Christians can preach the gospel to them. As we have discussed, *"faith comes by hearing"* (Rom. 10:17). After making this statement, Paul offered a series of cause-and-effect relationships:

> *How then will they call on Him in whom they have not believed? How will they believe in Him whom they have not heard? And how will they hear without a preacher? How will they preach unless they are sent?*
>
> (Rom. 10:14-15)

Only God can give the grace that saves a person, but others can play a significant role in creating faith—faith through which the grace of God comes into the heart. This puts significant responsibility into the hands of God's people.

BIBLICAL PROGRESSION OF THOUGHT:
CAUSE-AND-EFFECT RELATIONSHIPS

Sola Fide

Teaching and testifying about Jesus create faith in the hearts of people. Of course, people may resist the truth they are being taught, but Paul was clear concerning how faith is created. The concept that teaching creates faith is very significant. What parents teach their children does result in faith in the hearts of those children. What teachers teach their students also creates faith. Evangelists can effect a change in the hearts of people.

This truth removes the mystical element that many people imagine is part of faith. Faith is not a mystical endowment with no basis in experience, reason, or logic. Believing is not a blind step into the unknown. Faith is a natural response in heart following teaching and testifying about Jesus.

Someone who is consistent with Reformed theology cannot accept this truth. Their concept of God sees Him as the sole Savior in the sense that what humans do is totally ineffectual in salvation. Their understanding of faith is as a mystical gift from God alone. Their understanding of grace is of an efficacious favor of God which no human being can resist, influence, or vary. Therefore, a person consistent with Reformed theology carries no sense of responsibility to share the gospel with non-Christians.

Of course, there are many Christians who attend churches that teach Reformed theology, and they still share their faith. They simply do not live consistently with Reformed theology.

Christians who understand the principles being taught here realize that they can play a very important and significant role in the salvation of others. God has commissioned believers to preach the gospel. In fact, God has given all Christians *"the ministry of reconciliation"* (1 Cor. 5:18). It is what believers are called to do.

Point 428: We Have the Power

Earlier we made a comment that reading the Bible through the eyes of Western philosophy yields a form of godliness but denies the power. Here we see another area in which this proves true. Reformed theology leads people to believe they cannot do anything to help another person be saved. People are impotent to do what God alone does, according to Reformed theology.

Yet, the Bible teaches us something very different. Paul declared that the *"gospel is the power of God for salvation"* (Rom. 1:16). This means

Systematic Theology for the New Apostolic Reformation

that someone who preaches the gospel of God is releasing the power of God. The power is in the words. The power of life and death is in our mouths. Furthermore, the Holy Spirit has been given to us to empower us as witnesses for Jesus. We are not impotent, as Reformed theology leads people to believe. We have the power of God entrusted to us.

Point 429: Faith and Works Are Inseparable

One final subject important in soteriology is the relationship between faith and works. To understand this, we must go back to the foundations of Western thought versus Hebraic-biblical thought.

The separation between the spiritual and natural worlds in Western thought allows people to easily separate faith from works. In contrast, there is no disconnect between faith and works when someone builds on the Hebraic-biblical foundation. The spiritual and natural realms are totally integrated. What happens in one realm influences what happens in the other. The idea that a person can have faith without works is foreign—inconceivable—to the person with a Hebraic-biblical worldview. Whatever is in the heart comes forth. It is impossible to have a change of heart without having a change in behavior. Where there is faith, there will always be corresponding works.

Faith Cannot Be Separated from Works

Sola Fide

Bible students know about James' determination to keep faith united to works (Jas. 2:14-26). John was also interested in teaching this truth, because his missionary work was primarily in the region of Asia Minor, the center of Greek philosophical thought. With a strong separation of the spiritual and natural worlds, Greek people thought they could become Christians and still live in sin. John made several statements to correct this error, including the following:

> . . . *make sure no one deceives you; the one who practices righteousness is righteous, just as He is righteous; the one who practices sin is of the devil; for the devil has sinned from the beginning.*
> (1 John 3:7-8)

There was no confusion in John's mind. He had no separation between the spiritual and natural realms. John stated that *"No one who is born of God practices sin"* (1 John 3:9). Of course, everyone sins from time to time, as John also stated (1 John 1:10), but making a *practice of sin* and *sinning occasionally* are vastly different. John made it clear that a person who knows God will act righteously.

The relationship between faith and works may be understood by thinking of a fruit-bearing tree. The roots represent faith growing in the heart of a person. If the tree is alive it will support a tree trunk and branches. Those branches will produce fruit. Comparatively if faith is alive in the heart of a person, corresponding works will be produced in the life of that person.

Faith cannot be separated from works. Knowing this, we should reconsider Bible verses such as Ephesians 2:8-9:

> *For by grace you have been saved through faith; and that not of yourselves, it is the gift of God; not as a result of works, so that no one may boast.*

If we read this passage through the eyes of Western Christianity, we may conclude that Paul is separating faith from works (or grace from works), but Paul held a Hebraic worldview. He never would have made that division. It didn't exist in his mind.

We must try to understand Paul's words in their historical context. Paul was addressing a major conflict between Jews and Gentiles at that

Systematic Theology for the New Apostolic Reformation

time. Jewish leaders were demanding that the Gentiles be circumcised and follow the Jewish religious traditions. In that passage, Paul went on to explain:

> *For He* [Jesus] *Himself is our peace, who made both groups into one and broke down the barrier of the dividing wall, by abolishing in His flesh the enmity, which is the Law of commandments contained in ordinances . . . .*
>
> (Eph. 2:14-15)

Notice that this was the context in which Paul wrote that we are saved as a gift and *"not as a result of works"* (Eph. 2:9). Paul was explaining how the Jewish religious laws had been done away with. People cannot be saved by keeping *"the Law of commandments contained in ordinances."* Paul was not separating faith from works. He was separating faith in Jesus from the Jewish religious laws.

It is impossible to separate faith from works. James explained that faith that doesn't result in works is not real faith—not the kind of faith that accompanies salvation.

This does not mean that people are saved by their good works. God looks at the heart. Faith is of the heart. Faith is *the response in heart following the natural outworking of proof, revelation, seeing, hearing, or reading.* That kind of faith always results in good works.

Volume VII
Ecclesiology and Basilology

Ecclesiology is the study of the *ecclesia* (or spelled, *ekklesia*), which is the Greek word usually translated in the NT as "Church." In systematic theology, ecclesiology typically follows an explanation of the atonement and the gospel, because one of the primary purposes of the Church is to proclaim the gospel. We will discover several other purposes of the Church, along with characteristics of the Church and God's future plans for the Church.

Basilology refers to the study of God's Kingdom. The Kingdom is the domain over which Jesus reigns.

In Section A we will explain how the Church and the Kingdom differ from, yet relate to, one another. Section B will focus on ecclesiology, and Section C will focus on basilology. Then in Section D we will discuss how our understanding of the Church and the Kingdom are related to our understanding of the gospel.

Section A: Distinction between the Church and the Kingdom
Section B: Ecclesiology
Section C: Basilology
Section D: Founded in the Gospel

• • •

I will capitalize *Church* when referring to all believers across the world and write *church* when referring to a local body of believers.

Volume VII
Ecclesiology & Basiology

Section A
Distinction between the Church and Kingdom

The Church is not the Kingdom of God. Let's identify the difference.

Point 430: God's Promise to King David

In 1 Chronicles 17:12, God promised King David that one of his descendants:

> ... *shall build for Me a house, and I will establish his throne forever.*

Notice two distinct entities over which one of David's descendants was to be the head forever: a house and a kingdom.

Solomon was the descendant of David who built a house, i.e., Solomon's temple in Jerusalem, and established a kingdom encompassing the lands surrounding Jerusalem. However, Solomon's temple and kingdom were destroyed, so we know that Solomon did not fulfill the promise that was given to King David.

Jesus was also a descendant of David (born of man and born of God). Jesus came declaring that He will build a house and establish a Kingdom. The house that Jesus is building is the Church, being made of living stones, which refer to His people. Jesus also ascended into heaven, and Father-God turned all authority over heaven and earth to the Son (Matt. 28:18). Jesus has been reigning over God's Kingdom for about 2,000 years.

It is helpful to look at Solomon's temple and his kingdom, then compare them with Jesus' temple and His Kingdom. As Solomon's temple was meant to be a place where God dwells, so also Jesus' temple, i.e., His

Systematic Theology for the New Apostolic Reformation

Church, is a place where God dwells. As Solomon's kingdom was the region over which Solomon reigned, God's Kingdom is the region over which Jesus reigns.

The theologian George Ladd explained well the difference between the Church and Kingdom:

> In Biblical idiom, the Kingdom is not identified with its subjects. They are the people of God's rule who enter it, live under it, and are governed by it. The church is the community of the Kingdom but never the Kingdom itself . . . The Kingdom is the rule of God; the church is a society of men.[254]

The Church is a community indwelt by God's Spirit. The Kingdom of God consists of everything in heaven and on earth over which Jesus reigns.

This means the Kingdom of God is much bigger than the Church. This is true because the community of believers may go out into society and establish the Kingdom of God wherever they go. Paul explained that the Kingdom of God consists of righteousness, peace, and joy (Rom. 14:17). As believers submit their lives and actions to King Jesus, they can bring the righteousness, peace and joy of Jesus into every area of society, including business, education, politics, and so forth. We will have more to discuss about this later, but now it is important to see the Kingdom of God as the reign of Jesus which is meant to extend beyond the walls of the Church.

Point 431: Seeing the Kingdom Separate from the Church

Identifying the distinction between the Church and the Kingdom is important for several reasons.

The first reason becomes evident as we study the Church during the Middle Ages. During that period, the Roman Catholic Church equated herself with the Kingdom of God. As such she could justify certain questionable actions that she never would have been able to justify had she understood that she was not the Kingdom of God. To see this, consider how Jesus said, *"From the days of John the Baptist until now the kingdom of heaven suffers violence, and violent men take it by force"* (Matt. 12:13). From these words and from the Medieval understanding of a natural kingdom,

---

[254] George Eldon Ladd, *A Theology of the New Testament*, (Grand Rapids: Eerdmans, 1974), p. 111.

Distinction between the Church and Kingdom

Church leaders in the Middle Ages reasoned that God's Kingdom could be advanced by violence. Hence, thousands of Christians went to war with Muslims during the Crusades. The Church also rationalized the killing of heretics since she saw herself as having the authority of God's Kingdom.

How the Church sees herself determines how she will act.

If the Church is thought of as God's Kingdom, then leaders may lose site of her most important role as a community and a dwelling place for God.

Consider, again, the distinction between the temple and the kingdom in OT times. Solomon knew God was with him when he was in the temple or out making war to expand his kingdom. However, Solomon certainly acted differently in the temple than he did as he was expanding his kingdom.

The distinction between the Church and Kingdom does not correspond with a distinction between the sacred and secular. That is not what we are identifying here. Everything Christians do for God is sacred, whether in the Church or in the Kingdom. Those who work primarily in the Kingdom of God are just as called of God as those who work primarily in the Church. The distinction between the Church and Kingdom is one of function and purpose, not sacred or secular.

Point 432: People Need Community

The Church is a community. People are created with the need to be part of a community. That need is meant to be met within the Church community. We can see how this has always been God's plan. In the OT, we see how God made the Hebrews into a united people. In the NT, we see Jesus declaring that He is the Good Shepherd who will gather His sheep together as one. When the Holy Spirit came upon the early believers, they became of one mind and heart. Paul wrote that all who believe in Jesus become members of one Body (1 Cor. 12:13 ; Eph. 4:4).

People are created by God to be in community relationships. Of course, people may find some of their needs for community met in organizations separate from the Church. Some may join clubs or service groups. Some may find camaraderie in the military or sports teams. Others may find like-minded friends in bars or pubs. All people need community, but God

Systematic Theology for the New Apostolic Reformation

intended for those needs to be primarily met in the community over which Jesus is the Shepherd, Head, and Husband.

This reveals another reason why it is important to see the distinction between the Church and the Kingdom. If they are equated, then Christians who see themselves as members of the Kingdom may see no need for themselves to be members of a local church community. Yet, God created people to need community and also to be part of something larger, i.e., the Kingdom over which Jesus reigns.

Point 433: The Church Has the Keys to the Kingdom

The Church and Kingdom are different entities, but they are intimately related to one another. Both the Church and the Kingdom have the same Head, Jesus Christ. All who are members of the Church are also citizens of the Kingdom.

An interesting relationship between the Church and the Kingdom results from the fact that the Church has the keys to the Kingdom (Matt. 16:19). Keys represent authority to open and close doors (Rev. 1:18). Church leaders can use the keys of the Kingdom by what they teach and do. If a church leader instills doubt and unbelief in people, those people are not likely to walk in the peace, joy, and power that is available in the Kingdom of God. On the other hand, if a leader boldly declares that Jesus is Lord and Jesus will help all who follow Him, then the people will rise in faith. They will walk in the authority of the Kingdom. They will carry out the will of King Jesus on earth. Hence, we see how the Church has the keys to the Kingdom and, therefore, is able to release the King's will into the earth.

Jesus rebuked the religious leaders of His day because they were locking the doors of the Kingdom so people could not experience it (Matt. 23:13). Lest Church leaders today fall into the same error, they must help rather than hinder people from experiencing the Kingdom. When Christians attend a church meeting they should become filled with faith and courage rather than be beaten down and discouraged. Church leaders must empower their people to go out and establish the reign of Jesus in every area of society.

Section B
The *Ecclesia*

Jesus Christ founded the Church. He is the Architect, Builder, and Chief Cornerstone. This gives the Church validity that no other community has. *"Christ also loved the church and gave Himself up for her"* (Eph. 5:25). Jesus is the Head, and He gives His Church authority. Also, the Church is the temple for the Holy Spirit to indwell. So what is this divinely founded, loved, led, empowered, and indwelt Beauty? Let's see.

Point 434: What Is the Church?

The Greek word *ecclesia* comes from two Greek words: *ek*, meaning, "out of," and *caleo*, meaning "to call." Hence, *ecclesia* originally referred to "the called out ones." More specifically, it refers to people who are called out of the rest of humanity, gathered together, and assembled together for a specific purpose.

In NT times the word *ecclesia* was used to refer to various types of groups. For example, in Acts 19:32, 39, and 41, the word *ecclesia* was used to refer to a mob that came against Paul and his preaching. In the Septuagint the *ecclesia* referred to the assembly of the people of Israel. As the word became associated with the Church in NT times, it referred to God's people, and especially as they were gathered together.[255]

---

[255] Recently some leaders have been teaching that the Church should be a ruling body, engaged in making decisions that govern secular society. They try to support this teaching by associating the NT use of the word *ecclesia* with how the word was used three centuries earlier when the Greek city of Athens was in power. At that time, the *ecclesia* referred to an assembly of citizens who came together to make governmental decisions.

Systematic Theology for the New Apostolic Reformation

Within the first 200 years of Christianity, the word *church* also became associated with the building where God's people met. However, it is not used that way in the NT, and we will not use it here to refer to the building. *Church* refers to all people around the world who believe in Jesus Christ and confess Him as Lord. However, the word *church* can also be used to refer to any local group of Christians who have formed a community.

Point 435: The Nature of the Church

As a worldwide community, the Church is portrayed with many different metaphors in the NT.[256] For example, the Church is called *"the people of God"* (2 Cor. 6:16). This terminology is borrowed from the OT references to the Jews. It reflects the idea of God calling a people to Himself. Those people belong to God (1 Peter 2:9-10).

The people of God are also called the elect, the saints, or holy ones. They are called believers, brethren, disciples, and the flock. The apostle Paul made much use of the imagery of the Body of Christ, teaching that each Christian is a unique member of the Body.

Also, the Church is referred to as the *"temple of God's Spirit"* (1 Cor. 3:16). In the minds of the first Christians, this would have inspired thoughts of how God was associated with the Jewish temple in OT times. Now since Jesus has poured out the Holy Spirit, the Spirit inhabits each Christian individually and corporately as they gather together.

Finally, the image of the Bride of Christ stirs thoughts of intimacy, commitment, and enduring love. Each of these metaphors sheds light on what God intended His Church to be.

Although most Christians today will agree with these metaphors and this description of the Church, they may have visions of the Church which are very different from what was just stated. For many generations the Church has been an institution with rituals and traditions, some written and some not. For this reason, when most Christians think of a church, they can't help but think of a church building or people sitting in a sanctuary. Yet those images cannot be found in the NT. Nor should they be equated with the word *church* as it was used in the NT.

---

[256] Paul Minear refers to 80 different terms and images that are used in the NT to refer to the Church. Paul Minear, *Images of the Church in the New Testament* (Philadelphia, PA: Westminster, 1960), p. 173.

The *Ecclesia*

If we are determined to understand the Church independently of our Western cultural influences, we would see the Church as a community—a unique group of people, separated from the world, cared for by God, indwelt by the Spirit, and intimately related to Jesus.

Point 436: The Foundation of the Church

Paul explained that the Church is built on:

> ... *the foundation of the apostles and prophets, Christ Jesus Himself being the corner stone.*
>
> (Eph. 2:20)

With the foundation of the Church being laid by the apostles and prophets, modern church leaders are called to build according to the truths already laid down by the apostles and prophets. The records we have of their teachings, thoughts, and actions are written in the Bible, so the Bible has also become a foundation upon which all of Christianity rests.[257]

Point 437: The Government of the Early Church

As we discuss the government of the early Church, we should be careful not to impose our modern concepts that may be foreign to the NT understanding. For example, when we ask about the government of the early church, we have already assumed that the NT Church had a government. Indeed, we see leaders who had some authority to oversee certain activities within the community, but the word *government* is typically associated with a nation or a large institution. That particular concept may not be appropriate for the community of God's people.

To see this, consider a family unit. In one sense we can identify certain leaders, usually parents, who have the governmental authority. However, the word *government* is not typically used to refer to the role of parents over a family unit. We do recognize some type of authority as necessary to bring order to the family, but the word *government* is a bit strong.

---

[257] Some church leaders who believe in modern-day apostles and prophets understand Ephesians 2:20 is referring also to the modern-day apostles and prophets.

Systematic Theology for the New Apostolic Reformation

Instead of a government that rules over a nation, think of a shepherd who leads a flock of sheep. This corresponds more closely with the titles used for leaders in the NT and with roles fulfilled by the early Church leaders. Of course, a shepherd may at times exercise authority in dealing with some straying sheep, but the shepherd's primary role is in guiding and caring for the flock.

This is essential for a healthy community for several reasons, one being the biblical concept that all believers are priests unto God, having direct access to God. Similarly, in a family unit, each family member should have access to the parents. In contrast, the government of a nation or institution may create several levels of authority that form a barrier between the common people and the leaders at the top. That dynamic is contrary to the biblical revelation of all believers being members of a family. Rather than distancing people from God, the leadership of a church should see themselves as guiding the sheep into closer communion with God. Each believer is responsible to follow the leading of the Holy Spirit. Therefore, community leadership, in contrast to institutional government, is an important distinction.

Unfortunately, some Bible translations distort God's heart for leadership by translating key verses using English words that are more heavy-handed than the original Greek words. For example, the KJV of Hebrews 13:7 says:

Remember them which have the rule over *you* . . . .

In contrast, more accurate translations, such as the New American Standard Version, say:

Remember those who led *you* . . . .

(Heb. 13:7)

The KJV terminology, "rule over," implies a greater exercise of authority than "led." Words that support the use of authority more than the original Greek manuscripts are common in the KJV (e.g., Heb. 13:17, 24).[258]

---

[258] This was in accord with the 15 rules King James gave to the scholars who developed the KJV. Several of those 15 rules reveal King James' desire to have a version of the Bible that supported the Church of England, along with its authority and structure. For more information concerning this, see my book entitled, *Living and Dying with the King James Bible*.

The *Ecclesia*

We must free ourselves of such influences if we are going to determine what the leadership of the early Church was like. Of course, modern leaders who want to have more authority may resist this, because it may undermine some of the authority they have already claimed for themselves, but if we are going to develop our understanding from the Bible then we will have to be faithful to what the Bible actually reveals.

We know the early believers formed into united congregations, and the apostles appointed elders (*presbuteroi*) to oversee each flock (e.g., Titus 1:5 ; Acts 14:23). The elders (corporately called the presbytery) were to shepherd the flock, but they also had some authority to oversee the local church funds (Acts 11:30) and to make the decisions necessary for the community.

Some congregations chose deacons. In the church in Jerusalem the deacons were chosen by the congregation and confirmed by the apostles. Those Jerusalem deacons primarily served the physical needs of the widows.

We also see apostles, prophets, evangelists, pastors, and teachers in the early church. These leaders are mentioned in Ephesians 4:11 and often referred to as the **five-fold ministry gifts**.

We will discuss these leadership gifts more later, but now we should identify the *nature* of these leaders in the sense that the early Church was a community rather than an institution. This is important because a rigid government can change a community into an institution. Consider a military commander running his family like he directs the soldiers under his charge; that family is likely to lose the nurturing and caring atmosphere that should be in a loving home. Similarly, some types of leadership in the local church can change a community into an institution unlike the community seen in the NT.

Point 438: The Ongoing Development of Church Government

By the beginning of the 2nd century, bishops (*episkopoi*) are mentioned in the writings of the Church fathers. The bishops were elders who rose to prominence, and they gradually replaced the first apostles who were dying out. Most local congregations continued to have a group of elders, while a bishop in the region oversaw one or more congregations.

Church government began to significantly change after 325 AD. In that year, Constantine, the emperor of the Roman Empire, called all of the

Systematic Theology for the New Apostolic Reformation

bishops together in the city of Nicea in the Roman province of Bithynia in order to develop a set of doctrines around which all of Christendom could unite. One outcome of that gathering was the Nicene Creed. Another outcome was the authority granted to bishops by the Roman government. They became officially recognized by the secular world.

Although the bishop of Rome did not attend the Council of Nicea, he sent two priests to represent him. The significance of their role is debatable. Historians who favor Roman Catholic tradition tend to elevate the role of the bishop of Rome (in their mind, the pope) and see him as the one who officially affirmed acceptance of the Creed. In contrast, non-Catholic historians tend to see the bishop of Rome as having no more authority than any other bishop.

Protestant and Orthodox historians usually identify 325 AD as the time during which the Roman bishop began exalting his position above all other bishops; hence it is seen as the time when Roman Catholicism began as an independent part of Christendom. Roman Catholics disagree and say that the Roman Catholic Church started when Jesus spoke to Peter, as recorded in Matthew 16:18,[259] and that there has been an unbroken succession of popes from Peter to the present.

In the 4th and 5th centuries, Christianity grew rapidly throughout the Roman Empire. The imperial authority in Rome became more and more involved in appointing regional bishops. With a gradual union forming between the Church and State, the bishop in Rome, i.e., the pope, became more powerful, eventually appointing a complete hierarchy of authority under him to govern Western Christendom.

The Eastern and Western portions of the Church became increasingly distant from each other resulting in the Eastern half becoming identified as the Eastern Orthodox Church and the Western Church as the Roman Catholic Church. Rather than a pope, the Eastern Orthodox Church appointed *patriarchs* who held authority over regional bishops.

Point 439: The Three Traditional Forms of Government

The Protestant Reformation of the 16th century broke the Western Church into many denominations, each with their own form of government. Of course, all groups claimed that Jesus is the Head Shepherd of the

---

259 *"I also say to you that you are Peter, and upon this rock I will build My church . . . ."*

The *Ecclesia*

Church, but questions repeatedly arose how Jesus should rule through His under-shepherds. The forms of Church government that resulted are usually divided into three different categories: episcopal, presbyterian, and congregational.

The **episcopal** form of government is that which recognizes one leader, usually called a bishop, as the final authority over the local church or over a group of local churches. This form of government developed in the early Church, and today we see it among such groups as the Anglicans, United Methodists, and Pentecostal Holiness Churches.

The **presbyterian** form of government recognizes a group of representative leaders, called the elders or presbytery, as the authority over the local church. This form of government is practiced among the Presbyterian and Reformed Churches. With their own unique modifications, some Pentecostals, including the Assemblies of God, have a presbyterian form of government.

The **congregational** form of government places the authority over the local church in the hands of the people and is run much like a democracy. This is used by the Congregational Churches, some Baptists, and some independent churches.

A problem with any of the forms of government that we have mentioned is that they are not clearly seen in the NT church. This does not mean we should automatically reject them. God has guided His people throughout history. Therefore, we should consider the possibility that God guided each of the different denominations of Christianity to develop the type of government that they have today.

Yet, it is also possible that the secular culture and traditions influenced church government in negative, unbiblical ways. For example, it is reasonable for us to question if the Roman Catholic Church patterned its government after the Roman Empire, with its strong value for demanding hierarchal order. We can ask if the Anglican Church chose the episcopal form of government because it allows authority lines to be traced all the way up to the King of England, who was given authority over the Anglican Church. We should also ask if churches that have a congregational form of government were influenced by the democratic ideals that were coming to the forefront of philosophical and political thought during the same period in history when many congregational churches were being founded.

Systematic Theology for the New Apostolic Reformation

Point 440: The Apostolic Form of Church Government

It is the belief of this author that the form of leadership most in line with the NT pattern is neither episcopal, presbyterian, nor congregational. Rather, it is that which is laid out by Paul in 1 Corinthians 12:28:

> And God has appointed in the church, first apostles, second prophets, third teachers, then miracles, then gifts of healings, helps, administrations, various kinds of tongues.

Because the apostle is mentioned first, this form of leadership is often referred to as apostolic leadership.

In the modern Church, adherents of apostolic leadership number in multiple millions, but the related issues are controversial. Those who oppose apostolic leadership typically argue that the gifts of apostle and prophet ended in the 1st century. That view, called **cessationism**, refers to the belief that those gifts ceased when the original twelve apostles of Jesus died and the NT was completed.[260]

In response to this, proponents of apostolic leadership will first clarify that the original twelve apostles who walked with Jesus (including Matthias who replaced Judas) had a unique place in God's plan. Indeed, their names will be on the twelve foundation stones of the wall around New Jerusalem (Rev. 21:14). However, there were more than those twelve apostles in the NT. There are at least 22 apostles named in the NT. In addition to the original twelve, there were Matthias (Acts 1:26), Barnabas and Paul (Acts 14:14), Andronicus and Junias (Rom. 16:7), James the Lord's brother (Gal. 1:19), Epaphroditus (Phil. 2:25), Apollos (1 Cor. 4:6-9), and Silvanus and Timothy (1 Thes, 1:1 ; 2:6). Some Scriptures imply there were more (Rom. 16:7).

In Ephesians 4:11, where the five-fold ministry gifts are mentioned, we are told that Jesus gave these gifts *as He ascended into heaven* (Eph. 4:8). This means these gifts were given after Jesus lived, died, and resurrected. Jesus gave apostles, prophets, evangelists, pastors, and teachers to the Church as He was leaving earth and ascending into heaven. Therefore, these five-fold ministry gifts mentioned in Ephesians 4:11 do not refer to the 12 original apostles. They are *in addition* to the original 12 apostles.

---

[260] The word *cessationism* is also used to refer to the view that says the miraculous gifts of the Holy Spirit, such as tongues, prophecy, and healing ended when the canon of Scripture was completed.

The *Ecclesia*

Ephesians 4:11-13 tells us that Jesus gave the five-fold ministry gifts to the Church, and then we are told why:

> ... *for the equipping of the saints to the work of the service, to the building up of the body of Christ; until we all attain to the unity of the faith, and of the knowledge of the Son of God, to a mature man, to the measure of the stature which belongs to the fullness of Christ.*
>
> (Eph. 4:12-13)

Unity and maturity. These goals have not yet been reached. Therefore, proponents of apostolic leadership believe that all five-fold ministry gifts will be with the Church until the Church attains that which is promised in these verses.

Fully discussing this form of leadership is beyond the scope of this book, but currently on the Christian book market there are dozens of books explaining it.[261]

Point 441: The Work of the Church

The work of the Church may be divided into that which is upward, inward, and outward.

The upward ministry of the Church is toward God. This pattern was set in the OT times when God's people worshiped Him in the temple. In the NT, we can read how the first Christians prayed and worshiped God when they met (Acts 2:47-3:1 ; 16:25). One of the clearest examples is in Acts 13:2, where we read how the leaders in Antioch were *"ministering to the Lord."* This concept that people can minister to the Lord assigns great value to our praise and worship.

The inward ministry of the Church is first of all to love and care for one another. We can see many examples of this in the NT, such as when the early Christians sold their possessions and shared with anyone who had need. The ongoing care of one another is in line with the nature of the Church as a community.

The Church's inward ministry also includes equipping and teaching. Paul explained that equipping was for the purpose of training people for ministry (Eph. 4:12).

---

[261] This includes my own book, entitled, *The Complete Wineskin.*

Systematic Theology for the New Apostolic Reformation

The Church was also commissioned by Jesus to go outward:

> *Go therefore and make disciples of all the nations, baptizing them in the name of the Father and the Son and the Holy Spirit, teaching them to observe all that I commanded you.*
>
> (Matt. 28:19-20)

Historically, the Church has embraced this commission for Herself. She is to go into the whole world. She is to make disciples of all nations. She is to baptize and teach everyone to observe the teachings of their Leader.

In addition to evangelism, the Church should be involved in helping the poor and needy. Indeed, She has done great works throughout history in building hospitals, orphanages, and charitable organizations. Christians are also called to transform society, a topic we will address when discussing the Kingdom of God in Section C.

Point 442: The Meetings Conducted for the Community

The work the Church sees as her inward ministry is directly tied to her understanding of humanity's problem and God's answer to humanity's problem.

As explained earlier,[262] Reformed theology sees humanity's primary problem as sin. All people are guilty. Because God is just, He must punish the guilty law-breakers. That punishment is administered via the wrath of God, and therefore, people must be saved from the wrath of God.

Since the Church sees herself as helping humanity on behalf of God, leaders in the Reformed tradition see their most important responsibility as making listeners aware of their own sins and then the answer that God is offering—namely, the penalty paid through the suffering and death of Jesus. The message concerning humanity's sins and Jesus' death is so important within the Reformed tradition that leaders typically teach about these at almost every public meeting.

ACCORDING TO REFORMED THEOLOGY

Humanity's Problem	God's Answer
Sin/Guilt/God's Wrath	Death of Jesus

---

[262] VI:A:349.

The *Ecclesia*

Since leaders in the Reformed tradition see these as foundational stones, they typically try to lead attendees at their meeting to the feet of Jesus, where they are humbly conscious of their sins and grateful for the death of Jesus on the cross.

In contrast, church leaders coming from the perspective of Father-Son theology have a very different emphasis in their ministry toward their own community. God is a Father. As we discussed earlier,[263] from His perspective humanity's first problem is broken relationship with Him. Second, it is death, which includes all of the consequences of sin. And the third problem is the darkness of this world in which humanity lives.

The first problem—broken relationship—is resolved in the new covenant that was established through the death of Jesus. The second problem—death—is overcome through life, and in particular, the life of Jesus.[264] The third problem—living in this dark world—is overcome by living in the reign of God's Kingdom.

ACCORDING TO FATHER-SON THEOLOGY

Humanity's Problem	God's Answer
1. Broken Relationship	New Covenant
2. Death (Consequences of Sin)	Jesus' Life
3. The World	Kingdom of God

In a community that embraces Father-Son theology, discussions of the new covenant will be at the forefront. Not only are sins forgiven, but Father-God has opened His arms to receive His children. Believers are children of God in covenant relationship with Him. Through the new covenant, believers have a new spirit and heart. God is at work within them, causing them to walk in His ways.

God has also given to believers the answer to death. Death is overcome as believers receive the life and grace flowing from Jesus through the Holy Spirit (Rom. 5:17). Believers can even be set free of the darkness of this world by living in the light of God's Kingdom. There they will experience righteousness, peace, and joy.

With this perspective, leaders in a community that embrace Father-Son theology will focus on God's love for humanity and endeavor to give life to the community. They will encourage the congregation to walk in the

---

[263] VI:A:352.
[264] This was explained in VI:C:372-381.

Systematic Theology for the New Apostolic Reformation

love and warm embrace of the Father. Flowing from the pulpit will be life, in the sense of encouragement, hope, and vision. Leaders will also release the life of God through blessings, prayer, and the laying on of hands. At a typical meeting where Father-Son theology is embraced, people will not be brought to the feet of Jesus where they are conscious of their sins. Instead, they will be encouraged to meet with Jesus who lives and reigns from His throne in the Kingdom.

Point 443: The Tenor of Life Established by the Church Meeting

The differences between communities that embrace Reformed theology versus Father-Son theology should be evident in how participants are impacted during church services. That impact should be carried with participants as they leave a church meeting and then carried with them throughout their week.

Participants at a meeting corresponding with Reformed theology will exit the building at the end of a typical meeting humbled and solemn because of an awareness of their own sinfulness, yet thankful to God for His mercy. That tenor should be carried with them throughout their week.

In contrast, participants at a community in tune with Father-Son theology will exit the building filled with a sense of God's acceptance and love. They will be filled with joy, energy, and life. They will also have an optimistic, victorious confidence, knowing that Jesus reigns from heaven and will be with them throughout the week.

Of course, these are very generalized observations. Every church meeting is unique, but here we are noting the general impact that theology has on church meetings and the believers who attend those meetings.

Point 444: The Sacraments/Ordinances of the Church

The Church also considers the administration of the sacraments as one of her responsibilities. During the Middle Ages this became the primary role of local churches and parish priests. Some older mainline churches continue to embrace this as a primary responsibility, but recently formed Protestant groups tend to have less and less connection to the sacraments of the historic Church.

The *Ecclesia*

Over the course of many years, the Roman Catholic Church developed seven sacraments: Baptism, Confirmation, Communion, Penance, Extreme Unction (Anointing of the Sick), Holy Orders, and Matrimony. These rites are also called ordinances, but only two of them are accepted by most Protestants: baptism and communion. Most Protestant teachers will say that only these two were established by Jesus.

The Greek word *baptizo*, from which the word *baptism* comes, means to "dip under" or "submerge." In keeping with this, water baptism was first practiced by submerging people under water and then raising them out. Some of the writings of the early Church reveal how submersion was, at times, replaced by pouring water over the head of each person.[265]

The rite of baptism signifies the person's identification with Christ. Paul explained that going under the water indicates a symbolic burial because the believer has stopped breathing and died to his old way of life. Then coming out of the water indicates that the person has been raised to newness of life through Jesus' redemption (Rom. 6:2-5).

Most Church leaders have followed the pattern of Matthew 28:19, which instructs Jesus' disciples to baptize new believers in "*the name of the Father, Son, and Holy Spirit.*" Certain groups, such as the Oneness Pentecostals, baptize "in the name of Jesus," only, according to the pattern in Acts 2:38 and 10:48. However, those who insist on this second pattern usually reject the doctrine of the Trinity. Father-Son theology embraces the Trinity, but I agree with Martin Luther that disagreements over the wording used in baptisms are pedantry.[266] Not the words, but the proper intent is essential.

Infant baptism has been another issue that has stirred much debate. We do not have any clear evidence of an infant being water baptized in the NT, but proponents argue that whole families were baptized, including infants, when there is mention in the NT of entire households being baptized (Acts 16:15 ; 16:33). The Church father Origen (c. 184–254 AD) mentioned that infants were being baptized in his time, while Tertullian (c. 160–225 AD) wrote that they should not be baptized until they are old enough to understand. After the Roman Catholic Church accepted Augustine's understanding of original sin, the practice of infant baptism became common, thinking that baptism could remove the stain of Adam's sin. Various Protestant groups have developed their own unique ideas

---

265 For example, the *Didache*.
266 Luther wrote this in his *Prelude on the Babylonian Captivity of the Church*, published in 1520.

Systematic Theology for the New Apostolic Reformation

and practices with water baptism, but a large percentage of evangelical groups only baptize those old enough to have made a profession of faith in Jesus Christ.

The other ordinance accepted by most Protestants is communion, also called the Lord's Supper. Before Jesus died, He shared a meal with His disciples at which time He took some bread, broke it, and gave it to them saying, *"Take, eat, this is My body"* (Matt. 26:26). Then He blessed a cup of wine and gave it to them saying, *"Drink from it, all of you, for this is the blood of the covenant which is poured out for the remission of sins"* (Matt. 26:27-28). When Jesus said, *"Do this in remembrance of Me"* (Luke 22:19), He established this as a practice to be repeated by His followers.

The Roman Catholic Church developed a view of communion called **transubstantiation** (affirmed at the Fourth Lateran Council of 1215). This view sees the bread and wine actually becoming the body and blood of Jesus as the priest consecrates them. During the Late Middle Ages this understanding gave the Catholic Church unprecedented power over its followers, since it gave the priests the power to actually offer Jesus to the people in the form of bread and wine.

After Martin Luther broke with the Catholic Church, he rejected the doctrine of transubstantiation but still taught that the presence of the body and blood of Jesus was with, in, and under the bread and wine. This view became known as **consubstantiation**. John Calvin rejected both the Roman Catholic and Lutheran understanding. Calvin taught that the spiritual presence of Jesus was "with" the Lord's Supper.

Other variations of the Lord's presence at or with communion have been developed by different denominations, but it is the belief of this author that the most important expectation is that the recipients of communion make personal contact with Jesus, Who is always willing to meet those who seek Him.

Point 445: The Authority to Impart Grace

Roman Catholics and most Protestants practice baptism and communion, however, Catholics call them **sacraments** while Protestants are divided over whether they should be called sacraments or ordinances. The word *sacrament* is usually associated with a ritual that actually imparts

The *Ecclesia*

grace to the recipient, while an **ordinance** is a ritual that is symbolic of grace that has already been obtained by the individual.[267]

This understanding of an ordinance has roots deep in Protestant thought. During the Protestant Reformation, leaders were attempting to break free of Roman Catholicism, and one of the strongest holds that Catholicism had over the people was tied to the belief that the priests had the authority to impart God's grace through the sacraments. As long as people believed that such benefits came through the Catholic priests, they were highly unlikely to abandon the Roman Catholic Church.

The Reformers not only wanted to break from Roman Catholicism, but in order to get away from the idea of man's control, they emphasized God's sovereignty in a way that negates humans playing *any* role in administering grace. Even their definition of *grace* as "unmerited favor" implied that humans play no role, even in accessing God's grace. In the Reformed understanding of grace, God and God alone gives grace to individuals.[268]

As a consequence, Christians from different traditions have very different expectations when it comes to receiving grace through the Church. Typically Roman Catholics have high expectations that they can receive some spiritual benefit by accessing what the Church offers. This becomes very evident to missionaries who travel to regions of the world where large numbers of Christians have converted from Catholicism to Protestant Christianity (such as the Philippines and South America). When those missionaries invite people to come forward at the end of a church service for prayer, they are often overwhelmed at the sight of how eager people are to respond. In contrast, Christians raised in many non-Charismatic, Protestant traditions are more reluctant to respond to altar calls because they have no frame of reference for going forward at an altar call to receive some grace or blessing. Evangelicals consistent with Reformed theology may go forward at a church service to commit their own lives to Jesus, but not to receive something from God.

In reality, there are numerous examples in the Bible of various blessings being imparted through Church leaders. Those blessings include healing, spiritual gifts, authority, empowering, and anointing for ministry. For example, in 1 Timothy 4:14, the apostle Paul wrote to Timothy:

---

267 Some modern Protestant churches are inconsistent at this point, calling communion and baptism sacraments, while teaching that grace is given sovereignly by God with no human involvement.

268 John Wesley taught that the sacraments are a means of grace.

Systematic Theology for the New Apostolic Reformation

> *Do not neglect the spiritual gift within you, which was bestowed on you through prophetic utterance with the laying on of hands by the presbytery.*

For another example, we can read how the apostles in Jerusalem went to the people of Samaria and *"they began laying their hands on them, and they were receiving the Holy Spirit"* (Acts 14:17). Paul wrote to the Christians in Rome that he was longing to come visit them *"so that I may impart some spiritual gift to you . . ."* (Rom. 1:11). In this verse, the word *gift* has been translated from the Greek word *charisma,* which refers to a gift associated with grace.

This truth that the Holy Spirit and various gifts are imparted to individuals through the laying on of hands is fundamental to biblical Christianity. The writer of Hebrews includes *"the laying on of hands"* as a foundational and elementary teaching of the faith (Heb. 6:2).

Today, Pentecostal/Charismatic churches tend to be more active in the practice of laying on of hands with prayer. As a consequence, Christians trained in other Protestant traditions who join Pentecostal/Charismatic churches may have to make significant changes in their patterns of thinking concerning how God works in this world and what authority He gives to His people. Some of those changes in thought are in accord with what is being taught here in Father-Son theology. God is in a cooperative relationship with humanity, and He grants much authority to people to bless others. This includes the impartation of God's grace.

Point 446: Preaching the Word of God

In addition to administering the ordinances (or sacraments), communicating the truth of Scripture is considered a ministry and responsibility of the Church. This has precedence in the Jewish practice of reading the Scriptures before the congregation. In the NT we can read Paul's instructions to Timothy to:

> . . . *give attention to the public reading of Scripture, to exhortation and teaching.*
>
> (1 Tim. 4:13)

Teaching and preaching from the Word of God was practiced from the day of Pentecost onward.

The *Ecclesia*

Generally speaking, churches that are more liturgical place higher value on the ordinances than the presentation of the Word. By *liturgical* we are referring to those churches which follow a format during their services that was standardized by leaders of a denomination that has been in existence for many years. This is in contrast to *non-liturgical* churches that conduct their services as unscripted or improvised.[269]

Different churches value the Bible for different reasons, and those reasons change over the course of time. Churches that value the Bible as the very Words of God believe that the hearers are actually hearing God speak as the Words are being read out loud. In such churches, it is believed that the congregational members are literally receiving the grace of God as they listen. In other churches, the focus is on the Bible's value as *"the pillar and support of the truth"* (1 Tim. 3:15), and therefore, leaders feel responsible to continue repeating the same fundamental truths of the Bible over and over. Other churches focus on the Bible's role in forming the character of each church member (Jas. 1:23-25 ; 1 Tim. 3:16-17), so the listeners are expected to apply the truths they hear as the Bible's message is being communicated.

Reading and preaching the Word also plays a significant role in helping congregational members simply feel okay about themselves. People want to know that they are right with God. In addition, people want to develop a worldview that is consistent and all encompassing. They feel a sense of satisfaction whenever they hear a bit of information that fills in the unknown or closes the gaps in their thinking. Further, they want to hear again that God loves them and is pleased with them.

Although we may not want to admit it, some preaching is done to help the preachers fulfill their own personal goals. There is also much entertainment value as charismatic preachers share their stories, which may or may not expound upon the meaning of the Scriptures.

Point 447: Present Challenges of the Church

The present-day Church is facing great challenges concerning what she actually has to offer to individuals and society as a whole. Before the last

---

[269] Many teachers object to this distinction because, in reality, churches referred to as non-liturgical usually have a set pattern by which their services are conducted, but that pattern is simply not acknowledged publicly.

Systematic Theology for the New Apostolic Reformation

three or four generations, most people living in Christian nations believed the Church actually imparted grace to the recipients, especially through the administration of the sacraments and the preaching of God's Word. Church attendees believed that they were pleasing God and garnering His favor which would give them an advantage in this life and the next.

Undermining that belief have been secular attacks on the reliability of the Bible. Also there has been a major paradigm shift that has occurred in the minds of most Western people. Lying at the foundation of that shift is the same dualism that we have discussed throughout this book. Plato laid down the Western cosmology with a gap of infinity between the spiritual and natural worlds. That gap became fixed during the scientific revolution of the 16th century. Today Western education is built on that foundation, with faith being associated with the spiritual world and knowledge being associated with the natural world. With only knowledge of the natural world available, Western people tend to think of the natural world as the real world or at least the only world with which we have to deal. Over the course of the last 200 years, the spiritual world dwindled to a place of insignificance in the Western secular mind.

This has become the foundation for the dominant worldview of Western civilization. People who have not absorbed it by osmosis are under pressure to conform. Pressure is especially strong in Western institutions of higher learning. Students who continue to think of the spiritual world as close to and influential in this natural world are thought of as unenlightened and uneducated. Students who try to bring God into the picture of daily life are sometimes ridiculed.

With the dominant dualistic worldview, Western people try to isolate themselves from God. This fits well with people's natural human desire to shun God so they may continue in sin. For those fully indoctrinated, God's existence is a non-issue. If God exists, people reason that they will deal with Him when they face Him after they die.

Secular Western people have tried to convince themselves that the spiritual world has no influence upon the natural world. For them, no one, not even the Church, can bring the things of God into this world. As a consequence, a great percentage of the population in Western society does not perceive that the Church has anything to offer them. In many countries of Europe, the Church is primarily seen as a historic institution, only serving people for marriage and funeral services.

The *Ecclesia*

MODERN SECULAR WORLDVIEW

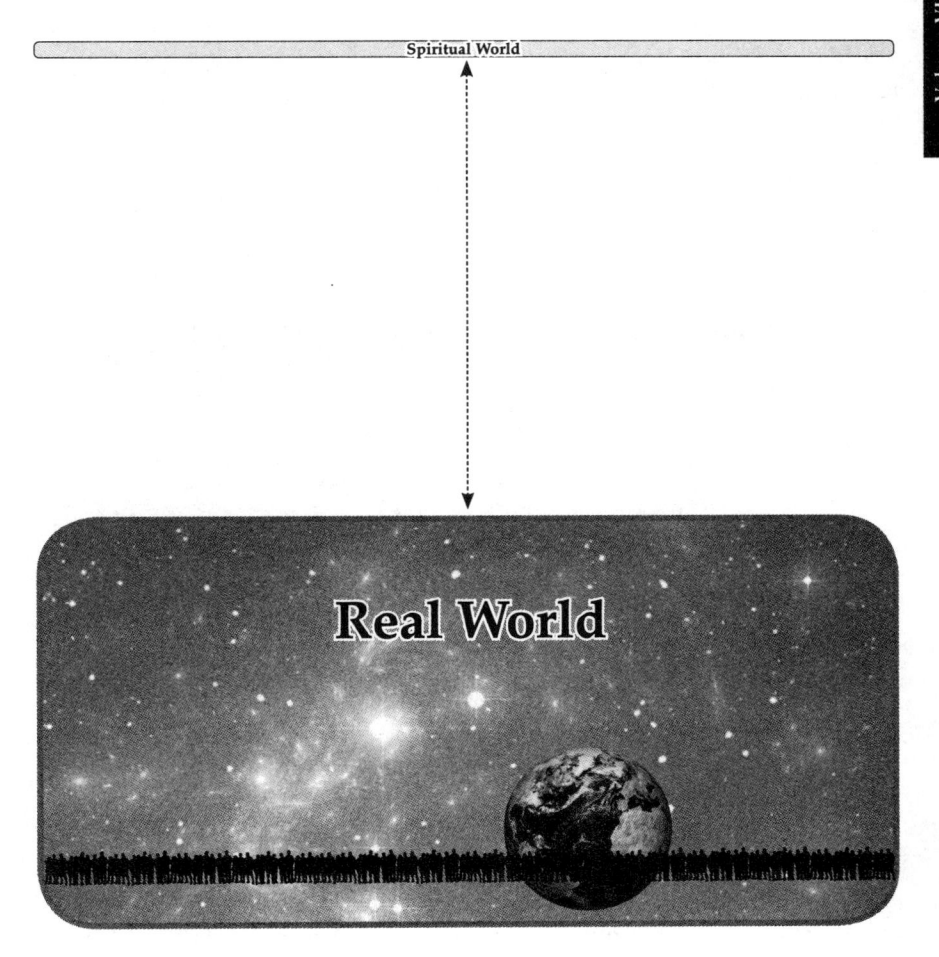

Spiritual World

Real World

Point 448: Recreating the Modern Church

With these and other challenges facing the Church, leaders are having to reevaluate their own work.

Of course, the Church remains *"the household of God, which is the church of the living God, the pillar and support of the truth"* (1 Tim. 3:15). Without the

Systematic Theology for the New Apostolic Reformation

Church continuing to faithfully speak the truth, individuals will have no solid anchor in the midst of humanity's ever-changing opinions and views.

The Church must also offer to humanity a biblical worldview. That worldview begins with a cosmology in which the spiritual and natural realms are completely integrated. There is no gap between the two realms. God is very close. He desires relationship with people. And the Church is still God's instrument to administer His grace to humanity.

THE CHURCH:
GOD'S INSTRUMENT TO ADMINISTER GRACE TO HUMANITY

As church leaders reevaluate the role of the modern Church, they are seriously reconsidering Jesus' original intentions for His Church. Of course, this does not negate the importance of preaching biblical truths, but it does elevate in importance the original intentions of Jesus for the Church, first and foremost, as a place to meet with God. This calls church leaders to provide that place and cultivate an atmosphere in which God's presence may manifest.

In reevaluating Jesus' original intentions for the Church, leaders also recognize the centrality of community. This requires loving and caring for one another. Leaders sensitive to community make opportunities for community development, especially in small groups.

The *Ecclesia*

As for ministering outside of the Church, leaders are seeing the importance of helping the poor and influencing society in positive ways. Influencing society is best explained through the expansion of the Kingdom, which we will discuss in the section to follow, but Church leaders should realize that they are using the keys of the Kingdom (to lock or unlock doors) every time they minister to their people.[270]

Point 449: The Temple of the Holy Spirit

Another distinction of the Church is her role as the temple for the Holy Spirit. Of course, we know that each believer is a temple for the Holy Spirit, but there is also a corporate fulfillment of this role.

One of the most profound witnesses of the Holy Spirit is a presence that manifests across the world wherever God's people gather. Personally, I have ministered in more than 25 countries, and in every country, no matter what the culture of the people, the presence of God is experienced in a similar way. That presence cannot be explained in words, but I have taken many people to the nations on missions trips, and they often sense the same Holy Spirit manifesting in those far away places as He does in their home churches.

Some Christians have been trained to be skeptical of spiritual experiences, and instead, they judge a church's validity only by the soundness of its doctrine. Those Christians may be skeptical of my observation that manifestations of the Holy Spirit are similar around the world. Yet, the apostle Peter had a similar experience, noting that the Gentiles who came to Jesus received the same Holy Spirit that the Jews who received Jesus did (Act 10:47 ; 11:17-18).

Paul wrote that believers are *"all baptized into one body"* by the Holy Spirit (1 Cor. 12:13). Paul also described how this union results in the many members of the Church functioning as a unit comparative to how all the members of a physical body function as a unit (1 Cor. 12:12). Ephesians 2:22 describes how we *"are being built together to become a dwelling in which God lives by his Spirit."*

The Bible offers God's promises to abide with His people. Jesus promised:

---

[270] Discussed in VII:A:433.

Systematic Theology for the New Apostolic Reformation

> *For where two or three have gathered together in My name, I am there in their midst.*
>
> (Matt. 18:20)

This promise of God's manifest presence cannot be overemphasized. When Moses went up to meet with God on Mount Sinai, he prayed:

> *Is it not by Your going with us, so that we, I and Your people, may be distinguished from all the other people who are upon the face of the earth?*
>
> (Ex. 33:16)

Notice how Moses wanted the presence of God to be prominent enough among God's people so as to be evident to outsiders.

Jesus also talked about the love among His people that should be a distinguishing mark:

> *By this all men will know that you are My disciples, if you have love for one another.*
>
> (John 13:35)

These two things—God's manifest presence and love among His people—set the Church apart from all other groups.

It was for these things (along with protection from evil) that Jesus besought the Father in His priestly prayer offered before His death (John 17). For the Church today to have the priorities that Jesus had, She must pursue the presence of God and love for one another.

Point 450: The Destiny of the Church

Will the Church ever become all that Jesus desired? Our Lord prayed to the Father:

> *... that they may all be one; even as You, Father, are in Me and I in You, that they also may be in Us, so that the world may believe that You sent Me.*
>
> (John 17:21)

The *Ecclesia*

Two verses later, Jesus prayed that His followers may be *"perfected in unity"* (John 17:23). He prayed that this goal would be fulfilled so the world would know that He was sent by the Father. This means that Jesus expected this prayer to be fulfilled while the world was watching.

Paul wrote that the five ministry gifts were given to the Church to equip the saints *"until we all attain to the unity of the faith"* (Eph. 4:13). Not only unity, but Paul gave the goal for the Church to become the *"mature man, to the measure of the stature which belongs to the fullness of Christ"* (Eph. 4:13).

Will the Church ever attain such a place of unity and maturity? Jesus seemed very confident when He said that He will build His Church and the gates of hades will not prevail against it (Matt. 16:18). He also confidently stated that His followers will do the same works that He did and greater works (John 14:14). Jesus certainly had an optimistic view concerning the future of His Church.

Volume VII
Ecclesiology & Basiliology

Section C
The Kingdom of God

Jesus is building His Church and reigning over a Kingdom. Let's examine the Kingdom now.

Point 451: The Reign of Jesus

God sent a Savior into the world. Jesus died on a cross, resurrected, and ascended into heaven; then He sat down at the right hand of the throne of God. All authority over heaven and earth was given to Him (Matt. 28:18). For 2,000 years, Jesus has been reigning. Everything over which He reigns is the Kingdom of God.

Point 452: The Kingdom of God versus the Kingdom of Heaven

It is important to know that the Kingdom of God is the same thing as the Kingdom of heaven. We know these are synonymous because of how they are used in the four Gospels. Each Gospel records some of Jesus' parables, many of which start off saying, "The Kingdom of God is like…" However, in the Gospel of Matthew, several of the same parables start off by saying, "The Kingdom of heaven is like . . . ." Bible scholars typically explain this difference by saying that Matthew was writing to Jewish people, who considered the name, "God," too holy to ever speak or write. Since Matthew knew this about his Jewish audience, he was being sensitive to them and wrote "Kingdom of heaven." In the parallel passages, Mark, Luke, and John refer to the Kingdom of God.

Systematic Theology for the New Apostolic Reformation

So whether we call it the Kingdom of God or the Kingdom of heaven, we are referring to the same Kingdom over which Jesus has been reigning for approximately 2,000 years.

Point 453: Thy Kingdom Come on Earth

God intends for the Kingdom to manifest here on earth. For this reason, we are instructed to pray, "*Your Kingdom come. Your will be done, on earth as it is in heaven*" (Matt. 6:10).

Notice in the Lord's prayer that the Kingdom coming to earth is equated with the will of God being done here on earth. For this reason, the Kingdom manifests wherever people are in submission to the King. Businesspeople who submit to King Jesus will bring the Kingdom into their businesses. School teachers who have a heart to please God will bring the King's will into their classrooms. Artists who desire to glorify God will have the anointing of the King's Spirit upon their work. Whenever and wherever people are doing the King's will, His Kingdom is manifesting.

Paul explained that the Kingdom of God consists of righteousness, peace, and joy (Rom. 14:17). In another passage, he explained that the Kingdom consists in power (1 Cor. 4:20). Therefore, we should expect the righteousness, peace, joy, and power of God to manifest wherever people are living in submission to King Jesus.

Point 454: Faith for the Kingdom Is Influenced by One's Cosmology

People's understanding concerning *how* the Kingdom manifests on earth is profoundly influenced by their cosmology. Therefore, when Classical/Reformed Christians pray, "*Your Kingdom come. Your will be done, on earth as it is in heaven*" (Matt. 6:10), they are envisioning a Kingdom which is located far above us crossing the gap of infinity and, as such, seldom manifesting in the natural world. With the Kingdom way up in heaven, Western Christians have a more difficult time seeing the Kingdom of God influencing this world.

The Kingdom of God

"Your Kingdom Come"
Seen Through the Dualistic Cosmology

Volume VII
Ecclesiology & Basilology

Heaven
Kingdom of God

(INFINITY)

Earth

Systematic Theology for the New Apostolic Reformation

In contrast, the Hebraic-biblical cosmology sees heaven as here and fully integrated into the natural realm. Jesus spoke to the Jewish religious leaders from the perspective of the Kingdom being very close:

> *The kingdom of God is not coming with signs to be observed; nor will they say, "Look, here it is!" or, "There it is!" For behold, the <u>kingdom of God is in your midst</u>.*
>
> (Luke 17:20-21)

The Kingdom of God is already here, around us and within us. Christians who have embraced this Hebraic-biblical cosmology have a much easier time envisioning the Kingdom of God manifesting in this world, thus they have more faith for it. They see that the Kingdom of God is here and available. As Jesus and the disciples preached, "It is at hand!"

"Your Kingdom Come"
Seen Through the Hebraic-biblical Cosmology

Point 455: The Kingdom Is a Domain of Grace and Life

Paul wrote that Jesus *"rescued us from the domain of darkness, and transferred us to the kingdom of His beloved Son"* (Col. 1:13). From this we

The Kingdom of God

know that the Kingdom of God is opposed to darkness. God's Kingdom is a Kingdom where sin, death, and Satan do not reign. Instead, Jesus reigns. His Kingdom is a domain of light and love.

JESUS TRANSFERRED US FROM DARKNESS TO THE KINGDOM

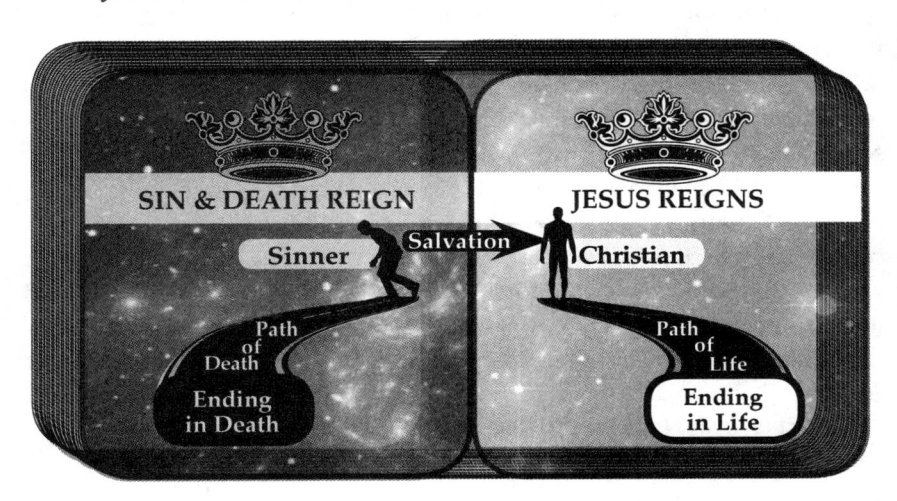

As we explained earlier, Adam released sin and death into the world, resulting in sin and death reigning over humanity. Jesus released grace and life into the world, which are powers greater than the power of sin and death. Therefore, those who walk in the Kingdom of God will experience victory over sin and death.[271]

Point 456: Jesus Governs the Kingdom via the Spirit

All Christians are citizens of God's Kingdom, however, not all Christians are experiencing the benefits. When Paul wrote that the Kingdom consists of righteousness, peace, and joy, he associated these benefits with the Holy Spirit (Rom. 14:17). This is because living in God's Kingdom is inseparable from living in the Holy Spirit.

To see this from another perspective, consider the words Jesus spoke to Nicodemus:

---

[271] This victorious Christian life is explained in XII:E.

Systematic Theology for the New Apostolic Reformation

> *Truly, truly, I say to you, unless one is born again he cannot see the kingdom of God.*
>
> (John 3:3)

Most Christians tend to read these words with a mind already trained in the gospel of salvation;[272] therefore, they interpret Jesus' words to mean that a person must be born again to get to heaven, but Jesus was not talking about getting to heaven. He said a person must be born again to *"see the kingdom of God."* The Kingdom of God is something believers can see and experience right now while alive.

Unless people are born again, they cannot see this. On the other hand, if people believe in their hearts that God raised Jesus from the dead and confess Him as Lord, then they can understand that Jesus is King right now. He is ruling over a Kingdom. Whoever is born again can see this, and it makes sense to them.

Jesus spoke further to Nicodemus:

> *Truly, truly, I say to you, unless one is born of water and the Spirit he cannot enter into the kingdom of God.*
>
> (John 3:5)

Here Jesus added to His previous statement. Not only can people *see* the Kingdom of God, but they can enter and walk in it.

What is required for a person to walk in this Kingdom? To be *"born of water and the Spirit."* Teachers often equate being "born of water" with natural birth,[273] because Nicodemus had just asked Jesus:

> *How can a man be born when he is old? He cannot enter a second time into his mother's womb and be born, can he?*
>
> (John 3:4)

Nicodemus equated the first birth with his natural birth from his mother.

Jesus explained the second birth, saying:

> *The wind blows where it wishes and you hear the sound of it, but do*

---

[272] The gospel of salvation in contrast to the gospel of the Kingdom is explained in VI:E.

[273] Some teachers equate being born of water with water baptism and others with being born of the Word of God.

The Kingdom of God

not know where it comes from and where it is going; <u>so is everyone who is born of the Spirit</u>.

(John 3:8)

Jesus compared the Spirit to a wind and said that the person who is born of the Spirit will be *borne on that wind*. This makes sense when we learn that King Jesus governs His Kingdom through the Holy Spirit. When people yield to the Holy Spirit, they are yielding to King Jesus. Therefore, whoever is borne on the wind of the Spirit is walking in the Kingdom of God.

Point 457: Walking in the Holy Spirit

We can equate walking in the Kingdom with walking in the Holy Spirit, but we are not referring to individuals walking the earth with their eyes glazed over while trying to sense some mystical wind from heaven. Jesus' government over His Kingdom is much more tangible than that.

God gives believers new hearts, and He is at work within them, causing them to will and to work for His good pleasure (Phil. 2:13). Once people yield their hearts to Jesus as Lord, He governs their lives through the Holy Spirit working in their hearts. Therefore, people may not even know that they are being carried along by the Spirit of God. Many times believers do God's will by simply doing what He has put in their hearts, such as caring for children, starting a business, talking to neighbors, and so forth.

Furthermore, we are told that God puts His Spirit in believers and causes them to carry out His will (Ezek. 36:27). Of course, there may be times when individuals sense God's nudging to act in a certain way, but at other times, they will be borne on the wind of His Spirit without being conscious of His leading.

The good news is that Jesus is King. He will govern His Kingdom and cause His will to be done in the earth. Believers can be a part of that through the Holy Spirit.

Point 458: The Kingdom in the Seven Mountains of Society

When we talk about establishing the Kingdom of God on earth, we are talking about more than leading people to Jesus. Of course, the salvation of souls is part of it, but establishing God's Kingdom is doing the will of King Jesus throughout the world.

Many of those who teach about the Kingdom of God talk about establishing the Kingdom on the *seven mountains*. These mountains refer to the seven spheres of authority that influence all of society:

1. business
2. government
3. media
4. arts/entertainment
5. education
6. family
7. religion

These categories are not presented anywhere in the Bible, but they have become helpful in identifying where God's people need to advance in order to influence society. Christians who teach about the seven mountains encourage other Christians to work toward becoming the major influencers in these areas so the Kingdom of God can be established throughout the world.

This understanding can be very surprising to Christians only trained in the gospel of salvation. For them, getting people saved is the big push. Many Christians only trained in the gospel of salvation have never even considered the possibility of establishing King Jesus' will on earth in any practical ways. Tragically, many Christians have given up hope for the world. They see the world as so corrupt that they do not believe it is possible for God's Kingdom to make any advancements in this world. They are simply trying to rescue people from a dark world that is spiraling downhill toward destruction. That way of thinking must change.[274] To embrace the gospel of the Kingdom is to embrace the authority and responsibility to establish the Kingdom on earth today.

Point 459: What Will the Kingdom on Earth Look Like?

As the Kingdom of God is expanded into the world, what will that look like? Righteousness, peace, and joy will reign. For the believer, the

---

274 This victorious and optimistic view of the future is explained in Volume VIII, *General Eschatology*.

The Kingdom of God

power of sin and death will be broken. Believers will not be enslaved to sin. Christians will walk in the fruit of the Spirit, including love, joy, peace, patience, kindness, and so forth (Gal. 5:22-23).

The King's will shall also be revealed in society as a whole. Systemic poverty and oppression will end. Racial tensions and class divisions will disappear. Corruption in government will cease, and justice will be accomplished for all. Isaiah 2:4 describes a world where Jesus reigns:

> *And He [Messiah] will judge between the nations,*
> *And will render decisions for many peoples;*
> *And they will hammer their swords into plowshares and*
>   *their spears into pruning hooks.*
> *Nation will not lift up sword against nation,*
> *And never again will they learn war.*

No more war. No more strife.

As people learn to govern their individual lives in accord with the King's will, business will be conducted in a win-win fashion, with businesspeople serving one another. The arts, entertainment, and media will glorify God. Children will be instructed in the truths of life and the ways of God. People will be free to exercise their gifts and talents for the benefit of society. As a result, society will make huge advancements in technology, medicine, agriculture, and every other area of human need. Food will be abundant. Medical workers will bring relief to millions. People will care for one another. Most importantly, *"the earth will be full of the knowledge of the Lord"* (Is. 11:6-9).

Volume VII
Ecclesiology & Basilology

Section D
Gospel of Salvation or Gospel of the Kingdom?

It is helpful to see how our understanding of the Church and Kingdom are related to our understanding of the gospel.

Point 460: The Orientation of Believer's Lives

In the preceding volume, we studied soteriology and saw how the gospel of salvation is associated with most of evangelical Christianity while the gospel of the Kingdom is what Jesus and His disciples preached.[275] Typically, Christians who only know the gospel of salvation do not understand the present reality of the Kingdom. Many adherents of the gospel of salvation equate the Kingdom of God with heaven, so they believe their only experience of the Kingdom will be after they die. Other adherents of the gospel of salvation believe God's Kingdom will only be available during a future millennium.[276] In contrast, Christians who understand the gospel of the Kingdom realize the Kingdom is available today.

Since most adherents of the gospel of salvation do not believe the Kingdom is available while they are alive, they tend to orient their spiritual lives around the Church—rather than the Kingdom of God. In contrast, Christians who are aware of the present reality of the Kingdom tend to orient their spiritual lives around the Kingdom.

---

275 The two versions of the gospel are discussed in VI:E.
276 This millennium is talked about in VIII:B-C.

Systematic Theology for the New Apostolic Reformation

Point 461: Commitment to Church versus Kingdom

Christians who orient their lives around the Church, endeavor to be good church members. Those who desire to be good Christians will endeavor to support their church and do what other good church members do. They will serve in the church, support the church financially, and help other people come to church.

In contrast, Christians who know the gospel of the Kingdom and desire to be good Christians may serve as members of a local church, but more importantly, they will endeavor to bring their lives into alignment with the King's will, which is particularly important to how they serve King Jesus outside of the local church.

This entails more than just trying to be model citizens. Kingdom-minded Christians endeavor to bring the will of Jesus into the realm of society where they have authority. For example, Christian business people try to bring the righteousness of Jesus to their business. Christian teachers who understand God's Kingdom try to establish the peace and joy of Jesus in their classrooms. Those in the arts and entertainment orient their work toward glorifying God. A Kingdom mindset includes an awareness of serving God in every area of society—that includes *outside* the church walls too.

Point 462: The Work of the Christian

Christians who only know the gospel of salvation tend to place all responsibility to accomplish God's work on the local church. In contrast, Christians who know the gospel of the Kingdom are more likely to see Christians accomplishing much for God as citizens of His Kingdom.

For example, Jesus gave the Great Commission, in which He told His disciples to go and make disciples of all nations. Christians who are only aware of the Church will conclude that it is the Church's job to fulfill this commission. On the other hand, Christians who know the gospel of the Kingdom are right to believe that the Great Commission should be fulfilled as a Kingdom task by going out into the world.

This opens a whole world of possibilities. For example, musicians may plan on sponsoring a concert that magnifies God before the city. Local carpenters and tradesmen may organize a program by which poor

Gospel of Salvation or Gospel of the Kingdom?

widows can have their residences repaired at little to no cost. Athletes may host an event for youth during which they testify of their commitment to Jesus. A group of businesspeople may get together and plan on how they can change laws, serve the poor, build a hospital, decrease crime, or impact their community in other ways.

A Kingdom mindset awakens God's people to how they can serve the King in innumerable ways outside of the local church. Of course, believers should desire and seek the blessing of the church, because the church has the keys to the Kingdom. However, Kingdom-minded Christians don't feel restricted to accomplish all of God's work through a local church.

When Christians embrace the responsibility to establish the will of King Jesus throughout society, the local church can focus more on its primary responsibility to host the presence of God and be a community for the saints.

Point 463: Equipping and Honoring the Saints

Christians who have yet to understand the gospel of the Kingdom tend to see people who serve God in the church as having greater significance than those who serve God outside the local church. But those Christians who know the gospel of the Kingdom recognize that people called to work outside the local church are just as *called of God* as those who work inside the church.

This sacred versus secular way of thinking is tied to the dualism which separates that which goes on inside the churches from that which goes on outside and then exults the "sacred" as more pleasing to God. Even if Christians are taught to avoid dualism, the feelings associated with dualistic thoughts linger. Those who only know the gospel of salvation have more difficulty escaping that dualism.

Dualism is also seen in how church leaders equip the saints for the work of service. Leaders who only know the gospel of salvation see their primary role as equipping their church members to serve in the local church. In contrast, church leaders who understand the gospel of the Kingdom see their role as primarily equipping the saints to work successfully outside of the local church.

This difference will be marked by how church leaders recognize and honor congregational members. Pastors who see church service as having

Systematic Theology for the New Apostolic Reformation

higher value than working outside of the local church will tend to honor those who faithfully serve in the church. They will even promote church workers by mentioning them from the pulpit and leading special services during which the congregation thanks and prays for church workers.

In contrast, church leaders committed to the gospel of the Kingdom will just as fervently honor, recognize, and pray for those who serve God outside of the local church.

Point 464: The Willingness of Christians to Labor

People's beliefs determine where their energy will be directed.

Christians who only know the gospel of salvation tend to be more committed to a local church than Christians who are Kingdom-minded. Of course, this is a generalization, but it is obvious enough to cause frustration in the lives of pastors who want to grow their churches. It is difficult to keep Kingdom-minded Christians committed to just one local church.

Christians who know the gospel of the Kingdom tend to be more desirous of unity among all of the churches in a region. Because they see God's Kingdom as bigger than the local churches and encompassing all of the churches, they more readily work toward bringing local churches together.

Point 465: The Social Gospel versus the Kingdom Gospel

The gospel of the Kingdom that we are explaining is sometimes associated with the *social gospel*, but that is a misunderstanding.

By **social gospel** we are referring to the message and value embraced by many Christians that the Church's primary role is to solve social problems such as poverty, hunger, poor education, alcoholism, crime, slums, war, and so forth. Many churches across the world have embraced the social gospel, but the label *social gospel* became especially popular with certain American churches in the late 1800s and early 1900s.

At the other end of the spectrum, American fundamentalism arose in the early 1900s, criticizing those who embraced the social gospel. American fundamentalist Christians preached that the Church's primary role must be leading individuals into a personal commitment to Jesus resulting in personal salvation.

Gospel of Salvation or Gospel of the Kingdom?

Proponents of the social gospel taught much about the Kingdom of God rather than the need for personal salvation. As a result, when informed people today hear others speaking about the Kingdom of God, they wonder if the social gospel is the message being preached.

Indeed, a person cannot embrace the gospel of the Kingdom without embracing the King's will to help the poor and disadvantaged. However, the gospel of the Kingdom is still calling for the personal salvation of every individual. Jesus is the only means to that salvation. Each person must acknowledge Jesus as Lord. Furthermore, the Kingdom of God is meant to penetrate all areas of society. The successful advancement of the Kingdom of God will not only help the poor and disadvantaged, but it will bring righteousness, peace, and joy to families, the workplace, entertainment, and all other areas of society. Therefore, it would be wrong to equate the gospel of the Kingdom with simply the social gospel.

Most importantly, the two should not be equated because the gospel of the Kingdom is still the *gospel*. This means it is good news. In particular, it is the good news concerning what God has done for humanity. Jesus came to save humanity. Salvation entails salvation from sin and the power of sin. Christians are forgiven. Jesus established a new covenant through which believers become one with God!

These elements of the good news are often lost in the social gospel. Rather than the message being one that brings the good news concerning what God has done, the social gospel focuses on the responsibilities Christians have to change society. In that message, the good news is often lost.

In contrast, when the gospel of the Kingdom is preached, a personal response is expected. People need to repent. Unless people are born again, they cannot see the Kingdom of God. Unless they are born of the Spirit, they cannot walk in the Kingdom of God.

Volume VII
Ecclesiology & Basilology

Volume VIII
General Eschatology

Eschatology refers to the study of last things, and it is typically broken into two categories: **general eschatology** (or simply, **eschatology**) and **personal eschatology**. General eschatology is the study of the major end time events that happen to the entire world, including the second coming of Jesus, the millennial reign, the final judgment, and the new heavens and earth. Personal eschatology is the study of events that happen to individuals as and after they die.

In this volume we will deal with general eschatology. In Volume IX we will study the personal aspects.

This area of theology has not been as profoundly influenced by ancient Greek philosophy as other areas of theology have been. The non-biblical influences upon our understanding of eschatology are of more recent development. In particular, we need to be aware of dispensationalism, which is a lens through which most evangelical Christians today study eschatology. I will be encouraging you to look at eschatology through a more progressive lens.[277] The distinctions between these two lenses will be explained in Section A.

In Section B, C, D, E, F, and G, we will study key Bible passages and see what conclusions we can draw concerning the Kingdom of God, the millennial reign of Jesus, the future of the Jews, the Tribulation, the rapture, Jesus' second coming, the marriage feast, the final judgment, the new heavens and earth, and other topics important in general eschatology.

---

277 When we talk about the progressive lens, we are not referring to any political, social, or economic points of view which tend to be liberal views. Our subject here is eschatology.

Volume VIII
General Eschatology

Section A
Dispensational or Progressive View?

Everyone reads the Bible through a specific lens. Here we will examine the dispensational lens which is predominant today in evangelical Christianity. Then we will modify that lens to a more progressive view which yields a more accurate understanding of the Bible.

Point 466: The Dispensational View

Dispensation means "time period." When Christians read the Bible through a dispensational lens, they divide the Bible, history, and future into distinct time periods. Teachers of dispensationalism begin each time period at the point at which God intervenes in history in a way that alters the course of civilization. Then they teach that God relates to humanity in different ways during the different dispensations.

Various dispensational teachers divide time into a different number of periods, but most often they envision seven dispensations. The first dispensation begins with creation and ends with the fall of Adam and Eve. The second begins with the fall and ends with Noah's flood. The third dispensation begins with the flood and ends with the time God made a covenant with Abraham. The fourth begins with Abraham's covenant and ends with the death of Jesus. The fifth begins with the death of Jesus and goes until the Second Coming. Other dispensations follow the Second Coming, and we will identify those as we continue.

Dispensational teachers have developed names for each of their dispensations. The two names that will help us in our discussion here are the Jewish Age and the Church Age. The Jewish Age goes from the time

Systematic Theology for the New Apostolic Reformation

God made a covenant with Abraham to the time the Jews rejected Jesus and had Him put to death. The Church Age goes from the death of Jesus to the return of Jesus.

The Dispensational View:
God Working in Distinct Time Periods

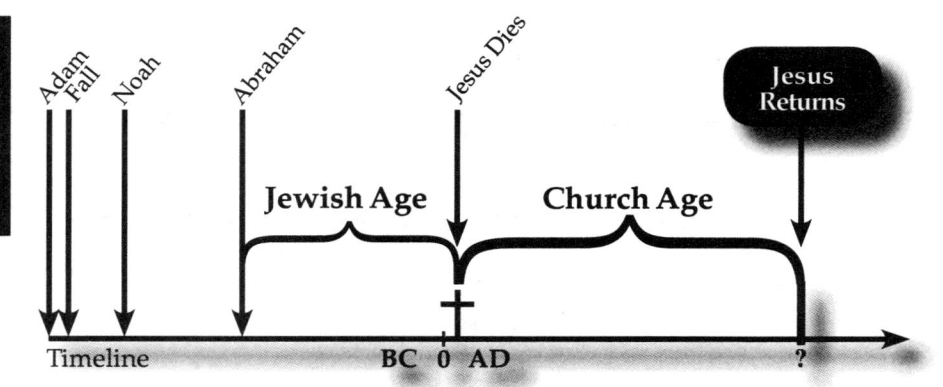

Timeline showing: Adam Fall, Noah, Abraham → Jewish Age → Jesus Dies (BC 0 AD) → Church Age → Jesus Returns (?)

The dispensational view was first seen in the writings of John Nelson Darby (1880-82) and the Plymouth Brethren movement. It was propagated through the Scofield Reference Bible (first published in 1909), which provided marginal notes that clearly marked where each dispensation began and ended. After World War II, the Scofield Reference Bible was used in many Bible colleges and became one of the most popular study Bibles in the Western world. Today dispensational thinking dominates evangelical thinking about eschatology.[278]

Point 467: The Progressive View

In contrast to the dispensational lens is the **progressive lens**. By progressive,[279] we are referring to how God gradually works out His will

---

[278] There are several possible variations on this dispensational view that we will not be discussing.

[279] When we talk about the progressive worldview, we are not referring to any political, social, or economic points of view which tend to be liberal views. Our subject here is eschatology.

Dispensational or Progressive View?

throughout history in a progressive fashion. Rather than seeing distinct blocks of time during which God relates to humanity in different ways, the progressive view sees God working throughout all of time with one ultimate goal in mind.

To see this, we must first determine where God is taking humanity and the world. What is His end goal? We have established the fact that God wants sons who are holy and blameless.[280] In Ephesians 1, where Paul stated this truth, he went on to explain that God does His work:

> ... *with a view to an administration suitable to the fullness of the times, that is, the summing up of all things in Christ, things in the heavens and things on the earth.*
>
> (Eph. 1:10)

A day will come when every knee bows and every tongue confesses Jesus as Lord. Then His will shall be done throughout all of creation and Jesus *"will come to have first place in everything"* (Col. 1:18).

God acts with His ultimate goal in mind. He intervenes, acts in history, guides, and influences the direction of the world toward the goal of bringing all things into submission to Jesus. Paul expressed this saying that God *"works all things after the counsel of His will"* (Eph. 1:11). Everything God does is *"with a view to . . . the summing up of all things in Christ"* (Eph. 1:10).

When God created Adam and Eve, He had His end goal in mind. After Adam and Eve sinned, God promised that He would send a Savior to crush the head of Satan, which fits into His overall plan. When God acted in the days of Noah, the world was moving in a direction contrary to His will, so He intervened with a flood. When God covenanted with Abraham, it was with a view of moving humanity more in the direction of the future day when all of humanity would bow to King Jesus. When God promised David that one of His descendants would build a Kingdom that would endure forever (1 Chron. 17:11-14), He was speaking of Jesus who would come and establish the Kingdom. When Jesus came into the world, it was according to the Father's plan to bring all things into submission to Jesus. Everything God has done throughout the last 2,000 years of Church history has also been for the purpose of bringing His ultimate will into fulfillment.

---

[280] Of course, this is a major theme of this entire book, and it was first laid out in I:A:1.

Systematic Theology for the New Apostolic Reformation

The Progressive View:
God Is Progressively Working Out His Will

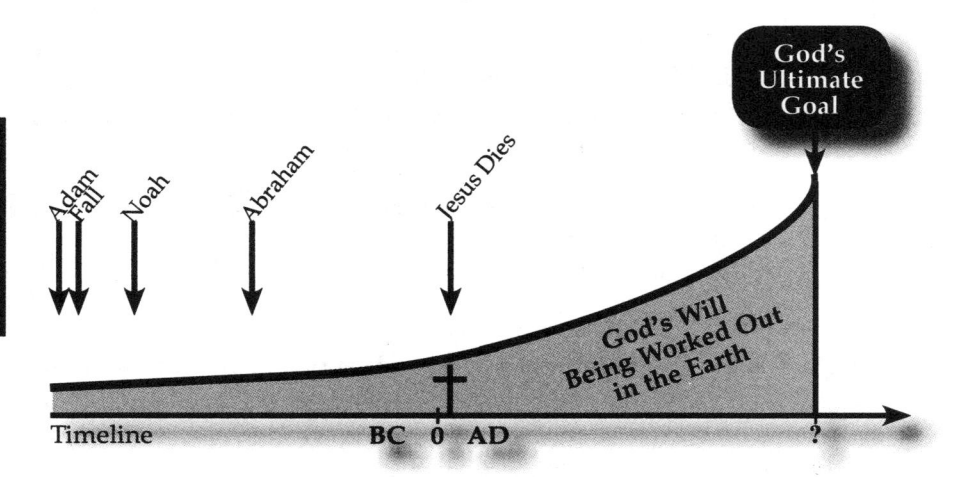

In the diagram above, I have shown the will of God growing in the earth in a progressive fashion, with growth accelerating the closer we approach the return of Jesus. This is in keeping with the parables Jesus told about the Kingdom growing like seeds in soil. Seeds multiply through generations rather than just adding. Therefore, they grow exponentially. Furthermore, the harvest at the end is the greatest.

Point 468: Dispensational Versus Progressive

An important distinctive of the progressive view is that it sees God always winning. In contrast, the dispensational view sees God enacting a different plan during each dispensation and more than one of His plans failed. For example, during the first dispensation, dispensationalists see that God commissioned Adam and Eve to subdue and fill the earth, however, Adam and Eve sinned so they will never fulfill God's commission. After the fall, God promised to send a Savior to crush Satan's head. According to dispensationalists, God enacted a second plan and a different way to relate to fallen humanity.

Dispensational or Progressive View?

In contrast, we discussed earlier how God's words to fill and subdue were a blessing, not just a commission.[281] With God's spoken words to fill and subdue, He released power to cause humanity to move in the direction of filling and subduing. That power is still at work today. Humanity's sin is never great enough to stop the power of God's word. So God's promise to send a Savior did not replace God's first way of relating to humanity. The promised Savior was step two, not plan two.

For another example, consider when God made a covenant with Abraham and promised to bless him and all of humanity through him. Dispensationalists see this as the start of the dispensation when God worked with the descendants of Abraham. However, dispensationalists know that the Jews rejected Jesus as the Messiah, and they see that rejection as the end of the dispensation of Jews and the start of the Church Age.[282]

In contrast, the progressive view recognizes that the Jewish rejection of Jesus is not strong enough to stop the power of God's blessing upon Abraham. The blessing of Abraham is passed to Jesus Christ and through Him every family on earth will be blessed. What happened after Jesus is not a different dispensation. It is another step forward in God's unfolding plan.

One implication of this distinction is that dispensationalists do not believe that the blessing of Abraham is upon Christians today. In contrast, Christians with a progressive view do believe that the blessing of Abraham is upon them. Not only the blessing of Abraham, but Christians also have the greater blessings of the new covenant.

With the progressive view, God's acts are cumulative. Nothing God does ever fails. His work goes on. It does not end with the end of a dispensation. With each act, God moves the world closer toward His ultimate goal of summing up all things in Christ.

Point 469: Where Is Evil in the Progressive View?

With the progressive view, it is helpful see the place of evil in the world. In Matthew 13:37-43, Jesus told a parable, explaining that His will is growing in the earth like seeds in the soil, but an enemy has also planted his evils seeds which are also growing in the earth. Both good and evil will continue growing until a future harvest day:

---

281 IV:C:202-204.
282 Most dispensationalists believe that the Jews will get another seven years of God's favor beginning at some future date.

Systematic Theology for the New Apostolic Reformation

Jesus explained that future harvest:

> . . . when the Son of Man will send forth His angels, and they will gather out of His kingdom all stumbling blocks and those who commit lawlessness, and will thrown them into the furnace of fire.
> (Matt. 13:41-42)

When Jesus returns with His angels, He will eliminate evil. Then He will fully manifest His Kingdom on earth. As Jesus said, *"the righteous will then shine like the sun in the Kingdom of their Father"* (Matt. 13:43). From then on, Jesus will reign with His people.

THE PROGRESSIVE VIEW WITH GOOD AND EVIL GROWING

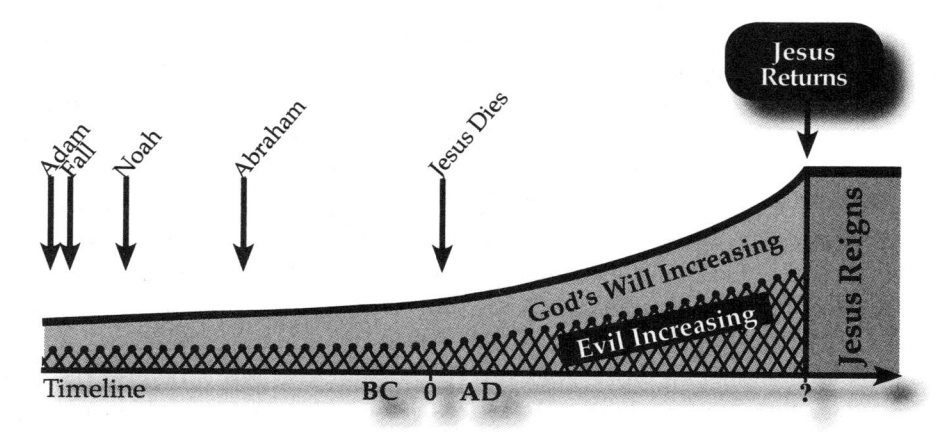

Point 470: Asking You to Be More Progressive

To this point, we have considered generalized descriptions of the dispensational and progressive views. Although I believe the progressive view offers a lens through which we can understand the Bible more accurately, it is not my intention to get you to completely abandon dispensational thought. I simply want to move you more in the direction of progressive thought. In some contexts, it is actually helpful to think in terms of dispensations. There are some truths (examples will be given later) that are more clearly revealed through that lens.

Section B
The Millennial Reign of Jesus

Now it will be helpful to identify the millennial reign of Jesus. Revelation chapter 20 is where the millennial reign is mentioned. There it is called the *millennium*, a word that simply means "1,000 years." Traditionally the millennium is understood in one of four different ways: **dispensational premillennialism, historic premillennialism, postmillennialism,** or **amillennialism.**

Before we describe these four views, it is helpful to know that the number 1,000 does not necessarily have to be understood literally. It can be, but Hebrew people in Bible times often understood the number 1,000 as referring to a large, indefinite number. For example, Psalm 50:10 tells us that God owns the cattle on 1,000 hills (Ps. 50:10), but this does not mean God only owns the cattle on exactly 1,000 hills; He owns all cattle everywhere. Similarly, the psalmist said that one day in the house of God is better than 1,000 elsewhere (Ps. 84:10); again we see the number 1,000 being used in a non-literal sense (cf. Ex. 20:6 ; Deut. 1:11 ; Ps. 68:17 ; 90:4). So in Hebrew thought, 1,000 years may be taken literally, it may refer to a great, but indefinite number of years, or it can even mean forever.

Point 471: The Dispensational Premillennial View

The view of the millennium most commonly held by evangelical Christians during the 20th century is called the **premillennial view** or simply **premillennialism**. The *pre* inserted before *millennial* means "before." In keeping with this, the premillennial view sees Jesus returning to the earth before the 1,000-year reign.

Systematic Theology for the New Apostolic Reformation

We already identified this view when we studied dispensationalism in the previous section. As we explained, dispensationalists envision Jesus ruling in heaven since He sat down on His throne about 30 AD. He will establish the Kingdom on earth when He returns. According to dispensational premillennialists, that future period of Jesus' reign on earth will be the millennium. Adherents consider that millennium to be the dispensation that follows the Church Age.

DISPENSATIONAL PREMILLENNIAL VIEW

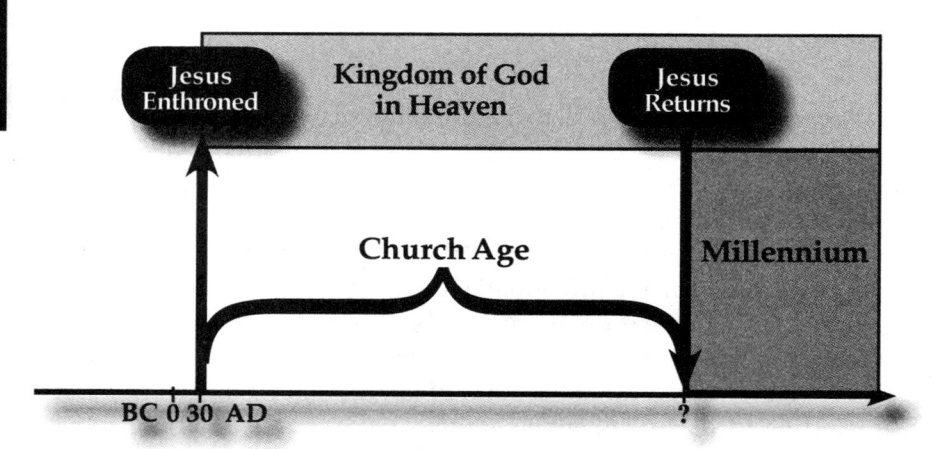

This **dispensational premillennial view** was the most predominant view among evangelical Christians during the latter half of the 20th century.

Point 472: The Historic Premillennial View

There is another form of premillennialism not associated with dispensational thinking. This second form is called **historic premillennialism.** It is referred to as historic because many leaders throughout history taught this view.

The difference between dispensational premillennialism and historic premillennialism is primarily that the historic version has no association with dispensational thinking. This distinction becomes important when

The Millennial Reign of Jesus

we talk about the rapture, Tribulation, future of the Jews, and other eschatological events. We will see later that dispensational thinking determines much of what Christians believe about these events.

It is helpful to think of historic premillennialism as the stripped down version of dispensational premillennialism. It agrees with dispensational premillennialism that Jesus will return to establish His Kingdom on earth, but historic premillennialism does not add on the other eschatological events (which we will discuss in coming pages) that are predetermined by dispensational thinking.

HISTORIC PREMILLENNIAL VIEW

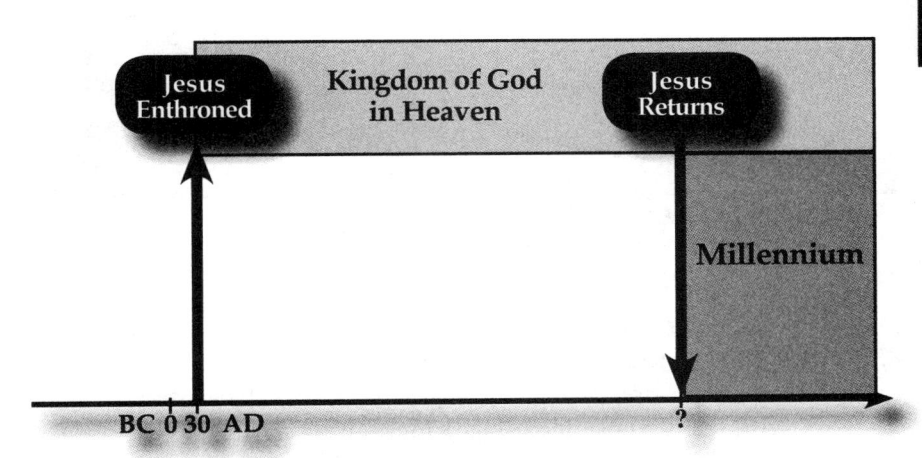

[Diagram: Timeline showing "Jesus Enthroned" at BC 0 30 AD, "Kingdom of God in Heaven" spanning the middle, "Jesus Returns" at a "?" point, with "Millennium" following.]

Some teachers of the premillennial views (dispensational or historic) believe the millennium will be exactly 1,000 years in length, while other teachers see it as a long indefinite length of time.

Point 473: The Postmillennial View

The next traditionally held view of the millennium is the **postmillennial view.** This view sees that Jesus will return after (post) the millennium. Postmillennialists believe the Kingdom of God has been here since Jesus sat down on His throne in 30 AD. Since that time, the Kingdom has been expanding. Postmillennialists typically believe that the successful

Systematic Theology for the New Apostolic Reformation

preaching of the gospel will usher in a golden age in which Christianity will be the predominant influence in the earth. That golden age will be the millennium.

POSTMILLENNIAL VIEW

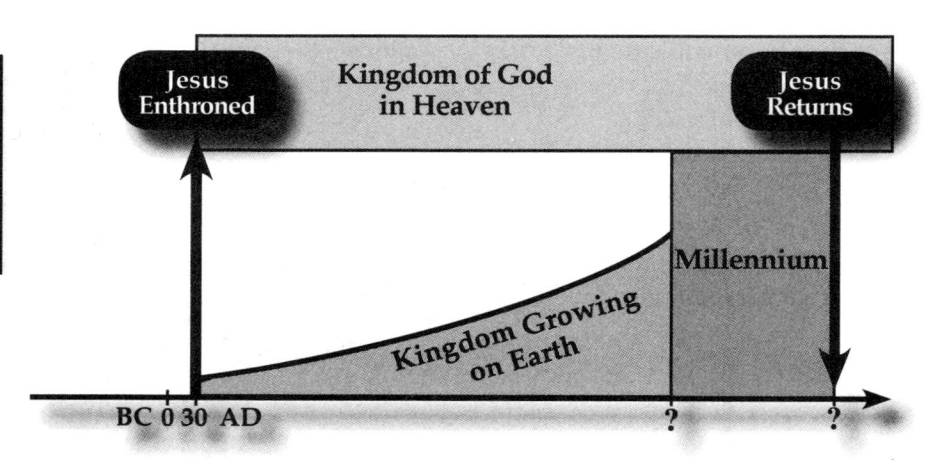

The postmillennial view was the most popular view among evangelical Christians during the 19th century. This had a positive impact upon society, because postmillennial Christians saw themselves as responsible to work with Jesus to establish His Kingdom on earth now before He returns. As fruit of this view, some of our major universities that were established during the 19th century have in their founding documents statements about being established for the furtherance of the Kingdom of God on earth. With that perspective, Christians were behind many great works including the building of hospitals and schools, along with active involvement with governments.

Point 474: The Amillennial View

The final commonly held view of the millennium is called the **amillennial view** or **amillennialism.** The prefix *a* means "no," so amillennial refers to no future millennium. Amillennialists believe that Jesus has been reigning since He ascended into heaven. However, most amillennialists think

The Millennial Reign of Jesus

of the reign of Jesus on earth as spiritual, and they believe the Church is the vehicle through which Jesus reigns. They typically equate the Church with the Kingdom of God on earth.

AMILLENNIAL VIEW

```
Jesus Enthroned | Kingdom of God in Heaven | Jesus Returns

Jesus Rules through His Church

BC 0 30 AD                                                  ?
```

The amillennial view was established in Western Christianity by Augustine in the 5th century. Today it is the dominant view of most liturgical, mainline denominations, such as Roman Catholic, Orthodox, Anglican, Lutheran, and Methodist.

Point 475: Choosing One of the Views of the Millennium

We have identified the four major views of the millennial reign of Jesus.

1. Dispensational premillennialism
2. Historic premillennialism
3. Postmillennialism
4. Amillennialism

Indeed, these four views identify one's understanding of the millennium, but in the next section we will see how important it is to arrive at one of these views by first developing a broad understanding of Scripture.

Volume VIII
General Eschatology

Section C
Kingdom Theology

Kingdom theology is another understanding of God's Kingdom and the millennial reign, but it deserves to be separated from the already mentioned, traditionally held understandings of the millennium. Rather than trying to choose one of the four (dispensational premillennialism, historic premillennialism, postmillennialism, or amillennialism), Kingdom theology offers a way to step back from the millennium talked about in Revelation 20 and then develop an understanding of the Kingdom before developing an understanding of the millennium.

It seems to me that this approach is most reasonable and helpful. It is difficult to start with the millennium in Revelation 20, because that is comparable to trying to fix a puzzle by beginning with pieces that should be inserted toward the completion of the puzzle. It would be better to start by building the frame of the puzzle, then fitting in the interior pieces (including the millennium) when the correct space appears. This is the approach that I embrace. Please let me explain . . .

Point 476: Expectations of the First Century Jews

In building a puzzle frame for understanding the Kingdom of God, it is helpful to know the historical context in which Jesus talked about the Kingdom. The Jews living in the time of Jesus commonly believed:

1. That a Messiah, born of the family of David, would come and establish a Kingdom.

2. That Messiah would conquer all enemies, which would usher in an age of worldwide peace and prosperity—known as the Messianic Age.

This was the most common understanding of Jews living in the 1st century. They were looking for a Messiah to come and usher in a Messianic Age.[283]

FIRST CENTURY EXPECTATION OF THE COMING MESSIAH

Messiah Enthroned on Earth

Kingdom Growing

Messianic Age: Peace & Prosperity on Earth

Into a Jewish population that held to these beliefs, Jesus came announcing that the Kingdom of God is at hand. The Jews would have understood this to mean that the Messiah had arrived and it was time for God to establish His Kingdom on earth.

Point 477: Jesus as King Over Heaven and Earth

The 1st century Jews were looking for a kingdom on earth. They were envisioning a kingdom in which they could reign over their enemies.

In contrast, Jesus explained that He was given authority over heaven and earth (Matt. 28:18). He sat down on His throne in heaven about 2,000 years ago. That enthronement established His Kingdom throughout heaven. Now it is being established on earth. Christians who read the Bible with a progressive view will conclude that the Kingdom is growing on earth like seeds growing in the soil.

---

283 Three of the many places which offer this understanding are:
B. *Talmud* Sanhedrin 98a;
Talmud Sanhedrin 97a;
Maimonides, *Commentary on Mishnah*, Sanhedrin 10:1.

Kingdom Theology

ADDING THE REVELATION OF JESUS RULING IN HEAVEN

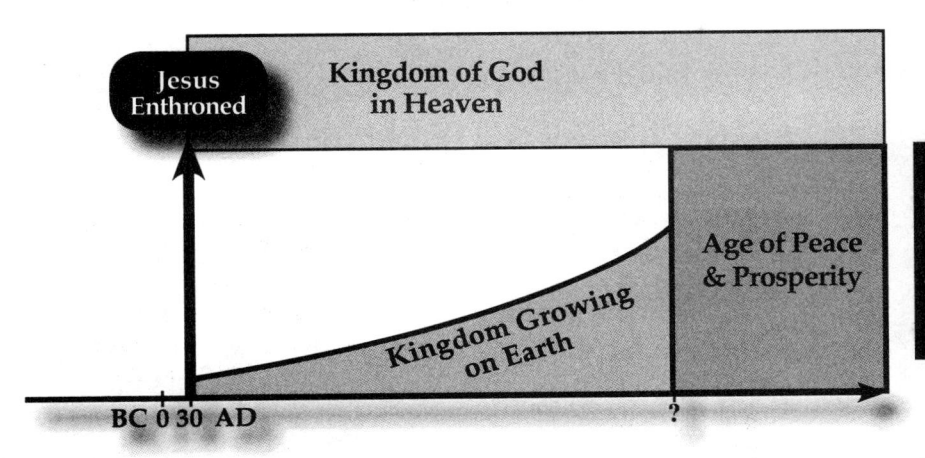

[Diagram: A timeline showing "Jesus Enthroned" at BC 0 / 30 AD, with "Kingdom of God in Heaven" above, "Kingdom Growing on Earth" as an upward curve, leading to an "Age of Peace & Prosperity" at a future point marked "?". Side label: "Volume VIII – General Eschatology"]

Indeed, the Kingdom has been growing for 2,000 years, but we also know that there will be a future day when the Kingdom of God will be fully manifested on earth. For this reason, Jesus also told His disciples to pray to the Father, "Your Kingdom come, Your will be done on earth as it is in heaven." This leads us to conclude that there will be a greater manifestation of the Kingdom on earth sometime in the future. There will come a day when the Kingdom does fully come, and the King's will shall be completely accomplished on earth as it is in heaven.

We have identified two Kingdom periods: the growing period and the Messianic Age of peace and prosperity.

Point 478: Kingdom Theology: Already and Not Yet

We have just explained the fundamentals of Kingdom theology.

With Kingdom theology, the growing period is often described with the principle of "already" and "not yet."[284] This means that the Kingdom is already available on earth for those who have faith, but it has not yet fully manifested for all.

---

[284] Typically a Princeton theologian, named Gerhardus Vos, is given credit for initiating this idea in the early 1900s.

Systematic Theology for the New Apostolic Reformation

All proponents of Kingdom theology hold to the already, but not yet principle. Concerning the Kingdom manifesting fully in the future, they vary on whether Jesus will return before (pre) or after (post) the millennium. In other words, Kingdom theology is compatible with historic premillennialism or postmillennialism.

KINGDOM THEOLOGY WITH HISTORIC PREMILLENNIALISM

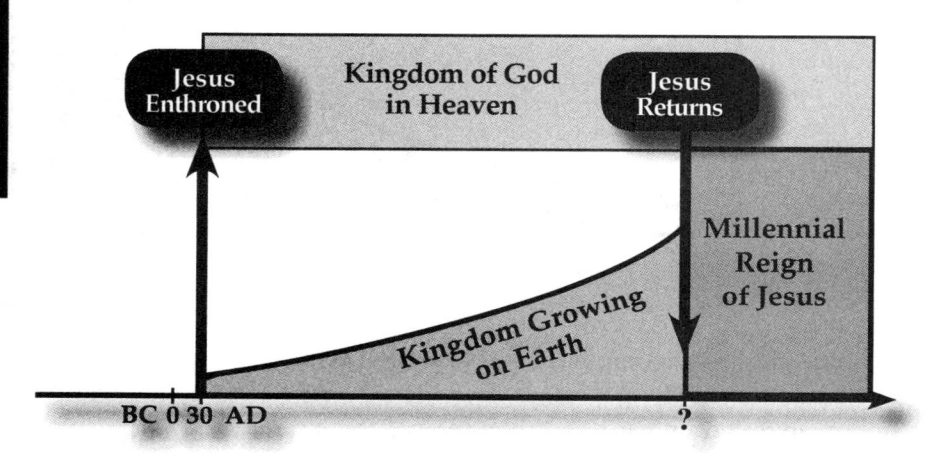

KINGDOM THEOLOGY WITH POSTMILLENNIALISM

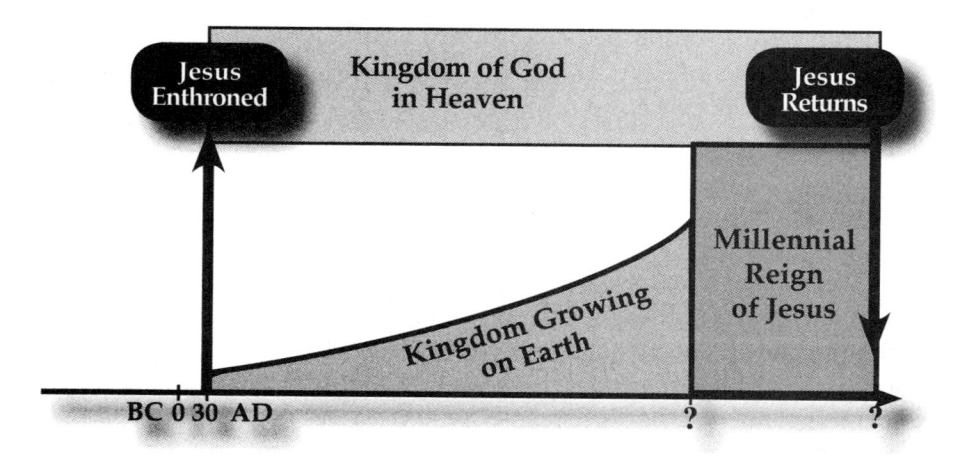

Kingdom Theology

Point 479: The Distinction of Kingdom Theology

How is Kingdom theology different from or similar to the traditionally held views of the millennium? Most importantly, it is a different approach to eschatology. It does not start by choosing a view of the millennium. Instead, it builds an understanding of the Kingdom, then fits in the millennial reign. It is also different in other ways.[285]

It is different from dispensational premillennialism because it does not break history and the future into distinct blocks of time. Unlike dispensationalism, proponents of Kingdom theology also say the Kingdom of God is available to believers on earth now.

Kingdom theology is different from amillennialism because it does not limit the present reign of Jesus through the Church, and it sees a future day when Jesus will fully reign on earth.

Kingdom theology is compatible with historic premillennialism so long as one adds the growing period during which the Kingdom is available to all who have faith now. Kingdom theology is also compatible with postmillennialism.

I hold to Kingdom theology with historic premillennialism, rather than postmillennialism, because I understand the Book of Revelation as reporting consecutive eschatological events. I see the events of chapter 20 (where the millennium is described) happening after the events of chapter 19 (where Jesus returns and celebrates the marriage feast). In contrast, postmillennialists see the millennium in chapter 20 overlapping the events of Revelation 4 through 19. I cannot find in the text any break that leads me to believe chapter 20 is a recapitulation of chapters 4 through 19. That seems to me to be a forced interpretation. Therefore, I favor historic premillennialism.

Among other leaders, Kingdom theology with historic premillennialism was taught by John Wimber, the founder of the Vineyard Churches. It has also been embraced by thousands of Charismatic churches and many leaders of the New Apostolic Reformation.[286]

---

285 By pointing this out, I do not mean to imply that the other views fail to take this perspective. They do, but Kingdom theology relies more upon an overall view of Scripture and could be developed without even considering the millennium.
286 The New Apostolic Reformation was explained in the foreword of this book. It refers to a major move within Christendom today, noted for the acceptance of the gifts of apostles and prophets functioning in the modern Church.

Systematic Theology for the New Apostolic Reformation

Point 480: Distinction of Dominion Theology

As explained, Kingdom theology can be summarized with the simple statement that the Kingdom is "already" and "not yet."

Some Christian leaders have added to Kingdom theology, and as a result, taken it another step. For example, **Dominion theology** is a form of Kingdom theology, however, adherents see themselves as ambassadors for the Kingdom with a mandate to take dominion of the earth (Gen. 1:28). The Great Commission is key in Dominion theology. Adherents want not only to convert individuals throughout the world but also to *"make disciples of all the nations"* (Matt. 28:19-20), in the sense of teaching national leaders how to govern and lead their nations into the ways of God.

Indeed, these are biblical goals, however, there is a characteristic of Dominion theology that often catches the attention of critics. It is evident in the label *Dominion,* which offers visions of a group of people in positions of authority dominating other people. Of course, this criticism is not warranted in all cases, but some vocal proponents of Dominion theology teach that Christians are to take dominion in all areas of society in the sense of fighting their way into positions of influence and then enforcing Kingdom principles from those positions. Such an aggressive posture is seen by critics as contrary to the Kingdom of God.

Proponents of Dominion theology will defend their position and often quote the King James Version of Genesis 1:28 for support:

> *And God blessed them, and God said unto them, Be fruitful, and multiply, and replenish the earth, and subdue it: and have <u>dominion</u> over the fish of the sea, and over the fowl of the air, and over every living thing that moveth upon the earth.*

Indeed, this verse tells us to have dominion so it can be understood as God's mandate to His people to take dominion of the earth.

However, Genesis 1:28 tells us to have dominion *over the animals* and not over people. It also delegates dominion to humanity by saying, "have dominion," rather than "take dominion." There is a difference.

Of course, some proponents of Dominion theology will have a difficult time with me pointing out this problem, because they are currently trying to change the image of Dominion theology and make it more acceptable. Indeed, some teachers are endeavoring to cultivate the proper attitudes of Christians reigning in the world with the right heart.

Kingdom Theology

When considering the right heart, we need to take into account Jesus' response to His two disciples who wanted to sit one at His right and the other at His left in His Kingdom. Jesus explained how His Kingdom operates differently than the kingdoms of this world in which people in authority lord it over others. Jesus explained that those who want to be great in the His Kingdom must become servants to all (Matt. 20:25-28). With this teaching, Jesus revealed the spirit in which ambassadors of His Kingdom should operate. Of course, positions of influence should be desired and sought after by Christians, because large numbers of people can be positively influenced from those positions. However, ambassadors of the Kingdom should be operating in a spirit of humility and service to others. With the proper attitude, Christians should be in decision-making positions, but they should also humbly help others see the benefits of doing their work in submission to King Jesus. So rather than Christians seeing themselves as the conquerers, it is better to envision Jesus as the Conqueror and His people bringing their lives and work in line with His will.

Personally, I can agree with Dominion theology in its goals and I will work whole-heartedly toward fulfilling those goals, but I pull my support when it is being taught with a conquering, oppressive spirit. When I see it being taught in the wrong spirit, I simply tell people that I believe in Kingdom theology without taking the next step to embrace or reject Dominion theology.

Point 481: Two Forms of Dominion Theology

There are two major forms of Dominion theology. The first is called **Reconstructionism,** which envisions Christianity taking dominion over society and governing according to the laws of God as given in the OT. Reconstructionism is most often associated with Reformed authors such as Rousas J. Rusdoony and Gary North.

The second form of Dominion theology is called **Kingdom Now theology**, which also sees Christianity taking dominion over society, but governing in a much less strict sense. Kingdom Now theology is most often embraced by Pentecostals and Charismatics and, in keeping with their theology, the future government is seen as more Holy Spirit guided. Earl Paulk is often considered the father of Kingdom Now theology.

Systematic Theology for the New Apostolic Reformation

Unfortunately, Paulk ended his ministry in disgrace, so most Christians today do not like to be associated with Kingdom Now theology.

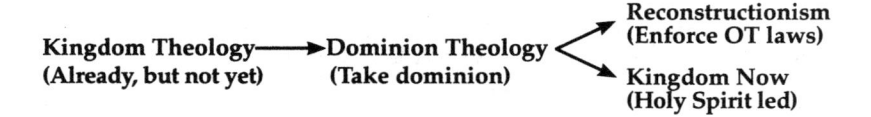

```
                                                    Reconstructionism
Kingdom Theology ──▶ Dominion Theology  ⟨           (Enforce OT laws)
(Already, but not yet)   (Take dominion)            Kingdom Now
                                                    (Holy Spirit led)
```

Informed readers may say that I am oversimplifying these views and, indeed, that would be correct. Proponents of each view have much to teach to present their own view in a more positive light.

Point 482: The God of the Kingdom

Kingdom theology emphasizes the role people can play in establishing God's Kingdom on earth. Of course, adherents believe that God will empower and guide His people, but a major theme of Kingdom theology is that people have a responsibility to establish God's will on earth.

This reflects back on our understanding of God and His involvement with this world. In Volume II, we discussed how Classical theology sees God in exhaustive control of this world, while Father-Son theology sees God as in charge but choosing to give humans some amount of free will.

The view of God associated with Father-Son theology corresponds with Kingdom theology. Jesus has all authority and can take control of anything He wants, however, He is not controlling everything at the present time. The Kingdom is growing. His will is increasing in the world, and there *"will be no end to the increase of His government or of peace"* (Is. 9:7). So Kingdom theology sees the level of God's control in the world as progressive and increasing.

This truth of the increasing Kingdom of God is a corollary doctrine to Kingdom theology. This means that if we teach someone about God's advancing Kingdom and they desire to remain consistent, sooner or later they will have to abandon the Classical/Reformed view of God being in exhaustive control. The Classical/Reformed view of God as being in control may fit with dispensational premillennialism or amillennialism, but if Christians are consistent with Kingdom theology, they will be led to embrace the cooperative understanding of God's relationship with humanity.

Section D
The Revelation of Daniel 9

Additional subjects related to eschatology include the future of the Jews, rapture, Tribulation, and Book of Revelation. One's conclusions about these subjects and others are determined by the lens through which a person reads the Bible. As explained in Section A, most Christians read the eschatological passages through the dispensational or progressive lens. In this section, we will consider Daniel chapter 9 through both of these lenses.

Point 483: The Revelation of Daniel Chapter 9

In Daniel 9 we read about Daniel praying for his people, the Jews, who were in captivity at that time. Their holy city, Jerusalem, was in ruins. Daniel knew that God would free His people from their bondage, for it had been promised through earlier prophets (Dan. 9:2). Daniel confessed the sins of his people and asked for mercy (Dan. 9:3-19). Then God sent the angel Gabriel to Daniel, and Gabriel told Daniel what would happen in the future.

The words Gabriel declared to Daniel revealed the future of the Jews and Jerusalem, along with some significant facts about the future of the whole world. However, Gabriel's words are understood differently by those who hold to dispensationalism in comparison with those who hold to a more progressive view.

Gabriel's declaration about the future began as follows:

> *Seventy weeks have been decreed for your people and your holy city, to finish the transgression, to make an end of sin, to make atonement*

Systematic Theology for the New Apostolic Reformation

for iniquity, to bring in everlasting righteousness, to seal up vision and prophecy and to anoint the most holy place.

(Dan. 9:24)

The angel revealed that the Jews and their holy city, Jerusalem, were to experience 70 weeks of God working with them, during which time the goals mentioned above were to be accomplished. Let's look at the 70 week time period, and then let's examine the goals.

Both dispensational and progressive Christians believe that God's promise of *"seventy weeks"* equals 490 years. This is because there are seven days in a week, and 70 times seven equals 490. A study of the prophetic language in OT times leads us to understand each prophetic day as a year (cf. Gen. 29:27 ; Lev. 25:8 ; Num. 14:34 ; Ez. 4:4-6); hence the Jews were promised 490 years of God's favor. Indeed, as we apply this period of time to the actual historical facts, it reveals some remarkable—obviously divine—predictions that are worth our attention.

As Gabriel went on speaking to Daniel, he divided the 490 years into three periods. First he talked about seven weeks (seven times seven, or 49 years), and then 62 weeks (62 times seven, or 434 years). Finally, he talked about the last week (seven years). Together these three periods total 490 years.

Consider Gabriel's decree concerning the first 69 weeks:

So you are to know and discern that from the issuing of a decree to restore and rebuild Jerusalem until Messiah the Prince there will be seven weeks and sixty-two weeks . . . .

(Dan. 9:25)

In this verse, Gabriel gave a precise time for the coming of the Messiah. He said that from the decree to rebuild Jerusalem until the Messiah, there would be seven weeks and 62 weeks, that is, 69 weeks or 483 years.

In 457 B.C., Artaxerxes, the king of Persia, decreed that the Jews were free to return to their homeland and rebuild Jerusalem and the temple (Ezra 7:12-26). If we add 483 years to that date, we come to the year 27 AD. This is the year when the course of history changed because Messiah Jesus was revealed.

The Revelation of Daniel 9

Most historians tell us that Jesus was born in 4 BC,[287] which means that He was 30 years old in 27 AD. That was the year in which Jesus was water baptized and a voice came out of heaven saying, *"This is My beloved Son, in whom I am well-pleased"* (Matt. 3:17). After a period of fasting in the wilderness, Jesus revealed Himself as the Messiah and began His public ministry (Luke 4:16-21).

DANIEL 9: FIRST 69 WEEKS UNTIL MESSIAH

```
Decree to          Jesus
Free the          Revealed
  Jews             27 AD


          69 Weeks
        = 483 Years


   457          BC  0 27 AD
```

Indeed, there were 483 years between the decree to rebuild Jerusalem and the revealing of the Messiah. Gabriel's prophecy was remarkably accurate and must have been inspired by God, seeing that it was given five and a half centuries before Jesus came into the world.[288]

Generally speaking, dispensational and progressive Christians agree on how to understand the first 69 weeks (483 years). It is the remaining one week (seven years) about which they disagree. They have different ways of understanding what has become known as "Daniel's Seventieth Week."

---

287 Historians know that Jesus was not born in the year 0 because Matthew 2 reveals that Jesus was born while Herod was alive and Herod died in 4 B.C. The confusion about dates is due to miscalculations made in the 6th century by Dionysius Exeguus, a monk who was commissioned by the pope to reform the Western calendar to center around the birth of Jesus.

288 The accuracy of this prediction is so remarkable that scholars questioning the trustworthiness of Scripture used to argue that the Book of Daniel must have been written after the prophesied events were fulfilled. The discovery of the Dead Sea scrolls between 1946 and 1956 proved that Daniel was written before the prophesied events were fulfilled.

Systematic Theology for the New Apostolic Reformation

Point 484: Dispensational View of Daniel's Seventieth Week

The angel Gabriel announced to Daniel that the Jews would have 70 weeks of God working among them to fulfill certain goals. We just discussed the first 69 weeks. Now we can look at the last week, which both dispensational and progressive Christians believe refers to a seven year period during which God promised to work with the Jews.

Dispensationalists believe that God has not yet given the Jews their last seven years, and, therefore, dispensationalists conclude that Daniel's seventieth week will have to come in the future. In contrast, Christians who read the Bible through a progressive lens believe Daniel's seventieth week already occurred, and, therefore, we are not still waiting for it to be fulfilled. Let's look at this more carefully.

Remember that dispensationalists break history and the future into distinct blocks of time. Therefore, it is easy for them to envision God working one way during one period and a different way during another period. As explained, dispensationalists identify the Jewish Age as the period from Abraham to the Jewish rejection of Jesus. Then they identify the Church Age as the period from Jesus' death to His Second Coming. Thinking in these distinct blocks of time, it is easy for dispensationalists to envision another block of time in the future when God will give the Jews their last seven years. In line with this, dispensationalists place that seven year period immediately after the Church Age.

DANIEL'S SEVENTIETH WEEK ACCORDING TO DISPENSATIONALISTS

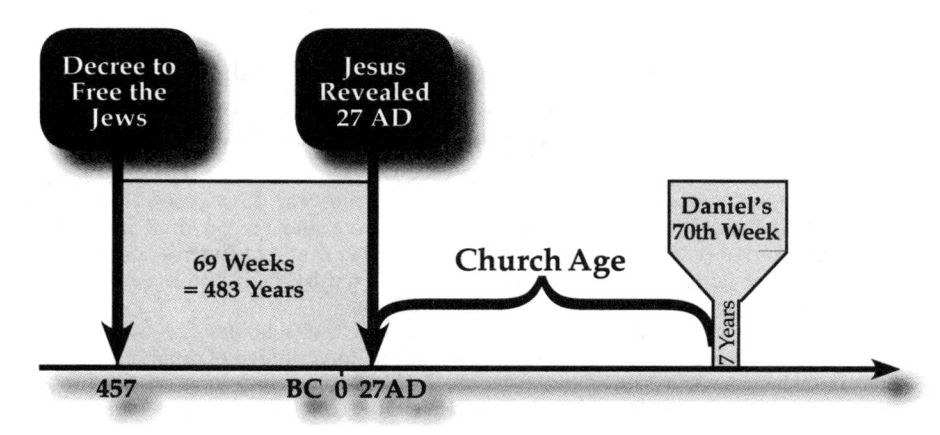

The Revelation of Daniel 9

Dispensationalists see a huge gap—2,000 years or more—between the 69 weeks and the seventieth week. They explain that in between those two periods God has been focusing on and dealing with the Gentiles during the Church Age, but at some point in the future, He will turn His attention back to the Jews and fulfill His promise to them.

Point 485: Progressive View of Daniel's Seventieth Week

Christians who read the Bible through a progressive lens conclude something very different about Daniel's seventieth week. Instead of inserting 2,000 years between the 69 weeks and the seventieth week, they see no gap. Teachers will explain that in Daniel 9, there is no gap stated or implied. The natural reading of Daniel 9 leads us to believe that the seventieth week follows immediately after the 69 weeks.

If Daniel's seventieth week began immediately after the 69 weeks, then it began in A.D. 27, the year Jesus was water baptized and began His public ministry.

DANIEL'S SEVENTIETH WEEK ACCORDING TO PROGRESSIVES

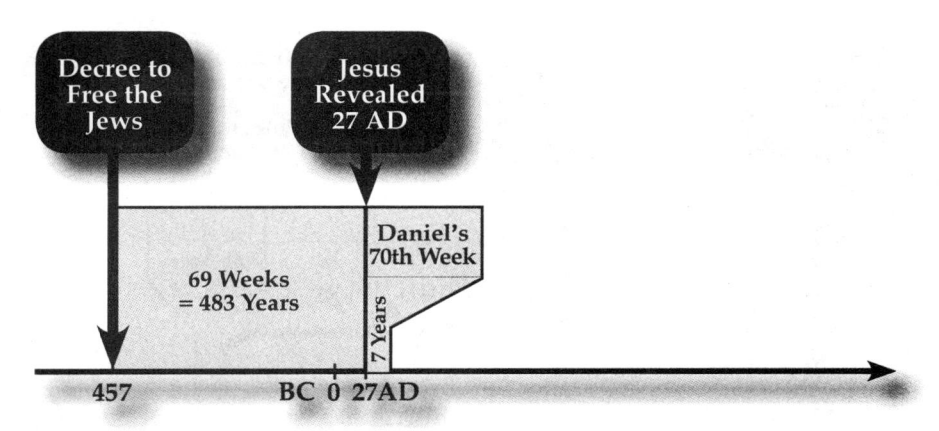

Most of our Church forefathers held to this view, seeing no gap between the 69 weeks and Daniel's seventieth week. In fact, seeing Daniel's seventieth week immediately after the 69 weeks has been the primary understanding of the historic Church.

Systematic Theology for the New Apostolic Reformation

Point 486: What Happens During Daniel's Seventieth Week?

What is supposed to happen during Daniel's seventieth week? Both dispensational and progressive Christians agree that the angel Gabriel answered this question in Daniel 9:27:

> *And he will make a firm covenant with the many for one week, but in the middle of the week he will put a stop to sacrifice and grain offering.*

Dispensationalists and progressive Christians *disagree* about the meaning of this verse.

Dispensational Christians understand that the pronoun "he" mentioned in Daniel 9:27 refers to the Antichrist who, at some point in the future, will make a covenant with the Jews, promising them peace and safety. But in the middle of Daniel's seventieth week—that is, three and a half years into it—the Antichrist will break his covenant, turn against the Jews, and put an end to their religious practice of offering sacrifices to God.

THE ANTICHRIST PUTS AN END TO SACRIFICES

[Timeline diagram showing:
- Decree to Free the Jews (457 BC)
- 69 Weeks = 483 Years
- Jesus Revealed 27 AD
- Church Age
- Daniel's 70th Week (7 Years)
- In the Middle of the Seven Years The Antichrist Puts an End to the Sacrifices]

As we explained, Christians who interpret Scripture through a progressive lens see Daniel's seventieth week as having taken place about 2,000 years ago. They also see the "he" spoken of in Daniel 9:27 as Jesus

The Revelation of Daniel 9

Christ, not the Antichrist. In the preceding two verses (Dan. 9:25, 26), the Messiah was the main subject, and therefore, it is most natural to conclude that the "he" referred to in verse 27 is the Messiah.

To see the fulfillment of this, first note that Jesus' public ministry was three and one half years in length. At the end of those three and one half years, Jesus gave up His life on a cross. On Passover, He shared the Last Supper with His disciples, during which time He took bread and said, *"This is My body,"* and then He took the cup and said, *"This cup is the new covenant in My blood"* (1 Cor. 11:24-25). After sharing that meal, Jesus fulfilled His words by dying on the cross. At that time, Jesus put an end to sacrifice and grain offerings. As the writer of Hebrews explained, Jesus made obsolete the Jewish religious system (Heb. 8:13). A new covenant was established, and the old system was abolished. Once the ultimate sacrifice had been made, there was no longer any need for further sacrifices (Heb. 8-9).

JESUS PUT AN END TO SACRIFICES

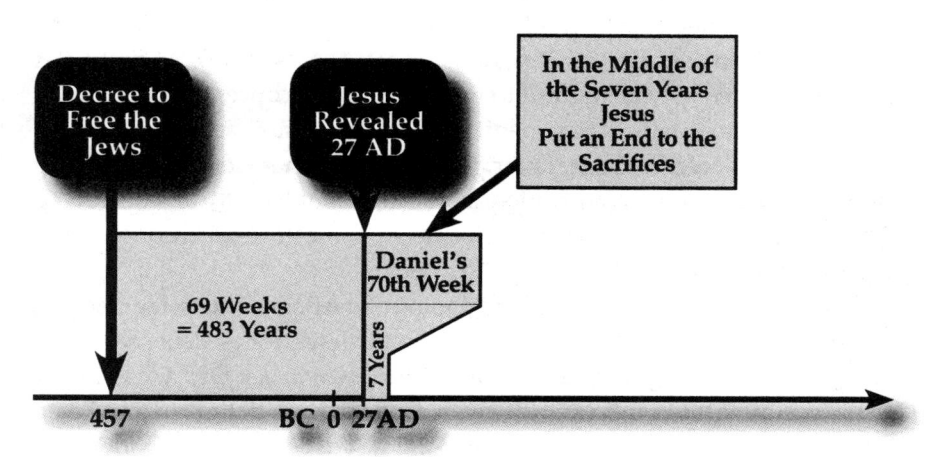

Notice how different this understanding is from the dispensationalists who are looking for the Antichrist to put an end to the Jewish blood sacrifices someday in our future. Christians who read the Bible through a progressive lens conclude that Jesus put an end to those sacrifices approximately 2,000 years ago.

That explains the first three and one half years of Daniel's seventieth week, but what about the last three and one half years? The Jews were

Systematic Theology for the New Apostolic Reformation

supposed to experience God working among them and the fulfillment of His promises during a seven year period. According to the progressive view, the Jews had the Messiah in their midst for the first three and one half years, but what about the three and one half years following the death of Jesus?

If we add three and one half years to the time when Jesus was crucified, we come to another historic event. Although the exact date cannot be proven, we know that three and one half years is very close to the time when Stephen was stoned to death (Acts 7:59-60). After Stephen gave a clear presentation concerning who Jesus was, the religious leaders rejected the Messiah. This event was especially significant because the high priest was among those who rejected our Lord (Acts 7:1).

Right after that, the focus of the apostles' ministry changed from the Jews to the Gentiles. In Acts 9:1-6, we read about Jesus revealing Himself in a blinding light to Paul; Jesus commissioned Paul to go and preach to the Gentiles (Acts 26:15-18). Then in Acts 10, we read about a vision that God gave to Peter in which all types of animals were presented to him. *"A voice came to him, 'Get up, Peter, kill and eat!'"* (Acts 10:13). At first Peter refused because he was faithful to the Jewish laws concerning abstaining from unclean animals. After meditating on the vision and witnessing a Gentile group receive God's favor, Peter realized that God was declaring that no longer were any people—including Gentiles—to be considered unclean (Acts 10:28). All were welcome to come to God through Jesus Christ (Acts 10:34-35).

What did all this mean? In the beginning of the Book of Acts, the disciples presented the truths of Jesus Christ only to the Jews, for as Paul said to the Jews, *"It was necessary that the word of God be spoken to you first"* (Acts 13:46). However, after three and one half years, God spoke to both Paul and Peter, telling them that now they were to present the gospel to all the world.

It is with this understanding that we see Daniel's seventieth week fulfilled. Beginning the day Jesus revealed Himself as the Messiah in A.D. 27, the Jews were given seven years: three and one half years during which Jesus walked among them, and then another three and one half years during which time the disciples preached the good news to them. In the middle of that seven year period, Jesus sacrificed His life which put an end to the Jewish sacrificial system.

The Revelation of Daniel 9

Point 487: Jesus Fulfilled Gabriel's Prophecy

It is important to realize how clearly Gabriel's words to Daniel were fulfilled 2,000 years ago. Gabriel said:

> *Seventy weeks have been decreed for your people and your holy city, to <u>finish the transgression</u>, to make an <u>end of sin</u>, to <u>make atonement for iniquity</u>, to <u>bring in everlasting righteousness</u>, to <u>seal up vision and prophecy</u> and to <u>anoint the most holy place</u>.*
> (Dan. 9:24)

These are the promises that Jesus fulfilled 2,000 years ago.

Consider the alternative explanation. Dispensationalists have to envision these things being completed during a seven year period in the future. How could the Jews "make atonement for iniquity" or "bring in everlasting righteousness?" They cannot because only Jesus is able to accomplish these things and He already did!

Point 488: The Future of the Jews?

The issues we are discussing raise questions about the future of the Jews. Dispensationalists envision the Jews as still having a special seven year period in the future. During those seven years, the Jews will have to *"make atonement for iniquity"* and *"anoint the most holy place"* (Dan. 9:24). To the dispensationalists, this means the Jews will have to rebuild the temple in Jerusalem and then reestablish the Levitical priesthood, along with the position of the high priest. This is because, in the Jewish religious system, the high priest is the only one who can make atonement and it must be done in the temple.

In contrast, Christians with a progressive understanding of Scripture believe Jesus has already accomplished those acts. Jesus is our High Priest, and He ascended into heaven where He is now in the very holy of holies. Jesus anointed that holy place. He made atonement for iniquity. Therefore, the Jews do not need to rebuild the temple in Jerusalem. Jesus already put an end to sacrifices and offerings. He has no intentions of restoring what He destroyed. He does not want anyone to approach Him through the Jewish religious system. Now, there is only one way to approach God, and it is through Jesus Christ.

Systematic Theology for the New Apostolic Reformation

Point 489: The Land Promise Made to Abraham

It is important to make a distinction between the Jewish religious system that was established through Moses and the covenant God made with Abraham. There was more than a 400-year separation in time between when these two were established. The religious system that was established through Moses was made obsolete as a result of Jesus dying on the cross (Heb. 8:13). However, the covenant God made with Abraham is an eternal covenant that can never be done away (Gen. 17:7-8).

God's eternal covenant with Abraham included the promise that his descendants would possess the Promised Land. Because that promise was part of an eternal covenant it cannot be broken. It is still valid today. However, how Bible-believing people envision the land promise being fulfilled is determined by whether they read the Bible through the dispensational lens or the progressive lens.

Recall how dispensationalists think in distinct blocks of time and they envision God working in a unique way during each dispensation. This also leads them to keep God's dealings with the Jews distinct and separate from His dealings with Christians. As a result, it is natural for dispensationalists to conclude that the promises God made to Abraham must be fulfilled in the lives of Abraham's natural descendants, the Jews.

Therefore, dispensational thinking leads one to believe that the majority of Jews around the world will migrate back to Israel for a future seven year period of God's blessings. Dispensationalists believe that once the Jews have taken possession of the Promised Land, God will raise Israel to be a leading nation in the world.

In contrast, Christians with a progressive understanding of Scripture see God working out His will in the earth with the ultimate goal of having a people for Himself and summing up all things in Jesus. Therefore, God does not have different plans for different groups of people. According to the progressive view, God has one plan He is working out throughout history and the future.

As a result, Christians with a progressive lens conclude that God will fulfill His promise to Abraham, but God is not obligated to fulfill the promise in the lives of the Jews. In fact, Paul explained that the Jews who rejected Jesus have been cut off from the promises made to Abraham and the other Jewish forefathers (Rom. 11:17-24). In Galatians 3, Paul went so far as to say that from the very beginning when God made the promises to

The Revelation of Daniel 9

Abraham, He always intended to fulfill them through Jesus Christ:

> *Now the promises were spoken to Abraham and to his seed. He does not say, "And to seeds," as referring to many, but rather to one, "And to his seed," that is, Christ.*
>
> (Gal. 3:16)

Here in Galatians 3, Paul further makes it clear that "*it is those who are of faith who are sons of Abraham*" (Gal. 3:7). Therefore, Christians are now the rightful inheritors of the promises made to Abraham. Paul also taught this in Romans 11, where he explained that believers in Jesus have been grafted into the family lineage of Abraham and the forefathers.

It is helpful to think again of the progressive view and envision how God works out His will throughout the ages. Nothing can stop the purposes of God. The Jewish rejection of Jesus was not strong enough to stop the fulfillment of what God has spoken. The Jews were cut off, but God will continue working out His will in the earth.

JEWS WERE CUT OFF FROM THE PROMISES BUT GOD CONTINUES WORKING TO FULFILL HIS WILL

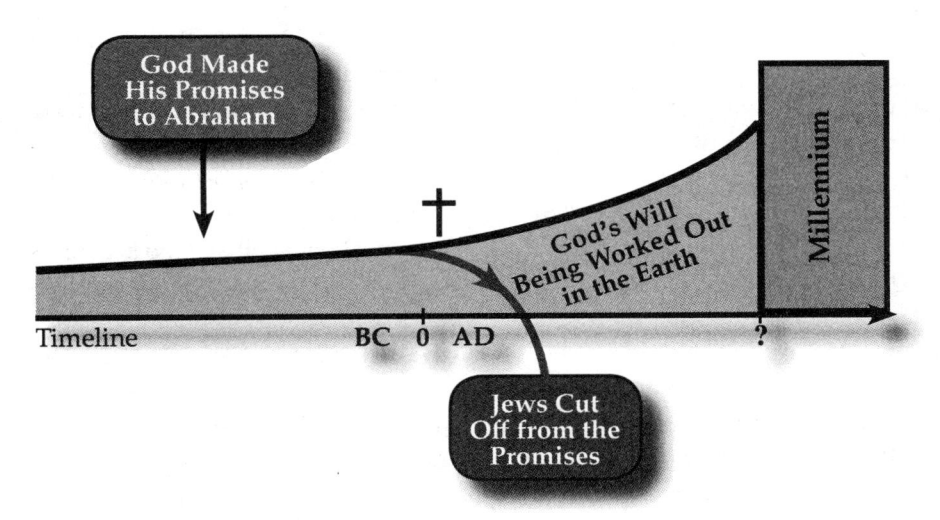

These truths are foundational in seeing what will happen in the future to Jerusalem and the Promised Land. God will fulfill His promises, but

Systematic Theology for the New Apostolic Reformation

He will do it through Jesus Christ and in the lives of all who believe in Him. At this point in our study we will not explain how the promises made to Abraham will be fulfilled, but it is enough to point out the vision the apostle John had of New Jerusalem coming out of heaven and onto the earth (Rev. 21-22). That New Jerusalem belongs to Jesus and all who believe in Him. Hence, we see the promises made to Abraham will be fulfilled through Jesus.

Point 490: Does God Have Only One Group?

Before we close this section and change our focus away from the Jews, it will be helpful to talk about how Christians should look at the Jews today. When Christians read the Bible only through the progressive lens, they may become too critical of the Jews as a people. Please let me explain.

Some Christians who are progressive in their understanding of Scripture tend to think in terms of God having only one group of people whom He is nurturing as His people at any one time. This vision of "one group" is developed in one of two ways.

The first way envisions God working with the Jews in the OT times, but because they rejected Jesus, God completely rejected them and replaced them with the followers of Jesus. So then, this view sees God only working with one group at time.

The second way in which the one-group vision is developed is by denying that God ever called the natural descendants of Abraham as His people. Instead, adherents of this view believe that God's people throughout the OT and NT have always been the *spiritual* descendants of Abraham, or in other words, those who have faith like Abraham.

Notice that the results of both of these one-group views is to see no special God-given value or role for the natural descendants of Abraham today. For this reason, critics often refer to such one-group views as **Replacement theology**. This terminology is used because the adherents of one-group views are seen as trying to replace the natural Jews in the sense of discarding them and inserting another group.

It is at this point that I must add a caution.

The Revelation of Daniel 9

Point 491: The Natural Descendants of Abraham

Earlier,[289] I explained how I believe that the progressive lens offers us the most accurate understanding of the whole Bible, but that does not mean we should completely reject all dispensational thinking. There are some truths to be learned by studying the Scripture with distinct blocks of time in mind.

Consider the following statements that correspond to the progressive and dispensational views:

> 1. Progressive statement: God does all things with the goal of summing up all things in Jesus.
>
> 2. Dispensational statement: God worked uniquely with the natural descendants of Abraham.

There is truth in both of these statements. Unfortunately, Christians who study the Bible exclusively through one lens or the other have difficulty in seeing the truth that may be revealed through the other lens.

God can do more than one thing at a time. He can work all things with the goal of raising a people and summing up all thing in Jesus. At the same time, God can work uniquely with the natural descendants of Abraham.

Let me repeat that I believe the progressive lens offers us the most accurate understanding of the whole Bible. However, any Christian who is not completely blinded by progressive thinking will still see God choosing and working with the natural descendants of Abraham throughout the OT. It was the natural descendants of Abraham who were delivered from slavery in Egypt, led through the wilderness for 40 years, and took possession of the Promised Land. It requires the rejection of much of the OT to believe that God never had the natural descendants of Abraham as His chosen people.

Similarly, we must look at the Jews during the NT period. It is true that most of the Jews rejected Jesus as the Messiah. As a consequence, they were cut off from the promises of God, but they could have never been cut off, if they were not first included in the promises of God. Indeed, the natural descendants of Abraham were chosen by God as His people.

So what happened when they rejected Jesus? Let's determine Paul's understanding by carefully examining his words on this subject.

---

[289] VIII:A.

Systematic Theology for the New Apostolic Reformation

Point 492: God Did Not Reject Those Who Rejected Jesus

Romans 11 is where Paul offered his most in-depth teaching on the relationship between God and the natural descendants of Abraham. In that chapter, Paul explained that most of the natural descendants of Abraham rejected Jesus (v. 15) and were cut off from the promises made to Abraham (vv. 17-19).

In order to grasp what Paul communicated, we must be careful to use the same terms that Paul used in the same way he used them:

(True) False 1. Most of the Jews rejected Jesus.

(True) False 2. The Jews who rejected Jesus were cut off from the promises of God made to Abraham.

When Christians read Paul explaining these two truths, they too often assume that God rejected the Jews because they rejected Jesus, but Paul was very clear that God did not reject them:

> *I say then, God has not rejected His people, has He? May it never be!*
> (Rom. 11:1)

Please note this, because it is a main point in Paul's teaching in Romans 11.

True (False) 3. God rejected the Jews who rejected Jesus.

To confirm that the Jews were cut off from the promises, but God did not reject the Jews, read Paul's explanation:

> *From the standpoint of the gospel they are <u>enemies</u> for your sake, but from the standpoint of <u>God's choice</u> they are beloved for the sake of the fathers.*
> (Rom. 11:28)

There is no doubt that in this verse Paul is talking about the natural descendants of Abraham who rejected Jesus. Paul even qualified his statement by referring to those Jews who are *"enemies of the gospel."* It is those enemies of the gospel who are still *"God's choice."* In the next verse, Paul said, *"for the gifts and calling of God are irrevocable,"* meaning that God

662

The Revelation of Daniel 9

did call the natural descendants of Abraham, and therefore, there is still a unique calling upon them.

Point 493: God Will Still Work Uniquely with the Jews

So what will be the future of the natural descendants of Abraham?

We know that they have been cut off from the promises made to Abraham, so God has no obligation to give them the Promised Land. We also know that Jesus made the Jewish religious system obsolete, so God does not want the Levitical priesthood reestablished or the temple in Jerusalem rebuilt.

However, God still sees them as His people because His calling is irrevocable. God will also treat them in a unique fashion because of their forefathers (11:28). What does this mean? The Bible does not clearly tell us, but our best indicator is Paul's heart for his people. Throughout Romans 11, Paul shared his passion for the Jews. He wrote about his desire to *"move to jealousy my fellow countrymen and save some of them"* (v. 14). Paul had God's heart for the natural descendants of Abraham.

Paul also talked about the possibility of the Jews being grafted back into the olive tree (vv. 23-24):

> *And they also, if they do not continue in their unbelief, will be grafted in, for God is able to graft them in again.*
>
> (Rom. 11:23)

The Jews will have to believe in Jesus into order to be grafted back in, but Paul talked about it being a natural fit: the natural branches being grafted into their own tree (v. 24). Paul talked about this as a real possibility, and even more, as his hope.

Paul's hope was in part based on God's future opening of the eyes of the Jews. Paul explained that God partially blinded their eyes so they could not understand who Jesus was, but there is a limit on how long that hardening will continue:

> *. . . a partial hardening has happened to Israel until the fullness of the Gentiles has come in.*
>
> (Rom. 11 25)

Systematic Theology for the New Apostolic Reformation

This implies that a day will come when the hardening will be removed. That day is after the fullness of Gentiles comes in. Then God will graft the Jews back into the promises.

JEWS WERE CUT OFF
BUT THEY WILL BE GRAFTED BACK INTO THE PROMISES

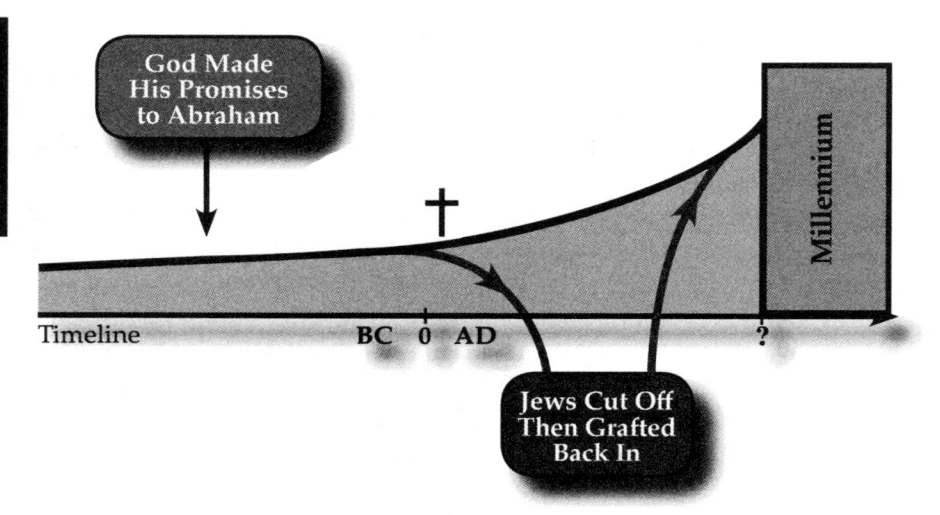

Further, Paul explained that the Jewish rejection of Jesus resulted in the salvation of the Gentiles, so how much greater will the Jewish acceptance of Jesus be? (vv. 12, 15). Notice how Paul had this great expectation for the people who rejected Jesus to accept Him at some point in the future. Furthermore, Paul implied that the Jewish acceptance of Jesus will result in some historic, world changing event that he referred to as *"life from the dead"* (v. 15).

No one really knows the future of the Jews. Paul said it is a *"mystery"* (v. 25). "Mystery" by definition means we do not know. However, Paul explained that the Gentiles were shown mercy even though they were once disobedient; so also the Jews will be shown mercy even though they have been disobedient (vv. 30-31). So, we do not know what the future of the natural descendants of Abraham will be, but we can be sure that God will give them mercy and open their eyes. This means something wonderful will happen with them.

The Revelation of Daniel 9

Point 494: Gentile Christians Honoring the Jews

Pertaining to the Jews, what is the most important lesson for Christians today? Christians need to maintain the proper attitude toward the Jews. Paul cautioned Gentile Christians not to be arrogant toward them (v. 18). We should also hold them in honor.

This is contrary to the view of some Christians who look at Scripture only through the progressive lens. They hold to the one-group vision and see the Jews as rejected from that one group. As a consequence, they see the Jews just like every other group of non-Christians in the world. According to them, there is nothing special about the Jews as a people.

In reality, there is something special about the natural descendants of Abraham. God worked among their forefathers for more than 1,000 years, developing a culture distinct from and more godly than that of the people groups around them. Paul commented on the distinct culture of the Jews referring to it as a cultivated olive tree in comparison to the Gentiles being a wild olive tree (vv. 17-24). Further, Paul compared the natural descendants of Abraham to the Gentiles, saying:

> *We are Jews by nature and not sinners from among the Gentiles.*
> (Gal. 2:15)

Notice that Paul was talking about the Jews of his day and, in particular, the Jews who had rejected Jesus as Savior. Those Jews were the cultivated olive tree distinct from the Gentile sinners.

This means Jews are not just like every other group of people. They do have a rich heritage like no other group of people. Plus, they are beloved for the sake of the fathers.[290]

---

[290] It is questionable if we should include all Jews in this since today there are some who are Orthodox, some Reformed, and others atheists.

Volume VIII
General Eschatology

Section E
Futurism, Partial Preterism, or Full Preterism?

Now we will talk about when some key eschatological events happen or happened in relation to the destruction of Jerusalem in 70 AD. It is difficult to over-emphasize the significance of that destruction. In 70 AD, approximately 20,000 Roman soldiers surrounded Jerusalem and cut off all supplies of food for four months so the city inhabitants would starve. Then the soldiers came into the city and mercilessly killed more than one million Jews. When the soldiers entered the temple, they slit the throats of over 2,000 Jews and then set the building on fire. Only 97,000 Jews survived that holocaust, and they were led away as captives to serve as slaves.[291]

The destruction of Jerusalem marks a turning point in history. How we understand that turning point determines much of what we believe about the Tribulation and the Book of Revelation.

Point 495: The Three Views

There are three commonly accepted views that are significant in this discussion: futurism, partial preterism, and full preterism.

In distinguishing between these three views, Bible teachers usually refer to the end time prophecies recorded in Matthew 24 and the Book of Revelation. Of course, there are many other Bible passages that talk about end time events, but Matthew 24 and the Book of Revelation are especially revealing. Revelation is the book where Jesus revealed the future to John. Matthew 24 is relevant because in verse 3 of that chapter, the disciples asked Jesus:

---

291 Flavius Josephus, *Josephus: The Complete Works*. Translated by William Whiston (Nashville, TN: Thomas Nelson Publishers, 1998), *The Wars of the Jews*, vi:ix:3.

Systematic Theology for the New Apostolic Reformation

Tell us, when will these things happen, and what will be the sign of Your coming, and of the end of the age?

When Jesus answered the disciple's questions in the rest of Matthew 24, He talked about false leaders claiming to be Christ, wars, famines, earthquakes, persecutions, tribulation, destruction, and so forth. The timing as to when those events are fulfilled is understood differently by futurists, partial preterists, and full preterists.

Point 496: The Futurist View

The most common view among modern evangelical Christians is the **futurist view**. It is referred to as the futurist view because adherents believe all of the end time events talked about in the Bible will happen at some undetermined date in the future. Those events may happen in our lifetime or during some generation that comes after us. Among those events are the rapture, Great Tribulation, Second Coming of Jesus, marriage feast, millennial reign, resurrection of the dead, Great White Throne Judgment, and creation of the new heavens and earth. Futurists are looking for the Book of Revelation and Matthew 24 to be fulfilled in the future.

Dispensationalists are futurists.

FUTURIST VIEW

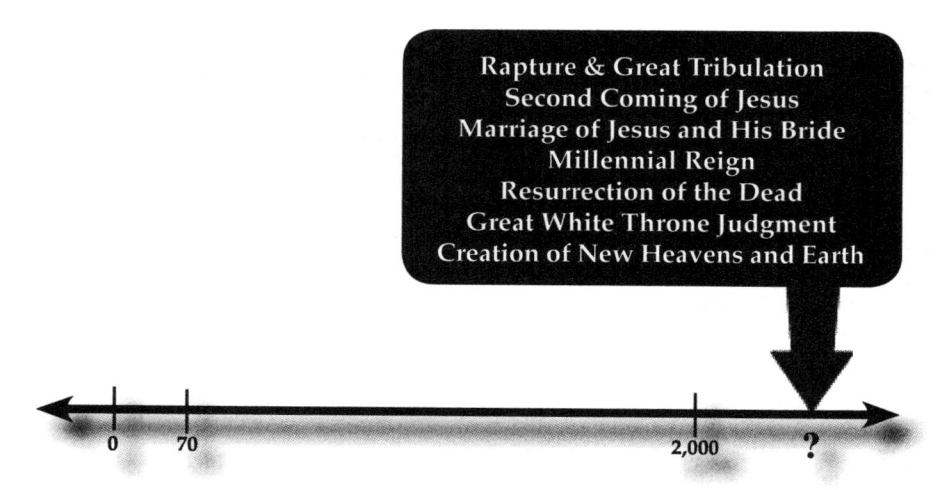

Rapture & Great Tribulation
Second Coming of Jesus
Marriage of Jesus and His Bride
Millennial Reign
Resurrection of the Dead
Great White Throne Judgment
Creation of New Heavens and Earth

0 — 70 — — — 2,000 — ?

Futurism, Partial Preterism, or Full Preterism?

Teachers of futurism are so prevalent on Christian radio and television today that most Christians who hold to futurism have never heard the alternative views of partial preterism and full preterism.

Point 497: The Partial Preterist View

The opposite of futurism is **preterism** (from the Latin *praeteritus*, meaning "gone by" or "past"). **Full preterists** believe all end time events recorded in the Bible happened in the past, while **partial preterists** believe that part of the end time prophecies were fulfilled in the past and part remain to be fulfilled in the future.

Let's look at the partial preterist view, which is the view I hold.

In order to understand the partial preterist view, it is helpful to reread Matthew 24:3, where the disciples questioned Jesus:

> *Tell us, when will these things happen, and what will be the sign of Your coming, and of the end of the age?*

Christians who hold to the futurist view read this verse and conclude that the disciples were asking Jesus about the events that will happen before the end of the world. Therefore, futurists read the rest of Matthew 24, thinking that Jesus was answering their question about when the end of the world will be.

In contrast, partial preterists read what the disciples asked in Matthew 24:3 and note that the disciples asked three questions, not just one:

1. *"When will these things happen?"*
2. *"What will be the sign of Your coming?"*
3. *"What will be the sign of the end of the age?"*

Partial preterists believe that Jesus answered each of these questions, one at a time, in the rest of Matthew 24.

The first question is, *"When will these things happen?"* Partial preterists point out that before we look at the answer to this question, it is important that we determine what "these things" are about which the disciples were asking. To make this determination, we must read the verses preceding the question.

Systematic Theology for the New Apostolic Reformation

Throughout Matthew 23, we see Jesus rebuking the Jewish religious leaders. Jesus ended His harsh set of rebukes declaring that judgment would come upon them (v. 35). Jesus declared that Jerusalem and the temple will be destroyed (vv. 37-38), and He said that the temple will be so completely demolished that not one stone will be left upon another (v. 2).

It was immediately after that pronouncement of judgment, i.e., the very next verse, that the disciples asked Jesus, *"When will these things happen?"* Therefore, adherents of partial preterism believe that when the disciples asked the first question, they were asking about when the destruction of Jerusalem and the temple would happen. Please do not misunderstand. Partial preterists recognize that the disciples asked two other questions, and Jesus also answered those questions in Matthew 24. However, the first question is not about the end of the world. It is about when Jerusalem and the temple will be destroyed.

Jesus said the destruction would happen within one generation:

> *Truly I say to you, all these things will come upon this generation.*
> (Matt. 23:36)

If we take these words of Jesus literally (which partial preterists do), we would expect that judgment to have happened by 70 AD, since Jesus made the pronouncement in 30 AD and a generation in Bible times was considered 40 years long.[292]

Indeed, the 70 AD destruction of Jerusalem and the temple happened exactly as Jesus declared that it would. As noted earlier, 20,000 Roman soldiers killed more than one million Jews and burned the temple in Jerusalem. The Jewish population was decimated. It was not until 130–135 AD that the Jews reassembled with enough strength to attempt one last rebellion against the Roman Empire. Then after three years of battling, the Romans were able to crush that rebellion, killing 580,000 more Jews, and Israel was no longer recognized as a nation (for the next 1,913 years, until 1948). It was also at that time that the Roman commander ordered the temple in Jerusalem to be demolished so completely that each and every stone was carried away and the land upon which the temple had stood was plowed over—exactly as Jesus prophesied!

Knowing these historical facts, partial preterists believe that the first question that the disciples asked in Matthew 24:3 was not about the end of

---

[292] For example, the Hebrews wandered in the desert for 40 years until a generation passed.

Futurism, Partial Preterism, or Full Preterism?

the world, but it was about the destruction of 70 AD. Jesus answered that first question in Matthew 24:5-28, where He talked about leaders claiming to be Christ (v. 5), wars (v. 5), famines and earthquakes (v. 7), tribulations and persecutions (vv. 9-13), and so forth. Therefore, partial preterists believe the events talked about in these verses preceded the destruction of Jerusalem in 70 AD.

This can be very surprising to futurist Christians who have never heard this explanation before. They have only been exposed to the views of other futurists who often talk about a coming Great Tribulation, preceded by wars, famines, and earthquakes. Yet, most of the historic Church before the 20th century understood Matthew 24:5-28 to be talking about events that took place during the 1st century. (For a full discussion about this partial preterist view, see a book I coauthored with Pastor Martin Trench, entitled *Victorious Eschatology*.)

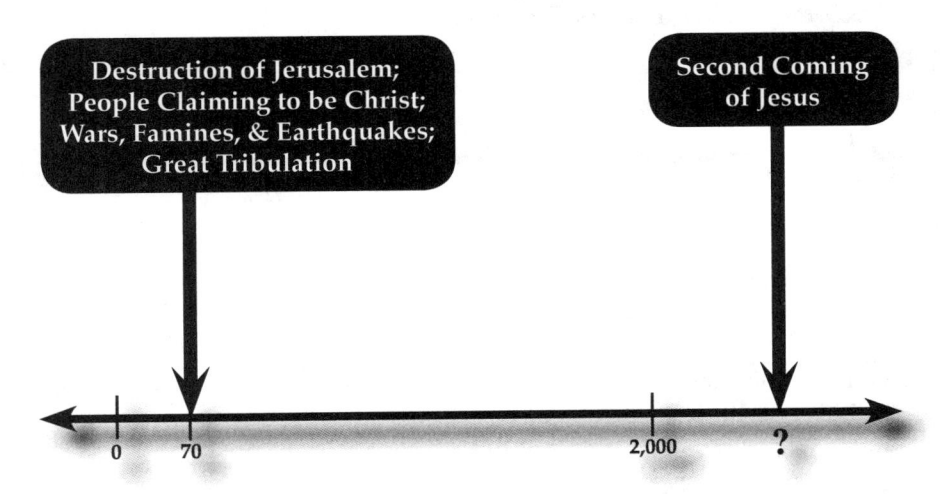

Concerning the second and third questions that the disciples asked Jesus, partial preterists have differing views. We will discuss those views shortly, but now we can point out what partial preterists hold in common. They believe the first question in Matthew 24:3 is about the destruction of 70 AD. Therefore, they believe the wars (v. 5), famines and earthquakes (v. 7), tribulations and persecutions (vv. 9-13) prophesied by Jesus occurred by 70 AD, but other prophesied events will happen in the future. Among other events that will happen in the future is the Second Coming of Jesus.

THE PARTIAL PRETERIST VIEW

Destruction of Jerusalem; People Claiming to be Christ; Wars, Famines, & Earthquakes; Great Tribulation → 70

Second Coming of Jesus → ?

0 — 70 — 2,000 — ?

Systematic Theology for the New Apostolic Reformation

Point 498: The Full Preterist View[293]

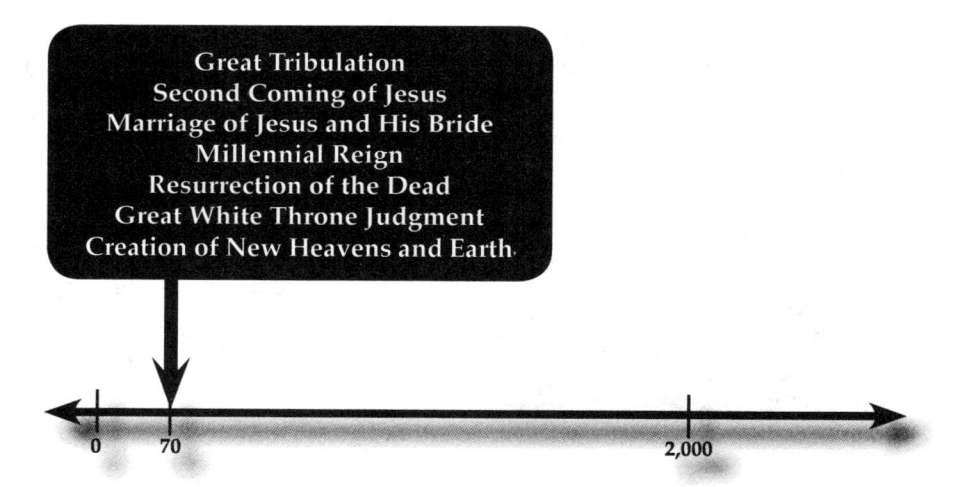

Teachers who hold to **full preterism** say that all three questions that the disciples asked Jesus in Matthew 24:3 are about the events that took place by 70 AD.[294] Therefore, full preterists believe that all of the events Jesus talked about in Matthew 24 happened in the 1st century.

Full preterists also believe the events talked about throughout the Book of Revelation happened by 70 AD. They believe the judgments poured out in Revelation were the judgments of God against the Jews in the 1st century.

In keeping with this view, full preterists believe the Great Tribulation, the Second Coming of Jesus, the marriage feast, the millennial reign, the resurrection of the dead, the Great White Throne Judgment, and the creation of the new heaven and earth have all taken place.

FULL PRETERIST VIEW

Great Tribulation
Second Coming of Jesus
Marriage of Jesus and His Bride
Millennial Reign
Resurrection of the Dead
Great White Throne Judgment
Creation of New Heavens and Earth

0 — 70 — 2,000

Although I am accurately explaining the full preterist's view, adherents would say that I am not offering a thorough enough discussion to make

---

293 Full preterism is also called consistent preterism, fulfilled eschatology, or covenant eschatology.
294 Some partial preterists see all three questions as pertaining to the destruction of 70 AD, but they are still considered partial because they see part of the book of Revelation to be fulfilled in the future.

Futurism, Partial Preterism, or Full Preterism?

their view seem reasonable. They would be correct in making that judgment. In a systematic theology, which is meant to offer an overview of different theological views, I cannot develop each position fully. Also, I do not want to give the full preterist view more credence, because I believe it is contrary to the biblical revelation—in particular, denying the future return of Jesus to earth. Those interested in further study on the subject can avail themselves of the many books that have been written by full preterists.[295]

Although I strongly disagree with the full preterist view, I can commend full preterists for making the modern Church more aware of the catastrophic events that took place in 70 AD. The destruction of Jerusalem and the temple marked the end of the Jewish religious system. God no longer wanted anyone to approach Him through priests or the sacrificing of animals. We have a new High Priest who has made the ultimate and final sacrifice!

Point 499: Variations on the Partial Preterist View

As I explained, partial preterists believe that part of the end time prophesies happened in the past and part will happen in the future. Unfortunately, the label "partial" does not specify what parts happened in the past and what parts will happen in the future. Therefore, Christians interested in eschatology sometimes make a finer distinction between two types of partial preterism: **historical preterism** and **modern preterism**.

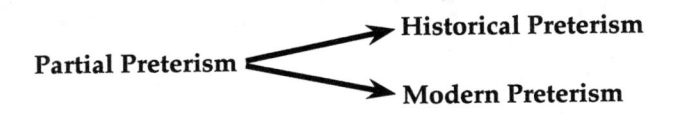

```
                              ➤ Historical Preterism
        Partial Preterism ⟨
                              ➤ Modern Preterism
```

Historical preterism sees the Book of Revelation being fulfilled over the course of history. More specifically, the judgments described in Revelation chapters 4 through 18 began in the 1st century after Jesus sat down on His throne; then those judgments are spread out over the course of history, which covers at least the last 2,000 years.

---

[295] Those interested in understanding the difference between partial preterism and full preterism can see my book, entitled, *The Comings of Christ*.

Systematic Theology for the New Apostolic Reformation

This historical preterist view was held by all of the major leaders during the Protestant Reformation, including Luther, Knox, Calvin, and Huss. Another well-known historical preterist was Charles Spurgeon.

The other form of partial preterism, often referred to as **modern preterism**, has been of more recent development. Adherents teach that the events of Revelation 1-18 happened by 70 AD, but some of the events in Revelation 19-22 will happen in the future. Among those holding to modern preterism are such noted authors as N. T. Wright, David Chilton, Gary DeMar, and Jonathan Welton.

I hold to the partial preterist view called historical preterism. I see some end time events (including the Great Tribulation) were fulfilled by 70 AD, but many of the events foretold in the Book of Revelation will happen in our future.[296]

The Partial Preterist View Called Historical Preterism

Destruction of Jerusalem
People Claiming to be Christ
Wars, Famines, & Earthquakes
Great Tribulation

↓ (70)

Second Coming of Jesus
Marriage of Jesus and His Bride
Millennial Reign
Resurrection of the Dead
Great White Throne Judgment
Creation of New Heavens and Earth

↓ (2,000 ?)

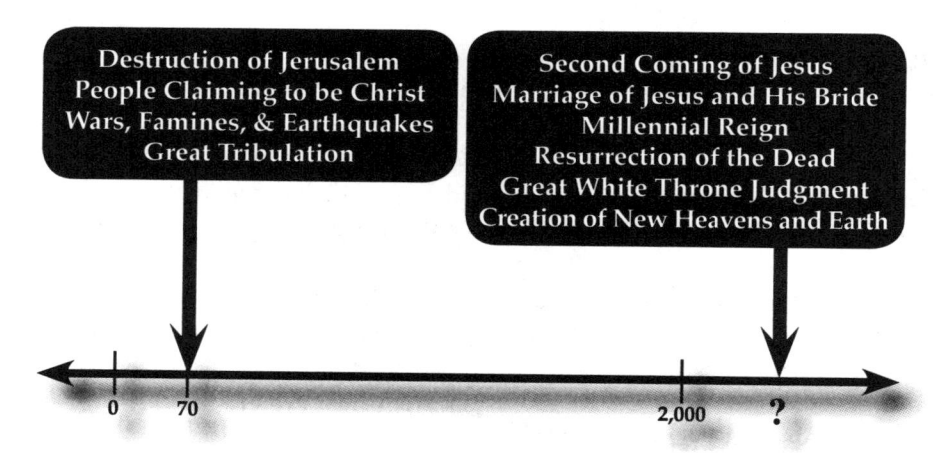

[296] For a thorough explanation of this view, see a book I coauthored with Pastor Martin Trench entitled *Victorious Eschatology*.

Section F
The Book of Revelation

In the previous section we identified the three views that identify when the major eschatological events happen with respect to the destruction of Jerusalem in 70 AD, i.e., futurism, partial preterism, and full preterism. We also saw the two forms of partial preterism: historical preterism and modern preterism. Whichever of these views Christians hold will determine how they understand the Book of Revelation. This will become clear in this section.

Point 500: Futurist's Understanding of Revelation 4:1-2:

Futurists, partial preterists, and full preterists generally agree concerning the meaning of the first three chapters of the Book of Revelation. Chapter 1 is an introduction, along with the account of Jesus' appearance to John. Chapters 2 and 3 record seven letters to seven churches that existed when the Book of Revelation was written.[297]

Generally speaking, futurists, partial preterists, and full preterists also agree that chapters 4 through 18 in Revelation describe a series of terrible judgments with their accompanying destruction. However, they disagree as to *when* those judgments recorded in Revelation 4 through 18 take place and *upon whom* those judgments fall.

Determining the time period of those judgments begins with how one understands Revelation 4:1-2. There John wrote:

---

[297] Some dispensational teachers see the seven churches as seven consecutive dispensations, rather than seven literal churches in the 1st century. That idea is rejected by the other views.

Systematic Theology for the New Apostolic Reformation

> *After these things I looked, and behold, a door standing open in heaven, and the first voice which I had heard, like the sound of a trumpet speaking with me, said, "Come up here, and I will show you what must take place after these things."*

Futurists see the Book of Revelation fulfilled in the future, and in keeping with this, they envision these verses (4:1-2) being fulfilled one day in the future when the Church will "come up here" or, in other words, will be raptured to heaven.

FUTURISTS' UNDERSTANDING OF REVELATION 4:1-2

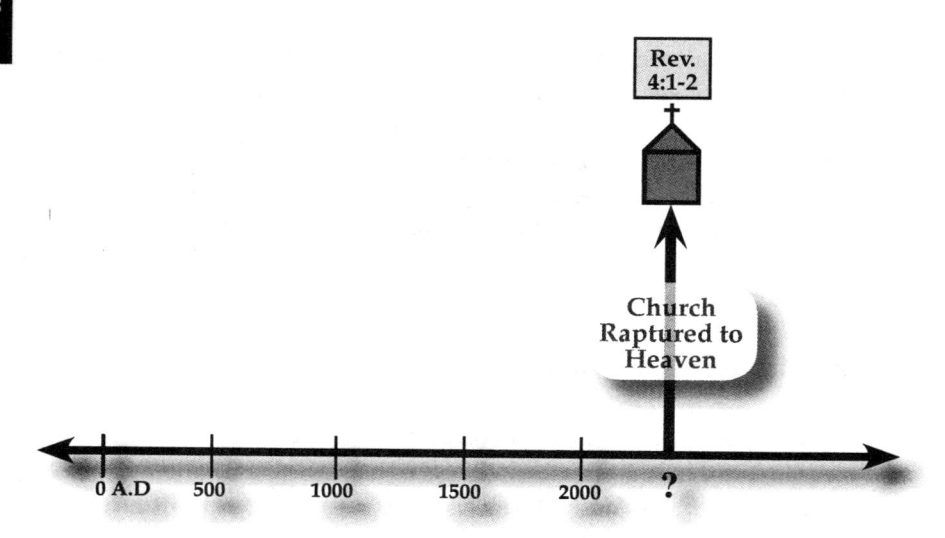

[Diagram: Timeline from 0 A.D. through 500, 1000, 1500, 2000, ? showing Church Raptured to Heaven at Rev. 4:1-2]

Building on this line of thinking, most futurists see the judgments reported in Revelation 4 through 18 occurring after the Church is taken into heaven. In particular, they envision those judgments taking place during a seven year period which they call the **Great Tribulation** or just the **Tribulation**. That Great Tribulation is thought of as a time when God will pour out His wrath on the whole world, killing at least one third of humanity. Because adherents of this view see the Church being raptured before, or *pre*-ceding the Tribulation, their view of the rapture is referred to as the **pre-tribulation rapture**.

The Book of Revelation

There are variations on this futurist view. Some futurists believe that the rapture of the Church will happen in the middle of the seven-year Tribulation, a view called **mid-tribulation rapture**. Others believe that the rapture of the Church will happen at the end of the Tribulation, called the **post-tribulation rapture**. Then there are other adherents of the futurist view that envision different parts of the Church being raptured at different times during the seven-year long Tribulation. These are all variations on the futurist view, the most common being what we mentioned first, the pre-tribulation rapture

FUTURIST'S MOST COMMON UNDERSTANDING OF THE RAPTURE:
PRE-TRIBULATION RAPTURE
(CHURCH RAPTURED TO HEAVEN BEFORE A SEVEN YEAR TRIBULATION)

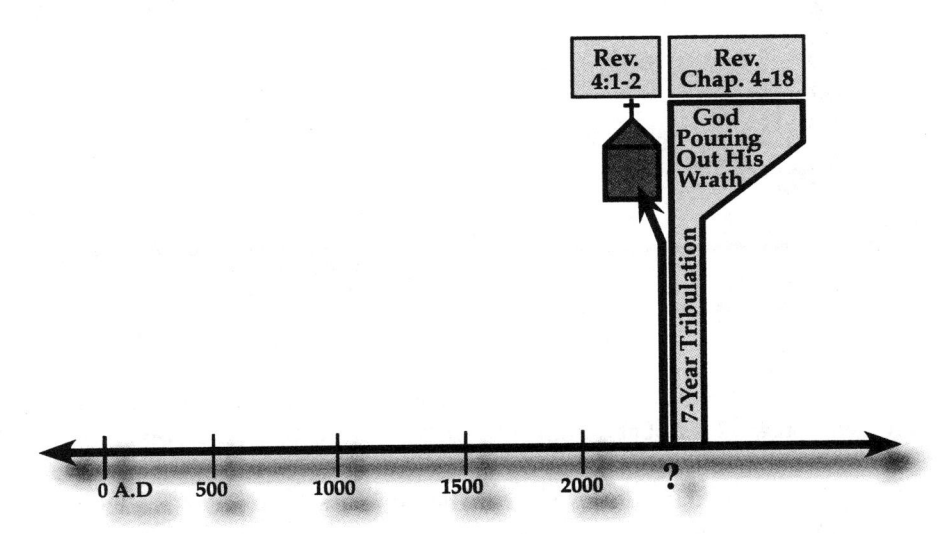

Point 501: Partial Preterist and Full Preterist Understanding

When partial and full preterists read "*Come up here,*" in Revelation 4:1-2, they note that there is nothing said about the Church being raptured to heaven. It was John who was called up into heaven:

> *After these things I looked, and behold, a door standing open in heaven, and the first voice which I had heard, like the sound of a*

Systematic Theology for the New Apostolic Reformation

trumpet speaking with me, said, "<u>Come up here</u>, and I will show you what must take place after these things."

(Rev. 4:1-2)

That event when John was told to *"Come up here,"* happened during the 1st century while John was on the island called Patmos (Rev. 1:9).

PARTIAL AND FULL PRETERIST'S UNDERSTANDING OF REVELATION 4:1-2

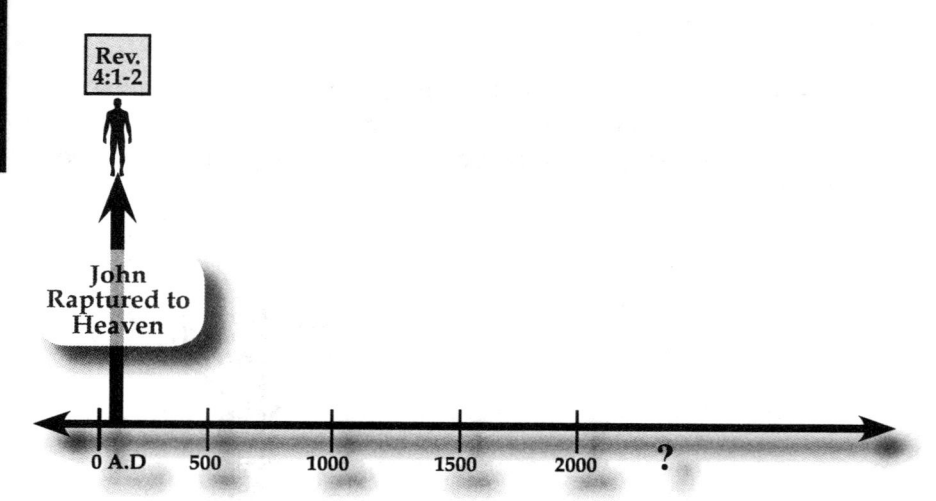

This changes how we understand the rest of the Book of Revelation. Revelation 4:1-2 is not about an event in our future, but it took place in the 1st century. John was taken into heaven and allowed to see what would take place from his lifetime forward. Therefore, the judgments recorded in Revelation chapters 4 through 18 began to unfold during John's lifetime.

Point 502: Historicist Understanding of Revelation

Although many Bible teachers agree that Revelation 4:1-2 is about John's rapture to heaven during the 1st century, they have various ways to explain the judgments recorded in Revelation 4-18. They agree that those judgments began to unfold during John's lifetime, but they disagree as to how long they take to fulfill and upon whom those judgments fall.

The Book of Revelation

Most of the leaders of the Protestant Reformation, including Luther, Knox, Calvin, and Huss, all taught that the judgments of Revelation are fulfilled over the course of history. The judgments began to be fulfilled in the 1st century and continue until the Second Coming of Jesus which is described in Revelation 19. This is called the historicist's view of the Book of Revelation.

HISTORICIST'S VIEW OF REVELATION 4-18
FULFILLED OVER THE COURSE OF HISTORY

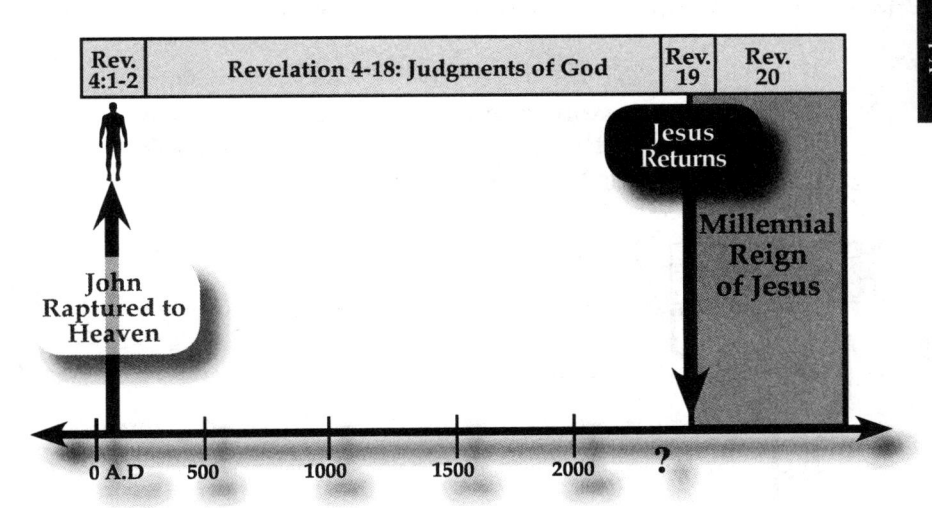

| Rev. 4:1-2 | Revelation 4-18: Judgments of God | Rev. 19 | Rev. 20 |

Jesus Returns

Millennial Reign of Jesus

John Raptured to Heaven

0 A.D   500   1000   1500   2000   ?

A distinctive of the historicist view of Revelation is that it sees all of the judgments of God in the Book of Revelation as God's actions of expanding His Kingdom over the earth. After Jesus ascended into heaven, the Father said to the Son:

> *Sit at My right hand,*
> *Until I make Your enemies a footstool for Your feet.*
> (Acts 2:34-35)

In keeping with this truth, Revelation chapters 4 through 18 record the judgments of God the Father subduing the enemies of the Kingdom so that by the end of chapter 18 everything is subdued, and then (chapter 19)

Systematic Theology for the New Apostolic Reformation

Jesus returns to fully manifest the Kingdom on earth for a millennial reign (chapter 20). This historicist's view of Revelation is the one that I have come to believe is most biblically accurate.

Point 503: Full Preterist Understanding of Revelation

Full preterists and modern partial preterists agree that John was taken to heaven in John 4:1-2, but they believe that the judgments recorded in Revelation 4 through 18 were released upon Jerusalem when it was destroyed in 70 AD.

**FULL PRETERIST AND MODERN PARTIAL PRETERIST VIEW:
JUDGMENTS OF REVELATION 4-18 HAPPENED IN 70 AD
AT THE DESTRUCTION OF JERUSALEM**

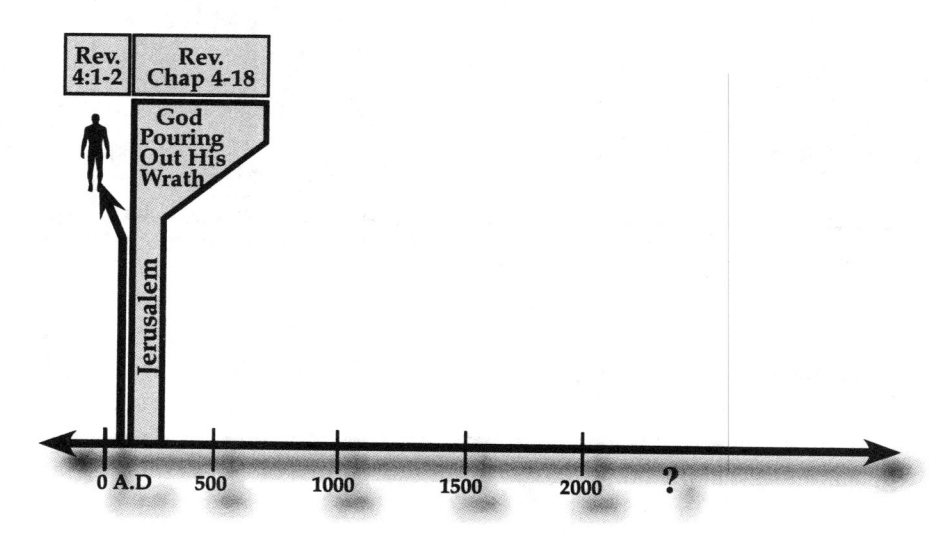

As I have mentioned, I cannot support this view, even though I respect sincere brothers and sisters who do interpret Scripture in a way that leads them to this view.

The Book of Revelation

Point 504: An Overview

To summarize, with hopes of not confusing any readers, let me say that I hold to Kingdom theology, with historic premillennialism and the partial preterist view known as historic preterism. I also agree with the historicist understanding of the Book of Revelation.

This means I believe the Kingdom of God is fully manifest in heaven, but is growing like seeds in soil on earth. While the Kingdom grows on earth over the course of history, God is judging the enemies of the Kingdom. After every enemy is placed under the feet of Jesus, *then* Jesus will return to earth to fully manifest the Kingdom and then reign on earth for a millennium.

KINGDOM THEOLOGY WITH HISTORIC PREMILLENNIALISM

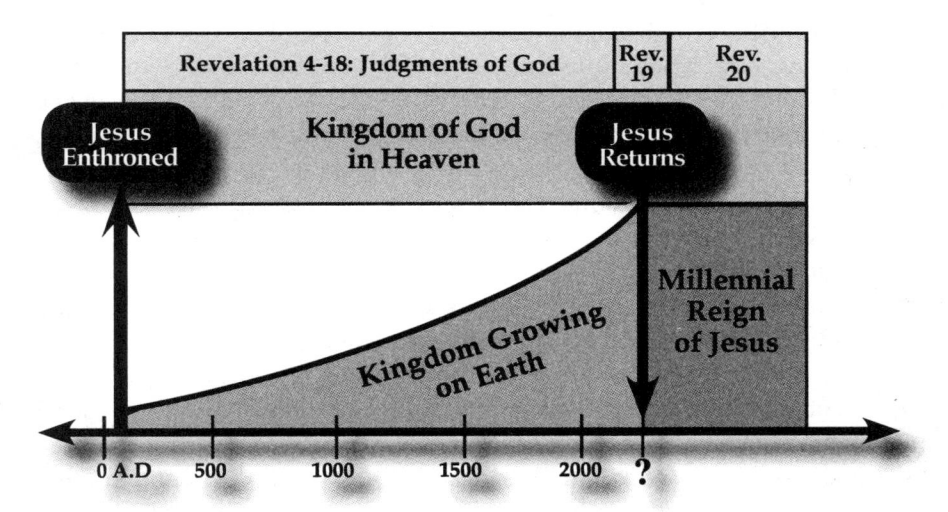

Point 505: Where Does the Rapture Fit?

Christians who hold to this or similar views believe in a future rapture of the Church, but they have a distinct understanding of the rapture. Aside from Revelation 4:1-2 which we just discussed, the Bible passage most often used to teach about the rapture is 1 Thessalonians 4:16-17:

Systematic Theology for the New Apostolic Reformation

For the Lord Himself will descend from heaven with a shout, with the voice of the archangel and with the trumpet of God, and the dead in Christ will rise first. Then we who are alive and remain will be caught up together with them in the clouds to meet the Lord in the air, and so we shall always be with the Lord.

This is the only passage in the Bible that speaks of God's people being *"caught up"* to meet the Lord in the air. It is from this passage that we get the word, *rapture*. This word is an English transliteration of the Latin word *rapio*. That Latin word appears in 1 Thessalonians 4:17 in the Latin translation of the Bible.

Futurists read 1 Thessalonians 4:16-17 and conclude that Christians will be lifted off of the earth and taken away to heaven for seven years so they do not have to be here on earth during the Great Tribulation.

In contrast, those who hold to Kingdom theology and the historicist view of the Book of Revelation read 1 Thessalonians 4:16-17 and conclude something very different. Indeed, we know from this passage that Jesus will descend from heaven and appear in the sky. Then God's people will be caught up. However, these verses do not say that Jesus will then take His people away to heaven. We are simply told that believers will meet Jesus in the air. Then 1 Thessalonians 4:17 says *"we shall always be with the Lord,"* but this does not mean we are going to fly away to be with Him in heaven. Jesus is coming to earth so we will alway be with Him here on earth.

Notice that with this view of the rapture, Christians are not taken into heaven for seven years. They are simply lifted off of the earth to meet the Lord in the air. Then they are brought back down to earth with Jesus.

Compare this meeting to meeting a friend who arrives at your local airport. You may meet that friend at the airport, but not to get on the airplane and fly away with him. Rather, you will meet your friend to bring him to your home. In a comparative way, Christians will meet the Lord in the air, not to fly away with Him but to accompany Him as He comes down to earth.

Because this understanding of the rapture is different than that proposed by the futurists (the dispensational, premillennial pretribulationists), those who adhere to Kingdom theology sometimes avoid the terminology *rapture*. So as not to confuse the issues, they will often prefer the terminology *caught up* rather than *raptured*. In reality, the phrase *caught up* is the literal meaning conveyed in 1 Thessalonians 4:16-17.

The Book of Revelation

THE CHURCH MEETS THE LORD IN THE AIR WHEN HE RETURNS

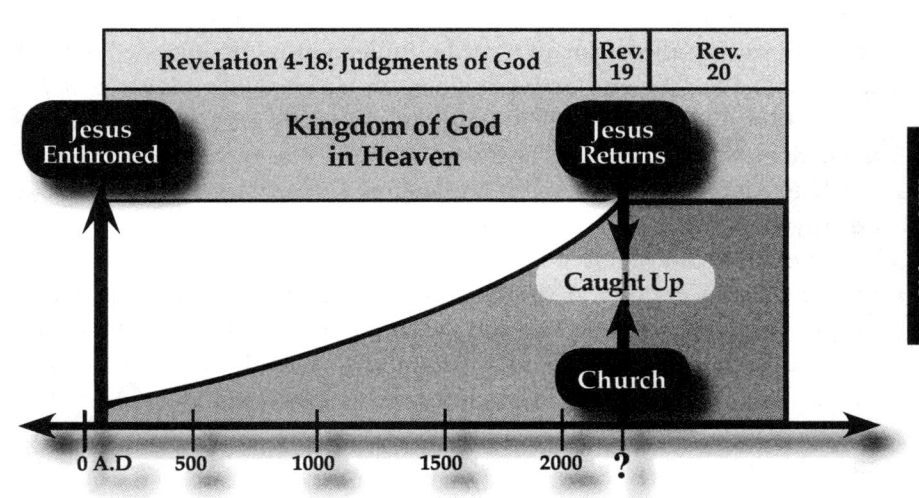

One final point in understanding this catching up is that Jesus will reveal His glory as He appears in the sky above. The radiance of His glory will judge all that is evil. Christians will be purged of all evil that remains in them and then be transformed into His image. At the same time, the world will go through a transformation, with the earth being purged of all evil. Then Jesus will continue descending down to earth to fully manifest His Kingdom on earth.

Point 506: The Marriage Feast and Millennial Reign

After Jesus removes evil and returns to earth, there will be a marriage feast for Jesus and His Bride (Rev. 19:7-9). Christians who embrace Kingdom theology and historic premillennialism believe that Jesus will then rule with His Bride for a millennium.

There are two events that will mark the millennial reign here on earth. In Revelation 20:1-3, John recorded what he saw:

> *Then I saw an angel coming down from heaven . . . he laid hold of the dragon, the serpent of old, who is the devil and Satan, and*

Systematic Theology for the New Apostolic Reformation

bound him for a thousand years; and he threw him into the abyss, and shut it and sealed it over him . . . .

We know from this passage that Satan will not have access to people on earth during the major part of the millennial reign, but then we are told that toward the end of the millennium *"Satan will be released from his prison"* (Rev. 20:7). Satan will attempt one last coup by trying to deceive the nations so that they rebel against our Lord. This, however, will simply result in identifying those who are against Jesus. They will quickly be destroyed by fire coming out of heaven (Rev. 20:9).

The Bible does not tell us why Satan is released and allowed to deceive the nations at the end of the millennium. Many teachers propose that Satan's release will be necessary for the fulfillment of God's original commission to Adam and Eve to fill and subdue the earth. The first Adam and Eve failed, but the last Adam (Jesus) and the last Eve (the Church) will succeed at filling the earth and conquering all evil.

Point 507: The Great White Throne Judgment

After the millennial reign, Jesus will take His seat on the Great White Throne of Judgment. Then all of the dead, the great and small, will stand before Him. Books will be opened, including the Book of Life. Then the people will be judged according to the things written in the books. Every human being will end up in one of two places: in the new heavens and earth or in the Lake of Fire, which is also called hell (Rev. 20:15). We will study hell in Volume IX, *Personal Eschatology*.

Point 508: The New Heavens and Earth

There is some debate among Christians as to whether the new heavens and earth will be the present heavens and earth that get transformed or whether God will totally destroy this present world and create a brand new heavens and earth.

The Book of Revelation

Judgment: People End Up in the New Heavens and Earth or Hell

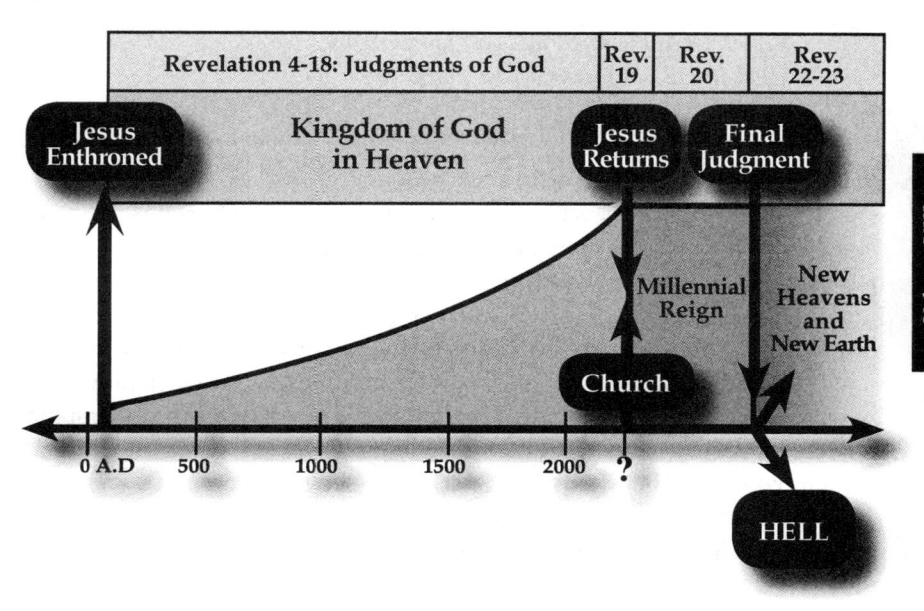

Much of the debate concerning the new heavens and earth is centered on two Bible passages:

> *Then I saw a new heaven and a new earth; for the first heaven and the first earth <u>passed away</u>* . . . .
>
> (Rev. 21:1)

> *But the day of the Lord will come like a thief, in which the heavens will <u>pass away</u> with a roar and the elements will <u>be destroyed</u> with intense heat, and the earth and its works will be burned up . . . the heavens will <u>be destroyed</u> by burning, and the elements will melt with intense heat!*
>
> (2 Peter 3:10, 12)

These passages talk about the world passing away and being destroyed. If we only consider these passages, it would be easy to conclude that the present heavens and earth will be obliterated and then replaced by a totally new creation.

685

Systematic Theology for the New Apostolic Reformation

However, we need to consider some other Bible passages. Some verses tell us that the earth will exist forever. For example, Psalms 104:5 says:

> *He established the earth upon its foundations,*
> *So that it will not totter forever and ever.*

Rather than this earth going out of existence, we must consider how it can go on existing forever (see also, Eccl. 1:4).

Second Peter 3:10-12 is the passage that says that the heavens will pass away, but if we read the context we learn that a comparison is being made between how earth was destroyed by the flood in the days of Noah and how the whole world will be destroyed by fire in the coming day of judgment. When the earth was judged by water, it was destroyed, but not in the sense of going out of existence. If the comparison between judgment by water and judgment by fire is carried to the point, we can understand how creation may burn up in the sense that all evil will be destroyed, but creation will continue to exist.

We also need to consider God's original intentions for creation. As discussed earlier,[298] creation was Father-God's love gift to the Son. He also established the earth as a place where humanity abides. Yet, because of sin, the world was *"subjected to futility"* (Rom. 8:20). However, Jesus came, not just to redeem people but creation itself. The apostle Paul explained:

> *. . . that the creation itself also will be set free from its slavery to corruption into the freedom of the glory of the children of God.*
> (Rom. 8:21)

Creation is destined for redemption.

The end goal is not to destroy creation but to bring all things in subjection to God, so that He may fill all and be in all (1 Cor. 15:25-28). This leads us to envision creation being totally brought into conformity to God's will. The new heavens and earth will not be subject to death, the curse, corruption, or futility. The Kingdom of God will be fully realized on earth, and Jesus will reign over heaven and earth forever and ever. This leads us to believe that the new heavens and earth will exist forever and ever.

What God's people will be doing for eternity is a subject we will discuss more fully in Volume IX, *Personal Eschatology*.

---

298 Discussed in III:B.

Volume IX
Personal Eschatology

Eschatology refers to the study of last things, but when we discuss **personal eschatology**, we are focusing on the events that happen *to individuals* after they die.

In Section A, we will discuss what happened to people who died in OT times. In Section B, we will discuss what happens after death to Christians. Section C will explain how the eternal dwelling place of believers will be in the new heavens and earth. Then Section D offers a study on the nature of hell.

**Volume IX
Personal Eschatology**

Section A
Old Testament Saints After Death

What happened to people who lived and died in OT times? We will discuss how they first went to hades, then those who believed were released from hades when Jesus descended and then ascended out of hades at His death and resurrection.

Point 509: Sheol, Hades, and the Place of the Dead

All people who died in OT times went to **hades**.[299] The word, *hades*, is the Greek word for "the place of the dead." The NT uses the Greek word *hades*, where the OT uses the Hebrew word *sheol*.[300] These two words, hades and sheol, refer to the same place where all dead people went before Jesus died on the cross. The New International Version of the Bible sometimes translates hades as "the grave," which is a helpful understanding.

Hades is not hell.[301] One way to see this is by reading about the final judgment day when hades will be thrown into the Lake of Fire (Rev. 20:14). That Lake of Fire is the final place into which the wicked will be thrown. The Lake of Fire is also called hell. Since hades will be thrown into hell, we know that hades is not hell.

Within hades there are two different regions. We can see this in the story of Lazarus and the rich man recorded in Luke 16:19-31. Both men went to hades when they died. However, within hades one region was

---
299 Exceptions to this are Enoch and Elijah who were taken up to heaven.
300 For example, Acts 2:31 uses the Greek word *hades*, when it quotes Psalm 16:10, which uses the Hebrew word *Sheol*.
301 One of the great errors of the KJV of the Bible is that it usually translates the Greek word *hades* as "hell."

called the "Bosom of Abraham" and the other was called the "Place of Torment." Lazarus went to the Bosom of Abraham and the rich man went to the Place of Torment. Lazarus and the rich man could see each other in hades, but there was a chasm separating the two regions, so they could not have contact with each other.

In OT Times, All People Went to Hades When They Died

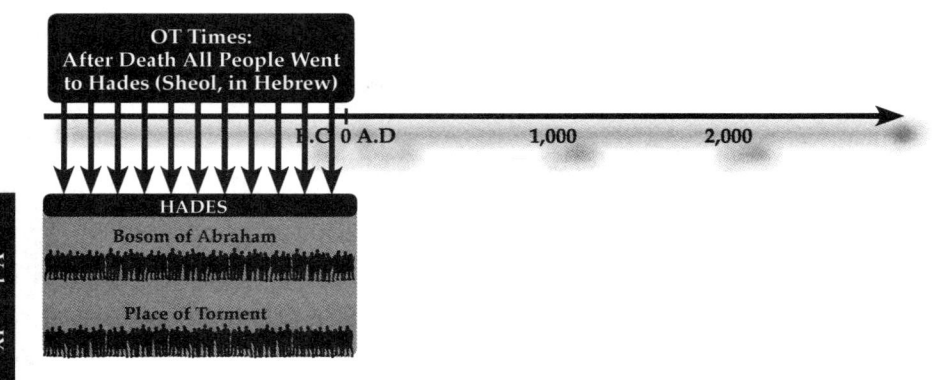

Point 510: Jesus Preached to Those in Hades

The NT reveals that Jesus descended into hades between His death and resurrection (e.g., Acts 2:27, 31,[302] and Eph. 4:9). While Jesus was in hades, He preached to the people there. Peter taught this, writing:

> *For Christ also died for sins once for all, the just for the unjust, so that He might bring us to God . . . also He went and made proclamation to the spirits now in prison.*
>
> (1 Peter 3:18-19)

Peter went on to explain how Jesus even preached to those who died way back in Noah's flood:

> *. . . He went and made proclamation to the spirits now in prison, who once were disobedient, when the patience of God kept waiting in the days of Noah.*
>
> (1 Peter 3:19-20)

---

[302] Here the King James Version wrongly says that Jesus descended into hell, where the original Greek NT tells us He descended into hades.

Old Testament Saints After Death

A few verses later Peter wrote:

> For *the gospel has for this purpose been preached even to those who are dead*, that though they are judged in the flesh as men, they may live in the spirit according to the will of God.
>
> (1 Peter 4:6)

Jesus presented Himself to those who died in OT times. Many had been waiting for hundreds of years, but once Jesus died and descended into hades, they had the opportunity to hear the gospel.

Point 511: Jesus Led a Host Out of Hades

Paul explained in Ephesians 4:8, that after Jesus descended into hades, He then *"ascended on high,* [and] *He led captive a host of captives."* We do not know how many actually came out of hades with Jesus, but Paul referred to a host, which meant a huge number.

JESUS ASCENDED AND LED A HOST TO HEAVEN WITH HIM

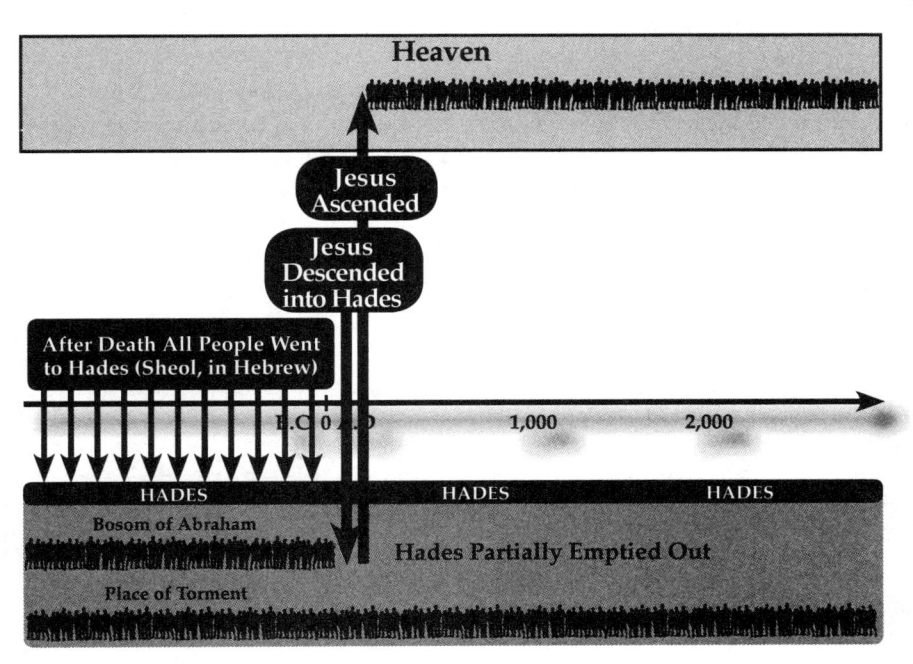

Systematic Theology for the New Apostolic Reformation

Matthew explained how some of those OT saints who came out of hades, stopped in Jerusalem before going on to heaven:

> *The tombs were opened, and many bodies of the saints who had fallen asleep were raised; and coming out of the tombs after His resurrection they entered the holy city and appeared to many.*
> (Matt. 27:52-53)

Jews living in Jerusalem actually witnessed people coming out of the graves and walking the streets.

It was at that time that the OT believers in God would have been "saved." Many already believed in God, and their faith was credited to them as righteousness, but they would not have experienced salvation until Jesus died, resurrected, and brought them out of hades into heaven.

There is some question as to what happened to those who were left in hades after Jesus ascended. They may have been left there to wait for the Great White Throne of Judgment when hades will be thrown into the Lake of Fire (Rev. 20:14). It is also possible that they have already entered into a final place of condemnation. This latter explanation is held by Christian teachers who hold that John 5:28-29 took place at Jesus' resurrection out of hades about 2,000 years ago:

> *Do not be amazed at this, because the hour is coming in which all who are in the tombs will hear his voice and will come out, those who have done good deeds to the resurrection of life, but those who have done wicked deeds to the resurrection of condemnation.*

We know the wicked will suffer condemnation, but teachers continue to debate if that condemnation started 2,000 years ago or will start after a future Great White Throne of Judgment.

Section B
New Testament Saints After Death

Now we can discuss what happens after death to Christians.

Point 512: To Die Is to Be with the Jesus

Paul expressed his understanding that he would be in a much better place after he died:

> For to me, to live is Christ and to die is gain. But I am hard-pressed from both directions, having the desire to depart and be with Christ, for that is very much better.
> (Phil. 1:21-23)

> ... we ... prefer rather to be absent from the body and to be at home with the Lord.
> (2 Cor. 5:8)

These verses indicate that Paul believed he would be immediately in the presence of the Lord upon his death. He wrote these words implying that all Christians will experience this when they die.

Point 513: Instantly in Heaven or Soul Sleep?

Christians will be immediately in the presence of Jesus when they die, however, there are two different ways of understanding this.

Systematic Theology for the New Apostolic Reformation

Most Protestant Christians have been taught that they will immediately appear in heaven upon their death, and there they will be in the presence of Jesus.

There is an alternative view called **soul sleep.** Soul sleep refers to the doctrine that Christians who die will *not* go immediately to heaven, but they will be at rest in the grave (in a sleep-like state) until a final resurrection day at the end of the world.

When adherents of soul sleep discuss the verses where Paul talked about being immediately in the presence of the Lord upon death, they say that after Christians die, they lay in the grave, but the presence of Jesus envelops them much as righteous people in OT times were in hades while being enveloped in the bosom of Abraham.[303] It is in this way that they will be immediately in the presence of Jesus.

I do not want to endorse the view of soul sleep or the view that Christians immediately go heaven when they die. I simply want to offer both explanations as reasonable for Christians who take the Bible seriously.

Adherents of soul sleep reference Scriptures that talk about dead people being asleep:

> *He said to them, "Our friend Lazarus has fallen asleep; but I go, so that I may awaken him out of sleep." . . . Now Jesus had spoken of his death . . . .*
>
> (John 11:11-14)

Several other Bible passages also equate death with sleeping (e.g., Acts 7:60 ; I Cor. 15:6, 18, 20, 51 ; I Thess. 4:13 ; 5:10).

This doctrine of soul sleep is often ridiculed and quickly discarded by teachers in mainstream Christianity today, because it is held by sects such as the Seventh-Day Adventists.[304] For some mainline Christians, the doctrine of soul sleep is guilty by association. Yet, many great Church leaders, such as Martin Luther, believed and taught soul sleep.

Also, there are some Bible passages that are difficult to explain without there being a gap of time between a person's death and resurrection. For example, Paul wrote:

---

303 The Bosom of Abraham was discussed in IX:A:509.
304 The Jehovah Witnesses have a similar view, but they envision people being annihilated at death, then recreated by God just before the future judgment.

New Testament Saints After Death

For the Lord Himself will descend from heaven with a shout, with the voice of the archangel and with the trumpet of God, and the dead in Christ will rise first.

(1 Thess. 4:16)

Proponents of soul sleep quote this verse and explain that Jesus will return at some future date then the dead in Christ will rise out of the grave. If all Christians are taken to heaven the instant they die, who are these who are dead in Christ until the Second Coming?

Opponents of soul sleep have several different explanations, but most often they will say that the resurrection being referred to in such passages is the future resurrection of the physical bodies of the saints. Since they believe that the souls of Christians go immediately to heaven upon death, they have to see any future resurrection as the bodies rising from the grave and being reunited with the souls of the Christians who are already in heaven.

Actually deciding which view is true, may be a non-issue, because even if believers sleep in the grave for a time, that period may seem to be only a moment. As people sleep in this world, they often do not know whether their sleep time lasted a moment or a full night; so also soul sleep may be a similar experience.

Many Christians make their decisions on this subject based on the testimonies of people who have died and come back to life. Yet, those who are trying to support one view or the other can find near-death testimonies supporting either view that they prefer. Besides, we are endeavoring to build our theology on what the Bible reveals. Christians who do take a strong stand on one side or the other should be cautious and willing to listen to the opposing view since noteworthy Christian leaders are on both sides of the debate. It is best to leave unclear what the Bible leaves unclear. Every person will know for certain once they themselves have died

Point 514: Contact Between the Living and the Dead

Whether Christians lie in the grave or immediately go to heaven, the Bible reveals how they have some awareness concerning what is going on with the living. An interesting example is from Matthew 2, when Herod had all the male babies in the region of Bethlehem put to death. We are

Systematic Theology for the New Apostolic Reformation

told that Rachel *"was weeping for her children, and she refused to be comforted"* (Matt. 2:18). Some Bible teachers take this as a figure of speech because Rachel had been dead for over 1,000 years, but it is worth noting that Rachel was buried in Bethlehem where the slaughter occurred.

For another example, we can mention the great cloud of witnesses discussed in Hebrew 12:1. The preceding chapter (Heb. 11) leads us to see those witnesses as dead men and women who believed God while they were alive; the cloud of witnesses are waiting and watching the people who are living fulfill that for which they believed God.

We can also identify a contact between the living and the dead in the incident when Saul had an medium conjure the prophet Samuel up from the dead (1 Sam. 28). That was an evil practice forbidden by God, but the fact remains that it did happen. Some Bible teachers try to explain that incident by saying that it was not really Samuel who appeared, but a demon pretending to be Samuel. In reality, we are clearly told *"the woman saw Samuel"* (1 Sam. 28:12, 14-15). If we take these verses literally, we have to conclude that it was Samuel who was raised from the dead and appeared.

We find further evidence that communication between the dead and the living is possible in God's command not to engage in such evil behavior (Deut. 18:11-12). If such communication was not possible, then God would not have forbid it. So we know the dead are somewhat aware of the living, but how much, the Bible does not reveal.

It is worth noting that Christians who embrace the dualistic cosmology of Western thought have a more difficult time conceiving of any contact between the living and the dead. This is because they envision the spiritual world as distant and separate from the natural world. In contrast, the cosmology developed from a direct reading of the Bible reveals the spiritual realm as close to and totally integrated with the natural realm. That Hebraic-biblical cosmology leads one to see contact between the spiritual and natural realms as plausible.

Point 515: An Intermediate State Called Purgatory?

At this point it is worth discussing the Roman Catholic belief concerning what happens to people when they die. Catholics believe that immediately upon death the most evil people are sent directly to hell,

New Testament Saints After Death

while only the holiest people go directly to heaven. That leaves the vast majority of humanity to go to an intermediary place called **purgatory**.[305]

According to Roman Catholic teaching, purgatory is thought to be a place where good people, who are not good enough to go directly to heaven, must spend time paying for and being purged of their sins before going to heaven. The length of time and amount of suffering people in purgatory will experience will be determined by how much they sinned while alive. A purging may take a day or it may take hundreds or even thousands of years, but once people have paid for their sins and been completely purged, they will be taken into heaven where they will live eternally with God.[306]

Catholics also teach that while alive, people can earn **indulgences**, which are allowances given to people to reduce the suffering they will have to experience in purgatory. Catholics believe that they can earn indulgences for themselves or for loved ones already in purgatory by praying or doing good deeds, such as giving financially to worthwhile projects.

The abuse of indulgences was the proverbial straw that broke the camel's back for Martin Luther. He watched a Catholic Dominican preacher named Johann Tetzel selling indulgences to raise money for the construction of St. Peter's Basilica.[307] Then Martin Luther posted his 95 theses on a church door in Wittenberg, Germany in 1517, which marked the start of the Protestant Reformation.

Today, Roman Catholics do not emphasize the earning or selling of indulgences as much as they did in the Middle Ages, but most Protestants continue to reject all of the teachings related to purgatory. Protestant teachers will point out that there is no biblical proof for the existence of purgatory, but the Protestant rejection of purgatory goes deeper than that. The teachings of purgatory are diametrically opposed to the Protestant belief that Jesus was the perfect sacrifice for sins. There is no further payment for sins that must be made. Therefore, people who have placed their faith in Jesus Christ will go to heaven without having to pass through purgatory.

---

305 An exception to this is babies who have not been water baptized. According to Catholic teaching, those babies which die go to a place called, limbo, which is a place of eternal happiness, but separate from the presence of God.
306 Roman Catholic doctrine is that no one can move out of hell once they have been cast there.
307 Money for St. Peter's Basilica is most often referenced in historical writings, but there is also historical evidence that Tetzel raised money for other projects.

Systematic Theology for the New Apostolic Reformation

Point 516: Passing through the Fire

Although Protestants reject the Roman Catholic doctrine of purgatory, many do recognize a purging that will take place before anyone proceeds to heaven. Paul wrote about a judgment when:

> . . . each man's work will become evident; for the day will show it because it is to be revealed with fire, and the fire itself will test the quality of each man's work. If any man's work which he has built on it remains, he will receive a reward. If any man's work is burned up, he will suffer loss; but he himself will be saved, yet so as through fire.
>
> (1 Cor. 3:13-15)

This passage does speak of a purging by fire that every Christian should expect to pass through.

Usually Protestants think of this purging as resulting from the revealed glory of Jesus Christ as each person stands before Him on judgment day. Contrary to the teaching of purgatory, this judgment sounds like a burning that will be instantaneous or almost so. Also, it is unlike purgatory, because Paul does not mention any suffering on the part of the individual, even though the works that were done with wrong motives will be burned away. On the other hand, works that were done for the glory of God will stand the purging fire, and hence, go on with the believer into eternity.

Point 517: Various Rewards for Various Deeds

After explaining that each Christian's works will be tested with fire, Paul wrote:

> If any man's work which he has built on it remains, he will receive a reward.
>
> (1 Cor. 3:14)

This and several other passages talk about the various rewards that will be given to believers for their deeds. Some of those are as follows:

New Testament Saints After Death

Deed	Reward	Verse
Suffer loss for Jesus	Many times more	Matt. 19:29
Caring for needy	Kingdom inheritance	Matt. 25:31-34
Suffer persecution	Great rewards	Luke 6:22-23
Building the Church	Reward	1 Cor. 3:10-15
Live disciplined	Imperishable wreath	1 Cor. 9:24-25
Persevere under trial	Crown of life	James 1:12
Shepherd God's people	Crown of glory	1 Peter 5:4
Overcome	Rule with Jesus	Rev. 2:26 ; 3:21

The concept of differing rewards for various deeds is incompatible with Reformed theology, because that view sees that God's actions are determined by His sovereign will, without influence of anything outside of Himself. Therefore, what people do is irrelevant. Everything God does for humanity is done by grace, and according to Reformed theology, grace is *unmerited* favor. Using this definition, there is nothing any person can do to merit any gift from God. If Bible students are consistent with the Reformed view of God, they will conclude that there are no such things as rewards for deeds.

In spite of this, some adherents of Reformed theology will talk about differing rewards that God will give out, but they are being inconsistent with their own theology (Augustine was inconsistent in this). For the most part, Christians involved with Reformed theology simply avoid the subject of rewards because it does not fit into their understanding of grace.

Yet, the Bible talks about all of the rewards for deeds that are mentioned above. Plus, the writer of Hebrews says God *"is the rewarder of those who seek Him"* (Heb. 11:6). It is God's nature to reward people for whatever good they have done. So then, Christians will go through a judgment in which their selfish works will be burned away and their righteous deeds will be rewarded.

What remains for us to see is *where* Christians will enjoy their eternal rewards. Where will they spend eternity? This subject is worth addressing in the section that follows.

Volume IX
Personal Eschatology

Section C
Our Eternal Destination

We ended Volume VIII with a discussion concerning how Jesus will be with His people forever in the new heavens and earth. This contradicts what most Christians believe. Most Christians have been taught that after they die they will be taken off of this earth and into a mystical, spiritual world called heaven. In that location, they will sing praises to God forever. So what is true? Will we spend eternity on earth or in heaven? And what will we be doing for eternity?

Point 518: Our Eternal Home in Heaven?

The early Church developed her understanding of eternity as Christianity was merging with the worldview of the ancient Greek philosophers. As we have explained, those philosophers held a dualistic cosmology, with God existing in a distant, timeless world, separate from the natural world. The ancient philosophers also thought of the natural world as a trap, inferior and insignificant. They envisioned their souls someday escaping their physical bodies and then ascending to God for their eternal existence.

Augustine and some other Church leaders were submerged in that cosmology when they began investigating Christianity. From the Bible they knew that Christians would spend eternity with God. However, they envisioned God up in a distant, timeless world, so it was only logical to conclude that Christians will have to go to that distant, timeless world. It was at that time in history when Church leaders began to teach a *bodiless eternity* with Christians floating up in the clouds forever.

Systematic Theology for the New Apostolic Reformation

THE CLASSICAL VIEW THAT CHRISTIANS GO TO GOD'S TIMELESS WORLD

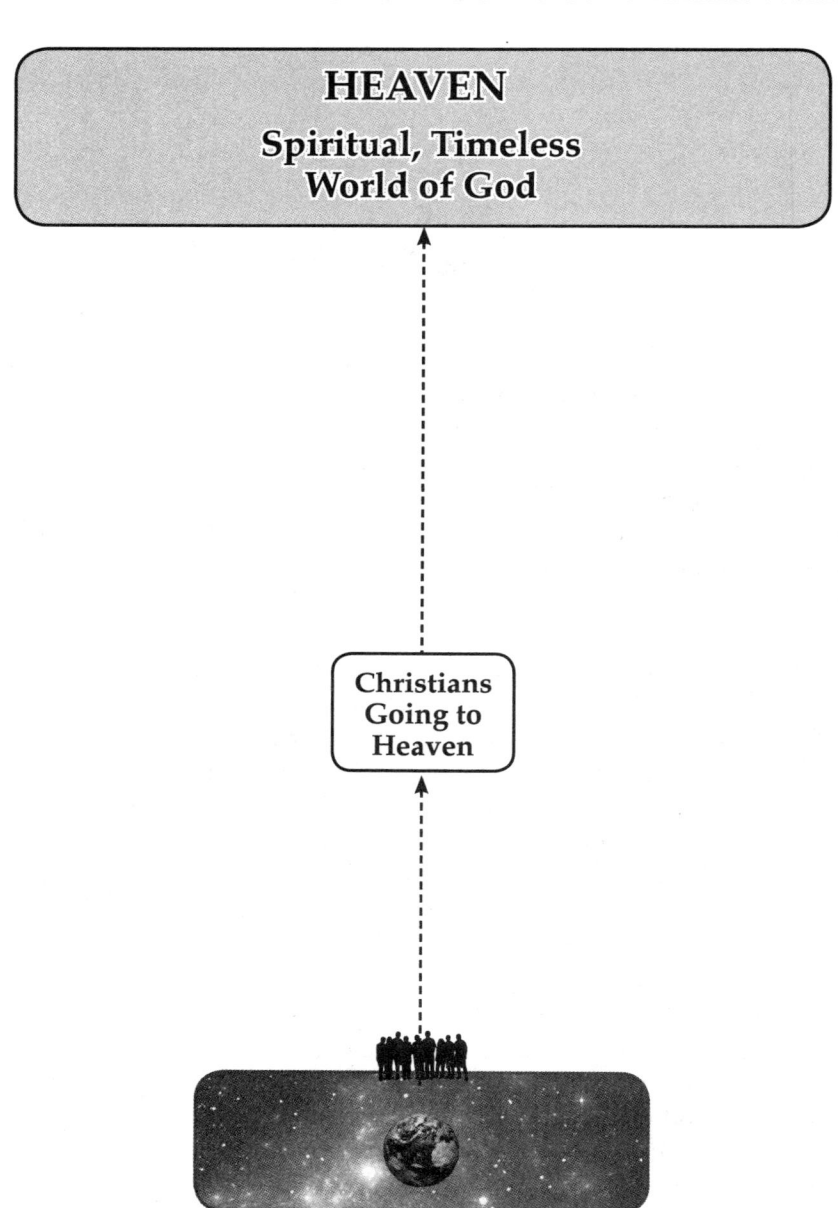

HEAVEN
Spiritual, Timeless World of God

Christians Going to Heaven

Our Eternal Destination

Christians trained in Classical/Reformed theology tend to envision saints floating in the clouds, praising and worshiping God, while in some type of trance-like state, forever intoxicated on God's glory. In reality, the Bible never gives us a picture of people living like that in heaven. Those visions are simply the product of trying to understand our eternal home while interpreting the Bible through a Western dualistic cosmology.

The Bible offers us a very different view of our eternal dwelling state.

Point 519: Our Eternal Home in this World

To develop a biblical understanding of our eternal home, we must start with a biblical cosmology.

A Biblical Cosmology

As we have stated many times, God created the heavens—plural. The heavens are within creation. Furthermore, God entered into and fills the heavens and earth. Christians do not have to leave creation in order to be with God. He has a throneroom within creation.[308] Already there are many saints with God in heaven, but that heaven is within creation.

---

308 This was explained in I:B:9.

Systematic Theology for the New Apostolic Reformation

When Jesus returns to earth, He will bring with Him, all of those saints who have died:

> For if we believe that Jesus died and rose again, even so God will bring with Him those who have fallen asleep in Jesus.
>
> (1 Thess. 4:14)

Jesus is coming to dwell with His people here on earth. He is not taking His people to heaven; instead, Jesus is going to make this world heavenly. He is going to manifest His Kingdom throughout creation and dwell with His people on earth forever.

OUR ETERNAL HOME IN THE NEW HEAVENS AND EARTH

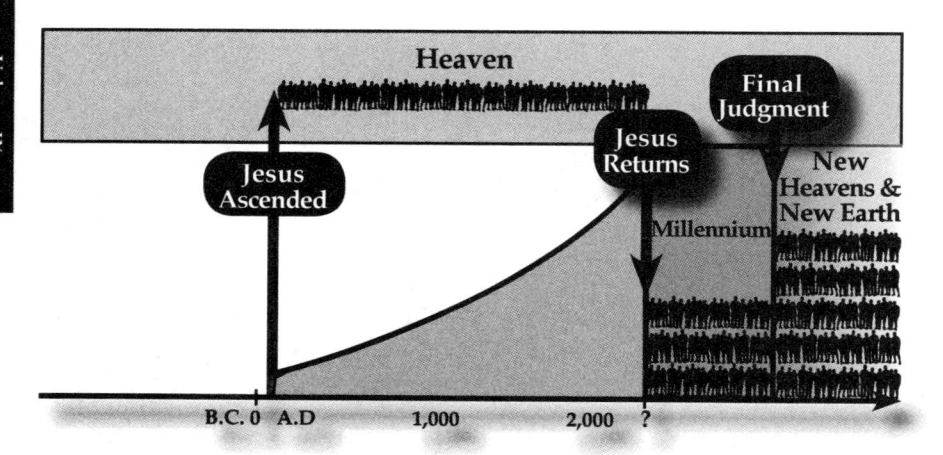

As we explained in the preceding volume, this world will go through a metamorphosis and there will be a new heaven and earth. With this perspective we must read Revelation 21-22, where the eternal home of believers is described.

Point 520: New Jerusalem

At the center of the new heaven and earth will be a city called New Jerusalem, where Jesus will dwell with His people. Many teachers under-

Our Eternal Destination

stand New Jerusalem in a non-literal, metaphorical sense, but there are several reasons that we should take the relevant chapters more literally.

One reason has to do with a literal interpretation fitting with the Jewish customs of betrothal and marriage. During the NT period, a man and a woman would be betrothed to one another, and then the man would go away to prepare a place for her. When the groom finished preparing that place, he was allowed to return, consummate the marriage, and live with her from then on. Jesus reassured His disciples that He would go away and prepare a place for His beloved (John 14:3). Revelation 21 describes that prepared place as a glorious city called New Jerusalem. John, the writer, described New Jerusalem coming out of heaven and then being planted on the new earth. Note again, the city will be on earth, not up in heaven.

The description of New Jerusalem implies that it is a literal, physical city:

> *The city is laid out as a square, and its length is as great as the width; and he measured the city with the rod, fifteen hundred miles; its length and width and height are equal. And he measured its wall, seventy-two yards, <u>according to human measurements, which are also angelic measurements</u>.*
> (Rev. 21:16-17)

The mention of angelic measurements being the same as human measurements is only worth mentioning if the city is the same size in the spiritual realm as it is in the natural.

If a city 1,500 miles by 1,500 miles was lowered down onto the middle of the United States, the city would cover most of the country. Envisioning New Jerusalem in this way, allows us to think of it as a real city that will actually be placed somewhere on this earth. However, it will probably be centered where present-day Jerusalem is located.

Point 521: Our Physical Bodies Will Be Transformed

Understanding our eternal home as on this earth also fits with the Bible's teaching about the resurrection of the dead. Christians will not be resurrected to live eternally in a mystical, bodiless state. Paul explained that the physical bodies of believers will be resurrected as immortal, imperishable bodies (1 Cor. 15:42-57). Every Christian's mortal, corruptible body will be transformed into an immortal, incorruptible body (1 Cor. 15:50-54). This transformation will happen *"in the twinkling of an eye"* (1 Cor. 15:52).

We can get an idea of what the Christian's body will be like by looking at the resurrected body of Jesus. He still had flesh and bones (Luke 24:39). He also had scars in His hands and feet from the crucifixion (Luke 24:40 ; John 20:27). Yet, Jesus was able to eat with His disciples (Luke 24:42-43), and He walked and talked with them.

In Matthew 12:25, Jesus explained that those who resurrect from the dead will be like angels in the sense that they *"neither marry nor are given in marriage."* From these and the testimony of other Bible passages, we can gain some understanding of what our resurrected state will be like. We will have glorious bodies. Our first bodies were made of natural substance from earth, but our redemption bodies will be made of spiritual, even heavenly, stuff (1 Cor. 15:42-49).

We will walk with two feet on the ground. We will not wander in the clouds in an intoxicated state. We will be joyful, but real and touchable. We will be able to look each other in the face and talk to each other. We will eat and enjoy many of the same blessings that we do now, but everything will be better.

Point 522: God Will Have Sons

On the new earth, Father-God will have what He has always desired—sons. Those sons will be transformed when they see Jesus. John explained:

> *We know that when He appears, we will be like Him, because we will see Him as He is.*
>
> (1 John 3:2)

Paul explained that believers will be *"conformed to the image of His Son"* (Rom. 8:29).

Paul also wrote how believers will be glorified (Rom. 8:30). Jesus said in His priestly prayer: *"The glory which You have given Me I have given to them . . ."* (John 17:22). What all this means has not yet been revealed, but it will be glorious. Father-God will have His sons, who are holy and blameless before Him.

Our Eternal Destination

God's sons will experience the fullness of God's Spirit. At the present time, Christians have the *"first fruits of the Spirit"* (Rom. 8:23), but God's intentions have always been to completely fill them. Then believers will have the fullness of the Spirit, including perfect love, joy, peace, patience, and so forth.

God's Spirit will also reveal the mind and will of the Father. No one will need to teach another person, for everyone will know God and have intimate contact with Him through the Spirit.

God's people will be the temples in which He abides forever.

Point 523: Jesus Will Have His Bride

Jesus will also have what He wants—a Bride. He has been waiting for thousands of years, and He will finally receive the one for whom He suffered and died. His Bride will know His love. She will not be ashamed in His love. She will know what it means to be loved. His love will make Her to be without spot or wrinkle.

The Groom will have His Bride forever. He will wash Her with the words of His love continually. They will dwell together in New Jerusalem where Jesus will be the light as His love floods the city.

Point 524: Sons of God Will Govern Creation

The Bride of Christ will own all that Jesus owns. We can express this same truth by saying that the sons of God will receive the same inheritance as Jesus does (Rom. 8:17). Revelation 22:3-5 also describes God's people as His bond-servants, and *"they will reign forever and ever."*

Over what will they reign?

First of all, over the earth. In Genesis chapter 1, we read about God's desire for humanity to fill and subdue the earth. Adam and Eve failed, but Jesus and the Church will succeed. However, this time *"there will no longer be a curse"* (Rev. 22:3), so the earth will yield its produce without humans having to work by the sweat of their brow. The earth will become a beautiful garden yielding an abundance for all.

The Book of Revelation also tells us of nations of people existing outside of the city of Jerusalem (Rev. 21:24). We are told of kings and other

Systematic Theology for the New Apostolic Reformation

rulers. Jesus made promises that believers who overcome will be given positions of authority over nations (Rev. 2:26). The earth will be filled with the knowledge of the Lord as righteousness, peace, and joy reign.

However, it is worth considering the possibility that God's people will not be limited for eternity on earth. Humanity was originally created to take dominion of the earth, but when Jesus ascended into heaven, He was given all authority over heaven and earth (Matt. 28:18). This means that the Bride and Groom will rule, not only over this planet, but all of creation. For this reason, all of creation *"will be set free from its slavery to corruption into the freedom of the glory of the children of God"* (Rom. 8:21). All of creation was subjected to futility because of sin, and all of creation will be liberated by the sons of God. In that liberation, *all things* will be brought into subjection so *"that God may be all in all"* (1 Cor. 15:25-28). Among other things, this means righteousness, peace, and joy will reign throughout the universe.

Point 525: Where Is Your Eternal Home

The description of our eternal home that is being offered here is different than what most modern Christians picture in their minds. Because Western Christianity is built on the dualistic cosmology of the ancient philosophers, tradition has handed us a vision of ourselves floating eternally in the clouds, singing to God. But think about that. If that eternal realm is really the immutable, timeless world of God, then there will be no changes there. In fact, there will be no changes in the notes that we sing. There will be no harmony. There will be no variation in sounds coming from instruments. It will just be one constant sound at the same volume coming from the believers for eternity. In addition, there will be no conversations going on. There will be no moving about. There will be no eating, no laughing, no planning, no work, no changing of thoughts or emotions. In a timeless world, everything always stays the same.

Instead of us going there, consider the possibility that God will come here. I mean fully here, so you can feel Him, walk with Him in a garden, and sit at His feet to hear Him talk. Revelation 22:1-3 says both the throne of God and the Lamb will be positioned in New Jerusalem. Imagine a God who is secure enough to come down from His throne and rub shoulders with His sons. One who wants people to call Him Father. Envision Jesus

Our Eternal Destination

who still has the same body in which He appeared to His disciples after His resurrection. Imagine One who enjoys playing ball and laughing. One who can pick up a handful of dirt and inhale the earthy fragrance. Think of Him smiling at you.

That is the heaven in which you and I will live forever.

Volume IX
Personal Eschatology

Section D
What Is Hell?

Now we can consider what will happen to those whose names are not written in the Book of Life. We are told that at the Great White Throne of Judgment:

> ... if anyone's name was not found written in the book of life, he was thrown into the Lake of Fire.
>
> (Rev. 20:15)

This Lake of Fire is also called the second death. Christians typically refer to it as hell.

Point 526: The Three Views of Hell

There are three commonly held views of hell: the traditional view, annihilationism, and ultimate reconciliation.[309] Adherents of each view claim that they develop their understanding from the Bible, yet their studies result in very different understandings.

The *traditional view* is that wicked people will be thrown into hell where they will be tormented, weeping and gnashing their teeth forever. That suffering is often described as eternal, conscious torment.

The second view is called *annihilationism*, which says that people who are thrown into hell will burn out of existence, i.e., be annihilated.

---

309 A fourth view which we will not be discussing is the metaphorical view which sees the suffering in hell as spiritual, emotional, and/or mental, rather than physical.

Systematic Theology for the New Apostolic Reformation

The third view is called *ultimate reconciliation*,[310] which is the belief that every person who is thrown into hell will eventually repent, be purged of their sins, and then enter into eternal happiness with God and all Christians.

Of the three views, the traditional view is the most commonly held view among evangelical Christians. In following pages, I will give the Scriptures that are most often used to teach this doctrine.

The second view, annihilationism, is a minority view, but in recent years it has become more accepted by evangelical Christians. In the following pages I will present it as a reasonable alternative view.

The third view, ultimate reconciliation, is a view of hell which I believe is unbiblical and a serious enough error that Christians should be warned about it.

Point 527: The First View of Hell: Traditional

As mentioned, the traditional view of hell is the most common view. However, the thought of it is so horrifying that Christians rarely talk or think seriously about it. Especially in modern times, Christian teachers rarely talk about hell as a place of eternal, conscious torment.

There are many Bible passages that refer to hell, but only a few can be used to teach the traditional view that hell will entail eternal torment. The most commonly used verse is the KJV of Matthew 25:46:

> *And these shall go away into <u>everlasting punishment</u>: but the righteous into life eternal.*

It is the term *"everlasting punishment"* that makes this verse effective in supporting the traditional view of hell lasting forever.

Another passage used by traditionalists is 2 Thessalonians 1:9, where we are told the destiny of those who are disobedient to the gospel:

> *These will pay the penalty of <u>eternal destruction</u>, away from the presence of the Lord and from the glory of His power.*

There are also two passages in the Book of Revelation that are used to teach the traditional view of hell:

---

[310] Also referred to as universal reconciliation, universal salvation, or universalism.

What Is Hell?

If anyone worships the beast and his image, and receives a mark on his forehead or on his hand . . . he will be tormented with fire and brimstone in the presence of the holy angels and in the presence of the Lamb. And the smoke of their <u>torment goes up forever and ever</u> . . . .
(Rev. 14:9-11)

And the devil who deceived them was thrown into the Lake of Fire and brimstone, where the beast and the false prophet are also; and they will be <u>tormented day and night forever and ever</u>.
(Rev. 20:10)

One more passage worth considering is Mark 9:47-48, where our Lord warned:

If your eye causes you to stumble, throw it out; it is better for you to enter the kingdom of God with one eye, than having two eyes, to be cast into hell, where <u>their worm does not die</u>, and the fire is not quenched.

In this passage, traditionalists focus on the phrase, *"their worm does not die,"* and they think of the worm as the soul of a person, which will wiggle in pain forever and ever in hell.

Although there are other Bible verses that talk about hell, the above five passages are the ones strongest in supporting the traditional view that each individual cast into hell will suffer forever and ever.

Point 528: The Second View of Hell: Annihilationism

Annihilationists believe that the people who are thrown into hell will burn out of existence, i.e., they will be annihilated. That annihilation may not be instantaneous, because the people may have to suffer for the sins they have committed, but annihilationists agree that every person thrown into hell will eventually burn out of existence.

Although annihilationism is a minority view, it has been around since the early Church. In recent times, it has become more commonly accepted, with certain prominent leaders embracing it or at least considering it as a biblically-based option. For example, in *Universalism and the Doctrine of Hell* (1993), the Anglican leader, John W. Wenham, rejected the traditional view in favor of annihilationism:

> I feel that the time has come when I must declare my mind honestly. I believe that endless torment is a hideous and unscriptural doctrine which has been a terrible burden on the mind of the church and a terrible blot on her presentation of the gospel. I should indeed be happy, if, before I die, I could help in sweeping it away.[311]

In his book *Essentials*, the noted Bible scholar, John Stott, wrote:

> ... the ultimate annihilation of the wicked should at least be accepted as a legitimate, Biblically founded alternative to their eternal conscious torment...[312]

The famous hymn writer, Isaac Watts, first believed in the eternal torment of the wicked but later came to believe that the wicked would be annihilated. The American evangelical scholar, Clark Pinnock, stated his belief in annihilationism in a book entitled *Four Views on Hell*.[313] These and many other Christian leaders have expressed their support of this view.

There are several Bible verses used to support annihilationism. The most used are the words of Jesus:

> *Do not fear those who kill the body but are unable to <u>kill the soul</u>; but rather fear Him who is able to <u>destroy both soul and body in hell</u>.*
> (Matt. 10:28)

To kill is translated from the Greek word *apokteina*. When applied to the physical body, it means to put to death, slay, or end the life of the body. We have no other interpretation when applied to the soul.

Other Bible verses warn that our God is a *Consuming Fire* (Heb. 12:29), and therefore, it is reasonable to think of His judgment fires as actually consuming rather than tormenting forever. Clark Pinnock pointed this out, writing:

---

311 John W. Wenham, *Universalism and Doctrine of Hell*, edited by N. M. S. Cameron (Grand Rapids, MI: Baker Book House, 1992), p. xiii.

312 John R. Stott, *Essentials: A Liberal-Evangelical Dialogue* (London: Hodder & Stoughton, 1988), pp. 320-326.

313 Clark H. Pinnock, *Four Views of Hell*, edited by William V. Crockett (Grand Rapids, MI: Zondervan Publishing House, 1996), pp.135-174.

What Is Hell?

The Bible uses the language of *death* and *destruction*, of *ruin* and *perishing*, when it speaks of the fate of the impenitent wicked. It uses the imagery of fire that consumes whatever is thrown into it; linking together images of fire and destruction suggests annihilation.[314]

Supporting this understanding, there are several Bible passages which compare wicked people to chaff that will be burned up on judgment day. For example, Jesus said:

So just as the tares are gathered up and burned with fire, so shall it be at the end of the age. The Son of Man will send forth His angels, and they will gather out of His kingdom all stumbling blocks, and those who commit lawlessness, and will throw them into the furnace of fire . . . .

(Matt. 13:40-42)

On judgment day, wicked people will be *"just as the tares"* which are *"burned with fire."*

Similarly, John the Baptist prophesied of the coming judgment saying:

. . . He will gather His wheat into the barn, but He will burn up the chaff with unquenchable fire.[315]

(Matt. 3:12)

The wicked are compared with chaff which is consumed when thrown into fire. The implication is that wicked people will be burned out of existence.

Notice that the fire of hell is called the *"unquenchable fire."* Some readers may take this to mean that people will suffer forever and ever, but that is not implied with this terminology. We can see the fire as unquenchable in the sense that it cannot be put out. Even today, firefighters sometimes encounter a building that is burning so ferociously that they cannot quench it. So they simply let the fire burn until it completely burns itself out. This understanding is supported by God's words in Jeremiah 17:27, where He said He would destroy Jerusalem by kindling *"an unquenchable fire."*

---

[314] Clark H. Pinnock, *Four Views of Hell*, edited by William V. Crockett (Grand Rapids, MI: Zondervan Publishing House, 1992), pp.145.
[315] Some Bible teachers consider this passage as referring to the destruction of Jerusalem in 70 AD.

Systematic Theology for the New Apostolic Reformation

Indeed, Jerusalem was destroyed in 70 AD. No one could quench the fire, but that fire does not burn today. It went out when Jerusalem was destroyed.

Think again of chaff being thrown into fire. In time it is consumed and utterly destroyed. Our natural experience with fire reveals how it consumes that which is thrown into it. If we see a house on fire, we know that it will be destroyed and only ashes will be left. Even human flesh burns up, rather than remaining alive while burning forever.

This corresponds with our understanding of God's nature as a consuming fire. His nature does not "heat up" those who come into His presence. It "consumes" them.

Malachi talks about that coming day of judgment, saying:[316]

> *For behold, the day is coming, burning like a furnace; and all the arrogant and <u>every evildoer will be chaff</u> . . . .*
>
> (Mal. 4:1)

Peter wrote of the coming judgment day, saying that it will be for the *"destruction of ungodly men"* (2 Peter 3:7). The word *destruction* is used rather than *eternal torment*. Similarly, Paul wrote that *"their end is destruction"* (Phil. 3:19). Further, he explained that *". . . the wages of sin is death . . ."* (Rom. 6:23). Paul did not say that the wages of sin is eternal torment.

Point 529: The Annihilationist's Answer to Matthew 25:46

Those holding to the view of annihilationism must deal with the verses used by those who teach the traditional view of hell.

Earlier I noted the favorite verse used by traditionalists to try prove their view of eternal conscious torment. The KJV of Matthew 25:46, says:

> *And these shall go away into everlasting punishment: but the righteous into life eternal.*

If, indeed, the wicked will go away into *everlasting punishment,* then the traditionalists are correct—hell will entail forever torment.

---

[316] Some teachers apply this verse to the destruction of Jerusalem in A.D. 70,, so they cannot agree with it being applied to the final judgment day.

What Is Hell?

But in this verse, the words *everlasting* and *eternal* are translated from the same Greek word, *aiónion*. The Greek root word, *aión*, literally means "age" or "dispensation of time." The Greek words, *aión*, and *aiónios*, can be difficult to translate because an age or dispensation of time can vary in length. The age in which God dwells is eternal, but there are other ages mentioned in the Bible that are limited in time. Romans 16:25 talks about *"long ages past."* Paul wrote about his current age, referring to it as *"this present evil age"* (Gal. 1:4). Other passages talk about ages in the future; for example, Ephesians 2:7 refers to *"the ages to come."* So the Greek word *aión* refers to an age which may or may not be an age lasting forever.

This puts into question our understanding of Matthew 25:46. The KJV says that the wicked go away into *"everlasting punishment,"* but the word translated as "everlasting" can also refer to "an age" of punishment. We know that the King James translators understood this because they translated *aiónion* in other ways in other passages. For example, the KJV of 1 Timothy 6:17, says:

> *Teaching us that, denying ungodliness and worldly lusts, we should live soberly, righteously, and godly, in this present world* [aióni].

"This present world" is not forever and ever. Similarly, in I Timothy 6:17 and Ephesian 1:21, the KJV translators translated *aiónion* as *"this world."*

So here is the problem: The King James translators translated the one Greek word *aiónion* in different ways. Even within Matthew 25:46 they were inconsistent, first translating *aiónion* as "everlasting" and second as "eternal." By saying that the wicked go away into "everlasting punishment," the translators were leading the reader to only one conclusion—that hell will entail forever torment. But, as explained, *aiónion* literally refers to a dispensation of time. It can mean everlasting, but it can also mean a dispensation of time which will have an end. Rather than tell us that hell is forever, the KJV of Matthew 25:46 tells us that the translators who developed the KJV already held to the traditional view of hell, and they were unwilling to let the reader come to any other conclusion.

Even if we accept this word *aión* in Matthew 25:46 as meaning "eternal," we must also consider how the words *eternal punishment* do not necessarily mean *eternal punishing*. The second implies ongoing torment forever and ever. But the first, *eternal punishment*, may indicate an event with eternal consequences. It may indicate the eternal judgment, in the

Systematic Theology for the New Apostolic Reformation

sense of being the final judgment. It will be a judgment from which no one can appeal. This understanding sees that people will be judged and God's sentencing will be final—never to change. Most Christians who believe in annihilationism understand this to be the actual meaning of *eternal judgment* or *eternal punishment*. Eternal judgment will be ultimate destruction.

Point 530: Annihilationist's Answer to Other Traditionalist's Verses

Now look at another verse which traditionalists like to use to support their doctrine of everlasting conscious torment. In 2 Thessalonians 1:9, we are told about the destiny of those who are disobedient to the gospel:

> *These will pay the penalty of eternal* [aiónion] *destruction, away from the presence of the Lord and from the glory of His power.*

In this verse, *aiónion* modifies *destruction*. This does not necessarily indicate a destruction that goes on forever, because it can refer to an event with eternal consequences. It is an eternal destruction in the sense that it is the final destruction.

This view is supported by other Bible verses. For example, Jude 1 verse 7 tells us that Sodom and Gomorrah were destroyed by *"eternal fire."* Even though the fire is called eternal, the fire which destroyed Sodom and Gomorrah is not burning today. That fire went out many years ago. It was eternal in the sense that it brought ultimate and final destruction upon Sodom and Gomorrah.

With similar reasoning, Christians who hold to annihilationism will explain the two verses in the Book of Revelation that traditionalists like to use to teach their doctrine of eternal conscious torment. Revelation 14:9-10 and 20:10, both use the phrase *"forever and ever,"* which in both passages has been translated from the two Greek words, *aiónios aiónon*. These words are literally translated as "ages of ages" or "dispensations of dispensations." Certainly a long period of time is implied with these phrases, and people thrown into hell may suffer for a long period before they burn out of existence, but ages of ages does not necessarily mean forever.

Furthermore, Revelation 20:10 only talks about the devil, the beast, and the false prophet; we know that the devil is a spiritual being, and

What Is Hell?

today there is much debate concerning whether or not the beast and the false prophet are human beings. Many scholars believe that these are spiritual powers behind certain people or that the beast is the personification of a totalitarian political system. The false prophet of Revelation may represent the voice of a false religious system rather than an individual. Acknowledging this, we realize that Revelation 20:10 does not tell us anything about how long *people* will suffer in hell.

Consider the other passage in the Book of Revelation that traditionalists like to use to support their doctrine:

> *If anyone worships the beast and his image, and receives a mark on his forehead or on his hand . . . he will be tormented with fire and brimstone in the presence of the holy angels and in the presence of the Lamb. And the <u>smoke of their torment goes up forever and ever</u> . . . .*
> (Rev. 14:9-11)

Christians who use this passage to argue for the doctrine of eternal torment focus on the phrase: *"their torment goes up forever and ever."* But actually it does not say their *torment* will last forever and ever; it says the *smoke* of their torment goes up forever and ever. What is meant by this smoke? The Book of Revelation is a very symbolic book, using apocalyptic language. *Smoke* sometimes refers to how things would vanish and *only the memory of those things would remain.* Such apocalyptic language was commonly used in declarations of judgment and end times.

To confirm this, we can see how the same terminology is used elsewhere in the Bible. In fact, the writer of Revelation may have borrowed the words of Isaiah as recorded in Isaiah 34:8-10:

> *For the Lord has a day of vengeance . . .*
> *And its land will become burning pitch.*
> *It will not be quenched night or day;*
> <u>*Its smoke will go up forever.*</u>
> *From generation to generation it will be desolate;*

In this passage, Isaiah was declaring the coming destruction of the city of Bozrah and the land of Edom. Isaiah said that the *"smoke will go up forever,"* but this did not mean that fire would continue destroying the region forever. In reality, that judgment came and went, plus the fires went out.

Systematic Theology for the New Apostolic Reformation

For further evidence of this, we can read Revelation 19, which tells us about the judgment of Babylon:

> *Her smoke rises up forever and ever.*
>
> (Rev. 19:3)

In the same context, we are told that Babylon will *"be burned up with fire"* (Rev. 18:8) *"and will not be found any more"* (Rev. 18:21). Hence, we see *smoke,* not as a sign of ongoing pain, but rather as the only thing left after judgment is complete. Babylon, we are told, will vanish and only the memory will remain.

Therefore, when we read Revelation 14:9-11, we should understand that people who received the mark of the beast will be annihilated and only a memory or a scent of them will remain. So then, rather than support the traditionalist's view, this passage actually supports annihilationism.

There is one more passage that traditionalists commonly use to support their doctrine of everlasting conscious torment. It is Mark 9:47-48, where our Lord warned:

> *If your eye causes you to stumble, throw it out; it is better for you to enter the kingdom of God with one eye, than having two eyes, to be cast into hell, where <u>their worm does not die</u>, and the fire is not quenched.*

Traditionalists typically think of the worm that does not die as the soul of a person which will wiggle in pain forever and ever in hell. In reality, the worm in this passage is *not* correlated with a person's soul. The worm is correlated with a worm that attacks a dead body and eats it. The worm is properly understood as a maggot that eats a corpse.

We know this because our Lord was quoting this phrase from Isaiah 66:23b-24, where God's judgment is described:

> *"All mankind will come to bow down before Me,"*
>   *says the Lord.*
> *"Then they shall go forth and look*
> *On the corpses of the men*
> *Who have transgressed against Me.*
> *For their worm will not die*
> *And their fire shall not be quenched . . . ."*

What Is Hell?

The *worm* works in unison with the *fire*. Both will consume. The worm (maggot) is not likened to the person, but the maggot comes from outside and eats the person. By saying the maggot will not die, Jesus was declaring that wicked people will not be able to outlive their devourers. With this understanding, we can see how the wicked people eventually will be burned, eaten, or consumed, even though the maggot may go on living just as the fire of hell goes on burning.[317]

We have just explained the primary passages which traditionalists like to use to prove their doctrine of eternal torment, but each of those passages can be explained through the eyes of annihilationism.

Point 531: Conditional Immortality

The question as to whether or not wicked people will suffer in hell forever hinges on the basic nature of humanity. Only if people are immortal beings can they—and will they—remain alive forever while suffering in hell.[318] If people are mortal, then we may expect the fire of judgment to end their existence.

Christians who believe in annihilationism understand that people become immortal beings when and only when they believe in Jesus. The Bible clearly declares that God alone is immortal. Paul wrote in 1 Timothy 6:16 about God *"who alone possesses immortality."* Therefore, people will only become immortal if and when they become partakers of divine nature by believing in Jesus.

Consider Adam. After he sinned, God told him:

For you are dust,
And to dust you shall return.

(Gen. 3:19)

Some teachers try to explain this as only referring to Adam's physical body, but God directed this toward Adam. He said *"you"* shall return to

---

317 An alternative understanding of this passage held by many Bible teachers is that the destruction being referred to here is the destruction which occurred when Jerusalem was destroyed in 70 AD. At that time, thousands of people were thrown beyond the walls of Jerusalem into the burning, maggot-ridden rubbish heap called *Gehenna*.

318 An alternative view which some traditionalists hold is that the wicked are mortal, but God will supernaturally sustain them forever while they suffer in hell.

Systematic Theology for the New Apostolic Reformation

dust. Furthermore, God closed off the tree of life so that Adam would not eat from it and then live forever:

> *and now, he might stretch out his hand, and take also from the tree of life, and eat, and live forever.*
>
> (Gen. 3:22)

Notice here the possibility for Adam to live forever. This means that Adam was not in a condition to live forever. This refers to his entire being.

If Adam ate from the tree of life, he would have become immortal. We can partake of Jesus, and hence, become immortal. It is the life of God that makes us immortal. The apostle Paul also wrote about the rewards awaiting those who *"by perseverance in doing good seek for glory and honor and immortality . . ."* (Rom. 2:7). It would make no sense for Paul to encourage people to seek for immortality if they already possessed it! The obvious point is that people (without the life of Jesus) are mortal. Humans only become immortal when they access the divine nature of God through Jesus Christ.

This is a central feature of the Gospel.

> *And the testimony is this, that God has given us eternal life, and this life is in His Son. He who has the Son has the life; he who does not have the Son of God does not have the life.*
>
> (1 John 5:11-12)

A person who does not have Jesus does not have eternal life.

This understanding, that only believers in Jesus are immortal, is called **conditional immortality**. Theologians refer to it by this name because there is a condition on being immortal. That condition is receiving the eternal life of God through Jesus Christ.

Some teachers use the terms *conditional immortality* and *annihilationism* interchangeably, but the focus is slightly different. Conditional immortality refers to the nature of humanity, with immortality being conditional upon one's acceptance of Jesus. Annihilationism refers to the nature of hell and the fires of hell having the ability to consume that which is thrown in there. These two doctrines are compatible with one another because non-Christians do not have eternal life, and therefore, they will be burned out of existence in hell.

What Is Hell?

E.G. Selwyn, the Dean of Winchester, wrote:

> There is little in the NT to suggest a state of everlasting punishment, but much to indicate an ultimate destruction or dissolution of those who cannot enter into life: conditional immortality seems to be the doctrine most consonant with the teaching of Scripture.[319]

Consider the most known verse in the Bible, John 3:16:

> *For God so loved the world, that He gave His only begotten Son, that whoever believes in Him shall not perish, but have eternal life.*

There are only two options: perishing or having eternal life.

What I hope you can accept is that the definition of *eternal life* is "eternal life." This may seem simplistic, but most Christians see eternal life as some mystical, unknowable God-quality of life. Of course, we become partakers of divine life when we receive Jesus Christ, however, that life also provides eternal existence. Eternal life is eternal life. Those who do not have this eternal life will not live forever.

Point 532: The First Century Jewish Perspective

Immortality is worth considering from the perspective of the 1st century Jews and their understanding of the OT.

In the OT, there are no verses that clearly say people will exist forever, but there are several passages indicating the opposite. Here are just a couple:

> *For the fate of the sons of men and the fate of beasts is the same. As one dies so dies the other; indeed, they all have the same breath...All go to the same place. All came from the dust and all return to the dust.*
> (Eccl. 3:19-20)

Then Psalm 146:3-4 says:

> *Do not trust in princes,*
> *In mortal man, in whom there is no salvation.*

---

319 Edward G. Selwyn, *The First Epistle of St. Peter* (London: Macmillian, 1961), p. 358.

Systematic Theology for the New Apostolic Reformation

His spirit departs, he returns to the earth;
In that very day his thoughts perish.

The truth that people's *"thoughts perish"* implies total extinction.

When the Jews in Jesus' day studied the OT, they were divided over this issue of human immortality. Most of the Pharisees believed that the dead would be resurrected from the grave by the power of God.[320] The Sadducees, on the other hand, concluded that people's existence ended when they died physically (Luke 20:27).

One day when Jesus was communicating with the Sadducees, He corrected their thinking, saying to them:

> *The sons of this age marry and are given in marriage, but those who are considered worthy to attain to that age and the resurrection from the dead, neither marry, nor are given in marriage; for they cannot even die anymore, because they are like angels, and are sons of God, being sons of the resurrection.*
> (Luke 20:34b-36)

Notice Jesus did not say everyone is immortal. On the contrary, He taught that only those worthy of the resurrection would be as the angels. Only those who are sons of God cannot *"die anymore."*

Point 533: Challenging Foundational Topics within Theology

The debates around the traditional view of hell versus annihilationism involve more than questions about certain key Bible verses. They reach deeper into people's theology and into their loyalties to certain key religious figures. Classical/Reformed theology corresponds most closely with the traditional view of hell. Therefore, challenging the traditional view of hell is challenging Classical/Reformed theology. Allow me to explain.

As we have shown throughout this book, Classical/Reformed theology was profoundly influenced by the ancient Greek philosophers. Those philosophers—especially Plato—believed that each person existed as a spirit being in eternity and descends into a physical body to inhabit and dwell on earth for a time—a time of imprisonment in a body. At physical

---

320 A significant number of Pharisees believed that the souls of good people are reincarnated.

What Is Hell?

death, people are set free from their bodies and go on living in a spiritual state eternally. This is according to the ancient Greek philosophers.

Some of the early Church leaders were influenced greatly by this Greek philosophical way of thinking. Although the concept of people preexisting (existing in eternity past) was rejected by most of the early Church, many embraced the idea that all people go on living forever.

Dr. William Temple, the late Archbishop of Canterbury, Primate of Great Britain, wrote:

> If men had not imported the Greek and unbiblical notion [from Plato], of the natural indestruction of the individual soul, and then read the New Testament with that already in their minds, they would have drawn from it a belief, not in everlasting torment, but in annihilation.[321]

Before the influence of Greek philosophy, the early Church did not commonly believe that all people are eternal beings. Some scholars who study the writings of the early Church fathers conclude that Clement of Rome, Ignatius, Polycarp, and Irenaeus each believed that wicked people will go out of existence. Others scholars who study these writings will debate some of these findings, however, there is no doubt that at least Irenaeus was firm on the mortality of humanity—soul and body.[322]

Embracing the immortality of all human souls was a gradual transition. By the 5th century, this doctrine became deeply seated into Classical theology. Therefore, modern Christians who question this doctrine are questioning Classical theology.

Furthermore, they are questioning certain heroes of Classical/Reformed theology. Adherents of Classical/Reformed theology have great respect for leaders who championed their way of thinking. Leaders such as Augustine, Calvin, Spurgeon, and Edwards kept the doctrine of eternal conscious torment as central to their worldview. Jonathan Edward's most famous sermon, "Sinners in the Hands of an Angry God," portrays God holding sinners by a thread directly over the everlasting flames of hell.

Just as revealing is the Reformed understanding of the atonement (the penal substitutionary view). At the forefront of Reformed thought is God

---

[321] William Temple, *Christian Faith and Life* (London: SCM Press Ltd., 1954), p. 81.
[322] For a list of dozens of Church leaders who believe in conditional immortality, see: http://www.specialtyinterests.net/champions_of_conditional_immortality.html.

Systematic Theology for the New Apostolic Reformation

taking His wrath out on Jesus. Nothing reveals more clearly the wrath of God toward sin or the seriousness of sin. Sin deserves damnation. People who reject the sacrifice of Jesus deserve eternal conscious torment—or so Reformed theologians teach.

Therefore, Christians who question the traditional view of hell have to consider the existence of a "nicer God." They must reconsider how serious sin is and if, indeed, it warrants everlasting torment. Those who question the nature of hell are also questioning the thoughts of past leaders. For Christians who have been taught to honor these leaders as the standard bearers of truth, that questioning can seem foolish or even blasphemous.

Reformed Christians who defend the traditional view of hell are defending more than a certain understanding of hell. They are defending the most fundamental beliefs of their worldview, i.e., their understanding of God, sin, and who the heroes of our faith should be.

Furthermore, considering the possibility that the souls of non-Christians may be annihilated in hell and, therefore, are not immortal, is to admit that our forefathers were profoundly influenced by the ancient Greek philosophers. That consideration shakes the foundation of Classical/Reformed theology and opens the door to every other thought contrary to Classical/Reformed theology that is taught throughout this book and other books like it. To soften on the traditional view of hell is to call into question the foundation of Classical/Reformed theology.

On the other hand, a Christian who has already identified the weakened foundation of Classical/Reformed theology will not be threatened by considering alternative views of hell.

Point 534: The Third View of Hell: Ultimate Reconciliation

Now we can consider the third view of hell, called ultimate reconciliation. This is the belief that all human beings will be reconciled to God, i.e., all people will ultimately go to heaven. Hell is not seen as a place of punishment, but rather purification. Some advocates go so far as to say that Satan and all the demons will some day see the light, repent, and be saved.

In order to embrace the view of ultimate reconciliation, one must accept the idea that people can be saved after they die, i.e., that God is not limiting the opportunities for salvation for this lifetime. According to ultimate reconciliationists, many conversions will take place the instant

What Is Hell?

people see Jesus after they die. Some ultimate reconciliationists propose that the vast majority of sinners will repent during the period of the new heavens and earth described in Revelation 21 and 22. They point out that in New Jerusalem the gates of the city will never be closed and people will be constantly bringing the glory of the nations into the city (Rev. 21:25-26). Ultimate reconciliationists take this to mean people will be constantly turning to Jesus and entering into eternal happiness with Jesus.

Ultimate reconcilationists use certain other Bible passages to support their position. One of their favorite verses is 1 John 2:2:

> . . . *and He Himself is the propitiation for our sins; and not for ours only, but also for those of the whole world.*

Through the reconcilationist's eyes, this verse declares that Jesus paid for all people's sins, and therefore, all people will be saved.

Another favorite verse of ultimate reconciliationists is Colossians 1:20:

> . . . *and through Him to reconcile all things to Himself, having made peace through the blood of His cross; through Him, I say, whether things on earth or things in heaven.*

Reconciliationists like to point out how this verse says "*all things*" will be reconciled.

Ultimate reconciliation was held by several of the early Church fathers, including Clement of Alexandria, Origen, and St. Gregory of Nyssa. Some popular modern teachers of ultimate reconciliation include Gregory MacDonald, Carlton Pearson, Thomas Talbott, Stephen Jones, and J. Preston Eby.

Point 535: What's Wrong with Ultimate Reconciliation?

Being someone who does not believe in ultimate reconciliation, I can point out some of the errors in their thinking. For example, Colossians 1:20, which I just quoted, says "*things on earth and things in heaven*" will be reconciled to God; it does not say things in hell will be reconciled.

We can also re-examine 1 John 2:2, where John tells us that Jesus is the propitiation for the sins of the whole world. Three verses earlier we are told that sins must be confessed and forgiveness received (1 John 1:9). So

Systematic Theology for the New Apostolic Reformation

even if Jesus made provision for the forgiveness of all people's sins, this is no guarantee that His forgiveness will be appropriated. One does not necessarily follow the other.

We must also look carefully at the ultimate reconciliationist's understanding of what will happen on the new earth. As mentioned, many ultimate reconciliationists envision people moving from hell into New Jerusalem and into the presence of Jesus. That explanation does not match what is actually described in Revelation 20-22. In chapter 20, the Great White Throne Judgment takes place, and all whose names are not written in the Book of Life are cast into the Lake of Fire (hell). Then after that Great Judgment, Revelation 21 tells us about a new heavens and earth. The Lake of Fire is revealed as a completely different place separate from the new earth and even existing before the new earth. There is no evidence that those who are in the Lake of Fire will be able to move from that place to New Jerusalem. It is possible that people on the new earth may move into New Jerusalem, but they are already on the new earth, not in the Lake of Fire.

There are other verses that reconciliationists like to use to support their doctrine, and many books have been written to discuss the counter arguments. Here I will simply point out two Scriptures that, to me, cannot be reconciled with the view of ultimate reconciliation.

First, Paul writes of the coming judgment:

> *. . . when the Lord Jesus . . . dealing out retribution to those who do not know God and to those who do not obey the gospel of our Lord Jesus. These will pay the penalty of eternal destruction . . . .*
> (2 Thess. 1:6-9)

This verse clearly tells of eternal destruction, not ultimate reconciliation.

A second passage that I cannot reconcile with ultimate reconciliation is Hebrews 11:26-27:

> *For if we go on sinning willfully after receiving the knowledge of the truth, there no longer remains a sacrifice for sins, but a terrifying expectation of judgment and the fury of a fire which will consume the adversaries.*

This idea that there *"no longer remains a sacrifice for sins"* contradicts the idea of ultimate reconciliation.

What Is Hell?

Point 536: Traditional, Annihilationism, or Ultimate Reconciliation?

Which view of hell one believes should also correlate with what a person believes about the nature of God. A person who believes that only good things (in the sense of warm and fuzzy things[323]) come from God will tend to choose ultimate reconciliation. A person who sees God as a wrathful Judge who must punish sin will tend to choose the traditional view of hell. These two views are polar opposites.

In this book, I have been trying to correct both extreme views of God. In Volume V, we saw biblical examples of how God was responsible for many things that cannot be considered warm and fuzzy. We have also discussed how God should not be seen as a wrathful Judge.

An accurate view is offered by God as He revealed Himself on Mount Sinai saying:

> *The LORD, the LORD God, compassionate and gracious, slow to anger, and abounding in lovingkindness . . . yet He will by no means leave the guilty unpunished . . . .*
> (Ex. 34:6-7)

God is full of goodness. He is love. Yet, there is also an aspect of His nature to be feared by those who live in disobedience to Him.

God stretches forth His hands all day long, wanting people to come to Him, but the Psalmist warns us:

> *He will not always strive with us,*
> *Nor will He keep His anger forever.*
> (Ps. 103:9)

God will ultimately judge those who continually reject His love. It is a terrifying thing to fall into the hands of the living God.

The NT warns us that past judgments reveal how God will deal with wicked people in the future (Jude 1:5-7). The wrath of God is a real aspect of His nature to be feared. To many He will say, "*I never knew you; depart from Me, you who practice lawlessness*" (Matt. 7:23). Peter wrote of the coming judgment day, saying that it will be for the "*destruction of ungodly men*" (2 Peter 3:7). Note that the judgment day is not for the reconciliation of ungodly men but for their destruction.

---

[323] This use of "warm and fuzzy things" is explained in V:B:280.

Systematic Theology for the New Apostolic Reformation

Point 537: Reformed Theology and Ultimate Reconciliation

Adherents of Classical/Reformed theology see God as a wrathful Judge[324] and, corresponding to this, typically embrace the traditional view of hell. However, there are some followers of Reformed theology who are reconsidering the relevant issues. Interestingly, adherents of Reformed theology who abandon the traditional view of hell are more likely to accept ultimate reconciliation than annihilationism. This is true for two primary reasons.

First, the concept of the immortality of all souls is deeply interwoven in Reformed theology. Therefore, ultimate reconciliation is a possibility, while annihilationism is not.

Second, followers of Reformed theology see God as sovereign in the sense that He is in exhaustive control of all things. According to them, God's will is always, in every case, accomplished. Corresponding to this, Christians consistent with Reformed theology do not believe that humans have (libertarian) free will.[325] If, indeed, God's will is perfectly accomplished, then a Bible verse that says God *"desires all men to be saved"* (1 Tim. 2:4) means that all people will be saved.

Most adherents of Reformed theology see ultimate reconciliation as unorthodox and even heretical, yet it is still more compatible with Reformed theology than annihilationism. For this reason, books that support ultimate reconciliation typically spend time defending the Classical/Reformed view that God is in exhaustive control of all things.

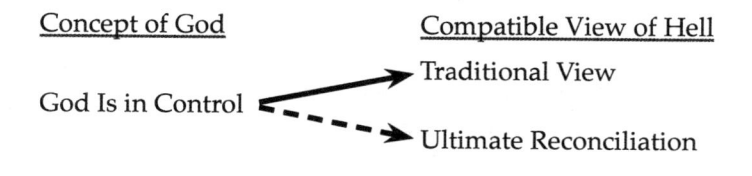

Concept of God	Compatible View of Hell
God Is in Control	→ Traditional View
	⇢ Ultimate Reconciliation

Point 538: Father-Son Theology and Hell

Father-Son theology leads to different conclusions.
First, Father-Son theology does not equate God's sovereignty with

---
324 Of course, they also see God as loving and merciful.
325 This is discussed in IV:M:267.

What Is Hell?

His exhaustive control of all things. Instead, His sovereignty means He can do whatever He wants to do whenever He wants. Further, God has sovereignly decided not to control all things. People have some amount of free will. So even though God desires all to be saved, this does not mean everyone will be saved. Because people have free will, they can choose to not be reconciled to God, which eliminates ultimate reconciliation.[326]

Second, we must consider if the human soul is immortal. If it is, then the traditional view of hell is a logical choice. On the other hand, if the human soul is only immortal as a result of receiving Jesus, then annihilationism is the logical choice, since mortal people can and will be burned out of existence in the consuming fires of hell. As I have already explained,[327] for me the Scriptural evidence reveals that people are mortal until they receive Jesus. This leads me to believe annihilationism is the most biblically accurate view.

A person's decision about the nature of hell is also profoundly influenced by that person's view of God. If God is as Reformed theology proposes, then our God is a consuming fire and He may, indeed, cause millions of people to gnash their teeth in agony for a billion years, wanting to die, but not allowed to die, experiencing pain beyond anything people have ever experienced, and then having a billion years ahead of them, and then another billion years, and then another. I must agree with Dr. Clark Pinnock that the eternal torment doctrine "... makes God into a bloodthirsty monster who maintains an everlasting Auschwitz for victims whom he does not even allow to die."[328] On the other hand, if God has *any* compassion and mercy in His nature, it seems to me that He will annihilate the wicked.

Finally, in choosing which view of hell is accurate, I must ask, "What does justice dictate?" The Bible reveals that God has instilled some sense of justice in us (Rom. 2:14-16). Paul encouraged the Corinthian Christians to exercise their sense of justice now while alive, because Christians will be called upon to judge the angels in the next life (I Cor. 6:1-3). Of course, God is the ultimate judge and we must wholly throw ourselves at His mercy, but we do have some sense of justice instilled within our nature by the God who created us.

---

326 Some teachers will still argue that God can eventually win the wills of all people, so for them, ultimate reconciliation is a possibility.
327 IX:D:531-533.
328 Clark Pinnock, *"The Destruction of the Impenitent,"* CTR 4 (Spring 1990): p. 253.

Systematic Theology for the New Apostolic Reformation

So what does justice dictate? Does 70 years of sin deserve ten trillion years of torture? I don't think so.

Still, I do not want to take an unshakable position on this, because it is possible that my sense of justice will be radically altered on judgment day. In the full presence of God, it may then become clear that rejecting Jesus Christ is so evil that it does deserve eternal conscious torment. Presently, I do not think so, but I might be wrong. So I am open to the possibility that the traditional view of hell is correct. However, presently I believe that the most biblically accurate view is annihilationism, corresponding to the nature of God and humanity as revealed in the Bible.

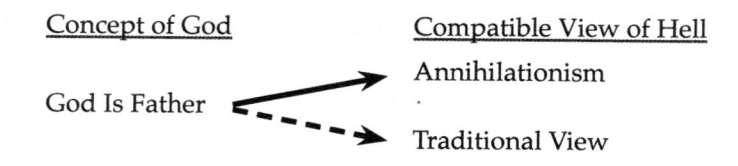

Concept of God	Compatible View of Hell
God Is Father	Annihilationism
	Traditional View

Point 539: The Bride Still Has Something to Say

Before leaving this subject we should consider one more factor in determining the eternal destiny of those who are cast into hell. Father-Son theology is firmly seated in the concept of a relational God who listens to His people and is capable of changing His mind in response to their requests. Closely associated with this is the relationship of Jesus with His Bride; they will rule together for eternity. These truths lead us to believe that God's people can and will influence future decisions.

Therefore, even if the traditional view of hell is correct, it is not fixed. It is possible that the sons of God will ask the Father to end the suffering of those in hell. It is possible that the Bride will ask Her Husband to annihilate the wicked. Of course, this is totally incompatible with Classical/Reformed theology, but as a believer in Father-Son theology, I am convinced that God can change His mind. Therefore, even if the traditional view of hell is correct, I hope that I will be among the saints who ask God to end the suffering by annihilating the wicked who refuse to repent.

Volume X
Trinity and Christology

The word, ***trinity,*** comes from *tri* meaning "three" and *unity* meaning "united as one." The word is not in the Bible, but it summarizes the orthodox Christian view that God is three Persons in One God.

In this volume, we will discuss this triune nature of God and **Christology**, which is the study of Jesus Christ. The reason we place Christology here is because the understanding of Jesus as both God and man has always been the most crucial element of our understanding of the Trinity. Establishing the fact that Father-God is God has been no problem historically, but the early Church fathers had to wrestle with their understanding of Jesus as both God and man. Similarly, today people have to grasp this truth in order to embrace the Trinity.

Knowing that the Holy Spirit is also God is just as important for understanding the Trinity, but we will dedicate Volume XI to our study of the Holy Spirit.

Volume X
Trinity & Christology

Section A
Biblical Witness to the Trinity

It has often been said that the NT reveals that which the OT conceals. This is true for the doctrine of three Persons in One God. Here we will see hints of the Trinity in the OT but revealed in the NT.

Point 540: The Singularity of God in the OT

The OT is very clear that there is only one God. Deuteronomy 6:4 declares:

Hear, O Israel: The Lord our God, the Lord is one.

God declares:

I am the Lord, and there is no other;
Besides Me there is no God . . . .

(Is. 45:5)

The idea that there are three or any other number of gods is unthinkable to those who take the OT seriously.

Point 541: The Plurality of Persons in the OT

In spite of the clear statements of there being only one God, we can find OT references that imply a plurality in one God.

Systematic Theology for the New Apostolic Reformation

In Genesis 1:1, we read how God created the heavens and the earth. As noted earlier,[329] the Hebrew word *Elohim* is plural, but the verb following this word is singular. Hence, *Elohim* has been translated as God.

In Genesis 1:26, we read, *"Then God said, 'Let Us make man in Our image, according to Our likeness.'"* Note the use of the plural verb, *"let us,"* and the plural pronoun, *"our."*

Some teachers have suggested that such usage of the plural forms may have simply been according to an ancient customary practice of using the plural when referring to any majesty, even human kings in ancient times. However, we have no examples in the Bible of the plural forms being used in that way. Other teachers have suggested that the use of the plural forms may have referred to the angelic beings who were with God. Yet, we have no reason to think that humans were created in the image of angels, since other passages only affirm that humans were created in the image of God.

Supporting the plurality within God are Bible passages in which more than one person is called God or Lord. For example, in Psalm 110:1, David says:

> *The Lord says to my Lord:*
> *"Sit at My right hand*
> *Until I make Your enemies a footstool for Your feet."*

David recognized two different Persons whom he called Lord. In the NT, we see Jesus quoting this passage and confounding the religious leaders of His day, who could not understand how there must be more than one Person worthy of being called Lord (Matt. 22:41-46).

For another example, look at Psalm 45:6-7:

> *Your throne, O God, will last for ever and ever . . . therefore God, your God, has set you above your companions . . . .*

Notice two Persons being referred to as God.

Although there are other similar passages, we will note only one more here:

> *The Spirit of the Lord God is upon me,*
> *Because the Lord has anointed me*

---
329 I:B:5.

Biblical Witness to the Trinity

To bring good news to the afflicted . . . .

(Is. 61:1)

Three divine Persons are noted here: "*the Spirit of the Lord God*," "*the Lord*," and "*Me*" (whom the NT reveals as Jesus: Luke 4:18).

Point 542: Three Persons Revealed in the NT

There are numerous passages in the NT that reveal the three Persons in the Godhead.

For example, Matthew explained the water baptism of Jesus as follows:

After being baptized . . . he [John the Baptist] saw the <u>Spirit of God</u> descending as a dove and lighting on <u>Him</u>, and behold, a voice out of the heavens said, "This is <u>My</u> beloved Son, in whom <u>I</u> am well-pleased."

(Matt. 3:16-17)

Here we see the Holy Spirit descending out of heaven, Jesus standing in the water, and the Father speaking from heaven.

Another clear example is from when Jesus talked about dying, ascending to the Father, and then sending the Spirit into the world:

<u>I</u> will ask the <u>Father</u>, and He will give you another <u>Helper</u>, that He may be with you forever; that is the Spirit of truth . . . .

(John 14:16-17)

We also have specific Bible verses that mention the three Persons of the Trinity. For example, Jesus told His disciples:

Go therefore and make disciples of all the nations, baptizing them in the name of the <u>Father</u> and the <u>Son</u> and the <u>Holy Spirit</u>.

(Matt. 28:19)

The apostle Paul wrote:

Now there are varieties of gifts, but the same <u>Spirit</u>. And there are

Systematic Theology for the New Apostolic Reformation

> *varieties of ministries, and the same <u>Lord</u>. There are varieties of effects, but the same <u>God</u> who works all things in all persons.*
> (1 Cor. 12:4-6)

Then in Ephesians 4:4-6:

> *There is one body and one <u>Spirit</u>, . . . one <u>Lord</u>, one faith, one baptism, one <u>God and Father</u> . . . .*

Peter wrote:

> *. . . according to the foreknowledge of God the <u>Father</u>, by the sanctifying work of the <u>Spirit</u>, to obey <u>Jesus Christ</u> . . . .*
> (1 Peter 1:2)

Jude exhorted his disciples, saying:

> *But you, beloved, building yourselves up on your most holy faith, praying in the <u>Holy Spirit</u>, keep yourselves in the love of <u>God</u>, waiting anxiously for the mercy of our <u>Lord Jesus Christ</u> to eternal life.*
> (Jude 1:20-21)

Paul closed his second letter to the Corinthians by writing:

> *The grace of the <u>Lord Jesus Christ</u>, and the love of <u>God</u>, and the fellowship of the <u>Holy Spirit</u>, be with you all.*
> (2 Cor. 13:14)

These are just a few of the verses that mention the three Persons of the Godhead.[330]

Point 543: Metaphors of the Trinity

Countless Bible teachers have offered their own metaphors to explain the Trinity, but no metaphor fully explains the relationship between the

---

[330] The King James Version of 1 John 5:7 is often used to support the doctrine of the Trinity, but it is based on a very small number of Greek texts that are from the late Middle Ages.

Biblical Witness to the Trinity

Father, Son, and Holy Spirit. Yet, Jesus used parables to help us understand spiritual truths, so it is appropriate for teachers today to use metaphors.

One of the most used metaphors is in comparing the Trinity to water, which is able to exist in three phases, solid, liquid, and gas. This metaphor is helpful because all three phases consist of water. Yet, the metaphor fails in explaining the Trinity because water does not exist simultaneously in all three phases.

Another metaphor is of a triangular prism made of glass. The three sides represent the three Persons of the Trinity, while all three consist of the same material—glass. This metaphor shows all three sides existing at the same time but does not reveal the truth of three distinct Persons.

The Trinity has also been explained using different dimensions of existence.[331] We can apply this to the biblical cosmology that we developed in Volume III, where we identified three heavens filling the same space. With that model, think of three Persons manifesting in the natural realm, but existing as one in the third heaven. This may be closer to explaining the relationship between the Father, Son, and Holy Spirit, but we have no way of actually knowing if this is true, so it is best thought of as a metaphor.

THE TRINITY SHOWN AS THREE PERSONS IN THE NATURAL REALM

---

[331] C. S. Lewis deserves credit for presenting a metaphor like this in his book, *Mere Christianity*.

Systematic Theology for the New Apostolic Reformation

No metaphor fully explains the Trinity, but Christians continue to hold to this truth because the Scriptural evidence reveals that there are three Persons in one God.

Section B
Jesus as Fully God

It is not enough to recognize the plurality of Persons and the singularity of God to develop the doctrine of the Trinity. We must also examine the nature of Jesus. We must see Jesus as fully God and fully man. After discussing the Scriptures most often used to teach that Jesus is God, I am going to take a less traditional path to explain His divinity. I will explain how Yahweh in the OT is the Preincarnate Jesus Christ.

Point 544: Jesus as God in the New Testament

The resurrection validated Jesus' divinity. Of course, He worked many miracles, and certain individuals such as Peter had already confessed, *"You are the Christ, the Son of the living God"* (Matt. 16:16). Others, like Thomas, did not believe until he saw the resurrected Jesus with his own eyes, after which Thomas confessed, *"My Lord and my God!"* (John 20:29). Jesus appeared in His resurrected body to His disciples, including more than 500 people at one time (1 Cor. 15:6), which gave witness to His divine nature.

The early Church wrestled with the related ideas, while studying the writings of the apostles. John's words made it clear:

> *In the beginning was the Word, and the Word was with God, and the Word was God.*
> (John 1:1)

John went on to declare that Jesus was Co-creator with the Father:

Systematic Theology for the New Apostolic Reformation

> *He was in the beginning with God. <u>All things came into being through Him</u>, and apart from Him nothing came into being that has come into being.*
>
> (John 1:2-3)

The apostle Paul added His authoritative words confirming that Jesus was Co-creator:

> *For <u>by Him all things were created</u>, both in the heavens and on earth, visible and invisible, whether thrones or dominions or rulers or authorities—all things have been created through Him and for Him.*
>
> (Col. 1:16)

Paul also declared Jesus' divinity:

> *. . . the Christ according to the flesh, who is over all, God blessed forever. Amen.*
>
> (Rom. 9:5)

> *. . . looking for the blessed hope and the appearing of the glory of our <u>great God and Savior, Christ Jesus</u>.*
>
> (Titus 2:13)

Anyone who accepts the NT as God's Word will conclude that Jesus is God.

Point 545: God Manifested in Flesh

It is the Christian belief that Jesus is God, yet, unbelievers often find this idea incomprehensible. It is most difficult when they think about an ordinary human being and compare that individual to their own concept of God. Their concepts of a human and God are simply too different from each other. In their minds, only an insane person could equate a man with God. As a consequence, those unbelievers may accept Jesus as a great teacher or leader—but not as God.

The perceived gap between Jesus as a man and Jesus as God is narrowed when we help people think in smaller increments.

Consider how God manifested in a burning bush to Moses. While God revealed Himself in the bush, we realize that He simultaneously

Jesus as Fully God

filled the heavens and earth. Next consider how God revealed Himself to the Hebrews in a pillar of fire. While God revealed Himself in the pillar, He simultaneously filled the heavens and the earth. God also revealed Himself in the Jewish temple, and while He manifested at that earthly location, He continued to fill all of creation. Most people who believe in God have no problems accepting these truths that God could manifest in one place on earth, while at the same time filling all of creation.

If, then, God can manifest in a burning bush, why couldn't He just as easily manifest in human flesh? Is it any more difficult for God to manifest in human form than it is for Him to manifest in a burning bush? God is sovereign, so we should not have difficulty accepting what the Bible tells us about God manifesting in human form. That is what happened. The very substance of God entered into the womb of Mary, and the Word became flesh. Then God as man walked among humanity.

Point 546: Yahweh as Preincarnate Jesus

Most Christians, who have studied this subject of Jesus being God, have examined the Scriptures already mentioned (and a few others). Many have also read through the history of the early Church noting how our forefathers concluded that Jesus is God.

There is another path to the same conclusion, a path seen in the writings of certain Church fathers, most notably Eusebius. Eusebius was a 4th century historian who is famous for having written *The History of the Church*. He also wrote to the Jewish people explaining how Christianity is not a different religion than Judaism, but the God whom the Jews worshiped in the OT was Jesus Christ.

Now as I take the same approach as Eusebius did, I will be talking about more than **theophanies**, which are manifestations of God to people. For example, God appeared in human form when He talked to Abraham and promised that he would have a son (Gen. 18:1-14). God manifested in a pillar of fire to the Hebrews as they walked through the wilderness (Ex. 13:21). Indeed, these events are accepted by Christians as theophanies, i.e., times when God manifested in the natural world.

However, I am not talking about theophanies now. I want to point out the evidence that Yahweh in the OT was the Preincarnate Second Person of the Trinity. For modern Christians who have never heard this perspective,

Systematic Theology for the New Apostolic Reformation

it can be surprising. Today Christians usually associate Yahweh of the OT with the Trinity or with God the Father. Consider the biblical evidence that Yahweh was Jesus Christ before He became flesh.

Point 547: Moses Met with the Only Mediator

The NT clearly tells us that Jesus is the only Mediator between God and humanity (1 Tim. 2:5). *Since Jesus is the only Mediator, then He must have been the One who met with Moses.* Please think about this.

The Bible tells us:

> *... the Lord used to speak to Moses face to face, just as a man speaks to his friend.*
>
> (Ex. 33:11)

Yet, the Bible also tells us:

> *No one has seen God at any time.*
>
> (1 John 4:12)

> *Nor does anyone know the Father except the Son ...*
>
> (Matt. 11:27)

> *No one has seen God at any time; the only begotten God* [the Son] *who is in the bosom of the Father, He has explained Him.*
>
> (John 1:18)

> *Not that anyone has seen the Father, except the One who is from God; He has seen the Father.*
>
> (John 6:46)

Similarly, Paul taught about God *"whom no man has seen or can see"* (1 Tim. 6:16). If no human being has seen God the Father, then with whom did Moses speak? He must have spoken with the Preincarnate Jesus. He must have spoken with the only Mediator between God and man.

This is exactly what Jesus said:

> *For if you believed Moses, you would believe Me; for he wrote of Me.*
>
> (John 5:46)

Jesus as Fully God

You search the Scriptures, because you think that in them you have eternal life, and it is these that bear witness of Me.

(John 5:39)

Moses did not write about Jesus in some hidden manner so the reader has to read between the lines to see Him. Moses was actually writing about the Second Person of the Trinity before He became flesh.

Think of Jesus when He took Peter, James, and John up to a mountain and was transfigured before them. There Moses and Elijah met with Jesus. This is just like the times in the OT when Yahweh met with Moses on Mount Sinai.

Point 548: Abraham Met with the Only Mediator

Consider the discussion Jesus had with the religious leaders concerning His relationship to Abraham:

Your father Abraham rejoiced to see My day, and he saw it and was glad. So the Jews said to Him, "You are not yet fifty years old, and have You seen Abraham?" Jesus said to them, "Truly, truly, I say to you, before Abraham was born, I am."

(John 8:56-58)

In this passage, Jesus revealed Himself as the I Am with whom Abraham talked. Because the Jews understood Jesus' statement as declaring Himself as Yahweh, they picked up stones to kill Him for blasphemy (John 8:59).

Point 549: Jesus, the Revealed Yahweh

In Volume I, Section D, we discussed the names in the OT that are associated with Yahweh. In the NT we see how Jesus revealed Himself as the fulfillment of those names. For example, God was revealed in the OT as Yahweh Rapha (Lord Our Healer), and in the NT we see Jesus healing the sick. The OT reveals God as Yahweh Tsidkenu (Lord Our Righteousness), and in the NT we learn how Jesus is our righteousness. The OT calls God by the name Yahweh Rohi (Lord Our Shepherd), and Jesus declares that He is the Good Shepherd. Similarly we can see Jesus as our Provider, Banner, and Peace.

Systematic Theology for the New Apostolic Reformation

In the OT, Yahweh is revealed as the Savior—the only Savior:

> *I, even I, am the Lord,*
> *And there is no savior besides Me.*
>
> (Is. 43:11)

The NT reveals that Jesus is the Savior—the only Savior:

> *Salvation is found in no one else, for there is no other name under heaven given to mankind by which we must be saved.*
>
> (Acts 4:12)

Paul explained:

> *... for, "Everyone who calls on the name of the Lord will be saved."*
>
> (Rom. 10:13)

This is most likely a quote of Joel 2:32:

> *And it will come about that whoever calls on the name of the Lord [Yahweh] will be delivered;*

When Paul declared that whoever calls upon the name of the Lord will be saved, he was referring to the name *Jesus* (or the Hebrew equivalent, *Yeshua*). When Joel declared that whoever called upon the name of the Lord will be saved, he was referring to Yahweh. They are the same Person. The name *Jesus* (*Yeshua* in Hebrew) literally means, "Yahweh saves." The Lord of the OT (Yahweh) is the Lord of the NT (Jesus).

Point 550: Elohim and Yahweh Elohim

The Preincarnate Jesus is not the only Person of the Trinity mentioned in the OT. The word *Elohim* is used to refer to God, and indeed, this is the fullness of the Godhead, three Persons in One God.[332] We know this because Genesis 1 tells us that Elohim created the heavens and earth. Other verses tell us that God the Father (Gen. 1:1), God the Son (John 1:3 ;

---

[332] *Elohim* is used over 2,500 times in the OT, but sometimes the word refers to the pagan deities or angels.

Jesus as Fully God

Col. 1:16), and God the Holy Spirit (Gen. 1:2) were involved in creation. So Elohim must refer to the fullness of the Godhead. The three Persons in One God created the heavens and earth.

> OT Use of Elohim
> *Elohim* = God, in the sense of the fullness of the Godhead

However, beginning in Genesis 2:4, *Yahweh Elohim* (translated as "the Lord God") is the one who actually came down to the earth. This One is the Mediator. This is the One who had personal contact with humanity. This One was the Preincarnate Jesus who breathed into Adam as he became a living being (Gen. 2:7). Yahweh Elohim is the One who walked in the Garden with Adam. Yahweh Elohim was the Preincarnate Jesus.

> OT Use of Yahweh
> Yahweh = Preincarnate Jesus
> Yahweh Elohim = Preincarnate Jesus who is God

In most of our Bible translations, *Yahweh Elohim* is translated as "the Lord God."

> OT Use of Yahweh
> LORD God = Preincarnate Jesus who is God

Point 551: Jesus, Fully God

Recall our earlier discussion concerning this universe being created for Jesus.[333] Once Elohim created the heavens and earth, it was all turned over to Yahweh (Jesus). Therefore, we should not be surprised to see Him as the One directly involved with creation and humanity.

Once we recognize Yahweh (Preincarnate Jesus) as the One for whom creation exists, it is easy to see Him as distinct (in personhood) within the Trinity beginning in Genesis 2. All Christians see Jesus as distinct in personhood beginning in Matthew chapter 1, but I am asking you to move that point of distinction earlier in time—to Genesis chapter 2.

---

333 III:B:146.

Systematic Theology for the New Apostolic Reformation

This simple change has significant implications. For example, if Yahweh is Preincarnate Jesus, then the Hebrews/Jews in the OT were following and worshiping Jesus. Paul testified to this truth:

> *For I do not want you to be unaware, brethren, that our fathers . . . were drinking from a spiritual rock which followed them; and the rock was Christ.*
> (1 Cor. 10:1-4)

The Preincarnate Jesus was the cloud and pillar of fire that went before the Hebrews in the wilderness. He was the One who led the Jews into the Promise Land.

This gives new meaning to Paul's explanation that Abraham believed in Yahweh and it was credited to him as righteousness (Rom. 4:9). Abraham got saved as a result of believing in the same Person that Christians believe in today.

This truth also settles the arguments that Christians sometimes have concerning the God of the OT being wrathful and Jesus in the NT being gentle and loving. If Yahweh is the Preincarnate Jesus then distinguishing between the two is impossible. They are one and the same.

Section C
Jesus as Fully Man

In the preceding section, we saw how Yahweh in the OT was the Preincarnate Jesus Christ. Now we can discuss the truth that Yahweh became man in the NT.

Point 552: Why Did Jesus Become Man?

Yahweh had to become man to fulfill several promises that He made in the OT.

First, Yahweh promised that the seed of Eve would crush Satan's head (Gen. 3:15). Yahweh made promises to Abraham that through his seed all of the nations of the earth would be blessed (Gal. 3:8-19). Yahweh also promised to King David that one of his descendants would sit on his throne and rule forever (1 Chron. 17:11-12). In order to fulfill these promises, Yahweh could not merely appear as a man (as in a theophany), but He had to literally be born of human seed, that is, He had to become man.

Of course, Yahweh did not have to make those promises. Therefore, we should consider how those promises were not the *reason* Yahweh became man, but rather they are promises concerning what He would do as a man. If we take this perspective, then we have to look for other reasons.

One reason Yahweh became man is because God gave dominion over the earth to humanity. Rather than taking away that delegated authority, Yahweh became man to redeem the earth as a man.

Jesus was also tested as all humans are tested.

For we do not have a High Priest who cannot sympathize with our

Systematic Theology for the New Apostolic Reformation

weaknesses, but was in all points tempted as we are, yet without sin.

(Heb. 4:15-16)

Yahweh desired to truly relate to His people by becoming one of them.

Unlike other men, Jesus lived the perfect life. It was the sacrifice of that perfect life that became an acceptable propitiation for humanity's sin. Furthermore, Jesus had to be both God and man to be a true Mediator between Elohim and humanity. It was the shedding of His blood that established the new covenant between Elohim and humanity.

Point 553: Jesus Lived as We Should Live

Paul explained how Jesus laid aside His divine attributes:

. . . Christ Jesus, who, although He existed in the form of God, did not regard equality with God a thing to be grasped, but emptied Himself, taking the form of a bond-servant, and being made in the likeness of men.

(Phil. 2:5-7)

Jesus emptied Himself. This does not mean that He ceased being God. Paul explained that Jesus continued existing in the form of God. However, while being God, He emptied Himself.

This truth, that Jesus emptied Himself, has profound implications upon how we should live. This is because if Jesus laid aside all of His divine attributes, then He lived without using His own divine power. This means Jesus had to depend upon the Holy Spirit to work in and through Him. Since Jesus lived successfully and powerfully depending upon the Holy Spirit, then we can live successfully and powerfully depending upon the same Holy Spirit.

To see this more clearly, envision how Jesus would have lived if He had maintained and used His own divine powers. If Jesus resisted sin and worked miracles out of the power of His divine nature, then we have no reason to think that we can do what He did. We are not divine, so we should not expect to live successfully or powerfully.

On the other hand, since Jesus truly set aside His divine powers, He succeeded at living without sin and working miracles without depending

Jesus as Fully Man

upon His divinity. Since we have the same nature that Jesus took upon Himself, then we should be able to do what He did.

Of course, we know that we all sin. We need God's grace to succeed. However, we have God's grace.

We also have the Holy Spirit who empowered Jesus. It was the Spirit who anointed Jesus (Luke 4:18). Jesus testified to how He cast out demons by the Spirit of God (Matt. 12:28). As believers, we have the same Spirit. Jesus told His disciples that they would do the same works that He did and greater works because He would send the Holy Spirit to them (John 14:12-17). Just as Jesus depended upon the Holy Spirit, so we can depend upon the Holy Spirit.

Volume X
Trinity & Christology

Section D
Who Is Jesus?

In the previous two sections we talked about Jesus being fully God and fully man. These are the topics that usually come to the forefront when Western Christians discuss who Jesus is. However, discussing these topics only offers us a sterile, abstract view of Jesus. Please consider a more personal and relational view.

Point 554: Jesus Is Near

For a more personal view of Jesus the first thing that needs to change is our Western cosmology. The dualism that sees Jesus sitting on a throne in a far away world removes Him from personal involvement in the daily life of individuals. On the other hand, people of cultures that see the spiritual realm as present and fully integrated into the natural realm are able to sense the nearness of our Lord at all times. Many Christians "practice the presence of Jesus" which involves keeping an awareness of Jesus nearby. Such a practice makes no sense to those indoctrinated into a dualistic worldview, but those who practice the presence of Jesus testify to experiencing a deep love for and intimacy with Jesus.

Point 555: Jesus Is Involved

Some cultures, such as the African cultures, not only think of the spiritual world as immediately present, but they also look for Jesus to be personally involved with daily activities. This allows them to see Jesus as

Systematic Theology for the New Apostolic Reformation

the One who assists them for protection on journeys, harvesting of crops, favor with others, and safe delivery of babies. African Christians are more likely to pray for their immediate needs and invite Jesus into their daily struggles.[334]

There are millions of ordinary people who live around the world and have discovered Jesus as their immediate Helper in time of need. Many have cried out to Jesus in a moment of crisis and now know Jesus as their Rescuer. Untold multitudes have sought the help of Jesus for their next meal or to feed their children and then found food left on their doorstep. Some have cried for the healing of their loved ones and witnessed our Lord's healing touch. Millions have mumbled a prayer to Jesus to help them find some lost item and immediately had their eyes opened to see what they could not previously see.

There are even some Christians with childlike faith who routinely pray for Jesus to give them a good place to park their car in a busy parking lot. Of course, such answers to prayer may be explained as coincidence, but those who are wise in the wisdom of this world may never know if it truly is Jesus who answers such prayers. As Jesus said:

> *I praise You, Father, Lord of heaven and earth, that You have hidden these things from the wise and intelligent and have revealed them to infants.*
>
> (Matt. 11:25)

Expecting help in the simple affairs of life is sometimes ridiculed by those "who know better," but Jesus may be finding in such innocent faith someone who is like the centurion who had greater faith than everyone in Israel (Matt. 8:10).

Point 556: What Is the Most Accurate Christology?

We can easily identify people in the NT who must have had unique but valid impressions of Jesus. The man who was born blind but healed knew Jesus as his Healer. The woman caught in adultery and brought before Jesus to be judged came to know Jesus as a loving, compassionate

---

[334] For an informed explanation of how modern Africans look at Jesus, see: Timothy C. Tennent, *Theology in the Context of World Christianity* (Grand Rapids, MI: Zondervan, 2007) chap. 5.

Who Is Jesus?

man of God. The man possessed by a legion of demons knew Jesus as his Deliverer. Zacheus knew Jesus as a holy man willing to come into the home of a sinner. The woman at the well identified Jesus first as a prophet and then as the Messiah. Many Jews understood Jesus to be the fulfillment of what the OT prophets promised. Peter recognized Jesus as the Christ, the Son of the Living God.

Each of these individuals came to know Jesus in their own unique way. Each of them had their own limited, yet valid, Christology.

Among other things this raises a question concerning what are the most important aspects of our Christology? Western theology has focused on Jesus as God and man. Certainly the related truths are important and profound, but we with our Western minds may have a distorted view of Jesus by focusing on truths upon which the Bible does not focus. Consider how the Bible does not spend much time discussing how Jesus can be both fully God and fully man. But the Bible does spend much time revealing Jesus as a servant and lover of humanity.

If we read the Bible with the innocence of a child, we may become most aware of Jesus' nature as a lover of the poor, orphans, and widows. Perhaps we will become more aware of His desire to heal the sick and set demon-tormented people free. We may see how Jesus hates religious pride and hypocrisy. We will certainly see how He desires people to understand who Father-God is.

How is it that Jesus wants to be known? Perhaps the woman who knows Jesus as the One who provides her with a parking space is the one with the most accurate Christology. Maybe she actually knows Jesus in a way that He wants to be known.

Volume X
Trinity & Christology

Volume XI
Pneumatology

Pneumatology refers to the study of the Holy Spirit. The English word comes from two Greek words: *pneuma*, meaning, "spirit," and *logos*, meaning, "word" or "teaching." Under pneumatology, we will study the person, the works, the anointing, and the gifts of the Holy Spirit.

Volume XI
Pneumatology

Section A
Person of the Holy Spirit

The Holy Spirit is God. The Holy Spirit is a Person. The Holy Spirit is the Third Person of the Trinity.

Point 557: The Holy Spirit Proceeds from God the Father

The titles, Holy Spirit and Spirit of God, are used interchangeably (*cf.* Matt. 12:28, 32). They are the same.

In several verses, we can see that the Holy Spirit comes from God the Father. Jesus described "... *the Spirit of truth who proceeds from the Father* ..." (John 15:26, see also Ps. 104:30). This proceeding from the Father reveals how the Holy Spirit is not a different substance from the Father. The Father and the Holy Spirit are one. Hence, we must see the Holy Spirit as divine.

When Jesus ascended into heaven, He received the Holy Spirit from the Father and poured the Spirit out upon the world (Acts 2:33). We see then that the Holy Spirit comes from the Father, through the Son. So in that sense, the Holy Spirit proceeds from the Father and Son.

Point 558: The Holy Spirit Is a Person

Next we need to recognize the Holy Spirit as a Person, rather than a force or energy emanating from God the Father.

There are several ways that we identify a person. One of the most significant is that a person has a will. We can see this with the Holy Spirit. When Paul explained the gifts he wrote, *"But one and the same Spirit works*

Systematic Theology for the New Apostolic Reformation

all these things, distributing to each one individually just as He wills" (1 Cor. 12:11). We can also identify the will of the Holy Spirit where the Holy Spirit forbade Paul from proceeding in his missions work to a certain region (Acts 16:6-7).The fact that the Holy Spirit has His own will allows us to see the Holy Spirit as a distinct Person.

We also see the Holy Spirit has His own ministry distinct from the Father and Son. This is most evident in Jesus' explanation concerning how the Holy Spirit would come to earth after Jesus ascended into heaven:

> *I will ask the Father, and He will give you another Helper, that He may be with you forever.*
> (John 14:16)

Having this distinct ministry, the Holy Spirit is called the Comforter, the Counselor, the Helper, and the Paraclete.

Paul writes about how *". . . the Spirit searches all things, even the depths of God"* (1 Cor. 2:10). This offers an image of the Holy Spirit acting as an independent agent, searching the depths of God the Father.

There are many references to the Holy Spirit in which He is shown as initiating certain actions. For example, in Acts 13:2 we read:

> *. . . the Holy Spirit said, "Set apart for Me Barnabas and Saul for the work to which I have called them."*

This does not mean that the Holy Spirit initiated actions contrary to the will of God the Father. It simply reveals the Spirit acting as a Person.

The Holy Spirit is also referred to with personal pronouns, such as "He" and "Him." Such terminology reveals the Spirit as more than a force emanating from God. He is the Third Person of the Trinity.[335]

Point 559: The Holy Spirit Is Co-Equal with the Father and Son

In Volume X, Section A, we identified several Bible passages that refer to the three Persons of the Trinity. We do not need to repeat that discussion, but it is worth re-emphasizing how the Holy Spirit is placed right along-

---

[335] Most of these points about the divinity and person of the Holy Spirit are simply a reworking and simplification of a discussion in J. Rodman Williams, *Renewal Theology* (Grand Rapids, Michigan: ZondervanPublishingHouse, 1996), p.137-154.

Person of the Holy Spirit

side of the Father and Son. In fact, there are some verses that name the Father first, some that name the Son first, and some that name the Holy Spirit first. For example, the Father is mentioned first in Matthew 28:19:

> *Go therefore and make disciples of all the nations, baptizing them in the name of the <u>Father</u> and the <u>Son</u> and the <u>Holy Spirit</u>.*

Jesus is mentioned first in 2 Corinthians 13:14:

> *The grace of the <u>Lord Jesus Christ</u>, and the love of <u>God</u>, and the fellowship of the <u>Holy Spirit</u>, be with you all.*

The Spirit is mentioned first in I Corinthians 12:4-6:

> *Now there are varieties of gifts, but the same <u>Spirit</u>. And there are varieties of ministries, and the same <u>Lord</u>. There are varieties of effects, but the same <u>God</u> who works all things in all persons.*

If God the Father was to be thought of as greater than the Son or the Spirit, we would expect Him to always be referred to first. Yet, that is not what we see in Scripture. Even though we recognize an order referring to the Son as the Second Person of the Trinity and the Holy Spirit as the Third Person of the Trinity, they are both recognized as co-equal with the Father.

**Volume XI
Pneumatology**

Section B
Works of the Holy Spirit

In Genesis 1:1-2, we see the Holy Spirit with God at creation (Gen. 1:1-2). From then on we see the Third Person of the Trinity involved and interactive with humanity.

Point 560: The Holy Spirit's Role in Convicting the World of Sin

In John 16:8, Jesus spoke of the coming of the Holy Spirit:

And He, when He comes, will convict the world concerning sin and righteousness and judgment.

How this verse is understood is influenced by a person's theological perspective. As discussed earlier,[336] Reformed theology is built around humanity's problem of sin and God's wrath concerning sin. As a consequence, Christians trained in Reformed theology are very sin conscious. They also espouse the gospel of salvation,[337] which teaches that in order for non-Christians to become Christians they must recognize their sinfulness, turn to God, and accept Jesus as Savior. Since recognizing one's sinfulness is the first step in this progression, the Holy Spirit's role in this is key in Reformed theology.

With the Reformed perspective, adherents tend to read John 16:8 and conclude that the Holy Spirit's primary job in the life of non-Christians is to:

---

336 VI:A.
337 We discussed the difference between the gospel of salvation and the gospel of the Kingdom in VI:E.

Systematic Theology for the New Apostolic Reformation

1. convict them of their sinfulness
2. convict them concerning how they fall short of righteousness
3. convict them that they will be judged for their sins

Seeing these as the primary works of the Holy Spirit reinforces the perspective of Reformed theology. Indeed, most evangelical Christians think the Holy Spirit's primary job is to convict people in the three areas listed above.

Point 561: People Know Good from Evil

In order to see things from a new perspective, we often have to challenge present ideas. Here we must challenge the evangelical understanding of the work of the Holy Spirit in convicting people of sin.

In John 16:8 (quoted above), Jesus told His disciples the Holy Spirit will convict the world concerning sin. Yet, people were aware of their sins long before the Holy Spirit came into the world. We can see this as we study how the Jews in the OT were very conscious of their own sins. They continually brought sacrifices to make atonement for their sins. Yet, in the OT times, the Holy Spirit had not yet been released into the world to do as Jesus said, "*to convict the world*" (John 16:8). How then did God's OT people become so aware of their own sinfulness? Of course, they had the Law of God to compare their own behavior to, but they also had their eyes opened to see their own nakedness.

To see this, consider when God spoke to Adam and Eve after they ate the forbidden fruit; God said, *"Who told you that you were naked?"* (Gen. 3:11). It was not the Holy Spirit who told Adam and Eve that they were naked. They knew it because their eyes were opened. God said, *"Behold, the man has become like one of Us, knowing good and evil"* (Gen. 3:22). Adam and Eve could see their own sins because they had gained the knowledge of good and evil.

All of Adam and Eve's descendants have had their eyes opened to know good and evil. Therefore, they know what sin is. In Romans 2:15, Paul explained that even Gentiles:

> . . . *show the work of the Law written in their hearts, their conscience bearing witness and their thoughts alternately accusing or else defending them.*

Works of the Holy Spirit

Every person has a conscience. That conscience is flooding their mind with *"thoughts alternately accusing or else defending them."* The point is that sinners have an awareness of sin even without the Holy Spirit's direct involvement.

Point 562: The Holy Spirit Speaks of Jesus

Once Christians understand that the awareness of sin is common to all of Adam's descendants, the Holy Spirit's role in this does not seem so essential. Then another perspective allows Christians to see the Holy Spirit's role differently. Most importantly, Jesus told His disciples that, *"the Spirit of truth who proceeds from the Father, He will testify about Me"* (John 15:26). Consider how the Holy Spirit's role is primarily about testifying about Jesus rather than testifying about people's sins.

Consider again our Lord's words in John 16:8:

> And He, when He comes, will convict the world concerning sin and righteousness and judgment.

If awareness of one's sinfulness is central to one's theology, then it would be advantageous to enlist the Holy Spirit in procuring this. However, we get a different understanding of the Holy Spirit's role when we read the explanation that Jesus offered in the very next verses:

> ... concerning sin, because they do not believe in Me and
> concerning righteousness, because I go to the Father and you
>   no longer see Me; and
> concerning judgment, because the ruler of this world has been judged.
>   (John 16:9-11)

Rather than teaching that the Holy Spirit's role is making people aware of their sins, our Lord explained that the Holy Spirit's work in the world is to:

1. convince people of their need to believe in Jesus
2. convince people that Jesus was perfectly righteous
3. convince people that the ruler of the world (Satan) has been judged

Systematic Theology for the New Apostolic Reformation

The Holy Spirit's primary role is to point to Jesus and His victory—not to people and their sins.

When this is first pointed out to evangelical Christians, they are usually quite surprised, because the idea that the Holy Spirit's primary work is to point out people's sins is deeply seated in evangelical thought. However, it is wrong. That wrong understanding results from a natural progression of thought when someone reads John 16:8 through the eyes of Classical/Reformed thought (and fails to read the next three verses).

Point 563: What Is the Holy Spirit Saying to Believers?

The primary work of the Holy Spirit in the world (toward non-Christians) is to testify about Jesus, but what is His work in the life of the Christian? Jesus answered this, describing the Holy Spirit as the Spirit of Truth who *"will guide you into all the truth"* (John 16:13). So we know that a primary role of the Holy Spirit is to reveal truth to Christians.

1. Truth

Jesus also explained that the Holy Spirit will be a Helper, Comforter, Encourager, and Counselor (John 14:16-26). This means the primary truths that the Holy Spirit inspires within the hearts of Christians are thoughts related to:

2. Help
3. Comfort
4. Encouragement
5. Counsel

In Roman 8:16-17, Paul gave us more insight pertaining to what the Holy Spirit reveals to believers:

> *The Spirit Himself testifies with our spirit that we are <u>children of God</u>, and if children, <u>heirs</u> also, heirs of God and <u>fellow heirs with Christ</u>* . . . .

Notice the positive nature of all that the Holy Spirit reveals. He is saying to believers:

Works of the Holy Spirit

6. you are a child of God
7. you have an inheritance from God
8. you will inherit all Jesus inherits

Paul explained that the Holy Spirit searches the depths of God and reveals those things to us *"so that we may know the things freely given to us by God"* (1 Cor. 2:12). So the Holy Spirit is revealing:

9. that God has freely given us all things

Furthermore, the Holy Spirit is trying to help believers understand what the those things are that are freely given to us. As Paul wrote, the Holy Spirit is communicating to believers that:

10. we may know the things freely given to us

Paul explained that the Holy Spirit reveals the thoughts of Father-God, and we know Father-God has forgiven His children and *"will remember their sins no more."* Since Father-God has no remembrance of the sins of His children and the Holy Spirit's job is revealing the thoughts of Father-God, the Holy Spirit will not be talking to Christians about their sins.

Of course, it is the job of the Holy Spirit to reveal truth to believers so, in that sense, He may reveal specific sins to Christians in order to set them free. However, revelation of personal sins will not come as judgment from the Divine Judge. Christians have passed out of judgment (John 3:18), and now there is no condemnation directed toward them (Rom. 8:1). If and when Father-God reveals sins to His children, it will be accompanied with a message of faith concerning how they are forgiven and how they can triumph over the enemy who has been defeated.

Point 564: Identifying the Work of the Holy Spirit

This discussion concerning the work of the Holy Spirit is key because so many Christians are confused about the leading of the Holy Spirit. Too many Christians remain sin conscious all of their lives. They think it is the Holy Spirit who is constantly reminding them of their sins, but they are listening to the wrong voice. Satan is the accuser of the brethren (Rev.

Systematic Theology for the New Apostolic Reformation

12:10). The Holy Spirit is primarily reminding Christians that they are children of God and telling them of the wonderful things Father-God has done for them.

Another reason it is important to clearly identify the work of the Holy Spirit is because many preachers think they are under the anointing of the Holy Spirit when they are pointing out people's sins. In reality, they may be putting condemnation upon the very people whom God has delivered from condemnation.

Point 565: The Pentecostal and Charismatic Christians

The Holy Spirit is doing much more than just revealing truths to believers. He is also involved in personal and dynamic ways to change and empower believers, but before we discuss these works, it will be helpful to provide some key definitions.

In the 18th and 19th centuries, there emerged a move in Western Christianity called the **Holiness Movement**. A major figure in that movement was John Wesley (1703–1791), who taught that the Holy Spirit would come to dwell within people when they become Christians. In addition, Wesley taught that the Holy Spirit will do another work called **sanctification**. This second work of the Holy Spirit was also called a **second act of grace** and described as an experience when the Holy Spirit would come upon Christians and free them from the power of sin. Millions of Christians claim to have experienced this second act of grace resulting in their instantaneous deliverance from the power of sin. They claim to have been made holy, or in another word, **sanctified,** by the power of the Holy Spirit.

In the late 19th and early 20th centuries, another movement called **Pentecostalism** emerged out of the Holiness Movement. In addition to the Holy Spirit's role in indwelling every Christian, Pentecostal teachers taught about a second act of grace, but they emphasized how the Holy Spirit would come upon Christians and give them power, evidenced by their speaking in tongues. In Section E we will discuss the gift of tongues, but here it will be helpful to understand who the Pentecostals are because of how much they contributed to the modern Church's understanding of the Holy Spirit.

The early Pentecostals were so adamant about a second act of grace through which the Holy Spirit empowers Christians that they began to be

Works of the Holy Spirit

identified as a separate branch of Christianity. During the first half of the 20th century, many Pentecostal denominations formed.

The Pentecostal Movement had little influence on the long-established mainline denominations until the mid-1960s. At that time, many Christians within mainline denominations began experiencing the gift of tongues as taught by the Pentecostals. Those Christians who spoke in tongues were also filled with new enthusiasm and, hence, had a significant impact on almost all denominations, even though the authorities in some denominations denounced the movement. Christians who spoke in tongues, but remained involved with denominations that did not embrace the Pentecostal teachings, became known as **Charismatics**. The Charismatic Movement had a major impact in almost all denominations and spread around the world. In recent years, the distinctions between Pentecostals and Charismatics have been diminishing. Some teachers continue to think of Pentecostals as more dogmatic than Charismatics, but many teachers use the terms Pentecostal and Charismatic interchangeably.

In coming discussions, I will refer to Pentecostal/Charismatic Christians as Christians who believe in a second act of grace in which the Holy Spirit comes upon Christians and enables them to speak in tongues.

Point 566: The Indwelling of the Holy Spirit

The most important role of the Holy Spirit in the life of the Christian is His indwelling. Paul explained that every Christian is a temple of the Holy Spirit (1 Cor. 3:16). This means that God's Spirit dwells in human vessels—a truth too profound for our minds to fully comprehend!

The evidence, or the proof, that the Holy Spirit is *within* a person is the *fruit* of the Spirit, which is listed in Galatians 5:22-23:

1. love
2. joy
3. peace
4. patience
5. kindness
6. goodness
7. faithfulness
8. gentleness
9. self-control

Systematic Theology for the New Apostolic Reformation

Jesus explained that if we make the tree good then the fruit will be good (Matt. 12:33). As the Holy Spirit works in the lives of believers, sanctifying them, then the fruit of the Spirit becomes more and more evident.

It is worth noting that the fruit of the Spirit is different from the gifts of the Spirit. We will discuss the gifts in Section D, but here we can note that the fruit of the Spirit grows in the lives of Christians as they mature.

Point 567: The Coming Upon of the Holy Spirit

It is not only possible to have the Holy Spirit "dwelling within," but the Holy Spirit will also "come upon" Christians. This difference is easy to see in the lives of the first apostles as we identify the difference between the time when the Holy Spirit came to dwell within them and when the Holy Spirit came upon them.

On the first day of the week after Jesus rose from the dead, He appeared to His apostles, and *"He breathed on them and said to them, 'Receive the Holy Spirit'"* (John 20:22). The time frame of this event is important. It happened three days after Jesus' crucifixion. That is when the Holy Spirit was released **into** the apostles.

It was after the *Holy Spirit came into* the apostles that Jesus told them to wait in Jerusalem until the *Holy Spirit came upon* them (Luke 24:49). It is one thing to have the Holy Spirit come within and a different thing to have the Holy Spirit come upon a person.

Fifty days after Jesus' crucifixion, the apostles experienced Pentecost Day when the Holy Spirit came upon them (Act 2:1-4). This coming-upon experience was also called being *"baptized with the Holy Spirit"* (Acts 1:5).

Point 568: The Evidence of the Coming Upon Experience

Pentecostal Christians typically say that the evidence of the coming-upon experience is speaking in tongues.[338] However, that is not entirely accurate. Jesus told His disciples, *"You will <u>receive power</u> when the Holy Spirit has come upon you"* (Acts 1:8). In Luke 24:49, we read how our Lord

---

[338] Pentecostals are known for their doctrine that speaking in tongues is the evidence of the coming-upon experience. Charismatics are less dogmatic on this and some have completely abandoned it.

Works of the Holy Spirit

promised that they would be "<u>clothed with power</u>" when the Holy Spirit came upon them. Please do not misunderstand what I am saying here. I believe in the gift of tongues, and I believe that it is an important gift for the Church today, but Jesus clearly told us that the evidence of the coming-upon experience is power.

The power Jesus referred to had to do with boldness to share the gospel. This is what Jesus told them would happen:

> . . . but <u>you will receive power</u> when the Holy Spirit has <u>come upon</u> you; and <u>you shall be My witnesses</u> both in Jerusalem, and in all Judea and Samaria, and even to the remotest part of the earth."
> (Acts 1:8)

Indeed, we can read how Peter and the other apostles were transformed from fearful individuals to totally confident ones.

Contrast this change with the change that happens through the indwelling of the Holy Spirit. The evidence of the indwelling of the Spirit is the fruit of the Spirit. The evidence of the coming-upon experience is power.

Work of the Holy Spirit	Evidence
Indwelling	→ Fruit of the Spirit
Coming Upon	→ Power

This explanation is different than traditional Pentecostal teaching. Because I take this stand, many Pentecostal teachers would not want my teachings associated with theirs. So I am not a traditional Pentecostal. Yet, I cannot back down from what seems to me to be clearly stated in Scripture. Jesus taught that the evidence of the Holy Spirit coming upon Christians is power.

Point 569: Multiple Coming Upon Experiences

I also disagree with the traditional Pentecostal teaching that Christians can only have the Holy Spirit come upon them once. Instead, I understand that the Holy Spirit may come upon individual Christians on many occasions and on each occasion endue them with new power.

Systematic Theology for the New Apostolic Reformation

Notice that this understanding of multiple coming-upon experiences only makes sense if we first abandon the Pentecostal association of the coming upon experience with speaking in tongues. This is true because a person can only *begin* speaking in tongues one time. Therefore, if we associate speaking in tongues with the coming-upon experience then a Christian can only have one coming-upon experience.

In reality, the evidence of the coming-upon experience is power, and Christians should expect the Holy Spirit to give them power on many occasions. This has been evidenced in the lives of millions of Christians. Millions have experienced the Holy Spirit coming upon them, and they indeed began to speak in tongues, but then at some later date those same Christians have had the Holy Spirit come upon them resulting in increased power for exercising other spiritual gifts, callings to various ministries, living victoriously, ministering under the anointing, and other works of power. In my own life, I can testify to many occasions when I have been standing before a strange crowd in a foreign land and the Holy Spirit came upon me, giving me power to preach more boldly than I could have without His fresh empowering.

Many Christians refer to these repeated coming-upon experiences as being "refilled with the Spirit." Indeed, it is biblically accurate to refer to each experience as being filled with the Spirit, because we can see the early disciples being filled with the Spirit on several occasions (e.g., Acts 2:4; 4:8, 31). Yet, it is also correct for a Christian to describe the experiences saying, "The Holy Spirit came upon me and I was filled with the Holy Spirit."

Section C
Anointing of the Holy Spirit

The word *anointing* means "having oil spread upon." In Bible times, oil placed upon the head of an individual signified the Holy Spirit resting upon that person.

Point 570: All Christians Have an Anointing

All believers in Jesus are temples in which the Holy Spirit dwells (John 7:38-39 ; 1 Cor. 6:19). The Holy Spirit not only helps Christians live holy lives, but also enables them to accomplish God's unique calling upon their life. John wrote to the early Christians, *"But you have an anointing from the Holy One, and you all know"* (1 John 2:20). So all Christians have an anointing. The anointing is the empowering of the Holy Spirit to help the believer fulfill God's calling.

As God places His Spirit within individuals they become transformed in heart and mind so they can carry out the will of God. The Holy Spirit causes them to will and to work for God's pleasure (Phil. 2:13). The apostle John also wrote *"the anointing teaches you"* (1 John 2:27). The Holy Spirit aligns the thoughts of a person so that person knows how to do what God wants accomplished.

Many Christians live their daily lives not aware of the Holy Spirit's guidance. They think the desires they have and the decisions they make are completely their own, but the Holy Spirit is at work in their hearts and minds, causing them to do God's will. Christians do not always yield to the leading of the Holy Spirit, but God is always at work within them.

Systematic Theology for the New Apostolic Reformation

Point 571: The Power of the Anointing

As the Holy Spirit moves in the life of an individual, He reveals Jesus Christ. In the presence of Jesus, every knee bows and every tongue confesses Him as Lord. This means that wherever the anointing is, there will be some tangible effect upon people, causing them to bow and yield to the Lordship of Jesus Christ.

For example, worship leaders can be talented, but that does not mean they are anointed. Talent enables worship leaders to make great music. In contrast, anointed leaders release the presence of Jesus. Those who sit under anointed worship will sense their hearts coming in submission to Jesus.

For another example, consider a teacher who is able to present truths in a very understandable way. If she is anointed, the listeners will also experience errors being broken in their thought processes.

Some people are anointed by God to succeed in the political arena. God will have them connect with the right people at the right time. They will find favor with the right individuals, and they will be raised up to positions of authority as if there is some supernatural elevation occurring.

Some people are anointed to make money. The presence of Jesus causes the right opportunities to come before them so they can make the best investments and most advantageous decisions.

The presence of Jesus manifesting through the Holy Spirit causes doors to open and people to fall into alignment. King David praised God, *"Who subdues my people under me"* (Ps. 144:2). That subduing is a supernatural work that God accomplishes through His anointing.

Point 572: Many Anointings

There are many different areas in which people can be anointed.

Exodus 35:31-35 tells us that the Spirit of God filled Bezalel causing him to have wisdom and understanding in all craftsmanship. This included the wisdom to know how to work in gold, silver, and bronze, cut stones, carve wood, engrave, design, and embroider.

Some people are anointed to work with children. Some are anointed to do secretarial work. Others are anointed to pray, and still others are anointed in art or communication.

Anointing of the Holy Spirit

<u>Examples of Areas in which People May Be Anointed</u>

    Worship Leading
    Singing
    Intercession
    Deliverance
    Public Speaking
    Secretarial Work
    Writing
    Children's Work
    Working with Teens
    Working with Adults
    Working with Disabled
    Business
    Politics
    War
    Art
    Craftsmanship
    Construction
    Business
    Making Money
    Counseling

We cannot find all of these areas of anointing specifically mentioned in the Bible, but the Holy Spirit may come upon anyone He chooses and hence, anoint them to do anything He wants them to do.

Volume XI
Pneumatology

Section D
Gifts of the Holy Spirit

We will not be talking very much about the individual gifts. Instead, we will identify some general truths that Paul communicated in 1 Corinthians 12 through 14. Then, in Sections E, F, and G, we will discuss in more depth three gifts that have become especially prominent in Pentecostal/Charismatic circles: tongues, prophecy, and healing.

In 1 Corinthians 12 through 14, Paul gave us the most in-depth teaching on the gifts that we have in the Bible. He began by saying, *"Now concerning spiritual gifts, brethren, I do not want you to be unaware"* (1 Cor. 12:1). This begins his great exposition on the subject. Here, we will draw out a few of Paul's major points.

Point 573: Lesson Number One: Glorifying Jesus as Lord

The first issue Paul addressed in 1 Corinthians 12 is how we can know what spiritual things are from God.

> *Therefore I make known to you that no one speaking by the Spirit of God says, "Jesus is accursed"; and no one can say, "Jesus is Lord," except by the Holy Spirit.*
>
> (1 Cor. 12:3)

Paul was explaining that if something is from God, then it will glorify Jesus as Lord. If some spiritual manifestation does not exalt Jesus as Lord, then that manifestation is not from God. Paul reassured the Corinthians that if they use this as their guide they would not be deceived as they

Systematic Theology for the New Apostolic Reformation

had been in the past (1 Cor. 12:2-3). The exaltation of Jesus as Lord is the basis of discernment.

Point 574: The Holy Spirit Manifests

After listing some spiritual gifts in 1 Corinthians 12, Paul explained:

> *But to each one is given the manifestation of the Spirit for the common good.*
>
> (1 Cor. 12:7)

The word *manifestation* is key. What does it mean? In this context it means something in the spiritual realm comes into the natural realm so you can see it, hear it, touch it, or have some other physical awareness of it. For example, if an angel was sitting next to you right now, you would not be able to see it, but if the angel manifested, you would be able to sense it with one or more of your natural senses. In like fashion, the Holy Spirit manifests, that is, He comes into this natural world, through His gifts.

This means that the gifts of the Holy Spirit are more than something the Holy Spirit does. They are expressions of the Person of the Holy Spirit.

THE HOLY SPIRIT MANIFESTS THROUGH HIS NINE GIFTS

Gifts of the Holy Spirit

For example, a crippled individual in a wheelchair may be brought to a Christian for prayer. That Christian should pray to God the Father, in the name of Jesus. If the healing and miracle-working power of God manifests, it will be the work of the Third Person of the Trinity. If the crippled person arises out of her wheelchair, then the onlookers will see the Holy Spirit's power and love. They may say, "Wow, did you see that!" Those who observed the miracle healing *saw* the Holy Spirit coming out of the invisible world and manifest in the natural world.

This truth is evident with each of the gifts of the Holy Spirit. For example, when a gift of faith is imparted to Christians, they will be transformed from being timid and unsure, to confident and bold. Those who watch a Christian being transformed in this way are watching the work of the Holy Spirit. They are also seeing the Person of the Holy Spirit making Himself known in this world through the life of that transformed individual.

So the gifts of the Holy Spirit are the expression of the Person of the Holy Spirit. For this reason it is essential that no one rejects the gifts of the Holy Spirit. Foolishly, someone may say, "I like the Holy Spirit, but I do not like the gift of prophecy," but that is like saying, "I like you but not your voice." Or someone may say, "I like the Holy Spirit, but not healing," which is like saying, "I like you, but not your face." The face of the Holy Spirit in this natural world is healing, miracles, faith, and so forth. The voice and thoughts of the Holy Spirit are revealed through prophecy, words of wisdom, tongues, and so forth. These are ways in which the Holy Spirit manifests.

Of course, this does not mean we should blindly accept every manifestation that someone says is from the Holy Spirit. We need to discern and reject those which are invalid. We also need to realize that the Holy Spirit is manifesting Himself through human vessels. People have all kinds of weaknesses and character flaws, but the Holy Spirit has chosen to reveal Himself through frail human beings.

Point 575: The Excellency of Love

Paul sandwiched a chapter on love (1 Cor. 13) between his two great chapters on the gifts. He made strong points that exercising the gifts without love is empty and useless. In fact, any exercise of the gifts without

Systematic Theology for the New Apostolic Reformation

love makes them annoying, like *"a noisy gong or a clanging cymbal"* (1 Cor. 13:1). Paul told the reader that love is the greatest of all. Of course, we could write volumes on love and, indeed, volumes have been written by others, but here I simply mention it hoping it is obvious to the reader.

Point 576: The Perfect Will Come

Paul inserted a few verses in 1 Corinthians 13 that have been used to cause some controversy concerning the modern use of the gifts. Paul wrote:

> *... but if there are gifts of prophecy, they will be done away; if there are tongues, they will cease; if there is knowledge, it will be done away. For we know in part and we prophesy in part; but when the perfect comes, the partial will be done away.*
>
> (1 Cor. 13:8-10)

Some Christian teachers have used these verses to teach that the gifts of the Holy Spirit have ceased, and therefore, any modern use of such gifts are mere counterfeits without the blessing of God. This viewpoint is called **cessationism**. Adherents promote cessationism by pointing to Paul's words, that the gifts of prophecy and tongues are to be done away with when *"the perfect comes."* They will typically say that the "perfect" Paul referred to in this passage was the completed Bible. Seeing how the Bible was completed during the 1st and 2nd centuries, cessationists say that the gifts of the Holy Spirit ceased at that time.

To be honest, this is a conflict that I dealt with so many years ago, I have a hard time even considering it seriously. Now that more than half a billion Christians around the world are a part of churches that operate in the Holy Spirit's gifts,[339] the arguments against their modern use seem trite and foolish. After using the gifts myself for so many years, considering the cessationist's argument is like telling the once blind man that Jesus does not heal. The most relevant answer is, "Once I was blind, now I see."

If it is necessary to offer an answer to the cessationists, I would point out that "the perfect" that Paul was talking about is not the Bible.

---

[339] The *International Bulletin of Missionary Research* gives the statistic at 628,186,000 for 2013.

Gifts of the Holy Spirit

For proof of this, all we have to do is read Paul's words where he said that knowledge will be done away with when the perfect comes (1 Cor. 13:8). Knowledge has not yet been done away with. I agree with most Pentecostal/Charismatic teachers that the perfect Paul referred to is Jesus Christ. When He returns, prophecy will cease because prophecy is only a partial revelation; Jesus will bring full revelation, so we won't need the partial any longer. Tongues will also cease, because we will have perfect communication between our spirits and God. Until that day, we need the partial, and so, we need to keep operating in the spiritual gifts.

Volume XI
Pneumatology

Section E
Gift of Tongues

Of the Holy Spirit's gifts, the gift of tongues has been especially controversial. For this reason, we will give special attention to this gift.

When we refer to "tongues," we are speaking about a supernatural gift through which Christians speak in a language that they never learned through education or any form of learning. Paul explained that tongues may be a language of men or angels (1 Cor. 13:1). That gift is the same gift experienced by the early disciples as recorded in Acts 2:4 and practiced in Pentecostal/Charismatic groups today.

Point 577: The Evidence of the Holy Spirit within a Person?

Part of the reason there has been much controversy around the gift of tongues is because many Pentecostal/Charismatic Christians claim that speaking in tongues is *the* evidence of being filled with the Holy Spirit. This implies that Christians who do not speak in tongues are not filled with the Holy Spirit. Of course, Christians who do not speak in tongues do not like to hear this.

As explained earlier,[340] tongues is not the biblical evidence of being filled with the Holy Spirit. Power is.

Jesus explained, *"He who believes in Me, as the Scripture said, 'From his innermost being will flow rivers of living water'"* (John 7:37). These rivers of living water refer to the Holy Spirit (John 7:39), so anyone who believes in Jesus has the Holy Spirit. Baptists believe in Jesus, so according to Jesus, they have the Holy Spirit. Nazarenes and Presbyterians believe in Jesus,

---
[340] XI:B:568.

Systematic Theology for the New Apostolic Reformation

so they too have the Holy Spirit moving within them like rivers of living water. It is not just Christians who speak in tongues who have the Holy Spirit. All Christians are a temple for the Holy Spirit.

For evidence of the indwelling Holy Spirit, we can look for the fruit of the Holy Spirit: love, joy, peace, patience, kindness, goodness, faithfulness, gentleness, and self-control (Gal. 5:22). All Christians who have the fruit of the Holy Spirit are showing the evidence of having the Holy Spirit. The plain truth is that many Christians who do not speak in tongues have more fruit of the Holy Spirit than many Christians who do speak in tongues. In other words, there are many non-tongue-speaking Christians who are more Spirit-filled than many tongue-speaking Christians.

For this reason, it is wrong for Pentecostal/Charismatic Christians to label themselves as *Spirit-filled Christians* and those who do not speak in tongues as *non-Spirit-filled Christians*. That terminology is biblically incorrect and divisive.

Point 578: The Pentecostal Desire for Tongues

Pentecostal Christians desire to help other Christians experience the Holy Spirit in the same wonderful way they have. This is the primary reason Pentecostals say speaking in tongues is the evidence of being baptized in the Holy Spirit. This doctrine allows them to point out the lack in the life of Christians who do not speak in tongues.

The motive of Pentecostals to get others baptized in the Holy Spirit may be commendable, but it is wrong to twist our doctrines to achieve our desired ends. In other words, it is wrong for Pentecostals to say that tongues is the evidence of the Holy Spirit coming upon a person for the purpose of convincing every Christian that they should speak in tongues.

Point 579: Gift of Tongues versus Prayer Language of Tongues

Although Pentecostal Christians often emphasize tongues to a point of distorting the truth about being filled with the Holy Spirit and the coming-upon experience, the gift of tongues is still a valid, important gift that offers great benefits to the modern Christian.

Gift of Tongues

Much clarification comes to our understanding of tongues when we contrast the **gift of tongues** with the **prayer language** of tongues. In 1 Corinthians 12, we read about the gift of tongues, which is one of the gifts of the Holy Spirit. Then in chapter 14, Paul discusses two different uses of tongues:

1. speaking in tongues out loud in the midst of the congregation
2. speaking in tongues privately as in a prayer language

The distinctions Paul makes in these two different exercises of tongues are key. As we look at these, I will refer to the public use of tongues as the "gift of tongues" and the private use of tongues as the "prayer language."

1. **Gift of tongues:** out loud in the midst of the congregation
2. **Prayer language:** privately as in a prayer language

Point 580: Who Listens?

The first distinction between the gift of tongues and the prayer language pertains to *who listens* to tongues. When Paul talked about the gift of tongues being used in the midst of the congregation, he said:

> *If anyone speaks in a tongue, it should be by two or at the most three, and each in turn, and one must interpret; but if there is no interpreter, he must keep silent in the church; and let him speak to himself and to God.*
>
> (1 Cor. 14:27-28)

From this we can see that the gift of tongues needs to be interpreted when it is exercised out loud in the congregation, so that the people can understand what is being said. This means that the congregation is to listen to the message. However, Paul said that if there is no one to interpret, then the Christian should not speak publicly but *let him speak to himself and to God*. Notice that if the Christian speaks privately in tongues, then God listens. So then, God listens to the prayer language of tongues, and the congregation listens to the gift of tongues.

Systematic Theology for the New Apostolic Reformation

Paul wrote more about the prayer language of tongues in the first half of 1 Corinthians 14:

> *For if I pray in a tongue, my spirit prays, but my mind is unfruitful.*
> (1 Cor. 14:14)

Earlier in that chapter Paul wrote:

> *For one who speaks in a tongue does not speak to men but to God.*
> (1 Cor. 14:2)

So again, we see that God listens to the prayer language of tongues, and the congregation listens to the gift of tongues.

Point 581: Who Is Speaking?

Another distinction between the gift of tongues and prayer language of tongues pertains to *who is speaking*. When the gift of tongues is used in the midst of the congregation, it is the Holy Spirit who inspires thoughts and words. It is God who speaks through the Christian.

In contrast, look at what Paul wrote concerning the prayer language: *"For if I pray in a tongue, my spirit prays . . ."* (1 Cor. 14:14). If we take this literally, then we will understand that it was not the Holy Spirit praying through Paul, but *his spirit* actually prayed. Paul made the same point in verse 2: *"in his spirit he speaks mysteries."* Please consider this seriously, because it clears up much confusion in the Church today. With the prayer language of tongues, the Christian's spirit speaks. In contrast, with the gift of tongues used in the congregation, the Holy Spirit speaks.

Pentecostals who are well-versed in the use of tongues are aware of this. In fact, this distinction can be heard when a message in tongues is interpreted. For example, tongues may be spoken out in the midst of the congregation, and the interpretation may start off something like this: "I, the Lord God, will bless you . . . ." Notice who "I" refers to: God.

In contrast, a Christian may pray in his prayer language, and if it is interpreted it may start off something like this: "I bless you, Lord God . . . ." Notice that "I" refers to the Christian who is praying.

Gift of Tongues

So then, with the gift of tongues God is speaking through the Christian to the congregation. With the prayer language, the Christian is speaking from within his or her spirit to God.

GIFT OF TONGUES VERSUS PRAYER LANGUAGE OF TONGUES

Point 582: Who Gets Edified?

The next major distinction between the gift of tongues and the prayer language is *who gets edified?* This word "edify" means to "build up, encourage, and strengthen." Paul explained that all of the Holy Spirit's gifts, including the gift of tongues, are to edify the whole Body. In contrast, Paul wrote in 1 Corinthians 14:4, *"One who speaks in a tongue edifies himself."* So then, the gift of tongues edifies the whole Body, while the prayer language encourages and strengthens the Christian who is praying in tongues.

Point 583: Who Can Do It?

Another distinction pertains to who can speak in tongues. First Corinthians 12 ends with several rhetorical questions, including, *"All do*

Systematic Theology for the New Apostolic Reformation

not speak with tongues, do they?" (v. 30). The obvious answer to this question is, "No, not all Christians speak in tongues." However, in chapter 14, where Paul explains the prayer language, he wrote, *"Now I wish that you all spoke in tongues . . ."* (v. 5). Paul knew that not everyone will have the gift of tongues to bring a message from God to the congregation, but Paul wanted everyone to have the prayer language of tongues.

Point 584: According to Whose Will?

Another distinction between the gift of tongues and the prayer language has to do with the use of tongues according to the will of the individual.

In 1 Corinthians 12, we are told about the Holy Spirit who gives His gifts, *"distributing to each one individually just as He wills"* (v. 11). When applied to the gift of tongues, we understand this to mean that Christians cannot decide when and where they will bring forth a message in tongues to be heard by the congregation. That happens as the Spirit wills.

In contrast, Paul explained the prayer language, saying,

> *What is the outcome then? I will pray with the spirit and I will pray with the mind also; I will sing with the spirit and I will sing with the mind also.*
>
> (1 Cor. 14:15)

Notice how Paul talked about his use of the prayer language as if he could turn it on or off whenever he chooses. In fact, Paul wrote, *"I thank God, I speak in tongues more than you all"* (1 Cor. 14:18). Indeed, this is the experience of Christians well-trained in the exercise of tongues. They find that the Holy Spirit will speak through a Christian to a congregation if and when the Holy Spirit wants, but Christians may use their prayer language whenever they want.

Point 585: When Do Tongues Need Interpretation?

Finally, we can note a distinction in when tongues must be interpreted. Paul explained that a Christian should only use the gift of tongues in the

Gift of Tongues

congregation if someone is present to interpret (1 Cor. 14:27-28). So then tongues need to be interpreted when used publicly.

On the other hand, Paul went on to say that if there is no interpreter, *"let him speak to himself and to God"* (1 Cor. 14:28). This means that if there is no interpreter, Christians should go ahead and use the prayer language of tongues privately without it being interpreted.

Of course, it is wonderful when Christians praying in tongues know what they are praying, but Paul mentions that he did not always know what he was praying:

For if I pray in a tongue, my spirit prays, but my mind is unfruitful.
(1 Cor. 14:14)

Even though Paul did not know what he was saying, he knew that *"in his spirit"* he was speaking *"mysteries"* (1 Cor. 14:2). God listens to those prayers of mystery.

Volume XI
Pneumatology

Section F
Prophetic Gifts

Much could be discussed about each of the spiritual gifts, but I am only including discussions that enlarge our understanding from the perspective of Father-Son theology. In this section, I will make several relevant points about the prophetic gifts.

Point 586: The Gift of Prophet

Many modern churches do not accept prophets as valid ministers in the Church today. This is in spite of the fact that Paul wrote that Jesus gave prophets to the Church to equip the saints until we all reach maturity (Eph. 4:11-13). We also read in the Book of Acts about several people called prophets:

> *Now there were at Antioch, in the church that was there, <u>prophets</u> and teachers: Barnabas, and Simeon who was called Niger, and Lucius of Cyrene, and Manaen who had been brought up with Herod the tetrarch, and Saul.*
> (Acts 13:1)

> *Now at this time <u>some prophets</u> came down from Jerusalem to Antioch. One of them named Agabus stood up and began to indicate by the Spirit that there would certainly be a great famine all over the world.*
> (Acts 11:27-28)

> *Judas and Silas, who themselves were <u>prophets</u>, said much to*

Systematic Theology for the New Apostolic Reformation

encourage and strengthen the believers.

(Acts 15:32)

In another passage we are also told that Philip, the evangelist, had four virgin daughters who were prophetesses (Acts 21:8-9).

A prophet or prophetess is a person who holds a unique ministry position in the church that should be recognized just like a pastor or evangelist. The primary role of the prophet or prophetess is to speak forth the will and words of God. The word *prophet* literally means advocate or spokesperson, so a prophet of God is one who speaks on behalf of God. Prophets or prophetesses speak under the inspiration of the Holy Spirit, and they must be able to sense God's leading and/or see visions of what God is doing. Amos explained that:

Surely the Lord God does nothing
Unless He reveals His secret counsel
To His servants the prophets.

(Amos 3:7)

Agabus is a good NT example of a prophet who foretold the future (Acts 11:28 ; 21:11).

Modern churches that recognize the gift of prophet will not allow just anyone to step into the role of prophet. Even if several members of a congregation show evidence of being able to prophetically speak forth the word and will of God, a local church may only release specific prophets and prophetesses to minister to their congregation. Usually these are prophets and prophetesses who have proven records and meet the qualifications that Paul listed for elders (1 Tim. 3:1-7).

Point 587: The Gift of Prophecy

It is important to see the difference between a prophet and a prophecy. As explained, a prophet is an individual who holds a specific position in the Church. In contrast, a prophecy refers to a specific message inspired by God.

The messages that prophets and prophetesses give under the inspiration of the Holy Spirit are prophecies, but prophecies may also be given by

Prophetic Gifts

Christians who are not prophets or prophetesses. This is true because the Holy Spirit may come upon any believer at any time to inspire a message from God. Paul wrote that he wished all Christians would prophecy (1 Cor. 14:5), but he also made it clear that not all Christians are prophets (1 Cor. 12:29).

The Holy Spirit's gift of prophecy is not a position in the Church. Nor is it a gift that stays with and abides with the recipient continually, as in the case of prophets. Instead, prophecy is a message that is given if and when the Holy Spirit sovereignly decides.

The gift of prophecy is for *"strengthening, encouraging and comfort"* (1 Cor. 14:3). Many leaders like to point this out because there has been some abuse of prophecy through the years in which some Christians have spoken prophetic messages giving rebuke or direction to people. When someone claims to have a rebuke or direction from God, they are claiming great authority behind that message and, therefore, it is incumbent upon the hearers to act in accordance with the message or to reject the message as not from God. Being placed in a position where that decision must be made is often avoided by teaching that the Holy Spirit's gift of prophecy must be limited to positive, general statements involving strengthening, encouraging, and comforting.

Point 588: Judgment of Prophetic Ministry

Paul gave instructions that every message brought forth by a prophet or through a Christian who is prophesying should be judged by other prophets (1 Cor. 14:29-33).

This judgment is different than that which was carried out in OT times. In OT times, what prophets spoke had to prove perfectly true or they were considered false prophets, subject to death by stoning. The OT prophets had to speak without any errors because they were the voice of God to humanity. Since the Bible was completed, we no longer look to prophets for the final or authoritative word of God. Now we look to the Bible as our final standard of truth. Therefore, if any person today is speaking by the inspiration of the Holy Spirit, we expect the message to agree with what is written in the Word of God.

The very idea that Paul instructed the early Christians to judge prophecy implies that church leaders must not accept any prophetic

Systematic Theology for the New Apostolic Reformation

message unless it passes their judgment. Someone who gives a prophecy that is rejected by church leaders is not stoned to death, but instructed and expected to remain in submission to other prophets (1 Cor. 14:29-32). When someone gives a message that is judged as coming from God, that message should be accepted, and if change is called for, then the hearers should change accordingly.

Judgment is made on the basis of agreement with the written Word of God, but also according to the spirit behind the message. Prophets must discern spiritually the message that is spoken to the church. Not only is the spirit of the prophetic individual discerned, but the message must correspond with the spirit of the church into which the message is spoken. In other words, church leaders must discern if the spoken message harmonizes with where the Holy Spirit is guiding that specific church.

Point 589: Partnering to Bring Prophecy into Fulfillment

How Christians judge prophetic messages is influenced by their concept of God. Those trained with the Classical/Reformed view of God will judge on a different basis than those who see God as Father.

Classical/Reformed theologians maintain that God is timeless, omnipotent, and sovereign, in the sense that He controls all things. Therefore, people trained in Classical/Reformed theology are less likely to see the need or purpose for prophetic ministry. If God is controlling all things, then what is the point? In contrast, if a Christian has an understanding that God is in a cooperative relationship with humanity, working out His will with His people, then prophetic ministry has an important function in revealing God's will.

Even if Classical/Reformed Christians accept prophetic ministry, they will judge it differently, in the sense that all prophecy must reveal predetermined truth. This is how they understand prophecy, because the Classical/Reformed view sees everything in the future as already fixed. If God is going to reveal something, then it has to be the revelation of what He already knows will happen.

In contrast, Christians who see God as Father understand that God may speak to His children as a Father. Often a father reveals his heart and his desires for his children. Therefore, a Christian speaking under the Holy Spirit's inspiration may reveal what Father-God desires to do with a

Prophetic Gifts

certain individual, church, or region. In that case, the hoped-for response is that the listeners will have faith rise in their hearts, and they will partner with God to see the prophetic message brought to fulfillment.

An interesting example of how this works is in Daniel chapter 9. Daniel read what the prophet Jeremiah had written about the desolation and captivity of the Jews lasting for 70 years (v. 2). Daniel realized that it was time for the 70 years to be completed, so he committed himself to fasting and prayer to see the fulfillment of what Jeremiah had prophesied (vv. 3-19). Daniel did not sit back and passively wait for God to fulfill what He had spoken of through Jeremiah. Instead, Daniel understood that he must play a role in bringing the prophecy to fulfillment.

God can speak in an inspirational way, or He can speak with absolute authority. Sometimes He wants His children to cooperate with Him, but other times He declares what He is going to do with or without help. For example, God spoke through Isaiah promising that He would establish Jesus in a Kingdom that would endure forever; Isaiah stated that *"The zeal of the Lord of hosts will accomplish this"* (Is. 9:6-7). This statement is made with total assurance that God determined to accomplish this with or without human cooperation.

God can even change His mind about something He has spoken through a prophet. For example, in 2 Kings 19:20, Isaiah said to Hezekiah:

> *Thus says the Lord, the God of Israel, "Set your house in order, for you shall die and not live."*

When Hezekiah heard this message, he prayed and God heard his prayer, healed him, and added 15 years to his life. In this case, we see that the Word of the Lord that first came through Isaiah did not come true, because God changed His mind.

Of course, Classical/Reformed teachers cannot accept this as literally true because they have decided that God cannot change His mind. Yet, God spoke through Jeremiah explaining that He often deals with people in such a fashion.

> *At one moment I might speak concerning a nation or concerning a kingdom to uproot, to pull down, or to destroy it; if that nation against which I have spoken turns from its evil, I will relent concerning the calamity I planned to bring on it.*
>
> (Jer. 18:7-8)

Systematic Theology for the New Apostolic Reformation

The idea that God decides something, speaks out His decision, and then changes His mind is in direct conflict with the Classical/Reformed view of God. Yet, this is what the Bible shows us to be true.

In order to understand the prophetic gifts, we must think of God as a Father. Then we can understand the various manners in which Father-God speaks to His people. Sometimes He speaks with total authority, declaring what He is about to do. Other times He speaks His desires, wanting His children to partner with Him to bring those desires into reality.

Section G
Divine Healing

In this section we will complete our discussion of pneumatology by looking at divine healing. Thousands of books have been written on this subject, so obviously we cannot cover the subject in-depth here. What we can do is offer a few key points.

Point 590: Purpose of Divine Healing

Everyone who takes the NT seriously will agree that divine healing was a central feature of Jesus' ministry. However, Christian teachers understand the purpose of that healing ministry differently.

Many Christians will say that the reason Jesus healed the sick was to prove that He was the Son of God. Once they accept that reasoning, it is easy for them to reject divine healing as a valid ministry for today. They simply restrict that healing ministry to the period when Jesus was still proving His divinity 2,000 years ago while He walked this earth.

But if we think more deeply about this subject we can see that proving the divinity of Jesus remained a valid purpose for healing after Jesus ascended into heaven. For example, Acts 4:30-33 shows us how the apostles prayed for God to demonstrate Himself with healing, signs and wonders, then we are told, *"And with great power the apostles were giving testimony to the resurrection of the Lord Jesus."* Healing serves the same purpose today. Indeed, many evangelists make it a practice to publicly pray for sick people. They pray in the name of Jesus. Then, if and when a visible healing takes place, it is presented as evidence that Jesus is alive and still active today.

Systematic Theology for the New Apostolic Reformation

Yet, our understanding of the purpose of healing should be expanded. Jesus healed not only to prove His divinity but also because He loves people. Matthew tells us how Jesus *"saw a large crowd, and felt compassion for them and healed their sick"* (Matt. 14:14). The heart of Jesus is the heart of God. Seeing God as a loving Father, we should expect God to continue healing people because He loves them.

Point 591: God Uses People

Certainly God can sovereignly heal anyone at anytime He chooses. God does not need the help of any human being.

Yet, we see God using His people in the Book of Acts. When Peter and John commanded a lame man to walk, the man leaped to his feet (Acts 3:4-8). When the apostles walked around Jerusalem large numbers of sick people were brought to them *"and they were all being healed"* (Acts 5:16). Similarly, Stephen was used in Jerusalem (Acts 6:8), while Philip was used in Samaria (Acts 8:4-7). Through Paul, *"God was performing extraordinary miracles . . ."* (Acts 19:11). So God uses His people.

James wrote to the early Christians:

> *Is anyone among you sick? Then he must call for the elders of the church and they are to pray over him, anointing him with oil in the name of the Lord; and the prayer offered in faith will restore the one who is sick, and the Lord will raise him up . . . .*
> (Jas. 5:14-15)

Notice that this is spoken as matter-of-factly as someone reporting that the sky is blue. James went on to talk about Elijah *"who was a man with a nature like ours"* and *"he prayed earnestly that it would not rain, and it did not rain on the earth for three years and six months"* (Jas. 5:17). The point James was making is that people can make a difference. In particular, *"The effective prayer of a righteous man can accomplish much"* (Jas. 5:16).

Many Christians who do not understand this truth may become sick and when asked if they want someone to pray for healing, they may say, "If God wants to heal me, He can do it without anyone praying." That response may sound like an expression of faith that God is able to sovereignly do what He wants to do without people being involved. In reality, it is based on a misunderstanding concerning how God works in this world. James

Divine Healing

explained that we do not have because we do not ask (Jas. 4:2). Many things God will not do unless people get involved.

Of course, this is incompatible with Reformed theology which teaches that God is sovereign in the sense of being in exhaustive control. If God is in control as Reformed theology teaches:

1. then God is the One who makes people sick in the first place
2. then God will heal whomever and whenever He wants whether or not people are involved in the healing process
3. then grace is unmerited favor which implies that humans can play no role in giving or receiving any healing grace from God[341]

Hence, followers of Reformed theology have much to overcome before they can have faith that God will heal them.

Point 592: Via the Word or Spirit in the Bible

Ministries of divine healing can be studied from many different perspectives. One that is especially helpful is to separate divine healing accomplished via the spoken Word in contrast to that which is accomplished via the Spirit. In making this separation, I do not mean to suggest that the Word of God can be completely separated from the Spirit of God. Of course, God is one, but we can see in the Scriptures different ministries of the Persons of the Trinity.

Consider how God acted throughout the Bible sometimes through His spoken Word and other times through His Spirit. During the first five days of creation, God spoke His Word and things came into existence, but then on the sixth day, God formed Adam's body from the dust of the earth and breathed His Spirit into Adam's physical body. At various times in the OT we see individuals like Abraham, who were changed because they believed the Word spoken to them by God. At other times, the Holy Spirit came upon certain leaders and changed them, i.e., Saul when he was *"changed into another man"* (1 Sam. 10:6).

In the NT we can see Jesus ministering divine healing and sometimes the spoken Word was emphasized while other times the Spirit was

---

341 Discussed in VII:B:445.

Systematic Theology for the New Apostolic Reformation

emphasized. The Word was emphasized when a centurion with a sick servant requested Jesus to *"just say the word and my servant will be healed"* (Luke 7:7). On another occasion, Jesus did not even say a word of healing, but a woman with a hemorrhage touched the hem of His garment, and spiritual virtue flowed out of Jesus to heal the woman (Luke 8:43-48).

We can see a similar pattern with Jesus' disciples. Jesus first *"sent them out to proclaim the kingdom of God and to perform healing"* (Luke 9:2). At that time, the disciples had not yet received the Holy Spirit because the Spirit had not yet been given (John 7:39). The disciples had authority to command that people be healed (Luke 9:1). Later in the Book of Acts we see that the disciples received the Holy Spirit and they did many similar miracles via the work of the Holy Spirit.

Point 593: Via the Word or Spirit in Today's Healing Ministries

As in Bible times, so also it is today. Some divine healing ministries emphasize the spoken Word and other healing ministries emphasize the Holy Spirit. For example, the spoken Word is emphasized by leaders who are part of the "Word of Faith" movement, e.g., Kenneth E. Hagin and Kenneth Copeland. In contrast, the Holy Spirit is emphasized by many healing ministers in the Pentecostal/Charismatic movement, e.g., Kathryn Kuhlman and Benny Hinn.

Ministers who emphasize the spoken Word talk much about the authority that God has given to His people. It is on the basis of that God-given authority that believers can command sicknesses to leave. Therefore, believers should rise up and take authority over sickness.

In contrast, ministers who favor the work of the Holy Spirit in divine healing show more dependency upon the Holy Spirit. They see healing as a gift of the Holy Spirit who distributes His gift *"to each one individually just as He wills"* (1 Cor. 12:11). In line with this understanding, ministers believe they can only release God's healing power if and when the Holy Spirit desires.

An important distinction between these two types of ministry is how much faith is required on the part of the sick individual. When Jesus heard the centurion request Him to *"just say the word,"* He commented that He had not seen such great faith in all of Israel (Luke 7:9). On several other occasions, Jesus spoke His Word in order to heal people, and He followed

Divine Healing

up saying, "Your faith has made you well." There was a clear association between the spoken Word and the recipient having faith to receive. Corresponding to this, modern ministers who emphasize healing via the spoken Word talk much about faith being required on the part of the recipient.

On the other hand, ministers who emphasize healing as a gift of the Holy Spirit rarely talk about the need for faith. Since healing is a gift, it requires nothing from the recipient. Corresponding to this, people who experience healing often have no faith before the healing takes place. In fact, some people who get healed under those Holy Spirit oriented ministries are very critical of divine healing until God supernaturally heals them.

Usually both types of healing ministries are rejected by Reformed Christians who have been trained to think God is in exhaustive control of all things. However, if they do accept divine healing, it will usually be that which is Holy Spirit oriented. This is because healing via the spoken Word places great authority and responsibility in the hands of people. Seeing that much authority transferred from God to people is a more radical departure from traditional Reformed thinking.

Point 594: One's Worldview Determines Their Faith

The successes and failures of divine healing ministries are profoundly influenced by the worldview of the people involved. As explained, the worldview of Western society is founded in a dualist cosmology. The spiritual world is distant from the natural world in which we live. With that worldview, it seems like a major work for the timeless Wholly Other to reach across the infinite expanse and bother to heal people in this natural world. Hence, divine healings are less likely to happen among people indoctrinated in the Western worldview.

The Western worldview is even more of a handicap when we add the Western concept of human nature. For atheists, people are less than microscopic specs of dust in an ever expanding universe. For Christians trained in Reformed theology, people are also dust, but even worse, totally depraved dust.[342] With such ideas deeply embedded into the psyche of Reformed Christians, it is difficult to conceive of God bothering with an individual's little problems such as physical sickness.

---

342 Discussed in IV:A:187, 193.

Systematic Theology for the New Apostolic Reformation

THE WESTERN WORLDVIEW IS COUNTERPRODUCTIVE TO DIVINE HEALING

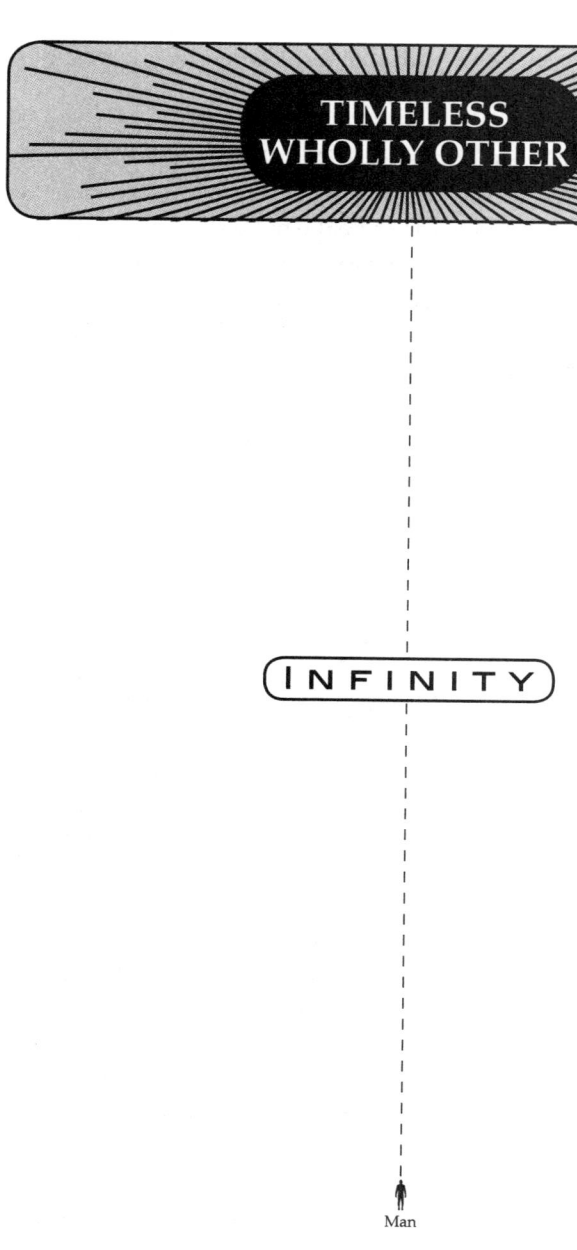

TIMELESS WHOLY OTHER

INFINITY

Man

Divine Healing

The biblical worldview is radically different, producing radically different results. It sees that God's realm is here, around us, and completely integrated into the natural realm. Plus, people are children of God, loved by Him. Furthermore, God is known as Yahweh Rapha. This is His identity. This is who He is.

THE BIBLICAL WORLDVIEW

For someone who is consistent with Reformed theology it is difficult or even impossible to conceive of God answering prayers to heal the sick. If and when they witness God supernaturally healing someone, they are typically challenged to rethink who God is, plus they are troubled about the inconsistencies in their own theology.

In contrast, for someone who is consistent with the God who is revealed in the Bible as Yahweh Rapha, the most troubling cases are those in which God does *not* heal the sick—something worth a few more thoughts.

Point 595: God Is Still Our Father

The fact that Christians do not see healing every time they pray for the sick is deeply troubling to those who embrace God as Yahweh Rapha. Millions of Christians have experienced the resulting disillusionment.

Systematic Theology for the New Apostolic Reformation

Some have totally given up on serving God. Many times members within a congregation have joined together to pray for a sick person in their midst, only to see that sick person die. Such incidents may lead to a crisis of faith.

Critics of healing ministries point to such cases as proof that God does not heal today. Then they hunker more deeply into their own powerless theology.

Yet, that will not work for those who believe God still heals today, because most of them have witnessed someone who did get healed as a result of prayer. So they cannot deny that God heals.

However, when Christians commit themselves to whole-hearted prayer for healing and the sick person dies, everyone involved is challenged to reevaluate what is true. They must ask questions such as:

1. Did they really believe?
2. Did they have sin in their heart that hindered prayers?
3. Did they lack persistence?
4. Should they have raised the sick person from the dead?
5. Did the sick person choose to die anyway?
6. Did God sovereignly override their prayers?
7. Is their theology wrong?

No answer, no matter how logical, will eliminate the emotional and spiritual chaos stirred when a loved one dies. However, there is a common thread in the lives of those who successfully navigate through unanswered prayers. It is seated in the primary message of this book that God is our Father. If this truth is settled in the hearts of God's people then they may be shaken, but they will not fall. When events of life do not turn out the way they are expected, chaos may overwhelm the mind, but the heart will remain anchored. If God was known as their Father before the experience of unanswered prayer, then He will still be known as their Father after the experience.

Volume XII
The Christian Life

Now we can see what our theology produces in the life of Christians. Classical/Reformed theology leads to one lifestyle and Father-Son theology leads to a different lifestyle. Of course, no one lives totally consistent with their theology, but their theology definitely plays an important role in determining how they live.

The most determining factor of Father-Son theology is in seeing God as Father. Not everyone has had a good natural father to represent the nature of God. So, we must talk about a father better than all natural fathers, when we talk about Father-God.

Volume XII
The Christian Life

Section A
Living as Children

A father loves his children. That love transforms them. Children desire to please their father. That desire influences their decisions and the course of their lives.

Point 596: Created to Be Loved

Classical/Reformed theologians maintain that God created all things for His own glory.[343] The logical outcome of that viewpoint is that we were created to glorify God. That is our highest aim according to Classical/Reformed theology.

In contrast, Father-Son theology is founded in God's desire to have sons, and His decision to have sons was based in love. This leads us to believe that we were created *to be loved*.

Allow me to offer an illustration from my own life. Earlier,[344] I talked about a young boy from a disadvantaged home, who began staying with us several days each week. We had him do some chores around the house, such as mow the lawn and empty the garbage, but that is not why we had him around. We had him around because we wanted to love him.

The idea that God wanted someone to love is inconsistent with Classical/Reformed theology because of their doctrine of God's self-sufficiency, which means God wants and needs nothing. In contrast, Father-Son theology recognizes that God opened His heart to humanity and He made Himself vulnerable. Now He desires to love us.

---

343 Discussed in III:B:144.
344 IV:D:217.

Systematic Theology for the New Apostolic Reformation

A corollary to this is that we are fulfilling our number one purpose by *letting God love us*. Of course, we should glorify God and serve Him. However, our highest purpose is to receive God's love.

Our Highest Purpose

Classical/Reformed Theology	Father-Son Theology
to glorify God	to receive God's love

Receiving God's love is different than knowing God loves us. We can see this in a troubled marriage, where the husband knows his wife loves him, but he will not receive her love. In a comparative way, we can know that God loves us but still hold His love away from our hearts. Letting God love us results in an experience of His warmth, His care, His protection, and His pleasure in us. If we are not experiencing that, then we are not receiving His love, nor are we fulfilling the number one purpose for which He created us.

Point 597: Transformed by His Love

God's love is the most transformative force in existence. As people receive His love, they are transformed into His image from glory to glory.

An excellent way to see the transformative power of love is to consider the dynamics in a family that has adopted a young girl. The adoptive parents may be taking in that child for the purpose of loving her, but she may or may not receive their love. She may not trust her adoptive parents, and therefore, she keeps up a wall in her heart. Another reason she may refuse the love of her adoptive parents is because she consciously or subconsciously knows that receiving love will change her. It will soften her. Remaining strong and holding on to her present identity may be so important to her that she would rather live isolated. She may also feel that changing will be disloyal to a parent she previously knew or wishes she could know.

Similar dynamics happen in one's relationship with God. People may hold God at a distance and not receive His love because they do not trust Him. Or they may consciously or subconsciously know that God's love will change them, and they may not want to change.

Living as Children

Point 598: Our Ambition to Please Him

Human beings are born with an instinctive desire to please their parents. This is a powerful motivation in human behavior. For people who see God as their Father, the drive to receive His approval is life molding.

Christians have varying beliefs concerning their ability to please God. Some have been taught that God sees "nothing but Jesus" when He looks at each child. While it is true that the righteousness of Jesus is given to each of God's children, He still sees individuals. Furthermore, Father-God is responsive to the behavior of each child. Paul explained:

> *. . . we also have as our ambition, whether at home or absent, to be pleasing to Him.*
>
> (2 Cor. 5:9)

People can please or displease God by their daily actions.

This truth cannot be reconciled with Classical/Reformed theology. If God is timeless, immutable, impassible, and self-sufficient, then there is nothing that people can do to add anything to God. The actions of people have no effect upon God if Classical/Reformed theology is true.

In contrast, a Father who is passible and going through time with humanity may experience pleasure or displeasure in response to human behavior. God's children can even please Him as Job did, as revealed in His conversation with Satan.

> *Have you considered My servant Job? For there is no one like him on the earth, a blameless and upright man, fearing God and turning away from evil.*
>
> (Job 1:8b)

God delighted in Job. He was proud of Job.

Christians consistent with the Classical/Reformed view of God must take such expressions as anthropomorphisms, but it is difficult to excuse all such comments of God, especially when we consider His words over His only begotten Son:

> *This is My beloved Son, in whom I am well-pleased.*
>
> (Matt. 3:17).

God doted on Jesus. Jesus hit the high mark. He pleased the Father.

Systematic Theology for the New Apostolic Reformation

Notice how our concept of God determines how we live our lives. If we envision God as timeless, immutable, impassible, and self-sufficient, then there is no reason to try to please God, because it is impossible for mere human beings to please such a wholly other God. On the other hand, if we see Him as a responsive Father, then we have strong motivation to live in a way that brings pleasure to Him. A strong motivation is to hear Him say, "Well done, good and faithful servant."

Point 599: What Pleases God?

Once we recognize that we can please Father-God, it is worth determining what pleases Him and to what He responds favorably.

Faith pleases God. Hebrews 11:6 tells us:

And without faith it is impossible to please Him . . . .

People who do not have faith are not pleasing to God. In fact, it is *impossible* for them to please God.

Further, we can say that God recognizes and likes our good works. The writer of Hebrews said:

And do not neglect doing good and sharing, for with such sacrifices God is pleased.
(Heb. 13:16)

We know that our salvation is based on grace through faith rather than the works of the Law, but God still likes it when people do good things.

In the Book of Acts, we are told about a man named Cornelius whose lifestyle was pleasing to God, and hence, he won God's favor. We are told that Cornelius was:

. . . a devout man and one who feared God with all his household, and gave many alms to the Jewish people and prayed to God continually.
(Acts 10:2)

In the verses following this description of Cornelius, we learn about an angel which appeared to Cornelius, saying:

Living as Children

Your prayers and alms have ascended as a memorial before God.
(Acts 10:4b)

God took notice, and we are told specifically what caught His attention: prayers and giving to the poor.

Humility is another quality that pleases Him: *"God is opposed to the proud, but gives grace to the humble"* (Jas. 4:6). James wrote this to Christians, reminding them that God treats individuals differently, based in part on their humility before Him.

Some readers may see this discussion as promoting a "works oriented religion." This is a special concern for Christians who have worked hard to grasp that God loves them just as they are. Yes, God has consuming love for each one of His children. Furthermore, our salvation is given by grace through faith. However, it is also true that there should be some performance orientation to our lives. Paul made it his *"ambition . . . to be pleasing to Him"* (2 Cor. 5:9). Paul had a works orientation to His walk with God. If we believe God is responsive to individuals, then we too will be motivated to do things that give Him pleasure.

The good news is that you and I can please the One we love.

Volume XII
The Christian Life

Section B
Healthy Relationships

People's understanding of God determines many of the dynamics within their relationships with other people.

Point 600: The Family Is God's Plan

God wants a family. This elevates the importance of every family on earth. Jesus wants a bride. This raises the value of marriage above any natural standards. Family and marriage are not just creations of humanity. Nor are they structures of convenience or temporary patterns for society to follow. The family unit came out of God's love. It is His plan. Family and marriage are the units patterned after the heart of God, in whose image we are created.

This does not mean that every individual living outside of a family and/or marriage is outside of God's will. Jesus talked about some who, for the sake of the Kingdom, left their family (Matt. 19:29) and others who made themselves eunuchs (Matt. 19:12). However, those are recognized as great sacrifices. God's plan is for the vast majority of people to live within healthy family units.

Furthermore, we can learn from God's love for His family and see how the orientation of His heart is fully toward His family. With God as our ultimate example, we can conclude that parents should be willing to do anything for their children—even give their lives.

So also, a husband should be willing to give his life for his wife.

Systematic Theology for the New Apostolic Reformation

Point 601: Jesus' Heart and Actions Toward His Bride

Jesus' heart and actions toward His Bride reveal how husbands should act toward their wives. Paul explained that Jesus is the model for every husband to follow (Eph. 5:25-28).

Jesus not only gave His life for His Bride, but His heart is to raise Her to rule and reign with Him. This is in contrast to that which resulted from Adam's sin, which was men ruling over their wives. That "ruling over" was part of the curse. The New Adam, Jesus Christ, redeemed humanity from the curse and established the proper role a husband is to take toward his wife, which is to raise her to walk alongside of him. Adam's sin resulted in men holding women down, while Jesus' example shows how a husband should lift his wife up.

Point 602: Nurturing the Image of God in Children

Father-Son theology sees all people as created in the image of God and children entering this world innocent, but vulnerable.[345] This determines the proper orientation parents should have in raising their children, which is to protect their children from evil and danger, plus nurture the gifts instilled within each child.

In contrast, Classical/Reformed theology see babies coming into this world as already totally depraved. If parents live consistent with that belief, they will orient their child-rearing toward controlling their evil children.

This distinction of nurturing or controlling that which is within is evident throughout the two theological perspectives. (In Section E, we will see how these two perspectives lead to different conclusions about living the victorious Christian life.)

Point 603: Relationships with Family and Community

When we recognize God's existence as Father, Son, and Holy Spirit, we see the One God existing in relationship. Being created in His image, humans are created to exist in relationship.

---

345 Discussed in IV:B, F.

Healthy Relationships

God declared that it is not good for a man to be alone, but man's need for relationship goes beyond a partner in marriage. Jesus declared that He is building His Church out of living stones. He is the Good Shepherd who will gather His sheep together as one. When the Holy Spirit came upon the early believers, they became of one mind and heart. Paul wrote that all who believe in Jesus become members of one Body. People are created by God to be in both family relationships and community relationships.

Point 604: People Complete Us in Our Areas of Vulnerability

When people open their hearts for relationship, they become vulnerable.

We can see this vulnerability even in God. Because He opened His heart for relationship, He is jealous of those whose hearts turn away from Him. Because He loves people, He can be grieved by those who hurt others. God is not only vulnerable, but He allows people into His vulnerability. For example, God was angry enough to destroy the Hebrews, but God allowed Moses to reason with Him. This allowance by God has profound implications.

Consider how some people are vulnerable to outbursts of anger. The best answer to their problem is not to hide their anger but to let someone into their life with whom they can talk. Psychologists know that there are many other emotional vulnerabilities such as depression, fear, and anxiety that are often solved by close, open relationships. The answer to people's vulnerabilities is not isolation but openness to others who will fulfill and complete them.

John explained the significance of relationships within the Body of Christ:

> . . . but if we walk in the Light as He Himself is in the Light, we have fellowship with one another, and the blood of Jesus His Son cleanses us from all sin.
>
> (1 John 1:7)

Walking in the light entails full exposure. True fellowship means hiding nothing. Those who walk in open relationships will have the supernatural intervention of God cleansing their innermost being. The only way to be healthy is to walk in open relationships with family and in community.

Volume XII
The Christian Life

Section C
Prayer

Prayer is communing with God. Our concept of God determines how we pray, what results we expect, and what results we get.

Point 605: God Does Answer Prayer

For adherents of Classical/Reformed theology, prayer serves as a means to connect the heart of the believer to God. However, God does not "answer" prayers. If God is in exhaustive control of all things as Classical/Reformed theology teaches, then God is doing His will whether or not people pray. If God is timeless, then all of His decisions were settled in eternity past. According to Classical/Reformed theology, God cannot change His mind about anything, so prayer cannot change God. Prayer only changes the person doing the praying.

The Bible teaches something very different. Jesus said:

> *Truly, truly, I say to you, if you ask the Father for anything in My name, He will give it to you.*
>
> (John 16:23)

There are several other similar passages in the Bible. James even says, "*You do not have because you do not ask*" (Jas. 4:2), which tells us that there are many things that God would do if we simply asked Him.

Systematic Theology for the New Apostolic Reformation

Point 606: Daddy Wants to Hear Our Desires

Many Christian teachers say that God answers our needs, but not our desires. They say this with good intentions, perhaps to reassure people who have prayed and not seen God give them their desires. Yet, Jesus told His disciples to pray their desires and wishes:

> . . . *ask whatever you <u>wish</u>, and it will be done for you.*
> (John 15:7)

Of course, there is nothing wrong with talking to God about our needs. Indeed, we read in the Lord's Prayer how we are instructed to pray, *"Give us this day our daily bread"* (Matt. 6:11), but in the same passage Jesus instructed us not to pray over and over for the things we need, because our Father knows what we need (Matt. 6:7).

This understanding comes into focus as soon as we see God as Father. Think of a father who tucks his daughter into bed every night. What would you think if every night the daughter asked her father, "Tomorrow can I have food? Tomorrow will you let me wear clothes and shoes? Tomorrow can I have a drink of water?" If we ever heard requests such as these, we would immediately wonder what was wrong with that father. A good father would never want his daughter to feel obligated to make such requests. He already knows what she needs, and he would be a bad father if he did not provide those needs without being asked.

What a loving father wants to hear from his daughter is what she desires, wishes, and dreams. If he heard his daughter say, "Daddy, I want to be a veterinarian when I grow up," then he would do whatever he could to make her dream come true. So too, God wants to hear our desires because He is Father.

Point 607: Praying According to His Will

John wrote:

> . . . *if we ask anything according to His will, He hears us.*
> (1 John 5:14)

Prayer

What does it mean that we must pray "according to God's will"? Do we have to bring our will in line with God's will before He answers? If so, why even pray, especially if He's going to do His will anyway?

These questions are especially difficult to answer for people who have the "sun like" image at the foundation of their concept of God. As we explained, Classical/Reformed theologians teach that God's will is eternally settled. With a concept of God radiating out His unchangeable will, the only logical understanding of "praying according to His will" is to bring one's own will into accord with God's will. According to Classical/Reformed thought, those are the only prayers that God answers anyway.

Consider a different understanding of the phrase, "pray according to His will." Think of it as praying "as God wills." Pray in the manner in which God wants us to pray. If we pray in the manner in which He wants us to pray, then He will answer. With this understanding, our efforts in prayer will not be to make our prayers match His will, but to pray our own desires as God wants us to pray our desires.

And how does God want us to pray? He wants us to have contact with Him. He wants us to dialogue as a child to a Father. God wants us to reason with Him as Abraham did (Gen. 18:22-33). He wants us to speak face-to-face with Him as Moses did. God wants us to know Him. He wants us to engage with Him. He wants us to call Him Father (Matt. 6:9).

This truth can be expressed by saying we must *abide* in Him. Jesus told His disciples:

> *If you abide in Me, and My words abide in you, ask whatever you wish, and it will be done for you.*
>
> (John 15:7)

Abiding in Jesus means living *in* Him and *with* Him. It is the relationship God wants. If His children walk in close relationship with Him, then He will answer whatever they ask.

Point 608: Living in Thankfulness

To abide in God is to live in His love. To know God as Father means accepting His care, provisions, watchfulness, and love. A lifestyle of prayer is a lifestyle of rejoicing in what Father-God is already doing. It is a lifestyle of receiving and, therefore, thanksgiving.

Systematic Theology for the New Apostolic Reformation

This pattern of life can be seen in Jesus' instructions to His disciples. After teaching them how to pray the Lord's prayer (Matt. 6:8-13), Jesus went on to explain that they should not worry about food, drink, or clothes. Instead, they should know that their heavenly Father takes care of the birds of the air and the lilies of the field, so He will certainly take care of them (vv. 25-34). Jesus taught them that if their eyes are single, meaning in this context that their lives are oriented toward the goodness of God, then their entire lives will be filled with light (vv. 22-23). It is this orientation of life that leads to a life of thanksgiving prayer. This is where God wants us to live.

Point 609: How Father-God Answers

Many Christians have wrestled with the supposed contradiction in God's promise to answer our requests and the fact that many prayers do not get answered. This does not require deep theological or philosophical reasoning. All we have to do is think of God as a Father.

A five-year-old boy who asks his father for an assault rifle probably will not get an assault rifle. That is not what a good father would do. Any five-year-old boy can figure out why his father will not give him an assault rifle.

Jesus reasoned with the Jewish religious leaders:

> *Which of you fathers, if your son asks for a fish, will give him a snake instead? Or if he asks for an egg, will give him a scorpion? If you then, though you are evil, know how to give good gifts to your children, how much more will your Father in heaven give the Holy Spirit to those who ask him!*
>
> (Luke 11:11-13)

This passage is actually speaking of giving the Holy Spirit when God's children ask, but the principle can apply to all requests. Father-God is good. He is not going to give a snake or poison to any of His children.

God answers prayers similar to how a natural father answers the requests of his children. If a son asks his father for financial help, his father may give his son a job and teach him how to work. A businesswoman who asks for help in her business can expect God to answer as a covenant partner, giving counsel and guiding her through daily decisions.

Prayer

If a Christian sees a poor beggar on the street and he asks God to help that individual, God may answer by saying, "You help him." Of course, there will be times when God sovereignly intervenes, and there will be times when God acts supernaturally. However, the primary way God wants to answer prayers is by working *with* His children.

Again, it is no mystery how God answers prayers. We simply have to think of Him as our Father, and then we understand.

Volume XII
The Christian Life

Section D
Worship

Another fundamental of the Christian life is worship. Why do we do it, how do we do it, and what should we expect as a result?

Point 610: The Nearness of God

Father-Son theology is built on a foundation where God's spiritual realm fills the same space as the natural realm. Therefore, God is always close to humanity and people are ever aware of that closeness.

FATHER-SON FOUNDATION:
GOD'S SPIRITUAL REALM FILLS THE NATURAL REALM

Systematic Theology for the New Apostolic Reformation

In contrast, Classical/Reformed theology is built on a dualistic worldview in which God exists in a world distant and totally unlike the natural world. This causes Christians trained in Classical/Reformed theology to maintain in their own mind a greater distance between themselves and God.

CLASSICAL/REFORMED FOUNDATION:
GOD'S WORLD IS DISTANT AND UNLIKE THE NATURAL WORLD

Spiritual, Timeless World of God

INFINITY

Creation

Worship

The distance which individuals maintain between themselves and God is reinforced by their life experiences. The most powerful influences are the prayers of others close to them. For example, if parents talk to God as if He is very near, then their children will grow up being comfortable with that same level of nearness. On the other hand, if parents use formal language, repeating standardized prayers and offering their words to a distant God, then children listening in will imprint that same level of respect and formality when they approach God.

Similarly, church leaders teach their members what is the appropriate manner in which to approach God. Not only are the tone and inflections of the leader's voice while praying determinative, but also the structure and arrangement of the sanctuary. Some church members tend to think of God at a distance from them which corresponds with their distance to the front of the sanctuary. For this reason, some church members who routinely sit in the front of the sanctuary tend to think of God as close. Others who think of God as far away feel uncomfortable sitting at the front of the sanctuary.

Of course, not every person is so influenced by the prayers of others or positioning within a sanctuary, but these are two of many influences acting upon the subconscious mind of each person.

Point 611: Drawing Near to God in Worship

Christians who have embraced the biblical cosmology will think of God as very close. If they have embraced a fatherly concept of God, they will know that He is instantly available.

Yet, they may also have an element of progression in approaching God during a worship service. This is expressed well in James' exhortation: *"Draw near to God and He will draw near to you"* (Jas. 4:8). However, it is not God who is drawing nearer in reference to distance, because God is always close. It is people's awareness and, hence, experience of God that changes as they focus more on God. As a consequence, many churches organize their worship services with a progression, beginning with exuberant praise and thanksgiving, followed by more reverent worship, culminating in a respectful awe of a God who is very close and intimate.

Such a progression is inconsistent with Classical/Reformed theology, which sees God as impassible and immutable, unmoved by what humans

Systematic Theology for the New Apostolic Reformation

do. For them, God is always at a distant, well-established position in relation to humanity. In a worship service, the "appropriate" distance is established with the first song. Classically minded Christians tend to maintain that same distance throughout their worship time.

The differing expectations of worshipers often cause conflicts. Some passionate worship leaders long to lead the people into contact with God where they know Him as their Lover and Romancer. Frequently, the senior pastor, who has the final authority over the congregational meeting, will not allow the worship leader to take the people to such a level of intimacy. This reluctance on the part of the senior minister is usually motivated by his awareness of his own congregational members, some of whom were raised in more traditional churches and, therefore, would be very uncomfortable with a deeper level of intimacy. The senior pastor's reluctance may also be due to his own level of comfort with God's nearness, a level established through his own upbringing and training.

The level of nearness in any one church service is not a matter of biblical dictate. Pastors should be aware of how desirous of and tolerant to the nearness of God the people are. However, a group of Christians who are becoming more and more aware of God as Father will tend to become more desirous of His closeness. Some levels of intimacy are not always appropriate in public meetings. However, in private, personal worship Christians should become comfortable with, and even long for, intimacy with Father-God.

Point 612: Exuberant Worship

What emotions are expressed or allowed in a worship service are also determined by the congregation's concept of God. Classical/Reformed theology teaches that God experiences no emotional variation, so people coming before Him tend to take on a corresponding demeanor and be subdued in their expression of emotion. On the other hand, if God is an emotional Being, and if we are created in His image, then worshipers should be free for a full array of emotional expressions.

If any emotions are allowed in a church teaching Classical/Reformed theology, they will tend to be awe, respect, and reverence. According to Classical/Reformed thought, we depraved human beings should bow to the uttermost of our being. We should feel humbled within ourselves,

Worship

while the songs that we sing should reveal our honor of the Transcendent Almighty One.

Thus Christians trained in Classical/Reformed theology tend to be more comfortable singing formal hymns *about* God rather than intimate songs *to* Him. Therefore, they would be uncomfortable singing words such as, "I adore You, Father. You are the Lover of my soul." They would feel much more comfortable singing to God in the third person with words such as, "God is great; He is our strength and the Caretaker of our souls."

If Christians trained in the Classical/Reformed tradition visit a modern Church where the worship service is very expressive with exuberant praise, dancing, and the raising of hands, those visitors are likely to be troubled and possibly offended. They may react as King Saul's daughter, Michal, reacted to King David when he danced publicly before the Lord with all of his might (2 Sam. 6:14-16). Someone trained in the Classical/Reformed view of God will see such expressive worship as irreverent. They may have a difficult time conceiving of how the Immutable, Transcendent One could approve of such disrespect from mere human beings. Classical/Reformed followers may wonder at the intimacy with God that is expressed and have to decide if such expressions are appropriate.

In contrast, Christians embracing God as revealed in Father-Son theology know that they should allow their voices to express what is in their hearts. They know that God takes pleasure in their expressive and intimate worship.

Point 613: Worship Gives God Pleasure

Does God benefit from our worship, or is it only for our benefit?

If God is immutable and self-sufficient, as Classical/Reformed theology teaches, then He benefits nothing from our worship. Christians consistent with Classical/Reformed theology do worship God, but they do it because He deserves to be worshiped; it is the right thing to do.

In contrast, Father-Son theology teaches that God takes pleasure in our worship. Several OT passages talk about sacrifices and worship ascending to God as a soothing aroma, which implies that God has a satisfying experience as a result of human worship. The pleasure that God experiences is in part related to His jealousy for the hearts of His people. As we explained earlier, the fact that God is jealous means that

Systematic Theology for the New Apostolic Reformation

He experiences anguish when the hearts of His people are turned toward other gods. On the other hand, worship that comes from devotion to God gives Him pleasure.

One of the most revealing examples is in Acts 13:1-2, where we read about the church leaders in Antioch ministering to the Lord. The word *ministering* entails serving God in a fashion that benefits Him.

Such thoughts are incompatible with a theology that holds to a self-sufficient God. We have nothing to give to that God who does not need or want anything.

Point 614: Giving God Glory

What can we give to God? Many Bible verses talk about giving Him glory (e.g., Ps. 29:2 ; 86:9 ; Is. 42:12 ; 1 Chron. 16:29 ; Rev. 14:7). This is a key feature of worship.

Before we explain how to give God glory, it is worth asking what *glory* is? Earlier, we explained glory as we talked about the glory that abides upon humanity. Of course, all people fall short of the glory of God (Rom. 3:23), but every human being still has a presence that demands respect. The Psalmist explained that God made humanity *"a little lower than God, And You crown him with glory and majesty!"* (Ps. 8:5). Paul also wrote about the glory that abides upon different aspects of creation. He mentioned the glory of the sun, moon, and stars (1 Cor. 15:41). As we consider that glory, we can identify it as that which stirs within an observer a sense of awe.

Of course, only God dwells in perfect light and glory. Sometimes it is referred to as the shekinah glory of God. So grand is His glory that Moses had to hide in a cleft of a rock while the glory manifested from the back side of God (Ex. 33:23). Such glory refers to God's radiance and brilliance, revealing His nature.

How then can we give glory to God? The Psalmist frequently gave God glory by *accrediting to Him the credit He deserves*. Some Bible translators referred to this as "ascribing to God" what is due Him:

> *Ascribe to the Lord, O sons of the mighty,*
> *Ascribe to the Lord glory and strength.*
> *Ascribe to the Lord the glory due to His name;*
> *Worship the Lord in holy array.*
>
> (Ps. 29:1-2)

Worship

Ascribing glory to God, included both speaking to Him and speaking to others about the greatness of God. We can see this when we read about people giving glory to God in response to seeing God work miracles:

> *So the crowd marveled as they saw the mute speaking, the crippled restored, and the lame walking, and the blind seeing; and <u>they glorified the God of Israel</u>.*
> (Matt. 15:31)

When we are thanking and praising God for what He has done, we are also giving Him glory. Simply giving Him the credit (in contrast to taking credit for ourselves or taking God for granted) glorifies Him.

Point 615: God Responds Positively to Worship

In the Bible we can read of many occasions when God responded positively to people who worshiped Him. For example, the writer of Hebrews explained that as a result of the offering that Abel made to God, Abel received God's confirming word that he was righteous and acceptable (Heb. 11:4). When Noah offered a burnt offering:

> *The Lord smelled the soothing aroma; and the Lord said to Himself, "I will never again curse the ground on account of man . . . ."*
> (Gen. 8:21)

In Acts 13:1-2, we read about the church leaders in Antioch *"ministering unto the Lord"* and immediately afterwards the Lord spoke and gave them specific direction.

Such responses from God should be expected. As the writer of Hebrews explained, everyone *"who comes to God must believe that He is and that He is a rewarder of those who seek Him"* (Heb. 11:6). God rewards, that is, He responds positively to people who seek Him. In the same way that God is a lover, He is a rewarder.

Volume XII
The Christian Life

Section E
The Victorious Life

Some of the most important distinctives of Father-Son theology are those pertaining to how Christians live the victorious life. We will explain the primary distinctives in this section.

As we discuss this, we will first need to define the "flesh." In some Bible passages this word is used to refer to the meat tissue of living organisms, as in the flesh of animals that people eat. Here we will not be using the word flesh in that sense. Instead, we will use the word flesh to refer to a person's corrupt, sinful nature.

Point 616: Victory According to Reformed Theology

Reformed theology teaches that, because of Adam's sin, all people come into this world with a nature that is totally depraved. That sin nature is inherited from Adam and it is called the "flesh." According to Reformed theology, people are justified in God's eyes when they become Christians, but they continue to have a sin nature, i.e., the flesh, all of their lives. Reformed theology also teaches that people receive a new nature when they become Christians, and that new nature is referred to as one in which the Christian has a new, recreated "spirit."[346]

This leads followers of Reformed theology to conclude that the ongoing Christian life is a battle between two natures, the flesh and the spirit. Teachers of Reformed theology support this view by pointing out Paul's description in Romans 7 of how his inner person wanted to please

---

[346] Some Reformed teachers define these terms slightly different, but they all conclude that the victorious Christian life is the result of a battle between two natures within the Christian.

Systematic Theology for the New Apostolic Reformation

God, but his outer person was a body of death, subject to sin and death. Reformed theology sees this struggle as the fate of all Christians. They must battle with sin and flesh all of the days of their lives. They must crucify the flesh. The amount of victory experienced in life will be the result of the spirit winning the battle over the flesh.

REFORMED UNDERSTANDING OF THE CHRISTIAN'S BATTLE BETWEEN THE INNER MAN AND OUTER MAN

Point 617: The Sin Nature Is Developed

Father-Son theology offers a different path to victory. To see this, consider again how Adam sinned, then sin and death came into the *kosmos*, i.e., into the whole world. Because of Adam's sin, all of humanity has fallen *under* the power of sin and death.

SIN AND DEATH CAME INTO THE KOSMOS

The Victorious Life

As people open their hearts to the evil in the world the sin nature is developed within them. A helpful illustration is to think of a slice of an apple that is being exposed to the air. In time that apple slice will turn brown. This is comparable to people in the world. All people are created in the image of God, but they are vulnerable. As sin and death reign over them, they become corrupted. Their sin nature is developed.

THE SIN NATURE IS DEVELOPED AS A RESULT OF CORRUPTION

Sin & Death Reign over Humanity

Corruption

Earlier,[347] we thoroughly discussed this subject of the sin nature being developed, so we do not need to repeat that discussion. However, it will be helpful to simply recall one revealing example of Paul's use of the terminology *sin nature*. In Galatians 2:15, Paul said to Peter, "*We are Jews by nature and not sinners from among the Gentiles.*" In this verse, Paul claimed that the Jews are *not sinners by nature*. If we maintain that Paul is speaking of "inherited nature," then we have to conclude from this verse that the Jews inherited a good nature from their fore parents while Gentiles inherited a sinful nature from their fore parents. This conclusion is unavoidable if we assume that Paul is referring to inherited nature.

The alternative explanation (which I hold) is that Paul understood the sin nature to be *developed*. With this understanding we can see from this verse (Gal. 2:15) that the Jews raised their children in a God-honoring

---
347 Explained in IV:F:228-233.

Systematic Theology for the New Apostolic Reformation

culture, and therefore, those children developed a nature that was more in line with God's will than the "sinners" who raised their children in an ungodly culture.

This understanding that the sin nature is developed is what Paul explained in Romans chapter 7. He talked about the corruption happening because we live in this corrupt world:

> *but I see a different law in the members of my body, waging war against the law of my mind and making me a prisoner of the law of sin which is in my members.*
>
> (Rom. 8:23)

Paul referred to "the law of sin." Then he identified the effects of sin and the law of sin upon his own life. He cried out:

> *Wretched man that I am! Who will set me free from the body of this death?*
>
> (Rom. 7:24)

Notice that the body of death of which Paul spoke developed as sin was at work in the members of his body.

The development of the sin nature is an ongoing process. Paul explained:

> *For the one who sows to his own flesh will from the flesh reap corruption . . . .*
>
> (Gal. 6:8)

As we discussed earlier,[348] whenever we live *"in the lusts of our flesh, indulging the desires of the flesh and of the mind"* (Eph. 2:3), we develop a nature that is opposed to God.

With this understanding, we can identify the flesh as the part of a person's nature that has become corrupted. The entire person is not flesh. They are not totally depraved. People are created in God's image, but the flesh develops in them as sin and death have their corrupting influence.

Notice the similarities and differences between this view and that of Reformed theology. Both acknowledge the sin nature within people. Both acknowledge that when a person becomes a Christian their inner man,

---

348 IV:F:233.

The Victorious Life

i.e., their spirit, is made alive and good. The difference between the view of Father-Son theology and Reformed theology has to do with *how a person gets a sin nature*. Reformed theology teaches that every person is born with a totally depraved nature. Father-Son theology teaches that the sin nature is developed.

FATHER-SON THEOLOGY:
THE SIN NATURE IS DEVELOPED AS A RESULT OF CORRUPTION

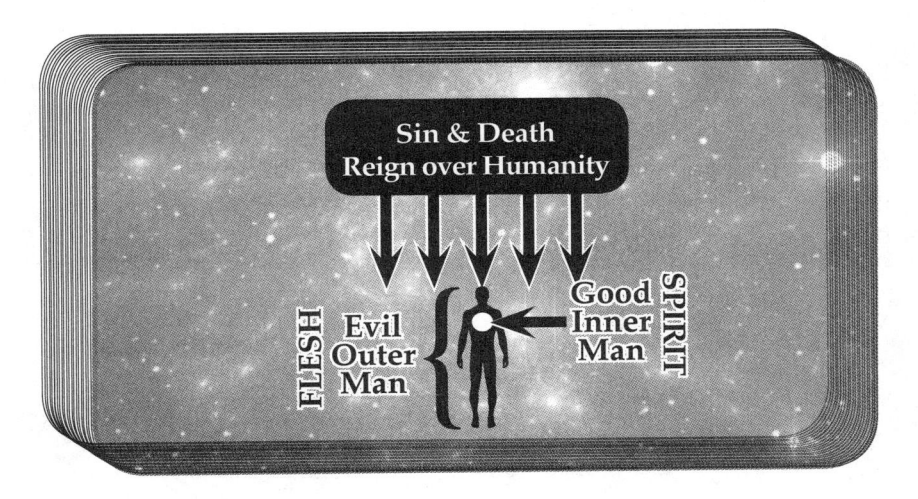

Sin & Death Reign over Humanity

FLESH — Evil Outer Man

SPIRIT — Good Inner Man

This may sound like a small difference, but it has huge implications. For one, Father-Son theology recognizes that some people are more evil than others. This is in contrast to Reformed theology that must insist everyone has the exact same amount of evilness within them since they all inherited the same evil nature from Adam. Second, if the sin nature is developed, then it can be "undeveloped."

Point 618: The Fleshly Part Becomes Spiritual

To understand how the corrupt sinful nature may be undeveloped or uncorrupted, consider again what Jesus has accomplished for believers. In Romans 5, Paul explained that sin and death came into the world through

Systematic Theology for the New Apostolic Reformation

Adam, while grace and life came into the world through Jesus. The apostle John also wrote about the abundance of grace that comes into this world through Jesus (John 1:16-17). Not only grace, but also life. When Jesus ascended into heaven, He became a life-giving Spirit (I Cor. 15:45). Jesus also received the Holy Spirit from the Father and is now pouring out the Spirit upon all humanity. Now grace and life are flowing forth from Jesus into the world.

Just as sin and death are forces that work upon humanity, so also grace and life are forces that work upon all who receive. Those who are living under sin and death will experience corruption. Those who are living under grace and life will experience **sanctification**. This means that a power will be activated to transform their nature from that which is fleshly into that which is holy. Fleshly desires will become holy, i.e., spiritual desires. Fleshly thoughts will become holy, i.e., spiritual thoughts. The Christian who lives under the grace and life flowing from Jesus will be sanctified by the supernatural power of God.

SANCTIFICATION RESULTS FROM LIVING UNDER GRACE AND LIFE

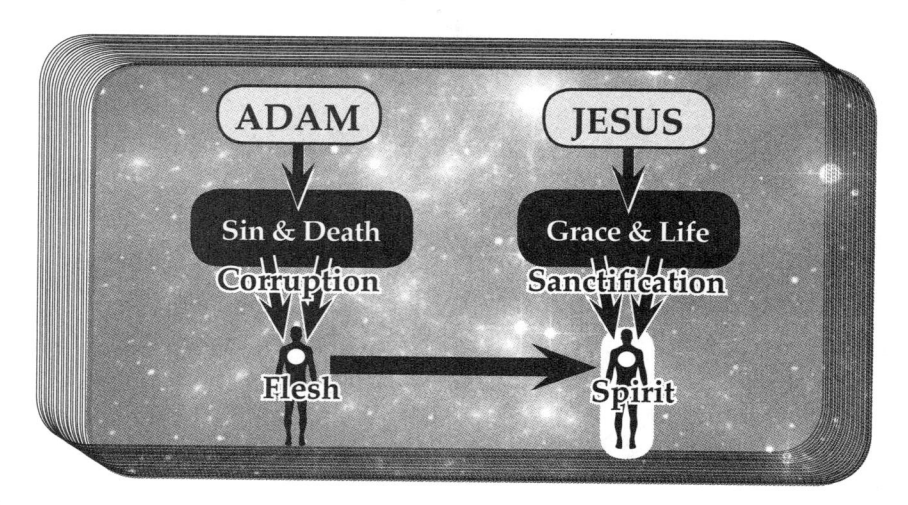

A helpful way to understand this is to think of a glass of water with an ice cube in it. The glass of water represents the person, while the ice represents the flesh part, i.e., the corrupted part, of that person. When that glass is placed in a cold environment, i.e., the environment of sin

The Victorious Life

and death, the ice increases. When the glass of water is placed in a warm environment, i.e., the warmth of God's grace and life, then the ice diminishes, i.e., the flesh melts away.

This truth that the flesh will "melt away" is profound. Paul explained:

> *However, you are not in the flesh but in the Spirit, if indeed the Spirit of God dwells in you.*
> (Rom. 8:9)

Notice that it is possible to be *"not in the flesh."* That is right. Flesh is not a fixed part of a Christian's nature. Christians may be transformed so the corrupt part of their nature is sanctified (1 Thess. 5:23).

When people change in nature, their behavior changes. Jesus explained that if the tree is good, the fruit will be good (Matt. 12:33). The fruit of the Spirit is love, joy, peace, patience, kindness, goodness, faithfulness, gentleness, and self-control (Gal. 5:22-23). A banana tree does not struggle to produce bananas. Nor does a spiritual person have to struggle to produce love and joy. All of the fruit of the Spirit, including patience and self-control, are the natural outworking of the sanctified nature.

Point 619: The Body of Death Becomes a Body of Life

The truth of the transformative power of grace and life is also explained in terms of the body of death becoming a body of life. Think again of Paul's dilemma in Romans chapter 7. He explained that his inner man, i.e., his spirit, wanted to do good, but his body was a body of death, not wanting to please God. Experiencing this conflict, Paul cried out, *"Who will set me free from the body of this death?"* (Rom. 7:24). In the next verse, Paul answered his own question, saying, *"Thanks be to God through Jesus Christ our Lord!"* (Rom. 7:25). It is possible to be set free of the "body of death!"

How can a person be freed? By receiving life. The spirit comes alive when it receives life. So also the body comes alive when it receives life. Paul explained these two steps in coming alive:

> *If Christ is in you, though the <u>body is dead</u> because of sin, yet the <u>spirit is alive</u> because of righteousness.*
> (Rom. 8:10)

Systematic Theology for the New Apostolic Reformation

Paul did not abandon the readers in that condition of having a spirit alive, while the body is dead. He went on to step two. In the next verse, Paul explained how Christians can also have their bodies come alive:

> But if the Spirit of Him who raised Jesus from the dead dwells in you, He who raised Christ Jesus from the dead will also <u>give life to your mortal bodies</u> through His Spirit who dwells in you.
> (Rom. 8:11)

God will give life to our spirit and to our mortal bodies. As a result, both our inner man and our outer man will want to please Him.

Some Christians want to assign this "coming alive of our mortal body" to a future date after they die, are buried, and then resurrect on judgment day. Indeed, Christians will come fully alive on judgment day, but in Romans 8, Paul was talking about a transformation that can happen now, while we are walking the earth. Christians can be set free from the body of death—or as Paul said, *"our body of sin might be done away with"* (Rom. 6:6).

How can our body of sin be done away with? The life that flows from Jesus overcomes death. As a result, Christians are not trapped to the miserable lifestyle described in Romans 7, where their inner man wants to please God and their outer man does not want to please God.[349] Instead, they can experience both their inner man and outer man being alive unto God, and therefore, their entire being wanting to please God.

Point 620: The Same Power that Resurrected Jesus from the Dead

To understand how our "body of death" may be made alive, consider Paul's explanation of the power directed toward believers. First, Paul said that he prays for Christians that they may get the revelation of this truth:

> *I pray that the eyes of your heart may be enlightened, so that you will know . . . what is the surpassing greatness of <u>His power toward us who believe</u>.*
> (Eph. 1:18-19)

---

[349] Reformed theology leaves Christians living in the dilemma of Romans 7 with the spirit fighting the flesh, because they see the inherited evil nature as a fixed element in human nature.

The Victorious Life

After this, Paul explained that the power directed toward believers today is the same power that resurrected Jesus from the grave and then ascended Him up into heaven 2,000 years ago:

> *These are in accordance with the working of the strength of His might which He brought about in Christ, when He raised Him from the dead and seated Him at His right hand in the heavenly places . . . .*
>
> (Eph. 1:19-20)

The same power that resurrected Jesus from the dead and ascended Him into heaven is directed toward us right now!

RESURRECTION LIFE IS POURED OUT VIA THE HOLY SPIRIT

Envision this: 2,000 years ago, Father-God looked down upon His Son who had died on the cross. Then the Father exerted His power, releasing life into that dead body and causing Jesus to get up and walk. That same power is being released into our bodies right now. As a consequence, Jesus who lives in our spirit, will resurrect within us giving life to our mortal bodies.

Read Paul's explanation again concerning the Spirit of God giving life to our mortal bodies:

Systematic Theology for the New Apostolic Reformation

> ... *He who raised Christ Jesus from the dead will also <u>give life to your mortal bodies</u> through His Spirit who dwells in you.*
> (Rom. 8:11)

The same power that resurrected Jesus 2,000 years ago is directed toward us who believe.

Not all Christians understand this. That is why Paul prayed for the Christians in Ephesus that the eyes of their hearts would open to this truth. We each need a revelation. You may want to pray for your own eyes to be opened. Pray that you will receive the revelation concerning what it means to have the same power that raised Jesus from the dead to be released in you.

Paul considered this revelation concerning the resurrection power of Jesus to be at the forefront of his heart. He wrote that he counts *"all things to be loss in view of the surpassing value of knowing Christ Jesus my Lord . . . and the power of His resurrection"* (Phil. 3:8-10). That resurrection power is directed toward us now!

Point 621: Living in the Spirit Flowing from Jesus

To access the resurrection power, what is required? To be filled with the Spirit that *"raised Christ Jesus from the dead"* (Rom. 8:11). What does it mean to be filled with the Spirit in this fashion?

Various denominations and branches of Christianity have their own unique way of explaining what this means, and there are many truths revealed in the different ways that the work of the Holy Spirit is explained. However, for right now, please set aside those explanations.

Consider the context of Romans 8. In the previous three chapters, Paul explained how sin and death came into the world through Adam while grace and life came into the world through Jesus. That grace and life is administered through the Holy Spirit. Jesus is pouring out the Holy Spirit upon all of humanity. To receive the Holy Spirit in the fashion being described here is to receive the grace and life of Jesus. It is to receive the love and acceptance of God. It is to receive all the goodness of God being freely given to you right now and continually.

This lifestyle is expressed in many different ways in the Bible. Jude tells us:

The Victorious Life

> *. . . keep yourselves in the love of God,*
> (Jude 21)

John quoted the words of Jesus:

> *I am the true vine . . . Abide in Me. . .*
> (John 15:1-4)

> *. . . abide in My love.*
> (John 15:9)

Paul encouraged the believers in Ephesus:

> *be filled with the Spirit, speaking to one another in psalms and hymns and spiritual songs, singing and making melody with your heart to the Lord.*
> (Eph. 5:18-19)

It is no mystery how to be filled with God's Spirit. Do not make it complicated or turn it into a theological conundrum. It is simple. Just be filled with Him and enjoy His love.

GRACE AND LIFE IS POURED OUT WITH HOLY SPIRIT

Systematic Theology for the New Apostolic Reformation

You are the receiver, and He is the Giver. Receive His love. Receive His grace and life. Let Him bless you.

Being filled the Holy Spirit in the way that is being described here is not a one time event. His blessings are new every morning. The Holy Spirit is pouring forth 24 hours a day, every day of the week. It is like a waterfall flowing from heaven. Receiving the abundance of grace and life is like standing under the waterfall of God's love.

You can do it right now. As you do, the resurrection power of Jesus will be instantly released into your nature. Your body of death will become a body of life. Your flesh will melt away. Your thoughts and desires will be sanctified. You will no longer be in the flesh, but you will be alive in both your inner man and outer man.

Point 622: Power to Reign in Life

In Romans 5, Paul contrasted sin and death with grace and life. As life overcomes death, grace overcomes sin. In other words, the power of God's grace is greater than the power of sin. Paul explained:

> . . . those who <u>receive the abundance of grace</u> and of the gift of righteousness will <u>reign in life</u> through the One, Jesus Christ.
> (Rom. 5:17)

Here we are told to receive the abundance of grace[350] and the gift of righteousness. Notice again, that our job is to "receive." It is not what we give to God or how we serve Him that transforms our nature. It is what we receive.

We will discuss how to receive the gift of righteousness shortly, but now look at receiving the abundance of grace. We are told that if we receive an abundance of grace we will *"reign in life."* I want to reign in life. Don't you? What is required? To receive an abundance of grace.

We are not talking about receiving a small amount of grace. Coming from heaven is more than a trickle of grace. It is more than a stream flowing from the throne. There is a waterfall of grace, and we can live in that waterfall.

---

350 Of course, this does not make sense to followers of Reformed theology, because their understanding of grace being "unmerited" means people can play no role in receiving or obtaining grace in any fashion.

The Victorious Life

Receiving grace is not a one-time experience as in the born again experience. Of course, the born again experience is the essential entry point into the Christian life. However, ongoing victory over sin and reigning in life comes as the result of continually receiving the abundance of grace that flows from Jesus.

Receiving an Abundance of Grace to Reign in Life

Sometimes Christians will say to me that they have been receiving God's grace but they are not reigning in life. My answer is always the same: You are not receiving enough. Be like a tree standing out on a sunny day. Let the light of His grace warm every part of your being. Let an abundance of grace flood into your nature.

Point 623: The Power of Grace

This understanding concerning how to live the victorious Christian life only makes sense if one embraces the biblical definition of grace.

Most followers of Reformed theology define grace as "unmerited favor." As explained earlier,[351] this is a weak, misleading definition of grace. It leads followers of Reformed theology to think of grace as a free

---

351 VI:H:406.

pass to heaven. That type of grace may cause Christians to be thankful to God for their salvation, but thankfulness is not enough to live the victorious Christian life. Christians must have more! To live the victorious Christian life, they need power.

Earlier,[352] we studied how *God's grace is an impartation that empowers the recipients to be all God created them to be.* Grace is literally a "thing," a "substance," an "energy," or a "power," that is transmitted from God into the heart of the believer. Grace works. Grace builds up and transforms. Grace is powerful!

Point 624: The Force Pushing toward Obedience

Grace not only brings us forgiveness of sins, but also power over sin. Look what Paul said in Romans 5:29:

For as through the one man's disobedience the many were made sinners, even so through the obedience of the One the many will be made righteous.

This truth is profound. Just as there is a force of sin at work in the lives of those who live under the power of sin, there is a force of obedience at work in the lives of those who live under grace.

This force of obedience is the fulfillment of the OT prophecies that God will put His Spirit within His people and *"cause them to walk in His ways"* (Ez. 36:27). Just as there is a power of sin at work in the world through Adam, there is a greater power that is at work in the world through Jesus. The power of sin is pushing people to sin. The power of the Spirit is pushing God's people to obey.

Tragically, many Christians have not been taught about the power of obedience. Some do not even believe in the covenant promise that God will *"cause them to walk in His ways."* However, they do believe in the negative power that pushes people to sin. How sad. Christians are being taught about the power of sin and death, but not the greater power of grace and life.

---

352 VI:H:407.

The Victorious Life

THE POWERS PUSHING PEOPLE TO SIN OR OBEY

Here is a metaphor that helps people understand.

There is a river flowing corresponding to the ways of the world carrying sinners toward destruction. Many Christians think of that river as powerful and at work against them. They reason that if they want to serve God then they must swim against the flow of the world's river.

That understanding is not entirely accurate.

There is second river flowing from God, and it flows in the opposite direction of the world's river. God's river is *much more powerful* than the river of the world. Any Christians who step into God's river will discover that the Christian life is not difficult. Of course, everyone faces trials and temptations, but Christians who get into the river of grace and life will be carried in the direction of obedience to God. They will discover the power that causes them to become what God created them to be.

Point 625: Two Different Views of the Victorious Life

The explanation of the victorious Christian life that is presented here is incompatible with Reformed theology.

Systematic Theology for the New Apostolic Reformation

Reformed theology teaches that the victorious Christian life results from the spirit fighting and conquering the flesh—a fight that must continue all the days of the Christian's life. Yet, followers of Reformed theology do not believe they can be very successful in that fight. They see themselves as always having to swim against the powerful, evil river of the world. They also focus on Paul's description of the flesh:

> ... *the flesh is hostile toward God; for it does not subject itself to the law of God, for it is not even able to do so, and those who are in the flesh cannot please God.*
>
> (Rom. 8:7-8)

Since followers of Reformed theology see the flesh as totally hostile toward God and as a fixed element in human nature, they conclude that it is only possible to experience a very limited amount of victory over sin during this life.

In contrast, Father-Son theology has great news. The victorious Christian life does not come as a result of the spirit fighting and conquering the flesh. Jesus already won that war. His victory becomes the victory of believers when they receive the abundance of grace that flows from Jesus. When believers receive that grace, the fleshly part of their nature is transformed. It is done away with. It no longer exists. More great news—when Christians bathe in that flow of grace and life, they will reign in life. They will step into a river that causes them to walk in God's ways. The power to obey will overcome the power of sin. Life will overcome death.[353]

Point 626: No Longer Crucifying Self to Live Victorious?

This understanding of the victorious life can be quite surprising when first heard by Christians trained in Reformed theology. They are trained to focus on conquering and crucifying the flesh. In reality, every verse in the Bible that talks about Christians and crucifixion, places crucifixion in the past tense as a work that has already been accomplished. For example, Galatians 2:20 says:

> *I <u>have been crucified</u> with Christ; and it is no longer I who live, but Christ lives in me.*

---

[353] This is further explained in my book, *Grace the Power to Reign*.

The Victorious Life

Then again Paul writes:

> . . . *our old self <u>was crucified</u> with Him.* . .
>
> (Rom. 6:6)

This means *Christians should not be crucifying themselves*. Instead, they should consider crucifixion a finished work.

There is one verse in the Bible that talks about putting to death the deeds of the body as an ongoing practice:

> . . . *for if you are living according to the flesh, you must die; but if by the Spirit you are <u>putting to death the deeds of the body</u>, you will live.*
>
> (Rom. 8:13)

At first glance readers may conclude from this verse that we should be actively crucifying ourselves.

Look more carefully at Roman 8:13. Note that it only tells us to put to death certain "deeds." In other words, it does not tell us to crucify "self." Also, Paul instructs us how to put those deeds to death. He did not say to do it by struggling and fighting against the flesh. Instead, he said, *"by the Spirit."* This exhortation is in the context of the whole teaching in Romans 5-8, about living in the Spirit that flows through Jesus Christ. When Christians receive the abundance of grace flowing from Jesus, the deeds of the flesh are put to death because Jesus conquered the flesh 2,000 years ago. The corruption of the flesh is not done away with by fighting or crucifying the flesh. It is done away with by the life flowing from Jesus 24 hours a day, seven days a week.

Think about it. How can we get rid of our body of death? Does it make sense that we should crucify it? More death will not make a dead body go away. Nor does crucifying the flesh make the flesh go away. Life overcomes death. Jesus not only gives us life in our spirit, but also in our mortal bodies. Who will set us free from the body of this death? *"Thanks be to God through Jesus Christ our Lord!"* (Rom. 7:25).

Point 627: Receiving the Righteousness of Jesus

There is one more key element in living the victorious Christian life. Read again Paul's declaration in Romans 5:17:

Systematic Theology for the New Apostolic Reformation

> . . . *those who receive the <u>abundance of grace</u> and of the <u>gift of righteousness</u> will reign in life through the One, Jesus Christ.*
> (Rom. 5:17)

Christians are to do two things in order to reign in life: receive the abundance of grace and the gift of righteousness. We have already explained the abundance of grace. Now let's look at the gift of righteousness.

Two thousand years ago Jesus came and lived the perfect life. Then He died on the cross and established the new covenant. Now all who believe in Him are joined to Him in covenant relationship. One of the benefits is that they are given His righteousness.[354] The righteousness of Jesus cannot be earned or purchased. It is a free gift of God that must be received by faith.

Why must we receive the gift of righteousness? Because grace and righteousness work in tandem. To see this, look at a comparison Paul made in Romans 5:21:

> . . . *<u>sin reigned in death</u>, even so <u>grace would reign through righteousness</u>.*

Paul said:

1. sin reigns in death
2. grace reigns in righteousness

Think about point number one. Paul specifically told us *where* sin reigns. He explained that the environment in which sin is king is the environment of death. Earlier,[355] we identified death as the consequences of sin, including shame, guilt, hopelessness, loneliness, sickness, fear, anxiety, broken relationships, lack of vision, purposelessness, self-hatred, sadness, deception, and so forth. When people are submerged in these consequences of sin, then sin will reign over them. In other words, when people are consumed in shame, guilt, hopelessness, etc., then sin will have authority over them. Then they will have no power to conquer sin. Sin will be rampant. Then they will be enslaved to sin. When people are lost in fear, sadness, and self-hatred, then they will discover that sin is a king reigning over their will.

---

354 VI:C:374-377.
355 IV:D:211.

The Victorious Life

This is evident in the life of the man who is drunk every night at the local bar. Usually positive thoughts about himself are not going through his mind. Often he will go to the bar trying to escape the constant bombardment of negative thoughts. Unfortunately, he is making things worse.

In contrast, Paul stated that grace reigns in righteousness. Where does grace reign? Where people are conscious of the righteousness that God has given them as a free gift. When people are aware of the righteousness of Jesus, then they will discover that the power of grace is activated in their life. Then they will sense the power to obey. The flesh will melt away. Their body of death will become a body of life. Jesus who lives within them will arise and give them His victory over sin. Instead of living under the reign of sin, Christians can live under the reign of grace.

WHERE SIN AND GRACE REIGN

Grace and righteousness work in tandem because one allows the release of the other. When Christians are conscious of the righteousness given to them, they can boldly go before God and receive His grace. In addition, when Christians are receiving God's abundant grace, they will receive His righteousness and know that they are fully accepted by God.

In contrast, if Christians are ever-conscious of their own sins, they will dwell in shame, self-hatred, and fear. Then they will not allow

Systematic Theology for the New Apostolic Reformation

themselves to fully enjoy the grace that is available. They will consciously and subconsciously feel unworthy to enjoy God's grace. They will also sabotage every grace opportunity that comes along since they limit their own access to that grace.

Point 628: Sin Conscious or Righteousness Conscious?

For many years I tried to live the victorious Christian life by conquering the flesh. I had been taught to be ever conscious of my own sins. My Christian teachers explained to me that every night as I fall to sleep I should review in my mind all of the mistakes that I made throughout the day. I was told to go to sleep humbled with an awareness of my sins, but thankful for God's forgiveness.

That never helped me overcome sin. It didn't work.

Through the years I have learned that it is counterproductive to make myself sin conscious. It only produces more sin. On the other hand, developing a righteousness consciousness does produce a victorious life.

When I am aware of the righteousness that God has given to me, I can understand Paul's declaration:

> *Therefore there is now no condemnation for those who are in Christ Jesus.*
>
> (Rom. 8:1)

God has no bad thoughts about us. Flowing from His throne into our hearts is His acceptance and love. There is no condemnation in His eyes. There is no scolding. No ridiculing. No judgment. He has given us the righteousness of His Son Jesus.

This does not mean we are denying that each of us commits sins. Of course, we all know our own weaknesses. However, when we become aware of any sin we can ask God's forgiveness and instantly be forgiven and cleansed from all unrighteousness (1 John 1:9). Since God *"will remember our sins no more"* (Heb. 8:12), we should remember them no more. He does not want us thinking about our failures. He wants us to think about the righteousness that He has given to us.

The Victorious Life

Point 629: Receive Grace, Righteousness, and Life

Right now there is a waterfall of grace and life flowing from heaven toward us. The same power that resurrected Jesus from the grave is directed toward each of us who believe. The empowering presence of God is flowing toward us right now.

Our job is to receive it. That is all. Receive an abundance.

We receive that grace and life in the same way that we received Jesus when we became born again. By faith. This is more than an intellectual assent. Receiving requires us to open our hearts and allow the grace and life to literally enter into our beings.

Recall our earlier discussion about receiving God's love.[356] It is one thing to know God loves us. It is an entirely different thing to receive His love. As we receive God's love we are simultaneously being transformed.

Similarly, receiving God's grace, righteousness, and life changes us. It enters into our hearts and reorients our lives. Grace and life overcome sin and death. The desire to sin fades and the desire to please Him rises.[357]

---

356 XII:A:596-597.
357 Living the victorious Christian life is further explained in my book, *Grace the Power to Reign*.

Volume XII
The Christian Life

Section F
Mature Sons of God

God gave His covenant promises to believers:

1. to remember their sins no more
2. to give them a new heart and spirit
3. to put His Spirit within them, causing them to walk in His ways

These promises assure believers that they will be transformed into the image of Jesus.

The process of transformation will take them from *téknon* to *huios*. *Téknon* is the Greek word translated in the NT as son or child. It refers to anyone who shares the same nature as their father. *Huios* is a Greek word also translated in the NT as son, but it refers to a mature son, one who has a position of dignity within the household, able to represent the father in all matters of business and government.

Point 630: Supernaturally Natural Sons of God

As I go on to explain what is entailed in being a mature son (*huios*) of God, I do not want this confused with a teaching known as the "Manifest Sons of God" teaching. That teaching is associated with an offshoot of the Latter Rain Movement, which grew out of a revival that began in 1948 in a Bible school in North Battleford, Saskatchewan, Canada. Thousands of leaders benefited from the Latter Rain Movement. Many brought the related teachings to their church communities, along with a fresh zeal and love for God. Some great revelations and insights came out of that revival.

Systematic Theology for the New Apostolic Reformation

However, there was also an offshoot of that revival that began focusing on Romans 8:19, where Paul wrote about all of creation longing for the revealing of the sons of God. Of course, there is truth in Paul's words that God's people will become the manifest sons of God. However, adherents of the Manifest Sons of God teaching began to see themselves as the first and soon coming group of people who would become these manifest sons of God. They envisioned themselves becoming immortal, invincible, god-like beings walking the earth, commanding creation to obey them and being God's ambassadors to usher in the millennial reign of Jesus on earth. Critics point out that such thinking led to exclusivity, pride, and isolation. Some adherents of the Manifest Sons of God teaching stopped functioning in normal everyday life, thinking that they should invest themselves entirely in spiritual activities that would qualify them to become those manifest sons. In reality, they never became what they thought they would become, no matter how much they prayed, fasted, and waited on God.

Of course, Christians should expect a continual progression in their own lives and in the life of the whole Church, but the manifestation of Jesus in us should be thought of as a corporate experience. The individual members will mature and be fitly framed together, so that each believer will supply that which is needed. However, no single person will possess the fullness of the Body of Christ, because each person is merely a part of the whole. Paul explained that the maturing Church is "... *the whole building, being fitted together, ... growing into a holy temple in the Lord*" (Eph. 2:21). Jesus is building and unifying His Church, not just a small group of believers. Together, the Church will reveal Jesus in the earth and manifest His fullness.

It is helpful to form a vision of what it means to be a mature son of God. Too often Christians desiring to become one of these mature sons focus on the supernatural aspects in the sense of working miracles everywhere they walk. Of course, mature Christians should expect signs and miracles to take place, but Jesus described characteristics of true sons of God and He focused on something very different:

> *But I say to you, love your enemies and pray for those who persecute you, so that you may be sons of your Father who is in heaven;*
> (Matt. 6:44-45)

Mature Sons of God

Blessed are the peacemakers, for they shall be called sons of God.
(Matt. 5:9)

From these verses we can conclude that the most obvious characteristic of a mature son of God is a heart like God's heart. More specifically, they will be peacemakers and lovers of their enemies.

Point 631: Given a New Spirit

Everything we need to become mature sons of God has been assured to us in the new covenant. The first benefit of our covenant is that our sins will be remembered no more. Most Christians are well-aware of this benefit, but many have not grasped the other benefits.

God promised to put a new spirit within each believer. Paul explained:

Because you are sons, God has sent forth the Spirit of His Son into our hearts, crying, "Abba! Father!"
(Gal. 4:6)

As the Spirit of Jesus is released into the hearts of the believers, their spirits come alive.

If Christ is in you, though the body is dead because of sin, yet the spirit is alive because of righteousness.
(Rom. 8:10)

That new spirit gives believers a nature like God's nature. This is part of the born again experience which makes believers children (*téknon*) of God.

Point 632: Given a New Heart

When people are born again, they also receive a new heart. It is a soft pallet upon which God writes His desires. This is in contrast to how God worked through the Mosaic covenant by giving His people His laws written on stone, then expected people to make their will submit to God's laws. Under the new covenant God works within believers causing them *"both to will and to work for His good pleasure"* (Phil. 2:13).

Systematic Theology for the New Apostolic Reformation

How long do Christians have to walk with God before their desires start to change? From the first moment of rebirth, desires start conforming to God's will.

Many Christians have never been taught this truth. They tend to think of their hearts as the enemy of God. Jeremiah 17:9 remains on the forefront of their minds: *"The heart is more deceitful than all else and is desperately sick."*[358] As a result, they live their entire lives mistrusting their own desires and trying to put their desires to death. In reality, the Christian's heart is *not* desperately sick. The believer's heart wants to please God. This is not to give credence to every desire that Christians have. Of course, each believer has some desires contrary to the will of God. However, this does not change the underlying truth that God is always in the process of conforming His children's hearts to His heart. The longer Christians walk with God, the more their hearts become like God's heart.

Some readers are so deeply seated in the teaching of the wickedness of humanity that they will not be able to accept this truth that Christians have been given a new heart. To reassure them that I am aware of how wicked people can be, I could spend several pages qualifying my positive statements about the Christian's heart, but I will not do that. Most Christians have heard the negative message over and over for many years. However, they have not fully grasped the promise of God to give them new hearts as part of the new covenant.

A good way to demonstrate that Christians do not have wicked hearts is to ask any group of Christians what they want for their community. Most Christians will say that they want revival, young people walking with God, strong marriages, a good economy, lower crime, and so forth. These desires are not contrary to God's desires. The plain fact is that Christians want what God wants. Their desires are very much like God's desires.

Of course, Christians should always watch out for desires that may conflict with God's desires, but the longer they walk with God, the more they should grow in confidence that their desires are God's desires. Therefore, the heart is not their enemy. Certain desires must be put to death, but the heart itself should not be put to death. Under the new covenant, the heart is an avenue through which God leads Christians to carry out His will. In fact, Christians will often discover that they are doing God's will when they are doing what they want to do.

---

358 This misunderstanding of Jeremiah 17:9 was discussed in IV:H:239-240.

Mature Sons of God

Someone may raise an objection to this understanding, referring to Jesus' own struggle in the Garden of Gethsemane. Before going to His death, Jesus cried out, "Not My will but Your will be done." It is true that Jesus had to wrestle with His own will before the greatest trial of His life, but Jesus did not live in the Garden of Gethsemane. Most days Jesus lived confidently knowing that the Father was pleased with Him. So, too, mature Christians should come to peace with their own desires and live in accordance with what God has written upon their heart.

Point 633: He Causes Us to Walk in His Ways

Not only do Christians receive a new spirit and heart, but God also releases His Spirit to cause them to walk in His ways. There is a real force at work in believers, pushing them to fulfill God's desires for their lives.

As the Spirit moves within believers, God can work with any amount of force that He chooses. He can gently woo His people or be more assertive, actually pushing them to obey. In some cases, Christians may grieve the Holy Spirit and resist doing His will, but that does not stop the ongoing hand of God nudging His people along His ordained path for their lives.

Point 634: Sons Are Led by the Spirit

How should mature sons (*huois*) live? A natural father wants his children to grow up and take responsibility for their own lives. That is what maturity entails.

I have three children. They are already adults, so I expect them to handle the situations of life that come before them. I hope they will always stay in touch with me and ask for my help when they need it, but they do not need minute-by-minute instructions. Rather, I want them to act out of a nature that is much like my own. I hope they share my spirit and heart. Certainly, I want them to have their own unique personalities, but I hope they will make similar choices to what I would make if I was in their shoes.

Similarly, God does not want us to ask Him about every decision we have to make. That would make us slaves of God, rather than His sons. Slaves take orders. Sons make decisions similar to what their father would make.

Systematic Theology for the New Apostolic Reformation

This does not mean God's sons should act independently of Him. Consider Paul's words:

For all who are being led by the Spirit of God, these are sons [huios] of God.

(Rom. 8:14)

Too often, Christians think of being led by the Spirit as listening to and then obeying minute-by-minute instructions from the Holy Spirit. Of course, Christians should listen and obey, but being led by the Spirit of God should be thought of as an internal guidance system switched on 24 hours of each day, of which Christians may or may not be conscious.

Paul explained:

But the one who joins himself to the Lord is one spirit with Him.

(1 Cor. 6:17)

This refers to Christians becoming so one in spirit with God's Spirit that they do not know where their spirit ends and God's Spirit begins.

Compare this to non-Christians being led by their flesh or by Satan. At the time they are being tempted, they usually do not know if it is their own thoughts or Satan's thoughts. So also, mature Christians are led by the Holy Spirit usually without knowing where their thoughts end and God's thoughts begin.

To see this from another perspective, envision Jesus walking around Jerusalem 2,000 years ago. He told us that He only does what the Father wants Him to do. This does not mean that Jesus was walking around with His eyes glazed over because He was so focused on hearing the Father's voice. Rather, Jesus was explaining how He was one with the Father. His will was the Father's will. So whatever Jesus wanted to do, the Father wanted Him to do. So if Jesus wanted to work a miracle, it was because the Father wanted to work a miracle. If Jesus wanted to be alone, it was because the Father wanted Jesus to be alone. If Jesus wanted to eat, the Father wanted Him to eat. Hence, we don't see Jesus struggling to hear the Father's voice. He was one with the Father, so He knew His will was the Father's will.

It is the same with mature sons. They have grown to a point where doing the Father's will means doing what comes naturally to them. All Christians will have times when they are unsure of what the Father wants,

Mature Sons of God

so then they will have to seek for His direction. However, for most of their ongoing decisions, they simply trust that God is guiding them.

Mature sons are not afraid of making mistakes, because they know that God will back them up. God will fix mistakes made from a sincere heart. Mature sons make decisions. Mature Christians take responsibility while being confident in Father-God's guidance. Mature sons can represent their father in all matters of business and government. This is implied in the Greek word *huios*. God is a Father who wants His sons to grow up.

Conclusion

Critics often focus on minor points and exaggerate the errors of people with whom they disagree. Yet, critics usually have some truth mixed in with their comments of judgment. The German scholar, Friedrich Nietzsche (1844–1900), was one of those critics. Among other statements, he is famous for saying Western Christianity is "Platonism for the people." If Nietzsche was alone in this criticism, we could justifiably ignore him, but other scholars have joined in with this evaluation and made their opinions known among the intelligentsia of Western society.

Nietzsche's criticism of Western Christianity has some truth in it, but it is also exaggerated beyond reason. Anyone within Christianity knows that our message is, above all else, centered upon Jesus Christ and His saving work accomplished for humanity. This is not Platonism. For 2,000 years, the historic Church has succeeded in trumpeting the greatest truth the world has ever heard.

Still, we should recognize that the message the Church heralds is tainted with the thoughts of Plato, Aristotle, and Plotinus through the work of Church leaders such as Augustine. Today in our Christian universities and seminaries, theologians continue to syncretize Western philosophy with the thoughts of the Bible. Many professors in secular universities are eager to point this out. Then they dismiss Christianity as irrelevant and leave their students wondering if it is even possible to distinguish Christianity from Platonism. The resulting confusion adds to their disrespect and distaste for anything Christian.

It is time to face this challenge. Indeed, I present this challenge before my learned brothers and sisters who are passionate for the life and success of the Church. Some may disagree with my conclusions on

Systematic Theology for the New Apostolic Reformation

certain points. Indeed, Bible teachers more intelligent and well-read than me will be able to point out my biases and errors, but if we work together we will be able to dialogue about these issues. We will also be able to bring to light the blind spots that each of us have. Through the process of working together, we will be able to offer a more pure form of Christianity to our family and to the world.

While Christian leaders endeavor to purify and reform the Church, the average Christian is not left in limbo waiting for the light to dawn. The good news is that the Word of God remains a shining light. The Spirit of God continues to work in the hearts of God's people. Those who stay close to our Father will enjoy life as it is meant to be.

Nothing has changed in God's original intentions. He wants sons. Through the shedding of Jesus' blood, God established a new covenant through which He joined Himself to all who believe. The new covenant is God's heart pouring forth forgiveness and acceptance. It is the aqueduct channeling eternal life into the spirit of each believer. It is the flow of grace transforming every child of God from glory to glory.

Through the new covenant, God's end goal will be fully accomplished. He will have offspring bearing His image and likeness, a family unique and yet united, diverse and yet devoted. He will have sons who are holy and blameless before Him.

Now, for Christians eager to start rebuilding their theology, I have some advice. During 35+ years of ministry, I have observed how new believers behold God as their intimate and loving Father. It is during those early days of falling in love with their Father that their understanding of Father-God is more innocent and pure than at any time later.

Learn from this.

Go back to the experience you had with God when you first encountered His love. His revelation of Himself to you is true. It is pure. Go back to the simplicity of Christianity and you will find a Father who loves you.

If you live in His love, your theology will be fine.

*God started as a loving Father determined to have sons,
and He will finish as a loving Father with sons.*

Appendix A: Major Differences Charted[261]

	Nature of God (Vol. I)	**God's Involvement (Vol. II)**	**Theodicy (Vol. II: Section D)**
Father/Son Theology	Eternal (no beginning/end) *Temporal within creation* Personal & responsive Covenant Maker Immutable in nature Mutable in decisions Mutable in emotions Sovereign (does whatever He wants) Holy Judge Acts in mercy Rewarder Love Like Jesus Father	Acts from within creation Predestines what He wants In charge (not in control) Answers prayers Influences via the Holy Spirit, angels, and relationships Disciplines His people Rewards Intervenes Selectively involved Limits Himself Works with humanity Influences via resistible or irresistible grace God's will is progressively accomplished as His Kingdom grows.	God is good, but bad things happen because God is not controlling all things, Satan & demons are active, this world runs according to natural & unnatural laws, sin is in the world, this world has been subjected to futility, people have some free will & do bad things, people make mistakes, & people have not taken responsibility to govern this world. Many evil things happen that are contrary to God's will and grieve His heart.
Classical/Reformed Theology	Timeless Immutable Impassible Perfect Omniscient Omnipresent Omnipotent Sovereign (controls all) Holy (which separates Him from sinners) Self-sufficient Transcendent Wholly Other Immanent Unknowable Incomprehensible	Acts from His timeless, distant world Predestines all things Exhaustively controls all things God only answers prayers that He predestined people to pray according to His will. Although there may be secondary causes, God is ultimately the cause of all things, including sin and evil. God makes people do what He wants by giving irresistible grace. God's will is always perfectly accomplished.	Because God is in exhaustive control of all things, nothing happens contrary to His will. God does not do evil, but He wills all of the bad things that happen (including sin, sickness, earthquakes, birth defects, pain, abortions, war...). God is good, but He wants to & will torture millions of people in hell forever (through no fault of their own, but only by His sovereign choice). Because all things happen according to God's will, He never grieves over anything that happens.

---

261 This table can only serve as a generalized summary, because some Classical/Reformed teachers will have variations on the views accredited to them here.

Appendix A: Major Differences Charted

	Nature of Creation (Vol. III)	**Nature of Humanity (Vol. IV)**	**Nature of Evil & Sin (Vol. V)**
Father/Son Theology	Created as a gift to the Son and for His own glory Spiritual & natural realms are integrated There are three heavens within creation. There is a throne room of God within creation. Running according to natural and unnatural laws Subjected to futility Creation will be redeemed & exist forever.	Created in God's image & likeness Blessed Of great value Not conceived in sin, but born under the power of sin & death Close to God and possessing the breath of God Sin nature is developed Possessing some free will Not everyone has a wicked heart. Able to do some good, such as agape-love their own Incapable of saving self	God created the world to run according to natural laws, which are good, but may result in suffering. God created the cycles of life & death within creation, but humans were not originally subject to death. God's judgments may cause suffering, but He does not want to cause His children to suffer. The world is about Father-God raising sons. Evil results from sin and the evil activity of spirits. Sin comes out of the heart of humanity. Sin and evil are things.
Classical/Reformed Theology	Created only for God's glory Spiritual & natural worlds separated Third heaven exists in a distant, timeless world. The throne room of God is outside of creation in a distant, timeless world. God is exhaustively controlling all things. World is fallen. Evil within creation will stand before God forever. Creation will be destroyed in time.	Image of God in people has been obliterated or so buried in sin as to have no positive influence. Cursed No intrinsic value Conceived in sin & born spiritually dead Born separated from God Born condemned & deserving of hell Sin nature is inherited. Totally depraved No free will to choose good Heart is totally wicked Incapable of any good apart from God's irresistible grace Incapable of even turning to God to ask for help	God created all things good, in the sense of there being no pain, sickness, or death in the Garden of Eden. Things became evil when they were distorted from God's original design. Evil is the absence of good. God created Satan & humanity good, but they rebelled and became evil. The world is about a war between God and Satan. Sin is law-breaking behavior. Since people are totally depraved, every thought, word, and deed, apart from God's grace, is evil. Sin and evil are not things.

Appendix A: Major Differences Charted

	Soteriology (Vol. VI)	**Ecclessiology & Basiology (Vol. VII)**	**Eschatology (Vol. VIII-IX)**
Father/Son Theology	*People must be saved now from broken relationship, death, and the world.* *Covenantal view of atonement: God is sovereign, so He can forgive sin.* *Jesus is the open door between us and a forgiving God.* *People are saved by Jesus' life.* *The gospel is: The Kingdom of God is at hand.* *Proper response to the gospel: Repent & believe Jesus rose from the dead & confess Jesus as Lord.* *Jesus died for all people and made provisions for anyone to be saved.* *The Grace of God is His empowering presence.*	*Church's primary roles: a community and an environment where people can corporately meet with God* *Apostolic government* *Church has the keys to the Kingdom* *Church can impart grace.* *The Kingdom of God is the reign of Jesus.* *The understanding of the Kingdom is a corollary to the truth of the gospel of the Kingdom (in contrast to the gospel of salvation).* *The Kingdom of God will continue growing until it fills the earth.*	*Church is maturing & the Kingdom of God is growing until it fills the earth* *Partial Preterist View (Futurist View cannot be reconciled with the Kingdom of God now being available)* *God's people will live forever in the new heaven and earth, rather than up in a spiritual world often called heaven.* *There will be varying rewards in heaven based on how people lived their lives.* *Hell: compatible with the traditional view or annihilationism*
Classical/Reformed Theology	*People must be saved first and foremost from God's wrath.* *Penal substitutionary view of the atonement: God is just so He must punish sin.* *Jesus is the wall between us and an angry God.* *People are saved by Jesus' death.* *The gospel is: Jesus died for our sins, so that all who accept Jesus as Savior will be saved.* *Proper response to the gospel: Accept Jesus as Savior.* *Jesus only died for the elect.* *Double predestination* *Grace is unmerited favor.*	*Various views on the Church and Church government* *Church cannot impart grace.* *The understanding of the Kingdom is difficult to reconcile with the gospel of salvation (in contrast to the gospel of the Kingdom).* *The concept of God's will increasingly being accomplished on earth as the Kingdom grows is in conflict with the Reformed view that God is already controlling all things & His will is already being perfectly accomplished.* *Various views on the future of the Church & Kingdom*	*Various eschatological views* *Heaven: God's people living eternally in a cloud-like world, separated from and distant from this natural world* *Varying rewards in heaven are difficult to reconcile with the Reformed belief that grace is unmerited favor in the sense that no person can play any role in obtaining God's grace* *Hell: traditional view that God will take out His wrath on unbelievers by torturing them forever and ever*

Appendix A: Major Differences Charted

	Trinity & Christology (Vol. X)	**Pneumatology (Vol. XI)**	**The Christian Life (Vol. XII)**
Father/Son Theology	Trinity: three Persons in one God Jesus is fully God. Jesus is fully Man.	Holy Spirit is the Third Person of the Trinity. Primary work of the Holy Spirit in the world is to convince people to believe in Jesus, that Jesus is righteous, and that Jesus has conquered evil. In the life of the Christian, the Holy Spirit is the Comforter and Counselor. The Holy Spirit indwells the believer, evidenced by fruit, and comes upon the believer, evidenced by power. Gifts of the Holy Spirit, including healing, miracles, prophecy, & tongues	People are created to be loved. Our ambition is to please God. Primary orientation of parents training children is to nurture the image of God God responds to prayers; He wants to hear the desires of His children, and He answers requests as a good father does. God is near and is blessed by our worship of Him. Living victoriously comes as a result of living in the grace and life of God, causing the flesh to disappear. Through the new covenant, Christians have a new heart & spirit. The Christian life is not difficult.
Classical/Reformed Theology	Trinity: three Persons in one God Jesus is fully God. Jesus is fully Man.	Holy Spirit is the Third Person of the Trinity. Primary work of the Holy Spirit in the world is to convict people of sin. In the life of the Christian, the Holy Spirit is the Comforter and Counselor. The Holy Spirit also indwells the believer, evidenced by the fruit of Spirit. There are various views concerning the gifts of the Holy Spirit, but most do not accept the supernatural gifts as valid today. It is difficult to reconcile any grace coming through the gifts since God alone gives grace.	People are created to glorify God. Impossible for people to please God or for God to take pleasure in anything people do Primary orientation of parents training children is to manage sin Prayer changes people, not God. God only answers prayers that He predestined people to pray according to His will. God is unmoved and gains nothing from our worship. Living victoriously comes as a result of the spirit fighting and conquering the flesh. Through the new covenant, Christians are forgiven, but do not have a new heart. The Christian life is difficult.

Appendix B
The Unholy Union with Western Philosophy

Throughout this book, I have explained how Classical/Reformed theology emerged from the marriage of Christianity with Western philosophy. Unfortunately, that marriage yielded a form of godliness that denies the power of biblical Christianity. Of course, Classical/Reformed theology recognizes the power that God exerts in controlling the affairs of this world. However, it denies the power God has made available to people. This deserves a fuller explanation.

One of the most obvious results of the marriage of Christianity with Western philosophy is the dualistic worldview which distorts people's perception, causing them to think of God existing in a world separate and distant from the natural world. Envisioning God in this way has impacted Western humanity in profound ways:

- When people think of God as distant, they can more easily put Him off and not deal with Him in present space or time. The thoughts of multitudes are, "I will deal with God after I die, if He exists at all."

- With God far away, it becomes more difficult for Western people to believe in the supernatural and miraculous.

- With the spiritual world and God's throne room far away, Christians tend to envision the Kingdom of God as far away. This is in contrast to the Hebraic-biblical worldview that leads believers to think of the Kingdom of God at hand, near, and within reach; this viewpoint allows believers to have great faith for the manifestation of God's Kingdom now in this world. Confusion about this issue hinders Classical/Reformed followers from having this faith.[359]

---
359 VII:C:453-454.

Systematic Theology for the New Apostolic Reformation

- The dualistic worldview of Classical/Reformed theology has no place for a second heaven that overlaps and exists within the same space as the natural realm. This greatly limits one's understanding of angels, demons, and spiritual energies associated with natural things.[360]

- Envisioning the throne room of God separate and distant from the natural world, it is difficult for Christians to fully grasp the biblical truth that they have been seated with Christ in heavenly places. Hence, it is difficult for them to fully embrace the authority that is theirs to rule and reign on earth.[361]

Each of these points reveals a way in which the marriage of Christianity with Western philosophy has diminished the effectiveness of Christianity. However, there's more.

The unholy marriage has caused Western Christians to define God's nature in abstract terms, such as omniscient, rather than relational terms, such as Yahweh Jireh. A God who is known in abstract terms will be experienced as distant and sterile. A God who is known in relational terms will be experienced relationally.[362]

The God of Classical/Reformed theology is timeless, immutable, impassible, omnipotent, self-sufficient, and sovereign (in the sense of controlling all things), which eliminates the possibility of people influencing God in anyway. [363] Think about it:

- If God is as Classical/Reformed teachers claim, then there is no possibility of people entering into relational covenants with Him.[364]

- If God is sovereign—in exhaustive control of all things—then all people are puppets, being moved about by the irresistible will of God.[365]

- If God is timeless and sovereign, then He has predestined all things from eternity past, which means people are impotent to change anything, let alone alter the course of history.[366]

---

360 III:A:134-139.
361 III:A:138.
362 I:H.
363 II:A.
364 I:C:22-24.
365 IV:M:267
366 II:A:93.

The Unholy Union with Western Philosophy

- If God is in exhaustive control, then people have no free will. There is no greater form of powerless religion than a religion that claims that people have no free will.[367]

- If God is in exhaustive control, then grace is irresistible, which means people have no power to resist it. Again, humanity is impotent.[368]

- If God is impassible, then God does not answer prayers in the sense of people initiating a request and God responding.[369]

- If God is sovereign in the sense that He is in exhaustive control of all things, then everything that happens—including sickness, pain, and death—are according to His will. Christians who believe that everything that happens is according to His will have a huge theological barrier to overcome if and when they want to resist sickness, pain, and death.[370]

- If God is impassible and self-sufficient, then there is nothing people can do to please Him. Then Paul's ambition to be pleasing to the Lord (2 Cor. 5:9) was seriously misplaced. If Father-God does not enjoy what we do for Him, why should any of us do anything?[371]

- If God is impassible, then He is not *"the rewarder of those who diligently seek Him"* in the sense of actually responding to people. If God is not a rewarder, then humanity has less reason to work for or seek Him.

- If Christians believe God experiences no emotional variation, then they will tend to suppress their own emotions. Yet, one of the benefits of emotions is as motivation for action. Emotionless Christianity is less motivated Christianity.[372]

Each of these points reveals how the Classical/Reformed understanding of God's nature undermines human initiative, passion, and confidence, but there are many more ways in which the marriage of Christianity with

---

367 IV:M:267.
368 II:A:94.
369 XII:C:605.
370 V:C:292.
371 XII:A:598-599.
372 I:B:18.

Systematic Theology for the New Apostolic Reformation

Classical Western philosophy has emasculated Christianity. Consider the implications of the Classical/Reformed view of human nature:

- According to Classical/Reformed teachers, people are born totally depraved, enslaved to Satan, cursed, and unable to do anything other than sin (apart from God's grace). It is hard to find a clearer description of human impotence than this.[373]

- Classical/Reformed teachers say that all people, including Christians, have a wicked heart that can never be trusted. People consistent with this view will never trust their own heart and, as a consequence, they will try to deny and war against their own desires. Human actions separated from desires are rarely powerful.[374]

- Adherents of Classical/Reformed theology claim that every person is born with an evil nature inherited from Adam. They believe that the evil nature is resident within Christians all of their lives, leaving Christians in a war between the spirit and flesh, a war that Christians can never win, sapping their energy and leaving them defeated. That view relegates Christians to live in the experience of Romans chapter 7, where Paul cries out in anguish, *"Who will set me free from the body of this death?"* Sadly, the Classical/Reformed view, i.e., that the flesh is inherited and continually resident within, disallows Christians to live in the experience of Romans 8, where Paul explains that it is possible for Christians to *"no longer be in the flesh"* (Rom. 8:9).[375]

The Classical/Reformed understanding of grace and faith also renders Christians impotent.

- If grace is unmerited favor, as Classical/Reformed teachers say, then there is no part people can play in obtaining, receiving, or giving grace.[376]

- If God is the only active agent in the administration of grace, then the Church has no authority or ability to impart grace

---

373 IV:A:193.
374 IV:H:239.
375 XII:E:616-625
376 VI:H:405-406 and VII:B:445.

The Unholy Union with Western Philosophy

through sacraments, blessings, laying on of hands, or prayer.[377]

- If grace is a work of God alone, then there is little to no value in Christians operating in the spiritual gifts.

- If faith is purely a work of God with no human effort involved, then people can play no role in helping others be reconciled to God. In other words, people are impotent to aid in the salvation process of others.[378]

Each of these points reveals how Classical/Reformed theology renders people impotent, but the destructive nature of Classical/Reformed theology goes even deeper.

- Classical/Reformed teachers insist that God wills and causes all that happens. Therefore, God is responsible for all things. If people live consistent with this view, they will tend to be irresponsible. For example, if a man honestly believes that God has predestined the day of his death, then he will not be as careful to care for his own physical well-being. If a woman believes God determines her career, her lifestyle, and who she will marry, then she will not be motivated to pursue the related benefits. If a couple believes that God determines how many babies they will have, then they will take no responsibility to plan for the size of their family. Of course, there are Reformed Christians who do take responsibility in these areas, but they are not living consistent with their own theology.[379]

- Teachers of Classical/Reformed theology have never been able to offer a valid theodicy. The only conclusion they offer for all of the suffering, pain, and evil in the world is that God wills it. With that as the only logical answer, Classical/Reformed Christians have nothing to say to the atheists who point out how evil the Christian God must be.[380] If, indeed, God wills all of the suffering, pain, and evil in the world, then the atheists have a valid point: "How can anyone believe in a God who wills all of the evil in the world?"

---

377 VII:B:445.
378 VI:I:427.
379 IV:M:267-273.
380 II:D.

Systematic Theology for the New Apostolic Reformation

> • If natural theology is a myth (as some followers of Reformed theology infer from their dualistic cosmology) and creation does not reveal the nature of God, then the world has no proof of God's existence. If there is no proof of God's existence, then there is no ultimate standard for right and wrong. With no standard, no human being has a right to declare what is right and what is wrong. Then the Church must, in good conscience, silence her cry for holiness and repentance.[381]

In these and other ways, the marriage of Christianity with Western philosophy leaves Christians sterile, weak, unmotivated, and helpless. People become victims of Satan, Adam, their own sinful nature, God, the world, and atheists. Yet, a direct reading of Scripture, without the filter of Western philosophy, yields a vibrant call to humanity to live powerfully as children of God.

So how can we have a vibrant Christianity with power and godliness? The first step is to divorce Christianity from Western philosophy. This does not mean that we should eliminate all philosophical thought. That would be impossible. The word *philosophy* means "love of knowledge." Christians should love knowledge. However, *Western* philosophy has been built on some fundamental assumptions that are incompatible with the Hebraic-biblical worldview. In this case, incompatibility is grounds for divorce.

If and when we need philosophical thought, we must depend upon that which is developed from the Bible. This does not mean Eastern thought which is built on an entirely different foundation. We are talking about biblical thought which is developed as we read the Bible within the original Hebraic-biblical context. Hebraic-biblical thought supports biblical Christianity. It builds on a cosmology in which the spiritual and natural realms are fully integrated. More importantly, God is close and knowable in relational terms.

The most important element of Western philosophy that must be overcome is its posture of arrogance. Although I did not address this in the body of this book, it is a more fundamental and deceptive characteristic of Western philosophy than what has already been discussed. The arrogance is stupefying.

Deception by definition means the person being deceived does not know it. I, for one, was seduced by the arrogance of Western philosophy.

---
381 III:C:147-149.

The Unholy Union with Western Philosophy

During my 35+ years of ministry, I took time to attend four different seminaries. As almost all scholarly seminaries in Western society, three of the four I attended were children of the union of Christianity with Western philosophy.

During each of my seasons of study, I thought I was accumulating knowledge that would be helpful in my ministry. Yet, each time, I experienced a negative transformation in my walk with God as I allowed my mind to be conformed to Western thought. As mentioned, people being deceived are never aware of it, but the truth is evident when, and only when, they step outside of the deception that once enveloped them.

The best way I can explain the deception of Western philosophy is by comparing it with a transformation I experienced during my undergraduate studies. My first degree was in wildlife management. I went into that field because I loved nature. As a youth growing up, I spent countless hours in the countryside were I was raised. Nature was my safe place. Trees and creeks were my paradise. So I pursued a career in the wilds.

When I completed five years of university study, I had a startling awakening. I was working on a government-funded job to maintain the health of the local forests. One day I looked up at a mountainside and realized that I could no longer see the beauty that had captivated my heart as a youth. Instead, my mind was examining the environmental dynamics related to insect damage, fire dangers, species competition, and future treatment methods. Because I had been trained to objectively analyze the environment, I could no longer see it's beauty and wonder. The realization hit me like a ton of bricks.

A similar transformation of my thoughts took place during my seminary training. One day I looked at the Bible and realized that I could no longer see or hear God who used to speak freely to me. I had lost my intimacy with Him. The more education I received, the more difficult it was to accept the reality of miracles. I was no longer a child who could listen and believe.

I know such a negative transformation does not happen to every seminary student. Some students draw closer to God and value their time at seminary as the most intimate time in their lives, but it was not that for me. Nor was it that way for many of my classmates. For us, it did more damage than good.

Seminary had trained me to posture myself "above" the Bible, the Church, and God in an analytical position. Higher education, by its very nature, requires the student to take that position. It is the position

Systematic Theology for the New Apostolic Reformation

modeled by the philosophers who laid the foundation of Western thought. The analytical position is helpful in many fields of study, but it can be very detrimental in religion because true religion is founded in a relationship with God.

No one can have a healthy relationship with another person while positioned in the seat of a critic. Nor can a person drink from a glass of water while that person is positioned above the glass. For the water to flow in, a person's lips must be lower than the rim of the glass. So too, people cannot read the Word of God and hear God's voice while they are objectively analyzing it. People cannot sit in a church service and hear God speak through the preacher, so long as they are critically analyzing the preacher's theology. Nor can Christians hear God speak when they are posturing themselves above God.

During the time I spent learning from Socrates, Plato, and other philosophers, I learned to sit next to them in the exalted seat of objectivity. That seat was far away from Jesus. Sadly, I learned about two different gods. Sitting next to Plato, I learned about a distant, omnipotent god. Sitting at the feet of Jesus, I learned about Yahweh Rapha. Sitting next to Aristotle, I learned about a timeless, sterile being. Sitting at the feet of Jesus, I learned about a God who cares for the sick, poor, and oppressed. Sitting next to Plotinus, I learned about a god who is wholly other. Sitting at the feet of Jesus, I learned about my Father.

Bibliography

All of the books listed below were used in gathering material for this book. However, intensive research on the Internet has also been the source of much information.

Augustine. *Confessions*. Translated by Maria Boulding. New York: Vintage Spiritual Classics, 1998.

Augustine. *The City of God*. Translated by Marcus Dods. Peabody, MA: Hendrickson Publishers, Inc., 2010.

Augustine. *On Free Choice*. Translated by Thomas Williams. IN Indianapolis, IN: Hackett Publishing Co., 1993.

Aulén, Gustaf. Translated by A.G. Hebert. *Christus Victor*. New York: MacMillian Publishing Co., 1979.

Barr, James. *Biblical Faith and Natural Theology*. NY: Oxford University Press, 1993.

Barth, Karl. *Christ and Adam*. NY: Collier Books, 1962.

Barth, Karl. *Church Dogmatics*. Peabody, MA: Hendrickson Publishers, 2010.

Barth, Karl. *A Shorter Commentary on Romans*. Richmond, VA: John Knox Press, 1963.

Bibliography

Behe, Michael J. *Darwin's Black Box*. New York: Touchstone, 1996.

Beilby, James and Paul R. Eddy, ed. *The Nature of the Atonement*. Downers Grove, IL: IVP Academic, 2006.

Berkhof, Hendrikus. *Christian Faith*. Eugene, OR: Wipf and Stock Publishers, 1985.

Boer, Harry R. *An Ember Still Glowing*. Grand Rapids, MI: William E. Eerdmans Publishing Co., 1990.

Boman, Thoreif. *Hebrew Thought Compared with Greek*. New York: W. W. Norton & Co., 1960.

Boyd, Gregory A. *God at War*. Downers Grove, IL: InterVarsity Press, 1997.

Boyd, Gregory A. and Paul R. Eddy. *Across the Spectrum*. Grand Rapids, MI: Baker Academic, 2002.

Brehier, Emile. *The Hellenic Age*. Chicago, IL: University of Chicago Press, 1963.

Cahn, Steven M., ed. *Classics of Western Philosophy*. Indianapolis, IN: Hacken Publishing Co., 1977.

Cahn, Steven and David Shatz, ed. *Questions about God*. New York: Oxford University Press, 2002.

Casalis, Georges. *Portrait of Karl Barth*. Garden City, NY: Anchor Books, 1996.

Calvin, John. *Calvin's Commentaries* (1847). Grand Rapids, MI: Baker Book House, 1984.

Chant, Ken. *Strong Reasons*. Romona, CA: Vision Publishing, 1994.

Clifford, Ross and Philip Johnson. *The Cross Is Not Enough*. Grand Rapids, MI: Baker Books, 2012.

Bibliography

Coplestone, Frederick S. J. *A History of Philosophy*. New York: Doubleday, 1993.

Craig, William Lane. *Time and Eternity*. Wheaton, IL: Crossway, 2001.

Crockett, William, ed. *Four Views on Hell*. Grand Rapids, MI: Zondervan, 1996.

Cullman, Oscar. *Christ and Time*. Philadelphia, PA: The Westminster Press, 1964.

Cummins, Bradley J. *YHWH, Preincarnate Jesus*. Enumclaw, WA: Winepress Publishing, 2010.

Davies, Paul. *About Time*. New York: Simon and Schuster, 1995.

Doniger, Simon. *The Nature of Man*. Plainview, NY: Books for Libraries Press, 1973.

Edwards, Jonathan. *The Works of Jonathan Edwards* (1834). Edited by Edward Hickman. 2 Volumes. Edinburgh: Banner of Truth, 1974.

Eusebius, Pamphilius. *The History of the Church*. London, England: Penguin Press, 1965.

Finney, Charles. *Finney's Systematic Theology*. Minneapolis, MN: Bethany House Publishers, 1994.

Fromke, DeVern. *Ultimate Intention*. Shoals, IN: Sure Foundation, 1963.

Ganssle, Gregory E. ed. *God and Time*. Downers Grove, IL: InterVarsity Press, 2001.

Gorday, Peter, ed. *Ancient Christian Commentary on Scripture: NT IX*. Downers Grove, IL: InterVarsity Press, 2000.

Grudem, Wayne. *Systematic Theology*. Grand Rapids, MI: Zondervan, 2000.
Hahn, Scott. *Kinship by Covenant*. London: Yale University Press, 2009.

Bibliography

Hordern, William. *A Layman's Guide to Protestant Theology*. New York: Macmillan Publishing Co., 1955.

Horton, Stanley. *Systematic Theology*. Springfield, MO: Login Press, 1998.

Intrader, Asher. *Who Ate Lunch with Abraham?* Peoria, AZ: Intermedia Publishing Group, Inc., 2011.

Jersak, Brad and Michael Hardin, ed. *Stricken by God?* Abbotsford, BC, Canada: Fresh Wind Press, 2007.

Kruger, C. Baxter. *Across All Worlds*. Vancouver, BC: Regent College Publishing, 2007.

Kruger, C. Baxter. *Jesus and the Undoing of Adam*. Jackson, MS: Perichoresis Press, 2003.

Kruger, C. Baxter. *God Is For Us*. Jackson, MS: Perichoresis Press, 2000.

McGrath, Alister E. *Studies in Doctrine*. Grand Rapids, MI: Zondervan, 1997.

McGrath, Alister E. ed. *The Christian Theology Reader*. Malden, MA: Blackwell Publishers Ltd., 1995.

Morgan, Christopher and Robert Peterson, ed. *Hell under Fire*. Grand Rapids, MI: Zondervan, 2004.

Noe, John. *The Creation of Evil*. Indianapolis, IN: East@WestPress, 2015.

Olson, Roger E. *Arminian Theology*. Downers Grove, IL: InterVarsity Press, 2006.

Pagels, Elaine. *Adam, Eve, and the Serpent*. New York: Vintage Books, 1988.

Pagels, Elaine. *The Origin of Satan*. New York: Vintage Books, 1995.

Pinnock, Clark. *Flame of Love*. Downers Grove, IL: InterVarsity Press, 1996.

Bibliography

Pinnock, Clark, Richard Rice, John Sanders, William Hasher, and David Basinger. *Openness of God*. Downers Grove, IL: Intervarsity Press, 1994.

Olson, Roger E. *Arminian Theology*. Downers Grove, IL: InterVarsity Academic, 2006.

Roberts, Alexander, and James Donaldson, eds. *The Ante-Nicene Fathers: Translations of the Writings of the Fathers Down to A.D. 325*. 10 volumes. Grand Rapids, MI: Eerdmans Publishing Co., 1989.

Rollins, Peter. *How (Not) to Speak of God*. Brewster, MA: Paraclete Press, 2006.

Ross, Hugh. *The Genesis Question*. Colorado Springs, CO: Navpress, 2001.

Rowlands, Rainie. *The Shining One*. Lyle, WA: Living Word Publishing, 2001.

Sanders, John. *The God Who Risks*. Downers Grove, IL: InterVarsity Press, 1998.

Simonetti, Manlio, ed. *Ancient Christian Commentary on Scripture: NT* Ib. Downers Grove, IL: InterVarsity Press, 2002.

Sproul, R. C. *What Is Reformed Theology?* Grand Rapids, MI: Baker Books, 1997.

Sproul, R. C. *Everyone's a Theologian*. Orlando, FL: Reformation Trust, 2014.

Tennent, Timothy C., *Theology in the Context of World Christianity*. Grand Rapids, MI: Zondervan, 2007.

Thiessen, Henry. *Lectures in Systematic Theology*. Grand Rapids, MI: William B. Eerdmans Publishing Co., 1996.

Verduin, Leonard. *The Reformers and Their Stepchildren*. Grand Rapids, MI: William B. Eerdmans Publishing Co., 1964.

Ware, Bruce A. *God's Lesser Glory*. Wheaton, IL: Crossway Books, 2000.

Bibliography

Weaver, Denny J. *The Nonviolent Atonement.* Grand Rapids, MI: William B. Eerdmans Publishing Co., 2011.

Welton, Jonathan. *Understanding the Whole Bible.* Rochester, NY: Jon Welton Ministries, 2014.

Williams, J. Rodmann. *Renewal Theology.* Grand Rapids, MI: Zondervan-PublishingHouse, 1996.

Witherington III, Ben. *The Problem with Evangelical Theology.* Waco, TX: Baylor University Press, 2005.

Wright, N. T. *How God Became King.* New York: HarperCollins Publishers, 2012

Wu, Jackson, *Saving God's Face.* Pasadena, CA: WCIU Press, 2012.

Yung, Hwa. *Mangoes or Bananas?* Oxford, UK: Regnum Books International, 2014.

Zahl, Paul F. M. *A Short Systematic Theology.* Grand Rapids, MI: William B. Eerdmans Publishing Co., 2000.

Other Books by Harold R. Eberle

Christianity Unshackled
Are You a Truth Seeker?

Most Christians in the Western world have no idea how profoundly their beliefs have been influenced by their culture. What would Christianity be like if it was separated from Western thought? After traveling the world and untangling the Western traditions of the last 2,000 years of Church history, Harold Eberle offers a Christian worldview that is clear, concise, and liberating. This will shake you to the core and then leave you standing on a firm foundation!

Compassionate Capitalism
A Judeo-Christian Value

As you read this book, you will learn how capitalism first developed as God worked among the Hebrew people in the Old Testament. The resulting economic principles then transformed Western society as they spread with Christianity. However, our present form of capitalism is different than that which God instilled in Hebrew society. What we need to do now is govern capitalism wisely and apply the principles of capitalism with compassion.

Releasing Kings
For Ministry in the Marketplace
By John S. Garfield and Harold R. Eberle

"Kings" is what we call Christian leaders who have embraced the call of God upon their lives to work in the marketplace and from that position transform society. This book explains how marketplace ministry will operate in your community in concert with local churches and pastors. It provides a Scriptural basis for the expansion of the Kingdom of God into all areas of society.

Other Books by Harold R. Eberle

Victorious Eschatology
By Harold R. Eberle and Martin Trench
(Second edition)

Here it is—a biblically-based, optimistic view of the future. Along with a historical perspective, this book offers a clear understanding of Matthew 24, the book of Revelation, and other key passages about the events to precede the return of Jesus Christ. Satan is not going to take over this world. Jesus Christ is Lord and He will reign until every enemy is put under His feet!

Jesus Came Out of the Tomb... So Can You!
A Brief Explanation of Resurrection-based Christianity

Forgiveness of sins is at the cross. Power over sin is in the resurrection and ascension. Yet, most Christians have no idea how to access the benefits of our Lord's resurrection and ascension. They are locked into death-centered Christianity rather than life-centered Christianity. This book empowers the reader to make the transition and "come out of the tomb."

Grace...the Power to Reign
The Light Shining from Romans 5-8

We struggle against sin and yearn for God's highest. Yet, on a bad day, it is as if we are fighting against gravity. Questions go unanswered:

• Where is the power to overcome temptations?

• Is God really willing and able to breathe into us so that our dry bones can live and we can stand strong?

For anyone who has ever struggled to live godly, here are the answers.

Other Books by Harold R. Eberle

God's Leaders for Tomorrow's World
(Revised/expanded edition)

You sense the call to leadership, but questions persist: "Does God want me to rise up? Do I truly know where to lead others? Is this pride? How can I influence people?" Through an understanding of leadership dynamics, learn how to develop godly charisma. Confusion will melt into order when you see the God-ordained lines of authority. Fear of leadership will change to confidence as you learn to handle power struggles. It is time to move into your "metron," that is, your God-given sphere of authority.

The Complete Wineskin
(Fourth edition)

The Body of Christ is in a reformation. God is pouring out His Holy Spirit, and our wineskins must be changed to handle the new wine. Will the Church come together in unity? How does the anointing of God work, and what is your role? What is the 5-fold ministry? How are apostles, prophets, evangelists, pastors, and teachers going to rise up and work together? Where do small group meetings fit in? This book puts into words what you have been sensing in your spirit. (Eberle's best seller, translated into many languages, distributed worldwide.)

Church History
Simply Stated

How did the Church get to where She is today? How did we get so many denominations? Who were the leaders who formed our thoughts? Where is the Church going? To fully answer these questions requires a knowledge of the past. Here is a simple, concise explanation of Church history. With two or three hours of reading, anyone can develop a clear picture of our Christian heritage.

Other Books by Harold R. Eberle

Precious in His Sight
A Fresh Look at the Nature of Humanity
(Third edition)

How evil are we? How can I love myself if I am evil? What happened when Adam sinned? How does that sin influence us? Where do babies go when they die? This book has implications upon our understanding of sin, salvation, who God is, evangelism, and how we live the victorious Christian life.

Thy Kingdom Come

The gospel Jesus and His disciples preached is not what we preach today. They preached, "Repent, for the Kingdom of God is at hand." We preach, "You are a sinner; Jesus died for your sins, and if you accept Jesus as Savior, you will be saved."

Why are these two gospels different? Who might be closer to the truth? Let's revisit Jesus' gospel and understand how to truly bring people into God's Kingdom.

Developing a Prosperous Soul
Vol. I: How to Overcome a Poverty Mind-set
Vol. II: How to Move into God's Financial Blessings

There are fundamental changes you can make in the way you think, which will help you release God's blessings. This is a balanced look at the promises of God with practical steps you can take to move into financial freedom. It is time for Christians to recapture the financial arena. These two volumes will inspire and create faith in you to fulfill God's purpose for your life.

Other Books by Harold R. Eberle

The Spiritual, Mystical, and Supernatural

The first five volumes of Harold R. Eberle's series of books entitled, *Spiritual Realities,* have been condensed into this one volume, 372 pages in length. Topics include how the spiritual and natural worlds are related, angelic and demonic manifestations, signs and wonders, miracles and healing, the anointing, good or evil spiritual practices, how people are created by God to access the spiritual realm, how the spirits of people interact, how people sense things in the spirit realm, and much more.

**To place an order
or check for current book prices visit:**

Website: www.worldcastministries.com

E-mail: office@worldcastministries.com

509-248-5837

Worldcast Publishing, PO Box 10653
Yakima, WA 98909-1653

On-line Bible College
Institute for Hope and Life

- Independent or group study
- Sensibly priced
- Study and proceed at your own rate
- Audit courses
- Earn a certificate, associates degree, or bachelors degree

http://instituteforhopeandlife.com

Other Books by Harold R. Eberle

Join in with great discussions about
Father-Son Theology.
Visit:

fathersontheology.com

At this site, you may
- ask questions
- add your insights
- debate related topics
- find out more information
- purchase more books